When I started to research and write this book nearly twenty years ago, the staff, friends, family—and foes—of both Elizabeth Arden and Helena Rubinstein who I had traced and interviewed were already elderly. Many of them have since died. I would like to take the opportunity in this new edition to raise a toast to the memories of those no longer alive and also to express gratitude to everyone who helped me trace this incredible story along the way.

I remain full of admiration that these two trail-blazing women built business empires before women had won the right to vote. They didn't break the glass ceiling—they created it. I'm often asked why I chose the topic, my answer being that I like stories about achieving women and writing about two at once was beguiling as no one had twinned them before. I felt their achievements were equal and thus inseparable and, although hostile rivals, their triumphs, talents, tribulations and tantrums were so similar that had they met, I do believe they would have truly bonded.

Yet behind the bickering, each had a respect for the other. Talking about Miss Arden, Helena Rubinstein said: "with her packaging and my product we could have ruled the world." I'm particularly proud that this quote, selected from my work in discovering it, made it into the *Oxford Dictionary of Biography*.

As an author, I'm also proud that this book (in print since 2003) has re-vitalized interest in the dazzling duo; inspired additional books on their achievement and been the basis of a well-crafted *PBS* documentary. Above all, I'm proud that it's now a Broadway musical starring Tony Award-winning legends Patti LuPone and Christine Ebersole, who, in stepping into the shoes of Helena and Elizabeth, bring their story to life in the city that the two female tyrant-tycoons made their own.

I felt a strong empathy in many ways when writing their story, not least because at the time I formed my own Public Relations business in 1973, even in London it was rare for a young woman (I was just 23) to open her own business—even more so if she was married. But my husband and I did things differently and by 1977 he had given up his job to come and work alongside me in the glossy world of international fashion that was the core of our business. I spent 25 years criss-crossing the Atlantic and travelling to Paris, Milan and Florence handling a stellar list of clients—amongst them Hermes, Louis Vuitton, Ferragamo, Valentino, Oscar de la Renta, Krizia, Cerruti, Wolford and Karl Lagerfeld. I spent four years working for the late, great Jim Henson (of Muppet fame) and hold the distinction of arranging for Miss Piggy to wear a Karl Lagerfeld hat on the cover of *Tatler* magazine! I often said the fashion industry was rather like the Muppet show in those heady years before it became a juggernaut. Crazy, but fun.

Juggling husband, home, children and a business is always demanding, often exhausting and—although often exhilarating—when approaching 50, I had reached a point where I craved to change direction. My choice was to write and the result was this, my first book, which I titled *War Paint*.
I hope you enjoy reading it as much as I did writing it.

Lindy Woodhead
Oxfordshire, February 2017

About the Author

Lindy Woodhead worked in international fashion public relations for more than 25 years before retiring from fashion to write full-time in 2000. Her follow-up book to *War Paint*—*Shopping, Seduction & Mr Selfridge* (2007)—the biography of the maverick American- retailer Harry Gordon Selfridge who founded London's Selfridges in 1909 was the basis for the successful international television *PBS/Masterpiece* drama series *Mr Selfridge*, starring Jeremy Piven. Lindy is currently completing her latest biography, the story of Kate 'Ma' Meyrick, London's notorious Jazz Age 'nightclub queen' (Weidenfeld & Nicolson, April 2018).

Married with two sons and a grandson, Fellow of the Royal Society of Arts (and keen gardener!), Lindy divides her time between homes in Oxfordshire and London.

Also by Lindy Woodhead

Shopping, Seduction & Mr Selfridge (Random House USA, 2013)

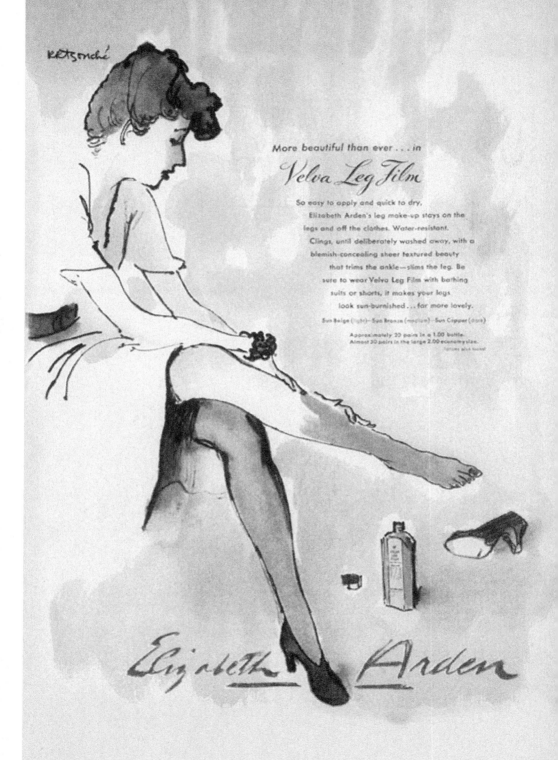

More beautiful than ever . . . in

Velva Leg Film

So easy to apply and quick to dry,
Elizabeth Arden's leg make-up stays on the
legs and off the clothes. Water-resistant.
Clings, until deliberately washed away, with a
blemish-concealing sheer textured beauty
that trims the ankle—slims the leg. Be
sure to wear Velva Leg Film with bathing
suits or shorts, it makes your legs
look sun-burnished . . . far more lovely.

Sun Beige (light)—Sun Bronze (medium)—Sun Copper (dark)

Approximately 20 pairs in a 1.00 bottle.
Almost 30 pairs in the large 2.00 economy size.
(prices plus taxes)

Elizabeth Arden

We'll be seeing more of you this summer!

what lovely limbs! MINUTE STOCKING FILM
for excitingly beautiful, slender-looking limbs. Flattering and sleek-
as-silk. It spreads and dries instantly. Resists water. And,
heavenly news—it's in a tube! A glorious sun-brown shade.
About 25 applications. 1.00. For hair-free, carefree legs and arms.
MINUTE HAIR REMOVER, 1.00

the sun is not your undoing!
LIQUID SUNSHINE. Protects your skin
when it is exposed to the sun.
Imparts an appealingly young, even,
golden tan. .85, 1.50

daily summer skin care
WATER LILY CLEANSING CREAM — the
perfect summer cleanser. Quick,
light, fragrant. 1.00, 2.00, 3.75

NOVENA NIGHT CREAM. Natural oils,
dried out by the sun are supplemented
while you sleep. 2.00, 5.00

HERBAL SKIN LOTION. Look and feel
delightfully refreshed. A summer
poise requisite. 1.00, 2.00

summer make-up magic
TOWN & COUNTRY MAKE-UP FILM.
Petal-smooth, all day foundation. Richer
summer tones — Mauresque, Rico
Tan. 1.00, 1.50

FACE POWDER. In the thrilling new
summer shades — Mauresque, Sun Tan,
Royal Tan. 1.00, 1.50, 3.50

LIPSTICK. Romantic, bright, young
reds — Apple Red, Cochinelle,
Red Coral. 1.00

plus taxes

Helena Rubinstein

War Paint

Madame Helena Rubinstein
and
Miss Elizabeth Arden

Their Lives, Their Times,
Their Rivalry

LINDY WOODHEAD

WILEY

John Wiley & Sons, Inc.

Published by John Wiley & Sons, Inc., Hoboken, New Jersey
Published simultaneously in Canada

First published in the United Kingdom in 2003 by Virago Press, an imprint of Time Warner Books UK.

Library of Congress Cataloging-in-Publication Data:
Woodhead, Lindy.
War paint : Madame Helena Rubinstein and Miss Elizabeth Arden : their lives, their times,
their rivalry / Lindy Woodhead.
p. cm.
Includes bibliographical references and index.
ISBN 0-471-48778-3 (cloth)
1. Rubinstein, Helena, 1870–1965. 2. Arden, Elizabeth, 1878–1966. 3. Businesswomen—
United States—Biography. 4. Cosmetics industry—United States—History. 5. Beauty culture—
United States History. I. Title.

HD9970.5.C672R859 2004
338.7'64672'092273—dc 22
[B]   2003062034

Printed in the United States of America
10 9 8 7 6 5 4 3 2 1

Dedicated to the memory of Patrick O'Higgins

In a country where wealth is constantly bringing new claimants for consideration into the arena of fashion — for it is, after all, no more than a struggle for notoriety, that may be more bloodless but is not less bitter than that of the gladiators — those who are in its possession contrive all possible means of distinction between themselves and those who are about to dispute their ascendancy.

James Fenimore Cooper, 1828

CONTENTS

Photo sections follow pages 102, 220, and 334

Introduction

ELIZABETH ARDEN AND HELENA RUBINSTEIN were, indisputably, the originators of the global, luxury, beauty industry as it exists today. They were able to achieve it due to the fact that women's hopes, those of becoming – or staying – attractive and looking younger, largely rest in creams. These two opportunist women, born in the late 1800s, had had no formal education, yet their instinctive knowledge that 'beauty culture' was a good idea meant they had already built their names into identifiable brands before the First World War.

Each established a flourishing international business, harnessing the emergent trend for skincare to the great commercial consumer growth of the twentieth century. That they did it at a time when women could expect little, if any, financial support from husband, family or banks, and even less from the male-dominated pharmaceutical industry from which they purchased supplies, makes their achievements all the more remarkable. They exercised autonomous control as sole owners and operators of their companies, which achieved multimillion-dollar turnovers, at a time when women rarely achieved commercial leadership, and job opportunities for women of their class were often limited to being a nurse, secretary or shop assistant, perhaps with the hope of making a suitable marriage.

When Elizabeth Arden arrived in New York from Canada in 1907, her name was Florence Nightingale Graham. It was a decade before women got the vote, a time when to show so much as an ankle was horrifying, when less than sixteen per cent of America's houses were wired for electricity, when a single woman might conceivably have a job, but definitely not a career, and on marriage was expected to retreat to her husband's side and look after hearth and home. Florence came from a small, agricultural homestead, where a bath would have been a Saturday night treat to prepare for Sunday church. Toothbrushes were rare, deodorants didn't exist and she and her sisters would have washed their hair every four weeks – sharing the same water, heated in a vat on the kitchen range. Stockings were lovingly darned, buttoned boots were expected to last for at least two years and there were few, if any, medicines to treat illnesses such as TB, pneumonia, influenza or measles. The only influence that her rival Helena Rubinstein achieved in her youth was in ruling the roost over her seven sisters in their cramped house in the Polish city of Krakow, where they lived a quiet, orthodox Jewish life, expected to work hard helping out at the family hardware store, leave school early, and marry whichever man their father told them to.

Despite the fact that both women were born into hardship, they had an innate understanding of luxury and showmanship. Rubinstein's was honed by world travel – she left Europe for Australia to find her fortune – and Arden's by her passion for nickelodeons and romantic novels. Their inherent marketing and business skills were formidable and each had an instinctive gift for persuading affluent and aspirational women to part with their money. Their intuition in taking 'beauty culture' out of the realms of snake oil salesmanship and into the realms of respectability was a masterstroke. But their real genius was to put their name above the door of their own beauty salons, creating shrines to the mysteries of the skin and the body beautiful, in a *mise-en-scène* that was as inspired a business move as it was inspiring to their clients. No other brand achieved this unique position. Big businesses ultimately *bought* salons belonging to other so-called experts, or opened salons of their own to give credibility to their retail offerings. Rubinstein and Arden, however, each started with her own tiny, luxurious salon, massage skills, a jar of cream, a heightened sense of salesmanship, and the knack of making clients believe in their magic. Their success was due to the fact that they did it better than *anybody* else.

Their visionary creative skills have become overshadowed by the vast size and power of the beauty business in the twenty-first century. By the time they died in the mid-1960s, both were old in an era when age was neither revered nor respected. Their contribution and achievement was quickly forgotten in the dynamics of consumerism and the emerging media markets that lionised the latest and the youngest, non-conformist style-setters. The death of two elderly, opinionated and seemingly dated ladies was noted by the media as 'the end of an era'. There was little time in the rebellious freedom of the 1960s to remember two women who represented the past, despite each having been a genius.

Like all geniuses they had their flaws. Both wielded immense power, which they used with misguided force against their hapless executives. Both were tyrannical, temperamental, obsessive, mercurial, despotic workaholics. Neither came from the school of business training that preaches you achieve more by not arguing. Both were bullies, often terrifying to their staff, and loved and hated in equal part by families, friends, employees, lawyers and bankers. They ruled imperiously, loath to delegate even the smallest decision. Fear and trembling – as well as excitement – echoed through the corridors of their perfumed offices when these perfectionist women arrived at work.

Helena Rubinstein froze out anyone she didn't care for. If they didn't get the message quickly enough, she had their desk removed. Elizabeth Arden turned on staff she felt were being stupid, reducing grown men to a quivering heap – and sometimes to tears – hiring, and more often firing, on a whim.

Working at Elizabeth Arden was often described as 'walking through a revolving door'. Both women led however by example, working harder than their employees and were inspirational teachers, earning tremendous admiration, particularly amongst their female counter-staff and factory workers. Male sales managers were, for the main part, less keen to accept their female leaders' divine right to rule their empires as they wished.

Both women knew the value of a dollar. Whilst Miss Arden would be wildly extravagant, she was also thrifty, whilst Madame – as Helena Rubinstein was always known – was mean to the point of obsession. She prowled the corridors of her buildings, turning off lights. 'Electrick is *so* expensive,' she would say, and often took her lunch to work in a brown paper bag, munching on a chicken leg at her desk, grumbling that the staff had gone out for their own break. 'Where *is* everybody?' she would yell at an empty office, shaking the half-eaten drumstick in her fist as she gestured towards the deserted desks. Madame rarely increased an employee's salary without a fight, and had a reputation for being tight about pay and benefits – except when she was poaching staff from Arden. Then she would pay whatever it took to get them. Miss Arden, however, always paid top salaries, her canny business instinct telling her that training up new staff would cost more. She took her pound of flesh by working them around the clock. A great insomniac, she would call her weary executives at all hours. 'Just for a little chat, dear,' she would say. As her little chats were wont to continue for nearly an hour, most of her senior management were seriously sleep-deprived.

Although always surrounded by people, both women were achingly lonely. They sacrificed their private lives to run their companies, and their friends and travelling companions were almost always on the payroll. Neither was fulfilled emotionally, nor physically, yet both married twice, late in life, the first time round to men who, although financially dependent on their wives, helped them commercially, and the second time to princes with dubious titles and, in the case of Arden's, even more dubious sexuality, but whose names helped them socially. Elizabeth Arden had no children and Helena Rubinstein's two sons grew up resenting the fact that, in their eyes at least, her business always came first.

These two women so dedicated to beauty were not beauties themselves. Diminutive in size (Rubinstein was a tiny 4'10" and Arden a petite 5'2") if not in ego, and certainly not in bank balance, they towered above their competitors in energy and vision. Always wary and vitriolic about each other, they were also paranoid about their competitors, in particular Charles Revson, of Revlon fame, who was called 'the nail man' by Madame and 'that man' by Miss Arden. Not known for his sense of humour, the industry smiled when Revson brought out an after-shave called 'That Man!'

Both women were born under the star sign of Capricorn and showed strong characteristics associated with that sign, being stubborn, resourceful and underneath all the outward bravura, quite shy. They loved their work and the businesses that bore their names, more than anything else – except possibly money. Their insecurities – both were the daughters of failed fathers and felt family rejection keenly – meant the acquisition of money became the driving force in their lives and both were recognised at the height of their fame as the richest, most powerful, self-made women in the world. Madame and Miss Arden both lavished their fortunes on their one great personal passion. For each of them, this obsessive passion – Madame's was collecting what she described as 'beautiful things' and Elizabeth Arden's was racehorses, which she felt were often more beautiful than humans – eclipsed family, home, husbands and friends. The affection they poured into their consuming hobbies compensated in no small part for their repressed sexuality.

Helena Rubinstein and Elizabeth Arden can claim to have created the beauty regimes we take for granted today and were decades ahead of any competitors in their ideas for developing product ranges. Their enlightened salon exercise and health treatments have rarely been bettered. Between them they manufactured hundreds of products, their first being a commercial range of moisturisers, nourishing cream, cleansing cream and astringents, all beautifully packaged, scented and labelled and promoted with the requisite 'scientific' claims that they would keep the skin 'young and beautiful and eliminate wrinkles'. Best known for their 'treatment creams', they soon expanded into cosmetics. Between them they packaged fine, tinted face-powders; light tinted foundation creams; soft, blended cream-rouge; lip-pencils; lipstick in a push-up metal container, developed from cartridge shell cases after the First World War. Their make-up ranges included coloured eye shadows in cream *and* powder form – in both bright and muted tones – eye-brow pencils; eye-liners and mascara – all at a time when most women would hardly have worn a dab of rouge, never mind full eye make-up. Helena Rubinstein can take credit for the world's first water-proof mascara and later for the precursor of the mascara wands used universally today when she bought and developed a business called 'Mascara-Matic'. They were the first to develop a professional range of sun-tan products, including fake tan, and to advocate sunblock. 'I have but this to say, sunburn is beauty suicide,' said Madame Rubinstein.

They weren't the first successful operators in the cosmetics business. Industrialists François Coty and Pierre Wertheimer, French businessmen *par excellence*, made their fortunes from fragrance and make-up, as had Eugene Rimmel before them. The two 'Beauty Queens', as they came to be known, were not the first to commercially offer coloured cosmetics. That accolade belongs to Leichner, the family firm from Berlin and Vienna, founded in 1853, which provided greasepaint for actresses. Neither were they the first to offer complexion soap, or shampoo, or dentifrice powder or cold cream. Such things were made by Ponds, or by Procter & Gamble who were founded in America in 1837, or Colgate Palmolive Peet. Procter & Gamble's soap was rather nice, especially 'Ivory', promoted as being 'nearly 100% pure'. In the 1920s they launched 'Camay', their 'complexion soap endorsed by dermatologists' – who were, naturally enough, on their staff at the time. Neither did Rubinstein nor Arden ever attempt to target the African American market. That was exclusively the fiefdom of two dynamic women, also great rivals, Annie Turnbo Malone and Madame C.J. Walker, whose hair treatment products had made them both millionaires by the early twentieth century.

Elizabeth Arden and Madame Rubinstein were however the first women to run their own global business, giving their personal name not merely to beauty salons and a luxury wholesale brand, but to a way of life. Both had huge personal magnetism and became so closely identified with the techniques they preached, that women consumers identified with them personally, much more than with the faceless power of a corporation.

They were the originators of selling prestige cosmetics ranges to department stores, whose 'toilet goods' departments in those days more usually sold rice powder, hairnets, soap and scent bottles. Both trained awesomely efficient, exceedingly attractive, demonstrators in their own beauty schools. They created cosmetics containers as a beautiful accessory, making jewelled powder compacts (one series of Rubinstein's designed by Dali and Dufy) and sensuously glamorous lipstick cases. Arden's ranges were available packed into travelling vanity cases in miniature sizes and if anyone went overseas and ran out of her favourite face cream it wasn't a problem. Devotees could pick up a jar at beauty salons, identified by their red doors, in London, Paris, the South of France, Madrid, Rome, Berlin, Buenos Aires, Rio de Janeiro, Sydney, Nassau, Toronto, New York and key cities across the USA, plus at beauty counters in all the world's finest stores.

By the 1920s, both Arden and Rubinstein were offering treatments in the salons which included oxygen facials, deep tissue massage, exfoliation, depilation, eyelash dyeing, freckle-bleaching, manicures, pedicures, self-tanning, metabolic testing, naturopathic water treatments, heat treatments, paraffin waxing, yoga, gymnastics, deportment, grooming, stretch and anti-stress classes and even fencing classes! Treatment staff were dressed in medically-inspired, crisp white uniforms and wore soft-soled white nurses' shoes, the whole atmosphere being one of a perfumed clinic. Light-diet dining rooms served delicious food and after several hours being pampered, clients could have a make-up lesson and finish off with the attentions of an in-house hairdresser.

Their public relations and customer-service skills were legendary. Between them, they pioneered special offers, customer mail shots, questionnaires and advice letters. Their demonstrators went into schools, colleges, factories and even the White House to preach the word of beauty.

Rubinstein intertwined her art collections and the creativity of artists with her business. Arden was the first tycoon to use sporting events for significant corporate client entertainment.

Their early product advertising was part of the creative process which spawned the growth of America's glossy, consumer advertising industry. They used the first – and the best – of the emerging fashionable photographers, illustrators, models, interior designers and creative directors. They helped, in no small part, to develop the amateur skills of many creative artists, enabling them to move into professional, financially rewarding careers. Ideas instigated by Arden and Rubinstein gave commercial work the requisite edge to seduce the fashionable customer. The effort of these two women has spawned industries now taken for granted. Product packaging, beauty advertising, consumer public relations – both women courted the press assiduously and were tireless at self-promotion – head-to-toe beauty salons, health spa holiday resorts – all of them can be more or less tracked back to concepts laid down by Miss Arden and Madame.

As the twentieth century unfolded, bringing untold economic opportunity, these two women seized the moment. Social historians writing about shifts in trends have written extensively about fashion designers who made their mark in changing the way women looked, amongst them influential women like Coco Chanel, Jeanne Lanvin and Elsa Schiaparelli. Chanel in particular having an enduring allure not just for the stunning simplicity of her early, directional, clothes, but because of the awesomely successful fragrance bearing her name.

But what Miss Arden and Madame fashioned helped give women a freedom of expression analogous to women gaining the right to vote. They lived and worked through two World Wars, adapting their products and promotional campaigns to the social change brought by these seismic events. Not to mention the invention of the motor-car, aeroplane, the cinema, radio, television, the telegraph and telex, commercial refrigeration, mass-distribution and the explosive growth of a consumer-driven, affluent society.

Despite working for over six decades in the same milieu, with much of that time spent in the same city – New York – and clashing head-on in business, Miss Arden and Madame never met. Madame, it's been said, once glanced at her rival, seated across a busy restaurant, and remarked to her lunch companion, 'Ha! Too much hair colour for a woman of her age', blithely impervious to the fact that her own blue-black tresses were by then professionally dyed each month.

These two innovative and talented women fought for most of their lives for supremacy in a field they made uniquely powerful. Their battles were an equal contest between two giant personalities. In the end, there was no outright victor. They were both triumphant, and the legacy these pioneering tycoons left behind – that when you wake up, you put on your make-up but *not* before cleansing, toning and nourishing the skin – arguably touches the lives of women throughout the entire developed world today.

The title 'War Paint' has the advantage of conjuring up powerful visual images, appropriate for a book about the cosmetics industry. Native American Indian braves, their faces painted with battle stripes ready for attack. The sumptuously made-up face of Queen Cleopatra, as she set out to conquer both Julius Caesar *and* Mark Antony with her painted beauty, both images indelibly printed in our minds thanks to that triumph of the creative arts in the twentieth century – the cinema.

Between the 1930s and the 1950s, the phrase 'war paint' became common usage to describe make-up. Putting on one's 'war paint' was part of the battle cry of women, often preparing themselves for their own battle, the seduction of men. The lyrics of a hit song in the mid-1950s went 'You don't need war paint, you're not going to fight a war, you're only going out with the boy next door!' The expression was not in common parlance prior to the 1920s because few Western women of refinement would wear much, if any, make-up in public life. Coloured cosmetics, particularly eye make-up, were the province of actresses – and whores. This social stigma lasted a long time. Stevenson's *Book of Quotations*, first published in 1934, says: 'Face: painted. See also under Whore'.

'Painting' inspires disdain and devotion in equal measure. For my part, I have always worn make-up and as a teenage rebel had the dubious distinction of being sent out of a history class at school to 'go and wash my face', having just discovered the delights of Max Factor's Pan Stick. As has often been reported, the most unlikely of high-flying career women, including doctors, lawyers, judges and MPs, are often as devoted to their cosmetics as any beauty editor, whilst conversely, even a top model waiting for a casting is likely to be barefaced. Most of all, girls of all ages, from four to forty-something, seem to adore lipsticks, having an entire wardrobe of salves, lip balms and glosses. Delighted manufacturers are obliging this seemingly recession-proof and insatiable desire (devotees admit to buying a new lipstick each week) by providing products scented with fruits, stress-relieving fragrances, circulation-boosting substances and even breath-fresheners. One enterprising manufacturer introduced 'Latte Lip' in 2000, which gives the wearer an energising shot of caffeine whenever she licks her lips. At £14 a time, such pleasures could come from a cup of freshly ground coffee a lot less expensively, but such is the power of lipstick that the product has been a phenomenal success.

Critics are fond of citing the fashion and beauty industry as being frivolous and superficial. Indeed, many aspects of the business are particularly unedifying, not least the behaviour of many of the people who control it. Kennedy Fraser, a perceptive writer, made the observation in her introduction to a book titled, *On the Edge, 100 Years of Vogue*, that 'The fashion world's a dangerous place. The most vulnerable don't survive it'. Not that Miss Arden or Madame were at all vulnerable. They were tough women. But they were fortunate in being able to create their businesses in a more gentle, and genteel, world than exists today. Both enjoyed the fusion of creative skills with a money-making process at a time when such things were a more pleasurable experience.

Increasingly today, there is a move towards a more holistic approach to health, beauty and lifestyle, which impacts on our psychological well-being and which is particularly relevant to the early vision of Miss Arden and Madame. Women who spend their valued leisure time at a spa, or having massage, or any form of 'alternative' therapy, are giving their immune system a treat. There is even a slow, but sure, move towards hospitals realising that patients respond to more subtle care and that the make-up advice given to patients recovering from strokes affecting their facial muscles, or from facial and cancer surgery, is of vital importance to their self-esteem. Beta-endorphins, generally associated with the pumping up process of the gym, can just as successfully be evoked by sensory and gentle moods. Music, massage, laughter, good sex, friendly companionship, fine food, meditation, prayer, scent – all stir the emotions.

Above all, beauty is uplifting. The quest for inner beauty is what Elizabeth Arden and Helena Rubinstein should best be remembered for. Not so much for the products they made which 'promised beauty' but in their underlying philosophy that women deserve time for themselves. That women need some pampering. That women who spend time on a beauty regime that makes them feel better about themselves are not being self-indulgent or vain. That a beauty regime, good grooming, 'putting one's face on', a healthy lifestyle, vitality and above all the confidence that these things give, are essential tools for coping with life in today's combative, competitive and often cruel world.

The urge to decorate ourselves is one of the most fundamental instincts in human nature. The dressing-table of a hundred years ago, just like today's, cluttered with bottles, brushes, jars and tubes is nothing new – the ancient Egyptians were inseparable from their make-up and took their brushes and eye-shadow pots with them into the afterlife. Elizabeth Arden and Helena Rubinstein made modern history out of an ancient pastime – and have left their names behind them.

CHAPTER ONE

RIVALS EVEN IN DEATH
New York 1965–1967

URING THE EARLY EVENING of Friday 29 April, 1966, in an atmosphere of tense, almost palpitating excitement, over seven hundred people were gathered in the Madison Avenue premises of New York's prestigious Parke-Bernet Galleries. There was a hush as auctioneer John Marion, the man known as a 'wizard run by an adding machine', took the gavel to start the Friday evening sale, the last in a series that had started the previous week. In the space of ten days, Parke-Bernet had placed under the hammer one of the largest – and certainly most famous – private collections ever to come on the market *en masse*. The belongings of their remarkable owner would, at the completion of the sales, fetch over $2,600,000 (more than $14,000,000 today).

There had been so much to catalogue, including as it did the contents of five homes in three countries, that it had taken over a year to complete, involving at least one change of auction house and a series of family arguments reported to be pretty lethal. Even as Parke-Bernet were launching their sales, it seems quite possible that they did not have the collections in their entirety – the owner's lawyer, himself an executor of her will, having received offers from interested parties to acquire favoured items, with, it seems, some prepared to offer the added inducement of payment to a Swiss Bank.

There had been much gossip and eager anticipation amongst specialist dealers about this particular sale. Many were absolutely purring with pleasure, in spite of – or maybe because of – knowing they would be going head-to-head with the steely determination of museum directors from all over the world. This then was no ordinary sale.

Observing the crowded rooms with a self-satisfied smile was Peter

Wilson, chairman of Sotheby's in London, the new owners of Parke-Bernet. His voracious skills in marketing and public relations were legendary, as was his tenacious grip on the firm's finances. Peter Wilson wasn't a man to stint if it meant winning a victory, all virtues he shared with the woman whose belongings were being sold – Madame Helena Rubinstein.

Just the week before, Wilson had conducted the opening sale of the series, 'Modern Paintings and Sculptures – Part One'. The total bids had reached just under $1,450,000, with Brancusi's polished bronze, *Bird in Space*, reaching $140,000 in just seventy-five seconds. A most satisfactory result for Wilson, who liked to get results, and had worked his legendary charm at the rostrum. Whilst the artists' names were amongst the most acclaimed and desirable in modern collectible terms, with works by Picasso, Juan Gris, Paul Klee, Bonnard, Degas, Marie Laurencin, Fernand Léger, Henri Matisse, Joan Miró, Modigliani, Monet, Tchelitchew, Utrillo and Vuillard, not to mention no less than five Renoirs, they were, according to some experts, not particularly inspiring. In the words of Conor Macklin of London's Grosvenor Gallery, 'The paintings were strong in names but not strong in quality'. Ray Perman, the gallery's managing director, puts it more succinctly: 'The paintings, with a few exceptions, were bin ends.' They were also, like many of the owner's other belongings, a little worse for wear. Frames had been described by one of her acquaintances as being 'chipped so badly they looked as though they had been gnawed by rats' whilst some pictures were frankly rather grubby.

There were however some contemporary gems in the collection, in particular Joan Miró's *Portrait* and Willem de Kooning's *Elegy* which experts say were particularly desirable. The distinguished art dealer David Nash, then working at Parke-Bernet, is more sympathetic in his appraisal of the pictures. 'She bought what she liked best' he says tactfully about Madame, 'and she had the most wonderful Matisse'.

Bravura collectors, smitten by the allure of lesser known contemporary artists, had found 'Modern Paintings and Sculpture – Part Two' more to their taste. Dealers identified the real bargains as pictures by Antoni Clave, Jean Fautrier and Antonio Music. This group included, according to Conor Macklin, 'what are regarded today as some of the best works by these artists'. As before, it was the sculpture which fired the buyers' imagination, with pieces by Ossip Zadkine and a collection of breathtakingly beautiful heads by Polish sculptor Elie Nadelman, fetching the highest prices.

But for the collector with good taste and an eye for beauty, the real treasures were to be found in the sale 'Modern Drawings and Prints'. Showing the same creative flair with which she had built up her business and buying with a more assured hand than when she had selected her paintings, there were dozens of sublime nineteenth- and early twentieth-century engravings, etchings, lithographs, drawings and watercolours. David Nash acknowledges the collection as 'really exceptional'. Madame was, however, as with so much of her life, ahead of her time in amassing these works, which fetched comparatively little. As Ray Perman explains, 'They were great quality, but it is only in recent years that drawing has been appreciated'. Artists included Léger, Brancusi, Buffet, Degas, Derain, Dufy, Juan Gris, Helleu, Marcoussis, Matisse, Modigliani, Pascin – and Picasso.

John Richardson, Picasso's friend and eminent biographer, acknowledges the pencil drawings as being 'quite, quite wonderful' and Conor Macklin cites the two 1907 gouaches which were studies for Picasso's masterpiece, *Les Demoiselles d'Avignon*, as being 'hugely important'. The sale list was a roll call of talent made all the more enticing by the fact that Madame had bought the majority of them from each artist privately. She had known them all.

Although Wilson wasn't taking the closing sale, he understood better than most the potential in what was to be sold on that rainy night, having observed with great satisfaction the astonishing result of the previous week's sale in the same category, when two pieces had sold for $24,000 and $27,000 respectively. Whilst not large sums, they were world records for their genre and he was even more confident of this, the second half.

As the public strolled through the galleries during previews, one can only wonder at their impressions of the person whose grand passion had been to amass such a plethora of possessions. What did they think when looking at the suite of translucent 'Lucite' furniture, which included her famous illuminated sleigh-bed from which she had long tyrannised staff at early-morning breakfast meetings?

It might have entertained them to know she had been an obsessive bridge player and, when paired against any new, or particularly gifted opponent, was wont to move one of the larger pieces from her African art collection to within a whisker of their chair before the rubber, realising that anyone playing a game requiring great concentration was likely to lose it when faced with a savage carved figure with a beard of human hair. Madame was a woman who liked to win.

And she was a winner, losing only her final battle – with death – on the first of April 1965. Those who knew her well thought, when they heard the news, that it must be a mistake. She had, after all, died on April Fools' day. Even then, she had defied the odds, living to her ninety-fourth year and working at a pace which was almost as demonic as her beloved African fetish figures. In death, she ruled as imperiously over her belongings as she had done in life. She decreed they should be sold, despite the fact that over a hundred eager relatives may have expected their share of the booty, almost all of them having worked for her at some point or another, some for their entire careers.

It was not to be. She made specific bequests, leaving paintings here and there to office managers and far-flung relatives, and specifically left to her sisters and a few favoured nieces some *extremely* important pieces from her fabled jewellery collection. The rest of this gorgeous, if sometimes gaudy, collection of jewels, an integral part of Madame's personality, had been sold by Parke-Bernet a few months earlier. The famous jewels, however, had fetched just under $372,000 (over $2,000,000 today), with some friends observing it was a fraction of what they were worth. Others at the auction like society jeweller Kenneth J. Lane acknowledges that 'a lot of the stones were flawed and settings often damaged' and as the big and splashy stones were not the fashion mood of the time, the disappointing result of the sale came as no surprise. As a significant number of particularly fine pieces, including a black and white pearl necklace, Madame's signature five string cabochon ruby necklace, not to mention her seven string necklace rumoured to contain the missing strand from the Maharajah of Baroda's legendary family pearls, were bequeathed to relatives, the sale it seems was merely the 'best of the rest'. Almost all the rest of her possessions, after a lifetime of collecting, a hobby she described as her greatest passion, were destined to go under the hammer. It was almost as though she could not bear for anyone else in the family to have them, or to squabble over them. 'Better they should go,' she might have said. And go they did.

Absent were certain pieces which today would be considered hugely important, in particular her clothes and furs. Madame was *very* particular about her furs, which included sables, chinchillas, minks and rare Somali leopardskins fashioned into a luxurious coat by Christian Dior. Her clothes were by Worth, Poiret, Chanel, Schiaparelli, Lanvin, Balenciaga, Fath and Dior. Their omission is perhaps understandable as, in the 1960s, such sublime items were not considered as collectible as they are today. Her clothes, like most of the fabled shoe collection of the great fashion icon Rita Lydig, simply disappeared. Possibly they found their way into the wardrobes of friends and relatives, the furs in her Paris house were said by someone close to her to have been 'stolen by her maid' who, presumably having suffered five decades of penny-pinching wages, simply helped herself.

The sale poised to start, however, was the one the experts had been waiting for. In John Marion's recollection, 'there were more prestigious dealers from Europe than we had ever seen in New York for this very specialised category of sale. It was a professional and sophisticated audience.' The cover of the catalogue simply said, 'The Helena Rubinstein Collection. African and Oceanic Art. Parts One and Two'. The endpapers showed the breathtaking view from the vast roof terrace of her Paris apartment on the Quai de Bethune, where Bruce Chatwin, protégé of Peter Wilson and then Head of Antiquities at Sotheby's, had spent several weeks cataloguing the collection. By her own admission, Madame Rubinstein had 'put out the best bits' in Paris, saying sagely, 'The French appreciate that sort of thing.' Bruce Chatwin didn't seem to appreciate it very much however, writing to his mother-in-law, 'Helena Rubinstein wore a lot of people out during her long life, and she retains that capacity in the grave. We work from 9 till 8 in the evening and we still get nowhere.'

The team at Parke-Bernet responsible for describing what, in 1966, was still a little-known genre of antiquities, took pains to consult with the few experts in the field anxious to establish sound provenance. Their task was not helped by the total lack of paperwork or reference notes on many of Madame Rubinstein's pieces – as a cash buyer, she cared little for receipts and seemingly less for historical data. One such expert was M. Henri Kamer of the Musée de l'Homme in Paris who became, it seems, an ex-officio adviser to the auction house.

The sale however nearly didn't happen at all – at least, not in New York. The French government were unwilling to grant an export licence, at the eleventh hour becoming surprisingly protective about losing treasures from its French-African colonial heritage, so it looked as if the collection would be stranded in Paris. Eventually a deal was brokered between the Rubinstein executors, Parke-Bernet and the French government, with Mr Kamer's museum the beneficiary of, according to David Nash, 'several meaningful pieces', whilst the rest was allowed to be shipped to New York.

Parke-Bernet's catalogue notes and bibliography included reference to MoMA's important exhibition 'African Negro Art' in 1935, which effectively launched interest in the topic in America. Helena Rubinstein lent seventeen pieces to this exhibition, although intriguingly only five of them were included in the Parke-Bernet sale. Chatwin also drew heavily from one of the most important reference books on the subject, *Sculptures Soudanaises*, published by the French traveller-collector F.H. Lem in the 1940s. The catalogue text said, 'Madame Rubinstein's collection had been acquired mostly in Paris, at auction sales and from dealers before the War and, to a lesser extent, after it.' It went on to say that 'her major purchases had been from F.H. Lem who had lived in Africa in 1934–35 and who had hoped to establish a museum in Dakar'. His plans collapsed when the funding failed to materialise, so, short of money, not to mention short of space, he sold virtually his entire collection to Madame, who was short of neither.

Most other reference books referred to in the catalogue were written in the 1950s and 1960s, in particular texts by William Fagg, whose career as Keeper of Ethnography at the British Museum qualified him to opine on the complex history of these often mysterious pieces. He described the most highly prized piece in the Rubinstein collection, her Cameroon Grasslands statue of a royal titled woman, otherwise known as *The Bangwa Queen*, glowingly. 'She bids fair to be the finest expression of movement in all African sculptures,' wrote the admiring Mr Fagg.

It is unusual, even in the hands of experts, for auction houses to get everything right. David Nash points out that 'in the early 1960s the state of scholarship was really not so terrific in auction houses. It was very difficult to assess both quality and provenance without making *some* mistakes.' Chatwin's strangest mistake was the inference that Madame Rubinstein had bought her African art before the Second World War, when she had already become a keen collector before the First World War. He clearly didn't know of her friendship with the sculptor Jacob Epstein in London as early as 1909, when, prompted by Epstein, she started buying African art. There was no mention that by 1925 the American media were already saying that her collection was 'coveted by museums' nor that she had, by 1928, masterfully inveigled *The Bangwa Queen* out of the man described as 'the dean of African art collecting', Paris *über*-dealer, Charles Ratton. This move was as brilliant and Machiavellian as the one Ratton had made when he had sent his colleague in Berlin to inveigle the piece out of the safe haven of the

Volkerkunde Museum, where it had been on display for over thirty years. To this day, curators at the museum find it hard to discuss this particular *faux pas* on the part of one of their long-dead directors.

In what was, for Helena Rubinstein, a remarkably forthright admission, she once wrote, 'I have always favoured the unusual and when I followed such sound advice as Jacob Epstein's, as well as my own "inner eye", my purchases were invariably good.' What she didn't say is that along with her glorious prints and her collection of Belter furniture, the African carvings were top of her shopping list, in the beginning at least, because they cost next to nothing. She would probably have had to pay no more than a few dollars for any item pre-1920.

At the Parke-Bernet Galleries, however, the idea of collecting such mystical treasures at any bargain price was about to end. That eventful night, 125 pieces fetched nearly $300,000. It was, the experts are unanimously agreed, 'a benchmark sale'. It was the night that a little-known niche sector in the art world crossed the line and became a major collectible. The Helena Rubinstein auction of African and Oceanic art established the genre in today's terms. A noted dealer in New York grumbled to David Nash a few months later about 'how difficult it was to buy in Africa now every villager had a priced copy of the Helena Rubinstein catalogue.' He wasn't entirely joking.

It was a fitting result for the woman who over sixty years earlier had taken a small niche sector in the beauty world – that of face cream, brilliantly imbued it with mystical properties and turned it into a multimillion-dollar empire. Her success inspired countless competitors to join the market, fuelling a boom that has grown into a global industry.

Whilst Helena Rubinstein had several rivals in collecting African art, in the beauty business she had only one. The two of them competed to see who could acquire the most accolades and the most profit. Neither could bear to say her rival's name out loud. To Helena Rubinstein, her competitor was always 'the other one'. To her rival, Helena Rubinstein was always 'that woman'. Between them, these formidable women created the luxury beauty business as it is known today. The 'other one's' name was . . . Elizabeth Arden.

A year before those eventful auction sales, on a sunny day towards the end of April, four people were walking up Fifth Avenue towards La Grenouille, a fashionably swell restaurant in New York, then the favoured lunch venue for the upper echelons of the fashion and media world. Moving at a brisk pace belying her eighty-four years of age, and with her listing gait, the legacy of a childhood hip injury, just visible, the hostess was marshalling her group in her normal, rather bossy manner. Her companions were Mrs Ernestine Carter, the distinguished women's editor of the *Sunday Times* in London, accompanied by her husband Jake Carter, Sotheby's roving consultant in America, and Count Lanfranco Rasponi, a public relations consultant of rather flashy good looks with a fine taste in camel cashmere overcoats. The woman bustling ahead was Elizabeth Arden, Rasponi's most valued client. He was somewhat confused by this late-morning exercise, as Miss Arden invariably used her chauffeur and Bentley, even for journeys of a hundred yards. Indeed, the British racing green Bentley had already been dispatched to the restaurant where her chauffeur, Charles, would wait until Miss Arden was ready to be whisked back to her office. He wouldn't have to wait long. She ate like a bird, taking a crisp forty-five minutes for lunch, often leaving her guests lingering over coffee.

Rasponi soon understood the reason for this orchestrated walk. The route from the Elizabeth Arden headquarters passed the doorway of 715 Fifth Avenue, the flat, limestone façade bearing the words 'helena rubinstein'. Here Elizabeth Arden paused, halting her guests. Madame Rubinstein had died three weeks earlier. Waving a hand for dramatic effect towards the beauty salon windows, Arden murmured, 'Poor Helena.' Mrs Carter later wrote, 'Her voice was sad, but her eyes were triumphant.'

The formidable and famous Ernestine Carter and the equally formidable and extremely famous Elizabeth Arden, had first met a year earlier. Mrs Carter had been invited for lunch at Miss Arden's penthouse apartment at 834 Fifth Avenue. It was a hot day, yet Mrs Carter, who felt the heat badly, was kept waiting in the overheated drawing room of Miss Arden, who felt the cold. Wilting in front of a roaring log fire, the central heating turned up, Mrs Carter felt her make-up melting, not an auspicious start for a *tête-à-tête* with a cosmetics tycoon. Following a delicious light lunch, served on a lace-covered table in front of the fire, the by now very uncomfortable guest was horrified when Miss Arden's maid arrived with a tray groaning under the weight, not of iced tea, but all the latest Elizabeth Arden cosmetics. 'I will now make you up myself,' said Elizabeth in her soft, whispery voice. The faster she applied foundation, blusher and lipstick, the faster it melted off Mrs Carter's face. Quite oblivious to her discomfort, Miss Arden, clearly in her element, started to apply eye make-up. Her struggling guest tried to explain she had an allergy to mascara. Instead of stopping, Elizabeth Arden asked which brand she had been using. Alas for Mrs Carter, she blurted out the terrible truth, 'Helena Rubinstein's'. Whereupon Elizabeth jabbed her eyelashes fiercely with another swoosh of her roll-on black mascara saying sharply, 'That's just boot black.' Her victim's cheeks were black with dripping mascara as she left, groaning gift bag in hand, promptly going to her hotel room to wash it all off.

Having met and written about both ageing doyennes of the beauty industry in the mid-1960s, it's clear Ernestine Carter had a penchant for Helena Rubinstein. Even that, however, was not an easy relationship, as when the two first met at Claridges in London in 1963, Carter describes Madame Rubinstein's conversation as 'uttered in grunts' ingeniously translated by Helena's urbane and charming *homme d'affaires*, Patrick O'Higgins. They met several times thereafter and, as befitted an ex-curator of New York's Museum of Modern Art, married to an eccentric expert on rare books and antiquities, Ernestine Carter and her husband Jake felt drawn to Madame Rubinstein, clearly fascinated by her collections. 'At Madame Rubinstein's,' wrote Carter, 'one never minded waiting as there was so much to look at. She was a magpie collector.'

Despite being in New York in April of 1965, Ernestine Carter would not have been at Helena Rubinstein's funeral, for it was strictly a family affair. Indeed, even her laying-out, which took place at Campbell's funeral parlour on Madison Avenue, the venue of choice for New York's Upper East Side grandees, was very nearly a minor affair. Oscar Kolin, Madame's nephew and executive vice president of the business, was in Japan when his aunt was admitted to the New York Hospital, travelling back immediately on hearing of her death. He found the family and her omnipresent lawyer Harold Weill had made arrangements with almost unseemly haste, planning what they said would be 'a very simple event'. The body of the woman who had lived surrounded by opulent beauty, was shunted up to a room on the fourth floor of Campbell's, described as 'looking like the comfortable sitting room of a Miami Beach hotel, complete with plastic armchairs'.

Used to the thrifty ways of his illustrious client, her lawyer had, it seems, taken the 'budget' option, a move which caused much grief to Patrick O'Higgins, who immediately lobbied Mala, Madame Rubinstein's niece, to help make the necessary changes. Her body was subsequently moved to the

Williamsburg Room which, at a cost of $1000 a day, was Campbell's finest. The family had already decreed that no flowers be sent. Instead, it was suggested donations be made to the Children's Blood Foundation, a favoured charity of Roy Titus, her son. Patrick, however, ordered a mass of her favourite flowers, including peonies, roses and delphiniums (holding his head high when Mr Weill later queried the bill) and had her dressed in her latest couture purchase, a brocade suit by Yves St Laurent, accessorised by her glorious black pearls. The best make-up artist at the Rubinstein salon was summoned for her *maquillage*, artfully applied using exactly the right shade of violet dusting powder, and her hair was freshly dyed and swept into her signature chignon. The stage was set for her final triumphant goodbye. During the two days Helena Rubinstein rested at Campbell's the people arriving to pay their respects and sign the books of condolence numbered several thousands. Madame would have been pleased.

By a strange twist of fate, there was upheaval too in New York that Friday and Saturday. Three thousand shop-floor workers at Bloomingdales and Stern Brothers had gone on strike, picketing the stores and demanding a $1.50 per hour minimum wage and a thirty-five-hour week. Almost all the department stores in New York were paralysed as shoppers stayed at home, avoiding the *mêlée*. As if on cue, a twenty-four-hour taxi strike caused even more chaos with the result that three senior fashion and beauty editors, more used to limousines, were obliged to take the bus up Madison Avenue to Campbell's, getting off at every other corner en route for a fortifying tipple. When the illustrious trio of Sally Kirkland (*Life* magazine), Nancy White (*Harper's Bazaar*) and Eugenia Sheppard (the *Morning Post*) finally arrived at 8.00 p.m. to say goodbye, finding Patrick O'Higgins still there keeping solitary vigil, they were decidedly merry. 'I bet this is the only time Arden didn't mind Rubinstein being ahead of her,' was Sally Kirkland's *bon mot* as she took a nip of scotch from her friend Patrick's flask. She was quite right.

The funeral was held at Mount Olibet cemetery, Queens, where Helena was buried in the same grave as her second husband, Prince Artchil Gourielli-Tchkonia, her gravestone saying she had been born in 1870. Having spent a lifetime bickering with her family, she would have another cause to grumble that 'they always got things wrong' as her birth records in Krakow show she was born on 25 December, 1872. Her fabled black pearls were not buried with her. A relative was later observed at a party wearing the Yves St Laurent brocade suit. Patrick O'Higgins was not invited to the funeral.

Some eighteen months later, when Campbell's were preparing for the funeral of 'the other one', the director pursed his lips in irritation as bouquet after bouquet in myriad shades of pink, highlighted with just a touch of baby blue, arrived. He had always felt that the Williamsburg Room was more suited to cream, but what could he do? Nothing very much, as there were soon so many floral tributes that the room was in danger of overflowing. The heady scent was becoming sickly sweet, causing one beauty editor to remark, 'Too, too floral, dear, just like her fragrances.'

Florence Nightingale Graham, otherwise known to the world as Elizabeth Arden, died on 18 October 1966, following a stroke, at the Lenox Hill Hospital, where she had endowed a room for her favourite children's charity. 'That woman' hadn't had to wait too long for 'the other one' to join her in the afterlife. The same group of magazine editors, publishers, beauty editors, advertising executives — ever on the alert for a change of agency — and department store management filed past the body of Elizabeth Arden. This time, however, there was no family squabbling about costs. Elizabeth Arden was leaving life as she had lived it, in a glorious haze of pink-filled extravagance.

Even her burial clothes were pink. She was laid out in a ruffled chiffon confection, made for her by Oscar de la Renta, the last of the designers – her *boys* – who had worked for the fashion floor at Arden's Fifth Avenue flagship. Her beauty salon's famous creative director, the world-renowned Italian make-up artist Pablo, for whom *Vogue* had coined the phrase *visagiste*, had taken a full two days to compose himself after a diva-esque attack when he heard the news of her death. It wasn't grief that consumed Pablo, more the suggestion that he might apply her make-up, ensuring that Elizabeth Arden looked every inch the beauty queen even in death. The idea horrified him, particularly as her face had 'slipped' as a result of the stroke, and he offered every excuse to avoid the task, eventually consulting his lawyers to ensure he wasn't in breach of contract in refusing. He wasn't.

After an undignified scramble for a replacement, Miss Harris, who had worked for Elizabeth Arden for over four decades, volunteered for the task. She worked wonders on her late employer's delicate skin, shading her with pink blusher and her favourite baby-blue eye shadow, finishing with her signature pink lipstick. Elizabeth Arden had lived suffused in pink, firm in her belief it was the single most flattering colour, for her and her clients. Her flowers were pink, her tapestry cushions were pink, her cashmere car rugs were pink, her silk lampshades were lined with pink, her lightbulbs were pink, her racing colours were pink, her linen sheets – changed every day and ironed after her early evening rest – were pink. Most of her clothes were pink, along with several dozen of her hundreds of pairs of shoes. Her product packaging was pink, the ribbons on her jars were pink. Over fifty shades of Elizabeth Arden lipstick were pink and even her favourite diamond earrings, purchased with the profits from the lipsticks, were pink. When the couturier Elsa Schiaparelli called her signature fragrance 'Shocking' and packaged it in a pink flaçon, Miss Arden said, 'Hmm. It won't work. When people think pink, dear, they think Arden.'

Miss Arden's eulogy at her funeral service at St James Episcopal Church was read by the Rev. Dr Kinsolving, the eminent vicar to New York's elite. The same words would be repeated a few weeks later at the memorial service held at one of London's most socially esteemed places of worship, St George's Church in Hanover Square. 'We thank Thee for the spark of creative imagination in Thy servant Elizabeth, as for her ingenuity, energy and enterprise. We thank Thee for her keen perception and her love of beauty, of flowers and of animals, for her flair for life and vitality in living it, for her many friends and kindnesses along life's way.'

It was remarked by one of her friends that Elizabeth would have preferred her coffin to be pulled by her beloved horses on its final journey to Sleepy Hollow Cemetery, where she is buried in the Graham family plot, alongside one of her three sisters, her sister-in-law, a niece and a great nephew. The adjoining plot is empty – almost as though she were waiting for someone she had loved to join her – only they never arrived.

Being incapable of delegation and somehow believing she would always be there to run her company, Miss Arden left no clear line of succession, although rumour swept the trade that her sister Gladys de Maublanc would take over. Worse, there were no real financial means left to manage it. Elizabeth Arden, unlike her old rival, died with her financial affairs in a woefully tax-inefficient state. She left $8.5 million in thirty-seven individual bequests from an estate calculated to be valued at over $30 million. Financial reporters stated that she had probably *earned* more money than any woman in American history. Given the millions she had spent on her horses, and the fortune spent on her houses, the amount she left was impressive. However, Miss Arden did not have the benefits of a Foundation such as the one created by Madame in the 1950s. Instead, her lawyer, one Howard Carter, presided over a will which resulted in the American government reportedly claiming over $35 million in tax. One thing after another went seriously wrong, with the estate becoming embroiled in bitter litigation, resulting in great distress to her beneficiaries, many of whom waited for over six years to receive their inheritance and then only after everything Elizabeth had held dear — her horses, her homes and above all, her business, had been sold to pay taxes.

A year after her death, the contents of her beautiful mansion house in Kentucky were auctioned in Lexington. The sale, held over two days, attracted over 5000 viewers with standing room only when the bidding started. Household effects were displayed piled up on cloth-covered trestle tables and buyers, reported by the local media as 'being particularly well dressed', snapped them up. Memorabilia included such diverse items as engraved bookends and even the carriage lamps from outside her porch, to a net-trimmed pincushion and a monogrammed Louis Vuitton trunk, which went for $9 minus its key. Evening sales were held to dispose of her Louis XVI and Sheraton furniture, along with a group of fine French country armoires. All in all, the auction from her 'ole Kentucky home' fetched $45,000.

Not for Miss Arden her own named sale at Parke-Bernet in New York, although they did sell some of her belongings a few at a time. In November and December of 1968, over fifty pieces of her charming antique furniture were sold in a group auction, simply listed on the catalogue covers as being from 'the Estate of Mrs E. Graham — Miss Elizabeth Arden'. Amongst the decorative items were Regency chairs, a William and Mary table, papier mâché trays, marble-topped console tables and several pieces of fine Biedermeier. Included were two directoire painted 'Lits de Repos' and an 18th century Italian painted bed — in shades of pink. The furniture fetched just $10,000. According to Miss Arden's friend Emily Hutchison, the furniture was put up for sale by Patricia Young, Elizabeth's niece who, Emily says, 'needed the money'.

It was a sad end for the poor girl from Canada who had worked her way up from nothing to become, during her lifetime, the richest self-made woman in the world.

CHAPTER TWO
———

THE KRAKOW CREAM
1872–1896

CYNICS CALL THE BEAUTY business 'selling dreams' and no one sold them better than Helena Rubinstein. She was a natural born saleswoman with a rare gift for embellishment, obsessively glossing over her past – some shade here, some cover-up there – quite appropriate for a beauty queen, and when it came to telling her own story, the embellishment she added to the first three decades of her life took exaggeration to an art form.

It's doubtful even her vast, extended family knew the whole truth and, as most of them worked for her, it wasn't in their interests to discuss it. No one ever broke away from the party line. 'What Madame says goes' was the mantra from her press officers, and the stories got repeated so often that they became fact. As she got older and most of the people who had observed her early life or helped her achieve fame and fortune had died, she was alone with her version of her memories.

What Helena Rubinstein perhaps failed to realise is that the truth about her brilliant career, her unquestionable achievements, her phenomenal success, is all the more awesome when told without the omissions and exaggerations. It seems rather poignant that with all her fame and wealth, with all her abilities and assertiveness, she lived with her past life shrouded in a veil of fantasy.

Helena Rubinstein, or simply 'Madame' as she became universally known, was in her ninety-third year when she commissioned her memoirs in 1964. A few months later she was dead. Sales of her book, *My Life for Beauty*, were very successful. People wanted to read the story of the legend whose lipsticks they had worn. And what a story it was.

'I was born in Krakow, Poland,' she wrote, 'and we lived in a large old house near the Rynek Square where oil lamps were used to light the rooms. Mama was one of those fortunate women who, despite a child a year, manage to grow more beautiful. Her figure was slim and magnificent.'

A picture in the family archives of the rather earnest-looking and frankly plump Mrs Rubinstein, surrounded by four of her younger daughters, demonstrates Helena's talent for embellishment. The book went on to describe the story of a wondrous face cream, apparently introduced to the Rubinsteins by a family friend, the actress Modjeska, and made to a secret recipe by a Hungarian chemist, one Dr Jacob Lykusky. It was said to be made from 'essence of almonds and the bark of a certain evergreen tree from the Carpathian forests outside Krakow'. Careful searches have shown no trace of the Lykusky brothers, the chemists who supposedly made the original formula. To be fair, this does not mean they never existed. Polish archives have many gaps and in an area, and era, where few people could write, proven business records are rare.

Patrick O'Higgins, who worked for Madame as her executive assistant and de facto public relations director for the last fifteen years of her life, was one of the few people who saw what he believed was the original formula. He described the moment as follows:

> A few months before her death, while sifting through masses of old papers in the cellar of her Paris home, Madame handed me the original Valaze formula. 'Here!' she said, 'you might need this one day.' I took the tattered piece of paper. There was no mention of rare herbs, oriental almonds or the bark of an evergreen tree. The formula listed a variety of common raw materials such as ceresine wax, mineral oil and sesame . . . the only thing lacking was the instructions . . .

Among the treasures of many central-European families would have been their own recipe for face cream. This was usually mixed in a large pot on the kitchen stove and packed into jars for preserving in much the same way as they would have made pickles and chutney. Even today, in remote regions where Western skin-care products are only available on the black market, many families make their own, and herbal-based natural recipes are handed down from generation to generation. Poland in particular has a long tradition of herbal remedies – everything from horsetail extract for 'maintaining elasticity of the skin' to senna leaf and rosehip tea, which combined are apparently a whizz for improving metabolism. Polish pharmacies of the time would have recommended chestnut ointment for bruises and circulation, pine-tar for eczema, comfrey for burns and calendula for general healing. Searching in a herbal record of that time, you can find that calendula, along with buckthorn fruit and borage amongst other herbs suggested for skin care, are all referred to as Lekarski . . . not too far away from Lykusky . . .

Apart from today's obvious pollutants such as smoking or the lingering effects of fuel emissions, the two most lethal things for the delicate balance of the fine layers of skin are sunburn and excessive cold. Generations of women from the Carpathian to the Caucasus Mountains were aware of this. It is baking hot in the summer and bitterly cold in the winter and the blistering winds cause thread veins in the cheeks. They soon worked out that their skin needed protecting from both extremes, as well as needing to be moisturised. Cream would be used morning and night. Women throughout Eastern Europe, alongside pharmacists and chemists from that area, the most skilled acknowledged to be Hungarian and Viennese, developed considerable expertise in making moisturising face creams.

The origins of moisturiser however date centuries earlier, specifically to the skill of Greek physician Galen, who worked in Rome at the court of Emperor Marcus Aurelius in AD 160. Galen was fascinated by skin care and, knowing skin craved moisture, experimented to perfect a cream that would provide it. He melted olive oil with beeswax to make a smooth paste and, when it had cooled, added rose water. The water stayed in the emulsion and the finished cream had a cooling effect on the skin thus, *voilà*, cold cream was born. Even with all the technology available today, experts admit that skin care is not an exact science. However, water is the essential ingredient if we are to keep our skin moist. Drinking it helps, and using a water-based cream helps even more, as the cream works to contain the moisture and ensure it is absorbed by the skin. The formula developed by Galen is still the base of most creams used today, the principal ingredient of which is always . . . water.

If the cream Helena marketed so assiduously was more beneficial than most, it was by virtue of the pine bark. The plant chemical extracted from pine bark – known as a *flavonoid* – is a powerful antioxidant, said to be fifty times more powerful than vitamin E and twenty times more effective than vitamin C. More significantly, in relation to use in a face cream, the product is water-soluble. *Flavonoids* work to repair connective tissue and boost the immune system – thus to slow the ageing process visible in the face by 'plumping out' collagen and improving the overall appearance of the skin. Certainly everyone who met the Rubinstein sisters is agreed on one thing – they all had the most beautiful skin.

Madame's enthusiasm for the story that she and her sisters shared the same beauty regime as the famous Modjeska, shone out in her memoirs. 'My mother told us women influence the world through love. This cream will make you beautiful and to be beautiful is to be a woman, she would say to each of us girls in turn.' One can visualise the eight girls, lined up in a row before bedtime, faces upturned for their dollop of cream, the powerful romance of which was their very own bedtime story.

Krakow has a long theatrical tradition and the legendary Modjeska was born there in 1840. She was a theatrical superstar of great beauty and, like all actresses, would have known how to apply cosmetics and take care of one of her greatest assets – her fabled complexion. It is hard to imagine Modjeska, however, as one of the Rubinstein family inner circle of friends, as their daily life was totally removed from Krakow's sophisticated and intellectual theatre world. At any event, by 1870, the actress was living in America, where, as late as the 1930s, there were still cinemas named The Modjeska. When Helena Rubinstein first met Modjeska years later, she was famous herself, scribbling a memory of it in her private notebook. 'I met Sarah Bernhardt and Modjeska. I knew them both – the impression they left on me I never forgot.' She met them, however, through her work – once apparently creating a custom-made hand cream for Sarah Bernhardt using no less than three pounds of butter – rather than through family connections.

By 1964, Helena Rubinstein had already put her name to three books on the beauty business called respectively, *The Art of Feminine Beauty*, 1930, *This Way for Beauty*, 1936, and *Food for Beauty*, 1938. The greatest omission in the latter was any form of credit to the brilliant work of nutritionist Gaylord Hauser, who had produced a series of outstanding books covering the same topic and who preached it at meetings throughout the US, often attended by the celebrity clients who swore by his diet and holistic health advice. Four years before Helena produced her missive about healthy food, Gaylord Hauser had created the light-diet menus for Elizabeth Arden's celebrated health spa, Maine Chance. Madame Rubinstein had a great affection for visiting spas: 'I was not any novice to health resorts,' she said. 'I think I have at one time or another, during my search for better advice to women, visited every spa, every spring, every sanatorium and cure in Europe and America. Whenever I heard of a new way to health and youthful vitality, I went to its source.'

Indeed, there were famous spas near Krakow, in particular Krynica, in the Carpathian Mountains, about 120 kms from the city, where treatments involved water from the hills cascading through a base of pine needles, which is beneficial for pain, joint-stiffness and circulation. Sadly, however much she may have wanted to check out the attractions of Arden's Maine Chance, it was off the list. Helena Rubinstein couldn't – wouldn't – be seen at a venture owned by Elizabeth Arden. She confined herself to reading Gaylord Hauser's books, referring to them as 'her Bibles', where she would have found Hauser's recipe for 'Prune Whip' created for Maine Chance in 1934 and dedicated to Miss Arden: 'Mix one-and-a-half cups pitted and chopped prunes with quarter cup black-strap molasses and honey, one tablespoon lemon juice, half teaspoon lemon rind and a pinch of vegetable salt. Fold in two egg whites beaten stiff. Chill.'

When Hauser wasn't writing his newspaper column or pushing his own make of vegetable juice extractor, he was advising his private clients such as Greta Garbo, Elsie de Wolfe, Lady Diana Cooper and the Duchess of Windsor, devising menus to keep them 'young, fit and thin'. The Duchess of Windsor in particular was a great Hauser fan. 'He keeps me slim,' she once said. This, coming from a woman who famously said, 'You can never be too rich or too thin', was a powerful endorsement. Rubinstein was rich but she certainly wasn't thin. A tiny, stocky woman, she struggled with her weight all her life and tried every known scheme to lose pounds. Sadly, dieting didn't come easily to someone with a weakness for Polish sausage and fried chicken.

Helena Rubinstein might not have practised what she preached, but what *Food for Beauty* shows is her gift of adapting the trend of the moment to suit her empire; of taking an idea already in the public arena and putting her exclusive 'Rubinstein spin' on it. Whether she was creating her own products, adapting concepts put to her by her network of advisers, or buying in an existing item and simply doing it better than the competition, she promoted that item aggressively and with such skill that inevitably her eager public would become devotees.

Given the myths surrounding her past, the notes about Madame on the back cover of *Food for Beauty* come as no surprise. 'Helena Rubinstein was born in Krakow of a long line of medical doctors,' the text burbles. 'In her teens, she studied medicine but afterwards specialised in chemistry. After studying in Vienna she went to visit Melbourne, Australia, where her dynamic personality and brilliant mind made her a popular figure in the social life centred around Government House.' People who knew Madame would have been amused – and bemused – when they read this. She loathed cocktail parties, didn't do small talk and was painfully shy in social situations, rarely uttering a word. She did indeed have a brilliant mind but it was mainly applied to her business.

Madame's earlier book, *The Art of Feminine Beauty*, had a similar introduction where she said:

It was in Krakow that I was born, the first child of my well-to-do parents. Both my mother's and my father's families were esteemed in the community, for they were enterprising, cultivated and aware of their own worth. My two grandfathers had extensive mining and banking interests in Poland and my father was in the exporting business. I spent my childhood and youth in the peaceful atmosphere of a large old house with rooms containing the collections of a father who had a passion for bibelots, antiques and books . . . After my courses at the Gymnasium [the fee-paying, private school] were ended, I prepared to enter the university. I wanted to be a doctor, but at my very first lesson in an operating room I quietly fainted at the sight of blood. I was not intended to be a doctor.

At the height of her fame, Madame revelled in the epithet the Beauty Scientist. She adored the status that the word scientist bestowed. It went well with the legend she had studied medicine at university in Krakow, along with training 'under the best specialists in Europe'. Madame's aura of a clinical background was the cornerstone of her early success. She had a doctor on the payroll during the launch period of her early salons in Paris, London and New York, and invariably wore a white doctor's coat for the pictures taken in her laboratories. Madame's scientific knowledge, however, wasn't obtained at Krakow's university, where Copernicus had studied and lectured. She couldn't have gone there for the simple reason their medical school did not then enrol women. Another hindrance would have been that students had to be fluent in not just Polish, but German and French, not to mention able to read Latin. Helena Rubinstein's linguistic abilities, or lack of them, are well known. She spoke four or five languages, most of them in a strange accent described as 'a mix of Australian twang and mid-European guttural'. In Krakow she would have spoken Polish, and Yiddish, and possibly a little German. English and French came a lot later. When Helena was angry, which was a regular occurrence, she used to muddle her grammar, shouting in a mixture of two, sometimes three languages at once. She had a rather endearing way of confusing words, describing the benefits of colonic irrigation, for example, by saying: 'very good for the skin those colonials'.

What is true is that Helena Rubinstein was born in Krakow, the renaissance gem of a city, where in the fourteenth century, the enlightened King Kazimierz III created Europe's most architecturally and culturally significant Jewish quarter outside of Venice. It was Poland's 'Golden Century' of religious tolerance towards its Jewish population and Kazimierz was a haven for Jewish refugees from the whole of central Europe. Poland's turbulent history reached a climax in 1815 following the Congress of Vienna, with much of the country coming under control of Tsar Alexander I of Russia. The Polish people rebelled – unsuccessfully – against Russian rule in 1830, against the Austrians in 1846 and against the Russians again in 1863. Galicia, the part of Poland including Krakow, was annexed yet again, becoming part of the Austro-Hungarian empire. Life for the Jewish population was becoming increasingly hard, and by the 1870s, many of Galicia's Jews moved on in the hope of making their fortune overseas. Amongst them were Bernhard, John and Louis Silberfeld, who left for Australia. Their sister, Gitel, stayed behind in Krakow, where she had married Hertzel Naftaly Rubinstein, giving birth to their first child in their small apartment on the second floor at 14, ul. Szeroka, overlooking the cobbled square in Kazimierz. If Gitel Rubinstein was disappointed her firstborn was not a son, she needn't have been. Her daughter, named Chaja, would become one of the most successful business tycoons of the twentieth century.

Gitel Rubinstein, always called Gusta, fulfilled her destiny of being a good wife and mother by producing a large family. She had twelve children, moving home as the family grew. Only eight of her children were to survive. Her two precious sons, Aaron and Abraham, both died young, leaving her firstborn daughter as the son her parents never had – one reason, perhaps, why Chaja would develop into such a driven personality. Her goal, it seems, was to provide for her entire family.

The Krakow city census of 1890 records that Naftaly Hertzel Rubinstein, born in Dukla, a small town some 200 kms from Krakow, was a 'dealer in kerosene' with a shop at 13 Jozefa Street, and that he had at that time, as well as eight living children, a servant. The lamps may have burned bright in the Rubinstein household, filled as they were with kerosene, but their house most certainly did not 'overlook the Rynek Square'. One of the largest squares in medieval Europe, the Rynek is a magnificent place. The *Sukiennice* or Cloth Hall was originally designed in the fourteenth century as a centre for the burgeoning textile trade and, following a fire, was rebuilt in renaissance style in the nineteenth century. For hundreds of years the Hall's ground-floor walkways have been flanked by booths selling semi-precious jewels, amber, glass, dolls, laces and linens. Even today, in amongst the gaudy offerings of the tourist trade, some of Europe's most magnificent amber can be found.

For young Chaja, tired of helping to care for seven siblings, her greatest treat and escape would have been to make the ten-minute journey from Kazimierz to the Rynek, where Krakow's wealthy residents would shop and sit at pavement cafés. Helena Rubinstein's lifelong passion was collecting jewellery, dolls, lace and glass. Her famous, and sometimes faux, jewels became part of her personality. She described them as 'her armour' and was convinced her signature ropes of cabochon rubies and her famous black and white pearls helped her win business battles. They certainly signalled she was rich, and in business that's half the battle. There could be no better influence on a young girl who loved beauty than visiting Krakow's Cloth Hall.

Helena was particularly fond of upgrading details on her family background. This habit of 'glossing and gilding' seems to be common amongst successful Jewish immigrants from central Europe who have a fondness for romancing their past. Some say it is a particularly Galician trait: 'You must remember,' says Richard Cooper, a Jewish genealogist in England, 'that people from Galicia in particular felt rootless and stateless. Poland had changed hands as it were so many times they didn't know where they came from. It gave them comfort to invent it.' Another school of thought is that selective amnesia as to whether forebears came from Hungary, Romania, Austria, Galicia, Lithuania or Russia is based on snobbery, with Vienna coming top of the list.

The Rubinstein family tree, however, can be firmly traced back to Kazimierz. Gitel Rubinstein was one of the many daughters of Rabbi Sale Silberfeld and his wife Rwfka. Mr Silberfeld's occupation is variously described in census records as 'moneylender', 'banker' and 'speculator'. He was clearly quite a character and it's a fair assumption his brightest grand-daughter was a chip off the old block. Gusta and Herz Rubinstein seem to have lived a quiet and dignified life, clearly to the frustration of their ambi-tious eldest daughter who yearned for more excitement. All the Rubinstein girls attended the local Jewish school in Kazimierz (contrary to her memoir, not even Helena made it to the local Gymnasium) and would have stayed there until the age of fifteen or sixteen.

The young Chaja learned to pack her belongings, a skill useful for a woman who was to own six houses and circumnavigate the world at least four times, due to the endless relocation to larger apartments more suited to the expanding family. From their original flat at 14 ul. Szeroka they moved to Bozega Ciala 25 when Helena was about six years old, then back to ul. Szeroka, this time to number 18; to 2 ul. Wazka and then to an apart-ment at 2 ul. Bartosza, one of the largest of their homes. All were within walking distance of Herz Rubinstein's shop in ul. Josefa. Although described as a kerosene dealer, he may well have expanded his business into a general hardware store. Whether he was also a food-broker as claimed by Helena, who writes about him selling eggs, isn't accurately listed, but she seems to have honed her emerging business skills in helping with the shop's accounts.

When Chaja was in her teens, there was a serious argument in the family. The trigger for the explosion is shrouded in mystery, but reported to have been because she fell in love, to the extent that she sold some family belong-ings, presumably to raise money in order to elope. She described her beau as a student at the university, called Stanislaw, 'who had blue-black hair and strikingly blue eyes'. Her parents were violently opposed. Girls in the com-munity were expected to marry a 'suitable' husband, often a relative, and usually fulfilled parental expectations when they were about seventeen. Chaja's beau may well have been a student, which is perhaps why she would cling to her romantic story of meeting him at university, but whoever he was, and whatever he did (and one can assume he wasn't Jewish), the ensu-ing battle would have been fierce. Girls did not break away from family traditions easily in conservative Krakow.

It's said at this point her father arranged a marriage with a much older man whom he felt would tame his wayward daughter, but Chaja refused the match. The rift between the young, unusually spirited girl fighting against her orthodox family was so bad that according to family sources, she was ordered out of her parents' home altogether and left to live locally with her aunt, Rosalie Silberfeld Beckmann. Chaja Rubinstein would never be reconciled with her parents.

There is a small hospital in Kazimierz which treats the local community to this day. In 1888 or thereabouts, it is quite possible that Chaja, searching for a way to earn her living with a job considered suitable for a girl, enrolled there to study nursing. This would be a logical explanation for her admission of an early phobia to blood. She would have been more likely to have seen blood at the hospital as a nurse than in her 'first year at medical school', where students of the time rarely saw a live patient.

There has always been speculation about Helena Rubinstein's time in Australia, particularly as she claimed to be nineteen when she left Krakow, which would have dated her journey as 1891. This means a twelve-year gap has to be accounted for between her arrival in Australia and the opening of her first beauty salon in Melbourne in 1903. The truth is that she did not leave Europe until the summer of 1896. She was twenty-four years old, nudging twenty-five, when she boarded the German ship, the *Prince Regent Luitpold*, at Genoa – not Hamburg as she always claimed – bound for Melbourne. She travelled saloon class and, true to form, could not resist playing fast and loose with the passenger list details, putting her age down as twenty. She travelled alone, and under occupation entered 'tourist'. She entered her name as 'Helena Juliet Rubinstein'. Chaja is Hebrew for Helena, but quite where Juliet came from, other than her romantic fantasies of doomed love, isn't known. The saloon-class fare at that time would have cost about £32 for a single ticket (over £2,000 in today's terms) and whilst there might be a mystery as to how she could have afforded it, not to mention why she left from Genoa instead of the more usual German ports of Bremen or Hamburg, there is no mystery as to why she went.

In the 'official' version of her life story, Helena Rubinstein wrote: 'Since I was a child, it had been one of my dreams to go to Australia. My uncles had settled there and my imagination had been fed on letters from this remote land. My relatives, who lived on a large ranch near Coleraine, were duly notified of my intention and when I arrived in Australia, I found a hearty welcome. The newness of the country stimulated me.' In her desire, or more likely necessity, to leave Eastern Europe, Australia was the natural haven for Helena. She would later write: 'Uncle Louis had emigrated to Australia after his wife, a lovely Polish girl, had died giving birth to a daughter. The child Eva had been left with us until her teens and we two had become close. When she rejoined her father in Australia, she wrote to me often. I felt that life in that part of the world sounded much more promising than in Krakow.'

Helena had difficulty remembering names. She had her own code to identify the hundreds of people who worked for her. For example, of her six stockbrokers in New York, her favourites were 'the broker with the nice wife' and 'the deaf one'. Her two accountants were 'the tall one' and 'the short one with glasses'. Friends, designers and rivals came in for the same treatment. 'The polite one who makes the nice shoes and gives me a discount' was the celebrated Roger Vivier in Paris. That trait worsened as she got older, so it is perhaps not unsurprising that she muddled the names of her three uncles in Australia, and which of them had fathered her cousin Eva.

Eva had been born in Krakow in 1867. Some three years later, her widower father Bernhard Silberfeld (not Louis, who was unmarried and childless) sailed to Melbourne, leaving his young daughter with one of his sisters. Bernhard sent for Eva some years later and she settled in Australia, marrying Louis Levy. Eva and Louis had three children: Reginald (born in 1890), Frederick (1891) and Theodore (1893). Baby Theodore was lucky to be born at all. The divorce petition filed by Eva against her husband in 1895 makes horrific reading. He was a violent, cruel and abusive drunk who tried to kill his wife twice, threatening to cut her throat, and had beaten her nearly senseless when she was pregnant with her third baby. The petition shows how desperate Eva must have been. Her husband had sold everything they owned to buy drink and she describes the loss of her 'linen, plate, furniture, clothes, silver and jewellery' with great dignity.

Eva's uncle, John Silberfeld, was a jeweller, and her husband, on the rare occasions he was sober, worked for him as a travelling salesman, more often than not pawning his samples. In time, Louis Levy was committed to an insane asylum and when released, simply disappeared. Divorce, particularly orthodox Jewish divorce, was complex in those days, but his wife found the courage to proceed, claiming custody of their children. When her cousin and childhood friend agreed to come out to help her look after the children, it would have given Eva a chance to recover her health. It's no surprise Helena kept this secret. When selling glamour, public perception is all that matters. She would not want the world to know she had a cousin whose husband was a wife-beating drunk.

By the time of her sailing, Helena had moved to Vienna to live with another aunt, Helena Silberfeld Splitter. Mr Splitter and his three brothers were furriers and, judging by an imposing photograph of Helena taken in 1893, swathed in astrakhan, this is where she developed her lifelong affection for furs. We can presume she spent two or three years in Vienna, no doubt helping out at her Aunt Helena's house and almost certainly working in her uncle's business. Any emergent interest she may have had in the subject of skin care would have flourished in Vienna, then the capital of advanced dermatology skills. Helena would later open a factory in Vienna and had several specialist suppliers there, including one woman referred to as 'the mascara countess'. This mysterious and well paid expert was reputed to hold the formula for 'the best mascara in the world' which would become one of the key items on the Rubinstein line.

Whilst extended, yet close, Jewish families such as the Rubinsteins, Silberfelds and Splitters were always ready to absorb a needy relative into their homes, they would also have had good reason to worry about Chaja, who, aged twenty-four, was not yet married. The Splitter brothers moved to Belgium to develop their fur business at around this time, so a cry for help from Cousin Eva in Australia would have been a Godsend for her. About to become homeless, with no job, estranged from her parents, clearly ready for an adventure, suddenly Australia was the solution to all her problems. We can imagine her spontaneously boarding the boat, possibly as a nanny/companion to a travelling family, or perhaps the comfortably off Splitters funded her travel. After all, it was also *their* niece in Australia who was in trouble. As Helena prepared to leave, the Silberfeld women may well have sighed with relief – at least Helena might find a husband in Australia.

CHAPTER THREE

THE BEAUTY WIZARD OF OZ
Australia 1896–1905

Helena Rubinstein would have the world believe she went to Australia to enjoy life with wealthy relatives living in comfort on a ranch, and to heal the wounds of a broken romance. She claims she took the prettiest clothes she possessed, a parasol against the sun, and twelve pots of her mother's face cream – which became the foundation of her fortune.

Peeling away the layers of Rubinstein's early life in Poland is hard enough; discovering the truth about her life in Australia is harder still. She rarely talked about it. Only the remotest of clues as to how unhappy she was there ever surfaced, and never in the stories offered to the many journalists who interviewed her in Melbourne and Sydney in the early 1900s. To them, she painted a glowing picture of her first, easy steps to stardom. Helena manipulated the media brilliantly and they lapped it up. Given the distance between Australia and Europe no women's editor was going to bother checking the story. Helena Rubinstein was their very own heroine, the 'young woman who made good in Australia', and their glowing copy endorsed every step she took.

She was quite shameless in her inventions, taking several years off her age, adding several rooms to her houses, fabricating her scientific qualifications and painting a better, more imposing picture of her family background. Yet although she made her first fortune down under and received a glowing press, it is clear that she did not like her life in Australia. Or rather, she didn't like her life in Coleraine, which is perhaps different.

In 1896, the voyage from Genoa to Melbourne took from fifty to sixty days, sometimes as long as eighty, depending on stopovers. By all accounts, Helena adored the journey, the first of hundreds she would make, revelling in the time spent cocooned in the luxury of ocean-going liners. She would say later that her many weeks spent commuting by ship were 'my only real holidays'. The *Prince Luitpold* seems to have been a modest ship, carrying 53 passengers in saloon class and 152 in steerage, built nowhere near to the grand scale of the famous liners of the era, but German ships had a reputation for being luxurious and she would have been very comfortable. Saloon class, whilst not as hedonistic as First, still meant silver service, dressing for dinner, music and dancing and deck entertainment like tennis and quoits. To the sharp-eyed Helena, it was also an opportunity to observe comparatively wealthy middle-class women at leisure. Exercise and beauty treatments were part of that experience, with ships of the period having a barber's, a beauty parlour and often a fully fitted gymnasium. Better still, there was the excitement of the stopovers, which on this route meant Naples, Alexandria, Aden, Bombay or Calcutta, Colombo and on to Perth, Adelaide and Melbourne en route to Sydney.

The stopovers will have had a profound impact on Helena. Beauty treatments having been part of Egypt and India's culture for thousands of years, experts were always on hand to pamper travellers, offering threading — using fine cotton to whisk off facial hair and pluck eyebrows — and aromatherapy massage with essential oils, like lotus. The lotus flower, part of the water lily family, is widely used in Egypt and India, the ancients having admired the effect of well-being and sexual relaxation it gives. Today, lotus is being developed as a potential cure for Alzheimers, and for impotence, and, like the gingko biloba plant, it is a free-radical scavenger, boosting the immune system. In later years, one of Rubinstein's favourite ingredients in both fragrance and treatment creams would be the water lily.

Helena will have seen kohl used for eye make-up, and henna for dyeing and skin-painting, Indian women in particular using it to colour their cheeks as well as dyeing their palms and soles. Best of all she would have found the most sensual, fragrant perfumes, sold by the 'ittar wallahs' who met every boat, offering their 'fayas', a flat, cotton bud impregnated with a glorious smell which women used in their wardrobes and lingerie drawers — and in steamer trunks on board the liners — to perfume their clothes and keep out moths. She would almost certainly have had an ayurvedic massage, an Indian treatment said to be more than 5000 years old and described by devotees as 'the science of life and longevity', and have been offered scalp massages with essential oils to boost circulation. Madame, perhaps influenced by ayurvedic methods, developed a lifelong affection for combining honey and mint in treatments, a known ayurvedic remedy. For a young woman interested in skin care, not to mention jewellery, India in particular would have been very near to heaven on earth.

Helena's early love of jewellery was almost certainly honed into a passion by her visits to India and Ceylon and she subsequently bought a copious amount of Indian jewellery. Lack of funds on her first trip meant she could only stare at the jewellery sellers, who laid out their pearls, with special sieves for grading their size, along with precious and semi-precious stones, in heaps on their red-cloth-covered folding tables. On later voyages, Helena bought sapphires and other stones in Colombo, probably from Louis Seigal, known as 'the jewel master of the quayside', who specialised in sapphires and star sapphires. She also bought uncut stones, along with her favourite cabochons, not to mention some quite important jewellery in India where, in the early 1900s, cabochon ruby beads could be bought for around $3 a piece.

Even without the means to buy jewels on her first trip to Australia, the journey gave her something much more valuable – the experience of world travel. She came back down to earth rather abruptly, however, as she reached the final part of her journey, in Coleraine. Helena's final destination was over two hundred miles from Melbourne, and although Coleraine was linked by rail, the usual passenger transport to what Australians considered 'local towns' was by coach and horses. She found herself in a typical, small, pioneering outback town. The Aborigines called the land around Bryant Creek, which flows through Coleraine, Koroit, which means 'land of ferns', and for miles and miles around all that grew was – ferns.

In 1896, Coleraine boasted a postal service, a weekly newspaper called the *Albion* and amongst the other facilities offered to the 2000 or so inhabitants were a telephone line, a money order office and several general goods stores, including the one owned and run by her uncle Bernhard, operating out of modest, clapperboard premises at 107 Whyte Street, which would be Helena's home for the next three years. Coleraine had four bootmakers, four store-keepers, two saddlers, a livery stables, a draper and a blacksmith. Miss Lily Nickoll was the local dressmaker and one John McLeod was the tailor. There was a butter factory, two bakers and an auctioneer. Mrs Crouch and her niece Miss Arrovoye ran the local private school and there were three hotels, presumably kept busy by travelling salesmen. Interestingly, there was a jewellers, no doubt also kept busy with the thriving trade in wedding rings as local farmers secured a bride to run the homestead and cook for their herders.

There were two butchers, and it helped if you liked mutton stew or roast lamb, as Coleraine and its neighbouring outpost Merino, some twelve miles away, where Louis Silberfeld, Bernhard's brother, owned the grocery store, were home to thousands upon thousands of sheep. A more dramatic contrast to the glamorous, bustling ports seen on her voyage to Australia, or to sophisticated Vienna, or even to Krakow (which although it might have seemed restrictive to Helena, still boasted wide boulevards, cafés, shops and an artistic community), could not be imagined.

Helena spent three miserable years in Coleraine. Her first challenge was to learn English so, suppressing her embarrassment, she enrolled at Miss Crouch's school, bravely slipping into English classes to join students at least a decade younger than herself. Her uncle's store, where she had to work before and after class, was a general goods emporium, covering local needs from clothing (advertising 'gents clothes made to measure at the shortest notice') to castor oil. Such stores opened at around 6.00 a.m. to take in deliveries and closed at around eight or nine at night. As her uncle's store fronted their living quarters, there would have been little private time. It was Helena's training in the hard school of retailing and she learnt well. In the beginning, Helena would have shared kitchen and child-care duties with Eva. A year later, however, Eva returned to Melbourne, leaving Helena alone with her uncles and thus expected to run the kitchen herself – no easy task for someone who couldn't cook.

She couldn't ride either, a disaster in Coleraine, where long journeys to visit friends were by necessity made on horseback, and the prime source of entertainment was the racetrack where the Great Western Steeplechase was run. There is one rare picture taken in Australia, of Helena on a horse, looking decidedly uncomfortable. Though her memoirs claim that 'I became a skilled rider and there was no phase of horsemanship I did not master', her family denied this, especially her sister Ceska, who was adamant that 'Helena loathed horses and was frightened of them.' Ceska would have known, as she joined Helena in 1905 to work for her in Melbourne. It's doubtful Coleraine was their favourite weekend treat – the Hamptons it wasn't – and the painful memories of Helena's time there meant she grumbled constantly to Ceska about everything she loathed most, including horses.

Even more than horses, Helena loathed the sun. She was never comfortable in the heat, preferring in later years to take her holidays, such as they were, at a retreat in the Swiss mountains or on the Italian lakes. Her complexion, which was quite beautiful, was her greatest asset and taking a long, hard look at the sun-dried, wrinkled faces of the women in the outback, she determined to protect her own, wearing big hats to shield her face. If she did take a parasol with her, it's doubtful she could ever have used it. In Coleraine, anything other than the simplest hat would have been thought a worthless affectation. If a young woman had carried a parasol, she would have been laughed out of town. Nevertheless, Helena would be relentlessly anti-sun all her life and became one of the first manufacturers to identify sunblock as an essential for skin care and protection against burn.

Legend *à la* Rubinstein has it that the women in Coleraine, all of whom admired Helena's complexion, urged her to import her mother's cream so that they could buy it. 'My own skin was soft and fresh and remained so even in that terrible climate,' Helena would later write. 'First one woman was asking to use it and then another and I wrote home asking that supplies be sent to me by the first boat.' She claims to have sold her cream from her uncle's store, which he objected to, causing friction between them.

That she argued with her uncle is indisputable. A local story from the time tells how she shocked her schoolteacher by coming in one day and asking: 'What's a bugger? My uncle calls me that.' It also seems that one or other of her uncles took an unhealthy shine to the attractive, buxom, shy and rather lonely Helena, resulting in fierce arguments and the necessity, once again, for her to flee her home. She claims she went to work for the local pharmacist, Mr Henderson, who taught her about mixing medicines and grinding powders, and that she sold her cream from his pharmacy with his blessing. Not only did she have no cream to sell, the business directory of the time has no record of a Mr Henderson. Mr John P. Nicholas was the chemist in the early 1890s and by 1899 it was Mr F. Spooner. Coleraine's residents had the services of a doctor, Alexander MacDonald, and a hairdresser, Thomas Spargo. Helena always wore her long black hair slicked back into a chignon, but it's unlikely she ever tried out the skills of Mr Spargo, as by 1899 she had fled, and never went back.

Whether it was Dr MacDonald, or the local pharmacist, regardless of name, who inspired Helena to develop her 'great idea' we will never know, but it was certainly instigated, if not fulfilled, in Coleraine. The key to unlock Helena's fortune was all around her. Sheep. Or to be more precise, lanolin.

One of the oldest known base ingredients for skin cream is lanolin, the natural oil sheep produce to protect their skin and which secretes into their wool. Merino sheep have very long curly wool and accumulate so much lanolin that it is often half the weight of their fleece after shearing. Lanolin, washed from the fleeces, is purified for cosmetic use and is one of the simplest, cheapest and most effective softeners in existence. By a happy fluke, Helena's travels had taken her to where she found her very own 'golden fleece', just a few miles from Merino.

It seems certain that Helena did arrive in Australia with a pot of nourishing skin cream. It's also clear her wonderful complexion was much admired and that she saw potential in making a similar product to sell to the dry-skinned local ladies. Coleraine gave her the inspiration – although she never had product to sell when living there – and Merino gave her the base ingredient. The only thing she lacked was the money to develop her idea.

Cynicism abounds in the beauty business. A plastic surgeon, once a cosmetics consultant for Helena Rubinstein Inc in New York, was unimpressed with the story of the 'Krakow cream'. He said, 'She invented that cream from Poland . . . nearly every so-called exotic person comes around with some strange family formula that was given to them by their old grandfather from Transylvania . . . Believe me this gal never knew *anything* in Poland. All she knew was how to make money and told a good story about it. She was a fascinating character. She could just as well have been in the machine tools business, or any other business and she'd have been a great success.'

Without capital or stock, Helena could not have sold cream in Coleraine. The journey for freight would take at least two months, plus the time involved in writing back home, plus clearing the goods through Melbourne's quite aggressive customs then shipping it to Coleraine; any repeat orders would have taken a long time to arrive, even if she could have afforded to send for it. To develop her big idea, Helena had to move to Melbourne. In order to do that, she needed a backer. Coleraine offered few investment opportunities, but she tried. Her first approach was to a teacher. Professor John Poynter of Melbourne University, who wrote the entry for Madame in Australia's *Dictionary of Biography*, grew up in Coleraine and tells a story of Helena's early entrepreneurial vision. 'The girl who assisted Miss Crouch at the Coleraine school was my step-grandmother,' he explains. 'She said that Helena suggested that she go to Melbourne with her and start a beauty salon. My step-grandmother turned the offer down. She didn't think there was any money to be made in face cream.' Turning down a partnership in Helena Rubinstein's business wasn't the brightest decision Professor Poynter's step-grandmother ever took, but Helena managed without her.

Once more, Helena was on the move. She didn't have too many choices. She could have stayed in Coleraine, where there would have been no shortage of suitors, but Helena was not cut out to be a farmer's wife. Her relationship with her uncles was frayed. She was almost certainly frightened. So she did what all good Australians do – she went walkabout.

At twenty-seven, her prospects were bleak, but the indomitable Helena was not put off. In her first version of her departure from Coleraine, written in the 1930s, she claims she went to Brisbane: 'I was invited to visit a friend whose husband occupied a political position on the staff of Lord Lamington, Governor of Queensland.' By the time her final memoir was published in 1965, she had confused the location. 'I had a good friend in Melbourne, a young Englishwoman I had met on the boat coming out to Australia, who was the wife of the Governor's ADC. She invited me to stay with her and I suggested I teach her two children German whilst I was her guest.'

As Helena was in her nineties when she oversaw this second version, and age may dim fact, not to mention her own fiction, it's no surprise she confused the Governor of Melbourne – at that time the Earl of Hopetoun – and the Governor of the entirely separate state of Queensland, thousands of miles away, Lord Lamington.

There is a long-held belief in Australia that when she fled Coleraine, she went first to Meltham, the home of the Fairbairn family, as nanny to their children. If she did work for the entertaining, ebullient Stephen Fairbairn, it would have been a rare treat after the rigours of the Whyte Street store. When the Royal Historical Society of Victoria published a feature on the 4500-acre homestead of Meltham in their magazine in the early 1950s, it said Steve Fairbairn's young sons were brought up there and their governess was the 'now celebrated cosmetics tycoon, Helena Rubinstein'. One of the best-known Anglo-Australian families, the Fairbairns owned estates adjacent to the famous 'Eton of Australia', Geelong Grammar School, where the Fairbairn sons were educated and whose most illustrious old boy is HRH The Prince of Wales. Meltham would have afforded Helena her first glimpse of the British upper classes at play, and Steve Fairbairn played hard.

He was a celebrated rowing coach, international oarsman, Cambridge rowing Blue and a legend at Henley. Fairbairn's wife Ellen Sharwood came from Aramac, about 750 miles from Toowoomba in Queensland. In Australian travel terms, 750 miles is 'just down the road' and the Sharwoods and Fairbairns would have had many friends in both Brisbane and Toowoomba, not to mention Melbourne, the nearest city to Meltham and Coleraine.

The 'Lamington legend' has been repeated often, adding credence to Helena's being welcome at Government House, where she was reputed to have learned her social skills. A book published shortly after she died, written with the full collaboration of her surviving son, niece and nephew said: 'Helena Rubinstein became governess to the family of Lord Lamington, Governor of Queensland, teaching their children French and German, languages she had learned in the Gymnasium in Krakow.' As the Lamington children, Victor and Griselle, were aged three years and six months old respectively in 1899, it seems unlikely they needed to learn German, even if Queen Victoria *was* their godmother. At any event, Helena didn't yet speak French and her German, although improved by her stay in Vienna, was nowhere near good enough for her to be considered a Fräulein, the traditional governess of British upper-class children of the day. It's obvious Madame's family were carrying on the family myths – or that they knew nothing about her early years in Australia.

The patrician Lord Lamington, who championed the cause of Aboriginal tribes in respect of the loss of their settlements, was very popular in Australia. The Lamington family nurse was the long-serving Miss Fanny Rod, and the children didn't have the benefit of a Fräulein until they moved to India, where their father became Governor of Bombay late in 1901. Lamington's friend and colleague, Lord Hopetoun, was close to the Fairbairn family, often staying at Meltham, as did the Lamington family. The observation of these 'great and good' aristocrats would have had a profound impact on Helena, who was able to interact with women of all backgrounds, the subject of beauty care being one that breaks down social barriers.

When, in 1907, Helena Rubinstein took out Australian citizenship, she was obliged to inform the authorities where she had been living since entering Australia. She declared she had arrived in 1897 (adjusted by the immigration officer in the margin back to 1896), that she had lived in

Coleraine for three years, in Toowoomba, Queensland for one year and in Melbourne for five years. It seems certain that from 1900 to 1901 she worked in Toowoomba as a nursery nurse and it's more than possible that she assisted Fanny Rod in caring for the Lamington children. There is nothing surprising in the idea that the nursery would, for the main part, be housed in the healthier environment of Toowoomba. Whilst Lord and Lady Lamington lived in Government House in Brisbane, they spent a lot of time in their cooler, hilltop retreat, Harlaxton House in Toowoomba, less than one hundred miles away. The charming, bustling town with its temperate climate was a pleasant escape from sweltering Brisbane and Lady Lamington enjoyed it there, writing endless letters to friends in Europe, giving her address as 'written whilst in Toowoomba'. Throughout her life, whilst brusque and impatient with adults, Helena had a great rapport with young children (other perhaps than her own) – and she adored babies.

Her time in Queensland would have been enlightening. The Aboriginal tribes have legendary – almost mystical – skills in herbal medicine and treatments and the lush sub-tropical forests of the Toowoomba area were a rich vein of supply for essential plant ingredients. More significantly in piecing together the jigsaw of Helena's successful start, the area was rich in pine trees, imported to the colonies in the early 1800s. Native softwoods of Queensland and New South Wales included the hoop pine (*Araucaria Cunninghami*), the bunya pine (*Araucaria Bidwilli*), Kauri pines (*Agathis spp*) and the Cypress pine (*Callitris spp*). Plants and trees native to Australia may have had little place in the official scientific hierarchy of the time, but the Aborigines knew exactly what powers they contained. Today, Australia is regarded as being 'one step ahead' in terms of natural cosmetics, due to innovative companies and a responsive holistic market, and Toowoomba is the largest grower of echinacea in the southern hemisphere. One ultra-fashionable Melbourne spa called Aurora, offers products from Li'tya, an Aboriginal spa line which uses native Australian plant extracts, clays and salts. A press interview with Madame when she revisited Australia in 1957, quotes her as saying her first local skin-treatment cream contained water lilies. It also contained lavender. Between water lily and lavender it would have smelt good, and as both have healing properties, it would have soothed too. Toowoomba, in particular, has long been known for its water lilies.

Being attached to the Lamington household would explain Helena's reason for returning to Melbourne in 1901, but not before experiencing two moments of living history. In January that year, Lord Lamington read the official proclamation in Brisbane of the merging of Queensland, New South Wales, Victoria, Tasmania and other individual states into one country – Australia. The people's wild excitement and parties to celebrate the formation of 'the Federation' came to an abrupt end on 22 January when Queen Victoria died, but resumed in May when King Edward VII's son, the Duke of York, arrived to open the first Australian parliament amidst scenes of great pomp and protocol. Shortly afterwards, the Lamingtons left for Bombay. It was time for Helena to consider her future, and she determined it would be back in Melbourne. On the move once more, and given that Australia's narrow-gauge railways of the time were mainly used to carry cattle rather than passengers, with the coastal service not yet open, Helena would have travelled to Melbourne by steamer, calling in at Sydney en route. When she arrived, she would have found some dramatic changes had happened in the four years since she last saw the city.

By 1901, Melbourne had well over 2,200,000 inhabitants in what was still largely an industrial city, with its finances built on wool, wheat, butter and shipping. Important secondary industries such as chemical manufacturing, wholesaling and the importing of supplies from the Orient and Europe were thriving. After the recession that had swept Australia a year or so before, the rewards of late-nineteenth-century engineering were paying dividends, and Melbourne was now connected to an efficient sewerage system, ridding itself of the nickname 'Smellbourne'. The city was proud of its telephone system, where the public switchboard, operative since 1880, had over 2000 subscribers. Job opportunities abounded for the female population, including retailing, newspaper publishing and journalism, export and legal secretarial work, the flourishing entertainment business, catering, hotels – Melbourne had nearly three hundred – and essential services such as the aforementioned telephone switchboards, where the central exchange had over eighty female operators working day and night shifts. Work for women existed in any number of light-industrial outlets, in dressmaking and millinery – and in the beauty business. So many young women poured into the city looking for work that the local newspaper, *The Age*, coined a phrase to describe them, calling them 'the bachelor girls'. A milliner could expect to earn around 40/– a week, and a dressmaker 60/– whilst a barmaid took home around 20/–.

As the new century turned and the Victorian National Council of Women was formed, a staggering 35% of breadwinners were women, with as many as 40% of working-age women in full-time paid employment. Their wages were still low – they earned only half of what men were paid – and their hours were long, but they were glad to be working. Amongst them was one special 'bachelor girl' – Helena Rubinstein.

In Melbourne, just as in Vienna, Helena was able to take refuge with the city's surprisingly large and close-knit Jewish community. This time, the supporting link came through the third of her uncles who had settled in Australia, John Silberfeld, and his business partner, Maurice Schaumer. John Silberfeld had left Melbourne by the time his niece arrived back in the city, having moved to Antwerp to establish his diamond business, but Maurice was on hand to advise Helena over a place to stay, and to help her find a job.

She moved into the St Kilda home of one of Schaumer's relatives, Mortiz Michaelis, as nanny to his children. Morty Michaelis was a kindly and successful man with business interests in Melbourne and New Zealand, and a pillar of respectability at the local synagogue. Helena, however, had had her fill of domestic duties, and knew her time was running out. If she was to make her business concept happen, this was her last chance. However kind the Michaelis family, the concept of a beauty cream was clearly so remote from their daily lives that Helena, initially at least, had to look elsewhere to find support. Firstly, she had to free herself from the stricture of living-in domestic work, so she took a room at Mrs Stern's boarding house in Grey Street, St Kilda.

Over fifty years later, in 1957, when Madame was on what her staff described as one of her 'royal tours', staying in Melbourne at the Menzies Hotel, her travelling companion, Patrick O'Higgins, watched with fascination as his boss shied away from a memory of her past, when an elderly, shabby man paid an impromptu visit to the Rubinstein suite. Introducing himself as Abel Isaacson, the visitor started to reminisce about knowing Madame in Melbourne *circa* 1902. 'We met nearly sixty years ago. She was one of Mrs Sensenberg's girls at the Maison Dore and used to give me two helpings of fish for the price of one.' Madame had by now retreated into her bedroom and slammed the door, but hovered near to the keyhole to hear what revelations Isaacson would come out with. 'Without Mr Thompson – he was the manager of the Robur Tea Company – she wouldn't have done what she did. He helped her. He taught her. He made her. Mark my words, he was the brains behind the little lady.' Having said that, Mr Isaacson departed.

Virtually the only thing Helena Rubinstein ever admitted about her time in Australia was how hard she had worked. Desperate for cash to pursue her dream, she had indeed been a waitress, with not just one job but two, working the morning and lunchtime shifts at Maison Dore and an afternoon and early evening shift at the Winter Garden tea room, a café with an artistic clientele and a lively atmosphere.

Today's public image of Helena Rubinstein is mostly influenced by the dramatic Graham Sutherland portrait of her as a fierce, domineering, hawk-faced old lady. Sutherland's powerful picture, described by London art dealer William Thuillier as 'one of the most iconoclastic portraits of the twentieth century', was painted in 1957, and gives no clue as to how pretty Helena was as a young woman. She had a curvy, hour-glass figure, a creamy complexion and beautiful, lustrous hair. A drawing by the Swedish artist Hagborg, executed in 1909, was used as her public relations 'hand-out' sketch for the Australian media. She looks very striking and at least a decade younger than her age.

The tiny, attractive, bustling waitress at the Winter Garden soon found friends and admirers, amongst them the man who effectively launched her career. It is generally held that Helena's first husband, Edward Titus, was the guiding hand that helped develop her business. Although he took on a crucial role as advertising copywriter, he hadn't arrived in Australia when Helena opened her first salon. Her original mentor was John Thompson, who ran the Robur Tea Company and who seems to have taught Helena exactly the right mix of marketing and visual skills.

Looking at advertisements in Melbourne's press of that time, such as *Table Talk*, *The Age* or *The Australasian*, the constant front-page placing for the Robur Tea Company shows they were large importers, probably from Ceylon, and had an impressive advertising budget. In a letter reminiscing about Madame, Abel Isaacson said: 'Mr Thompson helped her to merchandise her goods, he gave his brains and lots of hints on advertising. Other people tried to copy her but failed – they didn't know the secret formula.'

Helena's 'secret formula' was her closely guarded secret, as was, it seems, her relationship with John Thompson. It certainly looks as though the two were lovers, just as it seems likely it was a doomed relationship due to the inevitability there was a Mrs Thompson. Helena didn't care. By her own admission she had little time for relationships as she was too busy working, but with a beau of influence behind her, she was able to launch her first salon and hype her cream, which she called 'Valaze'. Whilst John Thompson helped her with marketing, however, he wasn't responsible for the formula. She had another helper to assist with that.

Helena Rubinstein applied for Australian naturalisation in 1907. On a form which sternly reminds applicants that 'persons making false declarations will be punished for wilful and abrupt perjury', Helena was listed as unmarried, described her occupation as 'importer' and gave her age as twenty-seven. The immigration officer who rubber-stamped her request failed to notice that on her first entry into Melbourne in September 1896 her age was listed as twenty and that miraculously eleven years later she was still only twenty-seven. In fact she was thirty-five. By 1907, she had become a successful salon owner in Melbourne, with a branch in Sydney and another in New Zealand. Her products were available over both countries by mail order and stocked at 'fine chemists everywhere', and she was a rich woman. How had she done it? The main clue is in the name of her naturalisation sponsor.

Mr Frederick Sheppard Grimwade JP supported Helena's application, confirming she was 'a person of good repute'. Mr Grimwade, as a JP, didn't have to list any other occupation. If he had, he would have put 'chairman, Felton, Grimwade & Co, pharmaceutical manufacturers and distributors'. By the stroke of his pen, Helena Juliet Rubinstein became a naturalised citizen of the Commonwealth of Australia, swearing 'true allegiance to his Majesty King Edward VII'. There could have been no better friend for an emergent beauty specialist in Australia than Victoria's leading pharmaceutical manufacturer. The firm of Felton, Grimwade would have been a godsend to Helena, just as the New York firm of Stillwell Gladding would become to her rival, Elizabeth Arden, in 1915.

In all probability introduced to Helena via Morty Michaelis, Frederick Grimwade's company will have shown her how to distil pycnogenol, a key flavonoid, from Australian pine bark. Anthony Edwards of Mega Nutrition, whose firm markets high potency pine bark extract pycnogenol today, says, 'All she would have needed would be a heat source capable of producing 400 degrees Fahrenheit, ether, pure alcohol, sodium, and the proper glassware for distilling, which would all have been available to her.' Through Felton, Grimwade, such knowledge would certainly have been available, enabling Helena to replicate the pot of her European cream, by now long gone, but whose formula Helena would have obtained. She had no need to import cream from Krakow — she had all the ingredients in Australia.

In an intriguing twist, a portrait of Helena Rubinstein, painted in Australia on her last visit in 1957, has been on a millennium tour and was shown at the National Portrait Gallery in London in 2001. William Dobell's rather fierce image of her is the property of the National Gallery of Australia, its purchase funded by the Felton bequest in 1964. Alfred Felton was Grimwade's close friend and partner. He died in 1904 and left half his estate to 'purchase works of art' for Victoria's National Gallery. Although he didn't live to see his partner's ambitious protégée become a serious art collector herself, it seems a fitting coincidence in the rich pattern of Helena's life, that a picture of hers is in an Australian gallery entirely due to the generosity of one of the partners in the firm that started her on her way. The irony would have amused her, particularly as she didn't like the painting.

The original Valaze would have been a 'water in oil' emulsion cream, the most basic formula for which would be wool fat (lanolin), soft paraffin and distilled water. Wool fat is actually a very complex mixture and pharmaceutical companies soon discovered how to take most of the crucial emulsifying constituents to make wool wax alcohols. Lanolin also has a distinctly unappealing smell – quite a serious problem for a face cream – but essential oils, such as rose or lavender, mask it well; in the early days, Helena seems to have favoured rose. Ceresine wax, as written on the old piece of paper mentioned by O'Higgins, was more normally used for moulded cosmetics, such as boxed rouge, or lipstick, so couldn't have been the Valaze formula. The 'secret' to the formula, mentioned by Abel Isaacson, would seem to have been pine bark extract, and the result would have been very good. Helena became fascinated with formulae, studying until she was extremely knowledgeable, and delighted in mixing and pounding.

The Rubinstein cream was originally promoted as both a cold cream *and* a barrier cream. Although after a few months of good sales Helena was to offer a range of creams under the same name, to begin with, Valaze was a 'catch-all cream'. It was even said to remove freckles. This happy side effect was more likely due to the addition of a bleaching agent such as hydrogen peroxide or citric acid – lemon – rather than any herbs it was supposed to contain. A basic recipe for a comparable cream would include lanolin, white paraffin, hydrogen peroxide, acetanilide and a trace of titanium dioxide or zinc oxide, both white pigments. The result would be a skin-softener *and* a skin-whitener.

Certainly it would have smelt good thanks to the addition of essential oils such as rose, orange, lily and lavender, all with the advantage of having healing properties. This is one key to the success of both the Rubinstein skin-care range, and Elizabeth Arden's. They were the first to delicately scent commercially available skin creams, which until then had an aura of the hospital. What woman would believe that a gloopy, medicinal-smelling cream would make her look young and beautiful? That premise was the foundation of the success of both Rubinstein and Arden – they gave women what they wanted most, the promise of fresh, scented youth.

Helena developed her early creams in the 'kitchen', as she called the small laboratory she would soon install in every salon. She remained in control of her 'kitchens' through choice, adoring every moment developing formulae. So much so that when she later met the distinguished physicist, fellow Pole Marie Curie, she remarked 'how much she must enjoy working in her kitchens'. The response from the Nobel Prize-winner who had discovered radium whilst working on magnetism and radioactivity in her laboratories is not on record, but one can imagine her confusion.

Mystery surrounds the origin of the funding essential to set up Helena Rubinstein & Company which opened its doors in 1903, operating out of a small suite of rooms at 138 Elizabeth Street, in the heart of Melbourne. In a practice she rarely changed, Helena lived there, quite literally above the shop. She claims she borrowed £250 from a friend made on the outward voyage from Europe, called Miss MacDonald. The passenger list shows no one named MacDonald, so the woman identified as her first backer is unknown – if she ever existed. It's possible she may have been Miss MacDonald from Coleraine. The local doctor's daughter would have had more faith in skin cream, perhaps, than the local teacher, whom Helena had lobbied unsuccessfully. It's also possible that as she became more committed to her dream, with a business plan prepared by the obliging Mr Thompson, Morty Michaelis stepped in to help his family's ex-nanny – he could easily have afforded the investment – or else Mr Thompson was her backer. Possibly even Felton, Grimwade considered supporting the venture.

Whatever the truth, she found the money, and amongst the pool of helpers whipped in to fetch and carry, unload deliveries from pharmaceutical suppliers, take boxes for mailing and all the other essential jobs, were several of her admirers, including Abel Isaacson.

Helena's business started advertising almost immediately, with the March issue of *Table Talk*, Melbourne's smart publication of the day, carrying the bold announcement:

'VALAZE' BY DR LYKUSKI, the most celebrated European Skin Specialist, is the best nourisher of the skin. 'VALAZE' will improve the worst of skin in one month. 3/6d and 5/6d. If posted, 6d extra. Available from Helena Rubinstein & Company, 138 Elizabeth Street.

Although the first to use such 'fear factor' led copy — few advertisers were as blunt about skin defects — Helena wasn't alone in using the media to reach out to Melbourne's beauty-conscious women. Competition in the field of treatments and products was already fierce. Practitioners of the time included Miss Stone who claimed she could 'remove moles and hairs by electricity, having 13 years' experience'. Clients could see her at the Victoria buildings, Swanston Street. Miss Chant, also in Swanston Street, offered 'hairdressing, manicures and face brushing', while Madame Bosseree sold Royal Hair Tonic and 'Reval Skin Food, scientifically proven for a fine complexion', at 2/6d a jar.

Melbourne women were spoiled for choice. The Oriental Massage Company, again in Swanston Street, gave 'scalp massage, singeing and manicures'. A Madame Frokjar announced that she was a pupil of 'Dr Clod Hansen, Masseur to the Danish Royal Family', and Madame Frokjar guaranteed 'special methods for face treatments and hair removing' operating out of Collins Street. A product called Eve's Shadine seemed to be the big thing in hair dye, and rather worryingly, Scrubbs Cloudy Ammonia was energetically promoted as perfect for both 'cleansing hair and restoring the colour of carpets'.

Editorial coverage featuring Helena Rubinstein started almost immediately. 'Miss Helena Rubinstein is being kept very busy,' trilled a journalist, 'as her cream and different preparations for the face are so soothing to the skin, that they are much in demand. Fresh shipments arrive by every mail and Miss Rubinstein is always ready to give any information to customers at 138 Elizabeth Street.' Helena was *very* keen on reciprocal editorial, being a firm believer that product endorsement on feature pages was crucial. Later, she would come to expect such largesse from wary magazine publishers in exchange for her valuable advertising budget, keeping a hawk-like eye on beauty editorial stories, particularly about her competitors. She put her public relations department under constant pressure to 'keep in the news' and they were drilled to cost-evaluate editorial copy against the value of paid advertising. Madame knew better than any just how important the power of the press was, and how much it had helped to establish her in the early days.

Thanks to the combination of aggressive advertising and glowing editorial – not to mention the fact that her cream was very good indeed – Helena's rise was swift. Her company made an application for a trademark to protect 'Valaze – a toilet preparation known as skin food'. The trademark registration form carries no listing of ingredients, but under the section 'the essential particulars of the trade mark are the following', in her careful copperplate handwriting Helena inserted: 'the distinctive label'. She didn't put that the label design was courtesy of the Robur Tea Company advertising and art department, but perhaps she should have done. She listed her occupation as 'manufacturer'. A few months later, she was ensconced at larger premises at 242 Collins Street, listed in the local business directory as 'agent and importer'. To the authorities she was a manufacturer, but in anything the public might have access to, she carefully described herself as an 'importer'. She clung aggressively to the romantic and more commercially alluring story that her cream was imported from Europe.

'BEAUTY IS POWER' blazoned the headline of a Rubinstein advertisement in 1904.

> Dr Lykusky's celebrated Valaze Skin Food makes a poor complexion good and good skin beautiful. It is compounded from rare herbs which only grow in the Carpathian Mountains and is of exceptional value to those who are disfigured with freckles, sun-burn, wrinkles, eczema, blackheads or skin-blemishes of any kind. Valaze gives the skin the soft, clear, transparent appearance of a little child. WARN-ING. Be aware of local imitations got up to resemble Valaze, the *only* imported skin-food.

Although it is charming to imagine Helena had endless supplies of cream arriving from Poland, according to Abel Isaacson she worked day and night in the back room, firstly at Elizabeth Street, then at Collins Street, and finally at her third premises in Little Collins Street, making up her stock. She packed the finished product into glass jars bought locally, and stuck on the beautifully designed black, gold and ginger labels by hand.

Melbourne women seemed to suffer from all the afflictions mentioned in Helena's advertising, as she increased her budget and started to produce beauty self-help and advice pamphlets called *Guide to Beauty*. One promotional trick she used was to say 'mention this newspaper and get *Guide to Beauty* absolutely free'. This simple but effective marketing tool is still in use one hundred years later. The often brutal 'fear factor' text was a technique she perfected, putting the customer down before building her up. It would be adopted by virtually every other cosmetics manufacturer.

When Helena opened her first salon in 1903, Nellie Stewart, arguably the most famous and beautiful of all Australian singers and actresses, was wowing her audiences at Melbourne's Princess Theatre in *Sweet Nell of Old Drury*. Less than two years later, Nellie Stewart would be lending her name to endorse Rubinstein products.

In 1905, the women's editor of *Table Talk* wrote glowingly about Melbourne's star beauty culturist:

Miss Rubinstein has a beautiful, clear complexion, which seems impervious to any change of climate. No secret was made of the fact that it had been her custom for some years to use a simple skin-food, very well known in Warsaw, and prepared by a very clever skin specialist. Miss Rubinstein introduced the idea to Melbourne and now has the endorsement of the actress Miss Nellie Stewart who writes 'it is the most wonderful preparation I have ever had'. Miss Rubinstein explains that 'I could make much more money by having a locally manufactured article, but that would never do. People are under the impression that I am making my fortune now, but with costs, freight, duty and so on, there is not much profit on each pot of Valaze.'

Helena Rubinstein, it must be said, knew very well that each pot cost a few pennies to make and was being sold at a large part of the average woman's wage, but this was hardly something she was going to admit to the press, neither was it what her clients wanted to hear. She concluded:

It is my intention to go to Europe shortly to personally learn all I can about the skin and its treatment from the foremost European specialists in each country. Then I shall return to Melbourne and establish myself in a larger way. Imitation may be the sincerest form of flattery, but I confess I have not appreciated it. In fact I have been worried and annoyed by the way some local manufactures have been got up to resemble Valaze. My advertisements even have been copied. It is very annoying, but in my opinion, such things cannot be satisfactorily prepared, except by a skin specialist.

The readers of *Table Talk* were thus indoctrinated by the mantra according to Helena, who was clearly seething with anger at local competition. She had also shifted location of her 'European' discovery from the Carpathian Mountains to Warsaw, and emphasised the need to have 'specialist treatment', implying that anything less was not merely inferior but somehow dangerous. The bold statement about imported cream shows her determination to cling to her version of the story, despite irrefutable evidence that she was making her product domestically.

Helena was always one step ahead in offering something new. She was the first beauty specialist to classify skin as 'dry', 'normal' and 'oily', talking about the three in print, where readers, starved of credible information about their skin and their beauty regimes, felt reassured. It was a stroke of marketing genius. The single pot of Valaze was the first of a whole raft of treatment creams the beauty-conscious – and presumably now terrified – consumer had to purchase. Women, only just becoming used to beauty preparations being commercially marketed, felt their skin conditions, anything from spots to shine, freckles to flushing, were indicative of something being *wrong* with them, and that buying creams would put it right.

In early June 1905, Helena Rubinstein & Company applied for another trademark to protect the name Valaze. This time, the forms were completed by her own trademark agents, Alfred and George Cummins, who held her power of attorney. She could not sign the application herself, because she had sailed to Europe, her first trip home in nearly ten years.

RISE OF A RIVAL
1839–1907

As HELENA RUBINSTEIN SET sail for Europe in 1905, the woman who would become her greatest rival was struggling to find a pathway out of Toronto. Romantic myths abound about Elizabeth Arden's parents. It's said her mother grew up in Cornwall, eloping with a young Scottish jockey she met at an Easter fair in Polruan. Legend has it the two of them went to Canada to start a new life and that their daughter, christened Florence Nightingale after one of her mother's heroines, 'grew up with a whinny in her ear' from the many horses her father kept on their farm in Woodbridge, outside Toronto.

Willie Graham may or may not have been a jockey in Britain, but his future wife Susan Tadd certainly never met him at a point-to-point in the Cornish countryside, for the simple reason that she was born and grew up in Liverpool. They didn't even marry in England. Susan Tadd emigrated to Toronto with her mother and stepfather in about 1863 when she was fifteen years old and married William Graham in York County, Toronto, on 11 July 1872. It is unlikely a woman of nearly twenty-five would be forced to elope, even if her mother did not approve of her husband. Susan's parents, however, Samuel and Jane Pearce Tadd, did have strong connections with Cornwall, particularly Fowey and Polruan.

The boats moored in Fowey's picturesque harbour today are more likely to be the yachts of the leisured rich, but throughout the eighteenth and nineteenth centuries, Fowey, Bodinnick and Polruan were home to the wealthy boatbuilders and master mariners of the time. These ports were the base for their business of transporting goods, in particular local china clay or imported coal, their schooners often crewed by two, if not three, generations of the same family, like the Slades, the Salts – and the Tadds. Daphne du Maurier wove the local families into her stories, adjusting their names to better suit her novels, but her 'Mr Tabb', the boatbuilder in *Rebecca*, was in reality one of the Tadds of Fowey.

Samuel Tadd married Jane Pearce in the charming church Lanteglos by Fowey in 1839, strolling just over the lane to celebrate at Churchtown Farm, Jane's handsome, mellow stone family home. Tadd was one of five brothers who shared the responsibility of running their family ships, including the well known schooner, the *Bedwalty*, on overseas voyages as well as their less exciting, but profitable core journeys from Fowey to Birkenhead. The Tadd business had a base in Liverpool, the family maintaining property there as well as in Polruan.

A progressive, enlightened, articulate man, well educated for the time, Captain Tadd kept detailed diaries, noting his despair of his young crew on one particular voyage he made to Rio de Janeiro. 'Our mercantile sea-men are the nursery for our Navy, which is the defence of our nation, but I find insubordination, drunkenness, desertion and other want of discipline.' The strongminded and courageous Captain Tadd had the potential to become a great reformer, but sadly died at sea at the age of forty-four, without his stirring papers coming to the attention of the Admiralty. His enduring legacy is that of his granddaughter, Florence Nightingale. Given that running an international business requires huge discipline, a virtue Captain Tadd valued above everything, her grandfather would have had every reason to be proud of her.

Rewards for nineteenth-century mariners may have been high, but it was a hard life. Observing shipping records in the Fowey library, it's evident it was also a dangerous one. Take, for example, 'Phillip Tadd, age 30. Rank of Master from Polruan. Died with Ship *Silverstream*. Lost with all crew in 1882.' Or, 'Samuel Tadd, age 32. Rank of Master from Polruan. Died with ship *Snowflake*. Lost with all crew also in 1882.'

For the one-year-old Florence Nightingale Graham, living half a world away in Toronto, the loss at sea of her young uncle, Samuel Tadd Jnr, or her second cousin, Phillip Tadd, had no significance. For her mother, Susan Tadd Graham, the news of her brother's death, so close after her cousin's, would have been a grim reminder of the risks of running ships, her own father having drowned in 1854 when she was only six, his body never having been recovered. Susan's mother, having inherited his estate, remained comfortably off in Liverpool, remarrying a few years later. Her new husband, Thomas Turvey, was a Church of England organist and Professor of Music. In 1863, the Turveys emigrated to Canada, taking their young son Thomas, along with Jane's younger children from her first marriage: Susan, Samuel Jnr and James Liberty.

By the 1860s, some 40,000 or so emigrants a year were moving from Great Britain to Canada, most of them leaving from the port of Liverpool, where the Allan Line Ships were amongst the busiest operating the Atlantic route. The Canadian government actively sought agricultural workers and paid a bonus per head to tempt them, a system which enabled impoverished farmhands to make the crossing. The Turvey family had no need for this financial assistance, but it would have been a lifeline for the many Scottish farm labourers hoping for a better life – amongst them William Graham.

The Turvey family would have felt at home in Toronto, at that time a city with a population of around 70,000 and referred to as 'Little England', sporting a Regatta Club, cricket ground, bowling green and race course. Better still, the city was primarily Espicopalian, well suited to the career aspirations of a Church of England organist. Jane Turvey was apparently furious when her daughter Susan met and married young Willie Graham. Breaking the Tadd tradition of marriage between mariners was one thing, but in Jane's eyes Willie Graham had little to offer her daughter – he was a pedlar. Graham earned his living selling household supplies to the local farmers, his dream of fine horses being mainly confined to the broken-down hacks pulling his cart.

The Grahams had five children: Christine was born in 1873, Lilian in 1875, their only son, William Jnr, in 1878, Florence Nightingale in 1881 and Jessie Gladys in 1884. There has been universal uncertainty about Florence Nightingale's date of birth. The most often quoted date is 1884. It has also been put at 1878, and even as early as 1876. Birth records and census data on file in Thunder Bay, Ontario, however, show her as being born on 31 January 1881. Years later, she would famously remark, 'My dear, I've lied about it so often, I can't even remember the date myself.' This denial of age was a trait she shared with Madame (which was followed years later by Estée Lauder. Mrs Lauder's son Leonard, when asked how old he was, replied, 'You'd better ask my mother about that, I'm not sure what date she's giving out this year'. For those interested, Leonard Lauder was born in 1933).

Miss Arden, unlike Madame Rubinstein, rarely talked about her family. If pressed, she would admit to growing up on her father's 'small farm' in

Woodbridge, today a suburb of Toronto, but in the 1880s a quiet, agricultural community some fifteen miles out of town. She admitted her mother died young, leaving Florence to make her way, under the care of her older sisters. It has always been said that Susan Graham was estranged from her parents 'back in Cornwall', no writer knowing that her mother, stepfather and brothers lived in the same city and that Jane Tadd Turvey ensured that her daughter and grandchildren were provided for, despite the strained relationship with her son-in-law.

When her mother died a painful death from TB in 1885, after a lingering illness, it left a profound effect on young Florence. She became so paranoid about the cold, rain and damp, in the fear that she would also succumb to the disease, that in later years she lived in overheated houses and dressed in multi-layers of clothes. As a child, Florence stuffed newspapers into her shoes to avoid getting her feet wet through the thin soles. Years later, when she was one of the world's richest women, no one but her maid knew that she still lined her expensive, handmade shoes with newspaper.

In 1876, the Turveys moved to Philadelphia. Whatever fragile truce existed between Jane and Willie Graham when his wife was alive, seems to have shattered on her death, and Willie was left with five children to bring up by whatever financial means he could muster. Young Florence did most of the family caring and household management, for the simple reason that she was better at organisation than anyone else in the family. She never readily admitted how long she spent in the leaking barn, tending to the horses. Nor that she took the reins of the cart when she went with her pa to market to sell vegetables, grumbling that the local women were wont to 'Jew down' the prices, struggling to ensure he didn't drink any profits away. But she was fond of her feckless father, doing her best to protect him during bouts of ill-tempered depression, never grumbling about having to take on responsibilities far beyond her years.

Lack of money meant the younger Graham girls had to leave school and work, rather than go to college, something Florence always regretted. There were a variety of rumours about the many early jobs that Florence took, including a period working for a truss-maker, and some time spent as a dentist's receptionist, the boredom relieved by endless escapist visits to the local nickelodeon, which she adored. Media reports put a lot of emphasis on Miss Arden's early attempts to train as a nurse — a very suitable career for a girl christened Florence Nightingale — but these, like the same attempts by her rival,

Helena Rubinstein, would fail. Neither could stand the sight of blood. In her lifetime Florence won countless business awards, saw one of her racehorses win America's most prestigious race, the Kentucky Derby, was given the medal of the Légion d'Honneur, and dined with presidents, princes and queens. Nothing, however, pleased her more than when she was made an honorary doctor of law by Syracuse University. The girl who left school at seventeen had finally got her degree. She revelled in it, adored lunching with the Chancellor, Mr Tolley, and donated generously to their funding appeals.

Florence Nightingale Graham left Canada around 1907, heading for New York, where her brother Willie had already made his home. A series of nondescript jobs had led nowhere. She craved success, but it wasn't going to happen with office work – she couldn't type. Her tentative medical career had hit the buffers, and her skills, apart from having a peaches-and-cream complexion, looking years younger than her age, good housekeeping skills and a fondness for horses, didn't account for much. If she was to make anything of her life, it wasn't going to happen in Toronto.

She arrived in New York just as 'beauty culture' was emerging from behind closed doors. An edge of respectability had been acquired by practitioners in the city who were claiming 'scientific skills' and promising 'skin rejuvenation' to their eager clients. Florence Graham, however, had no idea about her future. She had to find a job, any job, straight away and it was by a stroke of luck that the business of beauty was how Florence found her fortune.

When Teddy Roosevelt came to the White House in 1901, it was reported there were 4000 millionaires in America, at least one third of them living in New York. It was estimated that one half of the country's wealth was owned by 1% of its families. Living in Toronto, dreaming of making something of her life, Florence would have observed those statistics, this being the type of newspaper story she loved. She would also have enjoyed reading the column by Harriet Hubbard Ayer, a leading women's editor at *The World* newspaper, whose column was widely syndicated and hugely popular. Mrs Ayer had three full-time secretaries replying to an estimated 20,000 letters a year. As well as advising her fans on beauty, grooming and etiquette, Ayer wrote brave features on social injustice and women's rights, topics about which she was well qualified to comment, having been a victim of the first and the lack of the latter. In 1899, Mrs Ayer had published *Harriet Hubbard Ayer's Book of Health and Beauty*, some 550 pages of world-wise advice and practical knowledge, written from the heart, and based on the time when she was famous for her own range of skin-care products. Few people today, even amongst the beauty media, know much about Mrs Ayer. When she died in New York in 1903 aged fifty-four, the cosmetics company she had founded was sold by her heirs. The brand continued, but with little mention of the remarkable woman who had created it. Her story is illustrative of the way women could be treated, regardless of their intellect or achievements.

Following an acrimonious divorce, which left her with the care of three young children and the need to earn her living, the elegant and famously well dressed Mrs Ayer went into the beauty business. She marketed an expensive face cream called Luxuria, based on a formula claimed to have been made in Paris for the celebrated *salonniere*, Julie Recamier. Calling her business Recamier & Company, Mrs Ayer was financed by a rich, but ruthless, Wall Street financier called James Seymour. She used his money well, opening a charming shop on Union Square and expanding into wholesale. Ayer's committed coterie of friends and fans included Sarah Bernhardt, Lillie Langtry, Lillian Russell and even the exquisite beauty, England's Princess of Wales, who gave her a Royal Warrant. Mrs Ayer's own social background enabled her to enjoy the support of New York's formidable society matrons, and her business flourished.

The stresses of being a single working mother, of travelling extensively, of looking good at all times as a leader of fashion, and of coping not merely with the stigma of divorce, but the depression caused by the death of one of her daughters, meant that Harriet Hubbard Ayer became ill. Doctors prescribed her the panacea of the time for nerves and insomnia – morphine.

James Seymour wanted more than a partnership with the beautiful Harriet but fending off his advances, she fled to Germany, where her younger daughter was studying music. Seymour, to whom rejection was something to be avenged, determined to destroy Harriet. By a twist of fate, her eldest daughter had fallen in love with Seymour's son, and against Harriet's wishes, he not only encouraged the marriage, but financed the young couple. Whilst Harriet was in Europe, he laid claim to Recamier & Co and the next time she saw him was in Court, when she bravely went up against Seymour to try and win her business back. The press had a field day. Every scrap of Mrs Ayer's life was exposed, including accusations she was a drug addict. She won the case, but the formidable matrons of New York, who believed entries in the press should only appear on birth, marriage and death, were scandalised, and cut her completely.

Her reputation in shreds, her business destroyed and estranged from her daughter, just when she thought it could get no worse, it did. Her ex-husband, financed by Seymour, fought a custody battle for her youngest daughter and had Harriet committed to an insane asylum in Bronxville. She was incarcerated for a year and a half in solitary confinement, with a bucket for a toilet, allowed one cold shower a week and forbidden letters. Her only recreation was sewing, but the light was so poor she virtually lost her sight. When she was eventually released her flame red hair was completely grey and she was wearing the same dress and shoes she had been confined in, by now in shreds. Only forty-four years old, it's said she looked like a shrivelled, broken, old woman. Despite rallying and bravely forging a new career as a beauty writer and journalist, Harriet Hubbard Ayer never recovered her health. Florence Graham would have known her story. When she established her own business, there would be no male financial partners, she controlled her destiny alone.

Turn-of-the-century New York embodied everything Florence aspired to be part of. It was a titanic city, lusting for power and wealth, a dramatic, exciting, demanding, lively metropolis. The word 'millionaire' had first been used to describe New York's rich. The city was setting important trends in fashion and beauty, both of which intrigued Florence, and most importantly, it was the home of the great social hostesses of the day, whose every move she had studied.

As a young woman in Toronto, with a modest budget and even more modest prospects, Florence had read the gossip sheets avidly. As a devotee of the nickelodeons, she was captivated by the images of pioneering heroes leading exciting lives, and the books she read were romantic novels, whose heroines were drawn from the upper echelons of society. Florence yearned to become rich, and everyone who knew her agrees that she was an unmitigated snob.

For the past fifty years New York's social hierarchy had not been controlled by the men who made the money, but by the women they married, who had been every bit as ruthless in managing their place in society as their husbands were in managing their fortunes. This matriarchal group presided over phenomenal wealth and had created a rigid and powerful social structure.

By the early 1900s New York's lavish soirées were increasingly criticised by a media less deferential to the rich, but Florence Nightingale Graham had revered the 'gilded age' of the past and saw beauty culture as a way to carve her place in its evolving future.

In the late nineteenth century, women attending New York's parties wore the most ornate clothes and exquisite jewels, but whilst their hairdresser would visit an hour before to dress their hair, not one of them wore any make-up. That is to say, not one of them admitted to wearing make-up and certainly didn't seem to be wearing any. In fact, they would have worn a light dusting of rice powder and possibly the merest hint of rouge, high on the cheekbones. Their eyebrows would be plucked, brushed and waxed and they would have a touch of balm on their lips. A dab of perfume behind each ear completed their *toilette*. Not one of these ladies would have dreamt of painting their faces, that is using ceruse-based foundation creams and coloured eye-shadow. To do so would have meant social death.

They protected their skins by wearing vast hats and veils, carrying parasols and rubbing in a rather greasy, usually lanolin-based, cold cream at night. Such creams could vary from exceedingly expensive jars 'made to order' by a private perruquier who would often claim his unique formula was based on a 'European recipe', to something made up from an old herbal recipe by the family pharmacist. Perruquiers would also make up face-powder, usually scented with violets or rose, which was often pressed onto tissue sheets and used to dab shiny noses during the evening. Cleansing was with soap and water and their beauty regime would have included a cold water splash to 'freshen' the skin. One typical face-mask of the time was made from oatmeal and buttermilk, which would have a temporary tightening effect, and bathing in Epsom Salts was known to be a good diuretic. Puffy eyes were soothed with a witch-hazel eye-wash and spots were treated with extract of violet. Beauty treatments, almost always conducted at home, would include face steaming and massage. Any young beauty who had freckles would have used a cream made from elder-flowers and zinc sulphate, and for a ruddy complexion a mixture of orris root, white castile soap and cuttlefish bone was recommended. Almost all these preparations, along with hand cream containing almond oil, would have been made by their ladies maids and the same maid – skilled dressers being much in demand – would also have attended to manicures. Hands would be massaged with warmed fresh cream and corns were treated with extract of cannabis. Apart from their visits to the opera or ballet where the performers would wear theatrical greasepaint and kohl – these ladies rarely ventured anywhere near Broadway to see a musical comedy – they barely saw make-up.

Gossip sheets were required reading, even for New York's smartest set. Whilst these women claimed to abhor mention of their families, they still devoured the 'news' in the scandal sheets, even if they were delivered via the servants' entrance. The double-standards of these dowagers were noted by redoubtable feminist Cady Stanton Smith who said, 'fashionable women objected to the women's rights movement because they deemed it immodest to have their names printed in the newspapers.' Yet in the unlikely venue of Newport, Rhode Island, where the women's rights forces held their 1868 Convention, Mrs Stanton Smith watched those very same women scanning the morning papers to 'read the personal compliments and descriptions of their dresses at the previous night's balls'.

Gentle media coverage about balls and gowns however was one thing, the lavish costs of their parties, the foibles of their children, or sexual excesses of their husbands' being exposed by the media was quite another. The most feared publication of the day was a scandal sheet titled 'Town Topics' which delighted in exposing the antics of the gilded rich. Its owner was a kindly looking gentleman called Colonel William D'Alton Mann, whose long white beard and clerical frock-coat gave him an air of innocence that simply proved appearances are deceptive, as the Colonel's speciality was blackmail. His staff, on intimate terms with senior servants the length of Fifth Avenue and throughout Newport, were well trained to give him any necessary information, which he would parley into 'loans' from amongst others, J.P. Morgan and Willie K. Vanderbilt. The general public meanwhile viewed the antics of the super-rich with curiosity and even affection. Tourists visiting New York considered standing to view the Astor, Van Rensselaer, Belmont, Vanderbilt, Jones, Whitney, Huntingdon and Goelet mansions as an essential part of their tour, representing as they did the success of America's very own 'royalty' and visible evidence of the 'American dream'. These women of fashion, as a consequence, became extremely influential style icons.

Out-of-towners may not have been quite so familiar with the home of one of New York's most charismatic hostesses, Mamie Stuyvesant Fish, but her beautiful mansion on Madison Avenue and 78th St, designed by Stanford

White, was the more entertaining venue of choice than Mrs Astor's for *le tout* New York. Mrs Fish had an extremely low boredom threshold and was 'Queen of the one-liners'. Her patient husband was Chairman of The Illinois Central Railroad, much preferring their peaceful country house in the Hudson Valley, to the parties Mamie threw in New York or in their Newport summer house. Mr Fish however adored his wife and watched with fond amusement whilst she shrivelled her friends with her inimitable style. 'Make yourselves at home,' she would say on receiving dinner guests, 'and believe me, no one wishes you there more than I do.' When she had had enough of her party for the night she would have her orchestra play 'Home Sweet Home' and at her annual soirée in Newport, in pre-surgical face lift days, she famously greeted her friends saying, 'Here you are again, older faces and younger clothes.' Supremely confident of her role as an arbiter of fashion, she remarked about Teddy Roosevelt's wife, 'The President's wife it is said dresses on $300 a year – and looks it'. Her friends learned to be wary if they heard her start any conversation with the phrase 'sweet pet', knowing it was a signal she was angry. The Stuyvesant Fish summer house in Newport was called 'Crossways'. The social *habitué*, Bobby Van Cortlandt, annoyed at being left off her guest list remarked, 'I never can remember the name of your house, Mrs Fish. Isn't it Crosspatch?' She replied, 'Well, sweet pet, it's a patch you'll never cross.'

Stanford White, the architect who designed her houses, was no less an integral part of the complex New York society of the time. He numbered amongst his clients many scions of the greatest of 'Robber Barons' and his unfailing good taste and sense of style made him the gentleman designer of choice for everything from their mansions to their mausoleums. He came to an ignominious end, murdered by his friend, Harry Thaw, who was convinced that White was having an affair with his wife, Evelyn Nesbitt. Miss Nesbitt was a chorus girl in the famous musical revue, 'Floradora' and Stanford White who loved beautiful women as much as beautiful buildings was, along with most red-blooded men in Manhattan circa 1904, a devotee of the show. The chorus of six sexy and surprisingly petite girls, twirling their parasols and fluttering their eyelashes under vast black ostrich-feathered hats, were an incubator troupe for Florenz Ziegfelds's Follies.

The media image of the 'chorus girl' as a great beauty who led a charmed life was, if anything, heightened by the sensational murder of

Stanford White. Her appeal, at least among aspirational, working-class girls, who had dreams of conquering Broadway, was immense. Newspapers were full of stories about the Floradoras, who were intriguingly all brunettes, thus a momentary fashion for glossy, brown hair took hold. As with all successful showgirls, the Floradoras were a pivotal influence in fashion and beauty, inspiring a shift away from the previous vogue for blonde hair. This trend had reached epic proportions amongst fans of burlesque and musical comedy shows in the late nineteenth century in no small part due to a group of buxom, bouncy and bleached blondes from England who had taken America by storm. The all-girl group was the brain-child of a retired musical comedy star from London called Lydia Thompson, who recruited her dancers for their ample bosom and lack of inhibitions, along with their willingness to use the peroxide bottle. Calling them 'The British Blondes' their American tour was launched in New York in 1868 by Thompson, who ran successive troupes of 'Blondes' for over thirty years.

Although they spearheaded a major trend in beauty, neither The British Blondes nor the Floradoras were ever part of the charmed world of New York's society ladies. They would have abhorred peroxide. If their hair was dyed, it was with old-fashioned walnut juice, lemon juice or vinegar, treatments that had been used for hundreds of years. Other than that, they used wigs or false pieces. Mrs Stuyvesant Fish in particular had very fine hair and wore a switch. Adjusting her coiffeur one evening on arrival at a grand dinner party, her 'piece' fell to the floor. The implacable footman in attendance merely picked it up and handed it to her. Mrs Fish, happily reunited with her hair, remarked to her hostess, 'He'll have to go sweet pet, he knows my little secret.'

For three decades, America's most powerful fashion icon had been the 'golden haired Goddess' of musical operetta, the ravishing Lillian Russell. Famous for her pink-and-white complexion, skin reported to be 'as soft as a baby' and her voluptuous curves, Lillian Russell was a larger-than-life character. She had a big voice, a big heart and an even bigger reputation. Thanks to her gargantuan appetite, she had a big figure too. When the craze for bicycling hit New York in the 1890s, Miss Russell decided that as cycling was so good for the figure, she would take it up herself. She rode out in Central Park on her custom-made Tiffany gold-plated machine, with mother-of-pearl handlebars and her initials worked in diamonds on the wheel spokes. Miss Russell wore a cream serge leg-of-mutton sleeve cycling suit, with the skirt shortened by three inches, which caused a sensation and set a trend.

The media worshipped Lillian Russell. *The World* reported that when she went to the Café des Beaux Arts for a post-performance supper, dressed in shimmering silks, trailing her sables, smiling to the left and the right, 'it was a sight never to be forgotten'. The impact she made just about anywhere was so huge that the media came up with the phrase 'making an entrance' simply to describe her arrival. Russell was so often called 'the queen of American beauty' that America's favourite flower, the American Beauty rose, was named after her. When her fame was eclipsed, it wasn't by the type of rival even Lillian Russell could outmanoeuvre, because she wasn't flesh and blood. She was a drawing – and she came from the pen of the graphic artist, Charles Dana Gibson.

The Gibson Girl was officially launched in 1890 and for the next twenty-five years would be the most powerful female image in the United States. The tall, patrician, rangy young woman styled by Gibson was the antithesis of the curvy showgirl. Not that the Gibson Girl didn't have curves – he drew her with a full bosom and quite shapely hips, but she had a tiny, laced waist and a fine-boned, spare frame. Gibson's drawing in *Life* magazine became the weekly fix for literally millions of people who worshipped the Gibson Girl. Her casually up-swept hair and sportif clothes were much copied and she had a huge impact on fashion and beauty.

The Gibson Girl was the topic of much cultural debate. Argument raged as to who the role model was and clearly Dana Gibson was influenced to a great extent by his beautiful and very social wife, Irene Langhorne. The Gibson Girl ran, rather than walked. She rode a bicycle as well as a horse, played tennis, had a fresh-faced complexion, didn't wear make-up and was an eau-de-cologne girl rather than a perfumed woman. She was healthy and, naturally, given the place in society of Mr and Mrs Charles Dana Gibson – Irene's sister Nancy would soon marry Waldorf Astor – she was wealthy. But above all she was a natural 'all-American' beauty and a powerful force in how upper-class American women would shape their image, which has hardly changed to this day.

The Gibson Girl was indisputably 'a lady' and thus was a great favourite with Elizabeth Arden, who felt all women should be ladies.

Years later, in 1936, when Elizabeth Arden was invited to take over the

Colony Club's gymnasium, she wrote, 'The Colony Club is *the* aristocratic ladies' club of the world! I hope I will do a good job.' These words illustrate Elizabeth's love affair with New York's aristocrats, their roots deep in the city's nineteenth-century history, whose homes were on Fifth Avenue. Elizabeth Arden lived on Fifth Avenue, her beauty salon was on Fifth Avenue and her Red Door was always open to them, yet their drawing rooms had rarely been opened to her. The Colony Club was their inner sanctum and finally, Florence Graham had penetrated their walls.

The Colony Club was opened in 1905, when the wives, sisters and daughters of the men of New York who had the Metropolitan, the Union and the New York Yacht Club amongst others, yearned for their own exclusive bolt-hole. Mrs J. Borden Harriman, Anne Morgan, Bessie Marbury and Helen Barney became the founding committee of the Colony Club, hiring their friend, Stanford White, to build them a neo-Federal stone building on Madison Avenue. Five hundred and fifty members enrolled at $150 each and paid $100 annual membership. They got a swimming pool in the basement, a roof garden, card rooms, guest rooms, a gymnasium, Turkish baths, squash courts, a library, tea room, restaurant and, in a bold move for 1905 (when ladies hardly drank outside the home), a cocktail bar. The club also allowed women to smoke, a fact which seemed to cause more debate in the media than anything else.

Overseeing every nut and bolt of its décor, right down to the uniforms to be worn while doing exercises in the gym (white sailor blouses and navy blue bloomers) was Elsie de Wolfe. Her long-time lover, Elisabeth 'Bessie' Marbury – who would come to have a huge influence over the cultural and social aspects of Elizabeth Arden's life when they became close in the 1920s – was determined de Wolfe should get the job. Not all the committee approved, but the last word remained with Stanford White, who said, 'Give it to Elsie and let the girl alone! She knows more than any of us'. He didn't live to see the result, but her work was a triumph, particularly the tea room, with its tiled floors, wicker furniture and green-painted garden trellis. Elsie de Wolfe's greatest innovation at the Colony was using her favourite fabric, English chintz, at a stroke starting a trend for 'the English country house look' in smart New York homes. Being hired to decorate the Colony was a great social coup and it launched not just Elsie de Wolfe's career as a decorator, but arguably the profession of modern, interior design as it's known today.

Acceptance by the smart set at the Colony Club was a long way off when Florence Nightingale Graham arrived in New York in 1907. Ambitious as she was, she could have no idea that just two decades later she would be one of the most famous and wealthy women in New York. After all, at that time, she was working as a cashier in a beauty parlour.

CHAPTER FIVE

MADAME ON THE MOVE
Melbourne, London, Paris
1905–1914

HELENA RUBINSTEIN LEFT AUSTRALIA in 1905 a gifted beginner in the business of beauty and returned a consummate professional. Her first stop was Krakow, where she admitted to having an uneasy meeting with her parents. She would later write:

> When I returned to Krakow, I found it had not changed at all, yet to my eyes it had grown smaller. It was still a beautiful city, but I thought it quiet and dull and life there had become alien to me. I'm sorry to think I cut short my visit to my parents' home, but I had to hurry to Paris to begin my studies under the famous dermatologist, Dr Berthalot.

In reality, it seems likely she never saw her father at all, merely spending an hour or so with her mother, still clearly unable to comprehend the aggressive vitality of her eldest – and still unmarried – daughter. The deeply orthodox Rubinsteins were still living in Kazimierz, an area by now inhabited by people Helena considered depressingly poor. Her estrangement from her parents wasn't rectified by this brief visit. She was never to see either of them alive again.

Whether or not Helena studied with 'Dr Berthalot' isn't known, but she certainly went to Paris, where she found a bed at her sister Pauline Hirschberg's home. 'Aunt Hela's' visit clearly captivated the Hirschberg's thirteen-year-old daughter, Marcelle, who would later work for her aunt in Argentina, whilst her mother did 'family duty' by running Helena's first Paris salon which she opened in 1909. Helena knew expansion depended on good staff. Uneasy about employing strangers and in those early days unable to afford them, taking family on board was the better option. It was also a way of proving to her father that she could and would provide for her family. Before leaving Krakow, she enlisted her sister Ceska and cousin Lola Beckmann to Helena Rubinstein Ltd, arranging passage for them on the SS *Karlsruhe*, which left for Australia in September that year. All three returned to Australia as saloon-class passengers, Ceska, in true Rubinstein tradition, claiming to be seventeen when she was actually twenty-two.

The time Helena spent in Europe between July and September 1905 was an immersion in beauty therapy. Most of the treatments she was interested in developing were in practice at residential spas, so she investigated as many fashionable health resorts as she could. It would subsequently become one of Helena's most pleasurable pastimes and the base of much of her beauty knowledge. The late nineteenth century was the great European heyday of spas, made increasingly fashionable by King Edward VII, a devotee of naturopathic treatments, whose particular favourite was Marienbad.

Her first destination was Wiesbaden, a favourite of Queen Alexandra, where Helena formed a lasting friendship with Dr Kapp, Wiesbaden's celebrated medical director. He would keep her supplied with treatments for poor circulation and varicose veins which were used to great effect in her salons – and by Helena herself, who suffered badly with both.

As she considered other spas to visit she would have been spoiled for choice. The ultra-fashionable St Brides-les-Bains in Savoie was a favourite of theatrical agent Bessie Marbury and her close friend Anne, financier J.P. Morgan's daughter, who took an annual cure together there. Eugenie le Bains in South West France was created especially for the Empress Eugenie, who recovered there after the indulgences of Biarritz. Ischl, the renowned Salt Village Spa in Austria where the Glauber Salt Springs and Iodine-Sulphur Springs were renowned for circulation problems, was acclaimed by smart, medically-inclined travellers, as was the spa at Budapest, where the Duke and Duchess of Windsor would later retreat for anti-ageing injections and a de-toxing programme. Emperor Franz Joseph II adored Abano in Italy, while the Tsar of Russia preferred Franzensbad in Czechoslovakia. Elsie de Wolfe's favourite, in between bouts of shopping for European antiques for her clients, was Baden Baden.

Each spa had a 'physicus', a medicinal mayor, in charge of monitoring standards as well as promoting them to an audience eager to find a cure for modern illnesses by looking back at fifteenth-century skills. Spa bathing, especially in warm mineral springs, and hydrotherapy treatments as a cure for ailments were increasingly popular. When one considers that about half of all patients undergoing conventional surgery at that time died either on the operating table or of post-operative complications, water treatments were a very appealing alternative.

It wasn't all rest and relaxation however. Father Sebastien Kneipp, a Dutch hydropath, was very keen on pelvic hosing via an alternate warm and cold douche jet and kept his patients moving between treatments including electric baths, vapour baths, body wraps and magnetism. At most spas, the favourite cure for a sluggish circulation was to flog patients – both male and female – with wet towels or sheets. This treatment, along with roller-type electro-massage machines, combining massage with electrotherapy, was renowned for being very effective in 'renewing male sexual vigour'.

One of the most lucrative areas of the beauty and health business, then as now, was diet treatments. Most diet pills at that time were based on senna, a powerful purgative, usually combined with diuretics such as fennel, anise and juniper, promoted as a safe, herbal tablet. As usual, beauty came at a price. Prolonged use of senna caused intestinal and bowel problems and the diuretics would eventually cause kidney problems. German doctors were obsessed with 'reducing' cures and developed tablets based on thyroid extract for commercial use as early as 1880. Considered by most experts to be the most dangerous substance of all when used to excess, the thyroid craze swept to America where, by 1908, a diet product called Marmola was being enthusiastically marketed. Based on thyroid extract and cascara, Marmola damaged the health of hundreds of women, who ended up with malfunctioning thyroid glands, their endocrine systems shot to pieces, and severe menstrual problems.

Helena, being inclined to stoutness herself, was keen to explore the market potential of 'reducing' tablets. When she went home to Australia she took with her a large supply of diet pills, labelled as: 'Flesh reducing Tablets from King Edward VII's Favourite Spa, Marienbad', which were a bestseller at her salons in Melbourne and Sydney.

Helena's Grand Tour included London, where she admitted to 'experimenting by having had treatments at every salon in Bond Street'. Her West End shopping would also have meant a visit to Atkinsons, who had been selling their English lavender water since 1892. The *luxe* lavender label was of course Yardley, which had been operational since 1770 and had enterprisingly opened a wholesale outlet in Australia in 1905 and whose Bond Street stand-alone outlet opened in 1910. Other companies operational in London were Guerlain; Coty; Rigaud and Rimmel, owned by the French cosmetician Eugene Rimmel, who started his business in 1835, maintaining an important branch factory in Soho.

Another visiting essential would have been Mrs Henning's salon in South Molton Street, where the more discreet women could use the mews entrance so their friends wouldn't see them en route for face treatments or 'painting'. Given the Queen was such a fan of make-up, it's hard to fathom quite why upper-class society was still rigidly anti-cosmetics. Less than a century before, upper-class women were using lashings of make-up – and the Prince Regent and his set were no stranger to the powder puff – but the long reign of Victorian piety had put paid to the trend.

Queen Victoria had abhorred painting, and banned cosmetics at her court, but she maintained the services of a perruquier, who mixed her exclusive flesh-toned face-powder and made up her cold cream. The most famous of the Queen's cosmeticians was Willie Clarkson, an expert at making false eyelashes, but whose main claim to fame was his famous 'Lillie' powder, made for actress Lillie Langtry. It was a mixture of talc, melted lanolin, carmine, sienna and essence of violets. Mr Clarkson's mixture was a subtle combination and, rare for the day, given the toxic content of most cosmetics in use, totally harmless.

Helena would have observed the neo-baroque splendour of London's most famous department store, Harrods, which by 1905 was open on its present site in Knightsbridge. Shopping there, she would have found little in the way of cosmetics. The vast beauty departments and fragrance halls that are the integral part of department store shopping today were largely a 1920s development. In the early 1900s, the genteel world of 'toiletries' included hairbrushes and combs; travelling vanity cases; tooth powder; the ubiquitous hairnets, scented soaps and eau-de-colognes and new cleansing and cold creams, not forgetting Vaseline, launched by Cheesebrough in 1870 and used to slick down eyebrows, shine lips and add sheen to eyelids. It took a visionary American, Gordon Selfridge, to give fashionable London women the cosmetics they would come to crave, when in an imaginative move, on the opening of his mega-store in 1909, he offered powdered rouge from Bourjois amongst others, powder sheets to dab down shiny faces and tinted lip balm – an early lipstick.

Her induction into the European beauty business at an end, Helena sailed back to Melbourne, no doubt giving her sister and cousin induction courses in beauty techniques on the boat. In her luggage on board were her new clothes – Helena had visited Worth in Paris and ordered several outfits – along with wooden rollers for face massage, the aforementioned diet pills, a new formula for acne and, mindful of the Australian climate, one for sunburn. Her shopping was completed with dozens of terracotta plantpots bought in Genoa and Naples, for the gardens of her St Kilda house and as décor in her revamped salon in Collins Street.

Helena's new advertising played on the Australian deference for European status, milking respect for British connections for all it was worth. For example:

Mlle Helena Rubinstein of Valaze fame has just returned from Europe and her careful study in the most famous laboratories of the world's skin specialists has resulted in the enhanced Massage Institute at 274 Collins Street where fair woman finds a new skin. Mlle Rubinstein and her two Viennese assistants, co-jointly with a replete Electrical Apparatus, effect miracles.

Helena added face-powder in three different tints, including Rachel, to her Valaze range and had her *Guide to Beauty* pamphlets rewritten to include her 'European expertise'. Always the first to act on a trend, when a leading Melbourne newspaper published a report saying the city's top hospital confirmed 'massage had therapeutic, medicinal benefit for recovering surgical patients' and said that 'both surgeons and nurses of the future must have a knowledge of massage', she took even larger advertisements for her 'Valaze Massage Institute' and started to call her clients 'patients' and her treatment rooms 'operating rooms'. Large, ornate-framed certificates were displayed, reassuring Melbourne's women of substance that Helena and her new Viennese assistants were 'well qualified via top dermatologists in Europe'.

Co-tenants of Helena's at 274 Collins Street included Mrs Ward, who ran the Salon Charmazelie out of the basement; a piano importers; the

Melbourne Philharmonic society; the Musical Society of Victoria all on the ground floor and, in an adjoining suite of rooms, seventy-six individual music teachers were listed as giving classes. Amongst their clients was the famous Nellie Melba, who being curious, apparently climbed the stairs to Helena's seven-room suite on the second floor for a facial.

Helena was rarely out of the press. In an interview in *Table Talk* published in December 1905, the awe-struck women's editor wrote about Helena's salon: 'Carpets and corridors are in shades of green; the walls are white, the wicker chairs gilded, the whole very light and airy and everywhere flowers and beautiful terracotta pots.' Thrilled that her shopping in Europe had achieved such newsworthy results, Helena used the principle throughout her life, endlessly buying objects and bric-à-brac on her travels, charging it all to her business. Her houses, art and clothes were all 'gude for business' and presumably good for her tax returns too.

The same editorial feature said,

> The establishment here in Melbourne of a Beauty Institute, thoroughly equipped with the very latest systems and appliances, is an important event. Mlle Rubinstein's two Viennese experts, both dressed in red, look smilingly on and show the working of the appliances to remove wrinkles and to cure unduly flushed skin, but do not attempt much conversation as they have not yet mastered English. One has studied medicine I am told.

The reporter, blissfully unaware that the girls in question were sister Ceska and cousin Lola, was obviously impressed by Helena's uniformed staff. The girls, having been whisked from Krakow to Melbourne and transformed into 'red-uniformed Viennese experts', managed to smile their way through this media attention. As early learners in the Rubinstein school of public relations, they let Helena do the talking.

For a woman with little social small talk, Helena made up for it whilst she was doing treatments or selling her product. She had a way of bringing people 'under her spell' as buyers who knew her later would say, and a gift for 'establishing quick rapport'. Throughout her career, Helena worked the same magic on reporters, entrancing the media with her worldly-wise expertise, coupled with a homely, almost motherly approach. When she dispensed advice on skin care, proffering a jar of 'my own special cream, you *must* try it, I *know* it will work for you, you will *love* the result, believe me . . .', journalists left the interview in a euphoric mood.

A eulogising editorial feature in Melbourne placed great emphasis on Helena's 'European training', reporting Helena as saying:

> It was difficult for me to obtain permission to study with the best skin specialists, for on the continent women do not dream of going to a woman for skin treatment, they would only see a medical man. In Paris for example, I had to say I was a Russian lady doctor who was training to be a skin specialist. I worked with Dr Pashki in Vienna, under Dr Lasaar in Berlin who is quite well known in his way; with Dr Pokitonoff, a Russian doctor, in Paris and with Dr Una in Hamburg for the skin-peeling cure.

Skin-peeling was part of dermatological experimentation as early as 1886. The system involved the application of acid, using electricity to remove the upper layers of skin to eliminate scarring caused by acne or smallpox. It was risky, but effective. Early plastic surgery techniques included injecting paraffin under the skin to plump out cheeks and eyelids. Surgical treatment was available to reshape noses and for the brave there were facelifts, which all too often went wrong, leaving the patient with a lop-sided mouth or worse. Helena advocated plastic surgery, although it is doubtful she ever tried it herself, and the treatment she most favoured for instant effect was 'clipping': in a very advanced precursor of today's ultra-fashionable Botox injections, surgically 'clipping' the muscle between the eyes smoothed out frown lines. 'The muscles in the forehead,' explained Helena in her first book, 'which are the basic cause of frown lines, once being paralysed cease to contract, so in a short time the skin above, having nothing to pull it out of shape, smooths out.'

With business in Melbourne flourishing, Helena was keen to expand and in 1907 opened a branch in Sydney, at 158 Pitt Street, by now admitting to the public that her sister was on the team. Her advertising was showing subtle changes, the hard-selling tactics still evident, but pulled together in a more refined style, her favourite headline being: WHAT WOMEN WANT with copy saying, 'My cream gives a pearly lustre, imparting a *je ne sais quoi*'. 'THE BEAUTY OF VALAZE is that it works its wonders while you sleep' was another favoured copyline in the

Australian Home Journal, encouraging sales of Valaze night cream as well as the daytime moisturiser.

Her advertising always took the form of a personal message, or letter, designed as though Helena Rubinstein herself was actually talking to the reader, for example:

> I want to tell you – just in a personal little chat – about my Valaze Massage Institute. It is here in Sydney – I have one in Melbourne too, you know – and is fitted on the lines of the famous beauty institutes I have been to in Europe. Mind you come and see me when you are down in Sydney. Both I and my sister are to be seen at 158 Pitt Street.

The changes were undoubtedly due to the guiding hand of the new man in Helena's life, Edward Titus. Like Helena, Titus was both Polish and Jewish. His family had emigrated to the USA and Edward had an American passport and apparently a modest allowance courtesy of the family mineral water bottling plant. He was a 'journeyman' journalist when his travels took him to Sydney, probably meeting Helena at the end of 1906.

Without doubt, Edward Titus changed Helena's life, although in the beginning their relationship was strictly professional. He took over her advertising campaigns, developed design and packaging for new products, advised her on expansion – she opened a salon in Wellington, New Zealand early in 1908 – and had the satisfaction of seeing her turnover in Australia increase ever upwards. It's said he even wrote several of the glowing Australian editorial features which established Helena's reputation there, published under different bylines. He was not, however, the only male supporter and adviser in her orbit. Nor was he the only man who could lay claim to contributing to her success.

Between 1905 and 1908, Helena Rubinstein was 'on a roll'. Those three years were the defining ones in her climb to the top and she made the most of them. In early 1908, under pressure from Titus to accept his proposal of marriage, but fired by her insecurities, Helena did what gave her most comfort in times of stress – she went travelling.

For a 'Commonwealth' citizen like Helena, who had by now made a fortune from her three salons, not to mention her extensive wholesaling to chemists and a healthy mail-order business, London was the next international market. Sailing there in the spring of 1908, cash-rich and confident, she found a splendid building at 24 Grafton Street, part of the property portfolio of the Marquis of Salisbury. Every editorial, every advertisement and every beauty pamphlet from 1908 for the next three decades referred to the 'magnificent mansion' in Grafton Street. In her memoir she wrote, 'My London salon was the house of Lord Salisbury, one of England's great political figures. It was on four floors with twenty-six rooms, the rent was several thousand pounds per annum, more than I could really afford, but I gambled on my luck.'

The stucco house at 24 Grafton Street was indeed part of the Salisbury portfolio, but he had never lived there. As Conservative prime minister since 1895, 10 Downing Street was his London home and weekends were spent at Hatfield House in Hertfordshire. The present Marquis of Salisbury's librarian is keeper of an impressive archive of family papers. They show that Helena Rubinstein became the sole leaseholder of the property in 1924, paying a rent of £2000 per annum. Before that, she had sub-let the premises from Frank Collinson and Harold Crompton Bentley, a firm of interior decorators and architects, who were paying £950 per annum in rent. The elegant Georgian town house, with around twelve rooms plus servants' quarters and an attic flat, became her beauty salon. The first telephone line recorded in her name was put in during July 1908, the number was Mayfair 4611. Not that Helena was there to see the work done as she had gone back to Australia. Finally succumbing to his persistent courtship, Helena married Edward Titus in Sydney in July 1908. They returned almost at once to Europe, taking time to visit Nice on their honeymoon, an occasion fraught with drama, resulting in Helena rushing back to London without her husband. A few weeks later, Helena and Edward Titus moved into the attic flat in Grafton Street. Helena's relentless ambition was to conquer Europe as she had conquered Australia. She was helped by a personal fortune which she later explained to her family was over half a million dollars, and by her husband, who had very little money at all.

Helena's relationship with Titus, as she referred to her husband, was doomed from the start. Hesitant about him joining her business, nervous in case he had married her for her money, she nevertheless had become increasingly fond of him, was enthralled by his sophistication and education – and had ultimately fallen deeply in love. Oddly for such a strongminded woman, she was also curiously subjugated by him.

As astute as she was in business, Helena was unworldly and naïve in her personal relationships with men. If ever there was a couple less suited to marriage it was she and Edward Titus. American journalist Grace Davidson, who would become a close friend of them both, later wrote about Titus:

> He had great charm. He was attractive in a strange way, with good features, a shock of thick, smooth grey hair adding a note of distinction. He spoke precisely, incisively, in rather a florid style. He was at heart a loner. But it was not by preference. He aspired to people he could not have. He liked beautiful, important, talented, intellectual, well-bred people. Most of all he adored beautiful, sexy women.

So the man who loved the cultural highlife married a self-made, hard-working, poorly educated woman who had the means to provide it for him. There is no doubt that he admired his wife — indeed was dependent on her not just financially but emotionally; what he did not do however was *desire* her. He respected her as a businesswoman but never made her feel she was a *woman*. Neither did he make any effort to curb his flirtatious and sexually liberated attitude. From the beginning, Helena was bitterly hurt to find him turning the full force of his seductive charm towards other women. She later wrote, 'On our honeymoon I left him in France because he was carrying on with a woman. I was so inexperienced, had I had sense, I would never have lived with him again.' She never sent the letter. Her lengthy outpourings of grief were often kept to herself. Writing such letters was her way of ridding herself of her demons. When Helena experienced pain, or defeat, she picked herself up again; she could rise above the crisis, bury its impact and move on. Such letters were often filed away, where they would languish unread by the intended recipient, but the action made her feel much better.

Helena clearly felt sadness at what she perceived as her failure as a wife. She bottled this up, expressing her sexual and emotional frustration in shopping — giving herself 'treats'. Following arguments with Titus, she bought pearls, referring to them afterwards as 'quarrel jewels'. The French honeymoon débâcle resulted in Helena acquiring her first important string of pearls, later admitting that 'it soothed me to buy them'. Helena was very knowledgeable about precious stones and was also very superstitious, so possibly felt pearls were soothing because they are considered a calming stone, acting as an emotional balance and with a special link to the third eye. She would have known this, just as she knew her rubies gave confidence, energy, vitality and leadership and her emeralds improved relationships and were reputed to be relaxing, not to mention being a buffer against mental illness. Keen-eyed observers of her jewels could have spotted her moods each morning, based on her choice of stones. To Titus, such beliefs would have been pathetic. At any event, he wasn't too familiar with his wife's jewellery – she bought her own. Her impressive collection thereafter was largely the result of her frustrations and arguments with Titus. Their marriage followed a pattern of rage and reconciliation for the next twenty-five years.

By Christmas 1908, Helena was back visiting in Australia. This time she did her media interviews in a suite at the Grand Hotel in Melbourne, holding court with a flourish. The results of her press junket make entertaining reading. 'Mlle Rubinstein has compelled the grandest of London ladies into her salon. She herself is a student of history, of literature and of philosophy, who has studied chemistry and anatomy under the greatest experts in Vienna, Berlin, Paris and Russia . . . her astonishing capacity for unremitting work, combined with wonderful business acumen, have resulted in her owning a business which now covers the whole world.' Helena was waxing lyrical about her first trip away from home, 'by which I mean beautiful Vienna, on the River Danube,' explaining that she came to Australia with her range of luxury face creams so 'I could put them to the hardest test possible, that of a climate ruinous to the complexion. They all came out with flying colours.' Quite how Helena managed to keep herself composed as she told this version of her life story we shall never know.

The feature ended by informing readers of Helena's travel plans with all the status due to a major celebrity.

Mlle Rubinstein has come to Australia on what she calls a flying trip to visit friends and business establishments. She must be back in London for the next Season but will visit her New Zealand branches and proceed from there to India, where she is to complete arrangements for two branches on her way back to London. She has found time however to bring us out some of her new products, including one for the relief of tired eyes and Valaze snow lotion, the most refined of all liquid powders, which caressingly clings to the skin's surface, cools it and gives a delicate, sweet-scented tint.

Travelling back to London, Helena paused long enough in Paris to sit for her portrait, a graceful etching by Helleu. Delicate pictures of women and children by this society artist are the quintessence of elegance and his subjects were always well connected. It hangs today at the Madison Avenue headquarters of the Helena Rubinstein Foundation, where this light and gentle image is a key to the period when Helena was part of high society and when Europe was at one of its most social and decadent periods.

As Helena was an avowed workaholic, whose idea of socialising was to invite the family – most of whom worked for her – to a breakfast board meeting, or a dinner and bridge evening (proficiency at the game being described by Claude Forter, one of her sales managers as 'a sine qua non for admission to the upper echelons of management') understandably, those close to her never quite realised that, for a few years at least, she was part of the most glittering and glamorous group of the *haute bohème*. It's also fair to say that this era of extravagance in London and Paris from 1908 to 1914, when she was commuting between both cities, was probably her first and last real flirtation with the fashionable elite.

Titus collected books, Helena collected just about everything else, but in pre-war Paris and London, they were both collecting people – especially ones who could help Helena. Following some skilful advice from Titus, Helena launched her salon in London not with extravagant advertising claims about fantasy aristocratic clients, but by giving free treatments to a genuine aristocratic clientele. Word-of-mouth publicity from such a group would have been vastly helpful, even more so when she obliged them by settling the odd account here and there – a florist's bill or one from the caterers, especially if they were for parties attended by Mr and Mrs Edward W. Titus. She was happy to hire a guide through the complex hierarchy of Edwardian society and in London this role fell to the eccentric Baroness Catherine 'Flame' d'Erlanger, whilst in Paris the guiding hand belonged to Misia Edwards, who would soon marry Spanish artist, Jose Maria Sert.

Usually happy to let her husband handle their social life, Helena particularly enjoyed spending time with 'Flame' d'Erlanger, who lived in Byron's old home in Piccadilly. The baroness, an unconventional character, attracted London's *risqué* and fashionable elite to her drawing rooms, described by her friend Cecil Beaton as 'decorated with an eclectic display of shell-flowers, witch-balls and mother-of-pearl furniture, all picked up for a song at the Caldedonian market'. Flame had eccentric tastes in everything, including servants. Her daughter Baba was cared for by a Mameluke. As a consequence, young Baba – who grew up to become the Princesse de Faucigny Lucinge – was escorted to dancing class by a six-foot-six Egyptian in flowing robes and a turban, causing a stir amongst the other children who apparently adored him, but presumably causing annoyance to that other strand of impenetrable social hierarchy – Nanny.

Helena and Flame were drawn together by their love of trawling London's flea markets for treasures. Searching out 'beautiful things' at unlikely venues and bargain prices was already a Rubinstein obsession, and she would have been grateful to her glamorous guide.

Helena and Titus were at their best together when planning business. She was generous enough to recognise his part in shaping her career when, following changes in Australian company law in 1908, necessitating she incorporate her burgeoning business, she gave him an equal share. The Register of Companies shows that when Helena Rubinstein Pty Ltd was created on 25 April 1909, shareholders were: Helena Juliet Rubinstein with 46%, Edward William Titus with 46%, Ceska Rubinstein with 6% and two nominee directors with 1% each. Ceska was appointed managing director, leaving Helena free to pursue her European expansion – and her family expansion, for by now she was pregnant.

Titus's second wife, Erica Friedman, says that Titus always claimed he had invested in Helena's original Australian company, which is why he had a shareholding. In any event, Helena's rewarding Titus with equity at that point was well deserved. On one of his many trips to Paris, where he would buy books and manuscripts by, amongst others, Anatole France and Baudelaire, he came across an opportunity that would dramatically escalate his wife's career when he heard of a small beauty salon for sale on the rue St Honoré. The Russian owner, Madame Chambaron, had more to sell than just a salon – the package included the formulae for some important skin creams.

Helena Rubinstein's Maison de Beauté Valaze opened at 255 rue St Honoré in the summer of 1909. Amongst the preparations offered were the original Rubinstein Australian Valaze formulae with the addition of Madame Chambaron's herbal treatments and a new skin-toning lotion. The biggest moneyspinner was the Russian cosmetologist's range of 'pasteurised' creams thereafter promoted as 'Valaze Pasteurised – a delightful skin-refreshening wonder-cream – one of Helena Rubinstein's great masterpieces for improving the skin', and a treatment called 'Liquidine' which was promoted as 'subduing shine, eliminating redness and being good for circulation'. Unlike Grafton Street, the St Honoré premises were too small for production, so Helena opened a small outlet at St Cloud, where some twenty-five people were kept busy bottling and labelling.

Heavily pregnant, Helena relied on her sister Pauline to run the Paris salon whilst she remained in London. Her first son, Roy, was born at 24 Grafton Street in December 1909. On his birth certificate, under the column for 'father's occupation', Edward Titus entered 'of independent means'. As his only significant means at that time were gleaned from working for his wife, he could have put 'company director', but as an intellectual snob, the idea of public association with a beauty business was abhorrent to him. Titus, just like Elizabeth Arden's husband, Tommy Lewis, contributed to the family firm. But when financial independence relies on a wife's drive and bank balance, it takes an exceptional man not to be emasculated. Few men are capable of being happily married – and working for their wife. Titus was no exception.

Years later, Helena wrote that they 'entertained graciously' in Grafton Street, recalling memories of holding 'Polish suppers'. It is highly unlikely that Titus would ever acknowledge his Polish roots by offering regional food, and certainly Helena had neither the talent nor the time to cook. Any entertaining they did was catered; there might have been a small kitchen in their cramped attic flat, but the only 'kitchen' she was interested in was her large laboratory in the basement. Claude Forter has fond memories of the Grafton Street laboratory, having often visited it when his father, Boris, ran Rubinstein's British business. 'I remember the chief chemist, Herr Doktor Salfeld,' Forter says. 'He made wonderful coffee for his visitors, using retorts, bunsen burners and other lab equipment.'

Helena's salon offered, amongst other treatments, the revolutionary skin-peeling technique. Helena says she brought over 'the very talented Frau Doktor Emmie List' from Vienna. Dr List apparently worked miracles on the skin of a 'lady with a great English name' who had suffered from acute acne, leaving her face pitted and scarred, and as a consequence was a recluse. Quite possibly introduced to Helena via the Baroness d'Erlanger, this aristocratic beauty, having undergone 'skinning' sessions over a period of six months in Grafton Street, was duly transformed. Helena writes that 'her gratitude was touching and inspiring'.

This is another clue to her acceptance into the snobbish world of Edwardian London. It seems the grateful lady sent quantities of her friends to Grafton Street. Shortly afterwards, it seems the same benefactress opened up Pandora's box for her beauty saviour. Helena said, 'A year later, when she went to India with her husband in an official role, she sent me a number of Indian princesses, many with lovely features, but who were forced to hide their dreadful skins. I loved to see these colourful creatures in my salon, small-boned and graceful and adorned with sublime jewels. Around their necks they wore magnificent strands of pearls and their wrists were covered with emeralds and rubies.'

Pearls, emeralds and rubies were soon around Helena's wrists and neck too, Indian or otherwise. Based one can only suppose on glorious confidence, she set her prices at a stratospheric 10 guineas for twelve treatments or £200 for a weekly visit for the entire year, payable in advance. They paid. *Queen* magazine and other publications were soon full of stories about Madame Rubinstein of 'Melbourne, Sydney, Wellington and London'. They talked not only about her business, but also about her clothes.

Investing in a wardrobe became a seasonal ritual for Helena, who was savvy enough to know that appearance was everything in the beauty business and that important clothes impress important people. Her rich clients needed to trust the taste of their beauty queen and to be impressed by her. Helena did not let them down – but she didn't buy British.

London had its share of acclaimed fashion designers in the early 1900s, particularly Redfern, who maintained branches in London, Edinburgh, Paris and New York. Redfern's tailor, Charles Poynter, who was in charge in Paris, is credited as creating the first *tailleur*, made for yachting at Cowes, circa 1880, for the Princess of Wales, who remained exquisitely dressed by Redfern when she was Queen. Henry Creed, of the Creed family, ran their Conduit Street branch, and was famed for making 'Amazones' – tailored riding habits – for the Empress Eugenie and later the first tweed suit for the Duchess of Alba. Another famous – or infamous – client was Mata Hari who was executed wearing a Creed suit. Madame Pacquin, one of the first successful women in Paris haute couture, had opened a London site at 39 Dover Street in 1902, and style shoppers amongst the 'new women' were quick to adopt cycling suits with nipped waists, worn with huge white blouses with big sleeves and deep cuffs.

The softer alternative to all this tailoring was the ethereal 'tea-gown' trend, espoused by Lady Duff Gordon – London's own society dressmaker. Lady Duff Gordon, who called herself Lucille, was actually Scots Canadian, one reason perhaps why a few years later, Scots Canadian Elizabeth Arden would adopt the Lucille look.

Custom-made departments were buoyant in all the best stores: Harrods, Selfridges, the lavish marble-and-bronze Debenham & Freebody, and Swan & Edgar in Piccadilly, training place of the legendary Charles Worth. In any comment Helena made about her clothes, however, and in all of the extensive photographic records of her wardrobe, nothing was ever said about *le style anglais*. She was making her money in London but bought her clothes in Paris.

By the 1900s, couture was controlled by Worth, then run by his younger son Gaston, and their rival, Jacques Doucet. Whilst the Worths had extravagant tastes, which included entertaining almost as lavishly as their clients, the more intellectual and refined Jacques Doucet who dressed the aristocracy, actresses and *demi-mondaines* in a sensual froth of lace, silk and satin, spent his money on art. Doucet, unique amongst almost all fashion designers, was a true patron of the arts, and a friend of the artists. His gorgeous gowns, however, were too ornate for a working woman and Helena was, during the day at least, a *tailleur* woman. Her evening clothes were more dramatic. In the early years she liked the Grecian drape of Lelong and wore a lot of Lanvin, Chanel and Schiaparelli. In later years she owned a magnificent wardrobe by Balenciaga and bought at Dior. Her tastes were for the exotic rather than the ruffled, so in the beginning, her sense of drama coinciding with her first pregnancy, necessitating tunic dressing, she found the perfect source, courtesy of Paul Poiret in Paris.

Well trained at Doucet and following a brief, unhappy time at Worth, Poiret established his own business in 1904. A natural publicist, he was fast becoming known as a man whose tastes were as extravagant as his talent. He was driven around Paris in a beige Renault Torpedo by a chauffeur wearing uniforms tailored to match. Louis Sue, the designer described as 'the soul of French architecture', who would later mastermind the décor of all Helena Rubinstein's major properties, created the interiors of Poiret's houseboat, the *Nomad*. Max Jacob, the poet and novelist, a gifted amateur astrologer, predicted the colours his friend should wear in conjunction with the planets, his abilities enhanced by the pervading aura of ether around him. Yet another friend, the artist Raoul Dufy, designed his notepaper with an image and colour for each day of the week. Before the Great War, Poiret lived like a king, holding exotic parties for his courtiers as he was the newest 'king of fashion'. Poiret's lean look, with his narrow, hobble skirts, attracted the *haute monde* ladies in droves, amongst them Margot Asquith. In 1909, the fashion-loving Liberal prime minister's wife invited Poiret to show his collection at 10 Downing Street. The fashion presentation caused a furore in the press, with Mrs Asquith being accused of 'being a traitor to British fashion'. Reluctantly, Margot Asquith had to sever her connections with Poiret and turn patriotically to Lucille.

Helena admired 'mad' Margot Asquith, whom she met when Poiret brought his collection to London. She later credited the prime minister's wife with giving her business a boost. 'After successfully completing my first experiments with face powder,' said Helena, 'the next step was rouge. Only Margot Asquith had the courage to use it openly and I taught her how to dramatise her remarkable features.' In an early innovation of today's 'backstage at fashion show rituals', it seems more likely Helena will have offered her beauticians to co-ordinate the models make-up, taking charge herself and no doubt slicking a little rouge onto the ultra-fashionable Margot Asquith's cheeks before she received her guests.

Whilst Titus was more interested in carving out his literary career – he was by now buying and selling rare manuscripts – and happy to leave his wife to forge hers in beauty, together they delighted in their acquaintance with London-based artists. Jacob Epstein came into their orbit at this time, remaining a lifelong friend of Titus. In the intertwined circles of art and fashion, Helena's guiding hand in Paris, however, belonged to another Polish woman, whose name opened every door that mattered – Misia Sert.

Born Misia Godebski in St Petersburg in 1872, she was the daughter of a Polish sculptor who lived in considerable, if eccentric, style. Misia's stepmother, Matylda Natanson, was Polish, Jewish and very rich. One of her closest friends was Modjeska, the actress Helena metamorphosed into her own mother's life, and the Godebskis' extended circle of wealthy and bohemian friends in Paris in the late 1880s included Polish nobility like Prince Czartoryski and the Zamoyskas. Misia grew up in an extended family, marrying one of her stepmother's nephews, the intellectual and artistic Thadee Natanson, in 1893.

Thadee and Misia were a golden couple. He published the cult magazine of the day, *La Revue Blanche*, and Misia was soon absorbed into the world of its contributors, becoming close to Stephane Mallarmé and the poet Paul Verlaine amongst others. *La Revue Blanche* was an extraordinary magazine in an extraordinary time. Debussy was their music critic; Vuillard and Pierre Bonnard were hired to do an exclusive print for each issue; Toulouse-Lautrec painted their promotional posters. As the century turned, the Natansons were at the centre of the intellectual and artistic life of Paris. Closest in their charmed circle were the young writer Henri Gauthier-Villars – 'Willy' – and his writer wife Colette, along with Sarah Bernhardt, wowing audiences in l'Aiglon in 1900 wearing costumes designed by Poiret, and her fellow actress Rejane, a particular friend of Misia's. Misia was perfectly placed in Paris at that defining moment when art met fashion head-on.

By 1905, Misia had left Thadee Natanson and in an unlikely coupling married the decadent, vastly rich industrialist Alfred Edwards. Her social world shifted to encompass writers and the cutting-edge journalists of the day, by virtue of her husband's ownership of the Théâtre de Paris and the newspaper, *Le Matin*. His wife had a passion for jewels and Edwards indulged her. Her clothes became almost as extravagant as her jewels and she moved in fashionable circles when fashion designers were becoming famous, none more so than Misia's intimate friend Coco Chanel.

By 1907, Misia and Edwards were estranged. Her old friend Colette had also left her husband and was revelling in a very public lesbian affair. Their circle included Spanish artist Jose Maria Sert who introduced Misia to Diaghilev, watching with pleasure while the dandy and Misia became inseparable. Jean Cocteau, observing them at Diaghilev's Ballet Russes performance at the Théâtre du Chatelat in May 1909, when Nijinsky made his debut, wrote afterwards: 'It's impossible to think of Jose Maria Sert's golden ceilings, the sunny world of Renoir, Bonnard, Debussy, Ravel and the radiant dawn of Stravinsky, without seeing the face of the young, beribboned tiger, the double, cruel face of a pink she-cat that we saw in Misia.'

Picasso's biographer, John Richardson, observed Misia too, later in her life, when he visited her in Paris. 'I was taken to visit her in her ornate apartment on the rue de Rivoli – all mulberry coloured velvet and rock-crystal, dud El Grecos and bits of good Boulle – Misia was overwhelmingly awful and, according to Picasso, always had been. By the time I met her in 1947, she was on her last legs, totally addicted to morphine.' That Paris visit made a memorable impact on Richardson, who describes Misia as 'absolutely ghastly and not nearly as useful as people claimed'.

Helena, who saw Misia on and off for many years, keeping up with news about her from their mutual friend Coco Chanel, summed it up more succinctly by saying, 'She was a meshuggenah.' Students of Yiddish know this means 'crazy woman'. Crazy or ghastly, there is no denying her influence on artistic society in Paris.

In her memoir, Helena says: 'I had known Misia Natanson through mutual friends in Poland and I looked her up. Our common interest in art became an immediate link and our husbands became friends.' It's unlikely Titus would have had much in common with Alfred Edwards but the intellectual Polish community in Paris was close-knit and Titus would have admired Natanson and his magazine. Misia had already established herself as a powerful provider of introductions – for a price – to interesting and wealthy people who came into her orbit and Helena, encouraged by Titus, would have used the relationship. Misia was amongst those who introduced Helena to art, and Titus encouraged her. He dined with the artists and his wife bought their pictures.

Helena always claimed she cut back her work after her first son, Roy, was born, and took two years off following the birth of her second, Horace Gustave. Nothing could be further from the truth. She worked continuously, commuting monthly to Paris, and even managed to fit in another trip to Australia in 1911. She also claimed that, due to her expanding family, they needed a larger home in London. Her imagination fairly gallops along as she describes their move to a house she calls 'Solna'. 'It was in Roehampton Lane, near Putney Heath on the estate of J.P. Morgan,' she wrote. 'The house had twenty rooms and three unused Victorian hothouses. We turned one into a library for Edward and another into a billiard room.' In reality, Helena and Edward lived in a rather pleasant, larger-than-average Edwardian villa in south west London. Their address was number one, The Terrace, Richmond, and although their view was delightful, overlooking the park, there were no greenhouses. There was, however, a billiard room, the house having at one stage been a very substantial property, divided into two by a builder. There was a library for her husband's book collection, a dining room, butler's pantry and a double drawing room. A dressing room would have taken Helena's clothes, with a second one her husband's, who had just as strong a penchant for his own wardrobe as his wife had for hers. There were enough bedrooms for their baby Roy, his nursemaid, the cook, plus another Rubinstein sister, Manka, who was brought from Krakow to learn the ropes and help care for Helena and the London salon. Helena never cared for the house, but it seems Titus adored it, possibly as it meant he could visit their near neighbour, the Marchioness of Ripon. Gwladys Ripon lived at 'Coombe' on Kingston Hill, where she hosted glorious parties attended by Queen Alexandra, Nijinsky, Caruso (who sang at them), and Pavlova (who danced at them). She brought Diaghilev's Company to London in 1911 in a gala season to celebrate the coronation of King George V. Where Diaghilev went, so did Misia, and where Misia went, so did Sert, who was soon commissioned to paint fresco panels at Coombe. Inevitably, Misia will have brought along her 'cosmetologist' friend, much to the delight of Titus, with his craving for 'beautiful, important, talented, intellectual, well-bred people' – all of whom he would have found at Lady Ripon's.

Aged forty, Helena was pregnant again. Their second child was born at the Richmond house in May 1912, with Titus again describing himself on the birth certificate as 'of independent means'. Confined to home for a while, with time to consider redecoration, she didn't have Jo Jo Sert paint frescoes for the Richmond property, but she did commission Polish sculptor Elie Nadelman to sculpt large high-relief plaques, presumably to bring some light relief to the heavy, Victorian architecture. Helena had met Nadelman when he held his first exhibition in London at Bond Street's Paterson Gallery. A friend of Thadee Natanson and Gertrude Stein in Paris, Nadelman was as handsome as he was talented. Helena, having bought his entire show on the spot, became enraptured with his work, using his singular marble pieces in her homes and salons in London, Paris and New York.

By the autumn of 1912, the Titus family had made Paris their permanent base. Helena knew she had to conquer Paris and to do that she had to live there. London had become less appealing during the two years since the jovial King Edward VII had died and Paris was attracting the type of international traveller and cosmopolitan lifestyle suited to the fashion and beauty business. This is when she started clinical studies in dermatology, almost certainly studying at the St Louis Hospital on avenue Richerand, famous for treating skin disorders. Today, entering through the discreet and beautiful courtyard, visitors can look at over 4000 casts, drawings and sketches of skin disorders in the hospital's Musée de la Dermatologie.

Developing her Paris clientele, she was encouraged and supported by Misia, now living openly with Jo Jo Sert and seemingly happy to open her address book for the 'rich Helena Rubinstein'. Generally speaking, Helena left Titus to socialise, preferring work to partying, but as networking was 'gude for business' she went regularly to Misia's gatherings where she met an eclectic and influential group. Working too hard to be bothered by the antics of people she had little time for, sycophancy was never Helena's forte, and she managed to bring conversation about the grandest of fashionable grandees down to a basic level. Proust was an example. Helena met him at Misia's in Paris. Years later, struggling to remember his name, she described the incident to Patrick O'Higgins. 'Misia knew everybody – even that Jewish writer who slept in a room lined with cork and wrote the famous book I could never read. You know, Marcel something.' 'Marcel Proust?' replied Patrick gently. 'Yes, that's the one. Nebbishy looking. He smelt of mothballs, wore a fur coat down to the ground, asked heaps about make-up. Would a duchess use rouge? Did demi-mondaines put kohl on their eyes? How should I know? But then, how could I have known that he was going to be so famous? If so, I might have told him a thing or two.'

Misia turned her hand to sending clients for treatments at Helena's Paris salon. Her friend Colette, by now in the news for her lesbian cabaret shows, was dispatched to have a Swedish massage from the new supremo, Ulla. Helena claims she contacted a reporter and invited her to be in the area when Colette was due to leave. The idea was more likely to have come from Titus, who had a penchant for erotica, and it certainly worked. The press reported Colette as saying, 'Never have I felt so wonderful, now I am ready for anything.' In another report, Colette is reputed to have said, 'Massage is a sacred duty. The women of France owe it to themselves. Without it how can they hope to keep a lover!'

Helena would not have been surprised by Colette's enthusiasm. Years later she admitted, 'You know, it wasn't just an ordinary massage, they did little extra things.' In 1912, the 'extra' things Helena was referring to was the fact that it was perfectly respectable and presumably pleasurable to use vibrators whilst having massage.

Galen, the physician who worried about women's dry skin and gave them cold cream, also worried about their dry vaginas. He was convinced that a wide spectrum of women's conditions which were described as 'hysteria' were the result of uterine disease. This, in Galen's words, was 'caused by sexual deprivation, to which passionate women were particularly susceptible'. As a consequence, when he recommended 'genital massage therapy' for relief, his female patients readily responded. Galen was convinced that 'the resulting contractions and the release of sexual fluids from the vagina' were essential for a cure.

'Hysteria' was defined as a disease from the fourth century BC until the American Psychiatric Association dropped the term in 1952. Galen identified the symptoms as including menstrual problems, pre-menstrual syndrome, migraine, sweating attacks, temper tantrums, depression, anorexia, oedema and other conditions of tension and stress, all of which he believed could be cured by reaching orgasm.

A surprisingly large group of respectable doctors, obstetricians and gynaecologists, along with various naturopathic therapists, supported vaginal and uterine massage and were presumably relieved when in the 1880s a British doctor invented the electromechanical vibrator. Promoted as a palliative for female complaints and extensively advertised in respectable women's magazines and the Sears Roebuck catalogue, the vibrator joined various manual physical therapy devices, such as muscle beaters and Gustaf Zander's 'Swedish Movement' machines, as essential equipment in the physician's or therapist's treatment rooms, and at the fashionable spas throughout Europe.

By 1900, the electronic massagers were so popular that more than a dozen were on show at the Paris Exposition, including one so efficient it was called 'the Chattanooga'. This fierce-looking contraption could be used on male and female patients, apparently to great effect.

Whilst there is no evidence pointing to Elizabeth Arden ever using vibratory equipment in her salons, there is strong evidence that Helena Rubinstein did. She would have witnessed the demonstration of such technology on her spa tours, may well have installed it in Australia and New Zealand, almost certainly used it in London – but most definitely made it operational in Paris.

Small wonder then that Colette, most certainly a 'passionate woman' as defined by Galen, tottered from Helena's Maison Valaze in rue St Honoré with a satisfied flush to her face and gave such a glowing endorsement to the press. The system fell out of fashion by the end of the 1920s, perceived as 'unnecessary' by doctors and possibly distasteful to women, by now more in control of their own bodies. Colette, in a surprising move, opened her own

Beauty Institute in Paris in 1930. Her salon décor was based on Helena's premises, where she had enjoyed free treatments in exchange for her publicity value. No records exist as to whether Colette implemented the 'massage services' she had so enjoyed, but her salon in Paris, along with the branches in St Tropez and Nantes, closed down soon after they opened.

Helena's way of coping with her own repressed sexuality was by shopping – by now an addictive pastime – and she was busy at the antique and flea markets, not to mention the artists' studios. Her other addiction was work and the expansion of her empire. She realised she had to expand her horizons and, having been briefed by her family in America as to the acceptance of the beauty industry and the potential for profits, she set her sights on New York. With hostilities simmering, a Europe at war held little appeal for Helena. Sister Pauline was left running the Paris salon. In London, her manageress Rosa Hollay was put in charge of both the business and her precious formulae. It has always been said the Titus/Rubinstein family sailed together for New York at Edward's instigation, as he was concerned about the approaching war; but as they held American passports, there was no immediate threat to either of them.

In reality, Helena, showing her predilection for running away from a crisis, was once more at loggerheads with her husband. Leaving Titus and her two baby sons in Paris she travelled on 16 October to New York on the SS *Baltic* out of Livepool. Ellis Island records show she claimed to be just thirty-four. She may have *looked* thirty-four but she was forty-two when she set out to conquer America. Her husband and sons travelled six months later on the SS *Philadelphia* out of Liverpool, with a container load of her art, including her cherished collection of Elie Nadelman sculptures. By then, she had a New York salon to display them in. America had not yet joined the war, but battle was about to commence in New York, when Madame Helena Rubinstein invaded the territory of Miss Elizabeth Arden.

FLORENCE GRAHAM BECOMES MISS ELIZABETH ARDEN
New York 1907–1914

IT WOULD TAKE JUST three years for Florence Nightingale Graham to make her name, by which time she'd changed it. To begin with, when she was working her way up the career ladder, she called herself 'Mrs Graham', inventing a husband after the fashion of the time when 'nice girls' didn't go out to work. Florence strove all her life to follow such social niceties, adapting her clothes, jewels, manners, and her voice, to suit her aspirations. She wanted to be treated like a lady and was determined her business would only look after real ladies. She held fast to her ambition to serve the upper echelons of WASP society, and the Elizabeth Arden label, founded in 1910, once it had achieved prestige status, retained it for the rest of her life.

Florence Graham found her first job in the beauty business as a cashier at Mrs Eleanor Adair's on Fifth Avenue. Proud of her salons at 5 rue Cambon, Paris and at 92 New Bond Street, London, Mrs Adair's big idea was a complex system of 'muscle strapping' using a bizarre leather and canvas contraption which hooked under the chin and tied over the head, promoted as being able to 'lift the facial muscles and cure slack'. One unfortunate side effect was the total inability of her clients to talk, rather defeating the purpose of time spent in a beauty salon, where the intimate relationship between client and treatment specialist is all about chatting and gossiping, but Mrs Adair didn't take much notice of that. She promoted her strapping system, called Ganesh, enthusiastically, claiming that combined with her Ganesh range of treatment creams and oils it would 'make the face younger'. Her clients paid $2.50 a time for the privilege. The average working woman's weekly wage in New York during 1907 was around $7, but as there was nothing average about Mrs Adair's customers, price wasn't a problem. Despite a serious slump on Wall Street that year, business was brisk.

Florence quickly persuaded Mrs Adair to let her learn how to apply the treatments. She spent about a year there, absorbing every aspect of 'strapping', which would become the cornerstone of her own facial therapies. She also learned to give excellent manicures and studied massage, at which she excelled. She delighted in using her 'healing hands' on friends and colleagues. No one, it seems, was immune from her tactile approach.

Doyenne public relations consultant, Eleanor Lambert, recollects being with Miss Arden at a political fundraiser she held at her health spa, Maine Chance, towards the end of the 1930s. 'I remember we went up to Maine and Miss Arden was fluttering around. She would say, "You don't have to do anything, my dears – just vote Republican." She simply couldn't keep still. She'd push you onto a bed or a couch and start to give you a massage. People were there to give you all sorts of treatments. It was . . . exhausting. She pounced on Millicent Hearst – Mrs William Randolph Hearst – pushing her onto a bed and launched into a forceful massage. Millicent wasn't at all amused.'

When Florence had given all she could and taken all she needed to know from Mrs Adair, she moved on. She had met Elizabeth Hubbard (no relation of the unfortunate Mrs Hubbard Ayer), who had a modest range of her own preparations and was looking for an enterprising partner to open a salon. In 1909, the two formed an uneasy alliance, taking a lease on the third floor of a tall brownstone building at 509 Fifth Avenue and 42nd St. The location was perfect for the Fifth Avenue carriage trade, being near two of New York's most distinguished restaurants, Sherry's and Delmonico's, and not too far from Bergdorf Goodman, the small but exclusive womenswear store on 32nd St. It was Florence's first Fifth Avenue address and she revelled in it.

She insisted on imposing several strategies she had seen work well at Mrs Adair's and, in her inimitable way, improving on them. The duo's advertising was directly targeted at the smart market, the labelling on their jars of creams was very pretty and Florence came up with the name for their range – Grecian. She insisted an individual facial treatment be $2 rather than $2.50 and added the bonus of 'six treatments for $10', an offer she knew would appeal. They became busy virtually overnight, but Florence wasn't cut out to have partners and she parted with Mrs Hubbard within six months.

Just how the relationship deteriorated is not known, but Florence was in – she kept the premises – and Mrs Hubbard was out.

Florence was left with a beauty salon emblazoned with the name 'Mrs Elizabeth Hubbard' in gold lettering, the knowledge of how to formulate treatment creams, superb massage skills, limitless energy and enough experience to know she could carve a niche in the market. The downside was she had no trading name, no product name, no stock – and no money. First came the trading name. She stayed with Elizabeth, probably aware it would annoy Mrs Hubbard and almost certainly out of admiration for that great Queen, Elizabeth I, who had all the tenacious qualities Florence Graham admired – plus she used cosmetics. The surname was harder. There is a widely reported view that she chose 'Arden' from a poem by Tennyson called 'Enoch Arden', which apparently she was 'reading in a book of poetry at home'. The thought of Florence reading highbrow poetry is unlikely. Particularly as she was then doing nightly freelance manicures for cash and her bedtime reading was almost certainly women's magazines for ideas in beauty, or the society rags, to follow the lifestyles of the rich and famous.

The answer is more likely to be found in the latter. The railroad baron E.H. Harriman had died in September 1909 and Florence would have devoured the eulogies about the multimillionaire and his stables. Harriman had a penchant for light-harness horses, racing his thoroughbreds at his trotting track at Goshen, in the Catskills. More significantly, she would have read about his vast estate in nearby Orange County, where he owned 8000 acres of woodland and magnificent gardens, which he and his wife had called 'Arden'. A country girl at heart, Florence Graham had grown flowers on the family smallholding, bunching them up for sale at the market, and still nurtured seedlings in pots on the windowledge at her small apartment just off Riverside Drive. The name Elizabeth Arden suited all her aspirations, amongst them, owning a country estate.

Confusingly for her associates she would use a mixture of old and new names, sometimes signing letters 'Elizabeth Graham' and sometimes 'Elizabeth Arden'. As her alter ego, when she became a racehorse owner, she referred to herself as 'Mrs Elizabeth Graham', whilst her first stables were called 'Mr Nightingale's'. During her first marriage, she took her husband's name and was Mrs Lewis. At work, however, she was only ever 'Miss Arden'.

The name for her special line of creams was easier; she called it

Venetian. Throughout her career, Elizabeth Arden showed a rare gift for naming product, as well as developing it. Whilst never as passionate about spending time in her 'kitchens' as Madame, she was quite capable of handling her own initial production and in those early months did her share of mixing, blending and pounding, until she had perfected her first preparations. The packaging for her Venetian range was as exquisite as her salon's décor, lavishly redecorated in her favourite gold, white and pink with antique consoles in the main reception room. She even fitted her first Red Door, the gleaming entrance that would become the worldwide Arden signature, still used by the Arden company today.

The financing for Elizabeth's sole venture is shrouded in mystery. It's said that she borrowed money from her brother who was by now married and living in New York. But in 1910, the year she founded her business, neither her milliner sister Lollie, nor her china-salesman brother Willie, would have had anywhere near the funds required for a start-up loan. Her eldest sister Christine was married and living quietly in Canada and her father, as usual, was penniless. Her sister Jessie Gladys was still in Canada, poised to make a bad marriage and equally impoverished. There was a rumour in the Arden company that in her early days, Florence, who after all was a remarkably attractive woman, relied on the generosity of wealthy beaux for her survival. For example, following the acrimonious split from Miss Hubbard, when the penniless Florence mysteriously acquired the salon property she is reported to have said, rather ambiguously, 'The landlord preferred me.'

This early story about Miss Arden however, like so many, is impossible to confirm. What is true is that banks would have been unlikely to lend money to a single young woman with no collateral, so if she did get her seed money from the family, it could only have come from her uncle James Liberty Tadd in Philadelphia.

James Liberty, the youngest of Samuel Tadd's children, and named after a runaway slave his father had rescued in New Orleans, was a gifted amateur artist and director of the influential Adirondack Summer Art School and its associate faculty, the Florida Winter Art School in St Petersburg. His daughter Edith trained as an architect and ran her own design firm. Miss Arden would later be supportive to Edith's children, giving two of them jobs at the Fifth Avenue headquarters during the Depression, and she was particularly generous to Edith when she became ill with cancer, all kindnesses she might have felt she owed, if Edith's father helped her financially.

Looking for ways to increase her turnover and become self-sufficient, Miss Arden offered a spare room in her salon to the Ogilvie sisters, an enterprising group of young women, coincidentally also from Canada. Two of them were skilled hairdressers, already making a name in New York, and the third was a milliner. This association boosted profits at the Arden 'Salon d'Oro' – its name at that time – sufficiently for Elizabeth to survive the rigours of the start-up costs. The Ogilvie sisters soon moved on – and out – having also argued with Miss Arden. The parting of the ways had little effect on *their* cashflow, as they became the first importers of European pharmacist Eugene Schueller's innovative hair dye called L'Oréal Compound Henna. The mighty L'Oréal group is still controlled by Schueller's descendants in conjunction with Nestlé. In the endless circle of acquisitions and mergers that represents the luxury brands today, L'Oréal now own the Helena Rubinstein company.

The first full-time employee Elizabeth hired was Irene Delaney, whom she affectionately called Lanie. It was a good choice. Lanie stayed with the company for over forty years. Others who stayed for the long haul included Edward 'Teddy' Haslam, who ran the very profitable British division from 1921 until his death in the early 1960s, and American Gordon 'Gordy' Yates, who joined in 1928 and stayed until his retirement in 1968. Men like Haslam and Yates either devoted their lives to Elizabeth Arden, or left fast, often being 'bounced', Miss Arden's special word for firing somebody. When her temper flared people tended to bounce out faster than a rubber ball, so it was an appropriate epithet.

In those early days, there was little Elizabeth couldn't — or wouldn't — do to survive. Having invested heavily in salon décor, she saved money on a cleaner by doing the job herself. Budget problems meant choices, but when they were between advertising or technical staff, Elizabeth Arden always chose the advertising. After a day spent doing treatments and massage, she would go to the pristine laboratory at the back of her premises to make up stock, filling jars with their charming pink and gold labels by hand and tying her signature pink satin bow around the neck of each.

Packaging was crucial to the success of the range. She was lavish with this budget, identifying it as a key area, and designing it was her personal forte. Helena Rubinstein on the other hand often struggled with packaging concepts, never quite getting it right, torn between what she wanted and what she would pay for. She once astutely remarked about Arden, 'With my product and her packaging we could have ruled the world.'

Elizabeth was totally involved in every aspect of her business, including the copywriting. 'Beauty is one part nature and three parts care' ran one advertisement in *Vogue* during 1910, making a nod towards genetically inherited good skin. She wrote beauty pamphlets titled *The Quest of the Beautiful* and was quick to climb on the anti-ageing bandwagon, one copy-line in 1911 being: 'The Arden Salon d'Oro, where the spirit of youth is so all-pervading that you cannot leave without catching some of it.'

By 1912, Elizabeth's business was established enough for her to con-sider self-improvement. The Suffrage march on 6 May that year was an ideal opportunity to start her climb up the social ladder. She slipped out to join the throng of New York's great and good as they walked from 59th St to Washington Square. Susan B. Anthony and Elizabeth Cady Stanton had died, but new leaders had come forward to champion the cause. Over 20,000 women marched that day, joined by over 500 supportive men and watched with fascination by over half a million onlookers crowding their route. Their determination had inspired an intriguing figurehead to join their ranks, namely Mrs Oliver Belmont.

An unlikely convert to women's rights, Alva Belmont, the ex-wife of 'Willie K' Vanderbilt, having reached the pinnacle of her success as one of the leaders of New York and Newport society, was of an age where the delights of fashion were waning and she preferred to take up a fashionable cause instead. Oblivious to the rights of her own beautiful, if somewhat dutiful, daughter Consuelo, less than ten years earlier in 1895 Alva had insisted she marry the ninth Duke of Marlborough. Her daughter, looking back at those astonishing times, wrote that her mother had said, 'I do the thinking – you do as you are told'. Consuelo did as she was told and married her duke. Inevitably, they did not live happily ever after, theirs being a famously unhappy marriage. Mrs Vanderbilt herself subsequently divorced her own husband and married another rich and very attractive man, Oliver Belmont, son of August Belmont, the financial genius who ran the Rothschild interests in New York. Their marriage was cut short by his untimely death, leaving Alva very rich and very bored. Mrs Belmont was a born dictator, dominating events as much as people. Although she was nearly sixty when she took up the cause of women's suffrage, she threw herself into it with all the zeal she had previously expended on organising some of the most lavish parties ever seen in New York. Mrs Belmont founded The Political Equality League in 1909, throwing her not inconsiderable weight, not to mention her considerable fortune, behind, amongst other issues, the first major strike by New York's beleaguered young textile workers, most of them immigrant women, some as young as 14, and all toiling in shirtwaist sweat-shops.

The march was a triumph. Inez Milholland, a campaigner as beautiful as she was dedicated, led the parade riding a horse and marching behind were housewives, trade unionists and hundreds of female factory workers. The women, all dressed in white, made a strong visual as well as emotive statement: as a badge of courage they wore bright red lipstick.

The lipstick gesture was a particularly interesting one, given the strong political and social leanings of the marchers. For the grandees, it signalled they were able to wear lipstick because they now *wanted* to and they were not wanton women. Others were striking a blow against the deep, puritan ethic of 'anti-adornment' so prevalent then amongst American women.

Miss Arden's staff were astonished to see her leave to join the march, as she had rarely shown any particular interest in women's rights. She was, however, interested in being with the right women, using her involvement with the march, however brief, for years to come, telling people: 'I've always felt strongly about women's issues. I went on one of the key marches, you know, dear.'

When Miss Arden returned to her salon at the end of that afternoon in the company of ladies, she determined that not only would her salon look after such ladies but she would now start to live like a lady herself. Her first step was to move house. Vacating Riverside Drive, she took an apartment at the more fashionable location of West 79th St, until she made her victorious leap over the park in the late 1920s, settling into the beautiful apartment at 834 Fifth Avenue on the corner of East 64th St where she would live for the rest of her life.

Her second step was to enrol in elocution classes. Miss Arden's carefully modulated voice, often described as 'breathy' or 'child-like', was the result of very expensive lessons. The only trouble was that her new voice, rather like her new name, sometimes got confused and she forgot which was which. When her temper tantrums hit, her carefully modulated vowels, not to mention her carefully modulated grammar, slipped and Miss Arden became very unladylike indeed. Swearing like a trooper, her voice would rise to what long-suffering associates would describe as a 'squealing shriek'.

'Miss Arden wanted to be treated as the glamorous, beautiful, ethereal, ultra-feminine woman she dreamed about,' said Janet Leckie, an associate of New York advertising agency owner Henry Sell. Janet would have known, having spent most of her career working for Sell, creative counsel to Miss Arden from 1920 to 1966. The reality was that Elizabeth Arden was in reality Florence Graham, a tough little Canadian whose social skills came from books on etiquette, who had a steely determination to succeed, whose sexuality was repressed, who pushed away problems and never learned to control her violent temper. Florence and Elizabeth lived in the same person, often with turbulent results.

Miss Arden's next step was to expand her business and she opened a small branch salon in Washington DC. She also craved a little European polish and so, in the summer of 1912, set sail for Europe. Just as Helena Rubinstein had spent three months touring Europe in 1905, knowing the creative influences she would find there were essential for her expansion plans, Elizabeth knew she had to tour the beauty salons of Paris and London. Never a keen international traveller, even at the peak of her success, she was nevertheless aware that Paris, in those heady, pre-war days, was a crucial place for innovation. She later claimed she went to every salon in Paris, which would have included Rubinstein's Maison de Beauté Valaze on rue St Honoré, although she would always deny it. She had treatments, bought beauty products and fragrances, and observed the *avant-garde* 'full' make-up the sophisticated Parisian women were using, particularly eye shadow, liner and mascara. Pausing only to buy clothes at one of the best couture houses, Callot Soeurs, she booked her passage home. Elizabeth Arden returned to New York on the SS *Caronia* out of Liverpool which indicates she spent time exploring London en route home although, intriguingly, she never admitted to it. She did admit to packing myriad jars of beauty products – and to meeting her husband-to-be on the return voyage.

Elizabeth Arden would later claim that her first voyage to Europe was actually in 1914 and that she returned to New York on the SS *Lusitania*, where a fellow passenger was one Thomas Jenkins Lewis, a bank clerk whom she had met a year or so earlier when she had applied for a loan. The myth of Florence Graham applying for a bank loan can be laid to rest; no bank would have loaned a single woman without collateral any money in 1910. The question as to how or why a New York bank clerk could afford to tour Europe also springs to mind. There is no record of her name, nor that of Mr Lewis, listed on the *Lusitania*'s sailing records for that year, just before she was torpedoed off the coast of Ireland. Miss Arden, it seems, was romancing her journey.

More informed opinion as to Mr Lewis's early career puts him as a 'silk salesman'. This seems more accurate, as Tommy Lewis had a rare gift for salesmanship and an innate understanding of the fashion and beauty business, hardly the gifts of a bank clerk. It would also explain how he met Elizabeth Arden on her return trip via Liverpool – presumably he had been visiting nearby Macclesfield, then the centre of England's silk-weaving business. Apparently they dined and danced and formed a strong bond, so much so that he proposed marriage there and then, only to be rejected. The romantic heart of Florence Graham might have yearned to be married, but Elizabeth Arden was forging her career in which there was no space for a husband.

New York in the autumn season of 1912 was a booming place. The beauty market was growing and its potential was huge. In 1849, the wholesale value of manufactured toiletries throughout the US totalled the insignificant sum of $355,000. By 1914, the American Chemical Society announced domestic production of a shade under $17,000,000. Whilst Elizabeth Arden would never have admitted that Florence Graham's secret vice was watching the despised nickelodeons, she knew, as all fans of the 'penny pictures' knew, that she was witnessing the birth of a new phenomenon. As Elizabeth Arden, her beauty business was unquestionably helped on its way when that experience evolved into a new form of storytelling – the feature film.

Effectively born in 1912, the cinema industry brought glamour into people's lives. More importantly, it brought the close-up and close-ups required cosmetics. Theda Bara made her first film in 1914, but it was her lead role in *A Fool that Was* in 1915 that catapulted her to coast-to-coast fame as 'the Vamp'. It's no surprise that just two years after feature films began wowing audiences, the boom in the beauty business was so noticeable. Growth in spending power amongst American female consumers was seemingly untouched by President Wilson instigating America's first income tax laws in 1913. There was plenty of money to visit the cinema at the average price of $2 a ticket, with ample left over to buy cosmetics.

Not that Theda Bara, whose make-up as 'the Vamp' is said to have been created by Helena Rubinstein, would have appealed to Miss Arden. Her idea of filmstar feminine beauty, honed by her admiration of the British beauty Gaby Deslys, along with her heroine, Eleanora Duse, would have been Lilian Gish. When *The Birth of a Nation* starring Gish was shown at the White House in 1915, the first motion picture ever screened there, President Wilson said, 'It's like writing history with lightning.'

Charting the growth of the beauty business in the twentieth century is following history 'moving like lightning'. The core element of the first phase was in skin care and treatment creams. But the profitable icing on the cake, even then, was cosmetics. Elizabeth Arden knew the potential for coloured cosmetics, having witnessed it in Paris, but, in 1913, lacked the courage to promote it publicly. The gentle, tinted powders, creams and rouge she offered were not advertised commercially, she was too canny for that, but her salon would do special facials for favoured clients, which included as much make-up as she had in her range at that time. *Vogue* boosted her turnover by acknowledging that 'discreet face painting' would 'enhance a lady's appearance'. Once the social taboo against wearing make-up was eliminated, there was no looking back. Not everyone welcomed the emerging trend. The editor of the important magazine *Ladies' Home Journal*, Edward Bok, said in 1912 'that men continued to see rouge as a mark of sex and sin'. Bok banned advertisements for patent medicines and toiletries with extravagant therapeutic claims from his magazine, and discouraged glowing editorials about cosmetics for years. A manager at Macy's fired a saleswoman in 1913 for wearing rouge with the comment, 'Macy's was running a department store, not a theatrical troupe.' But the independent women of New York, who had come a long way since moralists bleated that 'painting' was wicked, were enjoying their new-found freedom in work, leisure and pleasure, and it pleased them to use cosmetics.

Arden's business in the two years since the suffrage march had been brisk. The fashionable New York department stores, Stern Brothers and Bonwit Teller, had started to stock her Venetian line and she had increased her advertising budget. Products promoted in 1914 included: 'Venetian Cleansing Cream; Pore Cream; Lille Lotion – to prevent freckles and keep skin from darkening – Muscle Oil; Velva Cream and her newest addition, Venetian Adona Cream for firming the neck and bust.'

As war broke out in Europe, Arden's salons were flourishing and her bank balance was escalating. In just four years, she had become the leading force at the top end of the emerging beauty business in New York. Her only competition was her ex-employer, Mrs Adair, who could not compete with

Arden's product innovation and tireless publicity campaigns, and the ex-showgirl Lillian Russell whose fame was fading fast. The legendary beauty whose skin had been described as 'all gold and cream and rose' had, appropriately enough, as her musical career declined, reinvented herself as a beauty queen. At one stage, Russell had endorsed Harriet Hubbard Ayer's Recamier Creams, but in the late 1890s, appropriately for the belle of the theatre, she opened a salon at 2160 Broadway and by the First World War was a star in New York's beauty firmament. Lillian Russell may have been a big star but the petite Miss Arden was a shooting star with a powerful aim; Russell's business would soon close down.

But Elizabeth Arden's peace and security was about to be shattered. Helena Rubinstein was coming to town.

Helena posing – and imposing – in astrakhan and ostrich feather trimmed hat for a photograph taken by Mertens, Mai & Cie in Vienna in 1893 – three years before she left for Australia

Helena's press handout photograph, used in the Melbourne publication *Table Talk* in 1904, just a year after opening her first beauty salon there. She was thirty-two, becoming famous and on her way to making her fortune

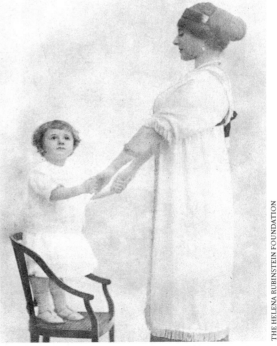

Helena, *circa* 1910, pregnant with her first son, Roy, and dressed by Poiret

Helena, *circa* 1912, living in London and pregnant with Horace, posing with her son Roy

One of the earliest pictures of Elizabeth Arden, *circa* 1910, when she had just established her own business in New York

Miss Arden and her husband, Thomas Jenkins Lewis, on their wedding day at the St Regis Hotel, New York, 29 November 1915

Miss Arden, *circa* 1922, with another of her beloved dogs – wearing an embroidered cheesecloth dress almost certainly by Babani of Paris, whose perfumes she was importing at the time

Elizabeth, *circa* 1925, in fantasy mode – dressed to impress for a costume ball – as Little Bo Peep, complete with her white poodle

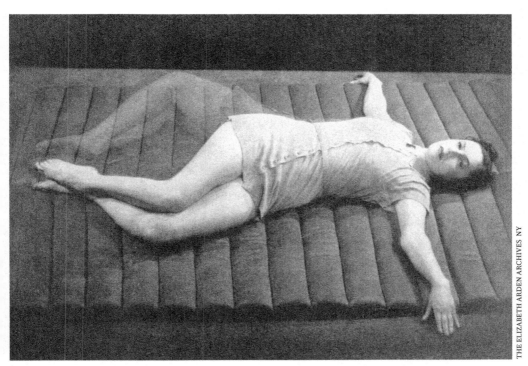

The Elizabeth Arden Salon exercise regimes were lavishly illustrated for clients to continue at home. This one is Arden's 'Hip Roll' reduction, *circa* 1928, 'counting 1 to 4 whilst contracting the abdomen' twelve repeats each morning

Madame Rubinstein's salons offered exercise and stretch classes too – neat navy blue gym clothes compulsory – this class is in her New York Salon, *circa* 1918

By 1935, Elizabeth had opened her first health spa, Maine Chance, described by Vogue as being 'like no other place under the sun, where you live a charmed and incredible life in Sybaritic surroundings, trained as rigorously as any athlete'. The Arden exercise demonstrators were put through their paces, working out with hoops for photography

Maine Chance offered tennis, water-skiing, swimming, sailing, badminton, riding and archery. Clients were never let off a minute of their exercise programmes – but there were cars to take them up and down hills, and a station wagon followed behind bringing mid-morning broth to drink

Miss Arden was *very* keen on deportment . . .
Once those spines were stretched, it was heads up
and shoulders back, going down the stairs with
books firmly balanced

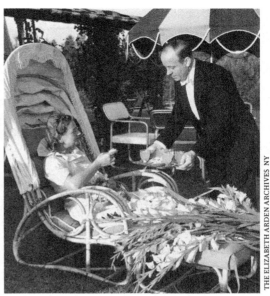

It wasn't all hard work at Maine Chance. Rest and
relaxation were part of the programme too. Miss
Arden's British butler, Frederick, was on hand to serve
diluted fruit juices from crystal glasses. The cane sun-
loungers had pink cotton scalloped hoods and
mattresses

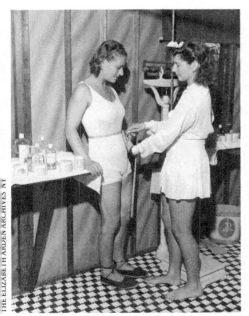

Measuring at Maine Chance . . . full
measurements were taken on arrival and
departure. The tables were stocked with Arden
products – as were the guest bedrooms. The
uniforms worn by the treatment specialists
included a pink *moire* bow in their hair

Merry Christmas and
Happy New Year
Elizabeth Arden
1933

Elizabeth's personal Christmas card in 1933 was a
photo-montage of everything she loved most – Maine
Chance, water-skiing, her New York salon – and, last
but not least, Elizabeth with one of her horses

A make-up class at the Helena Rubinstein Salon on Fifth Avenue, *circa* 1939. The marble head in the right-hand corner is by Polish sculptor Elie Nadelman

Exercises were done on miraculous machines like this awesome metal hip roller. Late-night sessions for working women were over-subscribed

By 1937, Miss Arden had opened a state-of-the-art 'Gymnasium Moderne' at her Fifth Avenue Salon, the colours and fixtures designed around a painting she commissioned at a cost of $10,000 by Georgia O'Keeffe called *Miracle Flower*. The fencing master Nadi gave classes, and clients 'unfurled' during stretching exercises on satin-backed cashmere yoga mats

Madame Rubinstein in her laboratory. She posed for similar pictures throughout her career, promoting herself as 'the Beauty Scientist'

With her factory workers, milling parsley for a skin tonic. Madame adored her laboratories and called them her 'kitchens'

Miss Arden, swathed in white mink, photographed by Cecil Beaton in 1930. They argued over the pictures and he thought she had destroyed the prints, but copies are still on file in the Arden archives in New York today

CHAPTER SEVEN

THE WOMEN AT WAR
New York 1914–1919

By 1914, HELENA RUBINSTEIN's payroll had reached a total of over a hundred employees. She was operating five salons in four countries, and was responsible for the livelihood of three sisters, several cousins and her husband. She was also the mother of two sons under five.

Wealthy couples travelling, leaving children 'at home with Nanny', was one thing, for a wife to leave her children at home with her husband while she went out to build her business was quite another. Helena, being an unconventional woman, cared little for what others thought about her behaviour. She had few friends – particularly women friends – outside her business which was by now an all-consuming force in her life.

Helena seems to have had few qualms about leaving her young sons – Horace was not even two – when, in October 1914, she sailed for New York. It was a logical move for her. At the back of her mind must have been the fear that everything she had worked so hard to achieve in Europe, now at war, was under threat and that America presented her with opportunities she could not afford to ignore. She would have been loath to admit it, but at forty-two she was starting to feel vulnerable about her age. That she sailed without Titus shows their marriage was at its usual *impasse*. Indeed, she left so abruptly it indicates yet another break in the relationship. Helena was able, however, to take advantage of the one really useful thing she reasoned he still had to offer her – an American passport.

She had been in Paris when the Great War started and was still there when French mobilisation began in early August and Germany invaded Poland. By the end of the month, the German army was advancing towards Paris and panic was setting in as people struggled to get out. Travelling to

London to brief her manager Rosa Hollay, Helena also collected funds from her British bank where she must have been a valued client. The Rubinstein business was reported to be making over £30,000 a year at this time with annual costs estimated at only £7,000.

A large part of Helena's growing art collection was left behind in Paris, whilst the artists she had bought from and fashion designers she had patronised joined up. Georges Braque joined the 224th Infantry and Fernand Léger fought at Argonne and Verdun, suffering bad gas poisoning. André Derain joined the 82nd Artillery Regiment and Roger de Fresnaye the Infantry, where he fought until discharged, having contracted TB. The tortured talent Modigliani apparently tried to enlist but as he was already desperately ill, his tuberculosis exacerbated by drugs and drink, he failed his medical, so had to watch as his friends like poet Blaise Cendrars and sculptor Ossip Zadkine went off to war. Moise Kisling was wounded at Carency and Guillaume Apollinaire, poet, art publisher and 'soul' of Montmartre had joined the 139th Division, albeit grumbling that his sky-blue uniform was too bright a colour. Poor Apollinaire got a bullet in his head, with the wound becoming badly infected. His health never recovered and he died at the end of the war. Not all the artists fought or fled – Brancusi, Diego de Rivera, Picasso and Juan Gris amongst them remained in France, whilst Nadelman, Francis Picabia and Marcel Duchamp saw out the war from the safety of New York.

With an airmail postal service established between London and Paris, and communications opened up between the USA, Australia and Europe by 'Marconigram', business activity, reasoned Helena, could be efficiently monitored from America. Not that she ever sent many cables. The costs horrified her and she instructed her teams around the world by the system she enjoyed the most, sending letters. She wrote from ships when she was travelling. She wrote from hotels. She wrote in the middle of the night. In fact she wrote whenever an idea or instruction came into her head, sometimes several times a day, and covered several sides of paper with her large sprawling handwriting. The cache of letters her London manageress alone kept when leaving her job fourteen years later ran into thousands.

Sister Manka was set to work helping establish the Rubinstein reputation in America's thriving retail sector. Manka, of all Helena's sisters, was perhaps the most beautiful, a fact of which she seemed very well aware. Her beauty stood her in good stead in her early years in the wholesale arm of the

Rubinstein business, but cut little ice with Helena, who despaired of her flighty sister, watching her marry, divorce and re-marry in rapid succession. The sisters eventually became estranged, in an argument as much about money as about men, with Helena being obliged to point out to Manka: 'You came to me green, raw, inexperienced. You have been handsomely paid for anything you have ever done. You know thousands are spent on your travelling. Yours has been the role of any premiere. Your vanity only is what keeps you from seeing it. I set the stage for you . . .' In fact, she set the stage for every one of her relatives, most of whom – including her own sons – rarely appreciated it and mostly resented it. Helena Rubinstein worked gruelling hours and led a lonely existence.

The Rubinstein legend would have us believe Helena opened a salon in New York almost immediately and graciously allowed retailers to stock her preparations. In fact, her salon didn't open until 1915, although when it did it caused a sensation. Prior to that, she set about touring America by train, deciding which cities she should target. Then she set about wholesaling her range. To make sure it was being properly presented, she often worked behind the counter herself. One such outlet was a store called E.T. Slattery's in Boston, where in 1914 Helena Rubinstein could be found plying her wares. Slattery's was owned by Patrick O'Connell, a big, genial, silver-haired Irishman who, although an ardent anti-Semite, rather liked Helena Rubinstein. Journalist Grace Davidson's mother shopped at Slattery's and met Helena there, later describing her as 'a kindly, homey, stout little woman who spoke with a strong accent'. Sixteen years later, when Grace, by then a reporter on the *Boston Post*, went to interview Helena, they reminisced about Slattery's. Grace told a friend, 'She talked with pride about those years,' Helena telling her, 'I worked around the clock. People today don't know how to work. Short hours they want. They think they have something more important to do afterwards. Work is the important thing.' She certainly worked – and it paid off. Australia was her testing ground, Europe her finishing school, but America was her goldmine.

The opening of Helena's sumptuous salon at 15 East 49th St attracted major coverage in the media in May 1915. By now her husband had arrived, bringing her sons, and crateloads of Helena's favourite art, including a cache of her African carvings and her treasured Elie Nadelman sculptures – the artist himself already being an expatriate resident, having fled to New York on the *Lusitania* in October 1914, his trip, it's said, paid for by Helena herself.

Vogue at that time had a column called 'On Her Dressing Table' in which they covered trends in beauty and fragrance. Mrs Chase and her team had no editorial credits system in 1915, so readers were invited to 'send a stamped addressed envelope' for more details. It's a safe bet the post room at the Condé Nast building was kept busy after their eulogy about Helena.

> The war has driven to New York a woman specialist whose handiwork is seen in the faces of the loveliest women both abroad and here. The *mondaine* no longer knocks at the door of her salon in Paris, for the Red Cross there has claimed the interest of even the most frivolous. In London, this specialist's salon is busy packing creams and lotions for Duchesses and Ladies, who come in their nurses' uniforms to receive their last complexion instructions before going to the front.

A public relations *tour de force*, this emotive editorial worked wonders, striking just the right note of awe and sympathy, creating a vision of these beautiful aristocratic 'angels of mercy' working in hospitals, complete with their make-up kits courtesy of Helena Rubinstein.

In fact, the feature wasn't so far from the truth. Young women in Paris and London, whose life had more recently evolved around dining at the Ritz and dancing in nightclubs, had turned their hand to nursing. Wining and dining became more difficult due to food shortages and Prime Minister Asquith asked the British upper classes to play their part by 'reducing their levels of servants'. Just in case they missed the point, he increased income tax on unearned income to 2/6d in the pound. The great hotels played their part, with Claridges giving space for ladies' sewing groups to make uniforms and clothes for the poor, whilst the Ritz in Paris turned part of the hotel over to the authorities as a hospital.

New York's female elite, who had long felt equally at home in Paris, felt a huge sympathy for the French, dozens of them volunteering for the Red Cross and leaving to work in both city and field hospitals during the First World War. Amongst them were Anne Morgan and Elsie de Wolfe, who offered their home, the Villa Trianon, to the French government as a base for making hospital supplies. Anne Morgan founded the American Fund for French Wounded and was later to receive the Légion d'Honneur. Elsie de Wolfe received the Croix de Guerre for 'bravery under fire' and later the

Légion d'Honneur for 'War Services'. Anne Morgan's colleagues at the Paris hospital were ladies more used to hosting gala parties than nursing the wounded, led by Madame Henri de Rothschild, who enlivened her uniform with a collar of real pearls, Madame Kiki Van Cleef of jewellers Van Cleef and Arpels, whose family firm may or may not have provided Madame de Rothschild's pearls, and Mrs 'Willie K' (Anne) Vanderbilt, who had her white pique uniforms tailored at Worth, accessorising them with a huge gold and ruby cross hung on a tassel, which *was* made by Van Cleef and Arpels.

These women may have been glamorous but their work was gruelling. The nurses often took up cigarette smoking, partly to calm their nerves, but mostly to disguise the stench of burning flesh. Many of them had led totally sheltered lives, but they were presented with unimaginable horrors of death and disfigurement. The innovation of plastic surgery, developed to help the victims of trench warfare, began in earnest. The legendary Dr Harold Gillies, who would later become a good friend of Elizabeth Arden, and only thirty-two years old when the Great War started, is credited as personally treating over 2000 cases of damage to the face of injured soldiers after the Battle of the Somme alone.

When facial disfigurement was so severe that the techniques on offer gave no hope, artists were on hand to assist, like Anna Coleman Ladd, an American sculptor, whose Paris clinic funded by the American Red Cross crafted 'portrait masks' made out of copper. Her finished masks were enamelled in skin-tones, human hair was added as needed and the shattered face of the soldier disguised, giving him a semblance of normality – at least in presenting his public face, if not his private one.

Carmel Snow, who would go on to work at *Vogue* and then edit *Harper's Bazaar*, also joined the Red Cross, arriving in Paris in 1915, where she promptly went to Creed to have her nurse's uniform tailored. Snow's war work didn't stop her eye for fashion. She was one of the first to discover Chanel in her emergent years, falling in love with her simple dresses made up in the jersey fabric that Coco acquired from the manufacturer Jean Rodier. Chanel's easy shifts, launched at the opening of her shop in Biarritz in 1915, struck an immediate chord with fashionable women. The French government had banned jewels and evening dress at the Opera and the Comédie-Française and for the chic women of *le tout Paris*, who were busy driving ambulances, riding round Paris on bicycles, nursing and working in canteens, Chanel's pared-down minimal clothes were exactly right for the time. By early 1916, the combined staff of her Paris, Deauville and Biarritz shops and ateliers totalled three hundred. In true peasant style, she liked nothing better than sitting at the till at the end of the day, counting the cash.

Helena confined herself to business, putting her husband in charge of finding a family home and becoming frustrated with the result, writing in a letter: 'If they know a property is for me, they double the price,' and in her memoir: 'Edward found the perfect house for us in Greenwich, Connecticut. It was 1910 Tudor, but I have known few country houses with the same degree of comfort and cosiness. It has remained my American country home ever since.' The Greenwich house, on Old India Chase Road, was indeed Helena's American country house, but she didn't take over the deeds until 1924 and Titus never lived there, as by then they were estranged. Their first family Manhattan apartment was on West End Avenue, which Helena hated, saying it was 'too Jewish'. Later, they settled in Central Park West, an apartment Helena kept until the 1930s. Helena herself, as she always did, maintained a suite of rooms on the top floor of her salon premises at East 49th St, where when she was working late she could take a few hours' sleep on site.

Controlling her European and Australian outposts at this time was a complex task. Madame, naturally, berated her staff at all times to cut back on expenses. Her early paranoia about the costs of electricity manifested itself in correspondence to Rosa Hollay whom she would nag to be economical with everything, even electric light. The Rubinstein technique was to convince her employees that business was hard and there was no money for a pay-rise. Her letters were always grumbling ones, peppered with gloomy news about her high tax bills – quite forgetting that her staff could easily calculate that in order to pay a tax bill of £750, she would have been enjoying a particularly high turnover. Tax was a word Helena abhorred. She would work out every conceivable way to avoid paying it, instructing her overseas staff to issue fake invoices and list a higher price for raw materials shipped. 'I had to pay nearly 12/– when I could have paid 12 pennies. I hope you will know in future,' she wrote.

The costs of running her husband, which Helena considered a burden, were also on her mind, although Titus more than earned his keep by his copywriting skills and childcare duties. At about this time they employed a tutor, John Oneal, who years later was remembered fondly, if modestly, by Helena in her will. Titus was more often to be found discovering the delights of the artistic and literary community in Greenwich Village, rather than Greenwich Connecticut, where the seeds were sown for his future publishing career in Paris. Described by John Richardson as 'a Greenwich Village intellectual' Helena's husband was unquestionably happier in 'the Village', by now an artistic haven for evacuees from the European war, than at his wife's beauty salon. While she checked sales figures, he would have preferred the cutting-edge liberal art and literary paper *The Masses* whose contributors were hip writers of the day, like e.e. cummings, or Chicago's literary magazine the *Little Review*. Cummings and his fellow American writer John Dos Passos would join the army and write the first, and many believe finest, war novels. Cummings would later become well acquainted with Edward Titus, and Helena used the lower case, modernistic graphics he affected in her own logo. She didn't care for books but she knew what was fashionable.

When Titus needed to escape from the rigours of writing his wife's advertising copy, a task he loathed, he could probably be found with the free-thinking, hard-drinking crowd at the Mad Hatter or the Purple Pup. Greenwich Village cafés, bars and tea rooms of the time catered for all tastes from the bohemian to the bizarre. Romany Marie gave artists free lunch at Bruno's Garret and read the fortunes of her rich, up-town visitors in the grounds of their coffee cups. My Tea Wagon and the Crumperie served tea, cakes and sympathy to resting writers and actors. Eugene O'Neill lived on Washington Square South, Man Ray at 47 West 8th St and Djuna Barnes on Greenwich Avenue. Leo Stein and curious, creative and rich Stettheimer sisters held court in 'the Village' and they all gathered to eat pasta at the raffish Bertolotti's on Washington Square South.

European expatriates flocked to Greenwich Village. Dada-exponent Gabrielle Buffet-Picabia wrote about them, 'they were a motley international band which turned night into day. Conscientious objectors of all nationalities and walks of life, living in an inconceivable orgy of sexuality, jazz and alcohol'. Leaders amongst them were the chic parvenu couple 'Baron' Adolf de Meyer and his cocaine-addicted fencing champion wife, who supplemented their income from his work as *Vogue*'s fashion photographer in residence by giving lectures in fashion and etiquette to nouveau-riche, social climbing women – a group not too hard to find in New York.

Helena, hovering on the edges of the 'Village people', as always, took only what she wanted and needed from the group. She was encouraged by her husband and by her friendship with the staggeringly handsome, if arrogant Nadelman – described by his friend Gertrude Stein as 'the coldest man I've ever met' – on whom she could always rely to attend her soirées, and to bring his eclectic friends, like Ettie Stettheimer, with whom he was madly in love, and her sisters. This heady mix of European art and money had the desired promotional effect. New York's media continued to rave about the Rubinstein beauty salon. 'The walls are covered with dark blue cloth, the skirting boards are deep rose pink, period mahogany furniture is upholstered in rose silk; and the sculptures are the work of a Russian, much praised in Paris,' wrote *Vogue*. In fact, the sculptures were all Nadelman's, and he was Polish. His sculptures were described by Helena as being like 'the scientific beautification of modern woman'.

They are astonishing pieces. A pair of cool marble figures, like ancient gods wearing modern, rounded military helmets, stand in pride of place in the New York apartment of Madame's great niece, Diane Moss, alongside a wonderful display of Helena's milky, shell-pink opaline glass. Three decades after her death, the wit, charm and modernity of these key collectibles Helena bought in the first years of the last century are reminders of how she got her money's worth from her shopping. The sculptures, art and jewels were a focal point for the press, enhancing her growing reputation as a collector.

Elizabeth Arden meanwhile looked at the intruder on her territory with loathing. She promptly relocated her salon to 673 Fifth Avenue, where she took five large rooms, with a private entrance on East 53rd St. The gleaming plaque by the equally gleaming Red Door by now simply said 'Elizabeth Arden'. She decorated in her usual 'sumptuous serenade' to the grand mansions of the rich; clients had consultations in the white and gold 'Oval Room' while treatments were given in 'withdrawing' rooms painted in sugar-almond pastels, with white voile curtains.

The treatment girls wore pink *moiré* ribbons in their hair, the only softening touch to their otherwise austere white uniforms and soft-soled white nurse's shoes. Treatments were given in an atmosphere of medicinal, yet luxurious, hush. Not to be outdone by her new rival, Miss Arden escalated her wholesale activity. A new department was established and a sales force hired. The man in charge was Mr Elizabeth Arden, Thomas Jenkins Lewis.

Elizabeth had finally accepted Tommy's proposal in 1915 and they were married in New York on 29 November that year, the bride aged thirty-four, her husband, it's said, 'a little younger'. A rare wedding photograph shows a slim and trim Elizabeth in a cloche hat, her hair bobbed, wearing a dark crepe suit, a silver fox stole and her signature pearls. Even her wedding didn't interfere with her very tight schedule. She apparently went back to work until 8.00 p.m. that evening, before joining her husband at the St Regis Hotel for their wedding night.

Theirs was no great, or passionate, love match. But she was lonely and he was charming, with a happy-go-lucky personality. He was also a good dancer; an important plus, as Elizabeth loved to dance. At the beginning of their relationship they seemed very happy. Tommy's rekindled interest in Elizabeth was perhaps due to his observance of the rise and rise of her business; since they had last met, she had created a production facility, developed a brand-strategy, doubled the floor-space in her salon and was becoming a media darling.

It is doubtful whether Elizabeth fully realised that when she became Mrs Lewis, she would have to find a job for her husband. He had enlisted shortly before their marriage and was not demobbed until early in 1919, so the first four years of their marriage were spent apart. Absorbed as she had been in her battles against the invading Helena Rubinstein, by the time her husband returned to New York she was glad to have an ally on board. The difference between the Arden/Lewis business relationship and the Rubinstein/Titus one is that Edward Titus had a shareholding in his wife's company and so, for a while at least, was actually on the board. Thomas Jenkins Lewis was merely his wife's employee.

A year after Elizabeth Arden started her married life, Helena Rubinstein decided to end hers. Serially unfaithful, Titus had played too close to home, having an affair with an Australian girl who was living in their family apartment and whom Helena was training up to run one of her salons. It's said Titus went off to Boston with the girl, ostensibly to check out the Rubinstein salon there. Helena quickly realised what was going on, threw him out and sought a legal separation, this latest affair being one too many.

The memorandum of agreement outlining their legal separation in 1916 and covering four pages of legalese included the words: 'They are now living separate and apart from each other and consent to do so in the future during their natural lives. Said parties have made certain financial and property settlements and Mr Titus has relinquished his claim of an *alleged* partnership with Mrs Titus and also his claimed interest in certain contracts and property.'

Helena bought out Edward's share in the Australian company and made a settlement in respect of other obligations, her lawyers no doubt concerned that Titus, a partner in Australia, could claim the same in America. Titus was left with an income and Helena was left with their two sons – seven and four years old – and her business.

Although her husband's infidelities were still some way off, 1915 was nevertheless a tumultuous year for Elizabeth Arden. Her pharmaceutical suppliers, Parke, Davis, were too involved with the war effort to be concerned about cosmetic ingredients and suggested she use Stillwell & Gladding, a smaller supplier, where she met the man who would be perhaps more important in her life than any other – Mr A. Fabian Swanson.

In the archives of the Elizabeth Arden Corporation's New York headquarters today, where much memorabilia of her life is filed away, amongst the diaries, letters and scrapbooks is a faded velvet-covered, gilt-encrusted photographic album. This is the record of a company dinner, held in 1918, presumably to celebrate in part the end of the war, and in part yet another year of success for the company. Her employees are all in Victorian fancy dress, their pictures captioned in beautiful script. Mr A. Fabian Swanson stares soulfully at the camera, looking rather subdued. Given how hard Elizabeth worked him, the poor man was probably exhausted.

Miss Arden was said to have an 'almost occult' ability to dream up the next big move in beauty products. She dreamt them up, but it was Mr Swanson who made them up. Her first major coup was a new face cream. She told Swanson she wanted it 'to be light and fluffy, like whipped cream'. He succeeded. The mousse-like confection was named Venetian Cream Amoretta and though it was manufactured in New York and had an Italian name, Miss Arden advertised it as a 'famous French formula, containing the perfume of delicate May flowers'.

Swanson's next development was a gentle astringent. Given that most similar alcohol-laden products on the market then were much like paint stripper, to perfect a subtle skin toner was an astute move. Women were getting used to the 'cleanse, tone, nourish' system as put out by Arden at this time and accepting the 'dry, greasy, normal' skin definitions as put out by Rubinstein. Between them, all they had to do was keep the products rolling out to meet the demand.

Mr Swanson's new skin tonic was more than a complementary product, it was the first in a whole new range. Elizabeth, using her innate marketing skills, called it Elizabeth Arden's Ardena Skin Tonic. Even if clients asked for Ardena Tonic, they were still thinking and talking Arden. This was the first move ever into subliminal product branding and it was utterly brilliant.

Even more brilliant was the cost-to-mark-up ratio. In 1932, several astringent lotions were analysed for their essential ingredients for 'consumer research' in Washington DC. Their cost was computed, based on calculations affecting the price of bulk-buying the raw materials. Ardena Skin Tonic then sold at 85 cents a bottle. Its contents were water, a small amount of ethyl (grain) alcohol, boric acid and fragrance: approximate cost, 3 cents per bottle. The bottle itself would perhaps have cost another 1 cent and the paper label less than 1 cent, leaving a surplus of 80 cents. Even after factory overheads — and at that time Arden product was made in a small, inner-city production space with nominal costs — there was still a vast profit.

Cosmetics manufacturers of course, then as now, claim that a large part of their profits go on promotion. Indeed, a glance through any glossy women's magazine will prove that the beauty business is the biggest advertiser. But even with the biggest colour budget in the world, cosmetics profits are immense. Elizabeth Arden knew that advertising was a vital tool and she brought as steely control to bear on her promotional campaigns as on her product. Like Rubinstein, she wasn't averse to 'fear factor' copy. One advertisement in *Vogue*, circa mid-1915, said:

> My dear, she looks so much older . . . those unkind remarks made over tea are frequently truthful, for a slight change in contour, a faint wrinkling or marking of the skin, a noticeable fading of the complexion . . . these add *years* to one's age. There is not an iota of an excuse for a woman of today to lose one bit of her youthful attractiveness. Every woman can do what Miss Arden's clients have done for years, by devoting ten minutes each day to proper treatments with her Venetian products.

Elizabeth took control over the copywriting of all her campaigns; even when the task had been handed over to her agencies, she vetoed anything she didn't care for, being chillingly ruthless in her criticism. When Henry Sell's

Blaker Agency handled her advertising, the account executive, Margaret Thilly, said: 'I can remember the tensions in the pit of my stomach. My most vivid impression is of taking a quarter-grain of phenobarbital before going up to see Miss Arden. Even then, the proofs always palpitated as I handed them to her.'

Henry Sell, an astute and charming man, along with A. Fabian Swanson and the urbane and wise Edward Haslam in London, who joined Elizabeth in 1921, were her 'three musketeers', all of them loyal, patient, and extremely well paid. When Tommy Lewis came back from the war, he became her d'Artagnan. For a while at least he tirelessly protected his wife's image and rolled out her wholesale division, until he had won immense victories and made his wife, already a wealthy woman, a rich one.

What power Lewis had, however, was restricted to his sales division. He did not dare interfere with his wife's beauty salons, or her advertising campaigns. Sell's chief copywriter on the Arden account was Leonore Buehler. Elizabeth, who managed to avoid ever learning Leonore's name, used to say to Henry Sell, addressing him with her affected version of his name: 'Hanque, I'm tired of Miss What's-her-name's copy. I think you ought to fire her and get someone else.' Sell would murmur agreement and do nothing. When he next presented Leonore's copy, Miss Arden would say: 'I like these words much better.' A few months later, it would be: 'You know, Hanque, I think I preferred Miss What's-her-name's copy. Perhaps you'd better hire her back.' This system went on for years, with Henry Sell allowing his capricious client to think that Miss Buehler had been hired and fired at whim. No one ever dared tell her the truth.

The rivals tilted at each other through their advertising. When Rubinstein's text said she was 'the greatest living beauty exponent', Arden retaliated with copy saying she had 'given her life to the study of her subject in America, Paris, London and Berlin' – a bit rich for someone who had never even been to Berlin at this point, and only spent a few weeks in Paris and London. Miss Arden, however, was by now facing the fact that Madame was a real threat.

In 1916, Elizabeth Arden finally took the plunge into making her own ranges, taking Mr Swanson out of Stillwell & Gladding, and setting him up in laboratory premises at 665 Fifth Avenue, with a wholesale and administration office in the same building. There followed a frenzy of product development, launching Ardena Orange Skin Food; Ardena Astringent

Cream; Velva Cream; Ardena Healing Cream; Ardena Spotpruf Cream; Ardena Bleaching Cream; Ardena Anti-Wrinkle Cream – the products fairly poured out, and by 1918 it was recognised that the Elizabeth Arden company had a larger, more diversified range than any other luxury cosmetics manufacturer.

The product pamphlets, mailed on request and handed to clients in her salons, were frothy confections, printed on flimsy tissue paper, a Fragonard-inspired lady on the front cover, swinging a basket filled with pale pink roses. 'Every skin should have a balanced diet,' ran the copy. 'For home treatment use Velva Cream in the morning and Orange Skin Food at night.' The health and diet conscious Miss Arden would soon be insisting that her clients 'only eat fruit in the morning and steer clear of all full-fat dairy products, including cream'. Feeding the body and feeding the face were two different issues in Miss Arden's mind. It is interesting that the word 'cream', with all its connotations of rich, luxurious, expensive, smooth, unctuous and delicious, is such a staple in the vocabulary of beauty. For years, 'creams' were promoted as 'skin foods'. Yet cream contains fat, and fat is fattening, so women have had to content themselves with putting it on their faces, with the illusion it will plump out their cheeks, rather than on their puddings, where it will definitely plump out their hips.

A second ripple on Miss Arden's pond came when cosmetologist Dorothy Gray set up shop at 734 Fifth Avenue in 1916. Gray's public relations machine inferred she had at one time been Elizabeth Arden's partner, and that Miss Gray's expensive treatment creams, apparently made up by her doctor father, were the same formula as Arden's. Elizabeth was furious, and took out advertisements in *Vogue* asking her clients to 'beware imitations' and to reassure them that hers were the 'only original formulas'.

In fact Dorothy Gray *had* worked at the Elizabeth Arden salon for a short time as a treatment girl. She had apparently been fired for 'living in sin' with her boyfriend, something the deeply puritanical Miss Arden could not tolerate, and subsequently sought her vengeance against her ex-boss by spreading the rumours. Gray took the easy way out when she sold her business in the 1920s to Lehn & Fink, a pharmaceutical manufacturer, whose most famous brand was Lysol. 'There goes another one I've made rich,' Miss Arden said, her voice stinging as sharply as disinfectant. She was right. Dorothy Gray; Marie Earle; Ruth Maurer of Marinello; Edna Albert; Peggy Sage and Kathleen Mary Quinlan were all part of the new wave of cosmetologists whose businesses had flourished on the back of Elizabeth Arden's initiative, all successfully sold out in the 1920s to conglomerates. Arden, on the other hand, remained resolutely a private company.

For relief from her work, Elizabeth's greatest pleasure was dancing. She prided herself on being a good dancer, as many of the attractive men who worked for her could testify, as part of their duties was to act as escort and dance partner to their boss. One of her foibles was to employ tall men – a trick which ensured that the diminutive Elizabeth looked even more fragile. Just as Rubinstein's higher management benefited if they played bridge, so did Arden's if they danced.

In 1914, with war sweeping Europe, artists' agent Bessie Marbury enticed Europe's star dancing duo, Vernon and Irene Castle, to cross the Atlantic, herself investing in the elegant Castle House dancing school and tea rooms which opened that year. Irene and Vernon Castle were the idols of Fred and Adele Astaire, and their talent was the incubator of modern ballroom dancing. The Castles danced with huge *élan* to the new syncopated music that was sweeping New York. Everyone seemed to be humming young composer Irving Berlin's 'Alexander's Rag-time Band' and couples on the dance floor were most definitely 'doing it, doing it' even if they weren't quite yet shaking their hips. Irene Castle also influenced fashion at an unprecedented level. When she bobbed her long hair, the nation – including Elizabeth Arden and Helena Rubinstein – bobbed theirs. Thanks in no small part to Irene Castle, dressed in floating chiffon by Lucille, liberated American women threw away their corsets, petticoats and hobble skirts and found freedom of movement.

It is doubtful that Miss Arden took dancing classes at Castle House, as clients had to be sponsored by a patroness and, in 1914, Elizabeth didn't move in those circles, however much she aspired to. It's quite possible that the dancing classes she did take were taught by a Castle-trained teacher. Elizabeth studied dancing, just as she did yoga and gymnastics, all her life, her diary recording in September 1960 that 'I went to my dancing class today.' She was nearly eighty years old. A year later she hired a dance duo to demonstrate the Twist after a dinner she held for designer Jean Desses at her Fifth Avenue apartment.

The Castles were not the only dancing stars in New York during the First World War. On 11 January 1916, Diaghilev and his Ballet Russes took the city by storm, followed by Nijinsky, who made his New York debut in

Le Spectre de la Rose and *Petrouchka* in April. There were other, huge talents dancing in New York, enthralling the public and inspiring artists and photographers. They represented a new, sinuous freedom of the body and quickly became a symbol for the New Woman. This group included Loie Fuller and Ruth St Denis, but it was Isadora Duncan who most captured the public's imagination. By 1916, Isadora, the American-born 'high priestess of dance', had moved back from France and was living quietly in Amagansett, Long Island, making occasional forays into New York to dance professionally. Duncan went back to Europe after the war, dying tragically in her car in 1927, strangled by one of her flowing scarves. Her spirit lived on, not only in dance but in art. In particular she had a profound influence on the world of American artist, Georgia O'Keeffe. Elizabeth Arden, who adored the free-spirited movement of gymnastic dancing, almost as much as she adored the flowing Lucille chiffon gowns inspired by Isadora, was later introduced to O'Keeffe by Bessie Marbury, developing a lifelong affection for the artist's work.

Helena Rubinstein had little interest in dancing and, in the war years in America, little time to watch it. She was involved in theatricals of another kind, developing her prestige product sites in department stores and training and dressing staff to work behind the counters. An uneasy reconciliation had followed the initial formal separation from Titus. With their relationship still hovering on the border-line of disintegration Titus was subdued but not bowed. He looked after the boys, whilst Helena toured America coast-to-coast, drumming up business. By now she had a collection of tinted rouge and lipsticks as well as her bestselling Water Lily Cleansing Cream, described as 'a rejuvenating cream de luxe for the ultra fastidious woman, containing the youthifying essence of Water Lily buds', and 'Georgine Lactee – a muscle tightener, which firms the contour and restores a youthful outline to the face'. Her original formula, Valaze, was being promoted for 'renewing skin cells' and Valaze Extrait was described as 'an exquisite anti-wrinkle lotion, which lifts all fatigue from the face and eyes'. Clients rarely left either her salons, or counters at stores like City of Paris in San Francisco, without buying Helena Rubinstein product, complete with instruction sheets for home use.

Helena had quickly detected the winds of change blowing in consumer awareness. It would be impractical and unnecessary to open salons in every major town, so a programme of wholesale development was essential. She instinctively knew it would only work if the salesgirls – the demonstrators of her line – who in those very early days were employees of the stores rather than the cosmetics house, were both enthused about her brand and expertly trained, and she opened a staff training school in New York. Emerging communication technology, like the telephone line between New York and San Francisco, assisted her expansion. Helena took to the road for the second time since her arrival in America, with her sister Manka, several assistants and a lot of luggage, knowing as she travelled the 4750 miles towards San Francisco for a personal appearance at City of Paris, that when she got there she could phone to check on activity in New York. Not that she used the telephone very much in person. She was, by her own admission, 'not very good with my fingers' and got into a muddle with the buttons and dials. Her staff got used to her picking up a receiver and just shouting – they would hastily get the number for her. She also had a deep, personal mistrust of the telephone, nervous that conversations could be held against her, and would insist that one of her executives listen in on an extension if the conversation involved contractual obligation. Finally, of course, she resented the cost, always insisting her travelling sales force use a telephone in the foyer of a hotel, never the bedroom, as it was cheaper.

The 'Rubinstein road show' travelled by rail and car throughout America, an adventure in itself, so that Helena had a first-hand view of all the cities that offered potential, plus a personal relationship with her speciality store stockists. The hawk-eyed Helena personally vetted each store, insisting that each one carrying her line not only put up the cash for a hefty minimum order, but sent their sales staff back to her in New York for 'intensive training'. She also insisted on prominent, branded counter-space, provided smart uniforms for the sales staff, and backed each store with initial local advertising. Business techniques such as Rubinstein's are taken for granted today, but in 1916 they were a revelation. She set up a network of agents to sell her basic lines – treatment creams, spot and blackhead removers, rouge, powders and 'reducing' (diet) jelly – to the most prestigious chemists in smart suburban areas, leaving the *crème de la crème* of her treatment ranges as the exclusive fiefdom of the top-quality stores.

In Australia, Helena's sister Ceska was having a crisis. She had been on a trip to London when war was declared, returning to Melbourne immediately, where she had applied for Australian naturalisation in 1915 so she could stay in Australia and travel freely to New Zealand, retaining her directorship of the Rubinstein business and her company shares (a new Commonwealth law had been passed affecting 'enemy subjects' holding shares).

Ceska wrote to the authorities, reminding them: 'I was born in Austrian-Poland but as the circumstances of Poland are very special and the fact that Austria controlled the portion in which I was born, I trust the minister will approve of my application.' Unfortunately for Ceska, the minister didn't approve and her application was rejected.

As the hostilities were escalating, with casualties inflicted during the ANZAC landings along the Gallipoli Peninsula fresh in the minds of Australians, there was a very real threat of Ceska being classified as an enemy alien. She stepped up her campaign for naturalisation, enlisting the support of her Uncle Bernhard Silberfeld, now retired and living in St Kilda with his daughter Eva. He swore a declaration that he had received information that his sister Gitel had married a 'young Russian Pole', paternity being key to Ceska's nationality, and thus her naturalisation. Next up to commit perjury was Ceska herself, abetted by Helena.

In order to convince the authorities that Mr Rubinstein was Russian, more documentation was needed, this time from Helena in America. It was company policy to keep communication by cablegram brief. Cablegrams and transatlantic telephone calls may have been becoming an essential part of business routine, but Helena had the thrifty soul's mistrust of these expensive messages. So Ceska, nervously mindful that even full stops cost money, put in an order for salon supplies at the same time as requesting crucial information, sending: 'Cable immediately where father born ship liplustre'. The reply, briefer, came back: 'Father born Lublin Russia Helena'.

Having moved Mr Rubinstein's birthplace from Dukla, on the Austro-Hungarian borders, to Lublin, in the Russian sector, Ceska wrote to the authorities again: 'I now append statutory declaration from my uncle and certified copy of cablegram sent to my sister in New York and her reply. These I trust will fully substantiate my claims to be a Russian subject as it is most resentful being classed as an enemy of Russia and the British Crown.' She reminded the authorities that her cousin, Eva Levy, was 'a tireless patriotic worker in Melbourne' and that two of Eva's sons were on active service: 'One has been in the firing line for some time and by cable last week he advises having been given a commission.'

No record shows if the consignment of Liplustre arrived safely in Australia, but Ceska Rubinstein was awarded her citizenship, obtaining a British and Commonwealth passport on 12 April 1916. Just two weeks later, Australia took part in the first 'Anzac Day', marking the fateful Gallipoli landings. Ceska married widower Edward Hastings Cooper a year later. Helena, in her memoir, describes Edward Cooper as 'being known in the Australian racing world for his fine string of horses'. Whilst he may have backed horses, he certainly didn't own any. Edward Cooper was a paper merchant, working from an office in Dalgety Street in St Kilda. Whether classified as Russian or Polish, Ceska and Helena were lucky not to be in either country, as atrocities against Jewish communities were frighteningly on the increase.

Back in New York, both Helena Rubinstein and Elizabeth Arden were benefiting from the trade boom sweeping America. Mass production techniques were not confined to Mr Ford's cars, but impacting on, amongst other sectors, munitions, shipbuilding and aircraft engines. Industrial success, all geared to the war effort of a country not yet in the war, had generated a massive increase in consumer spending. Both the emerging cosmetics tycoons were in the right place at the right time.

By 1917, when America finally joined the war, all-out war was also declared between Helena and Titus. Despite his compelling overtures for a reconciliation and his entreaties that he was celibate, she hired private detectives to follow him, discovering an infidelity in Chicago. Titus was followed to a hotel where he took a separate room from a companion, Mrs Bergman. The next day he was asked to leave due to 'reports of Mr Titus being seen coming from Mrs Bergman's room'. Unaware of the detective's report, Titus would have been even more horrified to know a copy was sent to Mr H.F. Schuettler, the head of Chicago's police force.

Helena held fire on the report but refused to answer her husband's letter, sent from Effingham where he was staying with friends. Plans she had made to join Titus for Christmas were put aside, but with his usual *élan*, on 16 December, he wrote to her regardless.

I am again, extremely frustrated. When your wire came I expected to hear from your lawyers. You said you could arrange Christmas, but that you would do no travelling. If that was to infer that you would meet me only in New York then it puts me again into the most disagreeable position of spending a lonely Christmas . . . I will not go back to New York unless I can do so on the basis of a perfect understanding between us. For mysterious reasons of your own you prefer to leave unanswered my letters – the purpose of which was to pave the way for our rap-prochement. I find myself a little over 32 hours travel distance from New York and fearing an expenditure of about $200 for the round trip which I cannot afford to incur without a very good reason. I would gladly spend ten times that amount if I could get nearer the sight of light at the end of the tunnel – but your behaviour is so puzzling that I can discover only uncertainty as its chief ingredient.

What had hurt Helena so much was that a few weeks earlier she had spent time with Titus in Chicago and they had slept together. To find out that just a week or so later he had been unfaithful yet again was more than she could bear. In blissful ignorance of the private detective's report, Titus told his wife:

After our *intimate* meeting in Chicago I should have thought that all fears of incorrect conduct or of compromising activity have been swept away. Your silence since our parting in Chicago is very much misplaced and not at all appreciated by me. It is the usual pain of arriving in New York and stirring up all the usual hysteria – I am not going through that performance again if I can help it and will meet you anywhere but in New York. Send me a wire, a straightforward yes or no with particulars, because I shall leave here when everyone is leaving – on Thursday – for the holidays. Should you wish to write, you might do so via Lola, where I would call on Friday. I received two sweet letters from the children. You can't imagine how much I want to see them. I don't know what to get them for Christmas. Do not disappoint me, Your Edward.

For Christmas that year, Helena sent Titus a copy of the detective's report. From that point on, they communicated via relatives and lawyers, but rarely met.

The First World War ended in November 1918. Much to the relief of Miss Arden, Madame left for Paris as soon as she could book passage, anxious to see what was left of her European outposts. She left Manka in charge of the US business and, once again, her estranged husband in charge of the children; travelling, as ever, being Helena's way of putting her troubled marriage behind her.

Titus spent the summer of 1919 in upstate New York with their sons, now seven and nine, also caring for Johnnie, Manka's son, and a young cousin, Helena Silberfeld. He wrote to Helena:

> We were naturally very glad to hear from you and of your safe arrival. There is practically a little kindergarten class here. With a house so full of children it is difficult to have a little time to one's self . . . I do not know to what an extent you are still interested in the market, but it may not be without interest to you to know that Crucible Steel has sold up to $200. Oil has reached high figures. This exhausts the budget of news, and as you probably do not care to read anything else I might wish to say of a more personal character, I will close with the sincerest wishes for your success, health and contentment. Yours, Edward.

Helena's health by this stage was fluctuating. She was developing the poor circulation that would haunt her for the rest of her life, causing phlebitis in her legs. She also suffered badly with stress-related headaches, in part a reaction to her violent temper tantrums. Soothed by being back in Paris, the city offering to her astute antennae a lot of appealing and lucrative post-war opportunity, she also urgently needed to re-establish lines of communication with her mentor, Dr Kapp, at Weisbaden Spa. Kapp provided her with many of her treatments, particularly varicose-vein lotion, thread-vein creams, reducing jelly and tablets, and a considerable debt had accrued during the time she had been unable to transfer funds.

Unfortunately for Miss Arden, her joy at her rival's departure was short-lived. Madame, enchanted with the American consumer culture, virtually commuted across the Atlantic. Every time she arrived in New York, the media had a new story to tell about what she was wearing, what she was selling and where she was living − although never with whom. Her estrangement from Titus was a closely guarded secret. To the outside world, they presented the perfect picture of a modern, if somewhat transatlantic, family unit. The truth, as usual *chez* Rubinstein, was different.

Elizabeth Arden, in the meantime, had decided it was time for the ladies in Europe to see what she had on offer. One sure way to annoy Helena Rubinstein would be to open salons in Paris and London, cities Helena thought of as her own. So that's exactly what Elizabeth did next.

CHAPTER EIGHT

MASTERS OF ART, MISTRESSES OF MONEY
Paris 1920–1926

L ONG-ESTABLISHED SOCIAL STRUCTURES that had tottered during the First World War finally collapsed in its aftermath. Largely thanks to war work, women had achieved an unprecedented level of independence and fashion rapidly evolved into the fluid, simple shapes that suited the way women now wanted to live their lives. Layers of restrictive clothing were peeled away, along with the layers of restrictive practices against women, the most objectionable of which was refusing them the right to vote which ended, in America at least, in 1920. Women in England had to wait until 1928 until they could vote equally with men, but freedom in fashion, with the elimination of corsets and petticoats, and finally servant-starched blouses, long skirts and buttoned boots, had long been achieved.

There was however one layer they added willingly – make-up. Cosmetics were perfectly positioned to capture the mood of women hungry for change. The face they displayed, carefully made-up, blushed and powdered, was a pleasurable way of signalling their newly gained personal freedom. The 1920s is probably the time in the twentieth century that women had the most unfettered fun.

Elizabeth and Tommy travelled to Europe in 1920, partly on belated honeymoon (although her sister Gladys travelled with them), but more significantly, to investigate competition and scout locations. In London, without hesitation, she chose Bond Street. Lobbying the stores to buy her product was unsuccessful, with the exception of Harrods, where a small order was placed. It wasn't actually that order that launched Arden into Britain, but rather the man who placed it, Edward 'Teddy' Haslam, a trained chemist, and the buyer for what was then quaintly called the store's 'drug department'. Just over a year later, having made up her mind to open a British salon, she headhunted Mr Haslam out of Harrods into Elizabeth Arden Ltd, where he stayed until the day he died. She went back to London in the summer of 1921 to firm up his employment contract, the *Harrodian Gazette* shortly afterwards noting 'Mr Haslam had been appointed European manager for a large American firm'. Teddy Haslam went to New York for induction training, returning to England six months later, and the Elizabeth Arden salon opened on the first floor at 25 Old Bond Street in October 1922, remaining there until after Miss Arden's death, forty-four years later.

The success of this venture was so crucial to Elizabeth that she moved to London for the three months leading up to the launch, and didn't return to New York until 8 October that year. She personally took over the recruitment and training of the salon staff and monitored the establishment of a small production unit in Coach and Horses Yard, just off Bond Street. She became close to Haslam, their loyalty and affection rarely wavering in the forty years he worked for her. At times he was pushed to the limit, and fellow executives sometimes witnessed Elizabeth's icy abuse reducing this gentle gentleman to tears. Miss Arden made a wise choice when she hired Teddy Haslam. Not just an astute businessman, he was also gracious, diplomatic and loyal. He found a way of working with his demanding boss, whom he clearly admired, responding to the better side of her nature and ignoring her whims. If the relationship hovered towards sycophancy on Haslam's part, it was because he learnt at an early stage that 'yes, Miss Arden' was an easier option than 'no, Miss Arden' and would bide his time to solve a problem his own way. It helped that he was based three thousand miles away across the Atlantic. Colleagues at her New York offices and factory were less lucky than Haslam in avoiding Arden's terrifying tantrums and inability to delegate. In modern-day parlance, both Arden and Rubinstein would be described as 'control freaks'. They simply didn't trust anyone but themselves to do the job properly.

Word of the Arden salon spread quickly around rival establishments in London, particularly as she paid exceptionally good wages to beauticians, the best of which were clamouring to work for her. Rosa Hollay, Rubinstein's manager, was by this time feeling rather remote from her mercurial boss. Helena, apart from a fleeting visit to London at the end of the war, had been in Paris and Germany since that time. Arriving in London in

1922, she was met by Miss Hollay requesting a pay-rise. Helena refused. 'Get it out of your head please that Arden pays such huge salaries to everyone, as I know better,' she later wrote crossly. Madame it seems was suffering cash-flow problems, and certainly during the immediate post-war period, when raw materials were hard to obtain and had increased in price, there may have been a glitch in the Rubinstein fortunes. It would have been a temporary one however, as America woke up to the joys of cosmetics in a remarkably short time and Helena Rubinstein Inc made sure they were there to provide them.

Whilst Elizabeth established herself in London, Helena and Titus bickered via transatlantic correspondence. In the spring of 1923, when Titus was en route to London, Helena was travelling the other way towards Paris, determined to avoid him. She sent a letter to Rosa asking her to inform her as to what her husband was doing at all times. She also said she was feeling ill, and would be going for a 'cure'. Miss Hollay was swept up into the machinations of the Rubinstein/Titus marriage, whether she wanted to be or not. Helena would plead with her to tell Titus she was ill, instructing her to 'pile it on' and telling Rosa her husband was 'a selfish beast'.

If Elizabeth and Tommy weren't bickering at this time it was because they were too busy. The period between 1920 and 1925 was significant in dramatic business expansion, both in America and Europe. By 1923, Haslam had located a charming suite of rooms on rue St Honoré, a step or two from the Rubinstein salon, a fact which entertained Miss Arden, and was a suitable starting-off point to tackle Paris. Gladys Graham, her first marriage in tatters, had been working in the New York salon, and was dispatched to Paris to take over. She also supervised the French wholesale division, hiring a chemist so that products could be formulated in Paris. Post-war import/export restrictions and high taxation battles between the US and Europe, and France in particular, made shipping unviable. Elizabeth, however, could not be content with a small salon in rue St Honoré; she wanted bigger and better – so in 1924 she relocated to 2 rue de la Paix, decorating the salon in her by now signature pink, cream and gold.

Elizabeth was delighted that 'sister', as she always called Gladys, had taken in such a big way to France and the French, as she herself found the people as complex as their language, didn't like the food and rarely drank, so was unimpressed with their wines. As far as Elizabeth was concerned, the English-speaking territories were the ones to conquer. Her challenge in

Europe was England, where she wanted to rule. As long as Gladys could keep the French loyal to Arden, Elizabeth was happy.

Coincidentally, 1924 was the year that Edward W. Titus established his own business in Paris, realising his literary ambitions by contributing to Ford Madox Ford's magazine *Transatlantic Review* and opening a charming bookshop at 4 rue Delambre (his mortgage arranged courtesy of Helena) where he stocked rare editions and valuable manuscripts, gaining a reputation as a bibliophile. Wambly Bald reported in his column 'La Vie Bohème' for the *Chicago Tribune* that 'Titus only sold books to those who loved them as much as he did.'

Many of the Greenwich Village radicals and rebels moved to France after the war, as much to enjoy their cash at a time when a dollar fetched around 26 francs – which went a long way in Paris – as to indulge their taste for wine. When Prohibition hit America in 1920, a lot of the fun went out of the street cafés and bars of Greenwich Village, who charged exorbitant prices for bathtub gin. Further up-town, speakeasies flourished, but their glitzy ambience was ill-suited to the literary lions of the Village, many of them decamping to Montparnasse.

Creative influence, the glamorous juice that fuels consumer growth, was everywhere in the booming jazz and dance decade. Fashion, music, dance, modern art and breaking-ground literature all blossomed. Artists in Paris were achieving cult reputations and poetry flourished – as did the poets. Jean Cocteau, Blaise Cendrars, Louis Aragon, Max Jacob and Tristan Tzara were all seen at the best salons. The film industry was bringing excitement to the masses and creating the first superstars. The boom in newspapers and the launch of radio in 1922 spread the creative word, but it was the development of fashionable, quality magazines, poised to capitalise on their readers' insatiable desire to be kept up-to-date with every trend, that gave the greatest boost to the prestige end of the glamour industry – fashion and beauty. One of their most powerful weapons was photography, and photography meant lighting, hairdressing – and make-up.

By the 1920s, magazines had become exceedingly popular and very powerful. By 1923 the aggregate circulation of all magazines in America was 130 million. Advertising revenues were equally astonishing. In 1909, it is estimated revenues in the US magazine market totalled fifty-four million dollars. By 1929, it was over three hundred and twenty million dollars with over twenty firms investing a budget in excess of a million dollars a year each. Magazines in the 1920s were the most influential vehicle in creating dreams, establishing trends and swaying consumer opinion.

Style icons of film may have been in America, but the superstars of the art world, the giants of the fashion world, experimental photographers and illustrators, writers and poets, were all in Paris, and at the centre of it all, sending a siren's call around the world, was Montparnasse.

Helena and Titus had experienced some of the earlier and earthier magic of Montparnasse when they had lived in Paris before the war, happy times for them, when they first started to collect art. She had dabbled with the Impressionists, buying eight Renoirs and work by Sisley, Degas and Monet, but her instinctive modernist tastes, like those that guided her through her triumphs in cosmetics development, had also taken root in those formative years in Paris. 'What's new?' was Helena's favourite greeting, and she meant it. She was a modern-minded, working woman in evolutionary times and her inclination was for modern art.

Despite their on/off marriage, she was often guided by Titus who, she would later admit to a journalist, 'had a nose for art, a nose for property'. Between 1908 and 1930, she acquired works by, amongst others, Modigliani, Matisse, Chagall, Bonnard, Brancusi, Georges Braque, Joan Miró, the ultra-hip Bulgarian painter Jules Pascin, the Polish painter from her home town of Krakow, Moise Kisling – and, of course, Picasso. She bought nineteenth- and twentieth-century engravings, etchings and lithographs until she had no wall space left, acquiring works by Derain, Helleu, Laurencin, Maillol, Marcoussis, and twenty-seven drawings by Matisse, her favourite artist. She bought several pencil and crayon drawings by Modigliani – some from him personally before he died in 1920, and others just after the war from her Polish friend, his passionately devoted dealer, Leopold Zobrowski. She bought illustrations by Juan Gris, watercolours by Kees van Dongen, Dufy and Fernand Léger, watercolours by Alice Halicka – Mme Marcoussis – and a cluster of very early pen-and-ink and watercolours by Picasso.

In post-war France, Montparnasse was the centre of the art-led euphoria sweeping Paris. Fernand Léger wrote: 'Man . . . lifts his head, opens his eyes and looks around, relaxes and recaptures his taste for life, his frenzy to dance, to spend money . . . an explosion of life-force fills the world.' This 'explosion' affected the Titus and Lewis families in different ways. When Titus moved to Paris he forged a transatlantic relationship with Helena which suited their circumstances. He kept an eye on her French investment property portfolio, reluctantly kept his hand in on her copywriting and supervised their sons on their frequent European visits. His wife, on the other hand, could still claim to be married, at a time when it mattered – for the benefit of the media at least – and remained free to work as she wished in America. With her husband 'abroad' she was able to travel to promote her business, albeit with a female companion.

For Titus, from a creative and social point of view, being back in France felt like coming home and he stayed there for the rest of his life. Helena, the inveterate traveller, rarely stayed in one place long enough to call it home, becoming bored if she did. When she had fled to France after the war, leaving her sons in America with her husband, business in New York was already being managed by a team of executives she had put in place – all men – including a chief accountant, company secretary, senior sales manager and a chemist. Sister Manka was still on the payroll, but Helena had little confidence in her ability to handle a crisis. The 'sister act' however was a good publicity angle and Helena worked it well. However, her sons were left without the guiding hand of either parent at a sensitive age. By 1922, with their father living in Paris and their mother constantly travelling, the boys, aged ten and twelve, had to make do with their tutor, two aunts and a variety of cousins as companions, shunted from home to home to suit their mother's hectic schedule. For Roy and Horace, there were Silberfeld cousins and even Manka's young son to play with, but they lacked what they craved the most, their parents living with them at home.

The early 1920s were as expansive for the fashion and beauty business as the literary and art business and people were talking and writing about both. 'Nobody represents the thin, factitious smartness of the age better than Jean Cocteau,' said Sisley Huddleston, the Paris correspondent of the London *Times*, a remark which could easily have been made about the beauty business. Magazines like Lucien Vogel's *Gazette du Bon Ton*, which had reopened after the war, *Jardin des Modes*, and the newly opened French *Vogue* were devoting more and more pages to fashion, smart women were ultra-thin and factitious means 'made for a special purpose, not natural, artificial'.

There was nothing natural about women's faces in 1920s Paris where the trend for cosmetics was enthusiastically adopted. The new lipsticks, eye shadows, kohl liners and rouge were entirely artificial, and women loved them. Sisley Huddleston, being a gentleman of distinction, commented wistfully about the new habit of women making up their faces in public: 'While speaking to you a lady will pass her lipstick over her lips, plant her mirror boldly on the table, and apply powder to her face. Sometimes she will even produce a comb,' remembering, perhaps, a more alluring time when a woman's *toilette* began and ended in her dressing-room.

But the brittle, carefree women of the day took no notice. They adored make-up and craved thinness, to the satisfaction of the growing band of fashionable dieticians. If diet alone didn't work, there were diet doctors, happy to prescribe amphetamines to kill the appetite, and for the ultra-stylish, who craved to be X-ray thin, the dieter's drug of choice was cocaine, which also boosted the frenzy to dance. Dance-crazy young women – flappers – took their passion seriously. With no room in their dancing wardrobe for a handbag, they put their make-up in jewelled rings with 'lift-up' centres, or in their shoe buckles, which were ingeniously designed as powder compacts. Confectionery manufacturers despaired, their profits plunging as sales of chocolate slumped.

In December 1922, the most sumptuous, romantic form of transport to the newly fashionable Riviera was launched – the Calais-Méditerranée Express, though from its inaugural run the gleaming, exclusively first-class train with its blue metal sides would be just *le train bleu*. When Coco Chanel disembarked from her lover, the Duke of Westminster's, yacht in 1923 with a deep sun-tan, women headed for the beach in droves.

Once the 'summer season' had taken off, there was no looking back. When couturier Lucien Lelong married the Russian Princess Natalie Paley in the summer of 1927, the fashionable duo placed the ultimate seal of approval on the new vogue for spending August in the sun – they went to St Tropez on their honeymoon. Such was the demand on the 'paradise route' that by 1929, *le train bleu* ran every day, all year round. For women wearing swimsuits, even covered by the ubiquitous beach-pyjamas, there was no hiding place for extra inches. A craze for exercise swept Paris, London and New York, where the Rubinstein and Arden salons both introduced eurhythmic exercise classes.

Passionate about yoga, which she would always say saved her from hip surgery, Elizabeth was a devotee of the regime, and fantastically supple as a result. She introduced classes in her salon, selling satin-backed camelhair yoga mats at $65 a time. As she adored dancing, her exercise classes were developed from dance routines. She took her research seriously and would have known that Isadora Duncan followed the system of François Delsarte, whose nine laws of gesture and posture were the key to freedom and relaxation for each part of the body. In 1920s New York, Elizabeth could sometimes be found conducting a masterclass in eurhythmic movement and stretch – and standing on her head.

Madame, in the meantime, never known to venture near an exercise class herself but identifying the trend as important, hired the ballet dancer Mikhail Mordkin to teach Rubinstein Rhythmics in New York. His technique was apparently *very* exacting, resulting in a high level of fall-out from his classes due to total exhaustion and quite probably a few pulled muscles, and his classes were quietly dropped.

Above all, there was the endless search for youth. For those who could afford it, Paris-based Dr Voronoff, who was experimenting with his anti-ageing process involving monkey glands, was the specialist of choice. Helena observed the trend with interest, telling a journalist from the *New Yorker* that she 'had studied with Voronoff'.

She also waxed lyrical about the benefits of plastic surgery. In an interview with *The American Magazine* in 1922 she advocated face lifts, explaining 'the commonest sign of middle age, and the most destructive of beauty, is the lost youthful contour of the face'. She told reporter Allison Gray about her association with Dr Kapp, who was experimenting with monkey gland serum, explaining a recent editorial on her bringing the wonder serum to New York had solicited over sixty thousand letters from readers who yearned for youth. 'Everybody wants to be young,' said Madame, who was fifty herself at the time. She went on to recommend that career girls take better care of their appearance, as 'natural good looks are an asset in business' and said overweight women could 'consider and operation to remove stomach fat'. Madame talked about oily skin and enlarged pores, about proper cleansing and nourishing and, above all, about not using alkaline soap on dry skin, 'as it strips away moisture and dry skin is already half-starved without that kind of soap being a thief stealing what little food your system provides'. By the time she had finished, the awed Miss Gray went away and wrote *six* pages on Madame's mantra, presumably nervously running her hands over her cheeks to check her complexion when she had finished.

Dr Gillies, the surgical hero of the Somme, had published his seminal book *Plastic Surgery of the Face* in 1920 and was at the forefront of development techniques, although cosmetic plastic surgery was still in its infancy and there were several unfortunate faces to be seen amongst society ladies who went to the wrong surgeon. Elsie de Wolfe, always at the cutting edge of experimental procedures, had a skin peel, which was remarked by her friend Gaylord Hauser to be 'very successful'.

It is generally held that Helena Rubinstein lived in Paris during the 1920s, but although she visited there several times a year, New York was her base and America energised Helena more than any other country she had visited. By 1920, she had established a meaningful wholesale business and her advertising listed outlets in Atlantic City, San Francisco, Boston, Chicago and New Orleans. Commuting to Europe was an obsession, and she usually found time to add a few days' exploring an exotic location on to her business trips. In 1921, the destination was Tunisia where she travelled with artist Jean Lurcat. Since her estrangement from Titus, Lurcat had taken on the role of art adviser to Madame. She posed for the ubiquitous tourist photograph riding a camel, looking rather *soignée* given the circumstances, in a cream pleated suit and cloche hat.

To begin with, Titus leased an apartment in Montparnasse, and by 1926 had opened his publishing imprint, At the Sign of the Black Manikin, from offices above his shop, where he published English language translations of cult books and poetry, most illustrated by the artists living in Montparnasse and many printed at Crete Printers, down the street at number 24.

The complex Rubinstein/Titus *ménage*, involving visits from their sons and the servicing of several properties, required a permanent staff and Gaston and Eugenie Metz were hired in the 1920s. Years later, Eugenie, by then working at Madame's Quai de Bethune apartment, told Patrick O'Higgins: 'I've been with Madame since this building went up. Before that, I worked for Monsieur Titus. He was a real gentleman. Their marriage broke up only because of money. Madame will tell you otherwise. She'll say he had mistresses. That's true. What else could he do? She never gave him a moment.' In fact, the break-up was about money *and* mistresses.

Much as Helena couldn't live with Edward Titus, she couldn't live without him either. She was obsessed by him, sexually and intellectually, dangling her power – that of her money – with exquisite cruelty. Clearly she needed and wanted to maintain the fantasy of their marriage. She obviously slept with him from time to time, from 1917 to around 1930, usually as part of a grand rapprochement on his part, and afterwards she despised herself for it. By now in her mid-fifties, the still striking-looking Helena was developing all the characteristics of a driven, menopausal woman, pushing herself too hard mentally and physically. She developed chronic insomnia, digestive problems, circulation difficulties, diabetes, high blood pressure, and seemed incapable of controlling her irrational and violent temper tantrums.

Helena Rubinstein was a workaholic. She thrived on stress – or thought she did – but more importantly, she thrived on money. Business, as far as Helena was concerned, was for one thing only, to make money. It wasn't to make friends. It wasn't even to earn prestige. It wasn't for indulgences of any kind. It was for cash. Titus seemed to her to lead an idle, charmed existence in Paris, enjoying his literary affairs, not to mention his romantic affairs. She wasn't far wrong. His leisure time was spent enjoying convivial conversations over a pastis at the Dome or the Dingo, just down the street in rue Delambre and the favoured haunt of Americans in Paris. Part of 'Kiki's Montparnasse' he spent time at the local artists' cult nightclub, the Jockey, in the rue Campagne Première, where on most nights Kiki could be found staging a pretty *outré* cabaret. Kiki's only rival was the sensational Josephine Baker, who having taken Paris by storm with her show, *La Revue Negre*, used to unwind by dancing at the Jockey in a white mink coat. When she got hot and peeled it off, she was stark naked. The Jockey, run by Hilaire Hiler who designed and painted the interiors in the style of a Wild West saloon, was fondly remembered by Ernest Hemingway as being 'the best nightclub that ever was'.

The celebrated 'muse of Montparnasse', known simply as Kiki, had moved to Paris just before the war, finding work as a sculptor's model, and never looked back. Kiki manoeuvred her way from hawking copies of Paul Husson's art magazine *Montparnasse* around café tables, to becoming a fixture of the *mise-en-scène* of Montparnasse itself. She started out modelling for Kisling and Foujita and was soon posing for Man Ray, with whom she had a passionate love affair lasting over six years. Ray encouraged her to paint, helped in no small part by Titus, who exhibited her paintings at his bookshop.

As Montparnasse boomed, property values surged. Entrepreneurs were able to buy buildings, many of them half derelict, knowing that after judicious haggling with tenants over eviction, a valuable freehold would be ripe for redevelopment. In 1927, an American-based property company called

Franc-Am Ltd, operating out of offices in rue St Honoré, went on a spending spree. Amongst their acquisitions was a row of crumbling buildings on the corner of rue Campagne Première, where one of their tenants was the Jockey, along with a plot on Boulevard Raspail, further property in Montparnasse and the freehold, subject to tenant eviction, of a superb building at 52 Faubourg St Honoré. It's doubtful that Kiki, or Man Ray, or Hemingway, Foujita, or any of the Montparnasse crowd who revelled at the Jockey, ever realised Helena Rubinstein, the owner of Franc-Am Ltd, was their landlady. She didn't like nightclubs and never ventured there; the nearest she came to Montparnasse nightlife was taking a nightcap with Titus at the Select or the Dome.

Titus was given a paid role to advise Helena on property acquisition and to liaise with her Paris lawyer, M. Levesque, her written and business French not being good enough for her to deal directly. Titus oversaw the purchase of an important plot on Boulevard Raspail and the hiring of Polish architect Elkuken to build a contemporary, eight-floor apartment building on the site with – in a publicity-generating move – a theatre-cum-cinema in the basement where Titus planned to have poetry recitals, to show modern plays and the surrealist films of his new friend Man Ray. Not surprisingly, since they were immediate neighbours, with pre-war New York in common, Edward Titus and Man Ray had become acquainted, bonding in particular over their admiration for Surrealism. Ray had a passion for African art and Titus loaned him key pieces from Helena's collection to use as props, such as in his celebrated 1926 picture of Kiki 'with mask' and his 1931 picture of ex-Poiret fashion model Ady, pictured with Helena's *Bangwa Queen* statue.

Titus was, in his way, as dangerously ambitious as his wife. He was clearly tuned in to the almost invisible mores of the arts world, which so often trigger the trends in fashion and cosmetics, and had a great fondness for his own carefully constructed wardrobe. As a consultant, he was still making a creative contribution to his wife's beauty business and lobbied Man Ray's friends, Marie Laure de Noailles and Louise de Vilmorin, to contribute to advertising copywriting. The rich Marie de Noailles was particularly influential. John Richardson, who knew her well, describes her as 'one of the most paradoxical women I ever met. Spoiled, generous, sly, fearless, manipulative, impetuous, bitchy, affectionate, childish, maddening and, not least, extremely cultivated'. In other words, she had all the talent to tackle copy-writing for the beauty business and her pedigree would have awed Titus.

It's doubtful that Helena ever appreciated what a coup this would have been to the fashionable set in Paris. Although she loved fashion, she was less than interested in the antics of the people who inhabit the fashion world. Hovering near the edge of their *milieu*, she would pull back at the last minute, never really comfortable with their brittle exotica. Nevertheless, copy by either of these two super-chic women – the type of women whose friendship Titus craved – would have added cachet to any promotional campaign.

As well as having a weakness for beautiful people, Helena's husband had a penchant for poetry. The Black Manikin Press published twenty-five titles in the seven years of its existence, including work by Paul Valéry, Ralph Cheever Dunning and Baudelaire's *Little Poems in Prose* translated into English by the sinister Aleister Crowley, a less appealing resident of Montparnasse.

There was only one problem – the list rarely made much money and Titus could not rely on Helena to sign the cheques. His confidence grew with the acclaim he received for publishing Ludwig Lewisohn's highly regarded book *The Case of Mr Crump* which, although it fell foul of American censors, was offered 'by private subscription' by Black Manikin, a system Titus operated successfully for his more controversial, often erotic, titles, sending them out to clients as individual parcels. Towards the end of the 1920s, keen to expand his business and wary of relying on consultancy fees from his increasingly erratic wife, he spotted an opportunity he felt too good to miss.

The concentration of talent in Montparnasse had spawned a flurry of literary and art publications, the 'little magazines' as historian Frederick Hoffman described them, 'designed to print artistic work which for commercial expediency is not acceptable to the money-minded periodicals'. The one the Paris-based international writing elite most revered was *This Quarter*. Launched in the early 1920s by the Irish American poet, Ernest Walsh, and his partner, the Scottish suffragette, Ethel Moorhead, the English-language magazine was committed to publishing contemporary writers – the first issue was dedicated to Ezra Pound, with photographs by Man Ray, and featured a tribute to Pound by Ernest Hemingway, who had recently taught him to box. Sadly the rather glamorous Mr Walsh, who suffered from TB, died soon after and although Miss Moorhead continued to operate the title, the situation was precarious. Titus, seeing the magazine as a natural extension of his business, bought the title in 1928. Helena thought it a folly and was furious, becoming almost irrational with anger and refusing him any financial support for his new baby.

By then, Montparnasse was becoming a victim of its own fame. Purists felt that publication of Hemingway's *The Sun Also Rises* in 1926 marked the beginning of commercialism in the 'Quarter', as the area was nicknamed. Travel companies were setting up guided tours to see 'bohemian artists at work', and 'writers' who were signing more autographs than writing prose seemed to be a permanent fixture at the Dome, the Rotonde and the Select, not to mention the newly opened la Coupole. American tourists flocked to see famous American sophisticates like Laurence Vail and his heiress wife, Peggy Guggenheim, the Hemingways, Gerald and Sara Murphy and Scott and Zelda Fitzgerald, who in turn seemed always en route either to or from their playground, the South of France.

Edward Titus, however, saw this as an opportunity. He adored being a magazine editor, imposing a structure on what had previously been a very informal operation, largely put together in local bars. 'Personal interviews with the editor may be had between 2 and 7 o'clock the fifteenth of every month, or otherwise by appointment only' was self-importantly printed underneath the index. Titus directed his marketing skills into a revamp of the ailing title. Some literary expatriates were not amused. *This Quarter* had been their baby, written and read by them. The problem was, it doesn't seem to have been read by anyone else *but* them. Titus, in nurturing their 'baby' into a 'grown-up', ran into a lot of artistic temperament.

The American writer and translator Samuel Putnam began working for Titus as associate editor of *This Quarter* in 1928, joining from his job at Sylvia Beach's Shakespeare & Company and staying with Black Manikin for two years. Theirs was an uneasy relationship and he would later write,

Titus was the perfect and most objectionable type of bourgeois, intensely disliked for his lordly airs and the impression he seemed to be trying to convey of being the owner of Montparnasse. Married at the time to Helena Rubinstein, who lived on the other side of the ocean, he was looked upon as being wealthy and niggardly, but most of all he was resented for having taken over the old *This Quarter* of Ernest Walsh and for having made of it something altogether different, giving another connotation to its name, even, which was really what he was buying.

Putnam's fallout with Titus had escalated over his refusal to publish short stories by American writer James T. Farrell, who Putnam felt had a significant talent. Looking at issues edited by Titus, it's hard to understand what Putnam was grumbling about. Articles were still being written by Montparnasse diehards like Hilaire Hiler and Natalie Barney and although Putnam complained that Titus only published works by famous, establishment writers, in fact he constantly sought out fresh work, appealing to new talent by offering $500 (nearly $5000 today) for the best short story by an English or American writer, an astonishing amount of money for the time.

Edward Titus clearly loved his magazine as much as he loved his books. He was a natural style innovator whose intellectual and academic gifts – he spoke, wrote and translated French, English, Russian, Polish, German and Hebrew – were sometimes at odds with his desire to combine more formal tastes in literature with new-wave art – and his desire to make money. It was his commercial edge that upset the diehards, many of whom, like Louis Aragon, had winced at the Black Manikin's exquisite 'luxe' surrealist art limited editions, described on their list as 'printed on heavy Montial Gris Rose hand-moulded paper, 250 numbered copies only'.

Much as Titus wanted critical acclaim for his title, he needed an improved circulation and was confident there was an international market for the only English-language magazine operating out of Montparnasse. He made changes to *This Quarter*, invested in promoting it and acquired distribution in New York and London. Helena viewed his business with suspicion; it didn't seem like work to her. She was quite wrong of course. Titus was, whether he cared to admit it or not, a natural marketing man, and the fashion and beauty world has long sought affiliation with art and artists. The brilliant strategies he introduced to his wife's business had positioned her as a world-famous name. He attempted to do the same with *This Quarter* which otherwise would have folded overnight, and if he was slow to pay bills, it was more likely because of the complex domestic arguments with Helena, who simply couldn't comprehend what it was about writers that excited her husband so much and grumbled about the costs, leaving him to struggle with funding.

Scott Fitzgerald famously called 1925 'the summer of 1000 parties and no work' but though Titus may have partied *and* worked in Paris, for Helena life had been all work. That year, she went to the Exposition Internationale des Arts Décoratifs et Industriels Modernes which was an inspiration for her, resulting in a radical refit of her salons. Along with the exhibition came not just the outpouring of 'art deco' but something more significant for both Rubinstein and Arden, the global vision of Paris as a 'woman's city', reinforcing its power-base as the centre of fashion and beauty. Paris was promoted as the city where the world's women of style, culture and sophistication would most enjoy their shopping, for everything from *haute couture* to the finest fragrance, from a flea market find to a treasured antique.

Helena loved nothing better than trawling flea markets and small workshops for treasures, knowing the best bargains were hidden there. On one foray at this time, she met the young Christian Dior, who long before his fashion fame had a partnership in an art gallery off the rue de la Boetie. Helena bought from him, forging a friendship that would continue in great harmony throughout his illustrious career, when she could always be found sitting in a favoured front-row seat at his fashion shows.

Her collection was an eclectic one. In her rush to buy quantity, she often slipped up on quality. Taking advice was not Madame's strongest point and she wasn't robust in the face of criticism. Besides Lurcat, another of her coterie of advisers in Montparnasse was Casimir Marcoussis, who did an etching of her in 1920. Marcoussis, whose critics accuse him of having questionable taste, had his patron's ear and escorted her to galleries and studios. 'Now, there's a painting to have,' he would say. 'It's a beautiful picture', the irony being he was probably right. Unfortunately Helena didn't listen to him, admitting she 'missed several beautiful pictures'. Translated from 'Helena speak' this means the price asked was too high, she couldn't beat it down, and suspected Marcoussis had built in a commission.

She sometimes made mistakes and occasionally bought fakes. The Rubinstein collection, however, was a spirited one – much of it representing a unique moment in time. Montparnasse, when Helena's favourite artists lived there, was a magical place for artists and art lovers. It seems sad in retrospect that she was so rarely there to see it and, when she was, couldn't relax enough to enjoy it.

CHAPTER NINE

ELIZABETH AND TOMMY
New York 1920–1926

ELIZABETH'S OBJECTIVE WAS TO open salons in Europe and Tommy's was to see the Elizabeth Arden brand established in prestige department stores in America – both set about their tasks, although not necessarily together. Miss Arden had been virtually commuting to Europe between 1920 and 1924, with Tommy remaining in New York, but whilst he was head of the wholesale division he could never encroach on his wife's sacred turf – her salons. By 1924, both Bond Street and rue de la Paix were established, and thanks to the support of Elizabeth's new friend in London, the well connected interior decorator, Lady Islington, who supervised the purchase of rugs, chandeliers and antiques for Bond Street, the anchor clientele was part of the smart set.

With Mr Haslam plotting a chart for European expansion, salons were opened in Biarritz, Cannes, Monte Carlo and le Touquet, Rome and Berlin. These elegant resorts and cities were a natural haven for Arden's clientele, and with the US dollar buying a lot of francs, France was a favoured destination for affluent Americans. Travelling on the great liners like the *Ile de France*, the *Leviathan*, the *Majestic* or the *Mauritania* was the ultimate in chic leisure activity. Travellers could relax, swim, play deck-sports, dance – and drink. When the gangplank lifted in New York, Prohibition was left behind, and the trip to France was a week-long cocktail party. At their destination, Miss Arden ensured there was one of her famous Red Doors waiting to greet them.

Tommy Lewis made himself very useful to his wife in the first half of the 1920s and is largely credited with creating the strong wholesale market for the brand. He had an appealing personality, a sunny sense of humour and was a natural salesman. Joseph Wile, now in his nineties, grew up working for the family store Wolfe Wiles in Lexington, Kentucky. His father often talked about the first time he met Tommy Lewis. 'They met in the early 1920s,' recalls Joseph Wile. 'When Lewis came in with their small range, my father bought $140 worth, and was most impressed. Tommy Lewis was her business manager and getting the wholesale line established. My father always said he was a most attractive and personable man.' Lewis, however, although giving the impression he was his wife's business manager, never held that title, much as he deserved to. Gordon 'Gordy' Yates was hired by Tommy in the 1920s, eventually becoming part of the team that opened up Europe for Arden. Yates had been destined for a career in law, but on meeting Elizabeth and Tommy was mesmerised by the sheer force of her personality and ambition and the brilliance of her husband's salesmanship. Yates's son, Tiki, says that his father would often reminisce about those glittering years and said Lewis was 'an utterly brilliant salesman – and my father knew a *lot* of salesmen'.

To maintain the status Elizabeth had created for her salons, Tommy determined which department stores were prestigious enough to carry the Arden line. He cancelled Stern Brothers in New York, initially insisting Arden would only sell on Fifth Avenue, kept Bonwit Teller and Best & Company, and opened at I. Magnin, the luxury west-coast chain of speciality stores. As the brand developed, boosted by the prestige of the salons, thus the wholesale figures escalated and the product range expanded. By 1925, Elizabeth Arden was producing over seventy-five individual products in three hundred shapes, shades and sizes in their own production facility, and was said to be turning over more than $2 million in the American wholesale division alone. Arden was stocked by Marshall Field in Chicago, made special offer 'large sizes' on an exclusive basis for Macy's and was introduced at Neiman Marcus, J.W. Robinson in Los Angeles, J.L. Hudson in Detroit and Halle Bros in Cleveland. Tommy kept well out of Elizabeth's way during working hours, basing himself at their sales headquarters, now at 212 East 52nd St, rarely setting foot in the salons. This gave both an excuse to travel – often in opposite directions across America or over the Atlantic – a situation which was beginning to suit them.

Elizabeth toured tirelessly, always with an entourage including treatment girls, selected not just for their beauty and charm, but their skills in massage and facials. These girls, immaculately made-up, dressed in crisp white uniforms with pink satin bows in their hair, all 'personally trained by Miss Arden', would do a guest week at a branch salon, creating excitement amongst the clientele and the local media, before returning to New York. By now, Willie Graham, Elizabeth's brother, was on board, working for Tommy in the wholesale division. He had been persuaded to give up his job selling porcelain, in which he had shown a certain flair; he was family and Elizabeth was extremely fond of his three young daughters. She was pleased to observe her husband and her brother becoming close. When the duo travelled, however, their entourage of beauticians and demonstrators making in-store appearances, dressed in pink crepe de chine smocks, to echo the pink and gold packaging on the Arden product, were no less attractive, and their massage skills were apparently put to very good use.

Outwardly, Mr and Mrs Thomas Jenkins Lewis put on a good show. They socialised tirelessly and Elizabeth had boundless energy. She often worked a ten-hour day, always starting early, taking a brief working lunch with a magazine editor, or a social celebrity, or quite often with her lawyer Robert Rubin, who had connections with the film industry. After a brief catnap in the early evening, ten minutes of yoga, and having swiftly bathed and changed, she was ready to enjoy her social life. Their friends at that time were drawn from the theatre and musical comedy world. Very often the women were Arden clients, actresses and emerging filmstars keen to enhance their beauty; for Elizabeth, there was kudos in dining with people as famous as Helen Hayes and Ethel Barrymore. She found two key members of her executive staff at the theatre. Genevieve Daily, who had been understudy to Arden's earlier rival, Lillian Russell, who stayed with her for thirty-five years, managing US salons, and Wellington 'Duke' Cross, whom she had spotted in the chorus line of *No, No, Nanette* on Broadway. Cross was persuaded to bring his matinee good looks into the business, becoming vice president of sales, and staying with Arden for over forty years.

Duke Cross fulfilled one of the most important criteria for an Elizabeth Arden man. He was tall. When she met him he was married and his wife Katie had just started working for the top society florist in New York, Irene Hayes. Elizabeth admired Irene Hayes, who had been one of Florenz Ziegfeld's showgirls before opening her flower shop, and immediately moved her account there, on the understanding that Katie Cross would manage it personally. This was practically a full-time job for Katie as Elizabeth was fastidious to a degree of paranoia about flowers. In later years, each employee would receive a packet of 'Elizabeth Arden Sweet Pea' seeds at Easter and friends and clients the world over would be sent tulip bulbs each Christmas, all from her Maine Chance farm greenhouses and gardens. Her favourite flower at the time was the American Beauty rose, seemingly a symbol for beauty tycoons. Named after Lillian Russell, it became Arden's signature flower and was later adopted by Charles Revson, who would send bunches of three or four dozen to editors, buyers, models, his girlfriends – and sometimes his wives.

It was as well that Duke Cross was already married, as Miss Arden let it be known to all her senior management that marriage was frowned on. Like Queen Elizabeth I, she had a penchant for bachelors. They could not only serve as her 'courtiers' readily available for escort duty when Tommy was away, but more importantly could be sent abroad on business at a moment's notice, or be transferred to some farflung territory, without a wife to complain about the upheaval. Her stance on this was even stronger in the 1930s following her own divorce. When Gordy Yates met his bride-to-be, Frances, they had to marry behind Miss Arden's back and managed to keep their wedding day, on 13 October 1935, a secret from her. When Yates was later sent to Germany, he insisted on being allowed to 'marry' and Frances had to go through the absurd ritual of a fake wedding.

Elizabeth and Tommy both enjoyed dancing and in 1923 would have been in the audience at a Broadway play called *Runnin' Wild* when the Charleston, which originated in its namesake city in South Carolina, found fame in New York, and effectively launched the 'flapper'. She also adored the Ziegfeld Follies. Their relentless round of dinners, suppers, shows, charity galas *et al.* meant they were constantly in the media eye. Considered a marketing asset, this was milked for all it was worth, and the 'smiling, happy couple' were never happier than when they featured in the social columns. Elizabeth shone in company, chattering endlessly about her business, handing out advice on health, beauty and exercise, rarely stopping to see if the recipient was interested. Both were natural salespeople, talking about 'Elizabeth Arden' non-stop. They saw all this as a way of promoting the business and the business was their lives.

Edna Woolman Chase of *Vogue* found this out early in her relationship with Elizabeth, who rarely relaxed enough to talk about anything except work. 'She's a remarkable woman,' wrote Mrs Chase about Arden. 'I remember meeting her in Paris. I didn't know her well at the time and we couldn't seem to get on any common ground. Topics introduced rose briefly and collapsed. I felt we were fencing through a façade of meringue until I said, "Tell me, Miss Arden, how did you start your business?" Her eyes lit up. Business! In a puff we were on solid ground.'

Prohibition had by now spawned the culture of the speakeasy, eclipsing the glamour of the great supper clubs, like the Sans Souci, where the Castles had danced. Never at her happiest in what she considered *louche* establishments, Elizabeth frowned on most forays to the 'speaks', with the notable exception of the Twenty One Club on West 52nd St, which was the most exclusive of the illegal watering holes and had great cachet. She lunched and dined at '21' for the rest of her life, often telling her guests with great glee about her early visits there. Tommy on the other hand, with his penchant for the racier form of nightlife, under the guise of 'looking after buyers', would have been spoiled for choice. By 1927 there were 27,000 illegal 'speaks' in New York alone. The absurd decision to enforce prohibition meant that huge numbers of America's leading citizens were breaking the law and the gangsters operating the production and smuggling of liquor were becoming the all-powerful new rich.

The most alluring watering hole was run by the peroxide blonde, Texas Guinan. At her club the music was good and her dancing girls and hostesses even better. Texas would greet her guests, about to be charged the most extortionate prices for mediocre champagne and weak whiskey, with a cheerful, 'Hello sucker!' By the time a host had bought his guests a boutonnière at $5 each, cigarettes at $1 a pack, not to mention a 'Texas Rag Doll' at $5 a time, all sold by girls wearing very little except a lot of make-up and a big smile, the bill was mounting. With a jug of tap water at $2, champagne at $25, plus tips for the maître d' and cloakroom girls, the city editor of the *Tribune* newspaper calculated that an evening for four cost $1500. Such costs didn't worry Tommy Lewis. The Arden corporate budget for lobbying buyers was a big one and Elizabeth's husband and brother made good use of it.

One of Elizabeth's greatest assets, rarely given the recognition she deserved, was her sister, Gladys. In Paris, Gladys had quickly become absorbed into the more sophisticated element of local nightlife and, like her brother and brother-in-law, used it to great advantage in promoting the firm. The two sisters were close, but with vastly different personalities. Emily Hutchison, who knew them both, describes Gladys as 'more brittle than Elizabeth, a little chilly, but quite soignée'. To avoid prohibitive French taxes, Elizabeth had, at an early stage, made the business in France over to Gladys, where she was very much in control. Gladys was her sister's 'secret weapon'. She had a nose for finding special, eclectic items, from jewelled lipstick cases to product formulae and chemists. When Arden moved into custom-made clothes, Gladys recruited the designers. When they left, as they did on a regular basis, she came up with a replacement. She worked hard but she liked to have fun. Her tastes were shaped by her extremely right-wing second husband, Henri de Maublanc, and she was a 'Right Bank' girl, who would rarely have made forays into the Left Bank clubs. Neither was she particularly interested in art or artists, the nearest to coming into contact with them would have been an evening at Le Boeuf sur le Toit, on rue Boissy d'Anglas, where Cocteau and Jules Pascin would play the drums, Jacques Doucet the piano and *le tout* Paris, artistic, intellectual or just fun-loving, would prop up the bar. At first, thrilled that her little sister's beau was the scion of an 'old' French family, Elizabeth considered Henri de Maublanc an asset to the family. Her regard would switch to distaste as his passion for the far right evolved into his pro-Nazi stance during the Second World War, but when he first met Gladys his social credentials were very useful.

Elizabeth Arden bestsellers at this time were Orange Skin Food, Venetian Bleaching Cream and Poudre d'Illusion, a liquid powder for a 'peach bloom' skin. Miss Arden was constantly irritated by her competitors stealing her ideas. When she launched June Geranium Bath Salts, Dorothy Gray launched June Geranium Bath Soap. Arden launched Orange Skin Food and the annoying Miss Gray launched Orange Flower Skin Tonic. However, Miss Arden was not averse to doing a spot of copying herself. In a take on the bestselling hand cream of the day, Hind's Honey and Almond, she created her own Ardena Milk of Almond Hand Cream. The only key item missing on the range at that time was fragrance. Until Chanel launched her No 5 in 1921, fragrance came from the leading perfume houses like Guerlain, Houbigant or even Coty. Either that or women, particularly in America, wore eau-de-cologne. Determined to win market share in what she saw as a lucrative niche, in 1924 Elizabeth sent a pleading message to her sister in France to find her a wonderful scent. Gladys responded with a range of fragrances from an obscure but interesting fashion house called Babani. Elizabeth subsequently imported what she described as 'a wardrobe of perfumes – six different scents by Babani only imported by Elizabeth Arden'. Despite her best efforts at promotion, assisted by the fact that actress Katharine Hepburn had married in a Babani dress the year before, the bohemian designer label never made enough impact in the US to sustain the recognition essential for success in sales of 'designer fragrance' and it would be over a decade before Elizabeth Arden successfully moved into perfume.

She did, however, successfully move into advertising. Elizabeth and Tommy were united in expanding their budget. Not until Charles Revson's dramatic post-Second World War advertising spend, which propelled Revlon into orbit, had any privately owned prestige brand invested so much in the media. To put this into context, the February 1926 expenditure by Ponds in major national magazines in the US was $60,000. By 1914, the original Ponds Extract, launched in 1846, was off the shelves and just two products, cold cream and vanishing cream, were the company staple. Ponds' advertising agency, J. Walter Thompson, under the direction of senior creative director Helen Landsdowne Resor, was quick to recognise the snobbish vitality of the salon-based beauty culture phenomenon created by Arden and Rubinstein, and set out to adapt its cachet for the mass market. In a move which did little for Miss Arden's blood pressure, Miss Resor and another famous J. Walter Thompson copywriter, feminist Frances Maule, co-ordinated a campaign for Ponds, one of their biggest clients, using the great social names of the day to endorse the product. Page after page appeared in *Vogue*, *Harper's Bazaar* and *Ladies' Home Journal*, with grandees like Alva Belmont, Queen Marie of Romania, Alice Roosevelt Longworth, Lady Diana Manners and Princess Marie de Bourbon all promoting Ponds, with side-bar copy which boosted their 'distinguished activities'. Elizabeth Arden rarely used celebrity endorsement (hers being the only famous name necessary), but if she had, it is unlikely she would have had the courage to ask such women to endorse Arden – she was too busy trying to get them to ask her for dinner.

One of Elizabeth's greatest beliefs in business was that you had to spend money to make money. In the month that the Ponds corporation spent $60,000, Elizabeth Arden, a tiny company by comparison, spent $20,775. 'Elizabeth Arden's Venetian Toilet Preparations – at smart shops everywhere', ran the end-copy line on the full-page advertisements in the glossy magazines. The 'smart shops' knew exactly what they were buying into – pure, unashamed, feminine, up-scale luxury, and how they loved it. It's unlikely that salon staff had any idea of the scale of the advertising budget, but if they had, they wouldn't have grumbled. A trained treatment girl could earn as much as $60 a week plus tips, not to mention commission on product sales, at a time when the average garment worker was earning around $18 a week and a retail store assistant, at most, around $30.

By 1925, Elizabeth Arden salons were open in Boston, Washington, Detroit, Newport, Palm Beach, San Francisco, Philadelphia and Los Angeles. Elizabeth also opened a salon at the Ritz Carlton in Atlantic City, a hotel which, in the fashion of the time, practised racial discrimination. Whilst no 'ethnic or minority' groups could cross the threshold, they accepted dogs, a great relief to Elizabeth who adored dogs, but was decidedly uncomfortable about ethnic and minority groups, including Jews, for she had a decidedly anti-Semitic streak. More guarded in public than in her private letters, in 1935 she wrote to Teddy in London: 'I saw the buyer from Fortnum & Mason at Hialeah races, she was with hopeless Jews.' In 1937, angry about a strike at her American factory, she again wrote to Teddy: 'The unions are going through the cosmetics business now. I think we have it fairly well squelched. If anything like this happens again, I will let a big Jew have the business.' Her management knew the unwritten rules. In 1949, Haslam contacted her about recruitment. 'Resumed search for two better hairdressers. Mrs Williams asks if you would employ a Jew?' Elizabeth's anti-Semitic tendencies were typical of the era in which she grew up, when such feeling was rife, but interestingly she drew her own distinction between personnel and personalities. She was, for example, a huge admirer of Leonard Bernstein, attending his concerts regularly and waxing lyrical about his charismatic talent. One of her diary notes says, 'Cocktails at the Ritz with Countess Mercati, dinner and concert. The symphony was conducted by Leonard Bernstein and this boy is a real genius.'

Many of Elizabeth's friends of the time, often exiled Europeans dangling a title, filmstars, actors and media tycoons, were drawn from café society, a phrase famously coined by veteran society reporter Maury Paul in 1919. Paul's column, published under the pseudonym 'Cholly Knickerbocker', was syndicated by his media baron boss, William Randolph Hearst, to over 120 newspapers throughout America. Maury Paul's readers devoured his gossip, covering the lifestyles of the rich and famous, and he became a celebrity in his own right, courted by the growing band of press agents, desperate for a client-mention in his powerful column. It was a tricky time to be a gossip columnist. The quiet confines of Fifth Avenue where the 'old' money families had always lived and where the Red Doors of the Arden salon were a token of her financial, if not yet social, success, gave him stories about charity balls and soirées at the opera, but he needed more. Paul was dining one night at New York's Ritz Hotel when he saw a powerful group of old money sitting with an equally powerful group of *nouveaux riches*, a group he likened to a 'sea food cocktail'. In his column the following day he called the phenomenon 'café society'.

Whilst generally speaking Fifth Avenue residents worked to keep their names out of the press, the new group, described rather scathingly by Cornelius Vanderbilt Jr as 'the Park Avenue set', were yearning to have fun and become famous. In the battle of Rhode Island v Long Island, Elizabeth Arden hovered in a social vacuum. Elizabeth was rich. Elizabeth was becoming very famous, but Elizabeth was in *trade*. Above all, Elizabeth was a snob. She was never happier than when the ladies from the formidable families booked appointments in her salon. But however hard she tried, and however much money she made, she couldn't seem to cross the line into their world. It was time, she decided, to follow her social aspirations to where she felt she belonged. Café society may have been fine for Tommy Lewis, but it most certainly did not suit his wife.

IN THE MONEY – HELENA
Paris and New York 1926–1930

P ARIS WAS WHERE MADAME enhanced her reputation, but America was where she relayed the message and it was falling on fertile ground. By 1927 there were over 7000 different cosmetics products on sale in the USA. One women's magazine survey estimated the average expenditure on grooming was $307 a year; the lipsticks sold at that time, laid end to end, would have stretched from Chicago to Los Angeles, via San Francisco. American women were annually buying 52,500 tons of cleansing cream, 26,500 tons of skin lotion, 19,109 tons of complexion soap, 17,500 tons of nourishing cream, 8750 tons of tinted foundation, 6562 tons of scented talcum powder and 2375 tons of rouge.

Rubinstein advertisements listed outlets in Boston, Newark, Newport, Atlantic City, Chicago, San Francisco, Palm Beach, Miami, Southampton and Detroit. Her product range had expanded to include seventy items, amongst them a lot of make-up such as Valaze Crushed Rose Leaves Rouge, Red Geranium Rouge and lipsticks in Red Raspberry and Red Geranium at $1 each. Madame's advertising promoted her as a 'scientist par excellence in the field of beauty', reminding her clients 'she has for over thirty years devoted herself indefatigably to the scientific study of the skin, absorbing herself in medicine, chemistry and dermatology.'

The European salons were supplied from the production unit at St Cloud, the small unit in the basement at Grafton Street, and a unit in Vienna. American production plants were operating in New York and Long Island, and a factory run by Helena's nephew, Henry Kolin, opened in Toronto. In Europe she had expanded to Berlin, Vienna and Cannes, where she bought an apartment and would later build a villa in the hills outside the town. Helena enjoyed Cannes and would take tea at the Negresco, although it's unlikely she ever required the services of the hotel's *danseurs mondains*. This group of good-looking young men, whose credentials had to include the art of conversation, a respectable dinner jacket, patent dress shoes and the ability to dance sublimely, were hired by the Negresco to twirl the wives of the visiting rich around the floor. Not to be compared with gigolos, who were hired to twirl rich women around the floor and on to their bedrooms — the *danseurs* relied on tips received from grateful husbands. When a flushed wife was returned to the table, breathless and happy from dancing the tango, her husband was more than willing to pay for her holiday thrill, hoping no doubt he could now go fishing in peace.

By 1925, she had relocated her New York salon to 57th St and Fifth Avenue, on the site where railway magnate Collis Huntingdon had built his mansion. Rumoured to have been involved in the deal over the demolition project, Helena retained an elegant slice of the building, which included a superb staircase. Helena adored important staircases, constantly praising the gracious sweep of stairs in both Grafton Street and New York. Her clients, she surmised, would be drawn to grand staircases, especially when they glided down them after a satisfying makeover, whilst for the diminutive Helena, standing on the stairs made her feel taller.

Staircases, it seems, held an allure for both Helena and Elizabeth who, in a rare personal endorsement advertisement, was photographed posing on the impressive curved staircase of her Paris salon on the rue de la Paix, *circa* 1930. The series of advertisements was used exclusively in French *Vogue* to promote the opening of her salon in le Touquet. 'In every age, the woman on a staircase invariably draws attention, especially if it's someone famous, someone you want to know . . . look how Elizabeth Arden is looking at you . . . whilst graciously leaning on the banister,' ran the text.

Whenever Helena arrived back in Paris she would find her husband entertaining the Montparnasse crowd, whom she observed, silently it seems, as they enjoyed hospitality she felt was funded by her fortune. In later years, she would comment dismissively about these parties with literary acquaintances of her husband's: 'Edward was always bringing these people home. They were easy to find — he always met the people who were hard up.' Patrick O'Higgins put it more bluntly, remembering Helena telling him, 'How was I to know all those writers were worth a sou . . . I never had a moment to read their books. To me, they were *meshuga* . . . and I always had to pay for their meals!'

What she did enjoy, however, was buying clothes and during the early 1920s Helena bought them as avidly as she bought art. She had a particular fondness for hats. Caroline Reboux, Schiaparelli, Agnes and Rose Valois made her originals, but she liked nothing better than finding a good designer copy – at a good price. Lilly Dache, the French milliner who lived in New York at that time, where her husband ran the American arm of Coty, witnessed Helena's fondness for copies. In 1925, Dache, along with Maud Moody, the millinery editor of *Women's Wear Daily*, was on board the SS *Paris*, en route back to New York following a trip to the Paris collections. Miss Moody had worn one of Dache's original 'dinner hats', a close-fitting evening confection, to the Talbot millinery show a week or so before. On board, Maud Moody nudged Lilly: 'Look, Lilly, look. There's Helena Rubinstein wearing your hat – it must be from Talbot!'

Post-war, the influence of the designer who had inspired many women including Helena, Paul Poiret, was waning. Times had moved on: skirts were shorter, the look was modern and the buzzwords were 'simple' and 'freedom'. All roads were leading towards Coco Chanel, and Helena, who had bought hats from Coco before the war, was an enthusiastic early client, favouring matelot-inspired jersey pants and *sportif* cruise-wear, which sadly did not flatter her curves.

As with art, she sometimes made mistakes with clothes, her brief flirtation with Irfe being one of them. The atelier in question was owned by the Russian Prince Youssoupof, famous as the assassin of Rasputin rather than for his dressmaking skills. The Irfe interlude was probably orchestrated by Misia Sert, who, struggling to find a niche in the late 1920s, promoted Prince and Princess Youssoupof in New York. Experimenting with most of the new Paris designers during the 1920s, Helena had Captain Edward Molyneux make her suits; she was an early adopter of Jeanne Lanvin and bought from Lucien Lelong, mainly to good effect. Vionnet's slinky bias cut didn't suit her stocky figure and there is no record of her wearing Patou, probably too much the rival showman for Helena's tastes. In a move that suited her well, Helena became one of Schiaparelli's first clients, ordering business suits with the requisite surrealistic twist.

Not surprisingly, Helena took advantage of every foray she made into fashion, posing for photographic studios like Kesslere and Lipnitzki on a regular basis. Each picture was carefully captioned, not to mention very often flatteringly retouched, and issued by her press officers in Paris and

New York. Her company paid for her clothes, she delighted in showing them off and the press pictures were proof to her accounts department of their 'value' in marketing terms, a useful buffer against intrusion by the tax authorities. A captioned print would be sent to each designer, ensuring a discount on the next round of shopping.

During this period, both Rubinstein and Arden put a message at the bottom of their advertisements, inviting customers to 'write to receive personal advice on any beauty problem'. Each letter received a personal reply, along with a pamphlet and list of new products, and drew the reader into the bosom of the company, at the same time giving valuable market research information. Elizabeth Arden took her market research very seriously and cleverly created a customer profile system which enabled her staff to cosset clients. Staff were instructed to find out as much personal data as possible about things as diverse as names of their clients' children – or dogs, where their country house was, or where they bought their clothes. All this information was put on to an index card and provided a fund of conversation, guaranteed to flatter the customer.

Although the Helena Rubinstein company targeted the affluent consumer – Arden preferred to think of hers as the company of choice for the *seriously* rich – the beauty playground was not confined to the wealthy few. By mid-decade, the middle-market was adopting cosmetics with enthusiasm. Max Factor, who developed specialist makeup for the film industry – 'flexible greasepaint' that gave a natural sheen under harsh lights – introduced his Society Makeup range in 1920. By 1927, the Max Factor label was being distributed coast-to-coast in the US. Maybelline, established in 1914, became the first company to specialise in mascara – a controversial cosmetic for decades – shaping it into a core product. Richard Hudnut, a conservative American manufacturer, was making fine-ground tinted face powders, much favoured by the *Vogue* fashion team in New York, Roger and Gallet had added lipsticks to their cologne and soap range, and the Paris-based Bourjois company, part of the Wertheimer empire, had established an important toehold in America.

The growth of the beauty industry created a boom in advertising, much to the delight of the media where the increased pages – and page rates – meant hefty profits. The whole 'beauty and toiletries' sector had moved to third place in categories advertised. Beauty was second in women's magazines and fifth in newspapers. Advertising agencies scrambled to hire staff with the creative background to cope with the growth, which given the whole industry was less than fifteen years old and commercial distribution had only been operational for a decade, was not easy. Poaching was rife and top staff swapped jobs rapidly. By this time, Rubinstein and Arden had become a seemingly unassailable duo, recognised as the top players in a powerful game.

There was an even more significant benefit to this rapid expansion; it created jobs, especially for women, at a variety of levels. Luxury cosmetics production was both labour-intensive and female-led. Women were managing all the specialist retail outlets, holding demonstration classes and training beauticians, as well as giving all the salon treatments. Helena, both as a woman in business and as an employer, was justifiably proud. 'The cosmetic business is interesting among modern industries in its opportunities for women,' she said. 'Here, they have found a field that is their own province, working for women, with women and giving that which only women can give – an intimate understanding of feminine needs and desires.' Needless to say, the enthusiasm with which employers, including Miss Arden and Madame, greeted their female recruits rarely resulted in an executive position. Directors in charge, whether of money or merchandising, were almost always male, even in a business targeting the female consumer.

By 1928 Helena was working to further the cause of female workers, particularly the women in her own family, all of whom were used to her being totally in charge and none of whom held any meaningful executive position. The payroll included her sisters Ceska in Australia, Pauline in Paris, and Manka in America. Cousin Lola had by now moved to America from Australia, setting up a fashion shop on Michigan Avenue, Chicago, where a thriving Rubinstein beauty salon operated from the first and second floors. Helena's sister Stella was apprenticed to Lola as a dressmaker in the Chicago shop, meeting her husband, a fellow Pole, whilst living there. Helena subsequently moved the newly married couple to Paris, where Stella was appointed titular head of the salon, taking over from her elder sister Pauline.

Various cousins and second cousins were on the workforce and many more would join in the 1930s, but the key female employee was her young niece and protégée Mala, who would prove to be a *tour de force*. Mala gave up a lot to work for her aunt, not least her name. She was always referred to as Mala Rubinstein and never by her real name of Kolin. Marriage to her cousin, jeweller Victor Silson — who had changed *his* name from Silberfeld — made no difference. Mala would always be a Rubinstein. Mala and her brothers Oscar and Henry were the children of Helena's sister Regina, who remained at home in Poland while three of her children worked for Helena and the fourth, Rachel, became an early settler in Palestine. Helena's habit of employing her family was well known. She had a curiously intense, almost obsessive, devotion to her relatives' welfare, operating rampant nepotism. Yet she was seemingly distant from all of them, as if she felt any intimacy might cause slacking. 'Better they work,' she snapped to *Sunday Times* editor Ernestine Carter when the latter remarked how many Rubinstein relatives seemed to be attached to the company. Elizabeth Arden, meanwhile, who had less luck with most of her relatives, always crossly referred to Rubinstein's troupe as 'the Polish Mafia'.

Not all Helena's female relatives joined the family firm, however. One notable exception was Michalina 'Lee' Libman, her sister Erna's daughter, who was starting a career of a different sort. When Lee Michelson left university with an economics degree, she became the first woman economist hired by the Department of Agriculture in Washington. Mrs Libman's distinguished career included working for the Roosevelt government on 'New Deal' farm subsidy programmes, working for the United Nations, and in her spare time she was a member of her County League of Women's Voters, working with minorities to overcome unfair laws. As a teenager, the headstrong and already socially minded Lee asked her famous 'Aunt Hela' what the value of cosmetics was in meeting the real needs of people. She admitted in an interview, years later, that the answer impressed her. Helena said, 'If my products help one young worker feel better about herself that day, then I feel I have accomplished something worthwhile.'

In June 1928, Helena was profiled by the *New Yorker* magazine. Their eulogy ran to four pages, the reporter obviously captivated by Madame Rubinstein's blunt speech and eccentricities and awed by her jewels. Helena had developed the technique of wearing what appeared to be all her jewellery at once. Ropes of pearls would jostle with strings of topaz and carved jade beads, charm bracelets of amethyst and garnets would rattle on her wrists and precious and semi-precious stones the size of gulls' eggs would gleam on her fingers. She was rarely without her diamond-and-pearl drop earrings, or cabochon emerald clips, and there was usually a diamond brooch pinned if not on her bosom, then on her hat. Her jewellery seemed to have a life of its own and was the stuff of legend. 'Gude for publicity,' Helena would remark when reviewing press comment about her baubles. When Cecil Beaton photographed her a few years later, he noted in his diaries, 'an old Polish frog . . . with a huge casket of jewels. I have never seen such a collection, and she clicks her teeth and shrugs "Only rubbish. Much more in Paris" – but they are jewels that would belong to a kingdom, not a private individual.'

New York's leading observer of society, jewellery designer Kenneth J. Lane, knew her quite well. 'She was a character,' he says, 'as far as wearing all those jewels . . . Well, she wasn't tall, she wasn't thin, she was dumpy and square and all that show suited her personality.' Kenny Lane confirms that her pieces were not always the finest. 'If you look at the Sotheby Parke-Bernet catalogue of the sale, you'll see there were lots of remarks about flawed stones and old settings – they weren't really serious pieces.'

In fact, her *really* serious pieces never made the sale. They were all left to her sisters and niece Mala, so presumably the fabled Rubinstein pearls are somewhere in a bank vault today. Helena herself didn't buy jewellery to keep it in bank vaults, she wore it, and she wore it well. She was passionately fond of large, showy settings and knew perfectly what she was doing when she bought stones that were less than perfect. She explained it once by waving her hand expansively and pointing to a huge, streaked red stone. 'That's a ruby. It would be worth $100,000 if it were perfect. If jewels are perfect you have to have too heavy insurance. I like to wear them, not leave them in the bank.'

Unfortunately she tended to leave them everywhere else, often forgetting where she'd put them. There was also her habit of carrying 'a few changes' in her vast handbag – then panicking when it was left in a taxi, with some hapless assistant left to sprint down the road and rescue it. Helena gave jewels away as part of her charm offensive, pulling off a ring, or an enamel brooch, and giving it to a journalist after a meeting. 'A small memento from me. I hope you like it,' she would say. The editors would leave, utterly enchanted, never realising Madame had carefully selected the items from her 'third-best' boxes a few hours earlier, and put them on especially so she could take them off again for presentation.

One of the most amusing and enduring stories about Helena's jewels is that the whole collection, including her 'best pearls', were at one point stored under her bed in an old Hattie Carnegie dress box, with corsets piled on top to deter robbers. Her favoured advertising manager, Sara Fox, was horrified when she found them, promptly rushing out to buy a filing cabinet and setting up a storage system: D for diamonds, E for emeralds, R for rubies, P for pearls and so on. Helena was enchanted. 'Very *klüger* [clever] that Sara,' she remarked fondly in German.

The *New Yorker* interview explained that her sons, aged eighteen and sixteen, were at tutorial college in London 'preparing for Oxford' – having mysteriously, it seems, already studied at Yale and Princeton at a remarkably young age – and that Helena spent 'four months of the year travelling with her French maid and German cook'. Her pioneering months in Australia were heavily romanticised and her business habits laid bare for the smart set in New York. These included her predilection for bombarding her staff with long, handwritten missives and spending a few days of enforced rest in a sanitorium after each salon opening, recovering from the inevitable nervous breakdown. 'She expects it, and looks forward to it, it's part of her schedule,' ran the copy.

After reporting glowingly about Helena's 'successful publisher husband' who lived in Paris and whom Helena commuted to visit 'several times a year', the magazine told how the directors of the Metropolitan Museum coveted her collection of 'African voodoo masks' and that she owned so many pictures she was running out of wall space. The feature closed with the information that Helena had rejected a recent offer from a French firm to buy her business: 'They calculated its worth in francs,' Helena said, 'and I work in pounds.'

She worked in dollars a few months later when she completed a business deal with Lehman Brothers which, although it surprised her competitors, left them gasping at the numbers. The story has become almost as much the stuff of legend as Helena's jewels. On 11 December 1928, Helena Rubinstein gave herself an early Christmas present and sold her American business to Lehman Brothers, retaining her European and Australian interests – about 25% of the company. Stock was floated with brokers Bauer, Pond and Vivian on New York's Curb market, offering one preference and one common share at $70 a unit, or common shares at $25 each. Her company pro-forma balance sheet as of 31 July 1928 had shown net profits of just under $960,000 on a gross of just over $2,000,000. The reward for Helena Rubinstein personally was reported to be an awesome $7,300,000 – nearly $72,000,000 today.

Madame always claimed that she sold in order to reduce her responsibilities and to spend more time in Europe with her husband in the hope of saving their shaky marriage. In her memoir she said: 'It was a sacrifice, for my business had always meant more to me than money. I had received offers before, but none so tempting. They promised that every one of my staff would be kept on. If I could free myself of the American business, my life could be lived happily in Paris, by Edward's side.' Her version was, of course, a complete fabrication. The deal she had carved out with Lehman Brothers was an awesome one, leaving her seriously rich at a time when people in the know were saying that the boom in the markets couldn't last. She had been fighting by remote control with her husband since the summer of 1928 and, when in Paris, stayed in her apartment above the salon while Titus stayed in his above his bookshop. By the autumn of that eventful year, they were – quite literally – at each other's throats.

Titus exerted a control over Helena unlike any other man – with the possible exception of her nephew Oscar Kolin – and managed to humiliate, frighten, awe and humour her in varying degrees. In August that year, Helena was staying at the spa at Wiesbaden when she received a letter from him, updating her on plans for a prospective purchase in Montparnasse. 'We have been figuring that the property is capable of a revenue close on 1,000,000 francs – around $40,000 – and being a new construction there would be no taxes to pay for several years. It is the most important piece of property in Montparnasse on the market at the moment and even if not built on, will certainly double in price before long.' He ended, conscious of her distrust of any deal she hadn't instigated herself, by saying, 'I would not for a moment try to persuade you to any deal if I did not think it a first class one.' He rather spoiled the effect by going on to say, 'Wiesbaden must be very beautiful just now. Although his lordship Dr Kapp did not see fit to come to see me on his several visits to Paris – because I am now a poor man I suppose – please remember me to him and his wife.'

Titus wrote to her again in London on 21 September. 'I am enclosing my cheque in your favour on New York for $250, which I would be obliged if you would deposit in sterling to the credit of my account at the Midland Bank – *immediately* – as my account there is getting short and I have payments to make. Only be sure please that you do it *immediately*.' Domestic niceties completed, he moved to business, reminding her about the property. 'I would like to know finally whether you have no interest in the studio hotel, say up to a million and a half. The sale takes place on the 11th October. Let me know definitely. Also, let me know please — equally definitely — whether I am to give up all hope of your agreeing to back my magazine to the extent of $500 a month, or $6,000 for one year only. I feel it would fit in nicely with the theatre scheme — and there would be enough glory for all.'

After this request came the reminder of his work for her. 'I take it you have no idea when you will again be in Europe. I ask this for a number of reasons, but the chief one is the plans for the office building which were left with me. Are you authorising anyone to decide the matter — and if so, who is it? Or is everything to await your return at whatever date that may come? The other reason is that I would like to go to New York — I must in fact — if I do not wish to avoid serious complications. I cannot just now afford the $500, or $600, which I suppose it will cost me.'

Helena's reply, scribbled initially on the back of her husband's letter before she felt composed enough to fire off her salvo, was simple. 'What do I have to do with your glory?' she wrote. 'I have always been your instrument and through me you achieved many things. All I care about is having a family home and being settled in one place. If it will help you I will pay the $600 for your trip.' Her tirade struck a sour note with Titus, who, by the end of the month, was desperate for a cash investment to secure the future of his magazine. He replied calling Helena, amongst other things, 'a petulant, spoiled schoolgirl' and said, 'concerning the magazine — it is undeniably your privilege to refuse although it would have been a greater privilege *not* to have refused to interest yourself in it. I feel I could have paid it back. There was no need, Helena, to add insult when replying — was it a criminal or dirty act of some kind I asked you to perform for my benefit?'

Titus was hurt and retaliated. 'It takes two, Helena, to share anything and you refuse to play. You don't have to sleep with one to share his or her life.' He refused her offer of a ticket to New York saying, 'Help thus extended is too bitter a pill to swallow. Thanks just the same.' He ended by telling her he had received the plans and estimate for the redevelopment of 52 faubourg St Honoré, which was designated to be not just her new Paris flagship salon, but offices and wholesale showrooms. 'The price has gone up just 1 million francs over what was said. Just about 50% more. Inasmuch as the tenants are not out, it is not so pressing to come to a decision and can wait till your return in November.'

The main reason for the bitter anger Titus felt is that he had discovered just who was to be put in charge of Helena's properties in Paris and didn't like it one bit. She handed the portfolio over to her sister Stella's husband, Osostowicz, putting Stella herself in charge of the salon. Titus bitterly resented his sister-in-law's husband dictating terms to him on the mortgage held on the rue Delambre property, albeit it was financed through Helena's Paris company, and raged at his wife about the 'insult'. Helena replied, 'I saw no reason why I should make an exception of the interest on the mortgage on the rue Delambre property. It's a business transaction and I see no reason why you should feel a loss of dignity at having the bill presented. It seems also apparently I did not select my words wisely in the matter of declining – at present – to interest myself in the magazine. You have manipulated my words until I do not recognise them.' She took a final side-swipe at him by saying, 'You come to me for help and go elsewhere for fun. Your interest in me seems to be limited to what I can do for you.'

Helena poignantly ended her missive by saying, 'I have had such a long siege of it, working like mad since I was eighteen, having to be in a dozen places at one time, always on guard to keep above water and seldom ever a resting time. I'm so weary of it all, yet what does the future hold for me but work? Perhaps I don't know how to play any more. I wonder if the boys will answer my need for consideration and understanding. Life hasn't held a great deal for me this far, but responsibility and work. You have rather had the best of it don't you think?'

Poor Helena. A part of her secretly craved calm, domestic bliss, once writing, 'I am getting quite old and have no home or home life which is very necessary to me. I can't possibly live much longer pick-nicking.' Poor Edward Titus too, who though he admired her, resented relying on her so much. Each had their own agenda and it didn't seem to include understanding each other. Neither of her sons answered her need for consideration – both failed to comprehend why she worked so hard, resenting her power and their parents' separation.

Oblivious of how much he had hurt his wife, Titus carried on supervising Elkuken's work on 'his theatre' in the boulevard Raspail property. His immediate cashflow problems meant the reluctant sale of his own flat – which he offered first to Stella, who refused it – and by November he was at loggerheads with Stella's husband, who he described to Helena as having 'an oily smirk and blinking little eyes'. Osostowicz was, it seems, the worst kind of puerile, petty-minded book-keeper, revelling in his moment of glory in acting for his illustrious sister-in-law and gloating with self-importance when he harassed Titus for interest payments on his mortgage 'due now to Madame Rubinstein'. Stella's husband was in fact so inept that he did incalculable harm to Helena's property company when he wrote to tenants about vacating terms using Helena Rubinstein Inc letterhead rather than Franc-Am's. At a stroke, they knew who their landlady was, which drove up the compensation they subsequently demanded.

This enraged Titus, who finally exploded about him, writing to Helena, 'I am not a worm to be eternally humiliated and suspected and put into a false light by spittle-licking understrappers, who even now do all their whoring and high and unaccustomed living by what my brain has produced. I have no more to say – you can chuck me out brutally and that means I could not hold my head up in Montparnasse. For the love of heaven, don't cable me any more shocking news. You might become a widow – albeit a merry widow – all of a sudden.' He ended by asking her to pay his bill at the Manhattan Storage Company and to 'empty my safety deposit box there'.

Edward and Helena had other problems that year besides their tenants in Paris and their squabbles. Their youngest son Horace was becoming a 'wild child' having been involved in the first of his many car accidents. At just sixteen, he had crashed a valuable motor in England. Titus wrote to Helena, 'The incident has a certain compensation for me, because it is for the first time as far as I can remember that you, over your own signature, recognised my paternity.' She had written crossly to Horace in London saying, 'Your father and I despair of your carelessness.' She had reason to despair. It was to be the first of many such accidents.

Titus didn't have the faintest idea his wife was in discussion with Lehman Brothers to sell her US business until the deal was completed. Cables fairly flew across the Atlantic, in one of which he pleaded for some personal shopping. 'Please send three suits Vassar combinations, sleeveless, size four cotton. Advise you strongly excellent future investment house containing my shop about seven hundred thousand quick action necessary. Have confidence and instruct me. Plans progressing well, your presence essential.' Helena rejected the building, also threatening to lay off Elkuken at boulevard Raspail.

Titus was horrified, replying, 'Ill from shock your cable can no longer stand such blows. If Raspail abandoned after all publicity you're seeking you will break Elkuken's heart and make me a laughing stock. This is playing fast and loose with people's livelihood. Consider and reassure me.' Her reply was not reassuring. 'Not coming to Paris this year, doubt if much use. Elkuken continuing working, shall sell both properties. Helena.' Left reeling by her venom and nervous about his beloved theatre, Titus moved to calm things by making helpful suggestions about faubourg St Honoré headquarters – and to help out with organising a new lease at the Jockey where, he explained, 'they take in an average of 5000 francs a night and outside taxes their expenses are practically nothing.' Helena seemed delighted with his suggestions about faubourg St Honoré.

Just a few lines in answer to your last letter . . . I think it is a very good idea . . . I have no idea what the Jockey people pay. I have not seen any agreement. But indeed I don't see why they should have the place for practically nothing. I ought to write these things to Mr Levesque but as I can't write a good French letter – and have so little time – I write to Mr Osostowicz. I felt through this medium I could carry out all my ideas, but as you did not seem to like having him come to you I have cabled him not to go near you with anything nor to ask you about anything. I can't come to Europe now . . . I've cabled the boys to come out here and I shall return with them later in the New Year.

In the end she didn't sell the Montparnasse properties – she sold her business instead. Her husband, most humiliatingly, heard about it via the Paris grapevine, writing to Helena on 21 December: 'A rumour has spread in the Quarter and I was asked if it was true that you had sold your business for ten million dollars . . . That rumour reached me the same day as your letter in which you said you had disposed of 75% of your interest, but were not as yet sure whether the deal will be consummated.' With remarkable restraint he said little else about it, but grumbled that 'Lurcat has been back for some days. Thus far the combinations I asked for have not been delivered. If they do not turn up tomorrow I shall call him as I am in need of the garments now.' There was no reply. Titus spent Christmas alone and, as he later informed her, 'ill and in bed, not knowing where you were. The combinations were delivered only I'm sorry to say they were useless to me. I wired distinctly I wanted Vassars 4 *cotton*. Those that were sent are *wool* and I can't wear them. I shall give them to someone who can.'

The fact that his wife had, at a stroke, become one of the richest women in America, didn't deter him from requesting she handle his shopping. 'If there should still be time for you to have others bought for me, please note they are to be *cotton, sleeveless and long legs*, not short, nor three-quarter length. Silk or cotton only, Helena, not wool . . .'

By the time he wrote this, Helena had sailed with her sons for Australia, partly to escape the dramas in Paris and partly to give herself time to think. She certainly had a lot to think about and the last thing on her mind was her husband's undergarments. She did not know that the lucky streak she had enjoyed for over twenty-five years was about to desert her. What had looked like a brilliant move in selling her American business was poised to turn into a near catastrophe, affecting her health and even threatening her bank balance. Rather than save her marriage — if that had ever been part of her rationale — it was the trigger that ultimately destroyed it.

By the end of the decade, a report published by the Women's Bureau of the Department of Labor in the USA showed that sales of cosmetics and beauty products, including money spent on hairdressing, totalled $2 billion a year at retail. The *New York Times* reported enthusiastically on the figures, noting that New York City alone boasted over three hundred 'beauty salons and hairdressers' and over 325 recognised schools and colleges across the USA were training 50,000 students a year to become experts in beauty culture. An industry offering excellent employment opportunity had grown up in the decade during the Jazz age when women had become beauty consumers. One woman who had helped to create the boom, however, was now without a proper job — and she didn't like it at all.

CHAPTER ELEVEN

END OF AN ERA
DEPRESSION AND DIVORCE –
HELENA
Paris and New York 1929–1934

WALL STREET WAS SWIMMING in debt. By October 1929, margin buyers were borrowing more than $8.5 billion and stock-market speculation had become an everyday pastime, not just for the super-rich but the middle classes and even the not-so-rich, convinced they would make their fortune in the greatest bull market of all time. Women, just as keen as men to gamble on the markets, held more than a third of the stock in US Steel and General Motors, 44% of the B & O Railroad and over 50% of the Pennsylvania Railroad. Women also held 80% of the stock of Helena Rubinstein Inc, a business which made its money from women, had been founded by a woman, was invested in by women, but was being run by . . . men.

The partners in the mighty Wall Street firm of Lehman Brothers had just begun to realise that the cosmetics business wasn't quite the easy ride they had imagined. Blissfully confident their expansion plans would more than justify the astonishing price they had paid Madame, they had anticipated a healthy return on their investment. They had also anticipated that Helena Rubinstein Inc's president, Madame herself, would enjoy a titular role, attending press soirées in America, for example, and making a state appearance at the AGM, but leaving them, complete with most of her original management team, to mastermind the business – whilst she enjoyed a life of leisure in Europe. She would, they reasoned, no doubt want to enjoy her semi-retirement and had earned a rest. After all she was now nearly sixty and exceedingly rich. They were in for a shock.

Everything started quite well. The concept laid down by Lehman

Brothers, fully endorsed by Madame, was to roll out a competitively priced Rubinstein range to capitalise on America's newly confident cosmetics consumers. Helena had always been fascinated by the volume market and shared Lehman's belief that taking the brand out of the exclusive fiefdom of speciality department stores and also selling to selected mainstream stockists would work. Cachet would be maintained by careful promotion of Helena herself as company president and reigning 'Queen of beauty science', creator of new products, and also by retaining quality in packaging and presentation. The New York, Chicago, Philadelphia and Detroit salons would be given the aura of the salons in London and Paris. Thus, it was felt, the brand would appeal to both luxury and volume markets. It was an interesting theory, but it didn't work. Luxury brands today, desperate to obtain added value via the 'trickle-down' effect, know that no matter how many diffusion ranges they own, it is essential to maintain gloss on the name at the top. The theory that rich women will buy the same brand as poor women is just a theory. They won't.

In fairness to Lehman's, their investment was soured by the Wall Street Crash a year after their purchase. When 24 October 1929 came, and $9 billion was wiped off the stockmarket in a matter of hours, financiers were reeling. The impact was not felt by consumers for some months, but major retailers were already jittery about recession, and with reason. Recession would soon turn into the Great Depression. Helena's enthusiasm for volume distribution faltered as she realised just how complex business was becoming as recession bit. Despite being cushioned by a lot of liquid assets, she was increasingly paranoid that her 'baby' was going to fail.

Ironically for Helena, had her brand remained hovering in the upper-middle market she had created for it, the company would have been more recession-proof. It was the urge to seek volume distribution that caused problems. Elizabeth Arden, on the other hand, relentlessly up-market, weathered the Depression remarkably well. Media analysts wrote explaining that affluent women, whilst resigned to spending less on clothes, would happily treat themselves to an expensive lipstick. Poor women on the other hand would have to sacrifice lipstick to buy food for their families.

The cosmetics industry has experienced many bad times since the 1930s, and the up-market glamour lines have each time taken less of a downturn in profits. What cheers women up, it seems, is their make-up, whilst what cheers the top-end cosmetics companies is their mark-up. Paul Cohen, a very distinguished senior partner at Lehman's today who has a personal interest in its archival history, says, 'Cosmetics was still a new venture for Lehman's. In hindsight, it was a woman's world and I guess the men just didn't know how to handle it.' More specifically, the men didn't know how to handle Madame.

America's financial crisis had found the Rubinstein sales team caught in a trap of their own making, spearheaded in part by Helena who was giving up-beat interviews to the American media, one of which is particularly illuminating. In 1930, *Sales Management*, a trade magazine for marketing executives, ran an in-depth profile on Madame Rubinstein, focusing on her staff training and marketing techniques, proving that she was as 'hands-on' as ever. Systems being implemented by Bernard Hoffenstein, her sales promotion manager for over ten years, had, she said, 'resulted in us having over 6,000 retail doors operational in the US *and* we are looking to expand'.

The level of this expansion irritated the brand's more prestigious retailers who were worried about trading conditions and could have done without the added problem of a local stockist – peeling off a sizeable chunk of margin due to lower overheads – taking their business. The speciality department stores needn't have worried; it seems that the consumer base of the local mid-priced stockist was rapidly fading away, with the result that neither retail sector was happy. Dwindling orders and dwindling sales meant the Helena Rubinstein company went into a seemingly unstoppable tailspin of losses. Madame put a brave face on the situation, but she was seething. Ironically for her, as the company she had nurtured started to flounder, her husband's started to flourish. She had always advised her family that 'hard work was the best cure for everything' and Titus was having to work harder than at any time in his life – and it was paying off.

His first break came in the spring of 1929, with the publication of *Lady Chatterley's Lover*, launched with an initial print run of 3000 and priced at 60 francs. This wasn't one of his usual *luxe* editions as Lawrence himself had already privately published his *Lady* the year before in Florence, as a limited edition of 1000 copies, printed on hand-made paper. John Worthen, Professor of D.H. Lawrence Studies at Nottingham University, explains about the Titus version. 'It was paper-covered, not on especially nice paper, but was a perfectly decent book.' Titus collaborated with Lawrence to make a 'perfectly decent book' of what, for most customs officials at least, was a totally indecent one; each putting down a deposit of 1500 francs, and they agreed a profit share of 8 to 7 in Lawrence's favour. The book was a great success, not before time for Lawrence, who was terminally ill with TB and desperately short of cash. Titus hadn't been the first choice publisher. Not unsurprisingly, Lawrence had initially approached Sylvia Beach. After the rigours of nurturing *Ulysses*, however, and not wanting to be known as a publisher of erotica, she turned him down. Beach, however, gracefully pointed Lawrence in the direction of Black Manikin Press, where Titus, who was unafraid of controversy, or any form of erotica, became an enthusiastic and generous supporter. *Lady Chatterley's Lover* went into a second printing in August, and a third of 10,000 copies in February 1930. A month before, Titus had been to Bandol, in Var, to visit the frail author. He never saw Lawrence alive again, as he died on 2 March that year. Titus was amongst the mourners at his funeral.

Titus achieved a second coup by publishing *Kiki's Memoirs* in English, translated from the French by Samuel Putnam. Ernest Hemingway wrote the introduction saying, 'She was wonderful to look at. Having a fine face to start with, she had made of it a work of art. She had a wonderfully beautiful body and a fine voice — talking voice, not singing voice — and she certainly dominated that era of Montparnasse more than Queen Victoria ever dominated the Victorian era.' In an innovative move, Black Manikin subsequently printed the introduction as a separate pamphlet. The book was illustrated with many of Man Ray's exotic pictures of Kiki and was subsequently bought by Bennett Cerf's Random House in New York. Samuel Putnam, however, was decidedly unhappy. He loathed the book and felt the whole project lightweight, arguing bitterly with both Hemingway and Titus over the English translation. To say that his relationship with Titus was fragile is an understatement, and by the end of 1930, Putnam exited swiftly to start his own magazine, titled *New Review*.

Kiki's Memoirs was a phenomenon. Titus revelled in his moment in the sun. He became, for a while, reconciled with Helena, who was quite pleased and proud about his success. It wasn't to last. Neither was the golden decade of Montparnasse. The chill wind of recession was sweeping in from over the Atlantic, and storms were sweeping over the remnants of the Rubinstein/Titus marriage.

While Titus busied himself with books, his wife busied herself with shopping. Invigorated by her success in striking a deal, she took on Charles Ratton, a Paris dealer specialising in African art and considered just as wily as any banker. Christophe Tzara, whose father owned one of the largest collections of African art, observed his father being consulted by Ratton on behalf of various clients keen to buy, including Peggy Guggenheim. 'Ratton', says Tzara, 'was the chief protagonist in African art circles at the time.' One senses he wasn't paying him a compliment. Ratton had originally acquired *The Bangwa Queen* by fairly nefarious means from the Volkerkunde Museum in Berlin. Helena wanted the statue and what Helena wanted, she got. She cajoled Ratton into swapping a bundle of her earlier African acquisitions for *The Bangwa Queen* without even a dollar changing hands, whereupon the glorious statue took pride of place in her collection.

Shopping alone, however, wasn't enough to keep her stimulated. Bored, Helena set about restructuring her European business, still her exclusive fiefdom. Rosa Hollay having left her employ after fourteen exhausting years, the sisters had to shift around and Ceska was moved from Australia to London to oversee a complete revamp of the Grafton Street salon. With some of her new wealth, Helena had ordered a lavish refit for her London base, applying to the Salisbury estate office for 'permission to undertake works' in 1930. She installed new lighting, put in black marble steps, covered the façade in antiqued silver metal with a surround of black marble and installed an 'electric automatic lift'. Having decided the ground floor was too large for her needs, and conscious of the value of prime retail space, she split the space into two, sub-letting the newly created area to an antique rug dealer. Ceska's husband, Edward Cooper, having travelled to England with his wife, took on the uneasy role of company secretary, a job perhaps not made any easier by the arrival of young Roy Titus, now aged twenty, sent as an intern to the business during his vacations from Oxford.

Helena had also made both her sons directors of Franc-Am Ltd, which conveniently acted as the source of their allowance. Not that Horace took much interest in property development. He had taken up writing and had his first story published in England, earning himself the princely sum of three guineas. Titus was thrilled. 'I only hope it won't go to his head,' he wrote to his wife.

Helena too had writing on her mind in 1930, having authorised the first book ghost-written in her name, *The Art of Feminine Beauty*, published by one of the premier companies of the time, Horace Liveright. From the text, it's quite clear that she not only knew her craft, but excelled in it. Helena told her readers to 'bath for beauty' using a long-handled exfoliating bath brush,

lashings of bath oil and the ubiquitous Epsom salts. She advocated moisturising cream be rubbed in *before* getting into warm — never hot — water.
She recommended scalp friction massage, the significance of a 'cleanse,
tone and nourish' regime for skin care, and warned that all women should
give special attention to their necks. Twenty minutes a day should be
devoted to exercise, gloves should be worn outside at all times — and at
night over a rich hand cream — and a Rubinstein anchor treatment, the face
mask, should be used at least twice a week.

She advised on a wardrobe of make-up brushes, lectured about grubby
powder puffs, and above all she warned about too much sun. 'The sun', she
wrote sternly, 'holds malice in its shining rays. One brief indulgent summer
can age the skin five years.' The book was a huge success and Helena went
on tour promoting it.

In the autumn of 1930, Helena was in Boston at the Ritz Carlton with
what was described as 'enough luggage to last an average person for two
years of travel', her wardrobe including apparently over two dozen hats and
as many pairs of shoes. Grace Davidson, an ingenue reporter on the *Boston
Post*, was assigned to interview her. The resulting story covered two pages,
vying for space with the great Boston Air Show (Helena won on column
inches), and was pictured on the front page, dressed by Poiret, wearing an
Agnès beret and several ropes of black pearls. Copy said her 'personal fortune is said to be over $20,000,000', a fact which will have intrigued the
paper's City editor and the partners at Lehman Brothers, who would have
surmised it a gross exaggeration, but which might not have surprised her
brokers nor indeed her accountants and tax advisers who were well aware of
her ever-increasing property and stock portfolio. The reality about Helena's
'personal fortune' is that she would often use the first figure that came into
her head, confident that no one could check it and knowing it would do her
image no harm to be seen as 'fabulously rich' — especially in America, where
they respected such things.

Helena as usual gave great copy. 'Women', she said, 'have a duty to
keep young. We should live adventurous lives, travel, work hard, earn
money, spend it, love someone deeply, have children. That is life.' In a curious gesture to her bizarre marriage, Helena went on to describe Titus as 'a
millionaire art dealer and publisher, who lives in Paris'. She referred to her
properties as including 'an apartment in Paris, a mansion in Mayfair, a penthouse in New York and a country estate in Greenwich', adding a fictitious

'castle in Vienna and villa in Italy' for good effect. The feature was a triumph. Madame clearly captivated the young reporter, who became a lifelong friend.

By dramatic contrast, in October Helena was back in Europe, in hospital. Titus, still paying royalties to Frieda Lawrence, wrote to her enclosing 10,000 francs, saying he was 'leaving for Vienna, where Mrs Titus was taken ill suddenly and had to be operated upon for appendicitis. She is quite all right now and I am going to bring her back to Paris. You can reach me at the Hotel Imperial.'

Helena wasn't 'quite all right' at all. Her surgery was more serious than an appendectomy. It seems almost certain that she had a hysterectomy, a gruelling operation even today and one necessitating a long recovery period. Then, as now, women were often unaware of the consequences of such radical surgery, particularly if it included removal of the ovaries, which plunges the patient into a hormonal crisis, often triggering not just exhaustion, very often a thyroid imbalance and weight gain, but also depression.

In a letter written in May 1931, Frieda Lawrence commiserated with him about Helena's health. 'I am sorry Mrs Titus has been ill. What a worry for you.' Titus was indeed worried, as were Helena's sons and her friends. Triggers that cause depression come from different angles, and in 1931 Helena was being hit everywhere. In Krakow, her father had died, followed just a few weeks later by her mother. In a pattern repeated throughout her life, Helena did not attend their funerals and took to her bed at Ceska's apartment in London. It was over forty years since her father had disowned her and bitter memories of that time will have flooded through her mind. Struggling to recover from complications following surgery, she was angry that she was obliged to rest, frustrated about events in America and literally making herself ill with worry. Titus kept in close touch, visiting and writing. 'I would have gone over to London this weekend, but the doctor told me I had better not for another week . . . I receive many enquiries about your progress . . . it is a mystery how news of your illness has spread.'

News of Helena's ill-health almost certainly spread courtesy of her sister Stella, who was incapable of discretion. Her main joy in life was to gossip, plot and complain. Helena wrote to her saying, 'I simply don't have the time to spend with such nonsense. You never see me wasting my time with friends, you come to me with criticism of everybody and frequently you have taken a negative attitude, causing difficulties at work.' Madame's

jump from wealthy woman to multi-millionairess had created a neurotic fris-
son between Stella in Paris, Manka in New York and Ceska in London.
While they anxiously waited to see how her recovery progressed, Helena
managed for the main part to ignore them all.

Bed-rest, however, wasn't part of her masterplan. She dwelled on the
prospect of the years ahead with nothing much to do and it didn't appeal.
Cushioned as she was by her private fortune, it wasn't the loss of money that
affected her so much as the loss of prestige, all the more bitter as Elizabeth
Arden's reputation was at an all-time high. Despite the Depression, Helena
knew that the real power was in America, and that was where her economic
future lay. Summoning a raft of soon-to-be-exhausted secretaries, Helena
set a plot in motion to get her American business back. She was in regular
communication with the men on the Rubinstein board in America — that is
her men, like Flateau, Burke and Cole, who had been with her pre-Lehman
Brothers. Flateau obtained a shareholders list and Helena wrote personally
to each of them — singling out the women as being particularly important —
persuading them that the business should, once more, be in the hands of the
woman who created it and offering to buy their shares, which were by now
virtually worthless. She is said to have spent $1.5 million scooping up stock
to regain majority control, leaving a profit on the deal of over $6 million.
Lehman Brothers acknowledged defeat, so angry that Madame Rubinstein
had not given time to their masterplan that they called her 'financially illit-
erate'. They were wrong. She may not have been an academic, but when it
came to finances, she was a genius.

The share-buying process had had to be handled discreetly and for a
while Helena thought she might not succeed. With so few people she could
talk to, and virtually no one she could trust, she turned to the one person she
knew would calm her fears. She wrote to Titus. His eloquent reply may not
have been what she expected.

> There is nothing I can say would convey to you the merest fragment
> of how sorry I am over the troubles you are having. If you win
> out — whatever it is that is involved — well and good. If it makes you
> any happier from the bottom of my heart I wish you would win out.
> But if you do not — and in that case I cannot quite see how you
> would lose all your holdings in the company — well look here, outside
> of wounded pride, which is not a wound that cannot be healed, if you

do not win, you will gain something more valuable. Three million dollars* – if entirely lost – is a fantastic sum, almost too fantastic to really and humanly know what to do with. You have two fine boys, whom you do not enjoy possessing, you have a husband if you would only once begin to really believe in him, who loves you truly and sincerely, whatever his faults are, you finally have yourself, to whom you have never, never given a real chance. These are the only things that substantially matter. The children's life, your life and mine, the combined life of the four of us. Everything else are only *things*, just *things*. At worst it means a money tragedy. Do not take things so tragically. Time and life slips by, almost gallops by, and we do not know it until it becomes too late to do anything about it. This is all I can say about your troubles. You take it harder than I would and I wish with all my heart that I could see a way to make this dreadful feeling disappear . . .

For Helena, whose passion for work was all-consuming, domestic stability did not appeal. She made her choice and she bought the business back. The chase invigorated her. Within a matter of weeks she was in New York, working once again. Titus was crushed. He had genuinely hoped that she might settle with him in Paris, albeit in cordial companionship. But it was not to be.

Madame's new friend Grace Davidson witnessed their odd relationship when, in June 1931, Helena sailed for Paris, taking Grace, who had never been to Europe and was hugely excited. What Grace did not realise, however, was that when Helena was in a troublesome situation she would use people as a shield between the antagonist and herself. The antagonist then was Titus, still bemused as to why she had bought her business back when he had felt she had a real chance to enjoy her life without it. He finally accepted what he had always really known, that Helena's whole life *was* her business. She was nervous about seeing him again. His pleas for reconciliation had been seductive and in her usual panic about confrontation, young Grace would be a useful buffer. Arriving at le Havre to collect his wife, Titus found her not with her maid as he had expected, but with a journalist.

* Nearly $30,000,000 today, although there is a discrepancy in the figures quoted, probably due to Helena exaggerating the cost to Titus in correspondence.

Grace Davidson recollected the visit as decidedly odd, writing about it later:

> Titus seemed a bossy, authoritative man. We drove in silence most of the way to Paris, with Titus now and again commenting on the landscape. When we got to Fbg St Honoré, he called a taxi for me, suggesting I stay at an hotel. Helena told me that this was because Titus was 'jealous' and that he wanted to be alone with her. Yet during the week, the three of us would dine at la Coupole and sit for half an hour or so afterwards at the Select, where various people would come up to talk to them. Helena seemed irritated by it all, and told me: 'This is the life he wants me to lead with him — with all these useless people, little zeros, idlers.'

Grace noted that the only time Helena brightened up was at a party when Brancusi came over and made a big fuss of her. 'Talking with him, all of a sudden she seemed happy.' Grace wouldn't have known that Brancusi had the most genial personality and went out of his way to be kind, rather than supercilious, to his clients, and Helena had just bought his marble sculpture *La Negresse Blanche*. Grace found the few days in their company strange and strained, although she too came under the spell of what she would later describe as 'the great, seductive charm of Edward Titus', remaining in touch with him even after his bitter divorce from her friend.

During the autumn of 1931, Helena busied herself in New York, struggling to put some order into the business, without much success. She was volatile, neurotic and for the first time in her career, seemed to lack intuitive direction. Her staff, confused by the impact of her buy-back, waited for instruction from the top. It wasn't to come. Tired and stressed, in early December Helena set off for France, having decided to be reconciled with her husband, hoping she would find some peace in Paris. Instead, she fell straight into the vindictive, gossipy circles of her 'friends' who were delighted to see the rich Helena Rubinstein back in a city by now sorely depleted of American dollars.

Wealth often means swapping one set of problems for another, one of the biggest being knowing whom to trust. Acolytes, sycophants, advisers, hairdressers, decorators, doctors, lawyers are all on hand to offer advice. Helena unfortunately listened to all of them, including those jealous of her husband's influence over her. The chief problem for Titus was the devious duo, the artist Marcoussis and the architect Elkuken. He had been vocal to Helena about costs on the Raspail property and scornful that Elkuken had fitted an expensive elevator which turned out to be only big enough to hold two skinny people. 'I warn you for your own good not to give Elkuken any more work to do. I also warn you to be careful when the buildings are to be finally accepted because hundreds of thousands of francs I feel convinced will be charged up for work not ordered,' he wrote to Helena. She promptly discussed what Titus had reported, with the result that the three men were at loggerheads. With Stella and her husband also bleating to Helena, Titus should have been more wary, but he didn't spot how vulnerable his position was until too late.

Elkuken was the first into the fray, bitterly angry that Titus had been interfering with the building budgets, particularly on the spectacular boulevard Raspail property, where the basement theatre was languishing empty as Titus had no funds with which to stage productions. Others surrounding Helena, like Lurcat, and the artist Tamara de Lempicka, were feeling the pinch of recession, bored, and keen to give Helena the latest gossip about her husband and his affection for a new woman in his life – Anaïs Nin.

Nin, at that time living in Louveciennes with her husband, was desperate to find a publisher for her first work and had been in discussion with Titus since the autumn of 1931 on plans to publish *D.H. Lawrence: An Unprofessional Study*. Obsessed with erotica, and with Henry Miller who had returned to Montparnasse, Nin was a fascinating subject for Titus, whose first love was for books, and their writers. Within days of arriving in Paris, Helena learned of their 'weekends away', and accused him of having an affair with 'that German lesbian'. It took just two weeks for Helena to threaten divorce, saying she would cite Anaïs Nin as co-respondent.

Helena refused to meet Titus face to face, having her letters delivered to rue Delambre:

> The whole situation since I arrived in Paris has been nothing but a nightmare to me. You are a strange creature. You never consider anyone. You consider me just the same as you do your maid. Little do you know how tired and worn out I was when I left New York. I hoped to get a pleasant welcome on my arrival in Paris from you, yet everything was to the contrary. Maybe you mean well, when you are sometimes alone, but the *minute* you pick up some acquaintance with

any woman, your habit is always to turn just ugly and nasty to me . . . You may miss me when we are away, but the minute we are together, you just hate me. I am sure that you know I am very sensitive, but I am afraid to speak, knowing I will be sneered at by you or not get an answer at all . . .

Titus denied the affair, writing to Helena that same night, the twelfth of December:

It is but fair to both of us that I should write you this note to say that it is only now that I seem to have discovered the reason for your astounding behaviour towards me since your arrival. If you had not been so obdurate, but frank instead, the whole thing would have been explained easily. You have listened to 'friends' again. I should not be surprised if it were Elkuken who has expressed himself to the effect that he would separate us to get even with me. Whoever told you that cock and bull story lacked one important element to support it, and that is the *physical possibility* either way. After my assurance you are, of course, still at liberty to drag yourself at your age and drag me at my age of 62 through the divorce courts, and gather a crop of ridicule, when the physical and physiological facts become known. If you wish any more light on the subject all you have to do is to ask me for it. Helena, this I ask you to remember, and this I would be ready to repeat if I were on my death bed, that all the letters of affection I wrote to you were sincere and I awaited your coming as one would for salvation. You have now done me a dreadful, irreparable wrong.

Helena replied:

I think it is no longer necessary to employ the melodramatic tactics of which you are so fond. Your affairs with other women I was reconciled to — because after all, I can see that a woman whose life is absorbed in earning the family's bread and butter, not through pleasure but through a necessity that was only due to my husband's neglect of a responsibility that was his — had no right to expect her husband's fidelity. Furthermore, I was under the impression that,

having passed 60, you would be prepared to give up these diver-
sions and devote your energy to establishing a pleasant family life
and to helping your sons to progress in the world. Your assertions to
people that I don't interest you as a woman, which is a public confession that all that *does* interest you about me is my material
resources, I was prepared to ignore, putting my own feelings behind
my aspirations for the boys. All this accumulation of indignities I was
willing to swallow, but there is a limit to endurance of such treatment
and when I became aware that, just preparatory to our living
together when everybody *knew* that we were going to bury the
hatchet, you were, if not *actually* in sexual intimacy with this
German woman, at least you were so indiscreet as to give people
every opportunity for believing the worst.

I know you too well to believe so easily the facts that you mention to me, trying to prove the *impossibility* of such a relationship. A
woman has *some* pride and to agree to play the part of the unsuspecting, admiring little wife in the face of such an outrage is too
much to expect from me. Now you know my grievances. The worm
has turned. If, in turning, she has upset a few of your precious plans
that is too bad. You'll get over it quickly enough, especially as I give
you credit for enough of the foresight of which you boast to believe
that you have in the course of the last few years feathered your nest
with ample provision for any such emergency. In view of this, I
would no more dream of having anything more to do with you than
I would dream of cutting my own throat after I have achieved my
freedom. Yours, Helena.

Acting quickly, as though if she lingered she might change her mind,
Helena had her brother-in-law write to Titus relieving him of his services to
Franc-Am Ltd, accusing him of impropriety in connection with its finances
and severing his consultancy fees. She also ordered the bulldozers into the row
of buildings on the corner of boulevard Montparnasse and rue Campagne
Première – and in so doing reduced the famous Jockey Club to rubble.

Titus, desperately angry and hurt, wrote to his son Horace:

By this letter I have been dismissed from the position of trust which
I filled for a period of three years or more in connection with the

properties of the company in which both you and Roy are share-holders. You may not have known of the dismissal — you may not have been consulted, I am more than certain that no one would have dared to consult you as to my dismissal. A dismissal so curt and cavalier from a position of trust carries a sinister implication. You have arrived at the age of discretion and I must ask you most earnestly not only to declare your dissent from both those utterly degrading implications but to insist that the letter of dismissal be expunged from the company's records and that I be duly reinstated and permitted to carry the work through to its final conclusions. It will make me very happy to hear from you. Your loving father.

In the spring of 1932, Black Manikin Press published *D.H. Lawrence: An Unprofessional Study* by Anaïs Nin, launching her writing career. *This Quarter* magazine announced that it was 'the first subscribers' edition, limited to five hundred numbered copies only, with two facsimile manuscript pages out of *Lady Chatterley's Lover*'. The September issue of *This Quarter* was an exclusive Surrealist edition, guest edited by André Breton, and featuring writing and poetry by Salvador Dali, Paul Eluard, Marcel Duchamp and Tristan Tzara, with illustrations by Max Ernst. It was to be the last. *This Quarter*, along with the Black Manikin Press, ceased to trade at the end of 1932.

Helena Rubinstein Titus could forgive her estranged husband a lot, but could not forgive him what she believed to be this final affair. She filed for divorce and cut him off without a penny. She never lived again in Elkuken's masterpiece building on boulevard Raspail with all its bitter memories, preferring to rent it out, giving her sister Stella the use of an apartment there. Instead, she purchased an imposing, albeit crumbling, property on the Ile St Louis from a debt-ridden Jo Jo Sert, the deal brokered by her old acquaintance, Misia. The house came encumbered with sitting tenants, but Franc-Am Ltd was used to removing them, and Helena was happy to wait.

The Depression heralded the beginning of the end for literary society in Montparnasse. 1932 also saw the closure of Nancy Cunard's Hours Press, after two years. American tourists could no longer afford their indulgent visits to Paris and most American writers had returned home in the hope of making their fortunes there. Depression had struck deep. Journalist Wambly Bald wrote 'Farewell to Montparnasse, I am tired of jiggling a corpse'. The glittering and beautiful people, like Gerald and Sara Murphy, had long gone. The divine Sara, who had sunbathed in her pearls on the beach and took her Helena Rubinstein pinkish red lipstick in its golden case everywhere with her, had returned to America with her husband. Hemingway was in Key West with his new wife, Pauline Pfeiffer. A few stalwarts remained, like Gertrude Stein and her partner Alice B. Toklas. Henry Miller, who had given up copywriting for the Sphynx brothel, was finally working on his book *Tropic of Capricorn*, and Sylvia Beach was now struggling to keep Shakespeare & Company afloat. Her friends launched a financial appeal, donations coming from Anne Morgan, who sent $460 and Helena Rubinstein, who gave $246.

Citing his ill-health, Titus moved to the artists' and writers' colony of Cagnes-sur-Mer, on the Côte d'Azur, taking most of his by now famous library with him. Helena went back to America, where she struggled to pick up the reins of her business and to explain to her sons why she had finally divorced their father. In one letter full of frustration she said,

> Your father is a cruel, wicked, bitter, disillusioned fool. He has books enough to last him a lifetime, but he loves to complain and be pitied. I hope that you will both see him – for my part I hope he will live another 20 years in real comfort. I honestly did not have one week's relaxation with him. Whatever was started, I had to carry through. I don't believe one woman in a million could have put up with all the tricks he played on me. That is why I always say, the more busy one is, the happier, as one has no time for mischief and stupidity . . .

In a letter from Cagnes, Titus said to Helena, 'Before leaving Paris, I entrusted to Eugenie two valuable beauty books to be given you on your return. One had been bought in 1928 for francs 1,400 the other in 1929 for francs 500, *taxe de luxe* included. I will be glad to receive a cheque for francs 1,900. Everybody is harassing me for money just now when things are at their worst for me, so please send the cheque by return. I hope that your health continues better and your business interests continue to prosper. Edward.'

That summer, Helena retreated to Germany, where she spent longer than usual in a clinic recovering her strength. She rallied, as she always did. In a move that signalled her return to health, she had her portrait painted, not once, but twice. Marie Laurencin painted her as a young Indian maharanee, wearing huge pearls and jewelled cuffs, whilst Pavel Tchelitchew's image shows her as a jewelled head, covered with gold sequins.

Retail therapy being a favourite cure, Helena also went shopping. In her case it was more wholesale therapy as she bought in bulk, adding a mass of significant pieces to her already acclaimed collection of African art when she bought the treasures collected in the Western Sudan by F.H. Lem, whose aspirations of opening a museum in Dakar dedicated to the 'art of Africa' had collapsed. There was no shortage of potential clients for Lem's magnificent collection in Paris — avid collectors would have been circling like hawks around the prey of Lem's treasures. Helena, however, swept in like a golden eagle, swooping up the lot.

Finally, before setting sail for New York, she hired the acclaimed architect designer Louis Sue to start work on her Paris mansion, giving him a significant budget to source important furniture. With the operating profits of her business in America at a paltry $228,371 for the previous year, she had work to do, chief amongst which was to sort out her staffing. Madame recruited the best man in the beauty business and charged him with getting the wholesale division back on track. His name was Harry Johnson and it's said she had to pay a fortune to get him. Fired with enthusiasm and an age-defying vigour — she was sixty-two — Madame went back to work.

CHAPTER TWELVE

LIPSTICKS AND LESBIANS
ELIZABETH AND ELISABETH
New York 1926–1934

O N 24 JANUARY 1933 promptly at 9.30 a.m., a long funeral cortège left Sutton Place. Sombre-faced men and women of the Democratic Executive Committee of New York, who had volunteered to make up the guard of honour, walked slowly ahead of the cars, muffled against the freezing weather, towards St Patrick's Cathedral on Fifth Avenue. The approach to St Patrick's had been cordoned off to the public, enabling cars bringing mourners to be waved through, and dozens of ushers greeted the 2000 guests arriving for the requiem high mass.

Despite the bitter weather, people were gathered outside, jostling for a view. New Yorkers were used to spectacle, but there had been little excitement in the city that winter and the impressive display of pomp and security had caught their attention. Over a thousand people were crowded on the pavements, their faces pinched with cold, and in some cases with hunger. The Depression had taken its toll. It was estimated that there were 34,000,000 people in America with no steady income and 'the middle classes had faces grey with worry about their rent and grocery bills'.

For those watching the event unfold, but who didn't know who had died, the meeting and greeting, laughing and hugging made it seem more like a party than a funeral. The honorary pallbearers for example, including Noel Coward, Gilbert Miller, Daniel Frohman and Condé Nast, were kissing a lot of mink-swathed ladies. When the cortège arrived, first out was Anne Morgan, followed by Anne Vanderbilt and Daisy Harriman. Then the crowd started cheering as Mrs Roosevelt herself arrived, without the President elect, but with their son James, who took his place with the pallbearers.

The coffin was carried into the cathedral, draped in a blanket of roses and lily of the valley, the glorious scent catching the attention of Elizabeth Arden who had been sitting quietly with her friends Henry and Anne Sell. It made her feel better. There was nothing more cheering to Elizabeth than the scent of fresh flowers, other perhaps than being in the company of people as illustrious as those at this funeral. Some of the people outside were starting to drift away. By now, they all knew the name of the deceased — Miss Elisabeth Marbury. They left thinking that she must have been some important woman. They were right. Bessie had been a very important woman. Above all, she had been a very popular woman, who would be much missed by her friends in politics, the Church, the media, the theatre and in Hollywood. But of all those who gathered to mourn her, no one was grieving more than Elizabeth Arden.

If anyone typified the cultural and social Zeitgeist of an era it was Bessie Marbury. One of the most brilliant and creative working women of the late nineteenth century, Bessie's influence lasted for over five decades. She was as respected in 1880s New York as in 1900s Paris, and as powerful in pre- and post-war New York. When Elizabeth Arden met her in 1926, Bessie was living both in New York and at her country estate in Maine. She had witnessed fifty years of the ebb and flow of the fame and failure of creative talent and knew *everybody*. Miss Arden, New York's own rich and famous beauty queen, was still a queen with no court. Bessie Marbury would soon change that.

Elisabeth Marbury was born in New York in 1856, the youngest of five children. Her parents came from Quaker and Huguenot lineage, imbuing young Bessie with a sense of history and a place in the hierarchy of New York's establishment families. Her grandparents lived in Oyster Bay, in the days when Long Island was a peaceful farming community, and Bessie's greatest childhood friend was their neighbour's son, Teddy Roosevelt. Her father was a lawyer; an intellectual, politically motivated man who saw nothing strange in teaching his youngest daughter Latin by the age of six and introducing her to Horace, Kant and Shakespeare. Bessie travelled constantly with her parents, spending time in London and Paris and meeting such diverse luminaries as Charles Darwin, Alma Tadema, George Eliot and Lillie Langtry.

If Bessie's parents had hoped for a brilliant marriage for their daughter, they were destined for disappointment. The gravel-voiced, quite plain and rather plump young woman knew from an early age that she was totally uninterested in men in any sexual sense and, at twenty-five, was still living at home with her family on Irving Place. Far too energetic to follow the genteel routines of spinsterhood, and blessed with pronounced commercial skills, Bessie started a profitable business as a poultry breeder. Apart from her lifelong passion for fishing, chickens were Bessie's greatest hobby and she became quite an expert, incubating the chicks in the city and moving them out to Long Island where the Marbury Oyster Bay home had enough space to build poultry sheds. However profitable it was, the poultry-breeding endeavour was a sideline to her other great love, the theatre, which in turn enabled her to meet the woman who became her greatest love of all, an ambitious amateur actress with pronounced social aspirations – Elsie de Wolfe.

Among Bessie's closest friends were Sarah and Eleanor Hewitt, daughters of one-time mayor of New York, Abram Hewitt. Their grandfather was millionaire philanthropist Peter Cooper. Known as the 'Amazons', the Cooper Hewitts seemingly shared Bessie's distaste for matrimony, surrounding themselves with literary and feminist women including the Duer sisters, Caroline and Alice. At a luncheon hosted by Sarah Cooper Hewitt in 1886, the young Elsie de Wolfe recited a poem by Caroline Duer. Bessie was smitten, the two became close and a year later were openly vacationing together. When Bessie co-ordinated an important charity production of a French play with Elsie in the leading role, her efficiency prompted New York's most successful theatrical impresario of the 1880s, Daniel Frohman, to suggest she go into theatre management. He introduced her to Frances Hodgson Burnett, whose bestselling novel *Little Lord Fauntleroy* was poised for production on Broadway, and Bessie Marbury's new career was launched. She took over the author's management, handling royalties, contracts, theatre leasing, casting and promotion, all of which she handled with aplomb. Sadly for Bessie, an entanglement with a confidence trickster who persuaded her to set up a joint production facility to take the play to Europe, ended up with her being swindled and she found herself in Paris, utterly penniless. Coincidentally, Elsie de Wolfe was in Paris taking drama lessons and was on hand to give consolation. The two women spent several months in Paris, living together openly in the city that was more sexually tolerant than any other at that time.

Bessie took advantage of her time in Paris to lobby Victorien Sardou and Ernest Feydeau to become clients, and never looked back. She handled the international rights for Sardou's play *Madame Sans-Gene* and signed a raft of leading French and British writers whose work was published or performed all over America. Amongst others, Bessie Marbury represented George Bernard Shaw, H.G. Wells, Clyde Fitch, Jerome K. Jerome, J.M. Barrie, Hugh Walpole and Oscar Wilde.

When the two women returned to New York, they set up home in a rented town house on the corner of Irving Place, near to Bessie's old family home. Elsie painted the house in pale shades, replacing the typically heavy Victorian furniture with light, decorative pieces, and created a modern, breezy look in total contrast to the dark opulence of New York houses of the time. The 'bachelors' as they were now known hosted Sunday afternoon salons, serving tea rather than dinner, partly to be different, partly as they were both thrifty, but mainly as they were on a tight budget. Their respective fathers having died in a less affluent state than either daughter had anticipated, each had to earn her own living, and they did it mainly through networking. As William Whitney said, 'You never know whom you are going to meet at Bessie's, but you can always be sure that whoever they are will be interesting and you will have a good time.' So, the little house on Irving Place became *the* port of call for everyone who was anyone living in, or visiting New York, such as Dame Nellie Melba, Oscar Wilde, Sarah Bernhardt, Ellen Terry, J.P. Morgan, Ethel Barrymore, Henry Adams, the Hewitts, the Harrimans and the great sensualist man of good taste, Stanford White.

By 1905, Bessie had started to take over the personal management of international stars, organising lecture tours and early sponsorship arrangements and cleverly adding up-and-coming, as well as establishment, journalists to her stable. The journalists she represented wrote about the stars she represented and the personalities she represented lectured at luncheons to the social ladies she knew. It was a cosy and very profitable arrangement. It was said that it was difficult to find a writer or performer who wasn't in some way connected with Miss Marbury. At about this time, Bessie had a passionate affair with Anne Morgan, financier J.P. Morgan's daughter, a shy person just coming to terms with her sexuality and at thirty-two much younger than Bessie, which meant her father was never seen at a Marbury salon again. Whilst her business flourished, however, Elsie's acting career was floundering. Bessie herself acknowledged that de Wolfe wasn't a particularly good actress and, showing her skill in re-invention, encouraged her to take up decorating. This she did with singleminded skill and, just as Elizabeth Arden and Helena Rubinstein were in the right place at the right time to satisfy women's needs for beauty, Elsie was available to satisfy their needs for beautiful houses. Bessie Marbury collected people as assiduously as Elsie de Wolfe collected French furniture and both had stunning collections.

As Marbury and de Wolfe were so at home in France and their business interests there were rapidly expanding, they closed up their New York house each summer, moving to the beautiful but run-down property in the park at Versailles they had bought together, called the Villa Trianon. Bessie had put down most of the money and Elsie took over the decorating, lavishing her skills on restoring the property and planting exquisite gardens. Their mutual friend Anne Morgan soon joined them in sharing the costs. Escaping from the oppressive society in New York, where her father had reluctantly realised his daughter wasn't going to give him grandchildren, Morgan became a fixture at the Villa Trianon, her trust fund paying for, amongst other improvements, a music pavilion and a superb cook. The women held court at Versailles, entertaining their friends like Princesse Edmond de Polignac, usually *sans* husband. The princesse was Winnaretta Singer of the sewing machine fortune, a famous lesbian and great patron of the arts in Paris where she lived in considerable style with her 'husband'. The prince cared little for the idea of a conventional relationship and in one of the many *mariages blancs* of the time, happily acted a charade which was a convenient disguise when women, and men, of a certain position and disposition didn't wish to live alone.

After the Great War, Bessie became deeply immersed in fundraising for the Democratic Party and an early player in the circle of talent forming in Hollywood. From being stout, she had become so huge that it affected her health and she travelled less and less. In 1920, she sold her share in the Villa Trianon to Anne Morgan and, looking for a home to truly call her own in New York, chose a run-down area called Sutton Place, on the East River between 53rd and 59th Streets. Other observers had spotted Sutton Place, amongst them Edna Woolman Chase, who longed to buy a house there. She made the mistake of asking Condé Nast to visit the area only to be told, 'Really, Edna! It's a slum. Why do you want to live in a slum?' His answer may possibly have been coloured by the fact that his wife, Leslie, was known to be fond of the ladies that frequented the Marbury home, and Mrs Chase living next door could have been a trifle embarrassing. However, Edna Chase should have listened to her instincts. For around $13,000 each, the town houses on Sutton Place, albeit next door to Burns Brothers coal yard, soon became the smartest enclave in New York. Elsie, naturally enough, decorated Bessie's house where for a while she kept her own *pied-à-terre*. Anne Morgan soon moved to Sutton Place, along with the group's friend Anne (Mrs Willie K. Vanderbilt) and her sister, Mrs Olins. The media were fascinated, calling the group 'the four horsewomen of the Apocalypse', and had a high time following the comings and goings of the great and the good to 'the girls' in Sutton Place.

Bessie's home became the focal point for a whole new wave of visitors, and café society came for tea, which included drinks, Bessie always having decent scotch to hand. She was no fan of Prohibition and would later campaign vigorously for Roosevelt, knowing he would abolish it. Her guests included the Prince of Wales, Somerset Maugham, Mrs Patrick Campbell, Artur Rubinstein, the Cole Porters and the Eugene O'Neills. George Gershwin played the piano and George Cukor came to talk about film scripts. Groucho Marx observed Charlie Chaplin, and Helen Hayes pouted at Constance Collier. It was a heady mix.

In about 1926, into this sapphic circle came 'pretty in pink' Miss Elizabeth Arden, with her little-girl voice and her baby-blue, blinking eyes. To be fair, she blinked because she was shortsighted. This difficulty was kept a huge secret and she loathed glasses, rarely wearing them, and being one of the first to use contact lenses. She was so prejudiced against glasses that she wouldn't hire people who wore them during interviews. 'Wearing glasses is ageing and we're in the youth and beauty business,' was her rationale. Canny staff learned to whip off their glasses when she was in the vicinity. Miss Arden took a long clear look, however, at the Marbury salon and liked what she saw. She was forty-five years old, looked thirty, admitted to thirty-nine and still acted as though she was twenty. Successful, ripe for development into the upper echelons of society that she craved, the rich Mrs Elizabeth Arden Lewis was ready to have some fun.

Her introduction to Marbury had come from her advertising agent and adviser, Henry Sell. Elizabeth met Henry Sell, who would become an important influence in her life, in New York in 1921. He had been a newspaper man, cutting his teeth editing the literary pages of the *Chicago Evening News*, before accepting the siren call to New York, and a job editing *Harper's Bazaar* for William Randolph Hearst. Sell's greatest coup at *Bazaar* was discovering Anita Loos, and publishing the adventures of her heroine, Lorelei Lee in 'Gentlemen Prefer Blondes'. *Everyone* adored Lorelei Lee. Even James Joyce had a weakness for her, persuading Sylvia Beach to stock the book at Shakespeare & Company. Sell, as editor of *Bazaar*, delighted in visiting Paris for the fashion shows, knowing that the favourable buzz was about his magazine.

The requisite shuffling of seats when the stellar names in the fashion media move from one title to another is nothing new. In the mid-1920s, the *Bazaar*'s line-up in Paris, besides Henry Sell, included their Paris co-ordinator *par excellence*, the great and well-connected beauty, the duchesse Maria de Gramont, and in a move that had made Mrs Chase of *Vogue* incandescent with rage, the leading society and fashion photographer, Baron de Meyer. The American *Vogue* camp was, at least once a year, dominated by the presence of the great Condé Nast himself, who travelled with Frank Crowninshield, the sparkling editor of *Vanity Fair* and a man of many talents, one of which was to translate for Nast, who didn't speak a word of French. Their editor in chief, Edna Woolman Chase, was accompanied by *Vogue*'s fashion editor, Carmel Snow, and their new star photographer, replacing Baron de Meyer, was the brilliant Edward Steichen. The rivalry between the two titles was intense. Sell, coming from a literary background, had the advantage of knowing writers like e.e. cummings, married at the time to cult *Vanity Fair* illustrator Ralph Barton's ex-wife Anne. The *Vogue* camp retaliated for a season or two at least when their prettiest and as it happens extremely wealthy Paris editor, Pauline Pfeiffer, fell in love with Ernest Hemingway, a star guest at any party. When he married Pauline and she left *Vogue* it didn't matter much any more because Henry Sell had moved on to edit what had been an influential but now ailing women's magazine, *The Delineator*. *Harper's Bazaar* entered a period in the wilderness, only recovering when Carmel Snow left *Vogue* to join them and revive the title. Cummings in the meantime, clearly a writer with an eye for beauty, started an affair with Steichen's favourite model, Marion Morehouse, and the two later married. The complexity of seating plans at fashion shows and planning guest lists for fashion soirées took on a delicacy of skill and tact akin to plotting a military manoeuvre over a minefield.

Paris was the capital of fashion, but New York was the capital of art-direction. Advertising as a creative force blossomed. Whilst it would take radio to take it to the next level and television to turn advertising into a full-blown industry, the up-market magazines were amongst its greatest early beneficiaries. Elizabeth Arden was an important client of *Bazaar* and known by everyone on the staff as a difficult one. As Henry Sell was charming and genuinely interested in commercial creativity, when his publisher suggested he lunch with Miss Arden to 'keep her sweet', Henry agreed. Happily, their rapport was instant and Sell soon added the role of creative consultant, advising the Arden company, to his full-time job. He introduced Elizabeth to Baron de Meyer, who took pictures for the campaign that Arden would run for years, using Madame Vionnet's star model, Roberta, as 'the face of Arden'. Roberta was also the favoured model of the greatest hairdressing genius of the time, Antoine, but probably to his chagrin, his skills weren't required for this particular photographic sitting. In a gesture clearly inspired by Miss Arden's passion for her 'muscle strapping' technique, Roberta was photographed in a rather sinister-looking picture by de Meyer, totally bandaged in white crepe, her beautiful face peering out rather as though she was recovering from plastic surgery.

As hair was of no consequence to this particular campaign, the de Meyer photograph of Roberta gave just the right hint of the medical aura beauty treatments were claiming to achieve. Elizabeth was enchanted with the results. To begin with, Baron de Meyer could do no wrong and Elizabeth, moved as much by his skill as by the rumour that his wife was the illegitimate daughter of King Edward VII, rarely used any other photographer.

At that time, hairdressing was of minor significance to both Arden and Rubinstein. Their clients had their hair swathed in turbans whilst they had treatments, and although such women enjoyed having treatments at a beauty salon, they often still had their hair done at home by their own maid. The very rich had their personal hairdresser, and ladies staying without personal maids at the great hotels around the world would find chambermaids well trained in dressing hair.

Specialist department stores had begun to open in-house hairdressing salons by the early 1900s, as part of their policy of offering 'everything under one roof' but women were often gifted at managing their own hair, and although it is hard to comprehend today, they often washed it only once a fortnight, using lavender water and hair powder as a stopgap. Even New York's most fashionable hairdressers, the Ogilvie sisters, were advocating washing the hair only once a month as late as 1928. False hairpieces were widely used and curls were often fixed with gum arabic, which could get them into very sticky situations if applied with too heavy a hand. It was quite normal for women to put curling papers in their hair each evening before going to bed and a dressing-table essential, along with hairnets, was a supply of long, brushed-steel hairclips for clamping curls flat to the head. There was a custom for middle-class women to 'set' each other's hair in the popular Marcel waves and they would often make an afternoon's leisure activity out of it.

Until the 1920s trend for short hair, hairdressers had been just that – they 'dressed' hair. Very few had specialist cutting skills and there were few schools where they could learn them. Two commercial developments and two fashion trends took the mainly amateur hairdressing profession into a full-time business. It started with the 'bob', what Chanel described as 'her shingle'. Young women who wanted bobbed hair went to the barbers and a great fuss was made about 'bobbing' versus 'barbering'. Many barbers immediately recognised there was greater profit potential in dealing with women's hair, and several 'Mr Jack, Barber' metamorphosed overnight into 'Monsieur Jacques, Ladies Hairdresser'. The invention of the portable hairdryer in the early 1920s, and with it a far less cumbersome range of hair salon dryers, made the process a little more appealing. Hair salons benefited even further when Charles Nessler's permanent wave machines were introduced, although at first the system was cumbersome to use, not to mention expensive – a permanent could cost as much as $100 – and very time-consuming as it took several hours. There was the added danger of the chemicals destroying women's hair, and the process only became consumer-friendly in the mid-to-late 1920s. The final boost to the fortunes of the industry was the craze for hair colour, which took hold in the late 1920s, helped along by Hollywood movie stars and their peroxide blonde hair.

If all else failed, women would simply put on a hat. No woman of the time was properly dressed without one, and star milliners had as much status as any leading fashion designer. Women had an entire wardrobe of hats, often wearing them all day at work, when out at lunch, and changing to a cocktail confection in the evening.

It was rare for a hairdressing salon to have real *cachet*, with the exception of Antoine in Paris, whose rue Cambon salon was the mecca for chic women. Antoine, a once-penniless Polish émigré who had come to Paris before the First World War, was a flamboyant star. Antoine simply adored white. He dressed in white. He dyed his hair white. He had his salon massed in white flowers and slept in a glass coffin. Antoine, who used to trial new dyes on his giant white poodle, was the stylist of choice for photographers, models and fashionable women like Elsie de Wolfe, whose white, lilac and even pale pink hair was dyed by Antoine.

Henry Sell knew Antoine, just as he knew Baron de Meyer, Elsie de Wolfe and of course Bessie Marbury, who had been a friend since his days on the *Chicago Daily News* when he published stories from her stable of writers. By 1926, Sell was moving out of magazines and was poised to buy the Blaker advertising agency which had fallen on hard times and whose largest client was the Elizabeth Arden Corporation. Having been in Miss Arden's orbit for six years, Sell was wilting under the pressure of devoting so much personal attention to his demanding boss, and the thought of handling her as a full-time client was worrying. He turned for advice to his old friend Bessie Marbury who advised him to introduce Elizabeth to important people with whom she could have a social or professional rapport, knowing this would create a useful diversion. 'I don't know any new fancy people except those she has either taken a bite out of and thrown back,' wrote Sell to Marbury, 'or the ones that are now her props.' The solution, they decided, was to introduce Elizabeth to Bessie, who would take care of the situation herself.

Bessie adopted Elizabeth almost immediately, the relationship flourishing fast. In fact, Marbury's new protégée had arrived at exactly the right time. Bessie had been shocked and hurt when Elsie had abruptly married British diplomat Sir Charles Mendl earlier that year, without even telling her. It was a *mariage blanc*, naturally, but they were a close couple and Bessie felt isolated by her lover's desertion. Friends of Arden's were mesmerised by the relationship. In the first instance there was the issue of Bessie's size. By 1926, she was so large she had to wear braces on her legs to support her weight and could only walk with two canes. Elizabeth was normally repulsed by anyone overweight and was obsessed with female physical beauty. Also obsessed with yoga, she loved nothing more than standing on her head: 'Let's shake up those little insides!' she would say. Arden was always active; Bessie could hardly get out of her chair.

Secondly, Bessie was an intellectual giant and Elizabeth's academic education was minimal. Rumours flew around that Arden was a lesbian. It's quite possible that she was a latent lesbian — or rather craved a more sensitive loving affection than she was offered by men. But Elizabeth bottled up her sexual feelings to such an extent, giving all her energies to work, horses, flowers, houses, social climbing and temper tantrums – in that order – that there was little left over for anything else. Her husband would claim she was frigid. But her lack of ability to love men – that is, to enjoy a loving relationship which included sex – came from the fact that she had been so bitterly wounded by the early death of her mother. Florence Graham had seen her mother worn out with childbirth, ill with TB and gradually withering away. She had sensed her mother's despair that her husband couldn't provide for his family and witnessed the struggles to feed and clothe her siblings. Thus, Elizabeth Arden doubted marriage, or any form of physical love, was worth the pain. She never met a man who could make her change her views.

She replaced reality with a fantasy about ideal love, growing up dreaming of courtly 'beaux' who would give a chaste kiss and need little else. Sex was too earthy for her. Elizabeth Arden's dreams were of a world where everything was pink and gold, happy, bright and beautiful. A world where ladies had maids and took a rest, wearing a rose-print chiffon negligee, each afternoon. Where tea was served in bone-china cups on a silver tray precisely at 3.00 p.m. A world full of flowers where the weather was always perfect, or if it wasn't, a chauffeur in a Bentley was waiting outside. She wanted that world so much that she created it *exactly* for herself, living a life of relentless perfection. There was just the one exception. If things didn't work out *exactly* as she wanted, she shouted and screamed, like a little child, and the genteel Miss Arden would become the foul-mouthed Florence Graham.

The truth about the unlikely pair is that they needed each other. They were tough and successful women, each pretending not to be. Bessie by this time was quite lonely, but still influential, and Elizabeth was desperate to learn. In Bessie, twenty-two years older than her, she found her ideal teacher. Bessie Marbury was part motherly figure, part teacher, part financial adviser and part mentor. Bessie's commercial brain was finely honed to spotting the benefits of a good deal. This would have been particularly welcome to Elizabeth, who had no one to discuss her business development with from 1928 since she and Tommy were by now virtually estranged. Bessie had run her own company, and that appealed to Elizabeth who admired successful working women. More importantly, Bessie could help her in her social goals.

Bessie indulged Elizabeth and clearly there was great affection between them. One can imagine Bessie treating her like a fond child, which was exactly what Elizabeth craved. From Marbury's position it is easier to understand the intensity of the relationship. In many ways, Elizabeth reminded her of Elsie. Now Elsie was living away from New York, Bessie was lonely. She had spent her life surrounded by people who needed her, and was the queen of organisation. Elizabeth needed organising. She also needed affection, a commodity in rare supply in the Lewis household, or the Arden offices. Bessie, used to giving affection to women and knowing how they craved it, eagerly adopted Miss Arden. The fact that Elizabeth was successful and very rich will also have appealed. Bessie liked to persuade her wealthy friends to make political donations, or to buy from some artist she was promoting. Money oiled the wheels of her life and appealed to her as much as the use of Miss Arden's chauffeured cars, Elizabeth by this time owning a Rolls Royce and a Duesenberg.

Of all the books Bessie may have encouraged Elizabeth to read, her autobiography, *My Crystal Ball*, probably wasn't on the list. Published in 1923, Bessie had written:

> I sometimes think that the prevalent use of external cosmetics eats out the internal brain if persisted in long enough. Were my crystal ball smeared with rouge and smirched with lipstick it would be of little value to me. The sale of rejuvenating creams or of restorative powders is always profitable. There is no town so small but that it cannot boast of a beauty parlour. There is no woman so poor who will not become its patron. The search for the Holy Grail never enlisted so much energy and so much faith as does this pursuit of youth by old age.

Despite Bessie's antagonism to cosmetics, she had been instrumental in placing several clients and friends into the Ponds 'celebrity' campaign, and was constantly on the search for other suitable placements, writing to Henry Sell, 'Do you know of anyone who might take an endorsement from HIH the Grand Duchess Marie of Russia? She has refused various people for perfumes and creams, but I have finally persuaded her to let me place her. She is great royalty, besides being young, chic and good-looking. I can sell her for $3,000.'

Under Bessie's guidance Elizabeth discovered art. She would never collect on the same scale as Madame, the bulk of her money going on her stables, but she bought pictures by Georgia O'Keeffe, Mary Cassatt and Marie Laurencin amongst others. She had her portrait painted by Augustus John, although as she loathed smoking the sittings must have been rather fraught. John was a compulsive smoker, who used to stub his cigarette out on his plate at dinner and, rarely noticing, happily eat it as he chatted. Arden wore an outfit designed by the great Charles James for her portrait. James was another member of the charmed Marbury circle and would go on to work for Elizabeth when she launched her fashion floor at the Fifth Avenue salon. She didn't like the first Augustus John portrait and insisted she sit a second time – only to realise when she saw the result that the artist had got the measure of her and she looked much steelier and tougher than in the original. Miss Arden kept the one she liked best, hanging it in pride of place at her Fifth Avenue apartment, sending the 'reject' to London, where it was hung in her management offices.

Elizabeth took to having her photograph taken at every possible opportunity, ordering dozens of prints of her favourite poses for the company press office. She was photographed in romantic pose in lace and velvet; as an altogether more hard-edged flapper with slicked-back hair; with cars and, invariably, with her beloved dogs. In 1929, possibly guided by Marbury, who had noted his rise with interest, not least because he had been given an exhibition at Elsie de Wolfe's gallery on Fifth Avenue which helped establish his name in New York, Elizabeth was photographed swathed in white ermine by Cecil Beaton. When Cecil went to see her to deliver his prints – delighted with her large order – he said she 'looked terribly tired, swollen and bunged up . . . a very bad advertisement for the shop.' Elizabeth, who was suffering with influenza and feeling sorry for herself, suddenly changed her mind about the pictures she had previously so admired, telling Beaton his work was odious, had a fit of hysterics and tore up the photographs 'in blind rage'. Beaton however wasn't aware that Elizabeth didn't destroy all the prints, and his picture of her, looking impossibly young for her age of forty-eight, remains in the Arden archives today.

Elizabeth embraced culture, joining the Opera Guild and the Friends of the Philharmonic, where she became a keen fundraiser and sponsor. No one knew better than Bessie that charity committees are the best place to meet women of influence. Most significantly, Bessie persuaded Elizabeth to buy the 750-acre estate next to her own property in Maine. The house had been gutted by fire, so when Elizabeth bought the land, Bessie organised builders and gardeners and naturally suggested Elsie do the interiors. Lady Mendl declined, claiming she was 'too busy'. She didn't care much for Miss Arden, whom she described as 'a dull little woman, pretty, but utterly lacking in spark'. Instead, Bessie suggested the wife of Chicago Orchestra conductor, John Alden Carpenter. Rue Carpenter, a great friend of Cole Porter (whose work Bessie had championed early in his career), was lively and talented, and a Chicago grandee with great taste. Elizabeth enthused about her new house, lavishing huge sums on it, naming it 'Maine Chance'. Mrs Carpenter's décor was beautiful — and Bessie watched happily from the wings, no doubt reminded of Elsie's early days in decorating the Villa Trianon.

Whilst Bessie often retreated to Maine, where weekends were spent fishing and talking politics, Elsie partied in Paris, aided and abetted by her close friend, Elsa Maxwell. Rapidly becoming known as café society's most famous 'Miss Fix-It', Elsa Maxwell had a nose for a trend and loved a party, coming into the orbit of Elsie de Wolfe in about 1921. She was a butch-looking, large, and larger-than-life dynamo, who preferred to fill her days — and nights — in the company of the gleaming rich. That they were often bisexual, homosexual or asexual, or just liked to observe people who were having whatever fun they preferred, was of no consequence to Elsa. If they had money and wanted a good time, she was there to provide it. She was particularly gifted at getting someone else to pay the bills — a skill she shared with Lady Mendl — and had an ability to create news for the social columns when promoting the people, places or products from which she earned her precarious living. To Elsie, Elsa Maxwell was a newer, raunchier, crude and lewd — and more exciting version of Bessie Marbury.

Elizabeth Arden was afraid to be alone. She was afraid of the dark and hated isolation, and to hide her fears she surrounded herself with people, masking her loneliness. Each weekend, guests would join her at Maine Chance, although her husband was rarely in the houseparty, spending less and less time in Maine. Her guests got superb service. She brought up hairdressers, beauticians and a masseuse from the New York salon and the highlight of the weekend would be when Anne Delafield, the head of the Arden exercise rooms, led her team of lithe and lovely exercise trainers, in their brief, Grecian-inspired uniforms, in a performance of acrobatic dance sequences to entertain Elizabeth's startled guests.

Tommy Lewis was delighted with Elizabeth's passion for her house in Maine. It meant his troublesome wife was out of town at least three days a week, and he could make excuses not to join her at weekends, preferring to roam alone in New York. Willie Graham and Tommy Lewis were able to be what they enjoyed best – men behaving badly. Tommy grumbled about his wife and Willie agreed with him, saying his sister had 'always been difficult'. Meanwhile they abused their relationship with Elizabeth by seducing the prettiest of her female staff, wining and dining them on the Arden expense account. Elizabeth, for the moment, was impervious, happy to be left to indulge herself at Maine Chance with her emerging hobby – her horses.

Her stables offered horseriding, and if visitors needed a lesson, Russian-born Prince Kadjar would teach them. The prince worked for the Arden Corporation during the week and was whisked to Maine Chance to take care of riding instruction at the weekends. He was very charming; Elizabeth was captivated by him, backing him in opening a riding stables in New York, not to mention financially supporting his mother. Unfortunately the prince was a drunk and Elizabeth, albeit reluctantly, had to let him go, first sending him to London, where Teddy Haslam refused point-blank to have him, whereupon she took him back in New York. Nothing worked and Miss Arden eventually fired him. A few years later, the prince was given a job with Helena Rubinstein in London, but the rot had set in, both in his attitude and his liver, and he was fired yet again. Whether Bessie appreciated the constant stream of activity next door when she was entertaining luminaries such as George Cukor is uncertain, but she had unleashed a fury in Elizabeth and had to put up with it.

Arden's business stormed ahead. Tommy opened wholesale outlets in Canada, South America, Africa, Australia and Asia, appointing agents locally to act as distributors, often on an exclusive basis. Elizabeth Arden salons, complete with Red Doors, were opened in Berlin, Madrid, Cannes and Rome, with Elizabeth always in attendance for their gala openings, accompanied by the prettiest member of her staff as travelling companion, along with her ladies' maid, her husband, Teddy Haslam, and often Gladys too. She sat for a photographic shoot with de Meyer, following which she briefed him to shoot her latest advertising campaign, a promotion for her very own fragrance. Fired with her fame, Elizabeth launched four signature fragrances in 1929 – La Joie d'Elizabeth, Le Rêve d' Elizabeth, Mon Amie Elizabeth and L'Amour Elizabeth – all exclusively available in Elizabeth Arden salons throughout the world. Baron de Meyer was instructed to find a model with 'the loveliest hand possible' and to shoot the well-manicured hand holding the fragrance bottles at a studio session in Paris. Unhappily, by the time de Meyer was in his studio, Miss Arden was back in America. She didn't like the proofs and ordered a re-shoot.

De Meyer was furious, writing to Henry Sell, whose agency had been in charge of the project, 'I might expect to be told what is wrong, so as to avoid making the same mistake again. I can assure you the picture is excellent, the hand charmingly placed.' Sell, interceding for his client, wrote back to de Meyer: 'Your letter finds the lady at Saratoga playing the ponies, so this one of mine must of necessity be guess-work, to be covered on her return. I'm a bit handicapped because *she* says that *you* say that I told you your prices were not high enough! I think that, being of a suspicious nature, she some-how suspects that I am in on the final accounting. Somehow this impression holds.' The storm clouds blew over and Elizabeth adored the results of de Meyer's second sitting. Sell wrote to him: 'Our Lady of the Lotions is pleased – my, my and how – with her new perfume prints.' The pictures may have pleased Miss Arden's vanity, but the fragrances didn't sell and were quietly dropped, along with Baron de Meyer, whose career was on a down-ward spiral and never properly recovered. He went to pieces after his wife Olga died, carrying her ashes around with him in an ornate box. It's said at one point he was so drug-addled that his cocaine-loving boyfriend, search-ing for a snort, found Olga's ashes and helped himself.

Miss Arden's fortunes, however, were founded on beauty treatments rather than fragrance, and a new treatment became a bestseller for her. She launched an innovate firming system called diathermy, involving the appli-cation of heat to the body via electric currents. She had seen the technique in Vienna, and, convinced it would be a magic cure for facial slack and lines, took the concept to New York, calling it the Vienna Youth Mask. She offered treatments at $200 a course, which were a sell-out.

Elizabeth was unconcerned about the Great Depression. She used to joke that sales of Arden's bath products had gone up; 'Our clients are coping with the stress of financial losses by soaking in a hot bath scented with my Rose Geranium bath crystals,' she wrote. She took a lease of a new building (which she would later purchase) at 691 Fifth Avenue at consid-erable cost, hiring Rue Carpenter to mastermind the décor. Mrs Carpenter, by now unwell and unable to direct the entire project, introduced Elizabeth to the Russian set designer and illustrator Nicholai Remisoff, who had been a discovery of Frank Crowninshield on *Vanity Fair*. His tastes were for brighter shades, and, as he adored Elizabeth's favourite pinks and yellows as much as she did, they bonded. Remisoff was one of the few people surrounding Elizabeth who could say, 'No, Miss Arden'. But although he occasionally put his foot down over excess in the salons he lost out at her Fifth Avenue apartment. Decorated by Remisoff but with Elizabeth's own taste predominating, a giddy display of pinks, blues and yellows in paint finishes and fabrics vied with quilted white satin furniture and pouffes tied with huge bows, the whole described by some visitors as like 'being in a bon-bon box'.

Whilst Elizabeth decorated her salons, Bessie worked singlemindedly to get F.D. Roosevelt into the White House. She still attracted visitors in droves. When Harold Nicolson made his first visit to New York he visited Bessie at Sutton Place. 'Miss Marbury', he wrote, 'is enormous, empathic, civilised and gay.' Two weeks later, in January 1933, the happy *and* gay Miss Marbury was dead.

Elsie de Wolfe did not return from Europe for the funeral. Her world was crumbling. First Bessie's death. Then her friend Alva Belmont died in Paris in the same week. Finally, news arrived that her friend Condé Nast was in deep financial trouble, his empire tottering. Nast wasn't the only one of de Wolfe's rich American clients who were no longer rich and she was uneasy about her own financial position. When she reviewed what she had been left in Bessie's will – who after making generous provision for her devoted servant and minor bequests to relatives and friends had left everything to Elsie – she moved fast to realise her assets, selling the art and furniture from Sutton Place and Lakeside Farm at auction, followed by the Sutton Place house. Elsie had inherited Lakeside Farm with the proviso that it be used as 'a home for working women'. But Anne Morgan was too committed to the American Women's Association to do much about it and de Wolfe never attended the committee meetings organised by Bessie's most efficient friend, Elizabeth Arden, to resolve the issue. Few were surprised at Elsie's boredom with the situation. Mercedes de Acosta said, 'When Elsie lived with Bessie, it was always Elsie who relentlessly got her way. It was Bessie who did all the giving in spite of the fact that she had more ability in her smallest and chubbiest finger than Elsie ever had all her life long.'

Elizabeth took charge of the various meetings, but no one came up with a constructive idea for funding Bessie's dream, so, patience snapping, Elizabeth bought Lakeside Farm from Elsie de Wolfe for $50,000 and promptly donated it back to the committee. At least that got Elsie out of the way. The only other donation to Bessie's dream of a women's refuge came from Eleanor Roosevelt and, in the end, Elizabeth re-purchased the property herself, merging it with her own adjoining one, and converted them into an exclusive health spa, Maine Chance. It was not the most apt memorial to the erudite, intellectual Miss Marbury, whose greatest hobby was fishing, who abhorred narcissistic self-indulgence and who was eventually too fat to walk unaided, but it was the only one she got.

Elizabeth Arden took over Bessie's house with its happy memories, but she had also inherited another precious memento. Bessie Marbury's will specified that her 'diamond and gold bracelet with the name Elisabeth spelt in diamonds be left to Mrs Elizabeth Lewis'. Friends who noticed Arden wear it may have assumed it was a relic of her marriage, or a piece she had commissioned herself. Post Bessie's death, Elizabeth moved into a different social set where few could identify the piece; Charles James perhaps, or Cecil Beaton, although Elizabeth didn't much care for him and they rarely worked together again. She often wore the bracelet, the true affection she had for its owner being one of her most treasured memories.

1933 was a depressing year for Elizabeth. Her patience finally snapped with Tommy, whom she suspected of having an affair with a treatment girl. She hired a private detective to shadow him and his reports of Tommy's infidelities and his louche behaviour in the company of his friend, her own brother Willie, devastated Elizabeth. She and Tommy were barely speaking but, ever-confident, he made a fatal mistake by cabling a senior demonstrator out on a provincial sales tour to send him the figures from the trip to a different address. The demonstrator, loyal to Miss Arden, called her to query the instruction, as it struck her as most odd. Tommy Lewis owned not one share in the business, nor had he any right to implement changes in policy. To Elizabeth it signalled that he was attempting to take over her business and it was the final straw. She called her lawyers.

By Christmas Tommy had moved out of their New York home and Elizabeth filed for divorce, citing 'cruel and abusive treatment'. The ending of their relationship was vicious. During their arguing, the issue of

Elizabeth's date of birth came up. It seems possible that Tommy may have thought his wife was younger – she certainly looked at least a decade younger – and Willie Graham, who rather foolishly sided with Tommy against his sister, was sent to Canada to track down the birth records, later making a statement to the court about her date of birth.

Nineteenth-century birth records are in longhand and in ledgers. Today, archivists and genealogists can see them on microfiche and if you look carefully in the listing under Florence Nightingale Graham in Thunder Bay, Ontario you will find the numbers run 12/31/1881/33. The last two numbers give a clue to Elizabeth's anger. It means an affidavit was sworn in 1933 to produce the birth records in court. When Elizabeth discovered her brother had been implicated in this low trick, she froze him out. At a stroke he was out of his job and out of her life. She never spoke to him again. She never even referred to him again. As far as she was concerned, William Graham did not exist.

Elizabeth's shrewd lawyer, J. Robert Rubin, was a vice president at MGM, so knew a lot about celebrity marriages and even more about celebrity divorce. Elizabeth filed her divorce in Maine, serving documents in July 1934. By October it was all over. For his fifteen years in his wife's business, during which time he had taken sales in her wholesale division from less than $200,000 to over $5 million a year, he got a settlement of $100 and was forbidden to work in the cosmetics industry in any way for five years from the date of their divorce. He took the deal.

Elizabeth blotted Tommy and Willie out and grieved quietly for Bessie. On two occasions over the next twenty years she would feel the tingle of pleasure in the company of a close companion – one male and one female – but she never had a relationship as close as the one she shared with Bessie; nor did she ever replace Tommy with anyone as skilled, nor who understood her so well in her business. Instead, she switched her affections to the ones she would come to love the most, who would never, ever let her down – her horses.

CHAPTER THIRTEEN

CHALLENGES AND CHANGES
America and Europe
1933–1937

How men hate a woman in a position of real power

—Eleanor Roosevelt

PRESIDENT ROOSEVELT'S DYNAMIC ADMINISTRATION brought challenges and changes for the booming beauty business in America. After a quarter of a century of freedom in terms of manufacturing, labelling and advertising, the industry was hit by new rules and regulations.

Firstly, Washington decided to levy a luxury tax on all products. The only surprise is that it had taken government so long to spot such a lucrative source of income from an industry reported to be worth $2 billion a year and growing. By 1931, a study of college women showed 85% of them wore lipstick, and at Macy's in New York, working women spent their lunch break in the vast beauty department, sniffing scented powder compacts and scrambling to buy lipsticks. The tax of 10% caused a furore amongst manufacturers who, in a rare moment of harmony, met to debate how to handle the levy. They were not alone in their annoyance. Women's groups took up the cudgels and protested that lipstick was as important to them as toothpaste, but the government was not to be moved.

Most companies, including Arden and Rubinstein, saw no problem in passing the cost on to their customers, whilst Dorothy Gray, Arden's *bête noire* from the previous decade, made a big issue about 'absorbing the charges', earning herself valuable press coverage. In the end, manufacturers decided that make-up lines – lipstick, rouge, powder and mascara – would carry the levy, whilst treatment creams would absorb it.

Next was the New York Federation of Women's Clubs who put forward a motion to license beauty parlours and salons. Elizabeth resigned from the Federation in protest, but whilst her own salons were impeccably run, she must have been aware that some form of control on cosmetologists was perfectly valid; and could not have been surprised when the New York State legislature passed a Standards Bill.

Then came a regulated working week. Both Miss Arden and Madame Rubinstein worked hours that would leave the most dedicated director today breathless. There is of course something of a myth about the 'tireless working woman'. As is so often the case, both of them had a vast infrastructure of support. There were domestic staff – Helena had a live-in couple at all her properties and was rarely without a relative or the daughter of an impoverished acquaintance as a general factotum. Her fondness for the latter had abated when her husband decamped to Boston with her Australian houseguest. Although she was divorced by 1934, realising her younger son Horace was following in his father's footsteps, attractiveness wasn't a major requirement in her female household staff.

From the beginning of the 1930s Elizabeth had a cook, butler, chauffeur and personal maid at her Fifth Avenue apartment, plus a full staff at Maine Chance. Employment patterns with domestic staff were no less erratic than with her business employees, although she was often much kinder to her personal staff, possibly because they were harder to recruit and she relied on them so much. Hedda Hopper, the famous show-business gossip columnist who worked for her briefly in the mid-1930s, describes a hilarious incident apropos Elizabeth's chauffeur. Misses Hopper and Arden were travelling in Elizabeth's Bentley when she glanced at the chauffeur, whom she had only hired that morning. 'Haven't I seen you somewhere before?' she asked him. 'Yes, Miss Arden,' replied the driver. 'You drove my friend, Mrs So-and-so, perhaps?' she queried. 'No, Miss Arden,' he murmured. Not to be beaten, she said, 'Of course, I remember now, it was Mrs So-and-so who suggested you come to me?' Hopper was riveted. The chauffeur replied calmly, 'No, Miss Arden.' Elizabeth's patience snapped. 'Well, who *did* recommend you?' 'No one, Miss Arden. I'm the driver you fired four weeks ago.' Elizabeth found this very funny, apparently, and Frank, the driver in question, stayed with her for fifteen years.

A full-time secretary at the office was supported by a second secretary working in shifts from her apartment handling social invitations and typing

Elizabeth's ritual daily diary notes. The Arden diaries covered her life in the most minute detail, recording her state of health, her breakfast, lunch, tea, cocktail and dinner engagements, all daily travel, dress fittings and personal purchases, beauty treatments and her frequent doctor's and dentist's appointments. Even letters received from any VIP were noted.

As her horseracing career developed, so did the section devoted to her horses. These included their health, racing engagements, travel arrangements, special treatments, notes from their vets, her grumbles about their trainers, plus any winnings, cups and other trophies. Elizabeth also kept notebooks at work, in which every single business lunch, bunch of flowers or gift dispatched, product tested, member of staff hired, or more often fired, was recorded in full detail. It's a wonder she ever had a moment to do half the things she wrote about.

Both women naturally had a troop of office staff who shopped for them, florists who delivered to them – and neither had to go further than one floor down to have a beauty treatment. Elizabeth enjoyed her 'daily treatments' much more than Helena, who always claimed she was too busy to practise what she preached. 'I'm a worker. I have no time for treatments,' she said. The truth is that Helena didn't enjoy having beauty treatments. She made her fortune out of them, but was the least relaxed and tactile person possible, wincing if anyone she didn't know well, or didn't like, touched her, and flinching when kissed. The exception was her long, glossy hair. Both women spent considerable time having their hair coloured – Arden's rather too gingery blonde and Rubinstein's inky-black were both high maintenance.

Helena never kept a diary, although her secretary kept a note of social functions, listing the guests invited. She kept her eye on every aspect of a party – particularly the budget – and wasn't adverse about complaining to the caterers if food didn't come up to her expectations, writing to one hapless firm: 'I just wanted you to know I was very disappointed with the last catering job you did for me. Some of the sandwiches tasted slightly stale and I personally felt there were too many bread sandwiches. Several of my guests commented on this. I was particularly disappointed because you always used to do such beautiful and interesting things. This time it just wasn't up to standard. Next time I know you will do a much better job.' The only list she was really interested in were the stockmarket reports in the financial press, after which she spent half an hour each morning on the telephone to her brokers – and the sales and salon figures from around the world which were her essential daily reading.

Elizabeth adored having massage, swore by Ardena Wax Baths and Vienna Youth Masks – the latter involving clients having their features cast in plaster and an individual satin padded mask created which was fitted with electrical currents to firm facial muscles. Miss Arden was very keen on firming facial muscles, printing a series of pamphlets illustrating the 'pulling in' and 'puffing out' exercises she advocated for devotees unable to book the expensive treatments. She also had a manicure twice a week, with a daily buff and polish, along with a weekly pedicure, daily massage, constant chiropody and a lot of depilation – Miss Arden *loathed* body hair – while managing to fit in her daily yoga and stretching exercises. Helena had a more modest morning ritual of a foaming bath and a simple exercise regime which included dozens of hand-pats under the chin. She never ran out of something scented for her bath. Samples of Rubinstein products were delivered in bulk to all her homes, usually piled up in half-open boxes, propped up against some valuable statue or pile of pictures waiting to be framed. Helena practised what she preached regarding moisturiser, faithfully rubbing cream on to her face, never forgetting her neck. 'The neck is important,' she would say, 'and when you put on cream, always upwards movements only, up, up, up, *lift* the face.' Finally she applied her *maquillage*, which given her fondness for make-up, took quite a long time.

Lady Weidenfeld remembers her late husband, the distinguished pianist Artur Rubinstein, being quite intimately aware of his friend and neighbour Helena's cosmetics routine. 'Artur's Park Avenue apartment was exactly opposite the windows of the room where Helena would apply her lotions and make-up,' says Annabel Weidenfeld, 'and he would often see her sitting there. She knew he might be watching and would sometimes wave at him. She always insisted it was best to put make-up on in natural light, it created a much better effect. There she was, this woman of considerable age, painting herself in the most precise way, ready to face her public . . . my husband could understand that.'

Staff in all beauty salons worked extremely long hours and would have been relieved when Roosevelt's National Recovery Administration established a forty-eight-hour week, with an eight-hour day. When a five-day working week later became mandatory in California, Elizabeth was furious. Not so much because of her staff rota, but because she was not in control of the situation. She wrote to her salon employees saying that for the benefit of the well-being of staff she was happy to announce a five-day week, indicating the decision was hers, and hers alone.

Consumer groups and market research organisations had mushroomed during the late 1920s, particularly in America, where the explosion of product sales targeted at affluent women had spawned a raft of experts. They had statistics at their fingertips, on everything from magazine circulation and readers per page to how often women washed their hair. Calvin Coolidge had said in a speech in 1928 that 'The requirements of existence have passed beyond the standard of necessity into the region of luxury.' He was absolutely right. Whether it was cars, clothes, lipstick or Listerine, the smart 'new woman' craved it all and teams of people observed her shopping habits. As a consequence, advertising agencies, armed with a vast array of data to convince their clients of the wisdom of increasing their media spend, took on an increasing importance, and even Harvard appointed a Professor of Advertising.

Consumer groups were critical of cosmetics, often with cause. One highly regarded organisation, Consumers' Research Inc, established in the late 1920s and rapidly achieving a subscription list for their newsletter totalling 50,000, published a book in 1934, written by M.C. Phillips, called *Skin Deep*. It was an early exposé on not merely the content of product, but the cost-to-profit ratio enjoyed by manufacturers and the dubious habit of selling illusions; 'as deleterious', claimed the author, 'as some cosmetics ingredients'. The philosophy of Consumers Research Inc was to 'develop a science of consumption so that consumers can defend themselves against the aggressions of advertising and salesmanship'. *Skin Deep* made powerful reading, particularly regarding the number of products on the market that were dangerous.

Claims against products like the depilatory cream Koremlu, containing a strong rat poison, and the equally toxic yet innocent-sounding Lash Lure, containing a dangerous analine dye, were heavily backed by the American Medical Association. Lash Lure, the highly promoted eyelash dye, was found to have caused burning and disfiguring, with at least one case of blindness attributed to the product. Eventually a woman died as a direct result of using Lash Lure. The book targeted cosmetics but acknowledged that it was hard to report scientifically on products like nail polish, lipstick and suntan oil in 1934, as there was little quantifiable data available. The industry hoped to keep it that way, but was coming under scrutiny. Fortunately for Charles Revson, his Revlon Corporation's dubious product 'Ever-On', a base coat so effective that it was suspected of destroying a good many fingernails and even, it's alleged, causing an amputation, wasn't on the market when Miss Phillips wrote her book.

The American Medical Association, which had been looking at quasi-medical claims by the cosmetics industry with growing suspicion, set up a board of standards, issuing guidelines for advertising. The board, for example, insisted that no 'allergy-free' claims could be made – an interesting move, inferring that doctors were fully aware chemicals in cosmetics might cause an allergenic reaction. The AMA was critical about tissue creams, stating that 'cosmetic creams cannot regenerate skin tissue', and even tougher on hair-care products, explaining therapeutic claims for 're-growth and enhanced texturing' were invalid. They insisted all ingredients should appear on packaging or be available to the consumer 'on request'. If manufacturers failed to oblige, their ability to use AMA 'endorsement' in advertising copy would be withdrawn.

By this stage, Arden and Rubinstein, along with several other manufacturers, were not particularly concerned about AMA endorsement anyway and tended to ignore what they felt was posturing. The AMA was an influential body however, and manufacturers who ignored their diktats soon discovered their mistake. The Federal Trade Commission was also taking notice of the more spurious claims made in the name of cosmetics advertising and started an investigation, recommending that medicinal claims for products must be substantiated.

The Food and Drug Administration's efforts to achieve revisions of the out-of-date 1906 Pure Food and Drug Act, started in the autumn of 1933, was one of the earliest initiatives of the Roosevelt government. The pro-change lobby included the AMA, the Joint Women's Congressional Committee, the Federal Trade Commission, Consumers' Research Inc and various influential women's groups including the American Nurses' Association, the National League of Women's Voters, the National Women's Trade Union League and the American Association of University Women. They were united over one issue, protecting the consumer against what the president had called 'dangerous fakes and quality chiseling'.

The most enthusiastic supporter for the proposed legislation was the First Lady herself. Mrs Roosevelt gave unprecedented backing to Ruth de

Forest Lamb for her book called *The American Chamber of Horrors: The Truth about Food and Drugs*. The book focused on toxic ingredients and exaggerated promotional claims and was based on an exhibition sponsored by the Food and Drug Administration which had been presented at the White House prior to a country-wide tour. There was an uproar against the legislation, with most of the noise coming from cosmetics manufacturers and pharmaceutical companies hotly followed by the advertising industry claiming that the media would lose millions of dollars' worth of advertising along with jobs. The need for a new law to replace the by now outdated Pure Food and Drug Act of 1906 was obvious, except perhaps to people who stood to lose money from it.

In the early 1900s, the pioneering chief of what was then called 'The Bureau of Chemistry', Dr Harvey W. Wiley, and his crack team of nine staff, had struggled to get Congress to pass a Food and Drug Act in a brave attempt to establish government control over the vast food and pharmaceuticals businesses flourishing at that time. Only 37 years old when he had taken on the job as America's 'Chief Chemist' in 1883 (auspiciously, the same year the cholera germ was isolated, proving it was transmitted via water and food), Dr Wiley spent the rest of his life championing the cause of unadulterated food, medicines and cosmetics. When he started his work, medicines containing opium, morphine, heroin and cocaine were sold over the counter, with no clue on their labelling as to their addictive contents. Unscrupulous travelling 'medicine men' were hawking horse liniment as a cancer cure and as ice was the only form of refrigeration, the essential ingredient in most products was preservative. Dr Wiley endeared himself to women everywhere when he spoke out on health and safety, particularly in respect of preservatives, which he considered particularly dangerous. He set up a 'poison squad' of young volunteers who sat down to dinners prepared from foods containing substances in daily use such as salicylic and benzoic acids and formaldehyde, the results of which were eulogies in the supportive press and fury from the manufacturers.

After bitter debate, his 1906 Act was finally passed, but sadly for women consumers, it failed to include cosmetics. Not particularly through Dr Wiley's choice. He had a deep mistrust of skin-care lotions in particular and several had to be re-labelled under the new Act, eliminating their most spurious claims. White lead – the highly toxic and dangerous ceruse – still widely used at the time, was banned. But the cosmetics industry in America then was so insignificant as to be virtually meaningless. Dr Wiley and his team had no idea what an explosion was about to take place. If they had, then maybe their 1906 Act might have been drafted in a different way. Experts then, however, were particularly uneasy about Benzoates. In 1909, a leading scientist wrote, 'the administration of benzoic acid, either as such or in the form of benzoate of soda, is highly objectionable and produces a very serious disturbance of the metabolic functions, attended with injury to digestion and health'.

Nearly a hundred years later, benzoic acid, sodium benzoate and related compounds – parabends – are still widely used in foods and cosmetics. They are called antimicrobial preservatives, which means they kill cells that might infect what we eat or put on our bodies. However, conclusive tests have shown they cause gastric irritation, hives and are a known asthma trigger. Because they dissolve in water or are soluble in oil, they are an invaluable tool for the cosmetics industry, which now has strict controls on potential microbe contamination. Dr Wiley would be a worried man.

In the 1930s, the weapon used to get consumers to part with their cash was advertising. Stories told by slick copywriters were often wildly inaccurate, with no legislation in place to stop them. Equally, unless cosmetics had medicinal claims, they were not subject to any Federal regulation. Congress had declined to take cosmetics seriously for three decades, largely ignoring the beauty phenomenon. Anxious consumer groups hoped this would now change, but by the time the new Act went to the floor in 1938, the additions were considered by many experts to be flawed. In respect of cosmetics, many felt it was a watered-down version of what had been lobbied for by those concerned with health and safety. It has remained in place, with only minor adjustments, particularly on listing contents, ever since. The Food and Drug Administration defines cosmetics as 'articles intended to be applied to the human body for cleansing, beautifying, promoting attractiveness or altering the appearance'. They define drugs as 'articles intended to cure, mitigate, treat or prevent disease and articles intended to affect the structure of any function of the body'. The mighty FDA is a powerful organisation, but they are 'only able to regulate cosmetics *after* products have been released on the marketplace. Neither products or ingredients are reviewed or approved *before* they are sold to the public'.* Apart from a short list of banned ingredients, including certain food dyes, there is

* FDA Centre for Food Safety & Applied Nutrition fact sheet. Italics, author's own.

no legislation in place to control what goes into cosmetics. Drugs, on the other hand, are rigorously controlled.

The book *Skin Deep* contained a questionnaire which thousands of consumers gladly returned. One woman, a teacher, wrote, 'I don't always keep regular hours and sometimes can't. I feel, in general, a mess. I buy Elizabeth Arden products and spend money out of all proportion to my salary. I don't really believe so much what saleswomen tell me as I *hope* that what they tell me will come true.' *Skin Deep* also explained what ingredients went into make-up. The list of chemicals, fixatives and compounds, with their potential allergenic effects, makes for uneasy reading. Women the world over however seem quite blasé about risk. Cosmetics throughout recorded time, just as in the 1930s and even more so today, have a compelling allure.

What did happen post-legislation, causing a furore in the Arden and Rubinstein boardrooms, was a series of strict rulings about what claims could be made on behalf of cosmetics and controls on what is stated on packaging – the crucial labelling and thus advertising – of cosmetics. What the 1938 Act meant in a nutshell was a flurry of name changes and some soul-searching in copywriting departments. Arden and Rubinstein were obliged by law to comply. Out went Elizabeth Arden's favourite cream, Orange Skin Food, not classified as a nutrient and forbidden as a name as cream cannot 'feed' the skin. She was livid, and started a barrage of correspondence with the FDA. One letter apparently enclosed a testimonial from a client saying her cook 'had mistakenly used my Orange Skin Food, always kept in the fridge, to ice a cake which the whole family enjoyed'. Elizabeth insisted all her products were nutritious and cited the case of a wealthy client who fed her dog with Velva Cream, insisting the pampered pooch was in marvellous health. The FDA refused to be moved by these entreaties and simply responded that it proved the product was largely composed of fats which would be harmless in small quantities.

Miss Arden knew when she was beaten. New labels were printed for every product, and although Helena Rubinstein had also responded by re-naming her Valaze Skin Food as Wake Up Cream, other products were deemed as incorrect and in 1937 when the Federal Trade Commission filed suits for malpractice against Yardley, Woodbury, Chanel, Richard Hudnut, Primrose House, Bourjois, Bristol-Myers and Helena Rubinstein, Elizabeth Arden remained unscathed.

To this day, the question of the safety content of cosmetic product rumbles on and even though, since 1977, principal ingredients are now listed on the exterior packaging in descending order of bulk content (which explains why the first item mentioned is often water), there is no requirement to list the breakdown of content of either fragrance or flavour. As there are over 1000 aromatic and perfume chemicals alone out of a total of 7000 chemicals used in cosmetics production, it's small wonder the consumer can become confused. Some facts speak for themselves. The value of the 'personal care' market in the US alone was, in 1996, calculated at $70 billion. The budget allocated to the investigation and supervision of the industry by the FDA is a tiny fraction of that. In 1984, when the 'personal care' market was valued at around $50 billion, the FDA Office of Cosmetics and Colours' budget was $2.5 million.

As recently as 1994 the FDA in America carried out a survey into allergies caused by cosmetics and toiletries; nearly one in four people claimed to have suffered an allergic reaction as a result of using a product. The same survey shows the public expect that a product labelled 'natural' should contain all natural ingredients. Nearly 50% of the people polled felt strongly on this issue. When asked if such products live up to their labelling claims, Dr John Bailey, director of the FDA's Office of Cosmetics and Colours admitted, 'Not necessarily. Image is what the cosmetics industry sells through its products and it's up to the consumer to believe the claims or not.'

Both Miss Arden and Madame would have agreed that 'image is what the cosmetics industry sells'. They each knew how important image was, especially since they were both so closely associated with their eponymous brands, and worked non-stop to promote their personal image in the style of their products. Madame's public relations campaigns focused on her as 'the queen of beauty science'. She was the 'international traveller', always finding some treasure for her beauty empire whilst moving around the world; the middle-European wizard of formulae, an international woman, a world-famous collector of art and antiques, and above all, a matriarchal, benevolent despot, 'strict' about beauty routines and 'strict' about business routines, but 'loved and admired' by her staff.

Helena's loving rapport with her employees is questionable. As the business at upper levels was so dominated by family members there was, recollects ex-employee Claude Forter, 'always a Rubinstein by blood, marriage or close association hovering in the wings. This caused internecine rivalries. There was great playing off of executives against one another and you always felt insecure working there.'

Madame practised the 'divide and conquer' method of management. She was particularly fond of trying to get her staff to send her critical memos about their associates, which she would then dangle as a weapon against their own management techniques. 'See what I've had to read about you. How can you two be expected to work together if you're squabbling like wild cats? Don't worry, leave it to me, I'll sort it out.' She never did sort it out, of course, rather left it hanging like the sword of Damocles, with the result that the executives never trusted each other again. But whatever her fractured relationships with family and executive staff, the difficulties rarely extended to the factory or retail sales workforce. Madame's rapport with those working 'at the coal face' was close. They admired her success and eccentricity and were inspired by her drive.

Miss Arden's staff by this time included a troupe of dancers, who toured with her making personal appearances in department stores as she launched her new lipstick palette. By the early 1930s, wearing make-up was firmly accepted at more or less every level of society, although *Vogue* still took the view that 'more make-up can be used for the eyes in the evening than in the day'. *Vogue* reminded its readers that 'nothing should of course be used for the eyes when in the country. A mere touch of rouge and above all, no vivid lipstick.'

'Vivid' meant red in dozens of shades. It took Miss Arden's lipstick colour palette, which she dubbed 'a wardrobe of lipsticks', to change perceptions. She introduced a kit of seven colours all promoted as 'toning with your clothes', giving them glamorous names like Coquette, Victoire or Carmencita. Miss Arden toured the stores, accompanied by her seven lithe and lovely ballerinas wearing Isadora Duncan-inspired costumes in muslin, dyed to match the lipstick colours. She rehearsed them in a routine, set up on a revolving mini-stage in beauty departments across the USA, to the music from the Gold and Silver Waltz, spotlit in pink.

The promotion was a spectacular success and Miss Arden brought it to Harrods in London in May 1932. 'Miss Elizabeth Arden will appear in person,' said the invitation ticket application form. 'Harrods, in collaboration with Elizabeth Arden, are presenting, for the only time in this country, a unique Beauty and Fashion exposition at 3.00 o'clock on May 3rd, 4th and 5th.' The invitation explained that 'the art of make-up and the art of dress are today inseparable'. Less than fifteen years earlier no lady would have shopped at Harrods even *wearing* make-up, never mind being able to buy it there.

To Elizabeth's annoyance, one of her favourite magazines, the *New Yorker*, failed to comment on her pet project. At that time, the beauty column, titled 'Lipstick', was written by ex-*Vogue* copywriter, Lois Long. Miss Long was fondly remembered by Carmel Snow who said, 'Lois joined us on *Vogue* in the 1920s. She had shingled hair, red lips and even wore nail polish!' Miss Long was clearly made for a career reporting on make-up, and her column was required reading. As the Arden company was an important advertiser, Elizabeth was furious to find 'Lipstick' ignored her lipstick promotion and demanded Henry Sell write to complain.

The advertising manager of the magazine was horrified that Sell was obliged to dangle the threat of removing advertising due to lack of editorial, knowing exactly what Miss Long's reaction would be. The beauty writer rose to the challenge, writing back to Henry:

> I'm not a quivering impressionable editorial flower, Henry. Possibly I have been neglectful of Arden, but if you, singlehanded, tried to cover the ground in three columns a week that twenty people on *Vogue* take a whole magazine to cover every two weeks, you wouldn't take time off to beg for more from anybody, however great. After seven years, the publicity department at Arden should know that anything new and good from them gets prior attention. I don't give a damn about Arden cancelling her advertising, but to get a letter like that from you — well it hurts.

Things eventually cooled down, but Arden's standing in the eyes of the *New Yorker* — not to mention her advertising agency — was diminished.

Miss Arden didn't care. She believed she was invincible. Her products were not merely designed to make you beautiful and keep you beautiful, they also *looked* beautiful, earning their place on the curtained dressing-table in the finest boudoirs. The 'world of Elizabeth Arden' was more feminine than *femme fatale*. It was also a world of wealth and status, of country leisure and refined city pleasure. The Arden vision of loveliness was the fragile, antebellum beauty with her pale face, large hats and ladylike manners. Rarely in the mix was the sultry vamp or what Madame Rubinstein described astutely as *jolie laide* — a French expression used to describe a woman of glowing personality rather than glorious beauty. Whilst Helena admired *jolie laide*, Elizabeth's heroines were all perfect beauties.

Rubinstein's women were urban, edgy, glamorous, while Arden's classic beauties were more likely women who had inherited or married great wealth and spent time on their country estates and vacationed at the watering holes of the upper classes. She knew her market. The Arden salon at the Lyford Cay Club in Nassau, whilst only open during the winter season, was a runaway success.

Miss Arden was the first person to tap into the genre of 'lifestyle' promotion. It rippled through her advertisements, which included a sidebar column devoted to such topics as 'Tally Ho!', a feature about horses as hunters, explaining that 'a woman is at her best in the hunting field, because that is one of the oldest sports. The uniform suits her, the stock and hard hat isolate her lovely features.' One particularly successful campaign used an illustration of a woman dressage rider, a silk top hat with discreet veil framing her perfect profile, gloved hands holding reins and crop, riding sidesaddle. Would an Arden woman do anything else?

Engrossed with her reputation, and her battles with Madame Rubinstein, Elizabeth Arden probably missed a small, ninth-of-a-page advertisement placed in the *New Yorker* in July 1935, and her staff would have been too nervous to draw it to her attention. At that time there were too few people at Elizabeth Arden Inc who had the courage to talk openly to her about competition or new trends, other than those Miss Arden deemed appropriate. The newest trend at the time was nail polish – one Miss Arden deemed deeply inappropriate. The boxed advertisement said: 'Sun Rose and Chestnut – the new exciting exclusive shades for summer. Originated by a New York socialite. Produced for her by the House of Revlon. Now available at Saks 5th Avenue and better beauty salons. Ask your manicurist.' The end-line address was 'Revlon Nail Enamel Corporation, 15 West 44th Street'.

The staff at West 44th St, in cramped, hot offices, pouring polish from large containers into small bottles, would have been surprised to hear their bare, bleak walls described as 'the House of Revlon'. Anyone close to Charles Revson, the man who conjured up the words, would have been astonished to think he might know a 'New York socialite' (he didn't) and readers of the advertisement, had they known about such things as budgets, would have been surprised, given the confidence of the words, to know that the $335.56 spent on that space was the total of Revlon's consumer advertising budget for that year. It is doubtful that Revlon nail polish was sold at

Saks, although as Revson well knew, the store operated a policy that if customers requested a specific product, they would buy it in. The advertisement was almost certainly positioned to create that demand.

Madame and Miss Arden ignored Charles Revson at their peril. They were so busy battling between themselves, they took their eyes off the competition. They disregarded him because he didn't make face creams. He didn't even make make-up. The Revlon company wasn't making *any* product they made at that time. Revlon only produced nail polish. But Charles Revson was hungry; he was a man in a hurry to make his name and his fortune. He was also singleminded, driven and the most devious and dangerous competitor the two women would ever have. He was in the 1930s as ahead of his time as they had been in 1910. Neither woman noticed.

Had Madame taken a little time out of her schedule to visit her old friend 'Flame' d'Erlanger, living in Venice in a rambling house called Villa Malcontenta with her amour of the moment, Bertie Landsberg, she might have beaten Revson at his own game. Amongst the myriad d'Erlanger houseguests was Diana Vreeland who then lived in London with her husband, Reed. The incomparable Mrs Vreeland – later fashion editor of *Harper's Bazaar* and subsequently editor of *Vogue* – became close to a friend of Flame's, simply called Perrera, who dabbled in investments, but whose greatest love was giving manicures. Perrera subsequently settled in Paris, becoming visiting nail-meister to the great and good of the fashion world as they assembled for the collections. Invariably accompanied by fashion artist Bébé Bérard who, having a penchant for observing his friend layer on the lacquer, acted as his assistant, Perrera would arrive for appointments carrying his fitted vanity case, complete with solid gold instruments, a gift from a devoted client, Queen Ina of Spain. Perrera's polish was made to a special formula which he alone knew, drying almost instantly to a rock-hard finish. From time to time he would give some to friends, and when Mrs Vreeland returned to New York in the late 1930s, she took two bottles with her.

The polish so impressed Mrs Vreeland's manicurist that she offered to have her boyfriend take a look at it. 'I think I can get him to copy it,' said the manicurist. 'Really,' replied la Vreeland. 'Who's the boyfriend?' 'Charles Revson,' came the reply. The Revlon range by this time had a great colour palette and a reputation for not chipping but, as Mrs Vreeland recollected, 'it took hours to dry and had no staying power'. She remained convinced that 'Revson studied Perrera's formula and evolved a product that dried faster than anything anyone had ever used in America', later writing: 'He became the biggest – the *most* – today the great varnish of the world that covers the *waterfront* is Revlon. Curiously enough, whenever I saw him, there was always something in Charles Revson's eye . . . I always knew that *he* knew that I knew that he had made this incredible fortune off one small bottle of mine, with maybe *this* much left in it.' Domination in the nail polish market remained the fiefdom of Charles Revson thereafter.

In the spring of 1935, Madame, much to her pleasure, was invited to exhibit the crème of her African art collection at New York's Museum of Modern Art, giving her the opportunity to show devotees of the genre just how skilled a collector she had become. MoMA's ground-breaking exhibition, 'African Negro Art', included seventeen of her key pieces and Madame was in her element. At the end of the exhibition she took her collection on tour across America, and at every opportunity posed with a work, explaining her passion for them. 'Today, Negro sculptures are no longer regarded as comic, grotesque or repellent beginnings of art. They are recognised as having a true aesthetic value and a peculiar beauty all of their own, entirely different, but no less interesting than the more conventional, long-accepted standards of Greek sculptural beauty,' ran her press release.

Miss Arden would have found the carvings grotesque, and no doubt shuddered at the publicity Madame Rubinstein got, particularly on her visit to Hollywood where she was pictured alongside Mae West and other stars. The cinema held a fixation for Elizabeth, so when an opportunity to develop a specialist range of cosmetics for film use was mooted, she took it enthusiastically, launching the project with her own visit to Hollywood just weeks after Helena's. Who lobbied Miss Arden to enter such a specialist market – one, after all, already dominated with great professionalism by the Max Factor corporation – isn't clear. One view is that it was the racing millionaire Jock Whitney, a major investor in Hollywood who knew Elizabeth from the racing circuit. It's possible it was Hedda Hopper, but it's more likely that her lawyer J. Robert Rubin, with his involvement at MGM, was the guiding hand. As usual with any new project, she waxed lyrical and invested heavily. And as usual with many of her pet projects, it was ill-thought-out, costly, and quietly folded.

The foray into film make-up started in March 1935 and she called the new division 'Stage and Screen'. She made energetic plans for the range, seemingly oblivious to the fact that Max Factor was the übermeister in the field. In December, Factor opened his cosmetics factory and 'beauty studio' in Hollywood – said to have cost over $600,000 – with a glittering party. He didn't have celebrities on his list – he had *stars*. Jean Harlow posed in the 'Blonde room' and Claudette Colbert in the 'Brunette'. Raspberry pink and chartreuse lighting swept into the sky above Factor's faux Greco-Roman shrine to glamour, and if guests were bored they could look at his display of cosmetics ingredients, cleverly displayed in little heaps, captioned with their Latin names as though in a pharmacy.

Supreme leader in the film niche, Factor, by now sixty-one, had come a long way since he left school in Russia to become an apprentice make-up boy and wigmaker with a travelling opera company. His powerful endorsements from movie beauties boosted his wholesale activities, and by 1936 the Max Factor company was reported to be the leading commercial cosmetics corporation in the USA, its reputation built on the association with Hollywood glamour. Whilst Elizabeth Arden dominated the market with her own top-end, luxury product, pitched against Factor, her Stage and Screen line never stood a chance.

Max Factor, like Helena Rubinstein, believed in employing the family and had four sons on the payroll. Davis ran the London office, Frank the USA chemical laboratory, Louis was the American factory superintendent and Sidney, the youngest, was studying science and chemistry in California ready to join the firm. One son-in-law, Bernard, was make-up adviser, whilst another, Max, was hair and wig adviser. Even Factor's stepbrother, nicknamed 'Jake the barber' was on the team, although whether Jake, who would go on to be arrested on fraud charges and was rumoured to be part of an organised crime syndicate, was a positive asset is debatable. Sadly, no mention of Factor's daughters or daughters-in-law appeared on company records. The Max Factor business didn't factor women in to their professional equation.

By early 1936, Miss Arden expected all satellite countries handling her distribution to wholesale Stage and Screen products and persuade retailers to display them next to their Arden counters. For a retailer to devote prime floor-space to a top selling name like Arden is one thing, but to extend that space, even if it meant getting a paid Arden demonstrator for the range, on an untried product line was a tough challenge for the sales team to negotiate. Elizabeth wrote to Teddy: 'We don't seem to be making any money on the venture yet, but we are getting wonderful publicity and it is so nice to have all those lovely actresses using our make-up. What a wonderful thing to have Mr Korda use it!'

Elizabeth didn't mean that the distinguished film producer Alexander Korda had taken to wearing lipstick, merely that he had used the range in a production, for which Arden had received a credit. She went on enthusiastically, 'The $1 lip-liner should have a good market . . . it's absolutely perfect! The Foundations, Eye Shad-O and Mascara should also sell well. I don't think the stores should have very much powder, it's better to use our own as the "Screen" one is too heavy for ordinary use.' The Arden corporation took advertising space in glossy titles to promote the new line, but even with Elizabeth's most experienced sales manager 'Duke' Cross, himself an ex-Vaudeville star, in charge, the venture never took off and she closed the company down a mere two years later.

The lure of show business, however, ran deep in Elizabeth's veins. 'Talkies' had tentatively started in 1926, but by 1929 Hollywood was totally converted and by the mid-thirties hardly anyone could remember the silent stars at all. Earlier forays into elocution not having been successful, her close friend Constance Collier, whom she had met at Bessie's, gave Elizabeth extensive voice-coaching lessons. The famous, if slightly fading, actress, known for her bi-sexual proclivities, was charging $100 an hour for her services, so it was an expensive exercise. The main reason she required coaching was to prepare for her Elizabeth Arden Radio Show. This was aired via CBS and had been the subject of bitter recrimination between Elizabeth and Henry Sell. Indeed it caused such a rift between them that Sell resigned the Arden advertising account – albeit on a temporary basis – in an attempt to prove his point.

Radio, launched in America in the early 1920s, had always had a fascination for Elizabeth. In 1927, when radio advertising was launched in the USA, the cosmetics industry invested $300,000 in buying air time. By 1930, it had grown to $3,500,000. When a voice enthusiastically announced that the 'show tonight is brought to you by so-and-so, the makers of America's finest soap/soup/sandwich filling', it was considered seminal product placement, about which agencies waxed lyrical to clients.

Agencies, that is, except Henry Sell's Blaker Agency, who bravely told their client, Elizabeth Arden, the truth. Radio was not for her because it was a medium for the middle and mass market. It was not, nor could be in the foreseeable future, the right vehicle for a tactile, luxury product like hers. She didn't listen. Sell managed to persuade her out of a very expensive thirteen-week contract with NBC and the Ritz-Carlton Hotel dance orchestra, but was obliged to find her another network and she took a contract with CBS, involving a shot on 'her' show read out by the king of the gossip columns, Maury Paul. Now Mr Paul may have been a tiger in print but he was a kitten in front of a microphone and according to witnesses in the studio suffered severe 'mike fright'. The fault wasn't entirely his. Paul's sources, often gleaned through the homosexual circuit, were impeccable. Apparently he would be poised to tell eager listeners the latest 'inside track' on a leading society beauty when Elizabeth would shriek, 'You can't say that, she's a *wonderful* client of mine!' Maury Paul was consequently reduced to a hasty rewrite, seconds before going on air. Small wonder his refreshment on set was dyspepsia tablets.

Elizabeth, on the other hand, appeared to be in seventh heaven, directing everything, confusing and disturbing everyone – and then blaming everything and everyone except herself when it all went wrong. The Elizabeth Arden show went out with Eddy Duchin's orchestra and Elizabeth personally covered a certain topic, the script having usually been re-written four or five times before she was satisfied. In her heart of hearts she knew she had made a mistake, telling Teddy Haslam in London, 'It is a little early to judge the radio results. It seems to me that Eddy Duchin is getting all the publicity and I do not know just what to do about it. We are working hard trying to get a program arranged so that it will be more Elizabeth Arden. Frankly, Teddy, we are now doing the experimentation that should have been done before we went into radio and it is such a shame . . .'

As Elizabeth's dabble with radio is reputed to have cost her over $200,000, and no experimentation was ever planned for the simple reason that her advisers had never planned for radio, it is perhaps Elizabeth who should have felt shame. The contract was not renewed. Sell withdrew from his contract too, following a telephone conversation with his client so verbally abusive it left him feeling 'quite weak'. Elizabeth was left more alone than ever. No Tommy, no Bessie, and now no Henry Sell, not to mention no further support from Maury Paul. As usual, she took consolation in her horses.

As her passion for racehorses developed, horseriding started to influence Arden advertising. After struggles to develop her own branded fragrances, Elizabeth finally hit bull's-eye, courtesy of sister Gladys. In 1936, Gladys found a charming scent at Fragonard, the French perfume house. Instinctively knowing Elizabeth would adore it, she took a provisional exclusivity agreement, which was eagerly confirmed as a formal licence by Elizabeth as soon as she could complete the paperwork. With her innate gift for marketing, Elizabeth insisted on calling her new treasure Blue Grass. Her sales managers were horrified, advising her that women would shy away from any fragrance associated with horses and stables, Kentucky Hills or not. Elizabeth, quite rightly, ignored them.

Launched in 1936, with advertising and packaging designed by Remisoff, Blue Grass was a phenomenal success, in its milky-blue bottles and boxes containing fragrance, eau de toilette, dusting powder, bath essence and scented soap cloths for travelling. Blue Grass, a floral scent with hints of lavender, orange flower, clove and nutmeg, dominated the fragrance market for over twenty-five years, and some sixty years after its launch is still available.

Blue Grass came at an opportune moment for Miss Arden, whose company finances were under strain. This was not a recession- or depression-led drop, although the value of Elizabeth's own stock portfolio was gloomy, but largely due to her lavish corporate and personal extravagance. Elizabeth's view that you had to spend money to make it was the right one; but she was spending money faster than she was earning it. In early 1936 following an investigation by the IRS into her corporate *v* personal taxes, she also discovered to her shock and chagrin that her company money wasn't necessarily her *own* money, something Elizabeth simply couldn't seem to understand. She wrote to Teddy in London explaining she 'had to find $100,000 by the spring to settle taxes'. Various ways were mooted to find the cash, including delaying the purchase of an essential new British factory – not an idea that appealed to the ambitious Mr Haslam, whose salary and benefits package was boosted by a performance-related bonus.

Britain was a major profit centre for the Arden company where the wealthy, largely upper-class women who frequented the Bond Street salon and who bought the product range at Harrods and smart outposts like Browns of Chester or Jenners in Edinburgh, created a comfortable market. It also created a comfortable standard of living for Arden's British managing director. Mr Haslam lived an elegant life, with a home in Harrow-on-the-Hill, a company car and chauffeur, and a working day that finished, in the style of the era, promptly at 5.00 p.m. The rigours of business were punctuated with luncheon at the Ritz, Claridges or the Connaught, all a gentle stroll from his Grosvenor Street offices, whilst essential trips to Paris, other European capitals, and beach resorts, to oversee salons, made an appealing travel schedule.

Travel to New York was always first class, with the Arden company favouring the Cunard Line. Poised to sail on the *Queen Mary*'s inaugural trip to London, Miss Arden cancelled in order to see one of her horses racing, catching up with the ship later that year. In Britain, as her racing stables gained increasing corporate as well as social importance, days out at Cheltenham, Doncaster, York and Ascot were part of Mr Haslam's working schedule, as were dealings with owners and trainers. The wives of these men, the elite of British racing, were all naturally encouraged to become Arden clients and were assured a cosseted welcome at Bond Street.

With the economic down-turn in Britain, increased domestic production was becoming a key factor to maintaining profit ratios, particularly since the British government had imposed the 'Abnormal Importations Bill' in 1931, adding 100% duty to certain imports. There had been a concerted government effort to encourage the public to buy British and the politicians harnessed the Prince of Wales to their cause, inviting him to make a radio broadcast pleading on behalf the 'Buy British' campaign. Teddy Haslam, who had virtually autonomous control over his territories, eventually got his way. Despite Miss Arden's panic, he succeeded in persuading her to purchase a factory in Acton, south west London, which was opened in 1937 and remained one of the principal European production centres for the company until it was closed in 2001.

Other suggestions the cash-strapped Elizabeth made to cover her looming tax bill included buying silver in England and jewels in Germany, although Teddy informed her 'family jewellery in Germany, i.e. diamonds with old gold mounting, has been looked at on your behalf, but others have had the same thought and the market has been swept.' Miss Arden visited Berlin in 1930, 1932, 1933 and 1936, her trip that year planned to coincide with the Olympics and to celebrate the opening of the Elizabeth Arden factory in Berlin. It was not the easiest of times to be running an international business in Germany. Back in 1933, a shiver of unease was rippling through Europe, centred on Berlin, where the Imperial and Nazi flags were flying side by side. Air Minister Hermann Goering may have been denying Germany's Jews were in any danger, but a boycott was issued against Jewish shops and businesses.

By 1936 it was clear events were running out of control and Elizabeth was starting to panic. 'I hear what you say, Teddy, about the decrease in unemployment in England,' she wrote, 'and it sounds encouraging until you stop to think that these people are being employed to make gunpowder to blow us all up! The whole European situation has me very worried.' The business of beauty, however, continued apace and not unsurprisingly, the Nazi Party High Command favoured the Elizabeth Arden salon, with Goering himself one of their best customers, buying dozens and dozens of boxed gift sets each Christmas.

Whether she was fully aware of the implications of events at that time we will never know. It's doubtful the move for compulsory sterilisation for disabled groups was dinner-party conversation on her visits to Berlin, likewise the fact that the intellectual and artistic elite of Germany, many of them Jewish, were being systematically removed from their posts and replaced with people who met with Nazi approval. It's also quite possible that the burning of books passed her by. Equally, the opening of Dachau and the plans announced in 1934 for a women's concentration camp at Ravensbruck may have seemed unimportant to her at the time – little realising that ten years later her own sister would be a prisoner there.

Along with many industrialists and British and American business leaders, all in dread of the rise of Communism, Elizabeth was quite impressed with overall activity and business efficiency in Germany. She was less impressed following a dinner in Berlin hosted in her honour by Air Marshal Goering and his wife. Having lectured him on the pitfalls of being overweight – apparently prodding his bulging stomach to make her point – she suggested an exercise regime. Goering took her advice and dispatched an official the next day to requisition an expensive exercise bicycle from her Berlin salon and had it set up in his office. Not quite what she had in mind. At any event, Teddy Haslam told her that 'Marks will soon be worth very little and property will be a useful investment', advising her to buy more property in Berlin.

Nowhere in Elizabeth's cost-cutting strategies did economies include cutting back on buying bloodstock. By now she had horse barns established at Saratoga and Belmont, the racetrack just outside New York. She had already hired and fired three trainers as none of 'her babies' had yet won a major race. In Elizabeth's mind, this was always the fault of the trainer, never of her horse. She rented a cottage at Belmont and another beautiful home at Saratoga, commuting to both by chauffeured Bentley, dictating to her secretary throughout the journey, with her cook and butler travelling ahead to get the properties ready for guests. 'I'm giving a beautiful lawn-party next Saturday and how I wish you and Budgey could be with us,' she wrote to Teddy in London. 'Saratoga is really a beautiful place and every-one has been so kind and wonderful that I did want you to share it with me.' The effect of this theoretical largesse was somewhat spoiled when in the same letter she said, 'I am so anxious to economise in every way possible. Spain, it seems to me, is such a bad indication of conditions in general and we must be particularly careful and conservative at this time. Just take in all the money we can and spend as little as possible . . . that's the rule we must follow!'

Fortuitously for Elizabeth, a second moneyspinner was poised to be unleashed onto the product line. Her loyal chemist, Mr Swanson, with over twenty years of service, came up with one of her all-time bestsellers – Eight Hour Cream. Described as an 'all-purpose beauty balm' the soft, glistening cream was reputed to have healing properties, so much so that Miss Arden insisted it be rubbed onto her horses' legs, so legend has it, to treat their bruises. Eight Hour Cream was definitely used at the Maine Chance stables, but it wouldn't have healed bruises. The knowledgeable Miss Arden used arnica for that.

Looking at the content of the emollient, still a top seller, is an interest-ing exercise. It contains petrolatum (a heavy oil extracted from petroleum), lanolin (sheep wool fat), paraffinum liquidum (liquid paraffin mineral oil), salicylic acid (a beta-hydroxy acid-BHA), tocopheral (vitamin E, an antiox-idant), BHT (E321, butylated hydroxy toluene, a synthetic antioxidant), zea mays (corn oil, a good emollient and solvent), ricinus communis (castor oil), propylparaben (a common cosmetic preservative for the oily components in preparations and a synthetic compound of the benzoate family) and some fra-grance and colourings, Cl 77491 and Cl 77492.

What it all adds up to is a very rich, yet light mixture that has exfoliat-ing properties, will soothe rough skin and help the healing process via the vitamin E. Eight Hour Cream not only made a welcome fortune for Miss Arden, its popularity to this day is a legend in the beauty business.

Despite the industry weathering the Depression better than most, during the 1930s the mainstream cosmetics and perfume sector was slow compared to the previous booming decade. Boris Forter, who ran Rubinstein's British company for nearly thirty years, was working in New York for Houbigant when the Depression took hold. He recollected that 'the business lived on deals. They sold lower and lower, some trading down instead of up. Some firms, like Bourjois, just disappeared in the US. Buyers wanted a deal. One box of powder meant a free lipstick. Selling then was a "gift with purchase" in reverse.'

For those firms who had the courage not to panic or compromise – Arden being one of them – sell-through at retail was still strong. Cosmetics, particularly make-up, have long been recognised as virtually recession-proof and encouragingly, sales of lipsticks and ornate powder compacts were buoyant. It was a time of opportunity or, in the case of an ailing business, of diversification. Not all luxury products survived, however, and one person suffering was Condé Nast, whose health eventually went the way of his wealth. *Vanity Fair* became a victim, although Condé Nast attempted to save the title by turning it into a magazine devoted solely to the beauty business, the company code name, aptly enough, being 'Arden'. It never got off the ground and *Vanity Fair* folded in 1936.

Germaine Monteil, a Frenchwoman living in New York where she ran a fashion company, diverted into cosmetics. Monteil and her husband had run into union problems with their small luxury clothing business. Boris Forter, who joined the firm in 1936, said, 'The workers in the dress business at that time had a powerful union and they could ruin you. They frightened the Monteil managers out of their wits because they didn't use union labour for her expensive line'. Cosmetics production being virtually outside the unions, the Monteil range, which only sold to specialist outlets, prospered and subsequently sold out to British American Tobacco for a sum large enough to finance a comfortable retirement for Madame Monteil in the South of France.

Members of the Arden elite staff in Europe also enjoyed themselves in the South of France, Biarritz in particular holding a special place in the upper echelons of vacation chic. *Harper's Bazaar* dubbed the town 'little Paris' and Molyneux, Vionnet, Lanvin, Hermes and Chanel all had branches there. These speciality shops sold resort wear to the rich and glamorous visitors, for whom protection against sunburn was becoming a major issue, almost as important as their wardrobes.

Never to be seen with a tan themselves, shuddering at exposing their skin to the sun, both Madame and Miss Arden witnessed the beach boom of the twenties and thirties at first hand and took their clients' cult of sun-worship very seriously. Each developed a moneyspinning range of products to capitalise on the trend, pouring considerable time, expertise and investment into the new market niche. Both took extensive advertisements in French *Vogue*. 'Neither wind nor sunrays will alter the purity and brilliance of your complexion,' said Arden's, 'sunscreen against sunburn and suntan oil ensure that your bronzed skin remains supple and retains its finesse.' Arden marketed Protectacream, a waterproof sunscreen 'whose virtues will fight against the disgrace of red patches even when you swim'. She launched Elizabeth Arden's Sunburn Cream and suggested using her Eight Hour Cream against sunburn and 'for when you have been imprudent'. The finishing touch was Elizabeth Arden's 'sun-bronzing cover makeup'. Rubinstein's offerings included Helena Rubinstein Sunproof Cream, Valaze Sunburn Oil, Crème Pasteurisée for 'wind-chapped skin', a range of foundation creams tinted for suntans including Terracotta, Tonique Solaire and Crème Solaire, and her Paris salon offered a solarium for pre-tanning.

The dangers of over-exposure to the sun were well known by the medical profession in the 1930s. In 1933, Professor Jansion of the Val de Grace Hospital in Paris issued a statement explaining that too much sun often resulted in skin cancer, particularly the variety long familiar to medical experts, found among fishermen and farmers. Beauty experts acknowledged care should be taken, advising people to tan gently and slowly, but the desire to tan often outweighed prudence. When Consumers Research Inc sent a variety of suntan treatment creams and oils for laboratory testing, their results showed that Elizabeth Arden's Sunburn Cream was amongst the most effective and that Helena Rubinstein's Sunproof Cream offered 'fair protection', whilst her Valaze Sunburn Oil was deemed 'very ineffective in screening out the light'.

Miss Arden and Madame were united in their distaste for the sun. Helena rarely took holidays, other than time out at her favoured spas, and if Elizabeth needed rest and relaxation, from 1934 she had the perfect place to go for it – her own health resort, Maine Chance.

The flat-fronted façade of the Helena
Rubinstein Salon at 715 Fifth Avenue which
opened in 1937 to great architectural
acclaim. The lower-case lettering was much
admired

Miss Arden cared little for architectural
acclaim, but believed totally in brand
recognition. Her bright-red lacquered doors
became part of her signature logo and were
used at every salon around the world. She's
photographed here, wearing silver lamé and
mink, outside the red door of her latest
salon on Fifth Avenue in 1929

Elizabeth Arden painted by Augustus John, *circa* 1930, at the suggestion of Bessie Marbury. She didn't care for the first portrait, so insisted on a second one – she didn't like that one much either!

Madame Rubinstein, however, adored having her portrait painted. This one is by Marie Laurencin, showing Helena as an Indian Maharani, wearing pearls and emeralds

Miss Arden on the cover of *Time* magazine, 6 May 1946. The prestigious magazine ran a major feature interview on her, titled 'A Queen Rules the Sport of Kings', devoting almost as much copy to her horse-racing career as her beauty empire

Helena posed for Salvador Dali in New York during World War II chained to a rock by her ropes of emeralds. Dali became a close friend and painted a series of murals for what he called the 'dream room' at Madame's Park Avenue penthouse

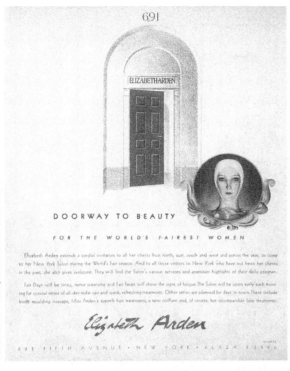

691

ELIZABETH ARDEN

DOORWAY TO BEAUTY

FOR THE WORLD'S FAIREST WOMEN

Elizabeth Arden extends a cordial invitation to all her clients from north, east, south and west and across the seas, to come to her New York Salon during the World's Fair season. And to all those visitors to New York who have not been her clients in the past, she also gives welcome. They will find the Salon's various services and amenities highlights of their daily program.

Fair Days will be tiring, nerve wearying and Fair faces will show the signs of fatigue. The Salon will be open early each morning for special series of all-day make-ups and quick, refreshing treatments. Other series are planned for days in-town. These include bodily moulding massage, Miss Arden's superb hair treatments, a new coiffure and, of course, her incomparable face treatments.

Elizabeth Arden

691 FIFTH AVENUE • NEW YORK • PLAZA 3-1940

Miss Arden's 'Doorway to Beauty' campaign ran in glossy magazines around the world. This version is from American *Vogue*, May 1939, and includes the famous Baron de Meyer photograph of Vionnet's favourite model Roberta, bandage-wrapped in white gauze. Miss Arden adored this image of virginal, faintly medicinal beauty, originally photographed in 1929, and ran the picture in various formats for almost two decades

Montezuma Red

Elizabeth Arden's newest lipstick colour — Montezuma Red . . . inspired by the brave, true red of the hat cord, scarf and chevrons of the Women in the Marines.

A vivid red to wear with black, white, gray, beige, navy and tweeds. A tribute to some of the bravest men and women in the world.

Free a Marine to Fight! Share the great traditions of the Marines. Join the U.S. Marine Corps Women's Reserve

Miss Arden was full of patriotic fervour in World War II and created a lipstick for the US Marine Corps Women's Reserve, advertising it extensively. Used in *Vogue*, April 1944, the copy said 'Elizabeth Arden's newest lipstick colour – "Montezuma Red" . . . inspired by the brave, true red of the chevrons of the women of America in the Marines . . . a tribute to some of the bravest men and women in the world'

Horses were taken as a theme throughout several major campaigns over three decades. This sleek and slick image for 'Saratoga Red', a new lipstick colour, was used in *Harper's Bazaar* in 1963

Brighten Lips and Fingertips

RADIANT PEONY, new Fall color . . . deep, dark and exciting. Crimson petals set against town blacks, fuchsias, purples, royal blues and hunter green. Wear Elizabeth Arden lipstick shades constantly. Love them every minute because they make people aware of the woman, not the make-up. Know these lipstick shades hold clear and fast . . . the lipstick is firm enough to define the shape of the mouth, soft enough to smooth on evenly . . . the brilliant nail polish matches . . . lasts indefinitely. All lipsticks are made under the personal supervision of Miss Arden for texture and high fashion color.

Lipsticks, 1.00 and 1.50; refills, .75 and 1.00 (plus taxes)

Elizabeth Arden

Czech-born fashion illustrator René 'R.R' Bouché was one of the most acclaimed illustrators of his era, earning admiration for his fashion drawings for French *Vogue*. When war was declared, Bouché joined the French army, was arrested by the Gestapo, but escaped and made his way to New York, where he became one of American *Vogue*'s most popular contributors. He was Miss Arden's favourite illustrator – his genteel, delicate style being used for several of her advertisements during the 1940s and '50s. This image was to launch a lipstick and nail polish called 'Radiant Peony'

Her lips are like a Red Red Rose

red coral...vivid, outdoor red
cochinelle...exotic, American Beauty
apple red...gay, bright, true-red
red velvet...deep, royal red
red raspberry...conservative red
orchid red...purplish, blue-red

Dewy
Fresh
Lasting
Bloom
Smooth
Protective
Texture
Fashion
Petal
Fragrant
Flower
Flurried

Lipsticks, .75, 1.00, 1.25.
Refills for your favorite case, .60, .75.
At leading stores everywhere. plus taxes

Helena Rubinstein

Meanwhile, Madame Rubinstein was also using flowers as a theme, and illustrating advertisements with, it must be said, slightly less élan than that achieved by René Bouché. Her advertising also had to work harder – this image for 'Red, Red Rose' featured six shades of red lipstick in one advertisement

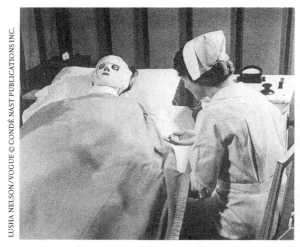

No, it's not plastic surgery, it's beauty salon treatments – Vienna Face Mask treatment at Elizabeth Arden, New York, in April 1937

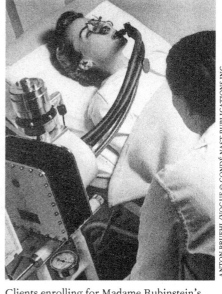

Clients enrolling for Madame Rubinstein's 'Day of Beauty' had their metabolic rate tested by the in-house doctor before they were given their diet plans

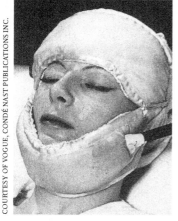

Face and chin being warmed with electric current pads wrapped in satin which begin the 'Firmo-Lift' treatment at Elizabeth Arden's Salon in New York, May 1939

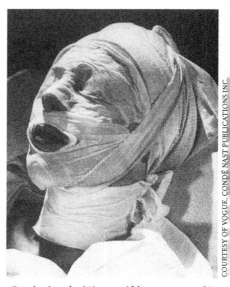

Continuing the 'Firmo-Lift' treatment, gel is applied and the face and neck are pressure-bandaged for half an hour

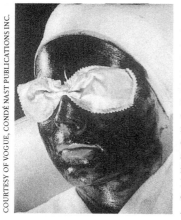

Helena Rubinstein's 'Pomade Noir' masque treatment, designed to 'firm the contours', in New York, March 1939. Each face masque treatment took at least one hour and 'hot' masques involved electric current. If a salon feature appeared in a January issue of a magazine on Rubinstein, by March, one appeared about Arden . . . and vice versa

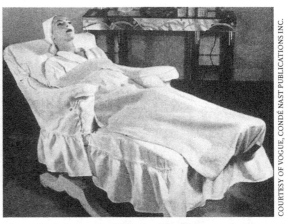

Rest and relaxation at Elizabeth Arden's New York Salon following a 'Firmo-Lift' treatment in 1939. The beds had special lifts under the knees to aid circulation

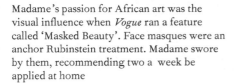

Madame's passion for African art was the visual influence when *Vogue* ran a feature called 'Masked Beauty'. Face masques were an anchor Rubinstein treatment. Madame swore by them, recommending two a week be applied at home

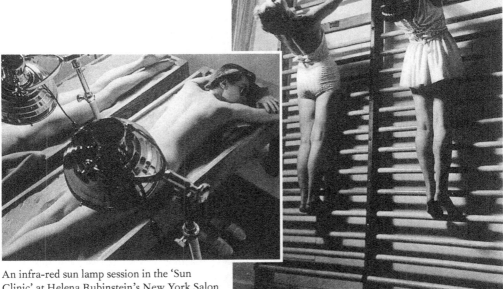

An infra-red sun lamp session in the 'Sun Clinic' at Helena Rubinstein's New York Salon in 1937. Clients stretched out on sun-loungers lying on real sand, heated by ultraviolet recessed ceiling lamps which 'bounced' back rays from an aluminium surface. An even, all-over suntan was guaranteed

The gymnastic bars at Helena Rubinstein's New York Salon in 1937. Clients were put through their stretching paces for half an hour at a time — skirted play-suits provided

THE DENVER DRY GOODS CO.
DENVER, COLORADO.

An in-store Elizabeth Arden product counter at The Denver Dry Goods Company, Denver, Colorado, *circa* 1935. Each counter was staffed by Arden-trained sales girls, who wore pink silk smocks and a big smile

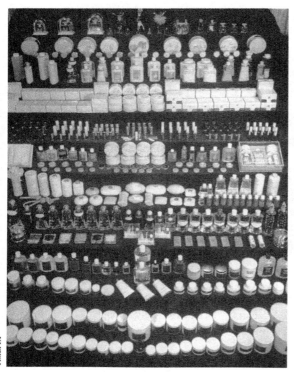

A Helena Rubinstein product display case, as used in their wholesale showrooms, *circa* 1938. Modified display cases would be provided to stockists such as local pharmacies and drug-stores, without the full counter space found in department stores

CHAPTER FOURTEEN

MAINE CHANCE AND MAKEOVERS
New York, London, Paris
1935–1939

AFTER BESSIE'S DEATH, ELIZABETH'S two properties in Maine held little attraction for her. As the estate was beautiful and, in Elizabeth's eyes, lent itself perfectly to rest and relaxation, she simply added 'reducing' to the equation and turned it into a business venture. There were several, mainly quite spartan, spas in America at that time but nothing to compare with the sybaritic charms of Maine Chance, America's first luxury health and beauty farm. Elizabeth poured energy and cash into the project, hiring Rue Carpenter to oversee the decoration, building guest cottages, landscaping the grounds, fitting steam rooms, exercise rooms, sound-proofed treatment rooms, vast kitchens and a sprung-floor dance studio. A beautiful swimming pool with cabanas and changing rooms with striped green-and-white canvas awnings was installed. She bought a teakwood motor launch and charming wicker hooded sunloungers. Butlers in formal dress would deliver fruit juices to guests taking the afternoon sun, serving them from solid silver salvers.

Maine Chance had a soft opening in the summer of 1934, when Elizabeth held a Democratic rally in Bessie's memory, bringing up her VIP guests by private rail car from New York and offering a choice of menus including her famous 'light diet' devised by Gaylord Hauser. Hauser's menus were so mouth-watering, it's hard to believe anyone went hungry.

One essential was that clients drank a pint of freshly made vegetable juice – usually 75% cabbage and 25% celery, both good diuretics. His famous 'Hauser broth' was made by adding a cup of celery, including leaves, a cup of shred-ded carrot, half a cup of spinach, some shredded parsley, a teaspoon of vegetable salt, a cup of tomato juice and a spoonful of honey to a quart of water. Clients who were seriously overweight fasted on this broth and the vegetable juice for a week with spectacular results.

There were forty staff on the payroll including six gardeners, a boatman, a dance instructor, riding instructor, fencing master, tennis coach and endless beauticians and masseuses. Exercise regimes were, as usual, under the direction of Anne Delafield who installed 'body-slant boards' in every bedroom. These tilting benches kept the head lower than the feet; two fifteen-minute sessions each day were recommended for lymphatic drainage and improved circulation. Clients had sitz baths, colonic irrigation, Ardena wax baths, skin exfoliation with organic oils and pumice spatulas, steam baths, seaweed baths and deep tissue massage amongst a host of treatments. A dentist was on site to advise on extractions and gum disease, Miss Arden sharing Hauser's belief that serious health problems, headache, sinus, blood disorders and toxic allergy were all attributable to bad teeth. She was obsessed with dentistry, visiting her practice monthly.

The twenty clients at Maine Chance had breakfast in bed on a beautifully laid tray: a pink linen napkin, bone china floral teacup – no tea, just hot water and lemon – half a grapefruit with a spoonful of blackstrap molasses, a small slice of wholewheat toast and honey, no butter. An old-fashioned rose cut from the flower gardens, placed in a crystal vase, adorned each tray. 'The poor dears get so little to eat I just had to make it all look lovely,' said Miss Arden. They were actually very rich dears, each paying a staggering $500 a week. They spent the morning having health treatments and the afternoon having beauty treatments, hairdressing, outdoor sports and deportment sessions. Synchronised stretch classes using tambourines to keep time, workouts with hoops and yoga, were held on the lake shore. Dinner, although light, looked even lovelier and was the moment for guests, who had spent the day in their uniform of Grecian-style exercise skirts and jersey vest tops, or towelling wrap tops and shorts, to bring out their jewels. Dressing formally for dinner at Maine Chance was compulsory. A pianist would entertain the ladies while they sipped fruit punch cocktails and tables were set up for bridge or backgammon after dinner. It was like being in a five-star hotel.

Elizabeth kept the resort open from May to September each year. In 1935 she had her grand opening, with Gaylord Hauser in attendance signing copies of his latest book, *Here's How to be Healthy*. The opening was combined with Elizabeth's second, and last, rally for the Democrats. Incandescent with anger about her tax bills, by 1936 she had conveniently forgotten Bessie Marbury's lifelong devotion to the Democratic cause and was back where she belonged, supporting the Republicans.

Elizabeth's temper was more evident than ever during the mid-1930s; indeed her mood-swings appear to have been so extreme as to be almost abnormal. As anger is often the insulation we wrap around our pain, it's also true to say Elizabeth was hurting. Although surrounded by acquaintances, she was short on friends. She was lonely, and behind her bravura she missed Tommy Lewis more than she cared to admit. Another reason could have been a chronic menopausal, hormonal imbalance. She was in her mid-fifties and operating a punishing schedule. Maine Chance was an outstanding success but although Miss Arden was often there, she rarely rested.

Post-divorce, she had taken over the wholesale division that had been her husband's, and personally managed the American and South American markets as well as controlling the salons and orchestrating the setting up of Maine Chance. Dealing with wholesale customers wasn't quite as easy as Elizabeth liked to think, and, just like Madame Rubinstein, she wasn't immune from forgetting people's names. Stanley Marcus of Neiman Marcus recalled 'although we were her largest customer, she had great difficulty in distinguishing me from Grover Magnin, the San Francisco dean of specialty store operators, despite the disparity in our ages. She irritated me by calling me Mr Magnin, so one day I replied, "Yes, Madame Rubinstein." Calling her by the name of her arch rival in the cosmetics industry did the trick. She was shocked sufficiently to call me by my own name thereafter.' Her inability to delegate caused the usual problems with staff recruitment. Miss Arden made up her mind on all appointments. If she had chosen well, she rarely gave the new executive a chance to show their worth and if she had chosen badly, the results spoke for themselves. A raft of new employees came on board in the 1930s including two notables, the actress Hedda Hopper and the advertising sales manager from British *Vogue*, Lawrence Schneider. She also enthusiastically foisted a junior trainee named Foster Blakely on to the long-suffering Teddy Haslam.

Blakely started his short career with the company as a protégé of Miss Arden's in New York, where his aunt, Grace Blakely, was already working. Elizabeth described young Foster to Teddy as 'intelligent and clever, beautifully educated, speaks French fluently and is a thorough gentleman. He's a friend of Barbara Hutton and is socially very well connected in London. He's working for Prince Matchabelli but the boy is too smart to grow up with any competitor of ours and I think he has every possibility of becoming the perfect inside man under you in London.' Poor Mr Haslam didn't stand a chance under the onslaught of praise for the young 'Ivy Leaguer'. Unfortunately, the gilded youth was finding it hard to live in the troubled world of the Depression, when family losses meant he had to work for a living. Elizabeth Arden, with her snobbish pretensions, was his ideal career 'sugar mummy' and clearly young Foster thought he had struck gold.

Miss Arden was enchanted with her protégé, telling Teddy, 'He is very quick and simply *hipped* upon advertising and even now, young though he is, has an arresting manner of putting his ideas across. He is delighted with the thought of going to London and I shall have him here for three weeks to train him and then send him to you and I want you to find a good place for him. Do let him go out and meet people as much as possible. He will, I am sure, bring us a great many clients.'

Elizabeth then left for Saratoga, leaving her niece Ginnie to inform the London office about the arrangements for Mr Blakely. Ginnie, and her sisters Patty and Beattie, were very much in favour with Elizabeth who adored them, despite her social and emotional distance from their father. From time to time Ginnie, who aspired to be a writer, was whipped in to do a little 'useful' work at the New York headquarters. Unfortunately, her copywriting technique didn't match up to expectations, and she often found herself in her aunt's office, handling personal letters which weren't in the main office filing system and were usually written on Elizabeth's private stationery.

Ginnie's letter of February 1935 explained that 'Foster is now receiving from us in New York the sum of $40 a week. We have also loaned him $175 for the crossing. The question of repaying this loan from his salary as well as the proportionate amount to pay him in London had best be definitely arranged with Miss Arden. Will you write her giving your opinion of it?' Interestingly, aunt or not, Elizabeth was always 'Miss Arden' to family working in the business.

So, Foster was foisted on to the London office with predictable results. It appears he took his remit to 'get out and about and meet people' as *carte blanche* to enjoy London's social life and just over a year later he had run up debts far over his official budget, without making the impact on business his mentor had hoped for. She blithely shifted the blame as usual, writing to

Teddy, 'I am very much upset about the Blakely matter. You engaged him and allowed him to take an expensive flat, and you will have to see him through as the money is not forthcoming from any other source. His family can cause me a great deal of worry here in New York so this matter has to be taken care of.' It was taken care of and Blakely left. Miss Arden's views on his next job aren't on record, but it's doubtful she was too thrilled. Foster Blakely joined the London office of Helena Rubinstein.

At least Haslam didn't have to cope with Hedda Hopper. The ex-actress whose career was on the wane had met Elizabeth through J. Robert Rubin. Knowing of Elizabeth's hopeless love affair with Hollywood and that she yearned to find an executive with glamour to take over the US salon division whilst she concentrated on wholesale, Rubin thought Hopper an ideal candidate. Observers of the two ego-driven, acerbic women might have predicted disaster. In fact, although Hopper's job with Arden ended a year or so later, their friendship endured, and when Hopper became one of the leading gossip writers reporting from Hollywood on the activities of movie stars and millionaires, Elizabeth was rarely out of her column. Although her indoctrination into the world of *haute beauté* was brief, Hopper later said, 'I'm glad I did it. It's fabulous. The profits would stagger a Maharajah.' Hedda was fascinated as to how Elizabeth ran her salons, particularly her New York flagship. 'Dozens of times a day girls sprayed perfume through it. As you lean back in a chair to have a treatment you see cream chiffon curtains, screening out the dust and dirt of the city. After an hour at Arden's you're bound to look more beautiful.'

Elizabeth and Hedda used to lunch out and make surprise swoops on the beauty counters at the nearby stores both to check out the Arden line and to look at the competition. One day they were in Saks where Elizabeth was thrilled that the buyers had recently placed an order for a gold-embroidered evening bag from her luxury accessories collection. The retail price for the Arden original in Saks was $20 but, this being American retail, they did a nice sideline in 'own label' copies. Pausing to admire her stock, Elizabeth asked the salesgirl if she had anything else. 'Oh yes,' the hapless girl said, 'we have one just as good for $5.95.' That was the first time Hedda Hopper witnessed Arden's temper. She said, 'To this day when Adam Gimbel – the chairman of Saks at that time – remembers what Elizabeth said to him over the telephone, his collar feels too tight for him.'

Poor Teddy Haslam's collar must have felt too tight following

Elizabeth's outrage about the departure of Lawrence Schneider, whose role at Arden began bathed in the rosy glow of anticipation on her part that she had finally found the right man. Schneider had been one of the original American crack team of advertising salesmen sent over by Condé Nast to run British *Vogue*. The dramatic downturn in the fortunes of Condé Nast was causing many executives to look for new jobs. Schneider's interview with Miss Arden in 1935 was brokered by his friend Henry Sell, and would no doubt have been discussed by Teddy Haslam and *his* friend, Harry Yoxall, the managing director of British *Vogue*. For Yoxall, the idea of his colleague joining a company so user-friendly to Condé Nast had a certain appeal.

Elizabeth offered Schneider a job at once. She was annoyed to learn that Condé had requested he stay with *Vogue* until June. 'Condé is being mean!' she wrote. 'He probably thinks that if I have to wait that long I'll have to get someone else.' By that summer Mr Schneider was on board, but had insisted on a contract of employment which Elizabeth delayed as she loathed contracts. Mr Schneider got off to a strong start, Elizabeth writing: 'Our business, thank goodness, is very good. What a difference having Mr Schneider . . . *everyone* adores him.'

In December, Miss Arden gave Schneider the title of vice-president in sole charge of wholesale activity, where he also enjoyed autonomy over advertising, and the selection of his sales team. His salary was an appealing $35,000 a year (worth $445,000 today), paid fortnightly, with a termination settlement of $17,500 to be paid in a lump sum should he leave, or presumably be fired. Elizabeth always felt mellow at Christmas, so even though Mr Schneider had had his contract prepared by his own lawyers, as her own document was not forthcoming, she merely glanced at it, signed it and had it sent to him with a $5000 Christmas-bonus cheque.

The honeymoon was soon over. On a trip to Los Angeles he was briefed to visit all her salons throughout America. The departure from his fiefdom, overseeing the 5000 established retail accounts from the Arden sales corporation headquarters, was bound to be difficult. To Elizabeth, her salons were sacred and she took offence at suggestions made in his follow-up report. The two had a major fall-out, and Lawrence Schneider left, having delivered his notice, effective immediately, claiming severance pay.

As usual, Teddy took the brunt of her wrath. 'I have never been more surprised than about Mr Schneider and I never tried so hard to co-operate with anyone in all my life. He expected me to give in once more to his ridiculous demands and give him more power over here. He is really a very nasty man!' Miss Arden could never accept any form of constructive critical advice from her senior management and was incapable of hearing that the heyday of the beauty salons was over. Schneider knew this. Other Arden management knew this too and hoped she would seek more profitable relationships operating in-store salons rather than try to maintain her own, which were beginning to leach money, were hard to staff, and whose appeal was waning as more and more women went to hairdressers, where they could get a tip-top manicure courtesy of Mr Charles Revson's Revlon nail lacquers.

She felt, not unjustly, that Lawrence Schneider had been out of order as far as the settlement was concerned. But then she had neither drafted his contract, nor properly looked at it. 'Now, Teddy, you must remember standing beside me when I, at first, offered three months' notice and Mr Schneider insisted on six months' notice and then I finally said, "I will give you six months' notice or six months' pay, but I expect the same from you." Do you mind telling me, Teddy, how you ever advised me to sign this contract? He deliberately went out and wrote the agreement with the absurd provision that he would get $17,500 — even if he walked out, with no notice to me! You really should have advised me to consult with a lawyer!'

In typical Arden style, she exonerated herself. 'I really feel better about my business now than I have in a long, long time. I never felt easy while Mr Schneider was here, and with very good reason. Well, Teddy, do make this a lesson for the future . . .'

A lot of Lawrence Schneider's report made sense, particularly his advice to incorporate luxury hairdressing. By the early 1930s it was estimated American women were spending over $4 million a year at the hairdresser's and clearly the time had come to bring a slice of that under the Elizabeth Arden banner. Arden already owned a small hairdressing salon on East 53rd St, called Au Printemps, where she had been monitoring results. But ordinary hairdressing was not the Arden way. She had to do it bigger and better. Off went another telegram to her sister in Paris and, as usual, Gladys came up trumps, hiring Guillaume. Whilst he was not as grand as Antoine, who by now had an in-store salon licence at Saks, Guillaume was a recognised star in the Paris hairdressing firmament and Elizabeth was thrilled.

Nicholai Remisoff was brought in to revamp the salons to incorporate hairdressing facilities and Elizabeth toured with Guillaume, recruiting hair stylists for Boston, Palm Beach, Nassau, Southampton, Chicago and Los Angeles, all of whom were subsequently promoted as being 'trained by Guillaume'. Elizabeth took advertisements in the glossy magazines promoting Guillaume's personal appearances and encouraged him to go out on photographic sittings for the magazine beauty departments to earn the crucial 'hair by Guillaume at Elizabeth Arden' credit.

She planned moneyspinning entertainment for her clients to amuse them whilst they were being coiffured, based around her phenomenally successful lingerie collection. Elizabeth's passion for the ethereal tea-gown style translated well into her couture lingerie collection. The Arden salons sold bed-jackets, peignoirs, negligees and other mysteriously delicate garments, typifying her ideals of feminine beauty. Elizabeth remained convinced that her 'ladies' spent most of their mornings – when not at Elizabeth Arden – drifting around their palatial apartments in a cloud of ruffled chiffon. As a consequence, five of the most beautiful models in New York drifted round the hair salon at Arden wearing clouds of ruffled chiffon. The captive audience adored it and the lingerie department, along with the salon modelling, became an Arden fixture for the next thirty years.

According to senior hair stylist, Maurice, who was personally hired by Miss Arden in the mid-1960s and is one of a surprisingly large core group who remember her still working at the Arden salon at 615 Fifth Avenue today, the lingerie modelling, which continued for several years after she died, was a phenomenon. 'The ladies *loved* it,' says Maurice, 'believe me, they would wave a hand and say, "I'll take that and that." It was shopping made easy for them. What else is there to do while you are sitting with rollers in?' Maurice is talking about the 1960s, but it was the same formula instigated by Elizabeth thirty years earlier. 'She made it special for them, they were pampered . . . it was another way of life,' says Maurice wistfully, his eyes clouding with emotion for just a moment . . .

The lingerie department was also important in London. Priscilla Moynihan, who worked at Arden's Bond Street salon from 1962 to 1967, remembers the lingerie with perhaps a little less enthusiasm than Maurice. 'The bed-jackets and silk nightgowns were in pale blue, pale pink and aquamarine. They were all lacy and frilly,' she says, 'and we had to put them away each night in tissue paper before we could leave.'

Miss Arden's passion for lingerie remained unabated all her life, and she knew the British royal family shared her tastes, dispatching gifts to them on birthdays and at Christmas, which were always accepted. 'The Queen has commanded me to write and thank you most sincerely for the pink dressing gown that you so kindly sent on the occasion of Her Majesty's birthday,' came one letter from Buckingham Palace in 1961, and from Sandringham the same year, a letter from Ruth, Lady Fermoy, on behalf of HM The Queen Mother, says: 'She bids me to write and thank you so very much for the lovely bed-jacket.'

Beauty journalists also came in for largesse at Christmas, with Elizabeth personally supervising the wrapping and ribboning of vast gift boxes of preparations and lingerie. Helena Rubinstein was also careful to acknowledge media support at this time and had an extensive list of press friends in her address book. Gift wrapping, however, wasn't an issue. She sent them cash.

The specialist designer for Arden's lingerie department in the 1930s was the Russian Princess Ketto Mikeladze. The princess, who had arrived in New York via Paris as a model in about 1931, working in Bergdorf Goodman's fine fashion department, would have been introduced to Elizabeth by Nicholai Remisoff, her interior designer, and *his* friend, Russian man-about-town, Serge Obolensky. The very charming Colonel Prince Serge Obolensky was, by virtue of his impeccable connections and one-time marriage to Alice Astor, the leader of New York's Russian society in exile. Elizabeth had a great fondness for the White Russians and, always happy to hire a titled lady, impoverished or not, was enchanted with Princess Mikeladze. The specialist pieces she designed sold at premium prices and were prized gifts when Elizabeth was feeling generous. 'Do give Lady Barker one of the Russian tea gowns,' Elizabeth said to Teddy when liaising over Christmas gifts suitable for the wife of HM the Queen's chiropractor – who just happened to be a non-executive director of the Arden London company.

The princess seems to have subsequently become a close friend of Helena Rubinstein, who thoughtfully left her $1200 in her will. As Helena's tastes in nightwear ran to $5 white cotton gowns, it's unlikely they met through lingerie designing. It's more than likely that she was a friend of Helena's second husband, the Georgian, Artchil Gourielli-Tchkonia.

Helena met the amiable Artchil in Paris in 1936 when he was partnered with her at bridge following a dinner party at the Comtesse de Polignac's. Marie Blanche de Polignac was the daughter of couturier Jeanne Lanvin, an old friend of Helena's. Madame Lanvin, as reserved as Helena, used to sit in silence at her daughter's parties, observing the beautiful people with gimlet-eyed interest. The comtesse was extremely social and held court at her beautiful house on rue Barbet-de-Jouy. Card parties were a tradition in Paris, where there was no shortage of elegant emigrés such as Artchil, many of whom earned a precarious living out of gambling (when they weren't driving taxis or making lucrative sums as gigolos) and were willing card partners in exchange for a good meal. Helena described him as: 'a big, hand-some, curly-headed man with a contagious laugh. I liked his frankness and his warmth as much as his gaiety.'

The prince seemed to show the world how to do charisma. After all, he was from Georgia, where the wine flows freely, the landscape is lush, and the people have a gift for telling tales of brave deeds and daring escapades. There is a view – not only expressed by Georgians – that the area was the original Garden of Eden. Whilst experts might quibble about that, they are united in acknowledging Georgia as the land of Colchis, where Jason and his Argonauts went in search of the Golden Fleece. Georgians used fleeces to trawl the rivers, scooping up alluvial gold from the river beds; hence the Golden Fleece. It must also be said that the saying, 'anyone from Georgia who owns a few sheep is called a prince' is not far from the truth. 'Prince' Artchil Gourielli-Tchkonia's title, however, impressed Helena, and for the first time in a long time she felt cheerful.

Helena's relationship with Gourielli developed despite her hectic schedule. Between 1935 and 1937 she was busier than ever. Firstly, she turned to new product development. Increasingly aware of her own age – she was now in her mid-sixties – Helena paid particular attention to hormone rejuvenation and poured money into developing radical hormone skin-treatment creams. The Rubinstein company launched Hormone Twin Youthifiers, a day-and-night cream to 'stimulate and rebuild new, younger skin cells'. She became obsessed with using female hormone extracts, and over the next two decades launched Estrogenic Hormone Cream with Progesterone, Estrogenic Hormone Oil for the throat, Young Touch Hand Lotion with estrogenic hormones and the most highly regarded of all, Ultrafeminine. Twin Youthifiers and Young Touch Hand Lotion fell foul of the new FDA legislation, but Ultrafeminine was one of the first beauty products to be approved as a drug by the FDA.

Rubinstein's hormone creams, particularly Ultrafeminine, which was subject to three years' testing, involving keeping skin tissue alive for eighteen months, were the pilots for today's fashionable 'cosmecuticals', the industry buzzword when marketing a 'pharmo/ cosmetic', a product claiming to have a scientific connection to beauty, and a division of the industry calculated in 2000 to be worth nearly $9 billion a year in its own right. As anti-ageing is the Holy Grail of the cosmetics industry, the use of hormone treatment creams has long been recognised as having a powerful benefit. Gaylord Hauser was effusive in his praise for hormone treatment creams in their embryonic years. 'I consider the addition of oestrogen to complexion cream one of the most helpful and interesting developments in the entire cosmetic field. It is my deep hope that all cosmetic manufacturers will embody and apply this newer knowledge and thus put healthier and younger-looking complexions within reach of all women in the second half of life.'

Not everyone was enthusiastic about hormones. In particular Dr Cramp, of the American Medical Association, said in 1934: 'Whether or not such hormones are present in the cosmetic is a matter of indifference, for there is not any scientific evidence to show that even if they were present, they would have the slightest effect in rejuvenating the skin. Such products are the ultimate in cosmetic quackery.'

Hauser also sang the praises of vitamins and minerals. Scientists in England and America were researching into vitamins in the mid-1930s and in another first, Helena Rubinstein launched a vitamin oil for skin rejuvenation. Elizabeth Arden also introduced hormone creams and valiantly tried one prototype on her own skin, resulting, to her chagrin, in a terrible rash. Coincidentally, Tommy Lewis became involved in promoting vitamins, introducing Henry Sell to a potential client involved in marketing them. The project fell through, but Sell, impressed by the concept, went on to open a business called Vitamin Plus. Stores like Marshall Field's of Chicago, Saks, and Lord & Taylor were enthusiasts, selling the vitamins on their cosmetics floor and Lord & Taylor sold nearly a thousand boxes at $2.75 each in the first week.

Instead of vitamins, minerals and hormones (although she had a product called Gland Cream which was hugely successful), Elizabeth's main focus was expanding her make-up ranges, in particular lipsticks, eye shadows with a palette mainly based on her favourite blue, foundation creams and concealers.

Arden's Beauty Cream was described as a 'concealer for the dark, brownish look that comes beneath the eyes when one is tired', and Eyelash Cosmetique was her own blend of mascara. She was a great believer in eye make-up, promoting Eyelash Grower, claiming it stimulated growth and made lashes thick and glossy.

She also spent time doing what she really enjoyed – giving parties. Fearful of loneliness, Elizabeth was a compulsive hostess. There were rarely less than ten guests a night, and often as many as a hundred once a fortnight in her apartment at any one time. Her lavish parties were often themed and she always had a pianist and often an accordian player and singers to serenade her guests. In 1935, Elizabeth took over the debut party of her niece, Beatrice 'Beattie' Graham, who was sharing her soirée with a well-connected schoolfriend. Incapable of containing her excitement at the idea of spending the evening in the company of swells at the Ritz Carlton, Elizabeth went into overdrive. Staff were kept busy wrapping table gifts for the guests and Elizabeth supervised the décor. Hedda Hopper had introduced her to the set designer Kate Lawson, and Miss Arden, lips pursed, eyes narrowing, apparently said, 'I want something like the stage setting of Gertrude Stein's operetta *Four Saints in Three Acts*, but I don't suppose you ever saw it.' Kate replied quietly, 'I did it.' It transpired Miss Lawson had worked on the innovative cellophane sets with the eccentric Florine Stettheimer, an old friend of Bessie Marbury's. That did it for Elizabeth, who immediately became enchanted with Kate Lawson and hired her to decorate the ballroom – and the Fifth Avenue windows too, Kate for a while becoming the company's window-display consultant. For the debutante ball she put up vast columns of pale pink cellophane, bunched around the walls, twisted into Prince of Wales feathers twelve feet high. The whole thing looked like a cross between a chocolate box and a meringue.

Irene Delaney, Miss Arden's most devoted employee, watched the event take shape with quiet pride, for she had known the Graham girls since they were babies and adored them. She was looking forward to the party; but Elizabeth didn't invite her. Hedda Hopper discovered this appalling slight. Realising Elizabeth couldn't countenance *staff* joining the smart set, Hopper didn't fight for Lanie. She knew she wouldn't win. So she took her to the hotel where she could see the room ready, the tables gleaming in the soft light, with their pink-ribboned gift boxes and everything poised for Beatrice to have the night of her life. Hedda and Lanie then retreated to the bar where they drank two sherries each in rapid succession. Lanie left, still hurt, but happier. Meanwhile, Elizabeth's more socially acceptable staff were arriving, along with the guests they had been instructed to put on the list. Princess Mikeladze had whipped in Serge Obolensky, the Grand Duchess Marie and Alexis Mdivani, the self-styled Georgian 'Prince' recently separated from Woolworth's million-heiress Barbara Hutton, along with 'Count' Kurt von Haughwitz-Reventlow, waiting to be married to the same Miss Hutton as soon as her decree was absolute. Of Miss Hutton herself, there was no sign. Beattie's ball guests weren't confined to European royalty. Grace Blakely, still on the payroll, used her connections in Palm Beach to rope in socialite Marjorie Merriweather Post and Palm Beach grandees, Charles and Dorothy Munn. *Nothing* pleased Miss Arden more than having her picture taken with Mrs Munn.

Helena was too busy for parties. Firstly, her glorious new home in Paris was nearing completion. The Quai de Bethune on the Ile St Louis is one of the most elegant addresses in Paris. Looking up at the imposing house that Helena built, you can just glimpse the roof terrace, said to have the 'best view in the whole of Paris'. She had bought the crumbling building, once the residence of the Hungarian prince, Nicholas Hesselin, from her friend Misia Sert's ex-husband in about 1931.

The property was rotting away, and came with elderly sitting tenants, but by 1934 Helena had contrived to remove the incumbents and hired master-architect and designer Louis Sue to supervise the gutting and rebuilding of her dream house. It had taken nearly three years, but Helena was now poised to occupy the magnificent penthouse where she was wont to describe the view as 'the most expensive one in Paris' referring to the fortune she had spent on the property. Grumbles apart, she loved her Paris home and was very proud of it.

Sue incorporated some of the Hesselin heritage into his re-working. The huge wooden Hungarian-styled coach entrance was retained and ironwork was copied from original seventeenth-century patterns. Helena's vast rooms included a library and several drawing rooms artfully lit to display her paintings, and her growing collection of African art. Helena's friend Marcoussis was part of her design team, with Sue rather graciously describing him as a collaborator. Marcoussis painted a huge, modernistic panel in the salon with a motif titled *Voyage* and repeated the theme and colour scheme of rugs and tapestries designed by Picasso and Joan Miró.

Madame's housemaid at Quai de Bethune, Marguerite, had the awe-some responsibility of caring for her mistress's possessions. When Patrick O'Higgins arrived to stay at the apartment in the early 1950s, Marguerite, who had worked there with Eugenie and Gaston Metz for well over twenty years, gave him a guided tour. 'There are two wings, monsieur,' she said. 'In the wing facing us, Madame has her bedroom. It is linked with this side of the apartment by *les salles de reception*, a salon, the library, card room, music room and the main dining room. There's lots for me to dust! *Pensez* – just think – six hundred and twenty-two blacks for a start . . .'

Louis Sue created an astonishing setting for his client's 'six hundred and twenty-two blacks'. He also supervised the arrival of a suite of mother-of-pearl furniture, which had been made for the Duc de Montpensier in 1835, a pair of Louis XIV boulle marriage caskets, a vast amount of Biedermeier, several malachite tables, dozens of Aubusson carpets and a black-and-white marble dining suite with twelve high-backed gilded Louis XIV chairs. He remained remarkably patient, and managed to restrain Madame's inclination for clutter, displaying her museum-quality furniture in minimal fashion. In years to come the effect would be blurred by her com-pulsive collecting, and it was hard to even find space on a table to put down a drink. Beds were covered with discarded furs cut up into rugs, and the whole was apparently quite hard to see after dusk, as Madame's phobia about wasting electricity meant she rarely put the lights on.

Her Paris house wasn't the only part of the Rubinstein empire to undergo a makeover at this time. In 1936, Helena had re-capitalised her business in the US and whilst it was still a public company, she remained the major shareholder, reportedly owning 52% of the stock. In the tit-for-tat battle she conducted with Elizabeth Arden, the stylish refit of Miss Arden's Gymnasium Moderne at her Fifth Avenue salon wouldn't have escaped Madame's attention. Miss Arden had opened her state-of-the-art gymnastics and dance floor to great press acclaim. She had fitted sprung floors, installed her by now famous tilt boards and set up classes in eurhythmics and fencing. The latter taught by fencing-master Nadi. To encourage her ladies to 'unfurl like a flower' Elizabeth commissioned her favourite artist, Georgia O'Keeffe, to paint a canvas for the opening. Titled *Miracle Flower* it cost an astonishing $10,000. The Gymnasium Moderne was, of course, under the direction of Anne Delafield, but Miss Arden so loved it she kept interfering, and the unhappy Miss Delafield left to join Richard Hudnut, launching the Hudnut Success School.

Commenting today about Rubinstein and Arden, Annette Green of the Fragrance Foundation in New York says, 'Both women were *it*. The only one who came near them in creative and marketing expertise was Anne Delafield at Richard Hudnut Du Barry.' Miss Delafield learned those skills working for Elizabeth Arden, who all too often seemed to train experts to work for the competition.

Helena's commercial acumen was strong enough to know she had to regain at least some of the leading-edge glamour that had been hers in 1920s New York. There was only one way to do it in a town that thrived on image and that was by putting on a show. Her New York salon was not just too small, it was tired. Her power base had suffered in the Depression and the gloss had cracked. In 1933, Helena had employed an astute, highly regarded sales director, with over twenty-five years' experience, called Harry Johnson. After a year or so of restructuring, mainly to cut back on the down-market 'pick and mix' outlets who had been allowed to buy the line, he reported that things were getting back on track. After the re-capitalisation of her business, she rewarded him with a seat on the board and her trust. His next move was to instigate a power thrust against Arden in New York and Helena needed little encouragement from Mr Johnson to authorise the investment.

Acquiring an elegant building at 715 Fifth Avenue, Madame set about creating her dream salon. Helena knew that the salon system was waning, but her strategic objective was to rebuild her brand, and she could not attempt to do so without a flagship. Paris also benefited from this largesse. The flurry of expenditure didn't go unnoticed by her family – nor by her ex-husband.

Sibling solidarity amongst the Rubinstein sisters, never strong, was wearing thin. Manka in particular, who wanted to retire, felt her share as a director of the American business was worth $100,000. Helena was furious, telling her sister:

I should have expected nothing else. You have some misguided friends who have flattered you so much that you have begun to think yourself a business genius. I want to tell you that your sole virtue has been that you could imitate me . . . and that you have carried out the plans I laid down. My nerves are too shattered and I will not subject myself to scenes any longer. Do exactly as you please. You can have your money tomorrow. You are so much younger than I am that these scenes do not exhaust you as they do me. You would have had so much more had your husband made less costly investments . . . You dismiss as nothing the half a million a year I spend in advertising. The thousands I have spent for formulas, for new businesses, that I have spent millions creating this business. I have made up my mind to spare myself for the few years left to enjoy what everyone – more than I – has profited by.

The loss of Manka was compensated for by the arrival of Mala, Helena's favourite niece. Mala had worked at every Rubinstein outlet in Europe and along the way had learned five languages 'plus a little Russian' as she told an awed reporter from the *Seattle Daily Times* on a promotional tour in 1934. Her sporting hobbies were listed as ice-skating, swimming and tennis, and other recreational activity included her fondness for sculpture. The multi-talented Mala did not tell the reporter that at one soirée in Paris, when she had been in the midst of a conversation on finances with a businessman, all of a sudden her tiny, dynamo aunt glided up and dug her sharply in the ribs. 'Act more stupid,' Helena hissed.

Madame Rubinstein was of the school of women who felt it was dangerous to show a man you had a brain. Women, Madame calculated, could achieve more if they said less, watched and waited. Mala, it's said, always yearned to be an actress. She never made it to drama school but she had a leading role on the stage of her aunt's company, running the New York salon, heading up the beauty classes and training schools, never really winning the encores she perhaps deserved.

Next in line asking for money was Edward Titus. He wrote a plaintive letter to Helena from Cagnes-sur-Mer telling her of his woes.

I have gone through a very hard winter. It has been raining and cold and the wet has got into my house . . . fortunately, that part where my books are has escaped without a trace, otherwise it would have ruined my collection . . . the doctor insisted I go to Morocco but the house could not be left unoccupied and I am too hard up to undertake the trip . . . my income from Paris has been reduced to about 30,000 francs per annum which does not cover my living expenses, so that I have been thinking of resuming my business in Paris . . . I have the catalogue of my collection ready for printing to be sent out to dealers in France, England and America . . . the printers want about £120, which I can't raise . . . I would need a whole trousseau before I could venture forth, because I have no decent clothes left . . . Also, I would have to have my teeth fixed up . . . you are therefore my last resort and resource. I don't know where else to turn . . . To finish this cheerless letter, let me say that I feel whatever your sentiments . . . you would not want me to spend my last days in need of most essential things. I am sixty-six years of age and naturally going to pot gradually, but my mind is still as fresh and nimble as ever. This emboldens me to make a last appeal to you. Can you make me an annual allowance of $2000, to be paid in a lump sum every year until I shall have no further use for the money?

Madame was probably relieved to be busy in New York, supervising the construction of her salon work as usual, so that she could put family dramas out of her mind. When her building on Fifth Avenue was completed, it wasn't just the beauty press who eulogised. A fierce architectural reporter, protective of the Manhattan skyline, wrote, 'The best recent shop front has appeared on Fifth Avenue, the new Helena Rubinstein salon between Fifty-fifth and Fifty-sixth Streets. The front of the Rubinstein salon is done in big limestone slabs and the shop's façade fits into the old-fashioned building above it without submitting to it. The design gets a good mark for tactful renovation.' The report noted the architect responsible was Harold Sterner and continues by saying about the façade, 'the widely spaced letters "helena rubinstein", all in lower case, are small, well-drawn, admirable. There is only one other mark on the front, the numerals 715 to the right of the building entrance. On the placing and size of these numerals, much depended, and I do not think that the result could have been improved.' He wasn't aware that the lower case lettering was a gesture towards the influence of Titus. Helena selected the lower case lettering because of e.e. cummings. The accolades were no doubt worth, in her mind, the allowance she made to her ex-husband.

The new salon was a sensation. *Vogue* ran a five-page feature in February 1937 reporting on the Malvina Hoffman sculptures, murals by Dali's protégé Pallavicini and rugs by Joan Miró. Helena's famous 'miniature rooms', created from the dolls-house furniture she collected, were displayed in recessed room-sets, back-lit as though they were priceless antiques. The library contained rare books on beauty treatments and the restaurant served exquisite food. With a nod towards Arden, clients were given peignoirs in silk satin to wear, rather than functional towelling robes. All this beauty before even one treatment . . . and what treatments . . .

The concept was promoted as 'a day of beauty at helena rubinstein'. There were milk baths, mineral baths, herbal baths and strong needle-showers, all followed with a pumice rub. There was electro-tonic treatment for deep-seated circulation. A doctor was on hand to give clients basal-metabolism tests. The exercise rooms had sprung floors and floor-to-ceiling wall bars. There were classes in specialised stretch, posture correction, deportment, and in an innovative incubator of today's stress-busting regimes, a 'ball' session where clients could toss a big rubber ball around with total abandon. The Rubinstein *coup de théâtre* was her San-O-Therm table. In a calm blue room clients relaxed on a calm blue table with an arched top generating infrared rays, heated from underneath. With cream gently massaged into the face, gauze pads over the eyes, half-an-hour of scented rest and relaxation, with the added advantage of drawing out toxins, was guaranteed. Facials, a manicure, a pedicure and a make-up lesson in a room described as 'having mirrors that are triumphs of lighting', were all part of the day of beauty, but the highlight was the time spent in the hairdressing salon. This session started with a scalp massage that *Vogue* described as 'setting your hair on end'. Buffed and fluffed, the ladies left feeling that whatever they had spent was definitely worth it.

Justifiably thrilled, Helena left immediately for Paris, where in April 1937 she presided over the opening of her revamped Faubourg St Honoré salon, equipped with San-O-Therm hot beds and gym equipment. She put a special emphasis on diet, much loved by the French, and installed the metabolic testing equipment that had caused such a sensation in New York.

Always keen to be thought of as informed in the art world, where she felt more vulnerable than in her business, Helena surrounded herself with experts. Her latest adviser was wealthy Marie Cuttoli, a patron of Picasso and a noted collector whose apartment in rue Babylon, according to John Richardson, 'was like an art gallery'. One of the first ideas they worked out together was the establishment of an annual art prize, the winner of which should be 'a mature artist of the French school who has proven by his work to be a lasting exponent of the modern art of today'. The inaugural winner in 1937 was sculptor Henri Laurens. Helena proudly posed with her judging panel on her Paris roof-terrace. The line-up was planned to show the world that she not only knew about art, but knew the artists: Henri Matisse, Georges Braque, Fernand Léger, Louis Marcoussis, Paul Eluard and Maurice Raynal represented art and literature, whilst Professor Henri Laugier, M. Dezarrois, Georges Henri Rivière, Jean Cassou and Marie Cuttoli represented education, development and patronage in art. The prize was 25,000 francs. As a public relations exercise it was a triumph, but for the artists a shortlived one. Two years later the award was suspended at the onset of war, and was never re-instated.

Whilst the Paris art world acknowledged Helena, the literary world was more cynical, which is hardly surprising given the abrupt closure of her husband's shop and printing press. Helena blithely ignored her critics and ventured out, on 25 May, to the cult literary event of the year, if not the decade. Sylvia Beach, still running her bookshop and library, albeit on a much reduced budget, was hosting an evening to honour Ernest Hemingway and Stephen Spender. Hemingway, back from Spain, was reading extracts from his latest book, *To Have and Have Not*, whilst Spender was to recite from his poems, also written in Spain. Talk that night was about the Spanish Civil War and what many believed was the inevitable war with Germany.

The salon was crowded. James Joyce and his wife were there, along with Natalie Barney. William Bullit, the new American ambassador in Paris arrived with Helena's friend Janet Flanner, the Paris-based correspondent for the *New Yorker*. Hemingway arrived with Martha Gellhorn and Beach was delighted with the turnout, noting in her private diaries, 'even that somewhat disdainful patron Helena Rubinstein was there, though she slept through most of the reading.' Never having cared much for poetry and given that Hemingway apparently spoke so softly he could hardly be heard, it's no surprise Helena nodded off. It may have helped her image that she was at Shakespeare & Company that night, but she would come to regret the extra month or so she squeezed out of her trip to Paris.

That same month, Elizabeth Arden, by now desperate to find a team of efficient, pro-active sales managers, headhunted Harry Johnson from Helena Rubinstein Inc. Mr Johnson 'crossed the floor' for a five-year contract reputed to be worth $50,000 a year plus incentive bonus. He delivered his own bonus to his new boss by arriving with *eleven* of Helena's crack team. A financial reporter assigned to the story, which had set trade tongues agog in New York, wrote with remarkable restraint about Mr Johnson's new job, 'It is a subject about which Madame Rubinstein herself is less than coherent.' Helena might not have been coherent when asked for a comment by the journalist but she was vocal enough around her offices when she arrived back in New York. 'That woman is stealing all my people,' she screeched. 'I'm going to get even.'

She took time to plot and plan. It is said that nothing beats a woman when it comes to revenge – Helena's was sweet indeed.

CHAPTER FIFTEEN

PRINCESS OF THE POTIONS v
LADY OF THE LOTIONS
1937–1939

'WHAT TO DO? WHAT to do?' When Helena was agitated, she used to mutter this to herself as she bustled around like the White Rabbit in *Alice*. Sometimes she would say it loudly, hoping one of her executives might come up with an interesting idea, but by the time any suggestions were forthcoming, she had usually made up her own mind what to do anyway. For a short while, though, when Harry Johnson defected, even Helena's spirit was crushed and she simply didn't know what to do.

In the end, she did what always suited her best, retreating to a place of isolation where she could recover from the blow. As the place in question was the Bircher Benner Clinic in Switzerland, it had the added advantage of a weight loss. Helena stayed there for about two months, on a regime of muesli and raw vegetables, and returned to the fray invigorated, fighting-fit and twenty pounds lighter. Madame's sojourn was quickly turned into a business opportunity. She adopted the concept of raw food, and her diet book, *Food for Beauty*, designed and illustrated by Robert L. Leonard, became a 1938 bestseller. Madame Rubinstein might not have had her own health farm, but she matched Miss Arden for nutritional advice with the cachet of a successful book, under her own name, attracting excellent publicity.

The restaurant at the Rubinstein salon on Fifth Avenue was adapted to offer 'Zurich raw food' lunches, where dozens of fruits and vegetables were carved and shredded into works of art. As usual, Helena's initial enthusiasm for a project ran out of steam if it didn't make a profit, and the extravagant lunches were quietly phased out. As far as her own eating habits were concerned, it was also noted she was soon back to munching cream-cheese bagels, smoked salmon, hard-boiled eggs and chicken legs with her usual trencherwoman's appetite. 'When you work hard, you have to eat,' she would say. An important writer invited to lunch with Helena observed her taking a leftover lamb cutlet from a guest's plate and eating it herself. Describing Helena as 'a plate-licker-cleaner' the reporter went on, 'Some of Madame's fastidious guests will call her a peasant for this, but it is the sound, natural instinct of a woman who saw enough poverty in her youth to have a horror of waste.' However embarrassing Helena's habits, however brusque her attitude, however tough her tactics, people *liked* her. She had the type of endearing charisma which enabled her to get away with some appalling behaviour.

Most of the next year was devoted to wreaking vengeance on Elizabeth Arden. *Life* magazine, at that time America's leading publication, reported that 'the rivalry with Arden is the chief spur in Rubinstein's life'. Madame had always enjoyed a special relationship with the media who liked her eccentricity and her 'made in America' success. They admired her clothes and jewels, and she always gave them a good story. Helena relished her friendships with editors of influence, in particular the ever-powerful Carmel Snow of *Harper's Bazaar*, whose name she had never quite mastered, pronouncing it 'Caramel', a habit the formidable Miss Snow apparently found enchanting.

Unfortunately for Helena, at about this time Elizabeth had forged a close personal relationship with Tom White, a very senior executive at the Hearst corporation which owned *Bazaar*, and irritatingly for Helena, he was Carmel Snow's brother. As a consequence, she mistrusted the lines of communication and turned her attention to *Vogue* and the Condé Nast magazines. At exactly the time that Condé Nast were reeling from financial losses, Helena substantially increased her budgets, earning herself friends in the publishing department. She invited *House & Garden* to photograph her new home in Paris and involved *Vogue* in all her New York activities, resulting in reams of enviable editorial. She was helped by the legend that had grown over the fortune she had made out of the Lehman Brothers sale and buy-back; also by the fact that every time she returned to New York from Europe, she brought back something interesting, from a rare Somali leopard coat to a new anti-ageing formula, guaranteed to attract media attention. 1938 was no exception. That year Helena arrived from Paris with something *very* interesting in tow – her second husband, the handsome, charming

Prince Artchil Gourielli-Tchkonia. How New York loves a title and how Helena loved being a princess. The pleasure was all the greater for knowing it was guaranteed to annoy the ultra-snobbish Elizabeth Arden.

Cynics disputed Artchil Tchkonia's right to claim the Gourielli title, although had they searched, it would have been a struggle to prove or disprove it. From a genealogical point of view however, the claim is somewhat vague. In the late 1990s, in the Georgian capital of Tbilisi, an historian presented a series of television programmes, all carefully researched, on some of Georgia's noble families. The transcripts state quite clearly that, 'Artchil Tchkonia's mother was Nene Shevardnadze. His father was Alexander, a famous Georgian literature critic. Nene and Alexander Tchkonia had four children, Ekaterina, Meliton, Maria and Artchil. When he married Helena Rubinstein, they decided it would be appropriate if Artchil changed his name to Gourielli, which was his grandmother's family name, thus becoming a prince.'

Even in Georgia where so many records were lost during the Bolshevik Revolution, it isn't that easy to 'become a prince', but it was very easy to *call* yourself a prince. There were many great princely families in Georgia, including the royal line of Bagrationi and the powerful Mingrelsky, Imeritinsky and Gourielli bloodlines. Many claimants to titles, particularly when they felt it would help their status in America, were fakes. General Zacharias Mdivani for example, who had briefly been an aide-de-camp to the tsar, was apparently resigned to his famous sons' social climbing and told a friend he was the only person in the world who had inherited a title from his children.

Prince Yuri Chikovani of the Georgian Nobility Association in Tbilisi published a book showing that the Gourielli family can trace their lineage back to 1260 through the dukes of Guria. A Russian Imperial Order dated 1843 qualified the sisters of the last reigning Prince of Guria to take the title 'Serene Highness'. What he can't say is that one of these sisters married a Tchkonia, because not all the husbands of the Gourielli princesses are listed. Interestingly the last Gourielli princess in direct descent was a leading chess champion. Artchil played that game too, but even a mutual aptitude for chess doesn't entitle a distant relative to take a title.

Searches by Timothy Boettger, an expert in tracing Russian and Georgian bloodlines, confirmed that the Tchkonia family was an 'aznauri' – untitled – although noble line from Guria. When a line was in danger of becoming extinct in Russia, there were incidences of adoption, which enabled a title to be passed on. Mr Boettger explains that 'Nicholas Tchkonia, for example, was adopted in 1920 by his grandfather, Prince Tchkotua, and his wife, Princess Nina Bekhlanovna Inalipa; and the head of the imperial family in exile, Grand Duke Kirill, authorised Nicholas to take the title in 1938.'

Mr Boettger also points out that 'after the Revolution, the system of royal permission on transferring titles was much less strict.' Presumably the shock of losing so many nobles prompted the imperial family in emigration to top up the list in case they all died out. At any event, genealogists would say that as the Russian Empire ceased to exist in 1917, neither the transfer of a title, nor the creation of a new one were valid anyway.

Amongst all the confusion as to the authenticity of the Gourielli-Tchkonia title, experts agree there had never been an incidence of the two, quite separate family names being connected before Artchil appeared. One wonders why, contrary to noble Georgian disciplines, Artchil used a double 'll' in the spelling. There were also irregularities in the coat-of-arms used by the prince, which was enthusiastically adopted by Helena when she packaged a prestige product line called 'Gourielli' in the 1940s. The rumour persisted that Helena's 'prince' had created and printed a page from the *Almanach de Gotha* to prove his lineage, but Artchil remained constant in his use of his princely epithet – Helena's 'best name' as she was wont to call it, like a Sunday suit – and he was so popular that little was said about it.

Prince and Princess Gourielli, which is how they styled themselves, seemed a happy couple. The age difference – Artchil was twenty-three years younger than Helena – didn't matter. Helena had more energy than women half her age and enjoyed being a princess whilst Artchil enjoyed being able to indulge his passion for gambling and his skills as a genial host. If some of her friends and family were surprised by Madame's second marriage, they should not have been. The timing of her union coincided with news reaching her that her ex-husband had fallen deeply in love and remarried, and there was also quite a difference in that happy couple's age: Titus was sixty-eight and his bride was . . . twenty years old.

Erica de Meuronurech, the daughter of a Swiss banker, met Titus in the autumn of 1938 at a lunch party at Jacob Epstein's house in London. A houseguest of the Swiss ambassador while studying History of Art, Erica had joined her host at the Epsteins, who were holding one of their informal gatherings where the crème of London's musical and literary society would meet for impromptu performances and readings. Too young and naïve to realise the importance of such a coveted place at the Epstein lunch table – and on this occasion Yehudi Menuhin, just twenty-two but already receiving worldwide acclaim, would play for the guests – Erica spent most of her time talking to two men who both, she recollected, 'flirted furiously with me. We laughed a lot and I particularly enjoyed talking to the older man, rather than his son . . . he was more . . . interesting.' These were Edward Titus and his son Horace, who was staying, as he often did, with his father. Horace, by the age of twenty-six, had married and separated, leaving his two young children with their mother in Woodstock outside New York, to travel the world.

Erica Titus Friedman, now in her eighties, lives in Cannes. Still a beautiful woman, tiny, chic and bursting with personality, she is surrounded by opulent beauty in her home full of paintings, sculptures and books, many of them the originals published by Edward Titus. She cherishes her library, and the memory of the extraordinary time she spent with Titus. She has vivid memories of their first meeting. 'The Epsteins' apartment was fascinating,' she says, 'full of wonderful art but completely untidy – dirty even.' The sight of the chipped china and glass was confusing to a wealthy girl brought up surrounded by crisp linens and gleaming Meissen. The food and wine, however, were delicious, served, says Erica, 'by an ancient butler as dusty as the windows'. She remembers the arrival of a late guest. 'He was *very* charismatic, dressed in a baggy linen jacket and soft trousers – rather crumpled-looking I thought – and he filled the room with his presence. Mr Epstein was dressed in a similar way and the man said, "Well, Jacob, we're never going to make the best dressed men's list are we?" It was – Winston Churchill.'

Titus and Epstein had been friends since before the Great War and conversation that day was about Epstein's commission to illustrate Charles Baudelaire's *Flowers of Evil*, Titus being an authority on the poet's work. He was clearly captivated with the young Erica, and despite their huge age difference they married soon after. She had very little contact with Madame, 'although the boys of course, particularly Horace, came to stay with us a lot in Cagnes. Edward told me how much he had done to establish her business in Australia and London in the early days . . . it was *his* idea to use British society women to promote her creams.' Edward and Erica, cushioned by an allowance from her parents, settled into literary domesticity in the South of France. 'I was always meeting such important writers with Edward,' says Erica, 'he knew such fascinating people.'

Meanwhile, in New York, Helena and Artchil were settling into married life. It's unlikely their relationship was founded on physical attraction, a situation which suited them both. Although Artchil sought sexual solace elsewhere, he was discreet about it. As it was generally acknowledged Helena had been uncomfortable faced with anything as intangible as humour, her family were delighted about her marriage to this genial man and were all fond of him.

Diane Moss, Helena's great-niece, remembers, 'He was very charming and well-mannered. He was a real sweetheart and wonderfully funny. The whole group came alive when he was around and had a lot of fun.' The 'whole group' Mrs Moss is referring to is, of course, Helena's extended family, the complexities of which may have come as a shock to her new husband. They could, it seems, hardly bear each other, and his humour, given the tensions amongst this bizarre bunch, would have been most welcome. Horace, for example, didn't see eye-to-eye with his brother Roy, and simply loathed his cousin Oscar, a feeling which was mutual. Madame on the other hand liked Oscar very much. Roy cared little for his brother, and even less for his mother, from whom he was virtually estranged, seeking solace in the company of his wives; his mother apparently liked neither daughter-in-law one, two, three- *or* four very much. Roy hardly spoke to his father or his stepmother; Horace did, but Helena of course did not. As far as her sisters were concerned, Helena was not particularly close to Erna, was virtually estranged from Manka, constantly at loggerheads with Stella, and was irritated by Ceska. All of the sisters were terrified of Helena. Various cousins kept their heads down and got on with their work. By the time Helena settled back in New York with Artchil, she had become used to spending most of her social hours within this odd family group. Mrs Moss admits, 'She didn't really count "non-family" and didn't like parties, she wasn't a social animal at all, she was actually quite homey and loved being at Greenwich.'

The prince on the other hand was very social indeed and so, for a few years at least, Helena joined in and they partied. First of all, they had to find a home to party in. Helena found a triplex in a delightful honey-coloured stone building just thirteen storeys high at 625 Park Avenue and 65th St. She made an offer, but was rejected. To say she was angry is an understatement, particularly when she heard she'd been turned down because she was Jewish. Ironically, Helena Rubinstein was the least Jewish person of all. She was never known to attend synagogue, and employees, excluding the family circle, were more often than not non-Jewish. Helena would often make disparaging quips about Jewish taste. The area where Mrs Lauder lived in the South of France, for example, was 'very Jewish'. The glittering box she was once shown for packaging was rejected as being 'too Jewish'. Even Proust had been 'the Jewish boy who wrote that book'. Madame however became very angry at this slight against her birth, so she made other arrangements. She bought the building.

Artchil's sense of fun would have been much appreciated in the Rubinstein household over that period, as Harry Johnson, flushed with his powerful new position at Elizabeth Arden, was holding court with the financial press on behalf of his boss. His efforts resulted in some powerful features extolling the success of the company, guaranteed to make Helena angry. Mr Johnson, having had experience in working with forceful women, presumably thought he knew which buttons to press to keep them sweet. Unfortunately, he miscalculated with Elizabeth Arden. One thing guaranteed to make her see red was her employees getting more publicity than she did and telling her how to spend her money. Harry Johnson did both. Firstly, he broke the golden rule of the Arden school of public relations which went something like 'only the name of Elizabeth Arden shall be used at any time, anywhere.' The fact that her newest director had taken a look at the books and realised things weren't in great shape, quickly moving to place corporate stories that presented a brighter picture, was completely lost on Elizabeth.

Fortune magazine, for example, profiled her company in 1938. The in-depth feature ran to an astonishing fourteen pages of triumphant eulogy to Miss Arden, quoting Elizabeth as saying, 'I am a famous woman in this industry,' and continuing with a blow-by-blow breakdown of her holdings in Brazil (held by foreign subsidiaries), of her wholesaling in the West Indies, in Canada and in Europe (all, as explained by Mr Johnson, run by separate limited companies). The type of intimate financial data that is required from a public company poured from the pages. The only trouble was that Elizabeth Arden ran a private company. If she didn't mind her business structure being exposed for her rivals, not to mention a testy IRS to see, she should have done. Johnson, naturally, was bathed in a rosy glow of success throughout the feature. Credence was given to a story that, in 1929, she had been offered $15 million for her business, which she turned down. Even the research skills of *Fortune* magazine couldn't find any evidence of this offer. Although she bordered on obsession about recording every detail of her life, extensive research in her family papers and other sources have failed to discover any record of it either. Such a story coming at a time when, although her business was performing well, she was cash-strapped, could have been a brilliant public relations ploy. At one time or another, both Arden and Rubinstein hired every major public relations adviser on the market and there would have been no shortage of experts ready with an opinion as to how to shift media emphasis towards or away from turnover.

By the 1930s, the art of corporate PR was evolving and Benjamin Sonnenberg was one of the earliest and most skilful of its operators. Mr Sonnenberg believed in presenting a polished and upscale image to his clients; if he showed his clients how well *he* lived, they would continue to hire him to ensure *they* lived just as well. To this end, Mr Sonnenberg moved into the Gramercy Park house of the late Mamie Stuyvesant Fish. As Mr Sonnenberg entertained the great and the good at his mansion, he could dwell on the fact his success came from making and breaking the reputations of the socially aspirational. Mamie Stuyvesant Fish did exactly the same, only she didn't charge fees for it. Whether Mr Sonnenberg worked for Miss Arden is not known, but he was certainly responsible for adding some polish to the early Rubinstein image in America, Helena admitting he had worked for her at a reduced fee as 'he was my friend'.

Elizabeth Arden didn't need much support from public relations efforts; her figures spoke for themselves. Her annual wholesale turnover by this stage was apparently $4 million, with her nineteen salons in America adding a further $1.25 million to the pot. The Fifth Avenue flagship alone was reported to take over $600,000. *Fortune* wrote it wasn't the volume of sales that made her special, nor the number of retail accounts, nor evenness of distribution. Elizabeth Arden, it said, was 'noted for being tops – absolute, unqualified, unarguably tops – in the "treatment" cosmetics business'. The journalist, with unusual perception for a financial writer tackling a relatively unknown area wrote, 'This was a chancy field of enterprise, ruled by high price, high style and high tension!' Miss Arden was described as 'the Tiffany of her trade' and no one, not even Rubinstein 'had been able to achieve the prestige of Elizabeth Arden's own particular business'.

Fortune did not know, however, that by 1937 Elizabeth's share portfolio had whittled down from $700,000 to $200,000 and she was already alerting Teddy Haslam, who held a large British portfolio for her under one of several businesses she used, including one called Beauty Art Ltd, that she might have to ask him for margin, knowing they could easily afford it. The rich in Great Britain were getting richer. In 1937, Inland Revenue statistics showed 824 millionaires and well over 85,000 people earning over £2000 a year. The Elizabeth Arden business in England was locked in to the 824 millionaires and was secure and profitable. Turnover was at $1 million a year, with higher salon prices and lower wages and distribution meaning Mr Haslam was able to operate on 'a 7 to 1 ratio of sales price to cost'. Haslam was also responsible 'for all the British Empire (excluding Canada) as well as South America and most of Europe'. For this, he was paid $24,000 a year, under half Mr Johnson's salary in America. A few weeks before the *Fortune* article was published, Elizabeth wrote to Teddy, 'Mr Johnson continues to increase profits and really looks ahead and plans carefully.' Not much that was favourable was ever said about him thereafter.

A little under a year earlier, in October 1937, echoing unrest amongst the garment workers' union, the cosmetics manufacturing workforce flexed their muscles. Arden's workers at her New York factory went on strike, some 70% of them having joined a union. She was livid, but rolled her sleeves up and waded in. 'I think we have it fairly well squelched now,' she wrote. 'We just saved ourselves from having these nasty unions come in and tell us what to do. Fancy, they wanted $27 a week to the last bottle washer.' The result of the settlement is not known, but it's doubtful that they got $27 a week. Whatever they got, they probably wished they had held out for more when headlines proclaimed their boss was drawing $75,000 in salary plus a further $200,000 a year for 'living costs' and that she had spent $54,000 on horses at one go.

She wasn't the only cosmetics manufacturer having trouble with the unions. Charles Revson was having battles with District Sixty-Five of the Distributive Workers of America, at that time a very left-wing organisation in New York. Revlon's pay talks, led by his bruising right-hand man, Mickey Soroko, eventually settled disputes and not before time, as some of their more militant workers had taken to putting little notes into product boxes saying 'Fuck you', which didn't go down too well with the ladies who bought them.

Although he had less of a union problem with the print workers, a stock-market slump of 1937 didn't help media tycoon Condé Nast, coming just as he was struggling to refinance his business. He still did his best to fly the flag in the way he knew best, by hosting parties. When Edna Woolman Chase's actress daughter Ilka was cast in the play *The Women*, by ex-*Vanity Fair* editor Clare Booth Brokaw, Nast gave an opening night supper dance at his Park Avenue home. His meticulous records show that out of 902 guests invited, 602 turned up. Even then it wasn't a crush. The opulent apartment, decorated by Elsie de Wolfe, took over one thousand people for a party. Ilka wasn't cast when the play was made into a film by the great George Cukor two years later, her role went to Rosalind Russell. Hedda Hopper won a part playing a gossip columnist. The opening scene of *The Women* is set in a beauty salon which, to anyone who knew about such things – particularly Hopper who had worked there – was obviously based on Elizabeth Arden's New York salon. Hedda took pleasure in inviting her great friend Elizabeth to visit the production and see for herself. However she loathed the set and lost her temper. 'It looks fake,' she screamed at George Cukor, 'I hate it and you can't use my name, I'll sue!' Cukor, used to dealing with difficult women, his production starring several of them, including Norma Shearer, Joan Crawford, Rosalind Russell, Paulette Goddard and Joan Fontaine, patiently explained, 'It doesn't show your name; it doesn't show *any* name, but of course we took our inspiration from you and I know you'll be pleased when you see the result.' When the film was released, making a big impact at the box office, Elizabeth forgot her earlier anger and adored it.

News guaranteed to please the social climber in Elizabeth came from London; Teddy told her that the new Queen was continuing her patronage of Elizabeth Arden. As the Duchess of York she had visited the salon, unlike Queen Mary, whose products were carefully mixed, blended and delivered to the palace. Now the duchess was Queen, her trips to Bond Street were curtailed, but treatment experts like Dinah Wall went to Buckingham Palace to visit their most illustrious client. When King George VI and Queen Elizabeth visited Paris, the Queen looking every inch the Winterhalter beauty in her Hartnell crinolines, her skin was glowing with Arden face treatments. Not everyone admired her taste in clothes. When

Wallis Windsor was asked what she felt her sister-in-law, the Queen, could now do to boost British fashion, the Duchess is reported to have said, 'stay at home'.

Unrest was rippling through Europe. Goering visited Vienna, claiming in a speech that 'Austrian Jews have nothing to fear'. That they had a lot to fear was becoming frighteningly clear and talk was of war. In a chilling move, by October 1938 the Jewish community in Berlin were given two weeks to hand in their passports. The date of 9 November became etched on the civilised world's memory as the date the Nazi Party declared their true colours. They called it Kristallnacht. Seven thousand Jewish shops were looted in Berlin that night.

President Roosevelt condemned Nazi anti-Semitism, but Hitler took no notice. As 1938 drew to a close, Jews in Germany were forbidden to deal in property, jewellery, precious metals or even to hold a bank account. Jewish businesses were closed down and assets confiscated. Helena presumably doubted she would ever see her salons in Germany again. With memories of her exodus from Paris during the last world war, she made plans to relocate permanently to New York. She also made additions to her staffing. Lunching with Elinor McVickar, beauty editor of *Harper's Bazaar*, in November, Helena asked what she thought of Thomas Jenkins Lewis. Elinor raised her sleek eyebrows. 'Arden's ex-husband? He was a good man.' Helena beamed. 'Fine, I've just hired him. He starts immediately. Don't tell anyone yet, I leave for Australia tomorrow.'

Elizabeth must have been weak with anger and probably wondered if it had all been worth it, especially as she was by now tiring of Mr Johnson, wailing to Teddy, 'I am crazy with the way my business is being run. We are selling a dollar's worth of this and a dollar's worth of that, which is cheapening our line. Mr Johnson controls everything and doesn't even call me when important buyers come in. I just hate her Rubenstein* methods.'

When Picasso unveiled his masterpiece *Guernica* in Paris in 1939, the Nazis condemned modern art as 'a decadent by-product of Bolshevik Jewish corruption'. Helena, astutely, had shipped most of her modern art to New York, where it was shown to the social set and the glossy media at parties hosted by Prince and Princess Gourielli to celebrate moving into their new, thirty-six-room apartment. Her business was back on track, and as a finish-

---

*Arden always deliberately misspelled Rubinstein.

ing touch, in a much-coveted publicity coup, April *Vogue* featured Rubinstein's Orchid Red lipstick on their cover.

New York was getting ready for the World's Fair to be held in June that year. There was tremendous excitement when it was announced that King George VI and Queen Elizabeth would visit the fair. Miss Arden became over-excited when she heard and wrote to Teddy, 'I wish Mrs Wonnacott could come over when the King and Queen come to follow them around and give quick, restful treatments. Could it be arranged she could always be at her disposal?' There was no further mention of this, so presumably Mr Haslam pointed out that it wouldn't be quite the thing for the Queen to turn up at Hyde Park to stay with President Roosevelt bringing her own masseuse. At any event, Elizabeth's grand plans for entertainment at the World's Fair crumpled when Madame stole her thunder by launching the world's first waterproof mascara as part of a synchronised water ballet called the Acquade Show. It was game, set and match to Helena.

Other cosmetologists were beginning to make a name for themselves in New York, among them the highly regarded Hungarian Dr Erno Laszlo, who, by 1938, was established as a serious, more holistic alternative to the Arden and Rubinstein salons and held court in a suite of rooms with the walls painted coal-black to induce tranquillity and eliminate wrinkle-producing tension. Silence and darkness was the Laszlo secret ingredient and his 'black makes you bloom' technique was proving vastly popular with his adoring disciple, Elsie de Wolfe and her set, including the Duchess of Windsor, several Whitneys and Rose Kennedy, who apparently took his treatment creams and soaps with her to London when husband Joe was appointed American ambassador.

Had the two women spent less time bickering they might have had their antennae more finely tuned to a far greater threat to their virtual stranglehold over the market in America. Their competition, however, wasn't coming from Dr Laszlo, nor Tangee, nor Dorothy Gray, Germail Monteil, Richard Hudnut, Max Factor or any of the other players in the field. Their real rival was the seemingly unstoppable Charles Revson. As Europe prepared for war, Miss Arden and Madame should have been preparing to do battle with Revlon, but they were still too busy fighting each other. They would come to regret it.

CHAPTER SIXTEEN

THE SECOND WORLD WAR –
PART I
London, Paris, New York
1939–1942

ELIZABETH WAS IN PARIS in the early summer of 1939 for the gala opening of her new salon in Place Vendôme, followed by a tour of her salons in the South of France and London. She took time out to visit the Paris couture collections, accompanied by Gladys, and even more time trying to persuade her sister to move back to New York to avoid the war in Europe. However, Gladys adored her husband, and since Henri de Maublanc welcomed the Germans, he insisted they were in no danger at all. The Elizabeth Arden company in France had been made over to Gladys several years earlier to avoid prohibitive French taxes on foreign ownership and it was now, somewhat reluctantly on the part of Elizabeth, made over to the name of Henri de Maublanc, where it would remain safe under Occupation, for the duration of the war. So supportive was Henri of the regime in Germany that during the late 1930s, when smoothtalking high-powered German visitors, members of Ambassador von Ribbentrop's 'charm squad', as they were called, visited London to spread the good word about Nazi Germany, they were apparently made welcome at Arden's Grosvenor Street offices. Such meetings were observed by a young employee called Joan Miller, who left shortly afterwards to take up war work as personal assistant to Charles Henry Maxwell Knight, aka 'M' – chief of MI5's B5 (b) Section. Miller later wrote about her experiences, in a book the government tried desperately to ban, saying, 'Elizabeth Arden's London head office was used as a pre-war rendezvous point by the Gestapo.' The outbreak of war put paid to any further Anglo-German hospitality via Henri, and it must be said that had Miss Arden known about such visits she would have been furious.

Edna Woolman Chase had also extended her summer trip to Paris and Europe that year and was lunching at Claridges with Teddy Haslam and Harry Yoxall, business manager of British *Vogue*, when a frantic message came through from her daughter Ilka, imploring her to come home. Mrs Chase sailed shortly afterwards on the SS *Manhattan*. The Americans in Europe seemed to take the threat of war more seriously than many of the British. Teddy Haslam wasn't alone in hoping it 'might not happen'. Boris Forter, Helena Rubinstein's newly appointed UK manager, was convinced nothing too serious would evolve, and failed to stock up on staple ingredients, most of which then became impossible to obtain for the duration.

Helena's sister Ceska, by now a widow and feeling isolated, was panicking to get out of London, convinced that bombing raids were going to start overnight. Her nephew Roy Titus, who had been working at the London office, was immediately recalled to New York and Boris Forter was, as he put it, 'left holding the fort' in the company of the Rubinstein chief accountant, Mr Slatter, while Ceska followed Roy back to America, remaining there in uneasy and underemployed exile throughout the war.

Helena planned as many safe exit routes as possible for close relatives still in Europe, in particular sending her sister Stella to Argentina and her young great-niece Regina, who had been working at the production plant in Vienna, to Australia. Regina stayed in Australia for the rest of her life, running the Rubinstein plant in Sydney and supervising business throughout Australia and New Zealand. When she married Fritz Garrett in the late 1940s, following the tradition of senior Rubinstein women working for Madame, she kept the family name. Regina's husband, like Mala Silson's, presumably accepted that such independence came with the family territory.

With her nephew Henry Kolin and his family in Toronto, and other relatives soon to be running the Rubinstein salon in Rio de Janeiro, Helena's 'operations map' of relatives was in reasonably good shape to see out the war, despite the more vulnerable position of her premises in Berlin, Vienna, Paris and London, the first three not places for a high-profile Jewish woman to be operating a lucrative business. Whilst her salons were confiscated, the Rubinstein property portfolio remained intact in Paris, Helena transferring ownership to her French lawyers, who managed her affairs astutely, just as the Bourjois corporation – along with their Parfums Chanel subsidiary, owned by the Wertheimer brothers, who had also moved to America, was managed by Felix Amiot, who fronted their business during German occupation.

One of their first tasks was to replace a tenant in one of Madame's Quai de Bethune apartments. Countess Johanna de Knecht, a wealthy and beautiful Dutch model, was exactly the type of tenant Madame liked: rich, organised and not often in residence – less work for the concierge. The countess had gone on a cruise with friends in the summer of 1939 and, stranded by the war, headed for New York. Visiting a beauty trade fair, she was lobbied by an exhibitor to come to their stand and have her nails painted. Six months later she married the manufacturer in question and became – Mrs Charles Revson. Madame Rubinstein did not renew her lease.

On 1 September, the Germans marched into Poland and the world of the Jewish life of Madame's youth vanished for ever. The Rubinstein family was more fortunate than most during this black hole of Europe's history. Helena's parents had died before the war and most of her immediate family had long left Krakow. Amongst relatives remaining, however, was Madame's sister Regina. She would never see her again. For most of the sixty thousand Jews in Kazimierz the future held unimaginable horror. Some 1200 however were lucky enough to survive. They were the ones selected to work at what had been a Jewish-owned factory — Deutsch Emailwaren Fabrik — making enamelled pots and pans where the new owner, who would become their saviour, was Oscar Schindler.

As the lights went out across Europe, and Britain and France declared war on Germany, supplying and staffing salons became hard to control. Elizabeth Arden remained open and fully functional in Berlin, and in France, where the brand was in favour with the German High Command. Madrid remained operational, and her salon in Milan was similarly lucky, although British staff working there when Italy joined the war were interned immediately. Elizabeth liked to think she kept her ear to the ground with power brokers in New York, and she was certainly wined and dined by European diplomats in Washington. Unfortunately, they weren't always the right ones. 'I have just heard, confidentially,' she wrote to Teddy in early June 1940, 'that Italy won't enter the war.' Well, she heard wrong. By 30 June poor Miss Mitchell Henry, the Milan salon manageress who had been sent out from London, was in an internment camp. Miss Arden was furious. Not just about her staff, but because revenues from Italy, along with those in France, Germany, Holland and Belgium were now frozen in war zones and could not be transferred to England. To overcome this hiccup in what had been a smooth channel of funding, delicate arrangements had to be made to safeguard the Arden assets.

Whilst most treatment staff in the European salons were recruited locally, Arden policy was to have an American sales manager in charge of wholesale activity, demonstrator training and overall liaison, assisted by a British assistant manager, all of whom reported to Teddy Haslam in England. The British contingent had to retreat rapidly back to London, where many of them volunteered for military service, leaving holes in staffing which were almost impossible to fill. As Elizabeth had always made a practice of seconding senior American management executives to Europe, the problem was less pressing in the early years of the war, as they were still free to travel within Europe. One of the American contingent was Bill Carlson, whose profile was typically Arden. Well-educated, speaking four languages, charming, well-dressed and well-travelled, Carlson was a senior sales manager for European territories, based in Germany and reporting to Mr Haslam in London.

Miss Arden, however, sent him back to America to sort out floundering figures on the normally profitable West Coast, leaving his French artist wife in Munich, where she became stranded by the war. On 17 September, the day Russia invaded Poland, Mrs Carlson got a letter out to Elizabeth from Germany, asking if she could contact her husband and get him to send her funds. 'I hope that the present conditions will not affect your business,' Valerie Carlson wrote. 'Here everything is quiet and peaceful and I shall return to Munich to work in a studio there.' Wishful thinking on her part. In 1940 Mrs Carlson was eventually given an exit permit and joined her husband in the US. In the meantime, Elizabeth, showing her customary generosity to staff she was fond of, but more significantly not wanting Carlson distracted from his job by worry about his wife, instructed Haslam to resolve the situation. 'I really do not see any point in making Mr Carlson change English money for German marks. The best solution would be to put her on the payroll in Germany for the time being.'

Gladys too was having a financial crisis. 'I had to send $10,000 to sister,' wrote Elizabeth, 'she seemed broke', and Elizabeth herself acknowledged that she had to sell $350,000-worth of shares to pay bank loans. Mr Haslam responded to the imminent crisis by laying off thirty-five staff, cutting the advertising budget by $30,000 and, in a move that would prove a false economy, cutting raw materials purchases by $75,000.

In early 1940, Elizabeth's financial troubles became even more gloomy, when she was presented with a tax bill which she said was for 'more than half a million dollars'. Despite entreaties to satellite countries to cut expenses, her own promotional costs were spiralling out of control and, to make matters worse, she was by now at total loggerheads with Harry Johnson. She was always grumbling about him. 'He's put on so much red tape it is just terrifying,' she complained to Teddy.

In Berlin, Gordon Yates, who had been running Elizabeth Arden GmbH since 1937, was safe enough, as an American, although he and his wife observed the situation in Germany with deep unease. Yates managed the business across Germany, Czechoslovakia and Austria, until he and his wife left at the end of 1940, driving their Mercedes across Europe to Scotland. The car, according to their son, Tiki, 'was packed to the gunwhales with valuables belonging to their Jewish friends who were desperate to get it all to England'.

Meanwhile, in America, after investigating the West Coast business in 1940, Bill Carlson found the courage to tell his mercurial boss the truth, feeling perhaps that, after ten years of working for her, he would be listened to. 'You simply must trust your loyal employees to organise your business on a sound, common-sense, ethical and consistent basis,' he wrote to her. 'If you do, you personally will have great satisfaction and pleasure and will own one of the most profitable businesses in the world.' Carlson enclosed a report critical of her sales representatives and of Henry Sell's advertising agency. He also said that the salons were becoming expensive to operate and pandered to an ageing clientele. Carlson was critical too about mass distribution – a policy implemented by Harry Johnson, whose sales targets at Rubinstein, which had seemed restrained at the time, were still far too aggressive to suit the relentlessly up-market Elizabeth Arden line. Showing remarkable judgement, Carlson said, 'merchandise is judged by the company it keeps', a policy revered by skilful brand-builders in the luxury sector for decades after Arden executives acknowledged its importance. One improvement deemed vital by Carlson was their own West-Coast warehouse to ease distribution.

'Rubenstein has recently installed such a distribution point and we must always be in a position to give better service than they,' he wrote to Miss Arden, making a gentle concession to his boss by also spelling her rival's name incorrectly. To be fair, Elizabeth did, for a while, try to fall in with Bill Carlson's advice. But she simply couldn't let go.

Looking for new ways to add to her turnover, Elizabeth decided to enter the area of nail polish, until 1940 virtually the exclusive fiefdom of Charles Revson. Acquiring a formula for what she described as 'the best nail polish in the world' she planned to sell it at 65 cents a bottle, and use it for manicures in all her salons. 'I'm sickened to think we can't get ahead of Revlon,' she wrote to Teddy. 'I hear that man sells $300,000 a month in polish.' She was talking about turnover at retail prices, but she wasn't far out. The Revlon wholesale figures were just under $1.3 million that year. In 1940, however, when Revson added lipstick to his range, his sales more than doubled to $2.8 million. During the 1940s, due to very aggressive selling techniques, well-positioned price points, an insatiable desire on the part of American women to wear lipstick, not to mention just a little luck, Revlon's turnover rocketed to around $17 million a year. An inveterate gambler who often took over an entire blackjack table, Revson was throwing all the lucky dice. His biggest stroke of luck came during the war, not least because he wasn't called up to fight in it.

Charles Revson managed to avoid active duty largely thanks to his chief *aide de camp*, Mickey Soroko, who was a mine of useful contacts and held a very flexible job brief. 'Mickey was a problem solver,' wrote Revson's biographer, Harvard Business School graduate Andrew Tobias. 'He had been a process server, tracking down people to serve with subpoenas. He had run a debt collection agency, frightening or threatening people to pay off their debts. He was the kind of guy who would go out of his way for a fight.' Soroko fought his boss's corner for twenty-five years. 'Charles liked street fighters, liked to think of himself as one, and had his man in Mickey Soroko,' said Tobias about the man who got things done for his boss. 'Soroko had signing privileges on a special Revson bank account and he sorted out fire regulations, particularly helpful in connection with the sale of nail enamel which was a flammable substance.' In one town, where there had apparently been a problem over this tricky issue, Soroko went in and, legend has it, the fire trucks were later seen delivering the delayed orders.

Mickey Soroko turned his charm and the full force of his personality on to people in government, the FDA, detectives, dermatologists, prominent Jews – anyone who could be of help to Revlon. 'Soroko managed to land some sizeable government contracts and somehow Revlon had an easier time than its competitors in obtaining the raw materials and packaging materials it needed for its cosmetics,' says Andrew Tobias. Having government contracts meant being excused from active service. Charles Revson was able to remain at the helm of his business and turn it into one of the most aggressive success stories in the second phase of the twentieth-century boom in cosmetics manufacturing. It also meant profits, which delighted him even more. His first two contracts were assembling first-aid kits and making dye-markers for the navy. The production was so successful that in 1944 Revlon were awarded an 'Award for Excellence', with its 'E' insignia, which was considered a great honour, although his staff, behind his back, murmured it was 'E' for ego. The third contract was apparently established whilst Charles was at a meeting in Washington with a Government Procurement Officer who asked him if he knew anything about powder. Charles replied, 'I know *everything* about powder' and before he knew it, he had a contract to make hand-grenades for the army. It didn't occur to the government official to explain he had meant gun-powder or to Charles Revson to admit he meant face-powder.

The Revlon corporation were fortunate in having a favourable position on obtaining raw materials, particularly as so many base ingredients used by the cosmetics industry were required for war effort production. It wasn't just what went into the product that was scarce, it was what the product went *in* as well: glass jars, metal lipstick cases, even the paper for labels, and the gum to paste them on the jars; tissue paper for wrapping soap, dyes for cosmetics and packaging, acids, fixatives, preservatives – it was all scarce or impossible to find – unless one paid the price.

In Great Britain, the government immediately placed a restriction on production, covering all goods it deemed 'non-essentials'. Cosmetics companies were allocated production quantities, ranging from a quarter to two-thirds of their 1938 production, depending on the status and definition of goods of the company in question. Scented soaps were considered favourable by the Board of Trade, enabling Bronnley to triumph, despite rationing. Bronnley reminded readers of the glossy magazines that they had been 'makers of the finest soaps for fifty years and the difficulties of output are being met by equitable distribution – the Quantity is governed by the nation – the Quality is guaranteed by the name.' Moisturising and treatment creams were considered an extravagance as base ingredients were derived from petro-chemicals needed for war use. This hit both Arden and Rubinstein hard, and both rushed out new products to get around government regulations.

Elizabeth stole a march on her rival with the launch of Velva Leg Film which quickly became a bestseller. A refinement of one of her suntan products developed over a decade earlier, Velva Leg Film was sold as the alternative to stockings. The sublimely talented fashion illustrator René Bouché drew the images for the magazine campaign. 'Elizabeth Arden's leg makeup stays on the legs and off the clothes,' said the advertising, 'water-resistant with a blemish-concealing sheer textured beauty that trims the ankle and slims the leg.' As the war took a grip, leg make-up, and drawing a fake seam up the back of the leg, became an everyday habit for many women coping with fashion shortages.

Advertising had a patriotic ring. Max Factor's pancake makeup was 'in keeping with the colouring of the Women's Service uniforms' whilst Tampax promoted their product as 'women's best ally, women's tasks today leave no room for disabilities'. Women were put under an obligation to take care of their grooming by the dictatorial tone taken by the beauty companies. Patriotic copylines appeared everywhere, such as 'Never forget that good looks and good morale go hand in hand' or 'There must be no giving in to careless grooming. We must not lower our standard to the enemy.' However hard manufacturers tried to cope with shortages, restrictions only allowed them to make a third or three-quarters less each year, so staff at every level were laid off – or were supposed to be.

Boris Forter at Helena Rubinstein UK drew the short straw. Interviewed by Helena in New York in 1938, he was told British turnover was 'over £100,000 a year', but when he arrived to take up his job in Grafton Street, he found the figures languishing at nearer £40,000 a year. As his pitifully low salary was augmented by a percentage payment that kicked in when targets over the house figure were reached, and the house figures were false, he could either starve, or improvise. He chose the latter.

The Rubinstein British quota was established at 25%, clearly not enough for Boris to maintain the lifestyle he aspired to, nor to properly support his wife Marisa and son Claude. The situation was further complicated by the fact that the sales manager responsible for top department stores was none other than Arden's ex-employee Prince Kadjar, as charming as ever but now showing more skill at opening a whisky bottle than riding horses or selling cosmetics. He was very popular with Helena's sister Ceska, who, presumably jealous that her sister was now married to a prince, at least had the satisfaction of employing her own prince. Following a stand-up fight with Kadjar outside Prunier's, however, Boris saw him off and took over sales himself.

The Board of Trade insisted that cosmetics companies 'doubled up' to save production facilities, thus releasing factories for the war effort, and issued quotas for production which could be bought or sold amongst manufacturers. Boris Forter had opened a factory in Surrey which was requisitioned, and they were twinned uneasily with Coty; a relationship not helped by the fact that Boris and the Coty managing director, Mr Valley, loathed each other. The Rubinstein chemist, Dr Salfeld, was becoming increasingly irascible — many of his family were in Germany — but whatever cheering spirit he lacked, the enterprising Boris made up for. With the Rubinstein sisters safely in New York, he had a clear run to re-build an ailing business. Madame might have been a huge success in the heady society decade before the First War, but by the time the Second came around, her British business was a casualty.

Unlike his counterpart Teddy Haslam, at Elizabeth Arden, Russian-born Boris, having lived most of his life in France and America, had little knowledge of how to appeal to the British personality. He had no entrée into the gentlemen's clubs Haslam was invited to, neither did he belong to the golf clubs his rival frequented. The Rubinstein camp also lacked an advertising budget, her product message being conspicuously absent from media pages during the war years. Even with a cut-back of 30%, Arden's budget bought a lot of pages, and Haslam ensured they went into *Vogue*, *Queen* and other useful publications.

Arden's advertising quickly took up the patriotic theme. Text in 1941 said: '*Many are the jobs a present day woman of the world does, but she talks of them seldom. Many are the pleasures she has given up. But one pleasure and also a duty she finds that she can still afford, a few minutes devoted every morning and evening to cleansing, toning and nourishing with Elizabeth Arden preparations.*'

Boris had no advertising budget, but he had personality, and that most valuable of weapons — charm — which he used relentlessly. He was tireless in wheeling and dealing his way around town, fraternising with people he determined could help him get the company back on target, and his own cash position, back on track. The fact that some of his associates were decidedly shady characters didn't worry Boris. He was, for example, able to 'accept a small gift' from the more entrepreneurial businessmen who came into his orbit with no hesitation. The first thing he did was to ensure Helena Rubinstein had some product, and he achieved this by buying quotas.

In theory, trading in quotas — what the Board of Trade deemed the 'rights to produce' – was perfectly legal, provided the quotas were official ones. In the early years of the war, the guidelines about such quotas were hazy. This played into the hands of most ambitious players in the beauty business, who rushed to buy and sell quotas, often on the black market rather than through formal channels.

Retailers were desperate for beauty products. All the department stores had customers ready and willing to pay whatever it took. There were always ways to fudge paperwork if it meant a supply of lipsticks or face-powder, and store buyers would rarely question the validity of stock quota. They just wanted the goods. Smaller, independent retailers and chemists could, and often did, simply buy outright on the black market, local women somehow divining at once when new stocks had arrived, happily queuing most of the morning for their lipsticks. As stock ran out, manufacturers started to encourage clients to conserve product and its containers. One of London's most successful companies, Gala, ran a campaign begging consumers to 'keep lipstick containers and buy re-fills to conserve metal for the War effort' and Cyclax implored its discriminating ladies to 'use our beauty preparations with a new economy'.

For those with neither the money nor the black-market access, help was on hand from an invaluable little book. A few years earlier, in the midst of deep recession, an unlikely bestseller went into a reprint, much to the delight of Sir Isaac Pitman & Sons, the publishers. *Cosmetics and How to Make Them* by Robert Bushby struck a chord with women everywhere whose budgets had been affected by the Depression. This invaluable guide to whipping up face cream went into a second edition in 1942, a third in 1943 and was reprinted yet again in 1945. Wartime shortages and rationing turned keen cooks into domestic cosmetologists.

Neither the Arden nor the Rubinstein customer, however, was a do-it-yourself fan. She wanted her product ready made. It's easy to imagine a smooth operator like Boris Forter turning on his charm to buyers and suppliers, over lunch or dinner at a glamorous restaurant. He would have been happy taking to the floor at supper clubs with lady cosmetics-buyers. Forter may have had a lowly salary but he had expensive tastes. He drew a generous expense account and milked the market for all it was worth. Before long he had increased the Rubinstein turnover to £100,000 a year.

To be fair, Helena understood sales costs, although she had a love-hate relationship with expenses – more hate than love. If sales were good, the budget was flexible. One sign of a problem, however, and costs were slashed. Travelling sales reps, for example, were apparently kept on a budget so tight that sometimes they hardly had cash to buy a meal for themselves, never mind a guest. She was a little more flexible with expense accounts in the hands of senior management, and her own family, but only just. In her will, she left her niece Mala a modest allowance of $5000 a year for life 'to enable her to meet the expenses of entertainment of clients and other persons in connection with the business of Helena Rubinstein Inc'. The result of this lifelong parsimony, according to Boris, was that staff became adept at fiddling expenses, and some executives, including Madame's own sister Ceska, became adept at fiddling their invoices.

Twenty-five years earlier, Boris had to manage on considerably less than Mala's $5000 a year, but with a four-course luncheon at Claridges costing 6s 6d, a little went a long way. Wining and dining at that level was far beyond the pay packet of the average junior civil servant, who could expect to earn about £12 a week. But Boris soon became experienced in dealing with British red tape and eased the path through it by ensuring minor officials were presented with a box of cosmetics 'for your wife, I do hope you'll accept it'. Due to his lobbying of officials at the Board of Trade, he obtained permission to manufacture 200,000 embossed and gilded drum-shaped powder boxes for Rubinstein's Apple Blossom talc. They were very pretty and very pricey, and Boris sold the lot at a premium.

But Boris's success was mainly due to buying and selling quotas, aided by a Hungarian acquaintance of dubious repute, called Mr Retty. Knowing Boris was keen to expand his activities, Retty introduced him to an ex-RAF 'officer' called Mr Mumford. All bristling moustaches and gleaming gilt blazer buttons, Mumford was very convincing and Boris was taken in, admitting to buying £30,000 of quota for £6000 in cash. Boris promptly sold some of it — at a hefty mark-up to none other than Mr Haslam of Arden, reserved a little for Rubinstein, and passed on the rest to Gala. Unfortunately for Boris, Mumford's quotas were fraudulent. A warrant was issued for the arrest not only of Mumford, but of Mr Retty and Boris too. They were all brought to trial with, as Boris relates, 'the Rubinstein family reluctantly it seemed to me paying for my defence'. Mr Justice MacDonald failed to be convinced by the Forter argument that (a) he was totally ignorant that Mumford was a crook and (b) cosmetics were essential for morale and he was only trying to help the war effort. The judge gave a grim summing-up, preaching about offensive and slack morals in wartime. The jury happily chose not to listen. Like most other people who met Boris Forter, they were captivated by his personality and were presumably swayed by his explanations about the machinations of provisioning stores with beauty products to serve the appetites of women starving as much for face cream as for fillet steak. Boris was found not guilty, but Mr Mumford was sentenced to eighteen months in prison. Eventually, the Board of Trade tightened up quota allocation by issuing stamped and witnessed documents, which apparently stopped the worst of the rackets.

Over at Arden, it was observed that Mr Haslam always found ways to hire treatment staff when hiring levels were supposed to be cut back. He was also flying in top personnel from the US, obtaining travel permits to visit France, and had secured a production quota at the highest level allowed, that of three-quarters of the previous year's production. His competitors could only watch with envy. No doubt there was many an official whose wife had a new perm, or a bag of cosmetics, to smooth the path of paperwork. Possibly royal patronage helped, it being generally well known that the Queen used Elizabeth Arden products, but the salon at 25 New Bond Street had many other influential clients, best described as 'the wives of the men who were running the country'. Perhaps the client with the greatest influence was Mrs Randolph Churchill, Winston Churchill's curvaceous and vivacious daughter-in-law, who was dedicated to her beauty regimes. Pamela had a close relationship with her father-in-law, who was sympathetic about his son's inability to pay the household bills, which, to Pamela's shame, resulted in her Harrods credit being cut off. There would be no such problem at the Arden salon, where Mrs Churchill was given open-ended credit, although such largesse was not extended to most of their clientele. Monthly accounts were cut back and clients encouraged to pay on the spot.

Miss Arden was very receptive to taking as many staff as possible across to America, exit permits permitting. Mr Haslam was keen she hire a top Swedish treatment expert, Mrs Kingston, but at the last minute, Elizabeth, fired with patriotic zeal, turned against the Swedes for being neutral and Mrs Kingston was left to fend for herself. Miss Arden had the last word on all employment, one of the main reasons her senior executives were in such despair. They felt they were doing their jobs with one hand tied behind their backs if they couldn't control the selection of their teams.

As the war took hold in Europe, causing severe staffing problems, what had been a 'crack team' for Arden in the USA was also starting to fall apart. Not only had Anne Delafield gone to Richard Hudnut, but Muriel Wedekind, group salon manageress in charge of hairdressing, had left to work for Seligman and Latz, who managed the hair and beauty concessions in all the American fine stores, including Neiman Marcus and J.W. Robinson. Miss Wedekind, who had been with Elizabeth for nearly twenty years, was worn out. She was never given authority to implement her plans and had no ability to hire and fire. One employee who did stay the course was Bert Chose, in charge of the West Coast. When his figures dipped and Bill Carlson was sent out to discover why, he quickly realised it had little to do with Mr Chose, and wrote to his old friend Teddy Haslam: 'Bert is a brilliant salesman. He knows the name of store buyers, their husbands, their children – even their children's birthdays. He knows everyone in the stores from the night watchman to the president. Bert is a joy to watch. He charms the waitresses in local restaurants, and is friends with the policeman on each street corner. He even had Rubinstein-paid demonstrators charmed to place our stock on their counter space.' In case Carlson had given Mr Haslam the impression that the charming Mr Chose was too close to the Rubinstein girls, he was quick to point out, 'It isn't sex appeal either, because Bert is a sincere Christian Scientist.'

The Revson sales team, on the other hand, followed their boss's example and relied heavily on sex appeal and aggression in meeting sales targets. They used every tactic in the book to gain counter space. Claude Forter, a sales manager for Rubinstein post-war, recollects one incident: 'The buyers I dealt with were most decent-size drugstores and pharmacies, and the reception we got was invariably good in the US and Latin America. I did happen on an instance where a Revlon rep was visiting a store while I was there. He was arrogant, domineering and vulgar and yelled at the quite civilised owner "to get that shit out of here!" pointing to a Helena Rubinstein display.'

Elizabeth's sales managers may have wanted her to run an ethical company, but the stakes in the industry were climbing, and with them the pressure that comes from making hefty profits. Harry Johnson, who had genuinely tried to make profits for Arden, was on the way out. 'Everyone in the country knows he's on the skids,' said Carlson, 'he's told all his buddies and news spreads like wildfire in this business. He can't do anything constructive now.'

Out went Harry Johnson. Out went Bill Carlson too, but for different reasons. As the war escalated he joined the US intelligence service, the OSS presumably delighting in his multilingual European expertise. Miss Arden's patriotic fervour diminished somewhat in the face of his resignation. 'I am very angry with Mr Carlson. Never in my life have I been very strong for him. Carlson comes first, last and always,' she wrote, somehow missing the point that it was America that had come first with her ex-employee.

She invited her Canadian general manager, Norman Dahl, to New York for an interview, hoping he would take on Carlson's responsibilities. He was less than keen, writing to her to explain: 'I have done every mortal thing I know how to serve your business, but under present circumstances there is no hope of success for anyone in the position of manager in New York, because he can do no more than be a rubber stamp for any important decision you care to make. There is no money in the bank because it has been used for the movie [Elizabeth's sponsored film *Young and Beautiful*], the Maine Chance house or for advertising a toothpaste promotion which has no chance of success. We can't pay our bills, let alone lay in enough stock of raw materials. Costs have risen and you are faced with increased taxation. Whoever follows Mr Carlson can succeed only if not interfered with by you.' Dahl ended this awesomely frank missive by saying, 'Nevertheless I hope you will accord me the privilege of remaining here in Canada.'

Elizabeth sent a copy of this letter to Teddy, but it took weeks for his soothing response to arrive. Haslam said, with masterful understatement: 'I hope you do not lose Mr Dahl, notwithstanding his somewhat insensitive letter.' Miss Arden kept Dahl on for a while, no doubt feeling he was safer ring-fenced in Toronto than visiting headhunters. He soon left to join Dorothy Gray, but not without holding Miss Arden to ransom for a three-month salary settlement. Mr Dahl got his cash because, as he ran a virtually autonomous territory with its own production facilities, he held the only copies of the Elizabeth Arden formulae. Paying him was one way of ensuring he didn't clear the contents of his office safe along with the contents of his desk.

At first, Miss Arden was merely shaken. She wrote begging Teddy to relocate to America, sounding like a little girl who had been told off by her teacher. 'All my loved ones are abroad. I feel completely alone. If only he had said a kind word to me. If he had given me a little praise it would have

been better. Teddy I *need* you here to help me. My dearest love to you all.'
Teddy tactfully replied that he could not get an exit permit. Miss Arden's
mood turned to righteous indignation, and she wrote again, defending the
renovations at Maine Chance and explaining how good the bookings were,
whilst agreeing that the pricey Savon Kennot toothpaste she imported from
Paris was not performing well. 'This is due to Johnson's bad management in
packaging and pricing . . . our lack of money is only temporary, Mr Dahl
forgot to mention we have paid off nearly all the $540,000 due on excise
taxes. He thinks he is talking to a dumbbell. I haven't a single broad-
shouldered, solid-thinking business man here.' She tried to defend her film,
but even Teddy Haslam knew it was a white elephant of the most extravagant proportions and that Elizabeth's fantasy of becoming a film producer
was turning into a fiasco.

The idea of making a film came to fruition in the aftermath of the col-
lapse of her Stage and Screen division. If Elizabeth couldn't have make-up
for the cinema, she would have a whole film to make up the stars for. The
idea may have come from Hedda Hopper but, given Elizabeth's social aspirations, it more probably came about through her friendship with John
'Jock' Hay Whitney. She had met Whitney through her developing passion
for horses, and no doubt adored being on friendly terms with one of
America's elite, especially one as charming, intelligent and influential as
Whitney. It was her love of horses and her success with horseracing that
enabled Elizabeth to break through the otherwise impregnable barriers of
America's super-rich families. Jock Whitney also had creative and artistic
talents not normally associated with killer-corporate skills.

By the mid-1930s, Jock was enjoying investing in his other great passion,
the cinema. His partnership with David O. Selznick resulted in such screen
triumphs as *Rebecca*, *A Star is Born* and *Gone With the Wind*; although his
enthusiasm for the latter caused several Whitney houseguests to nod off as
he insisted on screening the film every weekend at his home cinema, very
often to the same guests several times over. He was a trustee of the film
library at the Museum of Modern Art in New York and went on to chair the
motion picture division of the Office of Co-ordination of Inter-American
Affairs, set up by President Roosevelt. Coincidentally, Jock Whitney's first
marriage was ailing and by 1942 he was divorced and remarried to none
other than Betsey Cushing Roosevelt, the ex-wife of James Roosevelt, the
President's son who had been one of the pallbearers at Bessie Marbury's

funeral. Betsey Cushing Roosevelt Whitney and her circle were Arden clients and thus, as America was poised to enter the Second World War, Elizabeth Arden's beauty salons on both sides of the Atlantic catered to the needs of powerful women married to powerful men.

By the time war was declared in Europe, Jock Whitney was an established supporter of intervention; and Elizabeth echoed his views that too many Americans were isolationist. She actively supported projects dear to Whitney's heart and wallet, including the British War Relief Society, the American Field Hospital Corps and the Defence Recreation Committee for New York City. In all probability, it was her involvement in the former that triggered her intention to make *Young and Beautiful*, her first and last cinematic experiment.

The film was designed as a public relations triumph for the Arden company, but things didn't quite work out as she had planned. Shot in technicolor and eventually distributed in the USA and England via Warner Brothers, the plot line was charmingly simple and sickly sweet, based around a plain young woman who can't get a job because of her looks. It's suggested she go to a 'charm school' and the camera pans to see her going through Arden's famous Red Door where after exercises, make-up lessons and grooming – *voilà* – she is transformed into a beauty. Our heroine goes back to the employer who had previously refused to hire her, despite her lightning shorthand skills. He fails to recognise her and of course offers her a job, which she turns down. She bumps into an old boyfriend who is enchanted with her new look and immediately proposes. Cut to a party at her parents' house, to raise funds for war relief. Gracie Fields, glamorous in an evening gown, sings three patriotic songs including her signature 'Wish Me Luck as You Wave Me Goodbye'. End credits show that the film starred 'Duke' Wellington Cross, the Arden employee with matinee-idol looks, and that Gracie Fields 'donated her services for British War Relief'. The largest credit of all said, 'Produced under the technical supervision of Elizabeth Arden'. Titles were printed over a pink rose bouquet background *à la* Elizabeth Arden and the soundtrack featured the music from a popular song by Al Dubin for the 1934 film *Roman Scandals* called 'Keep Young and Beautiful'. The lyrics were entirely appropriate: 'It's your duty to be beautiful, Keep young and beautiful, If you want to be loved'. This homage to Elizabeth's dream of beauty lasted for just twenty minutes and is reputed to have cost in the region of $300,000, which in 1940 was a lot of dollars.

The room of 'our heroine's house' was Elizabeth's Fifth Avenue apartment, styled for the occasion by one William Haines. Haines, a successful silent-movie star whose career had declined with the advent of sound, was one of the major interior decorators in Hollywood, where he was particularly close to Joan Crawford amongst other screen goddesses whose houses he decorated. At a stroke, Elizabeth combined all her favourite things: film, glamour, patriotic pro-British fundraising, a Hollywood interior decorator of cult status, and 'unattractive girl makes good and gets her man by having a makeover at an Arden salon'. Elizabeth must have been in seventh heaven. Unfortunately for her, the complexities of dealing with film studios and filmstars caused her serious grief.

In early 1942, she wrote:

> Just when I thought everything was settled for Warner Brothers to take the film, cut it to meet their requirements and prepare for distribution, Monty Banks and Gracie Fields began to make claims, asking first for $20,000 then reducing to $12,500 to permit Warner to put out the picture. They are sticking to the letter of their contract which was for a non-commercial, even though the proceeds were to go to the British War Relief. Monty has done everything but help and has simply spoiled my plans as well as Warner's. In desperation I have just about decided to use my own film as is . . . giving all proceeds above the 30% allowed for expenses, to charity. Warner's were so annoyed they preferred to eliminate Gracie Fields from the picture entirely, but when I think of those beautiful living room scenes on which I worked so hard, I cannot bear to have them simply cut out and a new and unknown singer put in, with goodness knows what background. I worked so hard on that set.

Interestingly, Elizabeth makes no mention of William Haines, who presumably had just a little bit to do with how the set looked, but then she was never good at sharing credit. She went on to say,

> It would not be a good idea for me to appear in the movie . . . this would simply antagonise these two mercenary souls [Monty Banks and his wife, Gracie Fields] as they increased their original price because they claimed the picture was too commercial, although I

had eliminated many scenes just to please them. Frankly, I feel I have every chance of making more than $15,000 for the BWR and a goodly sum for other charities too, by showing the picture in clubs, colleges etc. Then too, the value to me in publicity will be much greater than if cut. You can use the picture for the same purpose in Great Britain.

This is a perfect example of the Arden philosophy that there was one rule for her but no one else. She could get 'great value out of the publicity', as her film was entirely about the Arden salon making dreams come true. Its stars, however, who had been told it was a war effort production, could not expect a commercial fee, even when they realised it was a commercial project. When *Young and Beautiful* was eventually released in Britain, it attracted a lot of praise. Ironically for Miss Arden, Bette Davis had just wowed international audiences in *Now Voyager* where she lost weight, fixed her hair and make-up, changed her clothes and got her confidence, along with her man. But by the time Miss Davis was winning critical acclaim for her role, Miss Arden had quietly forgotten about her own film and had become captivated with fashion.

In the face of staff defection, Elizabeth remembered her friends. By 1940, Haslam had been with her for nearly twenty years. At Christmas that year, by way of a reward for his devotion, she authorised him to take a staggering $5000 Christmas bonus with the message, 'May you soon have great victory and only happiness in the years to come. Love and affection to you all. Elizabeth Arden.'

CHAPTER SEVENTEEN

THE SECOND WORLD WAR – PART II

Go out and do your stuff
With a little powder and a puff

—*Young and Beautiful*

WHILST THE 'PHONEY WAR' simmered, Helena and Artchil, accompanied by Helena's devoted employee Sara Fox, journeyed leisurely by ship to Mexico, Panama and South America, the extended cruise by way of a working honeymoon, as Latin America presented an emerging market. As usual, Helena went shopping: a building in Buenos Aires, another in Rio de Janeiro, and an office block in Panama, where one of her relatives settled. She bought paintings by an unknown artist, Jesus Ray, in Mexico (where she also set up a sales agency), dozens of silver 'ballandangas', which are part of a Brazilian dancer's costume, silver-embossed water canteens as used by the Brazilian gauchos, and commissioned the inevitable portrait of herself, this time executed by Portinari.

As usual with Helena, everything was put to good use. Back in New York, Lord & Taylor made replicas of the small silver pieces, charms and gaucho canteens, selling them as 'inspired by the fabled collector's items of Helena Rubinstein, the Princess Gourielli', with all profits going to the Polish relief fund for the Red Cross. Helena also commissioned a sculpture of hands, titling it *Precision Hands* – 'grinding out vision lenses that spot enemy targets', exhibiting it at a press party.

In June 1940, with Italy declaring war and invading Southern France, swiftly followed by the French armistice with Germany, Edward Titus and his young wife Erica decided things were becoming uncomfortable and got passage in July on the last sailing of the SS *Manhattan*, bound for New York. What Madame thought of the arrival of her ex-husband and his beautiful child-bride isn't a matter of record, but it's a safe bet they weren't invited to make up a four at bridge. Roy Titus had by now joined the army, recruited to the OSS by virtue of his European languages. Horace failed his medical, so saw out the war handling advertising for Helena Rubinstein and bombarding her with long memos and reports about development ideas. Voluble and outspoken, his dream was to be recognised by his mother as having a meaningful role in her business, which, sadly, he didn't. When she failed to respond to his ideas, he drowned his sorrows in the jazz clubs springing up all over New York, a city now devoted to 'swing', that uniquely all-American youth-culture boogie music.

As for her new husband, Helena was beginning to get a shade frustrated about his daily regime. He lingered in bed, often not taking breakfast before noon — then possibly the Cavendish Club for bridge, the afternoon enlivened with a visit to his tailor, perhaps a leisurely game of high-stakes backgammon, before bathing and changing for cocktails and dinner. All far too gracious for Helena, who decided that Artchil must have a job, a goal, be *useful*.

Ironically, it was Thomas Jenkins Lewis who came up with the solution. Taking inspiration from the perfume line operated under the name Prince Matchebelli, he suggested a premium product titled 'Gourielli' using the family crest on packaging. Madame was enchanted. She bought a brownstone near the St Regis Hotel and opened the House of Gourielli. Artchil took little persuading to put his name to a distinguished-looking range of preparations, all beautifully packaged in vintage-style apothecary jars, resplendent with the Gourielli crest. In an innovative move, the products included creams for both men and women. The tastefully embossed jars — grey for the men and blue for the women — were displayed on polished wooden shelves, interspersed with original antique pottery. A white-coated chemist was 'on duty' to advise. There was a Blue Room for gifts, the shelves lined with early-American glassware — in blue, naturally — and the Pink Room was quilted in pink satin and decorated with pink and yellow early-American glass. The House of Gourielli's ground-breaking men's range was sold from the Grey Room. Gentlemen had their separate entrance leading to the barber's where they could have scalp massage and hair treatments, and could stock up on herbal and mineral compounds for skin, hair, teeth, body and bath. There were pick-up teas and tisanes and Vita-thin diet wafers, and the whole was a triumph of style.

Horace became enthusiastically involved in the advertising, but could not help giving his opinion about the sales promotion, the staffing and the product line, firing off memos to his mother about every aspect of the range except perhaps the one he should have been working on. His ideas, never taken very seriously by head office, included developing a 'men's soapless detergent cleanser', and, in a farsighted move, making part of the Gourielli range 'allergy tested'. Horace had a fascination with the laboratories and with ideas to use quasi-medicinal formulae. In this, he was supported by one of his few real friends in the business, Tommy Lewis, who also predicted that this was the way forward in premium-priced product.

Helena Rubinstein's tentative move into men's products was a clever one. Unfortunately, in the beauty business, where a good idea too early is merely research and development for a rival company, an innovation ahead of its time is often doomed to failure. The House of Gourielli never really worked. Madame's earlier foray into hormone creams having been expensive, in an effort to recoup her investment she packaged a Gourielli hormone cream called Estrolar. This was part of the problem with the Gourielli range, which was trying to cater for an up-market woman *and* an up-market man, with the prince and princess being photographed in his 'n' hers white coats, stirring pots in a laboratory. Despite a fortune invested, the combined use of the logo on women's ranges that included hormone treatments and men's that included scalp tonic, meant the definition of the brand was blurred. Horace did bring some influence to bear on the wholesale Gourielli division, where the range, sold at a premium price, had a clinical and pharmaceutical emphasis, with products like Sulfo-Collodic cream and Gourielli Cleansing Emulsion, and waxed lyrical on the subject of 'minimal packaging' from his Advertising House agency address at East 55th St, where he worked on Rubinstein's advertising and packaging development. Ostensibly, Advertising House was his own business, free to develop other clients. In reality, Horace worked exclusively for his mother, but she rarely took notice of his advice. The Gourielli flagship drifted off-course and it would take Elizabeth Arden and Charles Revson to capitalise on the vast market for men's toiletries and cosmetics. It should be remembered, however, that Helena Rubinstein pioneered it.

It was the war which led to the commercial production of men's toiletries. Military service transformed American men's formerly haphazard grooming habits. Soldiers had to have cropped hair, a close shave, a clean body and polished shoes, all subject to inspection. Army PX stores stocked aftershave lotions, skin creams, deodorants, fine-milled talcum powder, sunburn remedies, lip pomades and colognes. Eau-de-cologne was used by GIs when there was no bathing facility and, with the hugely subsidised prices, it's no wonder the soldiers were so popular when they arrived in Europe. They looked good, courtesy of terrific uniforms, and they smelled good, courtesy of their toiletries. Gifts for the girls were courtesy of Chanel No 5 and also Revlon, who had a lucrative contract to supply the PXs with lipsticks.

Soldiers in the Russian army were not so lucky; life held little luxury for them. For Helena's great-nephew, Majed Rubinstein, stationed in Samarkand, the thought of using his illustrious relative's Gourielli aftershave would have been an impossible dream. Majed's sister Regina, in Australia, was frantic for news of her young brother, lobbying government officials at every moment. To her great relief he escaped the war unscathed.

Men's toiletries at that time, in the US at least, were considered almost as morale boosting as women's products, but it was the women's products that were making money, and generating publicity, such as when the All-American Girls Professional Baseball League organised their players to take make-up lessons from Helena Rubinstein. Women war workers were particularly cosseted. Lockheed and Sperry installed beauty salons in their armaments factories and President Roosevelt, on meeting Helena Rubinstein and Elizabeth Arden (luckily for him not on the same occasion) told them to 'keep up their important war work by keeping lipsticks on the line'.

Whilst make-up for men was not part of Helena's plan when she put out a tentative range of men's toiletries, she was actually, for a moment, the world's largest supplier of coloured cosmetics for the exclusive use of the heterosexual male. The Helena Rubinstein company pulled off a coup during the Second World War when it was commissioned to produce supply kits for the American army for 'Operation Torch'. The soldiers poised to go on desert duty needed cleanser, sunburn cream and camouflage make-up. Operation Torch involved 60,000 troops; every soldier was issued a kitbox, with 'Helena Rubinstein Inc' discreetly lettered inside, with instructions on how to apply the cosmetics in desert conditions. The contract contributed a tidy sum to the Rubinstein finances and won Helena some influence in Washington.

Prevented from travelling, both Helena and Elizabeth were based in New York, putting a strain on their staff, magazine and retail executives, and social organisers, struggling to keep them apart. Helena, interviewed by *Life* in 1941, said carefully, to the great pleasure of the journalist who struggled to represent Madame's extraordinary accent: 'Vee haf been at zee same parties, yes, but vee haf nevair met — nevair.' Both threw themselves into fundraising. Helena adopted the Polish Red Cross and harnessed the support of such luminaries as Artur Rubinstein, whilst Elizabeth, as well as giving fundraisers for the British Red Cross, British War Relief and the War Orphans, also contributed to the New York Stage Door Canteen, the American theatre war service charity, giving food, music and entertainment to over 20,000 servicemen and women each week.

Helena, encouraged by Artchil, held dinners at the 'Rubinstein Hilton' as her lavish apartment was by now nicknamed, with her press officers issuing guest lists to the society columns. One list included 'Mrs Cornelius Bliss; Mrs Carmel Snow; Baron de Guinzbourg; the Duke di Verdura (society jeweller *par excellence*); Baron Kurt von Pantz and Monsieur de Brunhoff — although what the man who had edited French *Vogue* felt at being seated with the editor in chief of *Bazaar* is intriguing. The fall-out when she left *Vogue* had been fierce.

Madame loved showing off her apartment. Cocktails were in the French Modern drawing room. Dinner was followed by coffee in the Dream Room, whose walls were covered with tufted spun-glass fabric and had surreal panels painted by Salvador Dali, in artistic exile in New York, who would pop up for dinner *chez* Rubinstein. The combination of an African Gabon death mask carefully balancing on an ornate gilded Victorian blackamoor table must have caused a few raised eyebrows amongst her guests. Dali painted his 'n' hers pictures of Helena and Artchil. She was bound to rocks by her ropes of emeralds whilst Artchil looked uncomfortable in a pseudo-Russian costume. Helena's portrait by Dali hangs today with the rest of her paintings in New York, but of Dali's vision of Artchil there is no sign, Diane Moss admitting, 'We sold it . . . it was . . . an awful picture.'

Café society on the run from Europe at war at first gathered in New York where Cole and Linda Porter, Elsa Maxwell (writing a column called 'Party Line' for the *New York Post*), Emerald Cunard and Syrie Maugham were all living. But by 1941 a major group of *soi-disant* artistic people were ensconced in Los Angeles. Led by Lady Mendl and her husband, the group also included Gaylord Hauser, Artur Rubinstein and Cathy 'Flame' d'Erlanger. The Baroness was by now running a nightclub on Sunset Strip where she used to receive the guests in evening dress, her fabled emeralds (which Coco Chanel rather bitchily always said were chips of green glass) and tennis shoes. Others in the group included Anita Loos, Hedda Hopper and Aldous Huxley. Huxley was involved in script development at the time and had spent several months working on a treatment for a film about the great Madame Marie Curie. He was rather put out to say the least when a studio executive, having finally read it, rejected the screen-play saying: 'Jesus, who's gonna go for a dame who did chemistry?'

Ilka Chase, whose mother, aged sixty-five, was still editing *Vogue*, was now hosting a radio show called 'Luncheon at the Waldorf', recorded each lunchtime at New York's Waldorf Astoria. Chase was a sparky writer with a nose for gossip and scripted her interviews so her famous personalities were drawn into admitting more of the truth about their lives than they might have liked. Elizabeth Arden was persuaded on to the show in 1941. 'Elizabeth Arden is a lady of stamina and achievement,' wrote Ilka Chase in her autobiography, *Past Imperfect*, 'and one who hides her brains behind a bland, baby-face. She's one of the richest women in America who's built an industry independent of masculine aid and has held on to it against the encroachment of banks and other syndicates who wished to help lap up the gravy. Yet to meet her is to wonder whether she knows about coming out of the rain.'

Miss Chase was shrewd in her summing up. 'She burbles on so happily about her creams and lotions and her dear horsies in Kentucky, that you smile indulgently and think "funny little thing" and while you are thinking it, she's whipping up another million dollars.' Rehearsals on the radio show were frazzled, reports Chase. 'She chortled and burbled and fussed like a yellow chick and read her script so uncertainly we became alarmed for her performance. Then it occurred to me that probably a pair of specs would turn the trick. Miss Arden was reluctant at first, fearing glasses would dispel the glamour, but she finally hauled out the old hornrims from her handbag and our troubles were over.'

A few weeks after her successful radio broadcast, however, Arden could only watch in mute hatred as Madame produced a *coup de théâtre*, still remembered in the trade as one of the most original fragrance launches in its history. Rubinstein fragrances were light scents. For years Apple Blossom had been a bestseller, but in the early 1940s, Helena developed Heaven Sent. The bottle design was inspired by a Latin American angel, an effigy collected on her travels, and the fragrance, launched in 1941 exclusively at Bonwit Teller, was introduced to startled shoppers on Fifth Avenue when hundreds of miniature bottles packed in a charming basket, trimmed with an angel, floated down from the sky, suspended from pink and blue balloons. 'Out of the Blue for You' ran the lettering on the cards and if Hortense Odlum, Bonwit's august store president and a great friend of Elizabeth's, thought the pink and blue packaging was a steal on Arden's, she was too tactful to say so.

Mrs Odlum's tact was put to the test when Salvador Dali designed two special Surrealist windows for Bonwit's during the war. His themes were Midnight and Narcissus. The first showed a corpse reclining on a bed of coals, morosely surveyed by a moosehead, all shrouded in purple tufted satin. The second was a decadent-looking female, dressed in green coque feathers, stepping into a bath lined with Persian lamb, her bathwater resplendent with water lilies and an assortment of arms reaching up from under the surface. Very Surreal. Very Dali. Unfortunately not very Mrs Odlum, who ordered 'technical' changes — replacing the feathers with a neat tweed suit, taking out the naked arms, and having Dali's namecard removed. Later that week, the great man was strolling down Fifth Avenue and stopped to look at his handiwork. Dali was furious, burst into the store to grab the bath, fell forwards under the weight and crashed through the window, taking the bath with him.

The media continued to cover the fashion and beauty world, quite determined that 'the show must go on'. Lesley Blanche, features editor of British *Vogue*, wrote, 'It's one long battle against lapsing into dullness. We take our gasmasks everywhere. A string bag is as much a part of our equipment as a powder compact. We all look pretty tired, under-vitaminised as we are. Our grey look — and our grey hair — is due to nervous strain and deficiency in diet.' Miss Blanche and all her colleagues at the magazine, led by editor Audrey Withers, braved the bombing of their offices and bicycled to work, dodging the debris, but still looking soignée in suits from Creed, Goodbrook, Angèle Delanghe, Lachasse, Ravhis and Bradleys. *Vogue* urged its readers to 'make do and mend', encouraging everybody to raid their attics for vintage textiles. 'Toile de Jouy curtains are ideal for pretty house-coats' ran fashion copy, and wealthy women were encouraged to take care of what *Vogue* described as *the* most important person to cherish – a good dressmaker. Harvey Nichols came up with a handy addition to keep clothes pristine under attack, advertising: 'Especially designed gas protection costumes at a reasonable price of 40/– made in oiled silk and available in dawn apricot, amethyst, eau-de-nil and rose pink.'

Both in America and Britain, more women than ever were out at work. In Britain, if they weren't serving in uniform themselves, they had to take over jobs vacated by the men who were. Earning money, but with little in the way of new clothes to spend it on, beauty boomed. Hair was over-waved and over-curled, eyebrows were plucked and lips were – red. For the first time in a long time, America and England were totally cut off from Paris-led fashion influence. During the 'phoney war', the couture showed as usual, bravely trying to maintain its position, but it collapsed with the fall of France. A few Paris houses kept open, like Lelong, Balenciaga and Madame Gres, making the best of the circumstances, but they had to deal with new clients – German ones. Lucien Lelong led the Chambre Syndicale de la Couture Parisienne and managed to avoid the couture being moved piece-meal by the Germans to Berlin and Vienna. Several designers had already left France – Schiaparelli went to America as did Mainboucher, Molyneux went home to London, along with Angèle Delanghe. Chanel shut up shop completely, and didn't return to the fashion world for fifteen years, during which time her devoted clientele may have forgotten about her love affair with a man reputed to be a German spy.

Chanel's close friend Misia Sert stayed in Paris, apparently too drug-addled to know what was going on. She and her ex-husband Jo Jo were the type of collaborator who called themselves 'realists' – claiming that in supporting Germany they were helping keep the Communist threat at bay. Sert did however arrange for Colette's Jewish husband to be freed from an internment camp. If the Serts looked enviously at Helena's magnificent home, bought from them for a pittance, no one could blame them. The Gestapo looked upon it enviously too, according to Helena moving in several high-ranking officers to enjoy the luxury, where they spent many a happy hour taking pot shots at her valuable Greek statues.

The British textile industry struggled to cope with the demands of war. The Utility Scheme was instigated in 1941, coinciding with rationing for clothes. Women were becoming gifted at sewing and learning to live without what they had previously taken for granted – including metal lipstick cases and powder compacts. By January 1942 Elizabeth had reorganised her sales team along with her supply lines, having found a valuable cache of castor oil, crucial for cosmetics production, and was bursting with energy. 'We have sufficient of our beautiful metal lipstick cases to last until June, 140,000 on order,' she wrote to Teddy. 'When these are exhausted we will start on plastic cases, having half a million on order which should last us for a year and a half and then we will start to use our beautiful paper cases.'

Miss Arden had become very particular about checking her 'numbers', helped no doubt by her new office controller, Mr Danilek, who had experience in counting paperclips – he had worked for Revlon, where Charles Revson watched such things like a hawk. Checking invoices, Elizabeth discovered one of her purchase order clerks was playing fast and loose with her paperwork and paying 5c for soap wrappers instead of the 2c Elizabeth normally authorised. Convinced the clerk was pocketing the difference – on the usual ratio of 2c for her, plus 1c for the supplier for fixing the invoice – she was furious and immediately fired the woman, resulting in one of many suits for wrongful dismissal against her, most of which Miss Arden won. Such was the demand for staff that a few weeks later the clerk in question was working for Charles of the Ritz.

Purchase order clerks were in a prime position to cheat. All manner of packaging was needed in bulk and there were suppliers keen to help orders along by a direct bribe for an order or to fix an invoice and share the proceeds. It's said one Rubinstein manager made so much money he took early retirement and still lives like a millionaire today. Boris Forter admitted that even Ceska was not averse to fiddling company paperwork in her favour. He happily joined the scam, wilting when Helena discovered it. According to Boris, however, there was little recrimination – 'Madame merely insisted on being cut in to the deal.'

There is no doubt that Miss Arden was deeply enamoured of Tom White, the powerful and influential Hearst executive she had been seeing for three years. But there were two seemingly immovable barriers to their relationship; Mr White was a Catholic, and he was married. By virtue of his religion he couldn't get a divorce, and as Elizabeth was an unassailable episcopalian, she would never have married a Catholic anyway, never mind a divorced one. It was impossible for their affair to continue – if indeed it was ever physically consummated. Whether sexual or not, however, the relationship was a meaningful one. As Elizabeth had marched the moral high ground about 'living in sin' and other such abhorrent things all her life – firing Dorothy Gray, for example, for living with her boyfriend – the true romance she craved was a doomed romance, and she ended it.

A few months later, she took up with another man, one who claimed to have something Miss Arden found irresistible – a title. In the beginning, the relationship Elizabeth Arden had with Russian 'Prince' Michael Evlanoff was the height of her romantic dreams. Head waiters at her favourite restaurants and clubs bowed and said, 'This way, Your Highness' when they arrived. He sent her flowers – her favourite American Beauty roses – and, remembering she was superstitious about the number twelve, only put eleven or twenty-three in a bunch. Most important of all, he danced divinely. The icing on the cake for Miss Arden was that the 'Prince' even seemed to have an income. He didn't have a job, which made her rather uneasy, but he had money. That is, he *seemed* to have money, which he claimed was a part of a trust fund established in his name by the late Dr Nobel in gratitude for Evlanoff's services as his private secretary. The money was apparently paid to him, even in wartime, via a special dispensation from the King of Sweden. Her friends amongst the Russians in New York, like Serge Obolensky and Princess Mikeladze, were delighted, as they considered smoothtalking Michael to be one of them.

Michael Evlanoff should have won a Nobel prize for lying, but Elizabeth fell for it hook, line and sinker, and they married at Maine Chance in December 1942, the bride dressed by her old friend Charles James and the bridegroom wearing one of the dozens of new suits he had ordered on the announcement of his engagement to the millionairess. The happy couple went to Nassau, visiting Elizabeth's friend the Duchess of Windsor, and then on to Phoenix, Arizona, where Elizabeth had already identified an estate she wanted to buy to convert into a winter Maine Chance resort. Before she left, Elizabeth left instructions for the library at her Fifth Avenue penthouse to be converted into a bedroom for her husband, arranged for his luggage to be sent round, and sent her vast collection of exquisite linens to be monogrammed with her new 'royal' crest. She told her friends that Michael's title was of a better pedigree than Gourielli's and required her household staff to refer to her as Princess.

The marriage fell apart virtually overnight. Shortly after they arrived in Phoenix, Irene Delaney got a frantic cable saying 'Stop work on my apartment immediately' signed 'Miss Arden'. Her life as a princess had been shortlived. Stories as to why she panicked vary wildly. Serge Obolensky told a friend, 'Elizabeth rang me in tears and said her husband had "done awful things to her".' Evlanoff would later insist that such 'awful things' were merely claiming his conjugal rights, but even this seems doubtful. Apparently Evlanoff decided things were getting a little dull on his honeymoon and invited a friend to join them in Phoenix — one of his boyfriends! Elizabeth claimed she hadn't known he was homosexual. Used to the effete behaviour of her openly camp friends in fashion, hairdressing and interior design, she was less adroit at identifying the more subtle nuances of a man who preferred men for pleasure, but women for money. Elizabeth was appalled, sent for Bert Chose to join her from the West Coast to act as protection, and called her lawyers requesting an annulment. Obolensky later remarked, 'Evlanoff started thinking he could be boss and issuing orders. That was not very bright, you know. One thing you could not do with the cosmetics girl was to try to give her orders.'

There was a brief reconciliation on arrival back in New York, and she did eventually allow her husband to move into her apartment, where they lived uneasily together for a while, with Elizabeth moving around the country working and overseeing her racehorses and Michael Evlanoff running up bills in New York. These were now all coming for Elizabeth's attention, the 'Prince' claiming his 'allowance' had been delayed due to wartime administration problems. Elizabeth was becoming seriously worried.

In June 1943, Teddy Haslam travelled to New York using a lot of the legendary Elizabeth Arden influence to get an exit visa. During the month he spent in America, Haslam witnessed the final breakdown of the relationship between Elizabeth and Evlanoff. In August, when Teddy was back in London, Elizabeth wrote him a frantic letter. 'Evlanoff waited until you had gone to show his true colours. Just as soon as you had left, he did his best to break my spirit. He told me a frantic story about owing over $27,000 saying his debtors were pressing him. I set up an account with Mr Gladstone [the company financial controller] paying the money in and letting Gladstone give Evlanoff a blank cheque . . . he went straight to the bank and arranged to withdraw the money in cash the next day.' Elizabeth was then lobbied by a friend of Evlanoff's to offer a 'settlement sum' of around

$100,000, but instead of giving in to blackmail, she insisted that he leave her apartment. He took ten days to go, during which time his wife changed the locks, cut off his private telephone line and had her butler, Frederick, take him food on a tray to his room, rather than endure him in her dining room. Eventually her 'Prince' left in a huff, checking in to the Savoy Plaza hotel.

Elizabeth hired a detective to check out his background, discovering his title was fake, as was his allowance, not to mention his alleged friendship with the King of Sweden. He was heavily in debt, huge bills having been run up on the strength of his marriage. In a final humiliation, Elizabeth discovered he had claimed commission from jewellers and furriers for shopping she had done for herself, accompanied by him, and paid for herself. She filed for divorce in Maine in October 1943, citing 'cruel and abusive treatment'. When her case was heard in February the following year and she became a single woman again, her final act was to petition the court for legal permission to change her name back to Mrs Graham.

CHAPTER EIGHTEEN

THE SECOND WORLD WAR –
PART III
1943–1945

DURING THE FIRST YEARS of the war, both Miss Arden and Madame were distanced from events in Europe. Even after the Japanese attacked Pearl Harbor in December 1941, little actually seemed to touch their lives, or their families. All that was about to change.

In London, men like Teddy Haslam and Boris Forter, who were too old to join up, volunteered for approved war tasks. In Forter's case it was fire watching. People had become used to the gunfire over London along with the night bombing raids; Boris rather enjoyed sitting high on the rooftops, watching for fire damage after a raid, even though he felt the exercise was somewhat pointless. He had not expected Madame's Grafton Street building to be bombed and was working late in the top floor offices when it happened. 'Everything became black like the deepest dark of the night,' he said, 'and the staircase from the top floor collapsed and everybody fell on the floor. The bomb had hit next door where people were killed . . . but our staircase was falling to pieces and we had to scramble out with great difficulty.' Although the building wasn't badly damaged, it had to be evacuated. Boris had the foresight to evacuate possessions as well as people, taking typewriters and business papers. When the firemen arrived, he ensured they all got 'a personal gift' which meant he earned time to move out valuable stock. Such things were often looted when buildings were bombed. He set up alternative premises in Berkeley Square, using a small building Helena owned at number 48, offering a somewhat makeshift service, both in beauty treatments and wholesaling, for the rest of the war.

Neither Arden's Bond Street salon nor their Grosvenor Street offices were bombed, but something much more sombre happened and morale was low. It was inevitable that the bi- and often trilingual executives of companies such as Arden, with their knowledge of life in France, Italy, Spain, and of course Germany, would come to the attention of the authorities. One such was Sidney Jones, who had worked in France under Bill Carlson, spoke fluent French and was ready to serve his country. He joined one of the most courageous of all the wartime units, the Special Operations Executive – SOE. His intensive training would have been completed at a Group A centre in Arisaig, Scotland, where the young operatives learned to live off the land, sleeping rough. Parachute training followed, and finally, they went to a Group B centre in the New Forest, where they were taught how to look entirely natural and ordinary, so they could blend in behind enemy lines doing entirely unnatural and extraordinary things. They learned about coding, ciphering, counter-espionage and propaganda, how to use explosives – and how to kill.

Sidney Jones arrived in Southern France to undertake his first mission, establishing a sabotage circuit in Marseilles called 'Inventor' late in September, 1942. He was airlifted out of France in January 1943 and returned briefly to England for rest and recuperation. He dined with Gordy Yates and his wife in May that year, the night before he left again for France. They never saw him again. His new project, code name 'Donkeyman', was in the Loire Valley, where Jones was liaison officer and arms instructor. A young London fashion designer, Vera Leigh, was his courier. For over four months, Jones and his team worked in constant danger, and that autumn Vera Leigh and Jones's bodyguard became the victims of a lethal double-cross and were arrested in Paris. Jones himself held out a little longer, but was arrested in November and sent to Mauthausen concentration camp, where he lived for a year – a surprising feat given the treatment meted out to spies. Sidney Jones was executed on 6th September 1944, just a few days after the liberation of France. His colleague Vera Leigh was executed at Natzweiler concentration camp in July 1944.

Atrocities in Eastern Europe were gathering pace as Hitler moved towards the 'final solution'. In March 1943, the Krakow ghetto was destroyed with thousands of men, women and children slaughtered in the local camp at Plaszow, many more shot in the streets and the rest forced to make their last journey to the extermination camps of Auschwitz and Birkenau, less than an hour away from Krakow, amongst them relatives of Madame's. Young William 'Zew' Schantz, a great-nephew of hers by marriage, was amongst the fortunate on Oscar Schindler's list, surviving to make his way to Paris, where Helena found him work. Zew Schantz's uncle, Oscar Kolin, Madame's chief chemist in France, had been able to make his way to safety in New York, but for a while, his wife and two young children were left isolated in Paris, before finding passage to America.

For Miss Arden, the sad news that the long-serving and hugely popular head of her London salon, Dinah Wall, had been killed with her husband in a bombing raid was bad enough, but worse was to follow. In February 1944, her sister Gladys was arrested in Paris, along with Solange de Luze, who managed the Arden salon there. The only information about the arrest was a brief news item in the *Daily Express* on 6 March, informing readers that a 'round up of aristocrats belonging to the French Red Cross have been arrested'. The group in question, led by the Duc de Rohan, had been discovered caring for crashed allied airmen. Gladys was accused of 'espionage and communicating with the enemy' and shipped, along with six hundred other prisoners, in a cattle-truck bound for Ravensbruck. The newspaper said little else, except that 'the German high command considered English women more dangerous than Americans'. English women still living in France and not interned had to report to the police daily and were not allowed to own a bicycle – but were allowed to own a horse.

American women still in France had to report to the police weekly – and were allowed to own a bicycle, but not a horse. Apparently the Germans believed the Americans would try to escape by riding and the English by bicycle; they would then join the Resistance, whose mode of transport was a bicycle with a gun on the handlebars. Gladys spent two months in Ravensbruck, struggling to keep cheerful, as she later told her sister, 'by doing exercises'. In May that year, largely due to her husband's influence, Gladys was transferred to a prison camp in Vittel, where she would remain until the end of September. Poor Madame de Luze was not so fortunate, being kept prisoner in appalling conditions at Ravensbruck until the end of the war.

Frantic with fear for Gladys, almost everything in New York seemed to be going wrong for Elizabeth. She had wanted to buy a gift for Irene Delaney to mark her thirty-two years of working for Arden, and settled on war bonds. Miss Arden was very keen on war bonds and defence bonds, her advertising at that time in England actually saying: 'Review your budget. Think how much less you do – and can – spend nowadays on Elizabeth Arden preparations that you were accustomed to spend in days gone by.

What's become of the difference? See that it goes straight into 3% Defence Bonds.' Her financial controller, Mr Gladstone, was instructed to buy $32,000 worth of series G war bonds, representing $1000 for each year of the loyal Lanie's work. Gladstone instead spent the money on series F bonds, which were not only cheaper, but took twelve years to mature. He pocketed the $8320 difference. He also wrote fake invoices for work on her salon in Philadelphia, earning himself $22,000 on the side, and fiddled the Maine Chance Farm accounts by $6000.

The next man to cheat her was her English butler, Frederick. He had been with her for over fifteen years, so his behaviour was more of a blow than she cared to admit, but she wrote to Teddy and told him, as always, the whole story. She had never cared for Frederick's male companions, in particular one simply known as Bruce. When she wrote that 'Frederick turned out to be a terrible bounder' she was showing rare understatement. Her butler had found a new boyfriend called Jack, and her female staff in Fifth Avenue and at Maine Chance became fond of him too, allowing him in the house when Miss Arden was away, cooking him extravagant meals, starching his shirts and so forth. Elizabeth was then visited by the police, who were investigating the mysterious death in a supposedly domestic fire of Frederick's previous partner, Bruce. Her butler had taken out a hefty life insurance policy on his ex-lover's life, and was the beneficiary in the event of death. By this time Frederick and young Jack had disappeared, taking a fair amount of Elizabeth's possessions. The list she made for the police covered everything from a riding whip to jade beads, hand-painted china to antique lace bedspreads. Frederick had also made off with half the Arden wine cellar and most of her kitchen supplies – which in wartime were quite valuable, including imported olive oil, China tea and jars of foie gras.

Elizabeth blamed her housekeeper Chapelle for the theft, firing her at once and telling Teddy, 'I just cannot tell you what a slouchy, sloppy, lying woman she is. I was so indignant with her for not telling me the truth about Frederick. Also, you remember I told you Rubenstein knew what was actually going on in my house – well, Chapelle was going to dinner with Mr Lewis.'

'Mr Lewis' was of course her first ex-husband. Elizabeth had rarely, until now, mentioned his painful defection to Helena Rubinstein Inc. Inordinately successful in building up his wife's wholesale division, he had shown little evidence of such talent at Rubinstein. Her team didn't care for him – he didn't fit in – and Helena herself, quickly bored with her victory in hiring him, merely used him as a conduit for information about her rival. Lewis spent his time at Rubinstein spying on his ex-wife. He stuck it out for three years or so before moving on and attempting to regain a little of his old dignity and flair, but he never again found a role that suited his skills so well as when he had worked for Elizabeth.

Elizabeth had also been hurt by the publication of a book about the beauty business written by none other than Ilka Chase. *In Bed We Cry* was a novel, the central character being a thinly disguised Elizabeth Arden, whose beauty salons were entered through 'Green Doors'. She needn't have worried. The rather spiteful book, about large egos and shattered marriages, attracted attention amongst the fashion and beauty media, and Chase even wrote a stage treatment, but both book and play flopped. At any event, all publicity is good publicity and Elizabeth Arden's reputation was at an all-time high, so a book, however embarrassing, couldn't harm her business. Ilka Chase remained impervious to the furore. 'It wasn't about Arden anyway,' she remarked, and when congratulated on her research into the foibles of the beauty business said, 'Thank you . . . Helena Rubinstein was very . . . helpful . . . on that.'

In a morale-boosting commission for Miss Arden – both for her and for the soldiers – Elizabeth was invited to produce a make-up kit for the American Marine Corps Women's Reserve. She called the lipstick, rouge and nail-polish set, which exactly matched the chevrons on the women's uniform, Montezuma Red, and was so thrilled with the order that she took ads out in all the glossies, showing a uniformed Marine as the model. Miss Arden was invited to Camp Wilmington in North Carolina for the initial distribution and to talk to the Marines, and was beside herself with excitement.

I stood up and looked at the lovely, expectant faces of the girl Marines. I told them that seeing them before me in their uniforms, so eagerly devoting themselves to our country, I, for the first time, felt envious of their youth. It would have made me even more thrilled to have been one of them. The most thrilling moment of the day was the drill – arranged especially for me. Until you have seen such a thing you can never realise the overwhelming thrill of a lifetime to see three thousand young women marching by, in perfect order, all moving as one. It was such a lesson in discipline, symbolising what seemed to be classic beauty and order, that I will never forget it.

Another of her wartime initiatives was to set her laboratory in London to work on creating a special covering cream for her friend Sir Harold Gillies and his team of plastic surgeons. Known at his hospital as scar cream, it was based on hydrogenated coconut oil, isopropyl myristate, lanolin, zinc oxide and titanium dioxide. The Arden chemist added yellow ochre, burnt umber and Persian orange to the mix, and it worked wonders on battlescarred victims, covering shocking burns. Miss Arden would later develop the formula, improving it even more, and tour hospitals across America, particularly children's wards, helping facially disfigured people recover a little dignity, and proving just how morally uplifting make-up can be.

With Christmas, always the crucial selling time, looming, Elizabeth was ecstatic about her new discovery, a freelance copywriter who, she felt, had all the talent Henry Sell's agency writers now lacked. 'I am sending you my Christmas advertisement – I think it is beautiful. I have *at last* found a copywriter, and can accept everything she presents. Am keeping her as a freelance so that she will not become "contaminated". This young lady is Miss Fenton and she is doing a magazine, *Home and Food*, which used to be something awful. She practically redesigned the whole thing and now it is inspiring. We pay her $7500 a year, but she is well worth it.'

Fleur Fenton went on to set up her own agency called Pettingel and Fenton, but within a matter of months they resigned the Arden account, citing 'differences of opinion'. Elizabeth never mentioned her protégée again. Her ex-copywriter rapidly climbed the ladder of success, becoming Fleur Cowles, wife of millionaire publisher Gardner Cowles, and the editor of the cult 1950s magazine, *Flair*.

Elizabeth's social life was now organised around fundraising evenings such as the Toscanini Red Cross party, which she attended with Baron Rothschild in her box. Leonard Bernstein was conducting and the maestro's baton was auctioned after the concert, with the Marquis George de Cuevas (married at the time to Rockefeller's great-granddaughter) bidding $5000, only to be pipped to the post by Mrs Donohue for a staggering $12,000. The costs of a box at the Opera House and an expensive supper afterwards were nothing to Miss Arden. Her factory in Long Island had to take on 150 extra staff to cope with the demand for face powder and was making over 6000 boxes a day. During the 1940s, Elizabeth Arden was at the peak of her fame. Despite her rather breathy voice she was very articulate, and a confident, authoritative public speaker. She was invited to help put out one of the first-ever television shows in a link between Philadelphia and New York. She gave a talk and demonstration of make-up colours that worked best for TV studio lights, which was particularly important since all transmissions were in black and white, which cast difficult shadows. Television had begun in 1939, but had been suspended on both sides of the Atlantic because of the war. By 1944, progress was tentatively resumed, in America at least. Miss Arden was mesmerised by her time in the studio, writing, 'There will be *nothing* but television after the war, I feel sure, and it's good to get in on the beginning.'

Confident about controlling the faces and figures of her clients, Elizabeth now decided she wanted to manage their clothes. She had always dreamt about adding a fashion floor to her business, and was inspired by the success of her accessories and lingerie range. If Elizabeth Arden was going to do fashion, she had to do it with style, so she turned to Charles James. The mercurial and brilliant Charles James had first met Elizabeth when he was part of Bessie Marbury's circle. Born and educated in England — where he went to Harrow with Cecil Beaton, and from where he was expelled for 'unacceptable behaviour' with younger boys — he was the son of a British Army officer and a Chicago grandee. His entry into fashion design had been an erratic one. In early 1926, championed by interior decorator Rue Carpenter, he set up a millinery business in Chicago, operating out of a tiny boutique on Oak St. James moved to New York in 1928 where amongst his private commissions had been Miss Arden's clothes for her portrait by Augustus John.

Commuting relentlessly between New York, London and Paris in the 1930s, Charles James eventually began working out of his salon in London's Bruton Street. Horst photographed Joan Fontaine in a ravishing Charles James 'ribbon dress' for American *Vogue* in 1937, the caption describing him as 'a London designer'. His salon in London, like his businesses anywhere in the world, subsequently went bankrupt. Moving back to New York in 1939, he set up again, presenting his glorious silk taffeta evening gowns to Andrew Goodman at Bergdorf Goodman — wearing them himself! One can only wonder at the dignified Mr Goodman's reaction. He knew a good dress when he saw one, however, and placed an order.

By early 1944, James was short of cash. He was also short of a sponsor and very disdainful about the trend for streamlined, simple American 'sportswear' being designed in work-wear blue denim by Claire McCardell. McCardell, like all wartime designers on Seventh Avenue, was totally cut off from the dictatorial influence of Paris. She had evolved, to great acclaim, clothes for the modern American young woman: confident clothes, functional clothes, comfortable clothes. Neither Miss Arden, who clung to the belief all women needed decent underpinnings and a good ladies' maid, nor Charles James who was the king of occasion-wear, had any time for comfortable, functional clothes. Thus, James agreed to design a custom-made range for the Elizabeth Arden salon.

Elizabeth was hastened to move into fashion by the queen of Seventh Avenue herself, Hattie Carnegie. Miss Carnegie, a tiny Viennese dynamo whose stable of designers had included a rollcall of honour – Norman Norell in the 1920s, Pauline Trigere in the 1930s and Claire McCardell in the 1940s – had decided to expand into cosmetics. The minute Miss Arden heard that Miss Carnegie was launching lipsticks she picked up the telephone to Charles James. 'If that woman can do cosmetics, then I'll do fashion,' she screamed. James would have laughed. He adored gossip and intrigue and had a temper as violent, and a tongue as cruel, as Miss Arden's. This is the secret of their long-term friendship, which started before they worked together and would continue long after they parted professional company. James and Arden had a lot in common. They were both temperamental geniuses, made litigation a hobby, thought they were invincible and were obsessed with their work.

Whilst fashion would remain an Arden staple for the rest of her life, her professional partnership with Charles James was doomed. It began well. James wanted, and got, a newly decorated showroom, fitting rooms, cutting tables, sewing rooms and back-up staff. All this during the war, when resources were scarce. Miss Arden hosted a glittering benefit in May 1944 called 'One Touch of Genius' at the Ritz Carlton, to showcase his first capsule collection under her label. She wrote about the event,

> First, several Elizabeth Arden exercise girls showed how graceful the body is when under control, by demonstrating my exercises, which are also those of the fundamentals of dance technique. Then the fashion show – and the clothes were more beautiful than those *ever* shown in Paris before the war. *Vogue* is devoting four pages to the collection and I'll send you clippings. After the show, Leonard Bernstein the famous young conductor everyone is talking about, played some beautiful music. I had a wonderful time planning all the details – you know how I love to do just everything myself – and

always at the back of my mind was the determination to make as much money as possible for the Red Cross. After the accounts were straightened out, I was able to send them $5300! I was so thrilled.

The same letter breathlessly describes a lunch she had at her apartment for Alicia Markova and Anton Dolin, and that Constance Collier and Elizabeth's new *dame de compagnie* Madame Jean Hugo, the duchesse de Gramont, were there too.

Maria de Gramont was back in New York, the city she had taken by storm over a decade earlier, but this time things were different. She was widowed, had remarried and subsequently divorced, had a six-year-old son — and was penniless. Encouraged by their mutual friend Henry Sell, Elizabeth gave Madame Hugo a home at her Fifth Avenue apartment where she took on a more or less round-the-clock role looking after Miss Arden. In exchange, Elizabeth paid her handsomely and not only dressed and coiffeured her, but paid for her son's private education. All she asked, it would seem, was for her loyalty and companionship and attendance as a glorified lady-in-waiting at the formal galas, shows, dinners and operas Elizabeth so loved. There was one small detail. Miss Arden having lost her prince decided it was appropriate to gain a duchess, so Madame Hugo was asked to revert to her previously held French title. 'I do feel so many more people know you as the duchesse de Gramont,' wrote Elizabeth in a poignantly personal letter to Maria, in which her guard slipped for a moment, and it's clear to see how fond of the still beautiful Maria she had become.

Elizabeth steamed ahead with plans for the official opening of the fashion floor: 'I have been terrifically busy with plans for the Charlie James opening . . . and loving every minute of it. I think I am going to enjoy being in the dress business. You can imagine the turmoil of activity we are in . . . with plans for décor, draperies, dresses, publicity and advertising . . . to say nothing of the details of the parties. It is all terribly exciting.' Cecil Beaton, on a flying visit to New York in August, stopped by to see progress at the Charles James atelier and showroom. The two had never been really close, Beaton describing James as 'tricky and prickly', but he stayed long enough to do a ravishing drawing of the beautiful rooms coming together.

Miss Arden would not have been present that day. Beaton's rather supercilious humour made her feel . . . uncomfortable. But she was happy, particularly with the news of the liberation of Paris that month, feeling it couldn't be too long before Gladys would be free. She wrote to Teddy about a colour launch she had masterminded. 'We had a cocktail party for the press introducing Paradise Pink. Four models, gowned in variations of the Charles James "bow dress" – the one worn by Marlene Dietrich in *Vogue* – were made up in Paradise Pink colours, and all the guests were given little pink baskets holding samples of the new lipstick, rouge and nail polish, and of course the Paradise Pink powders. It seems to be a good colour, but I prefer it always over a *dark* foundation.' She enlisted Charles James as her escort to such functions. During those months he was roped in to accompany her to the opera, concerts and her favourite restaurants – 'extra mileage' as he was wont to call it.

In 1944, Miss Arden decided the time was ripe for property acquisition, first buying the building at 691 Fifth Avenue and then another in San Francisco. She also attempted to buy Floris in London. Much to her annoyance, her offer was rejected, but it prompted her to increase the search for a perfume chemist. Her first choice was an ex-Coty expert called Henri Robert, considered an outstanding 'nose'. He must have been, as he wanted $30,000 to join Arden which she rejected saying, 'I hesitate to pay the salary he is asking, as the essential oils are so hard to obtain, even though I'm told that this chemist would possibly save us roughly a hundred thousand dollars yearly.' She was talking about development costs in creating a popular perfume. The new technology in fragrances, that of 'aromatic chemicals', had become increasingly important to the perfume industry. Before the war, Grasse was producing some 7500 tons of flowers which were used in the extraction of essential oils, but the system was labour-intensive and expensive and supply lines were by now scarce. As early as the 1920s, artificial elements had become essential in many popular fragrances. Science had synthesised the aromas nature had started.

Perfume ingredients are not listed on the bottles, which is perhaps just as well; knowing the scent of rose comes from the chemicals rhodinol and geraniol acetate, violet from methyl heptine carbonate or hyacinth from phenylacetic aldehyde, does not make romantic reading. For companies producing perfume with a combination of scents however, synthetics were the way forward.

The official launch of the Elizabeth Arden fashion floor, planned for early autumn 1944, was delayed. Eventually Charles James said he would be ready on 30 October. Earlier that month, Miss Arden went to Chicago to attend a show for her favourite charity, St Luke's 'Cradle'. She took three of the newly finished James gowns to show at the ladies' luncheon – the only trouble was, she didn't take Charles James, insisting he stay in New York to 'get ready for the big show'. As Chicago was his home town, and the audience at St Luke's would be his mother's friends, James was incandescent with rage. Separating a fashion designer from the first presentation of his collection – even if only three dresses – was not a good idea. Miss Arden never quite grasped the fact that designers and their dresses are joined at the hip. When she got back to New York, James had decided to dress the Arden windows. He had found an antique cranberry glass vase and lit it with a lamp, the bulb coated with his favourite fragrance – Guerlain's 'Jicky'. Friends quipped that they didn't realise Elizabeth Arden was running a 'red-light house' and she flipped. A furious row ensued. The New York launch went on – without Charles James, and with no mention of his name on the programme. She had 'bounced' him.

Elizabeth, however, showing the twisty side of her nature, decided that he was perhaps just a little too influential to cut him off completely, so she arranged a cocktail party in his honour. She planned to wear a special gown he had made for her and was delighted when he suggested she send it back to him for 'freshening'. She never got the gown back. Instead, Charles James turned up at her soirée, accompanied by his black maid wearing Miss Arden's gown, holding a writ for 'wrongful dismissal and breach of contract' in her hand. 'Two birds with one stone,' James later remarked to a friend. The next season's collection was styled by Miss Arden herself. It was not a success.

Strained relationships, battles for creativity and clashes of ego were just as familiar at Helena Rubinstein's, even without her hiring fashion designers. The main problem was between Horace Titus and his cousin, Oscar Kolin. Kolin, who held a variety of significant titles within the company, seemed to specialise in soothing Madame's frazzled nerves, and was known as a charmer. He rarely wrote memos, preferring to visit her office for private chats. Horace, on the other hand, bombarded his mother with ten-page memos, never grasping that she had a low boredom threshold. He thought his cousin was a snake charmer.

With Roy at his desk job in the OSS, Horace had hoped his role at Rubinstein would be a way of proving himself in his mother's eyes – something he spent his entire life struggling to do. With Oscar's position increasing in importance, tensions were high. They boiled over when a sales manager by the name of Mr Scott was fired. Scott had been running a division called Tone, which Helena had bought several years earlier, convinced that its target, the younger woman, suited her portfolio. Mr Scott was a perfumier, not a sales manager, but he tried his best, and in the course of his work became close to Horace. When the axe fell, Horace was furious. 'Because Scott is a methodical person and endeavours to plan his activities accurately, qualities which are so rare and unique as to seem foreign to a management that has operated so long without them, it is decided to dismiss him without fair trial,' he wrote to his mother. In his defence of Scott, Horace let slip his true feelings about cousin Oscar. 'Your favourite nephew is very slyly and cunningly contriving to undermine the reputation of every worthwhile person in the organisation.' It's quite possible Horace was spurred on to attack Oscar by his father, perhaps worrying that his son's place in the inheritance line might be usurped. Horace felt increasingly isolated. Tommy Lewis had left, Mr Scott had been fired and his mother was spending more and more time in Mexico. 'Did you ever see a play called *Little Foxes*?' he wrote to her. 'It dealt with a family of clever, deceitful, underhand persons who were all angling for the major portion of a relative's fortune. I told you I was not interested in a "family business", unless I am convinced that the members of that family are the most capable and competent people to run that business.'

Running a successful business was also dear to Boris Forter's heart in London. He had some increased overheads to cope with by virtue of a new child on the way. Forter's private life was complex; the child in question was not by his wife, but by his mistress, one of two sons they would have together. Boris had taken an option on premises in Davies Street, calculating they would be ideal for the Rubinstein wholesale and managerial offices, and managed to get a seat on a flying boat out of Ireland bound for New York, where he intended to present the plan to Madame. His son Claude says, 'Boris wasn't sure if he was going to be decorated for distinguished Helena Rubinstein service, or shot by the flying squad.' In the end it was neither. He got to New York to find Madame Rubinstein unwell in Mexico. Thanks to his friend, hotel promoter Serge Obolensky, Boris found a room at the Plaza, where he stayed for three months waiting to discover if the Rubinstein family would agree to the purchase of the Davies Street lease. Eventually, Roy agreed the deal and Boris went back to England by boat. It would be the autumn of 1945 before Ceska returned to join him, confident by now she wouldn't be hit by a stray bomb. Her arrival was hotly followed by a telegram from her sister in German, the gist of which was 'What is missing there?' — not the best way to endear herself to Boris, who had guarded the Rubinstein interests, totally alone, throughout the war.

Helena herself got a passage to France in September 1945. What she found there gave her quite a shock. Her salon and factory had been appropriated by the Germans during occupation. Helena wrote to her nephew Oscar: 'The factory has hardly any merchandise. Everything is used up. We had to pay eight hundred francs a litre for sweet almond oil. No money ever goes into the bank. Madame Eliane claims one has to buy everything on the black market, which, to a certain extent, is true. I suppose you know the woman at the factory is a thief . . . I personally do not trust the book-keeper very much . . . I suppose he resents my asking questions.'

Apart from sorting out her business, Helena had to sort out her properties, reclaiming her country house, cleaning up her Quai de Bethune building and sifting and sorting the occupants of her other Paris properties, where tenants who had done the family a favour had been given favourable rates. Her companion throughout it all was Horace, Helena having decided that a European tour together would be a good moment to remove him from tension in New York (Artchil having gone to Hollywood, to stay with friends on Sunset Boulevard). She grumbled to Oscar, 'What is happening that you have not written? I presume you are ashamed to write, because you really should have come to Paris instead of me.' Helena told Oscar that the doctor — by which she meant company chemist — who was living in the Kolins' apartment had come to see her, requesting another apartment be made available to him. 'He was most rude,' said Helena. 'He claims since he saved your wife and children that you would give him any mortal thing he asked. Since then about six people have told me the same story.' It transpired that the doctor in question had a second Rubinstein apartment for his mother and Helena was furious.

'I do not see why she should have an apartment of seven rooms and pay only two hundred francs a month for it. Nowadays, one gets three thousand francs a year for a maid's room.' Helena also chastised Oscar for being over-generous with the refugees. 'No matter what beggar comes in for money, Eliane gives him something. She says you told her to. So please write her a note *not* to give anyone any money unless she has an OK from me. I don't see why one should give money to every Tom, Dick and Harry . . .' This was written when Paris was still suffering huge deprivation. Electricity was rationed, meaning shorter working days in factories, department stores, cafés and offices. There was little coal and heating was scarce; the rich were still burning sawdust in special stoves. A shocking drought raged throughout Europe. Street lights in Paris were dimmed, the metro worked restricted hours, meaning people walked to work – including Madame Rubinstein on occasion – and coffee was scarce. Luxuries, on the other hand, were always available to people who had the money to pay for them.

By that Christmas, Helena moved to London, to find new salon premises, taking the lease of yet another glorious building at 3 Grafton Street – the house of the Edwardian beauty Mrs Willie James – complete with requisite staircase. Mr Haslam was also busy evaluating property, and on his first post-war visit to New York that year, tried to persuade Miss Arden to buy the bombsite on the corner of Bond Street and Bruton Street. (The site was subsequently bought by Time/Life, and would have been the property investment of Miss Arden's lifetime.) It was a bargain, but she had extended herself in New York and, nervous of the left-wing government now at Westminster and set to impose tax increases, she ignored his advice, staying in her ageing and rather cramped salon premises.

The end of the war saw both Elizabeth Arden and Helena Rubinstein working as hard on redeveloping their businesses as they had done in originating them. Now, however, they were old. They had lived through two world wars; and younger, more aggressive rivals were encroaching on their territory, harnessing the new technology and employing, eager people with bright ideas. The years to come would not be easy. Their continuing battles for supremacy would be much harder to win. Both women were becoming used to dealing with Charles Revson, but soon they would have another woman to deal with, and that would be a little tougher. Her name was Estée Lauder.

CHAPTER NINETEEN

ALL THE QUEEN'S HORSES AND ONE OF THE QUEEN'S MEN
Mrs Elizabeth N. Graham
Racehorse owner 1932–1966

My business is to make women beautiful, my sport is to raise beautiful horses

—Elizabeth Arden Graham

As saturday 3 may 1947 dawned in Louisville, Kentucky, it was misty and grey. By late morning, racetrack officials had been looking anxious for hours, hoping the drizzle would clear and the sun break through. They needn't have worried. Rain wouldn't dampen the spirits of the people gathered at Churchill Downs – over 120,000 that morning, the largest crowd ever recorded in the history of the race. But this was no ordinary race. It was a mile and a quarter of pure, electrifying excitement – America's most famous horse race, the Kentucky Derby.

The crowd was behind Cornelius Vanderbilt Whitney's horse, Phalanx, the two-to-one favourite. Jet Pilot drew a surprisingly large vote, and when the field of thirteen paraded to the post, the Jet was second choice, with third on the list Calumet Farm's Faultless. Jet Pilot's owner had bustled around in the paddock, tense with excitement, yet as relaxed as ever when talking to her big, handsome horse. Gripping the arm of her young jockey, Eric Guerin, she said, 'Get out in front and go, go, go,' the words she used before every race. Guerin smiled down at her, clearly wishing she'd get out of the way. Jet Pilot merely tossed his mane as if he understood what she meant.

He probably did, for his owner was Elizabeth Arden Graham and she was known for 'talking to her horses'.

The strains of 'My Old Kentucky Home' drifted on to the track as the thirteen horses appeared from the paddock to huge cheers, their ears pricking up, acknowledging the applause. They were the greatest three-year-old thoroughbreds in America, each weighing in at around 1450 pounds, all gleaming muscle and sinew. Big, graceful beauties, all racing to win.

Jet Pilot's trainer looked on in his usual laconic manner, pulling slightly at the grey felt fedora he always wore. He'd seen it all before, his boss's excitement before each race, her babbling chatter to the horse, her last-minute instructions to the jockey. He'd been with her for three years – quite a record for one of Mrs Graham's trainers – but 'Silent' Tom Smith was no ordinary trainer.

Smith, a taciturn and wily old horseman, was nearly seventy when he took on Mrs Graham and her horses in May 1944, by which time Elizabeth was sixty-three herself and had already hired and fired well over twenty trainers. There was nothing 'Silent' Smith didn't know about horses. He'd learnt his craft working on the great American plains, growing up in a time when horses were not a hobby of the rich, but an essential way of life. The Indians had called him 'Lone Plainsman' and indeed, he seemed the ultimate loner, although he must have settled somewhere, because he had a son called Jimmy, who had followed his father's craft and was also a trainer. 'Silent' had done just about every job there was to do with horses, from breaking in mustangs for the army, to hunting deer; from being a ranch foreman to a mountain-lion tracker. He'd been a blacksmith and looked after circus ponies. Whatever work he'd done, he'd done it with horses, including training one of America's most famous horses of all, the mighty Seabiscuit.

Some people in horse circles said that taking on Elizabeth Arden Graham's stables was a harder job for Smith than the miracle he had worked on Seabiscuit. Mrs Graham and Seabiscuit, they joked, had a lot in common. Both were small and bad-tempered. They might have added that both were strong, brave, determined characters and both were natural winners.

Elizabeth had bought Jet Pilot as a chubby green yearling at the Keeneland sales in 1945, where her omnipresent horse manager and adviser on equine matters, Leslie Combs II, oversaw her investment of $41,000 on the colt. Combs had watched with glee in 1946, when the two-year-old made his winning debut in the first race on Derby Day, winning by an easy nine lengths, saying, 'There's next year's Derby winner.'

A year later, Jet Pilot rocketed out of the gate to assume command of the race from the very start. Every other horse changed place except 'the Jet', who grimly held on to his lead. Just over two minutes later it was all over and he had won. Only by a nose – in fact the finish between Jet Pilot, Phalanx and Faultless was so close the judges called for a photograph. Elizabeth was raking her hands with her nails until the result finally came in, when she was able to sweep into the winner's enclosure, fists clenched with proud excitement, as the famous 'blanket of roses' was placed over her sweating horse. He wouldn't be sweating for long. Mrs Graham's horses were rubbed down immediately, their grooms using Ardena Skin Tonic Lotion by the bucket load. They were then massaged – each leg for at least twenty minutes – shoes checked, tenderly covered with a cashmere blanket, whereupon her 'darling' could then relax.

Those who had backed Jet Pilot went to collect their winnings, amongst them Joseph Wile of Woolf Wiles, Lexington's premier department store. 'I felt I ought to place a bet,' he says, 'after all, our store did so well with the Elizabeth Arden range. I didn't win very much as I recollect, the odds weren't in our favour.' Elizabeth would have had a modest bet on her own horse; she rarely placed more than $5 to win. The horses were her passion, rather than betting, and she loved Jet Pilot more than most.

Her horse had been sired by Blenheim II, owned by the Aga Khan, and could trace his pedigree to Blandford, Swynford, Blanche and John O'Gaunt, the latter having been owned and bred by Sir Tatton Sykes at his Sledmere stud in Yorkshire, where John O'Gaunt had been mated with Lord Derby's prize mare, Canterbury Pilgrim.

Elizabeth would have been thrilled by the romantic background to those names. John O'Gaunt's progeny had been named after the Plantagenet royal duke, John of Gaunt's wife Blanche, Duchess of Lancaster, and his beloved mistress, the lowly-born Katherine Swynford, Chaucer's sister-in-law, whom the great Duke of Lancaster ultimately married in one of the most romantic stories in history.

For 'Silent' Tom Smith the victory was particularly sweet. Not merely for the bonus his ecstatic boss would give him, but because the suspension of his trainer's licence by the New York Racing Commission had meant that he had only been able to watch Elizabeth's three entrants in the previous year's

Derby, when sadly, none had been placed. Smith had been charged with 'hopping up' one of Elizabeth's horses, Magnific Duel, with ephedrine, classified as a stimulant, thus forbidden. He always claimed he had used the medication merely to treat the horse's cold, but William Woodward, Chairman of the Jockey Club inquiry found otherwise, and suspended Smith for a year. Mrs Graham had paid for his defence, hiring 'the Dean of vets', Dr Moehler, to plead his cause and subsequently hiring Smith's son Jimmy to take over her stables whilst his father was out of action. When two of her horses, Knockdown and Star Pilot, ran first and second in California's Santa Anita Derby, old Tom was keeping a paternal eye on the situation, precariously balanced up a eucalyptus tree, armed with powerful binoculars.

Of all her trainers in America, 'Silent' was the one she liked best. Shortly after hiring him in 1944 she wrote: 'I am thrilled with my new trainer, the horses look *wonderful* – their coats are smooth as satin. War Date has won three times now and I am out of the red.' War Date's winnings were a welcome relief as Elizabeth's stables, called Maine Chance after her celebrated health spa, had only made a miserable $6,865 in 1943. When Smith joined her in 1944, winnings went to $70,235, and the following year reached an astonishing $589,170, making Maine Chance the most profitable stables in America. Her winnings put her at the pinnacle of American racing, and Mrs Elizabeth N. Graham became almost as famous as her alter ego, Miss Elizabeth Arden. She was on the cover of *Time* magazine in 1946, captioned 'Elizabeth Arden – a queen rules the sport of kings' – and the issue devoted almost as many column inches to her success with horses as to her success with cosmetics. For the publicity-hungry Miss Arden it was a triumph, and a world away from the broken-down hacks that had pulled her father's pedlar's cart, when young Florence took the reins on their way to market.

Elizabeth had been introduced to the delight of fine horses in the late 1920s by a racing friend, Fred Johnson, who had invited her and Tommy Lewis for a weekend at his house in the beautiful spa town of Saratoga. This was the centre of the aristocratic horseracing community and Elizabeth felt as though she had 'come home', particularly when Alfred Gwynne Vanderbilt, a charming nineteen-year-old, asked her to dance at the most important racing ball of the season. If it was observed that the older woman and the younger man were getting on rather well, it was probably because they were talking about how he had enjoyed his last term at The Adirondack

Summer Art School, the very same college founded by her uncle, James Liberty Tadd.

The man who tipped her into owning horses, however, was the distinguished owner and breeder Samuel D. Riddle, owner of America's most successful racehorse ever, Man O'War. Acknowledged to be rather difficult himself, Mr Riddle rather liked Miss Arden and she rather liked the elegant, courtly, if somewhat crusty old man. Miss Arden rarely listened to a man, but when he advised her she needed a hobby, suggesting horses would be ideal, she took his advice. She installed stables at Maine Chance and took up riding again herself, buying several fine hunters and hiring Prince Kadjar to oversee her stables. Entering her horses for shows, however, wasn't enough and Elizabeth bought her first racehorse in 1931, spending $1000 at Saratoga on a yearling called How High. From that moment on she was hooked, bringing to racing the same dedication to detail and determination that had made her business such a success.

As affectionate as she was to her horses, she was less so to her horsemen. In her years in racing, from the early 1930s to her death in 1966 she hired and fired over sixty trainers, plus countless grooms and stablehands, and squabbled with almost all her jockeys. But Mrs Elizabeth N. Graham, as she was always known in racing (she called her first stables Mr Nightingale), was a generous owner and her trainers couldn't help being moved by the genuine love she had for her horses. Amongst the trainers she employed were some brilliant and important men – and, interestingly, one woman; Elizabeth Bosley.

Through the revolving door of Arden's stables went her first trainer, Clarence Buxton, fired for believing a horse should be treated . . . like a horse. As far as Elizabeth was concerned a horse was special. Louis Feustal, Man O'War's only trainer, managed to last two years. She engaged the services of, amongst others, Max Hirsch, Eddie Holton, George Poole, Monte Park *and* his brother Ivan, Jack Skirvin, Percy Garret, Alex Gordon, Tommy Queen, William Karrick, Tommy Grimes, Hugh Dufford, H.H. Battle and in England, amongst others, Captain Sir Cecil Boyd Rochfort, who trained horses for Marshall Field III, Ronald Tree, Lady Zia Wernher, William Woodward, and particularly appealing to Elizabeth Arden, the British royal family.

Her first few years as an owner were lacklustre and expensive. In March 1937, three of her most valuable horses were destroyed in a fire at her

Belmont Park barn. She bought a new yearling called Great Union, grandson of Man O'War, for $9200, and was ecstatic the following year when he came through to win the Merchant and Citizen's Handicap at Saratoga, despite being a 20/1 long-shot. Her first win, with a purse of $7600, was the trigger that turned her expensive hobby into an addictive passion.

Nothing was too good for Elizabeth's horses. Her foibles about the care of her 'babies' were as much a legend as her success in cosmetics. She lavished money, care and attention – but most of all love – on her horses and stables, and everyone on the payroll knew what to expect. When War Date developed a lump on his knee joint in the winter of 1945, which baffled his vet, Elizabeth rolled up her sleeves and went to work, massaging the swelling away with as much efficiency as she had used to massage her early clients. Music was piped into the stables. She remained convinced it soothed the horses and insisted on it wherever they were being prepared for a race. Her Eight Hour Cream was rubbed into their legs and hooves and zealously massaged into any cut or abrasion. Her horses were washed down with Ardena Skin Tonic – she was convinced they liked the smell. She shipped her product up to the stables in giant packs – Ardena Skin Tonic Lotion; Blue Grass for washing out their stalls and Eight Hour Cream. When she realised that her stable boys were operating a nifty sideline in selling off her preparations, she switched shipments to unmarked demijohns. She never knew her stable boys called her Mrs Mud Pack behind her back, but she probably wouldn't have cared.

Elizabeth fretted about their food. Her babies were fed with clover shipped at vast expense from Maine. She worried if they were getting too much fresh air on their morning gallops and she panicked about them being bitten by horseflies, fitting portable screens in their stalls and horseboxes. They had plants in hanging baskets over their stalls – she felt the oxygen was important. She loathed sheepskin nosebands, believing they made the horses sweat, and banned blinkers, saying they were ugly. Her jockeys were utterly forbidden to whip her fillies – colts yes, fillies never, and if they lost a race it was always the jockey's fault, or the trainer's – never, *ever* the fault of her horse. The Graham horsebarns were spotless, her grooms immaculate and her jockeys wore her cerise, white and blue silks – which their valets had to handwash in soap powder specially scented with Blue Grass after each race.

People may have laughed at Elizabeth's fanatical affection for her horses and her fanatical regime in looking after them. However, years later, experts agree that the massage and water treatments she advocated for swelling and muscle strain, including swimming and warm hosing, are of great benefit to a horse's well-being. Horses, as Elizabeth Arden knew only too well, have immune systems too . . .

She didn't seem to worry too much about her horses' travelling schedule, however, and they were moved rapidly from coast to coast for races, complete with grooms, trainer, kit, feed and Eight Hour Cream. She rented horsebarns at Saratoga and at Belmont, along with a cottage for herself at both tracks. This brought her properties up to five, as besides her apartment in New York and the 2000-acre estate at Maine, she also had a spectacular farm in South Carolina, at Summerville, not too far from the racetrack at Columbia. Her horses, however, didn't have a proper home until the late 1940s, when she leased her first horse farm in Kentucky. Pre-war transport to key tracks had been wonderfully comfortable, with special 'race trains' complete with horseboxes. The war meant the horses had to travel in more mundane cars attached to passenger trains, whilst Mrs Graham herself discovered the delights of interstate air travel. As her schedule was so crowded, she had her office make block bookings on several flights, causing expensive chaos when she didn't take up the seats. When Santa Anita in California was requisitioned as a military training ground, she lobbied John Clark, the owner of Hialeah racetrack in Florida, to build extra stalls for her. She was so persuasive that, despite the rush of owners wanting space, he couldn't refuse her.

Elizabeth's correspondence with Teddy Haslam became increasingly loaded with horse news, Haslam by now being her ex-officio racing consultant, obliged to look after her equestrian interests, although apparently he never understood much about horses. Filled with gloom about the poor performance of her darlings in 1943, she asked him about good mares. 'I must have good mares. Now I hear that you must not breed a mare until it is three years old – anything under that age is considered a child. What information can you get on this for me in England or Ireland?' Teddy lunched with an expert, V.R. Orchard, who said firmly: 'If Miss Arden is serious, I would suggest she make up her mind to trust some one individual and to confine all her communications to that individual. In a multitude of counsellors, there is unwisdom.' There was no more word about buying horses in England. If anyone was going to buy or sell horses for Elizabeth Arden Graham, it would be Leslie Combs II.

Elizabeth's horses were stabled for the main part at Combs's Spendthrift Farm in Kentucky. Combs was charming, and he was a good salesman. Miss Arden respected good salesmen and she had respect for Leslie Combs. It wobbled from time to time, as with all her relationships, and she grumbled about him constantly, but their affection endured and he retained a firm hold over her horses. Combs felt secure in his dominance over his client, once saying, 'Elizabeth didn't know a thing about the pedigree, soundness or conformation of a horse. The trainer and I handled all that for her.' However, he carefully waited until she was dead before making that statement.

The relationship with Mrs Graham was very profitable for Leslie Combs. In 1944 she paid nearly $300,000 for twenty 'babies', in 1945 a further $321,700 and in 1946 just under $250,000, all bought via Combs. He bred her winning acquisition Myrtle Charm (his own first stakes winner) in 1948, and would remain her chief adviser until her death.

To say that Elizabeth Arden Graham was opinionated is an understatement. She voiced her views on everything, from her trainers to her jockeys, from Leslie Combs to the state of racetrack hospitality. She was vocal about politics, politicians, gambling, Communists, Jews, blacks and her rivals in business, saying – and often writing – whatever came into her head. And she was careless whom she said it to. She had such belief in her own self-importance and such confidence in the power of her position that she felt above any form of criticism for her blunt approach. The press were generally kind to her, pithy talk giving good copy.

Elizabeth seemed incapable of tact: everything was black or white, wonderful or terrible, honest or dishonest. She behaved in this way all the time, rarely stopping to consider who might get hurt by her comments, and was so completely convinced that everything would somehow carry on as normal regardless of what she said, that it never occurred to her she might get hurt herself, or there might be retribution for her rhetoric. Jockeys in particular came in for her wrath. Writing to Teddy she said, 'I was hoping to tell you War Jeep had won last week, but the poor baby was very tired that day. The jockey actually held our horse so that the other one could go ahead. He certainly queered our ride. It's just a tragedy when these jockeys are running the track.'

In the autumn of 1945 in a letter to her dear friend Maria Hugo, who was in Paris on Arden business, she was even more blunt. 'I went to Chicago last week to see Royal Blood run and, as usual at Arlington, the gambling element oversaw to it that a long-shot horse won and my beautiful little one came in third. First, he was left at the post, then that nasty little jockey held him back until the last quarter. When the horse finally got his head of course it was too late. If this sort of thing continues, I shall withdraw all my horses from Arlington and take them where there is not so much dirty work.' She was forthright in her anger about Chicago's track involvement with organised crime and furious when the jockeys took money to swing a race, and as a result Elizabeth made some dangerous enemies in Chicago.

In May 1946, her barn at Chicago's track, Arlington Park, where twenty-eight of her horses were being stabled, burnt down in a shocking fire. Elizabeth lost twenty-two thoroughbreds and was crushed, visibly shrinking with despair when she was told. She wouldn't talk about it, unable to bear the thought of her horses burned to an agonising death. Only Blue Fantasy, Beaugay, Jet Pilot and War Date, along with a couple of non-starters, survived. Elizabeth's only consolation was that her Derby hopefuls, Lord Boswell, Knockdown (the horse she had bought at a bargain price of $1300 at the Alfred Gwynne Vanderbilt sale, buying it because she said 'he looked so forlorn') and Perfect Bahram were safely stabled in Kentucky at the time.

Arlington track director Ben Lindheimer issued a statement to the media: 'It was impossible to check the flames, because of the explosive nature of the fire.' The inquiry showed that both the grooms allocated to night duty at her barn had vanished. One was mysteriously 'out of town' and the other 'away from the barn' at the time. Even more curiously, a full investigation into the wiring showed that it was all in perfect order – although someone had noted that, unusually for night resting, the lights had been left on. Arlington Track night watchman Gilbert Jones was held responsible, and fined a meagre $50. Elizabeth received insurance, conservatively estimated at over half a million dollars, but nothing could compensate her for the loss.

I asked one of the most respected men in the world of racing today, James E. Bassett III, chairman of Keeneland, and also of the influential Emirates World Series Racing Championship, whether he felt the fire had been deliberately started as a warning to Elizabeth Arden to quieten down. The stalwart of Kentucky racing, at one time the director of Kentucky State Police, looked at me carefully and replied, 'It seems to me you may well be on the right track in thinking her barn was deliberately fired. She was outspoken and high-minded and there were some factions involved with racing at that time who were . . . dubious . . . to say the least. It was a difficult time.' Eventually representatives of the racing tracks went to J. Edgar Hoover and asked for, not merely protection, but a full investigation and cleaning up of the situation. Things improved, but sadly too late for twenty-two of Elizabeth's beautiful horses when the hard men of Chicago sent a warning to a talkative woman.

Mrs Graham busied herself buying new horses and getting 'Silent' Smith's licence back, grumbling that it was taking time and that people were gossiping about her. 'Some of the scuttlebuts, like Maxie Hirsch, are spreading the rumour that Tom Smith will not be re-instated,' she wrote to Teddy in September 1946, and by November the situation was worse. 'There is no chance of Tom getting his licence back until after December 15th. I am constantly working on the thing, as is Leslie, but we are up against a tough proposition.'

Ironically, it was Jet Pilot's Derby win that made Tom Smith decide it was time for a change. He had been particularly angry when, in the hour or so after the race, an over-excited Mrs Graham had kept coming up to Jet Pilot's stall with influential well-wishers – her corporate guests at the meeting – disturbing the horse's vital time to rest. 'Silent' actually asked a trade newspaper to publish a nugget that would lead to his dismissal – having signed another training contract in the meantime – and sure enough, when Elizabeth read the story, his bags were neatly packed and left outside his house at the stables. Yet he was genuinely fond of Elizabeth Graham and indulged her whims, even down to once having fired a groom she felt had a 'mean face'. 'Silent' recognised her abilities and, as an ex-blacksmith himself, was supportive one day when she had insisted a horse was limping only because his shoe was too tight. She had it taken off and was proven right. Smith would say about this time with her, 'I try not to hurt her feelings, yet do it my way.' His way, in 1947, was to leave.

His replacement was his son Jimmy. Elizabeth put on a brave face saying, 'The horses are simply wonderful, I never saw them more on their toes and Jimmy is a treasure. He is so normal and wholesome. When I think of what I put up with for so long when I had that old Tom Smith, I could kick myself.' What she had put up with was the most financially successful stable in America, and a Kentucky Derby champion, amongst many other winners. Elizabeth Arden Graham, however, had a short memory and felt 'Silent' had deserted her. Her resentment accentuated her need to be first and this had a knock-on effect on her relationship with Leslie Combs who, she felt, no longer valued her. 'He's so occupied with his own stables that my interests are secondary to him. I'm so mad with Leslie I can hardly bear to think of sending him a Christmas present,' she wrote. 'So many of those people are insincere and tricky that I really believe Sam Riddle is my only real friend amongst them.'

1948 was a tough year for the cosmetics industry, indeed for industry in general in the post-war period, and finances were tight. 'I'm having a hideous time here, manufacturing is at a standstill and the whole country is upset,' she complained to her sister. Yet her excitement was revived when Combs came on the telephone, offering her a special horse, Busher, coming up in the Louis B. Mayer sale in November that year. She bought it for a hefty $150,000.

Jimmy Smith was successful with her horses that season, Striker Pilot and Blood Royal both winning their races. He had tried to locate Mrs Graham to give her the good news, but she was delayed in San Francisco, wrapped up with plans for a fashion show, and had cancelled a trip to Chicago at the last minute – where Smith had left the message about Striker Pilot. Her staff were placed in a turmoil by her complex travel plans and Jimmy's message was forgotten. She was indignant. 'My babies won and I never knew anything about it. I sometimes think Jimmy Smith thinks he should run the horses for his own pleasure and not mine!'

The writing was on the wall for Jimmy. Elizabeth found cause for complaint at every turn. 'My beautiful little Lookout Jeep, who was my Derby hope, ran the day before yesterday and came in with his little leg lame. I could *murder* that brutal trainer who almost ruined him.' By September 1948 it was goodbye to Jimmy Smith and hello to Mr Moulter. He only lasted a few weeks, Elizabeth complaining 'the horses have got terrible chiggers'. Then came Mr Stauffer. By July 1949 she wanted Moulter back, but he backed off. She hired Mr Simpson, later described as 'a nice man but with no understanding of a stable such as mine'.

By the autumn she had persuaded Moulter to come back, and dispatched her company treasurer to inspect the horses which, as most were owned by Elizabeth Arden Inc, rather than Maine Chance Stables, seemed a good idea. He rather sensibly reported to his boss that 'they all looked wonderful'. Mr Moulter turned out to be a bolter, leaving late in 1949, when none other than 'Silent' Smith rode to her rescue, once again taking over. A year later he'd gone. Mrs Graham wrote to Teddy: 'When I got to Belmont, it was such a relief not to find Tom Smith there, I think I should have *murdered* him long ago. My new trainer, Monte Parke, has gone right to work on the horses and you won't *believe* the difference in them now.'

Mr Parke left shortly after arriving. His parting gift was to tell a story which Elizabeth's supporters furiously denied, but Parke swore was true. Mr Parke was asleep at his cottage at Belmont when the telephone rang. It was Mrs Graham, panicking because she had dreamt that one of her horses had escaped from her stall and was up in a tree outside the horsebarn. 'You will go and check she's all right, won't you, Mr Parke?' she said. 'Of course I will. I'll call you right back,' he replied. Having stayed in his room for about ten minutes he called her. 'You know, Mrs Graham, I climbed all the way up into that tree and I went in the stall, and I have to tell you that if she was up there, she got back down all right. Everything's fine.' Elizabeth was delighted. 'Thank you so, so much Mr Parke,' she said. Panic over, owner and trainer went back to sleep.

With her erratic behaviour including entering horses for races they weren't up to and pulling them when they were, it's no wonder her stables suffered. By 1951 her racing loss was over $200,000 and her breeding loss a shade under $165,000. In 1952, her racing loss had doubled and was little better in 1953 at nearly $350,000. Breeding losses were no better and it took until 1955 for Maine Chance Farm to show a profit and then only because she sold over $1 million dollars' worth of stallions and mares to Elizabeth Arden Inc.

In 1951 she was devastated when her greatest friend and supporter in racing, Sam Riddle, died, but she was soon being advised by another courtly and sometimes crusty gentleman – Captain Sir Cecil Boyd-Rochfort. Always known simply as 'the Captain', Sir Cecil and his beautiful, much younger wife, Rohays, met Elizabeth in Florida in 1950. The eminent trainer always wintered in the USA taking a break from his stables, Freemason Lodge in Newmarket, and spending time with American clients like Hope Iselin and lobbying for potential new ones, like Mrs Graham.

The Boyd-Rochforts kept in touch with Elizabeth through Teddy Haslam. At their suggestion, Haslam interviewed the Captain's nephew, Angus McCall, in 1950. A young major in the Irish Guards, McCall had been awarded the Military Cross whilst serving in Palestine. Mindful of army cutbacks, he resigned his commission at the end of the 1940s to find a job in civvy street. He joined Elizabeth Arden a few months later, staying there for over thirty years. Angus McCall was a natural fit into the Arden mould: tall, cheerful, attractive, his efficient disposition a legacy of nearly a decade in the army, most of which was spent at war. He was well connected and better still, through his mother who owned a stud in Ireland and his uncle, had a knowledge and love of horses.

Teddy Haslam was pleased, Elizabeth Arden was pleased and Sir Cecil Boyd-Rochfort and his sister were pleased. Poor Angus was slightly less pleased when his induction period in America was spent less at Elizabeth Arden Inc and more on escort duty for Miss Arden, visiting the racetracks of America. He was particularly worried when the London directors wrote quite crossly saying he should get back to his desk, feeling he was shirking. But Elizabeth liked him and, as she was temporarily bereft of 'walkers', being between fashion designers at the time – Angus McCall was excused duty in London and travelled with his boss, in considerable luxury, his trusty dinner jacket and cheerful smile to hand.

He might not have known as much as he'd hoped to discover about the Arden cosmetics line by the time he got back to London, but he knew more than he wanted to about Elizabeth's horses and trainers. To this day, he feels annoyed talking about it. 'She should have just kept six good horses with one decent trainer,' says McCall. 'She wouldn't listen, though, and wouldn't hear of cutting it back. It was such a foolish extravagance . . . quite ridiculous.' He recalls his concern for her horses. 'It was not a good thing at all to switch trainers like that . . . very unsettling for the horses . . . they were on the move absolutely everywhere, always in perpetual motion, and were worn out with it.' Sadly, Angus McCall's influence with his boss didn't extend to running her stables, or training her horses. In England at least, that rather dubious pleasure would go to his uncle.

In July 1951, Elizabeth bought a valuable breeding mare called 'Silence', leaving her, with her foal out of Lord Derby's famous Hyperion, at Muriel McCall's 'Tally Ho' stud in Ireland. She later sent the foal, called Hyperia, to the Captain's stables in Newmarket as a yearling, also asking him to buy her one of the royal stable's nine chargers that were coming up for sale – with a note not to spend more than £25,000. She was becoming quite addicted to buying in England, writing, 'These fine, big English horses are really glorious. I can't tell you how beautiful they are.'

She was also developing a fondness for young Englishmen, in particular Lord Montagu of Beaulieu, whom she'd met early in 1953 through the Elizabeth Arden company's new advertising agency, Coleman Prentice & Varley. Lord Montagu, whose sister was married to Colonel Varley, was working for Royston Vision, the PR arm of the agency, and had persuaded his boss to send him to America. It was coronation year and Lord Montagu felt it was a good idea, as he puts it, 'to drum up some excitement about our heritage', so his peer's ermine-trimmed robes went with him. Lord Montagu remembers that 'they were sent on a tour of the best women's department stores, while I stayed and worked in New York. Happily we re-convened so to speak!' He was seconded to spend a little time at Elizabeth Arden Inc, where Miss Arden took to him. She was always gripped with 'red carpet fever' when involved in any project connected with the royal family, or any member of the aristocracy for that matter and wrote excitedly to her London office, 'Lord Montagu has been urging me to create special coronation year preparations, colours, etc. He has all kinds of promotions in mind. Lord Montagu seems to be a very nice boy, so earnest in his work for someone so young . . . just plain smart I would say! It is too bad you did not get a boy like him for Elizabeth Arden, he is so well-connected. He said he would get me two seats for the coronation and do all kinds of helpful things.'

Lord Montagu doesn't remember it *quite* like that. 'I certainly wouldn't have said I could get her tickets – I couldn't do that – but I might have said something about getting her a couple of decent seats somewhere on the route from the Palace to the Abbey.' What he remembers very vividly is a luncheon at her Fifth Avenue apartment. 'My trip coincided with their presidential elections. She was fighting for Eisenhower in the Stevenson v Eisenhower campaign. She had one of those Maine Chance diet-menu ladies' lunches as a fundraiser, very minimal food as I recall. She was bobbing about and at one point said, "Now, ladies, be sure to vote for Eisenhower, you can't vote for Stevenson, the man's a queer!" I was quite shocked by that and left soon after. I was so starving I had to go for a hamburger.'

The election campaign was a dirty one. The Republicans were fighting for their first term for years, and Madison Avenue advertising supremo Rosser Reeves had been brought in to mastermind the campaign for Eisenhower in the first election to be fought via television. His 'We Like Ike' badges were a great hit, but he is unlikely to have told committee members like Arden that

Adlai Stevenson was gay. That slur was left to J. Edgar Hoover. As Stevenson was highly eloquent, Reeves had a fight on his hands. Television, however, accentuated Eisenhower's personality as a 'war hero', more seductive to the camera than subtle wit, and Stevenson lost. Elizabeth, who had worked hard and donated serious money, was delighted her friend the general had won.

She had hoped – in fact presumed – that because of her Anglo-American connections, not to mention her campaigning, she would be sent as 'ambassador to the coronation', an appointment within the remit of the president. To her abject humiliation, Fleur Cowles was chosen instead. Miss Arden's wrath when her ex-copywriter was seated as a VIP in Westminster Abbey was keenly felt. Mrs Cowles went to London with a tiara borrowed from Eleanor Lambert, who recalls, 'She was terribly excited about it all . . . yes, I believe Elizabeth was *very* upset, I seem to remember things got a little overheated.' In the Arden offices, the heat was better described as white hot. Cowles herself said, 'When the president announced my appointment, Clare Booth Luce may have beamed, but not everybody did. It caused a furore among certain of the older socialites waiting in line. Also raised in protest was the voice of that dyed-in-the-wool Republican, cosmetic queen Elizabeth Arden.'

Elizabeth did go to London during coronation year, and at least she got invited to lunch at Beaulieu, driven by the Hon. Mrs Varley who remembers Arden as 'wearing a beautiful black hat'. She also went to the Derby, which she adored, so much that Elizabeth Arden Ltd from that point took a hospitality box which seated twenty guests and filled it each year.

Her training relationship with Captain Boyd-Rochfort got off to a shaky start at the Coronation year Derby. Elizabeth could not resist handing out advice. When jockey Harry Carr, riding the Queen's horse, Aureole, failed to win, she took the Captain to one side suggesting he replace Carr with the American jockey, Edie Arcaro, to ride Aureole in the St Leger. The suggestion was not well received. Angus McCall remembers, 'The Captain was of course with the Queen and Elizabeth Arden had been told she might be presented . . . When they were in the paddock, Bruce Hobbs [ex-National Hunt jockey and assistant trainer at Freemason Lodge] was seconded to look after Miss Arden whilst the Captain was with Her Majesty. She was absolutely furious, thinking she'd been relegated to the second division.'

The young Queen must have been disappointed that Aureole lost the Derby that special year. Coronation day was on Tuesday 2 June, shortly after the Derby, and when one of her ladies-in-waiting asked her if all was well, perhaps thinking that the Queen was concerned about the elaborate ceremonies, or tired with the endless fittings for her Norman Hartnell robes, apparently the Queen replied that the Captain had just called her to say that Aureole had gone well in his last work and yes, all was fine.

Back in America, things weren't so fine with Miss Arden's trainers. Two trainers had been in and out, and in 1953 she called back 'Silent' Tom Smith for the third time. 'I must have someone in whom I can place my trust,' she wrote. 'Tom arrived yesterday and says it's wonderful to be home.' Sadly for 'Silent' he was by now quite ill and his season at Maine Chance Farm was his last in training for a large stable. He died in 1957, it's said still crushed by the ignominy of his racing ban.

Elizabeth's British horse Hyperia won his first race in 1954. She had been making two trips a year to England for some time, always visiting and sometimes staying at Freemason Lodge, beautifully run by Rohays Boyd-Rochfort, who organised splendid dinners where the wine flowed freely. As well as horses, cats and dogs, there were always young people about during the holidays. As well as their son Arthur, Rohays had four sons from her previous marriage to Henry Cecil. Her twins Henry and David were destined for famous careers in racing. Even in all the bustle, Miss Arden, according to Angus, 'fitted in quite well. She always brought bulbs from her collection – Arden sweet peas and tulips – which pleased my uncle.' Elizabeth was less pleased when she went to bed one night to discover that one of Rohays's prize cats had been sick on the eiderdown.

In December Angus McCall was whipped in for escort duty at the Newmarket sales where Elizabeth spotted a chestnut foal that took her fancy. She told Angus to bid for him. 'Teddy Haslam was looking over at me at the time looking worried,' recalls Angus, 'but Miss Arden was chatting away to someone, I can't remember who, and kept telling me to go for it. I was absolutely terrified.' By the time he'd finished, she was the proud owner of the colt at an all-time record price of 19,000 guineas, which caused a sensation in the press, and left McCall feeling quite weak. They named him Administrator. His brother went on to buy her a yearling filly, Mamounia, for another astonishing price of 17,500 guineas. The Captain and David McCall then spent *another* 13,000 guineas on a colt she named Tempest, bringing her British investment up to £50,000. As usual, she sent her own instructions on feed, insisting he used kelp, to the Captain's concern. 'He is needlessly worried about my using too much kelp,' she wrote to Teddy. 'He suggests a tablespoon a day . . . we give the horses one cup of kelp mixed with corn and molasses and they just love it!'

By 1956, Elizabeth had her own 'ole Kentucky home' as she liked to refer to her beautiful Bluegrass estate, and there had been an orgy of decorating, garden planning and designing of stables. She even attempted to commission illustrious architect, Frank Lloyd Wright, to design the stable complex but, after several heated meetings, he declined the commission. Her niece, Pat Young, was put in charge of the programme and commuted from New York to oversee the planting of trees, shrubs, new turf and thousands of bulbs. Elizabeth's tastes in furniture didn't run to Americana, so she bought French armoires, gilded Regency chairs, bamboo cabinets and crystal chandeliers. Her one concession to American country comfort was a series of giant red chintz sofas and awesomely efficient bathrooms, equipped with massage tables. Her own pale pink bedroom had spectacular views from windows draped with pink rose-print chintz and a wing chair covered with white satin. Her barns were red-trimmed and the miles of picket fences bordering the 725 acres where her 'darlings' grazed were gleaming white. She loved the place and held black-tie dinner dances the night before the Kentucky Derby with a guest list which, naturally, included people useful to Elizabeth Arden Inc.

Back in England, Mamounia was out of action with bad knees, Elizabeth pressing Teddy Haslam to send her details, and Cecil Boyd-Rochfort, in terrible pain himself with a torn knee cartilage, was having a bad time with her other two horses, Administrator in particular proving stubborn. Administrator was eventually shipped to Maine Chance Farm, but two days later he was dead. Angus McCall, remembering his expensive purchase, says, 'He spotted two frisky fillies and broke his neck jumping a fence to get at them . . . bloody useless great big horse.'

Elizabeth was considering switching trainers in England, writing to Teddy, 'I've been advised to put Tempest with Harry Wragg. He's winning everything just now and is a wonderful trainer. I'm thinking of putting all my horses with him especially since Cecil has knee trouble and can't properly look after horses.' That quip was rather unfair, as he had a successful operation and was soon back in action. In the end, she left Tempest with him, and was thrilled when he won at Epsom in April 1957. Cecil Boyd-Rochfort told Elizabeth that although Tempest needed two more good races, he could be entered for the Derby. Elizabeth was beside herself with excitement. Pierre Wertheimer, the cosmetics and fragrance tycoon owner of Chanel, had won the year before with Lanvin and she couldn't wait to have her own victory.

It wasn't to be. The Captain insisted Tempest run in the Newmarket Stakes and the Lingfield Derby Trial. Elizabeth utterly rejected the latter and the horse couldn't run in the Newmarket Stakes as the ground was too hard. As a consequence, Tempest went to the Derby green, running a decent but uninspiring race, and came in fourth. Elizabeth swallowed her disappointment, showered the girl grooms at the Lodge with boxes of Arden product, and watched his summer programme like a hawk. Her horse was second at Ascot, third at Goodwood and third at York, which was, as far as Mrs Graham was concerned, three losses too many. She was angry that Tempest was being cared for by a girl groom – she preferred men for her colts – and furious he had raced wearing a sheepskin noseband, firing off a hugely insulting cable about Boyd-Rochfort to Haslam, the gist of which was that she supposed Tempest was ruined, that the fault was probably his left front leg, and he was to be stopped from racing before he was *entirely* ruined. Quite how she could have divined the horse lost at York due to a bad front leg when she wasn't even there is hard to fathom. She was ill at the time, and sent the cable from her hospital bed in Chicago, which goes some way to explaining her curtness. Haslam, by now nervous about the whole situation between trainer and owner, panicked, and told Boyd-Rochfort exactly what she had said. It was an unwise move.

The Captain, a strong-minded individual, was not going to be told he had 'ruined' a horse by anyone. He wrote to Miss Arden at once.

I most strongly object to these insinuations because the horse has never had anything wrong with his leg and is as sound today as when I bought him for you. You seem to have no faith in me like all your other trainers and I certainly do not intend to be treated in this way. I have trained for our splendid Queen and for some of the greatest owners in England. I have had the honour to train for William Woodward . . . for Jock Whitney . . . for Joe Widener and I have never once had any insinuations made against me. I will keep the horse until the St Leger where he is quoted at 10-1 and the public have backed him so he should run . . . I will then ask you to remove him. You may be a great judge of your own business but you certainly know nothing about horses. You have the finest stables in America but you are making nothing except a mess of it.

Haslam was uneasy, but not nearly as uneasy as Boyd-Rochfort's nephew, who thought he might lose his job over the *fracas*. Teddy wrote to her on 23 August, pointing out that steps had been made to withdraw Tempest from the prestigious French race, the Prix de l'Arc de Triomphe, which Cecil Boyd-Rochfort had entered him for, and asked if she wanted the horse back in America or sold at Newmarket. She had calmed down by then, and agreed Tempest could run in the St Leger, but when Sir Cecil's letter arrived two or three days later, she exploded. The press got hold of the story, which made headlines on all the sports pages. 'Royal trainer shows Miss Arden OUT' and 'Elizabeth Arden in row with the Queen's trainer' – not conducive to a happy relationship with the Palace for Elizabeth Arden. Not used to being fired by her trainers – Boyd-Rochfort was the first to *ever* fire her – she took her horse away at once, sending him to Joe Lawson. The Captain watched as Tempest came in fourth in the St Leger on 11 September, and fielded questions from the press with dignity.

For Elizabeth, the story wasn't quite over. When she realised her precious horse had been scratched from the l'Arc de Triomphe she made contact with the Baron Louis de la Rochette in Paris, a man with considerable influence at the Jockey Club, to try and get him reinstated. In her vindictive but chatty letter she asked the baron if he had noticed her very successful horse in America, Jewel's Reward, which was making her a lot of money, and within a while would make headlines himself.

She had bred Jewel's Reward at Maine Chance Farm and the horse was one of her favourites, winning at Belmont Park in 1957, a year in which the horse won a shade under $350,000 – more money than any other two-year-old. In the winter of 1958, Elizabeth thought Jewel's Reward had won the Flamingo Cup at Hialeah, Florida's beautiful track. She headed towards the presentation area with her trainer Ivan Parke. The result, however, wasn't quite in and following a steward's inquiry, Jewel's Reward was disqualified. The *Miami Herald* wrote, 'at least when her number came down and her face turned the traditional Flamingo pink, Mrs Graham had the cosmetics to cover it'. She was consoled, but only just, by a telegram of sympathy from one of her best friends, Mamie Eisenhower, a devotee of

Elizabeth and her products. The First Lady was by now a regular visitor at Arden's Maine Chance health spa in Phoenix, jetting there on one occasion via Air Force One which led to a riot of unfavourable press comment about abuse of privilege.

Jewel's Reward was at Maine Chance Farm one day in the late spring of 1959 when Elizabeth went over to his stall. He apparently had a great fondness for oranges, but as she was giving her favourite his usual treat he bit the hand that fed him, tearing her little fingertip off. Her farm manager and groom looked on in horror, but Mrs Graham, for once staying remarkably calm, simply picked up the fingertip, told them to put it in ice and ordered transport to the nearest hospital. Her finger was sewn back on that night and, heavily bandaged, she went back to work.

A few days later in New York, Helena Rubinstein was giving a press luncheon at her Park Avenue penthouse when one of the beauty editors made excuses early, saying she had to go and see Elizabeth Arden. Glimpsing the expression in Madame's eyes, she explained, 'Well, you see, she's just back in town and there's quite a story because one of her horses bit her finger off.' Madame Rubinstein, drawing a deep breath, her face deadpan, replied, 'Oh dear. Such a shame. Do tell me, how is the horse?'

Jewel's Reward as it happens was fine. Elizabeth loved him far too much to be cross with him. 'The poor baby just got excited,' she told a reporter. The story flew around and Elizabeth had the opportunity of repeating it to the Queen Mother whom she saw in London at the end of May. Clearly, Her Majesty was as amused as Madame Rubinstein, as her lady-in-waiting wrote: 'Her Majesty was so glad to have seen you last week, and does so hope that your finger is growing!'

In the thirty-five years she spent in racing, Elizabeth Arden Graham may have been laughed at quite a lot, but she was laughed *with* a lot too. A lonely woman, she delighted in entertaining and was surprisingly popular with some of the most colourful characters in the sport. The irrepressible womaniser Prince Aly Khan, for example, took her dancing. Elizabeth used to look after his girlfriends when he was busy in New York; although sometimes to her shock he would deliver them two at a time to her apartment. Aly it seems was also careless about money, often the case with the super-rich — sometimes leaving bills unpaid at restaurants which the obliging Mrs Graham would have charged to her account. Then there was the even more colourful Sir Victor Sassoon. Arden had bred a horse from his Derby winner, Pinza, and they became firm friends. When the ageing multimillionaire, whose family had once owned all that was worth owning in Shanghai, to say nothing of the Sassoon Docks in Bombay and the Whangpoo River's most luxurious houseboat, married for the umpteenth time, his young bride was only thirty-nine. Still handsome at seventy-nine, Sir Victor was asked what his secret was. 'I credit it all to Elizabeth Arden,' came his reply!

Another friend who remembers her well is Emily Hutchison. Em Church, as she then was, first met Elizabeth Graham at a yearling sale in Saratoga in 1946. She has spent her whole life with horses and is a renowned horsewoman. At her elegant home in Middleburg, deep in Virginia's horse and hunt country, she reminisces about Elizabeth, particularly her extraordinary feeling for her horses. 'One of her horses, Jet Action, had run loose,' says Emily, 'and tore his chest really badly on a fence. Elizabeth was heartbroken when the vet said he would have to be destroyed. She wouldn't have him put down . . . she sat up with him for days . . . through the entire night sometimes, rubbing Eight Hour Cream onto his chest and talking to him like a child . . . She willed that horse better.' Emily recalls many kindnesses shown to her by Miss Arden. When she was feeling miserable following the end of her first marriage, Elizabeth sent her to have her hair done. 'Emily,' she said, 'go and get your hair cut by John at my salon in Washington.' She kept her shorn tresses and had them turned into a chignon. 'I had to, you see. I rode sidesaddle.'

Theirs was a professional as well as personal relationship, with Emily and her husband from time to time selling yearlings for Elizabeth. 'That was often a problem because you know she just *hated* to part with them, but she couldn't keep everything.' Being Elizabeth, however, she sometimes used to buy them back in the same sale, despite the furore this would cause, with accusations of driving up the value of a Maine Chance horse. The truth is, she could not bear to part with her horses.

Mrs Hutchison remembers Elizabeth always being surrounded by people, yet sensed she was lonely. 'I think all rich and successful women are lonely, don't you?' She also remembers her as being fierce about her product. 'I was in New York and went to see her at her offices. She said, "Emily, I love that lipstick, let me see it." When she realised it was Estée Lauder, she absolutely flipped. I scuttled out of the office very fast I can tell you . . . I never got the lipstick back.' Above all, Emily Hutchison remembers

Elizabeth fondly, despite her reputation. 'Oh yes, she had a fall out with lots of people, but to me she was always bright . . . and gay . . . and full of life.'

Ted Basset feels that, dearly though she loved her horses, they were a powerful marketing tool. 'Horses personalised Elizabeth in the eyes of the public,' he says. 'What she did by linking her racing name to her Maine Chance health farm was utterly brilliant. Whenever you read "Maine Chance Farm" you thought about her horses, but you know, the wives of the people who could afford to keep horses and the media too, they would always think of her other business, the Maine Chance Health spa at the same time.'

Mary Lou Whitney, a long-term racing acquaintance of Elizabeth's, always felt that racing was never a *business* with Mrs Graham, as it was with so many owners. 'Elizabeth had no children, but she did have a maternal instinct. So the horses were her babies, her children. She carried pictures of them in her billfold . . . She was the most practical woman in the world when it came to her cosmetics business, but when it came to horses, she was a sentimentalist all the way through.' Mrs Whitney adds sagely, 'She had an incredible amount of drive. Usually things like that start in early childhood, with people who have had to fight very hard and been hungry. I think that was her driving thing.'

Mack Miller, one of her last trainers, recalls that she used to have vats of olive oil shipped up to the stables with instructions to give the horses a cupful with their feed each day. 'You know what,' said Miller, 'they were the best-looking horses I ever saw. I never saw such coats in my life.' Miller liked her. 'She was a delightful lady, smart, a good businesswoman, but the horse business just defeated her. She wasn't practical in this business . . . she wanted horses treated like humans. She had a lot of luck as it goes, but if she had turned it all over to some man and said "Look, you run it" *and* left him alone, I'll tell you she would have cleaned up in this game.'

Trainers and managers all felt the same way about Elizabeth Arden Graham – if only she had left them to do their jobs, it would have been so much better. But she could never leave *any* of them alone.

CHAPTER TWENTY

POST-WAR WARRIORS
New York and London
1946–1950

IN 1908, THE YEAR after Florence Nightingale Graham arrived in New York, Josephine Esther Mentzer was born in Corona, Queens. At that time, Corona was an open-cast collecting ground for rubbish from the adjoining boroughs. The Brooklyn Ash Company piled ashes and cinders in vast mountains, and barges of manure docked at Corona's piers, waiting until the local farmers came to collect it. The all-pervading smell, leeching through Corona, especially in the shimmering heat of summer, was unforgettable. Josephine Mentzer would grow up to be responsible for perfuming a considerable number of American women.

In 1946, the year that Florence Nightingale Graham, aka Miss Elizabeth Arden, appeared on the cover of *Time* magazine, the *New York Times* reported that out of a survey of 1000 women, 99% of them used lipstick, 95% nail polish, 94% face powder, 80% a tinted foundation base, 73% perfume and 71% cleansing cream.

In 1947, after ten hard years spent demonstrating, giving facials and selling her product range, commuting between Miami Beach (where she had a concession at the Roney Plaza Hotel) and New York, Josephine Esther Mentzer, now Mrs Joseph Lauter, formed her own company. She called it Estée Lauder. She was chasing 71% of women who used cleansing cream – but she would soon be targeting the rest. Even if she had known about the incorporation, Elizabeth Arden would have taken little notice. Mrs Lauder was a one-woman band, assisted by her husband Joe (whom she had divorced and subsequently remarried) and teenage son Leonard, who apparently made store deliveries on his bicycle. She energetically hawked a small collection of products including lipstick and eye shadow but predominately based on her Cream Pack, All Purpose Cream and a cleansing oil, for the main part made up for her by her uncle John Schotz,

319

a Hungarian chemist who lived in New York. Neither Estée nor her creams had yet come into Miss Arden's orbit.

That same year, Revlon, riding high, was established in a glamorous suite of offices at the Squibb building, at 745 Fifth Avenue. Revlon were by then employing over 1000 people. Of the 95% of women wearing nail polish, at least two-thirds of them would have been wearing Revlon. Job security however, particularly amongst clerical staff, was tenuous. Secretaries lasted on average just seven months before they fled from the pressure. Receptionists were chosen to 'blend in with the décor', which made their tenure tricky as Charles was wont to repaint the area each time he launched a new lipstick colour. He would simply call up his personnel manager and demand he hire a blonde, redhead or brunette – whichever toned the best. As he changed the colours, thus he changed the girls, but like Madame Rubinstein, Charles Revson rarely fired anyone personally – it was considered to be bad luck – so he got personnel to do the dirty deed.

One staff member he never had fired was his press officer, Bea Castle. She was savvy and smart and the press liked her. Bea was also 'tenacious, dedicated . . . and tough', according to Grace Gilbert, a colleague of hers who says, 'Bea was a pain to many people in the business, but she held in there with Charles, so you had to admire her.'

Bea hadn't quite got the edge over Amy Blaisdell, Helena Rubinstein's devoted, and equally popular, press officer; but at least Rubinstein and Revlon had press officers. Elizabeth Arden had a press office, but it was rarely manned by a senior person long enough for her to form a lasting relationship with the media – Miss Arden preferred to control that element herself. She had a strong relationship with magazine editors and went to a lot of trouble to make life easy for them when they were travelling in Europe. Carmel Snow and Mrs Chase, for example, never lacked for a last-minute hair appointment in Paris or London, and were the first guests to be invited, with their families, to spend time at the new Maine Chance spa, in Phoenix, Arizona. Snow had seemingly forgiven Miss Arden's relationship with her married brother, Tom White, and even volunteered to take a carton of precious supplies to Gladys on her first trip to Paris after the war. In the end, Mrs Snow flew to France, thus avoiding the task, which is probably just as well as Elizabeth packed the trunks with everything from tins of fruit, soups, dried fruits, orange juice, coffee, tea, sugar, baking powder, malted milk, vanilla essence, hams, cigarettes and even candles –

all much appreciated by her sister in a city where such luxuries were desperately scarce. Helena also endeared herself to Carmel Snow at that time, by doing something more practical than offering trips to spas. She bought a car for Marie Louise Bousquet, the popular Paris editor of *Harper's Bazaar*, who was virtually crippled with arthritis. She also gave Marie Louise cash; 'They earn *nothing* on those magazines,' said Helena. It was well received.

The two years following the war had been particularly hectic for Miss Arden. There had been a scramble to hire staff, ready to cope with the anticipated post-war boom in cosmetics. In France, an attempt to headhunt a top man from Max Factor failed. 'Having stayed with the company so long in these lean years,' he said, 'I'm staying on to reap the rewards.' In Germany, desperate to find a salon manageress for Berlin, she was pleased that Lily von Hartmann, who had run the salon before the war, wanted her old job back. 'We heard she had become an enthusiastic Nazi,' wrote Teddy cautiously, 'but apparently that role has been discarded and she is now an interpreter with the army of occupation in Brunswick.'

Gordon Yates was sent to Australia and reported on the in-store salon at David Jones in Sydney, which had been in place for over ten years. Miss Arden had wanted the space expanded to include hairdressing, which, as the store had exclusivity on Arden products, was not unreasonable. Charles Lloyd Jones was less keen. He wrote to Miss Arden saying her brand was 'lacking management' in Australia and offered to release her from the store's obligation to operate the salon.

Australia was an important territory to Elizabeth, not just in profitability, but as it had been Rubinstein's original fiefdom, Miss Arden took success there as a personal issue. Her company had a flourishing wholesale division handled by Philip Keen and Scott Williams, and at David Jones alone she had a combined salon and retail turnover of $250,000 in 1946. Williams had just been poached to run Yardley in both countries, leaving a hole in the management structure handled by Teddy Haslam from London. Miss Arden decided to take over the territory herself, and whilst admitting she 'wanted to take his hide off', she wrote gracefully to Charles Lloyd Jones:

> I plan to bring Australia under my own personal supervision. I think it wise to go along quietly, making the present salon as beautiful and compact as possible. I am anxious to establish closer ties between our

publicity and promotion so you can have advantage of our newest ideas. I see advertising is less restricted in Australia than here . . . and ours can be changed to a broader type . . . although I do not mean to follow Mme Rubenstein's example . . . but to strike a happy medium.

Elizabeth couldn't resist the sideswipe at Helena, who had closed down her Australian salons and expanded mid-price wholesale activity. Elizabeth held passionately to her belief in higher prices, telling Mr Lloyd Jones, 'In both America and Canada I have found it necessary to substantially increase all salon treatment prices . . . there has been no resistance.'

Yates, bringing Philip Keen with him, went from Australia to New York to update Miss Arden, which was their opportunity to meet another new employee at head office, Jack Treat. Good-looking, and to Elizabeth's joy, very tall, Jack Treat was roped in for social escort duties as part of his sales manager's brief. She had also hired a general sales manager, now in charge of the entire wholesale department, called Ralph Lewis, via a recommendation from her friend Charles Luckman, the CEO of Lever Brothers US division, who felt Lewis had potential. He certainly did. By October 1946, Elizabeth was excitedly telling Teddy Haslam that Lewis and his team had sold a staggering $2 million of preparations in a single month (in the year when Rubinstein's entire American turnover was reported as being just $10 million). It was just as well, as Elizabeth was about to be given a tax bill for 1945 amounting to nearly $2.5 million. Panicking as usual when it arrived – Elizabeth rarely planned for tax bills – she sent out a barrage of letters asking for 'cutbacks in expenses'. This seemed unfair on London who had put in good profit increases, with wholesale up from the previous year by nearly 24%, the salon up by over 12% and hairdressing up by over 20%, all in a year when raw materials were scarce and rationing was still in place. Elizabeth did little about cutting back expenses herself, particularly where the launch of her new fashion collection was concerned.

Desperate to re-establish her 'custom-made' department, which had got off to a shaky start under Charles James, at the suggestion of Gladys Miss Arden hired Castillo in September 1945. Antonio Canovas del Castillo, a Spaniard who had been making his name in Paris, had been a protégé of Helena's friend, Misia Sert. Castillo had started out designing hats and jewellery for Chanel, and had spent the war in Paris, working for Paquin.

Teddy was dispatched to finalise details, reporting back: 'You may find him a handful from the point of view of management . . . but he has been conspicuously successful . . . there are difficulties in getting his permit from the US Consulate, complicated by the fact he is Spanish . . . interestingly, in Spain he was a qualified lawyer before he took up fashion . . . bear this in mind when he asks for a contract!'

Castillo got his contract and sailed to New York, getting ready to show his first collection for Elizabeth Arden on Valentine's Day, 1946, at the Everglades Club in Palm Beach. The show was a triumph, with Castillo presenting everything from swimsuits to a wedding dress. From this point onwards, the premier Elizabeth Arden salons in America added clothes to the ranges of cosmetics, creams, lingerie and accessories. It was a masterstroke by Elizabeth, who not only offered 'one-stop shopping' but could use her clothing collections in fashion shows at ladies' charity luncheons and evening events, where she controlled a 'top-to-toe' fashion and beauty experience, right down to the gift bags on the tables. The only thing that disturbed her equilibrium that season was losing her star hairdresser, Guillaume, to Lentheric.

Post-war problems in Europe involved everything from integrating women workers back into their home life as their men demanded their jobs back, to coping with the shortages of staple goods and continued rationing. The situation in Paris was grim and things were pretty bad in England too during the winter of 1947–8, where the worst weather ever recorded meant that electricity often failed and workers in freezing offices often toiled by candlelight. Roads were closed, trains were caught up in twenty-foot snowdrifts and the RAF had to make food drops to marooned villages. Women who had taken to Dior's 'New Look', launched the previous spring, probably welcomed their long, full skirts and swirling coats. At least they kept them warm. Import and export restrictions between Europe and the USA meant complications in shipping raw materials, and Elizabeth was particularly annoyed not to be able to receive Arden soap from England, where it was made, due to an export ban on soap imposed by the new Labour government. [*Soap rationing didn't end in the UK until 1950*]

After her win at the Kentucky Derby, her *Time* cover and her much reported divorce, Elizabeth had become, in both America and England, a *celebrity*. She was interviewed and photographed wherever she went, and started to be careful about what pictures were released via her offices.

They were all re-touched and they were always personally passed by Miss Arden. She revelled in the fame, yet interestingly turned down an offer by Scottish publisher Sir William Darling for an autobiography. She was not ready to discuss her past life – and as for her future, well, in her eyes it had hardly begun.

Elizabeth was, once again, beset with management problems. With key staff much in demand she was furious her American sales manager Ralph Lewis left, headhunted by Charles Luckman of Lever Brothers, who had just bought the Harriet Hubbard Ayer company, and poached Lewis to run it. Elizabeth felt bitter, sounding off to Teddy: 'When I think how hard I worked with him, teaching him . . . giving him my confidence and my friendship . . . not to mention a whacking good salary, it absolutely sickens me. What I've been doing is educating Lewis for Luckman – it wouldn't surprise me if this was planned from the beginning.'

She was even more upset when Lewis started to raid her office staff, and what's more, she had problems at home when her chauffeur, Frank Sanford, left abruptly after fifteen years. She had relied on him almost more than anyone, even sales managers, and his departure was a blow. A call to Rolls Royce, however, soon found her a suitable replacement. Miss Arden's new chauffeur, Charles, stayed until her death in 1966 and was so devoted he named his daughter 'Ardena'.

Nothing much seemed to be going right for Miss Arden. Even her friend Maria de Gramont let her down. In an interview with journalist Wambly Bald, Maria was critical of American women and Elizabeth was concerned. 'I feel he either misunderstood you or misquoted you,' she wrote to Maria, who was in Paris at the time. 'I am sure you would not be so foolish and undiplomatic as to say the things he attributes to you . . . remember what happened to Schiaparelli!' The blunt couturier had also been critical about American women and the furore over her unguarded remarks resulted in a downturn in her fragrance sales, to the annoyance of her American licencee. Fragrance was on Miss Arden's mind when she wrote to Maria, 'The perfume you mentioned never reached me and sister says you never told her about your perfume woman. This is too unkind, because you promised and it is important.' 1947 had seen the launch of 'Miss Dior', the first perfume from the newly formed Dior fragrance company, started by Christian Dior's childhood friend, Serge Heftler. Miss Arden knew that her own key perfume Blue Grass, successful as it was, had enjoyed a conspicuously good run, having been a bestseller for well over ten years, and was anxious to find a successor. In a nudge towards Maria de Gramont's role as company ambassador, she also said, 'I am delighted that everyone finds you so well dressed. I know this will please Castillo and inspire him to even greater heights.' Elizabeth missed her friend, and was feeling lonely. 'Enjoy yourself, my dear,' she wrote, 'and keep well. You are much loved and missed and it will be so nice to have you back . . .' Maria Gramont left Elizabeth's employ a few months later, without imparting the name of her 'perfume lady'.

Miss Arden soon forgot about Ralph Lewis leaving, even making a joke about it: 'If you *ever* hear about me getting mixed up again with anyone called Lewis, will you *please* recommend a good psychiatrist?' She was busy expanding what had been a custom-made fashion division into wholesale, which she calculated was the only way to make a profit on the department. The top stores were quite happy to stock Elizabeth Arden cocktail gowns by Castillo, with starting orders coming from both I. Magnin and Neiman Marcus. Elizabeth was getting on rather well with Castillo. 'He's very tractable and co-operative,' she wrote to Gladys, 'I hope it lasts.' She sponsored a ball at the Plaza Hotel where the fashion show resulted in orders worth $7000, which thrilled her. Castillo in the meantime had been commissioned to create the wardrobe for Judith Anderson in John Gielgud's production of *Medea*. For a while at least, creative peace reigned between designer and employer.

Always searching for key promotion staff, Elizabeth was particularly pleased to recruit Helen Golby to head up her advertising and promotion department – especially as she had been a star player at Revlon. She wrote excitedly, 'Helen worked for *that man* for eleven years and did all that wonderful business. She worked night and day until she couldn't bear it any more and said she would leave. She was so exhausted she had a nervous breakdown!' Henry Sell had been instrumental in sounding out Miss Golby, but Elizabeth then heard Henry had told Helen Golby that in leaving Revlon for Arden she was getting out of the frying pan into the fire. At any event, Helen took the job – at a salary not to be sneezed at of $2250 a month – and Henry Sell's agency was fired.

The honeymoon period with Castillo was also coming to an end. 'That little brat, Castillo, is a constant thorn in my side,' she said to Teddy. 'He can behave well for just so long and then the meanness comes out. I am getting very tired of his temperament and one of these days he is going to be a surprised young man! Gladys tells me she is *quite* sure we can have Balenciaga do some things for us in Paris, which would be far more satisfactory . . .'

Post-war expansion in some countries was countered by problems in others. For Elizabeth Arden Inc, the biggest headache was South America. 'Chile's restrictions are now down,' wrote Elizabeth in 1948, 'but we have already closed the salon there. Lima is improving all the time, but are still not out of the red. South America owes me over a quarter of a million dollars and I cannot get *any* money out of there . . . it is so hard having to finance all these places.'

South America was going remarkably smoothly, however, for Madame Rubinstein, who seemed able to cope with the variable situation in most of her Latin American territories with greater ease than Miss Arden. Claude Forter, who joined Rubinstein after the war, covering some of those territories, puts it down to the personality of the staff in place. 'The operational head of Argentina was Vittorio del Franco, an Italian Argentine of dubious antecedents and probity. None of us knew in which discipline he held a doctorate . . . my own opinion was that it was B & B – bamboozling and bullshit – yet New York worshipped this guy.' Brazil gave Madame Rubinstein one of her most trusted non-family employees, Richard T. Augenblick. Claude recollects, 'He was a successful Polish-Jewish lawyer who had fled from the Germans and somehow wound up in Brazil, via Africa and Argentina. During his stay in South America, he had come into contact with the local Helena Rubinstein people – her cousins – and came to the New York head office, where he was made export director.'

Forter has clear memories of the export department, staffed by a motley group whose international credentials entirely suited the business of exports. 'Nora Sullenberger was from Costa Rica, married to a Pennsylvania Dutch American; . . . there was a Cuban translator; a Colombian export document and typing tech; an assistant called Miss Fernandez, another assistant's assistant from Argentina and an American-Italian Rubinstein old-timer called Esta Shepard.' As for Claude, his father was Russian and his mother was French. It sometimes seemed that everyone was speaking half-a-dozen languages at once and, as Claude says, 'not often making sense in any of them'. One memorable meeting took place between Madame, a group of senior personnel, and Mr de Kolb, 'the packaging man', whose French/Lebanese accent was always hard to decipher. As Madame got more and more irate, Mr de Kolb tried to soothe her. 'Be quiet,' she yelled at him, 'I don't understand your English *or* your German.' No one had the courage to tell her he had been speaking French.

The most significant appointment at Helena Rubinstein was that of Oscar Kolin to the main board. Horace became almost incoherent with anger. 'Horace', says his stepmother, Erica Titus Friedman, 'had an artistic temperament . . . he was a . . . displaced person.' He certainly felt displaced by the elevation of his cousin to executive power and would not let go of it, worrying his mother like a dog with a bone. Madame on the other hand rather enjoyed pitting her team against one another, and seemed impervious to his anguish.

'What I would like to see,' Horace wrote to his mother, 'is a system whereby certain persons are given an opportunity to express their opinions *before* decisions are made, not after.' He enclosed a report on the state of the business, outlining his views for development and improvement. Madame – naturally – sent it to Oscar and pencilled a note in the margin saying 'pick out the most difficult and let him do it'. Incapable of realising that Horace was a one-man think tank, and in his eccentric way a visionary, she somehow hoped he would become practical. He never did because he couldn't.

Tucked away in the file of letters between mother and son is a draft note, possibly never sent, in which Helena tried to express herself to Horace.

I could not get to sleep on Friday after our talk, I kept thinking and thinking of all you say. There is a great deal of good in it but it goes on year after year. I have finally come to the conclusion that instead of putting all your efforts behind a given project and seeing it through, you dissipate your energies in talking. There are such people, Horace – you and I both know them – and I would hate to think that you are like that. Horace, I wish that you could prove to me that you can lay out a good program and see it through yourself. I wish you would!

Oppressed by his dominant mother, fuelled by resentment from his father, Horace suffered from low self-esteem, drank too much and ended up in therapy. It is clear that Helena loved her son very much, but couldn't show it. Someone close to her once said, 'The problem with Helena is that the people she loved had to die before her emotions got really involved, and even then, she often suppressed them.' Helena helped Horace in the way she thought best, by letting him be seen to mastermind development projects, but always copying the board on it as a back-up; in effect 'freezing' his ideas until someone else had costed them. She also did something which a lot of people would find horrific – she sent the anguished personal and business letters he wrote to her to his doctor, who was of course also Helena's doctor, and attached her own notes about Horace's behaviour to them, for background information.

One project Horace felt strongly about was the House of Gourielli. He was convinced the mish-mash product range was pointless and should be rebranded solely as a fragrance and men's range. He came up with a series of fragrance ideas based around classical gods and goddesses, his favourite being 'Juno'. He informed Helena that Juno, queen of the gods and wife to Jupiter, was a disagreeable woman, jealous of her husband's amours and vindictive to his mistresses. Juno, he said, was the presiding genius of the home, and 'Junoesque' had become a word used to describe the voluptuous sort of woman, with regal bearing.

When his report landed on Helena's desk, not unsurprisingly, there was a thudding silence. The by now Junoesque and often disagreeable Helena, who had had one unfaithful husband and now realised she had a second, didn't need names to remind her of it. She hadn't presided much over her home, she'd been out at work, she'd failed in love and was being lectured by her son about classical goddesses in stories she had never read as a child, nor had time to study as an adult.

Undeterred, Horace tried again. 'Instead of taking 100 items and expecting a moderately steady increase on all of them, and dividing our advertising and promotional efforts among all of them, would we not get greater results if we concentrated our advertising and efforts behind a selected number of items for which we know there is a ready acceptance?' He didn't say so, but he was referring to Revlon, who by now had an enhanced product range but were concentrating their advertising on just lipstick and nail polish. Competition was becoming increasingly fierce, with Revlon, Chen Yu and Max Factor all performing outstandingly. Horace told his mother, 'We are no longer catering to the one woman who has $25 to spend, but to twenty-five women who spend $1 . . .' This was also a sideswipe at the price positioning of the Helena Rubinstein range, which Horace felt was slipping downmarket. Turnover was winning over taste.

In fairness to Helena, competing in a growing market wasn't merely a matter of putting out stylish products. Stores craved promotional campaigns, ideas for windows, counter cards, expensive display units and better trained sales consultants. Store buyers craved higher turnover for their departments, exclusive lines and special discounts; and customers craved new colours for eyes and lips and new creams for their skin. All this demand meant that the companies providing the product had to have smarter packaging, better literature, slicker advertising, bigger budgets, wider distribution and increased production facilities. It was a world away from when Helena and Elizabeth had started, over four decades earlier, and Helena in particular was feeling the strain. '*Everything* is more competitive,' she often remarked.

In 1949, Helena took on board her son's advice about Gourielli for Men and, in a move which gave him a lot of pleasure, decided to launch a limited range in Paris. She toyed with the idea of a British launch, but withdrew at the last minute. British men, she calculated, were not yet ready for skin care. British women, however, were about to get a product from Rubinstein that would become a European bestseller and a media favourite – Silk Face Powder. Helena later claimed that Ceska discovered the formula in England, rather mysteriously writing that the 'powder was first used for hospital dressings during the war'. But the credit for this coup belonged entirely to Boris Forter and it happened three years *after* the war.

The formula for the Silk Powder originated in India. Not that Boris travelled to India to find it; in the late 1940s, he wouldn't have had to, as the scions of the great ruling houses – Jaipur, Kapurthala, Cooch Behar and Baroda – were living in London, showing off their prowess on British polo fields, and were regular fixtures at Europe's glittering resorts. In 1947, the year of Indian Independence, the princely state of Baroda, some 8000 square miles of India's west coast, was taking stock of its royal treasuries. By 1948, when Baroda State was merging into the 'new map' of India, a few things were missing. Firstly, the Maharaja. Secondly, his new, much younger and very beautiful wife, Sita Devi, and finally not just a considerable amount of cash, but most of the royal jewels.

Successive rulers of Baroda had acquired, via gift and purchase, one of the most highly regarded treasure troves in India; they were particularly fond of diamonds and pearls. One ancestor of the Maharaja, Pratapsingh, didn't just wear his diamonds, he took to killing people with them, by adding ground diamonds to their drinks. When Pratapsingh, a mature man with grown-up sons by his first wife, remarried in 1943, it sent shock waves through Indian high society. His capricious young bride, Sita Devi, was already married, but swiftly divorced and remarried the Maharaja, making her the subcontinent's very own Wallis Windsor. She certainly loved jewels as much as Wallis and, like the duchess, delighted in having her country's heritage broken up and remounted. Amongst the treasures she smuggled out when she and her husband moved to Europe in 1947 was a legendary pearl carpet, a diamond necklace reported to have belonged to Napoleon Bonaparte, another diamond necklace containing a vast Brazilian stone known as the Star of the South and the famous Baroda Pearls, a seven-stranded necklace with each pearl the size of a quail's egg.

In 1949, the Indian government demanded the return of the jewels. The Maharaja handed back, amongst other pieces, a Golconda diamond necklace, but only six rows of the seven ropes of pearls. The fabled carpet, along with trunkloads of jewels and gold, has never been seen since. Nor has the missing rope of pearls.

The Maharani of Baroda was spoiled and wilful and obsessed with her looks, wearing, in the fashion of the times, a lot of make-up. The very rich are apt to 'ignore' their tradesmen, often not paying their bills. One supplier Sita Devi ignored was a French chemist called Verdier, who had developed a system of pulverising silk into face powder. The effect was a translucent glow. The Maharani adored it, persuading her husband to invest in M. Verdier's project, promising him development funding, a factory and global distribution. M. Verdier would become rich and the Maharani would promote his powder. Unfortunately for Verdier it didn't happen as planned. The marriage was drifting apart; the Maharaja failed to deliver the promised investment, leaving M. Verdier angry, out of pocket, and with nothing but the patents on his formula. Then he met Boris Forter.

Boris had a variety of useful friends, ranging from wholesale furriers where Ceska sourced her mink coats, to moneylenders, where Boris (whose salary was modest) borrowed the cash to fund his passion for sports cars. Via one such acquaintance, he met the stud-groom who looked after the Baroda horses. The stud-groom had met Verdier, and *voilà*, Boris was presented with a unique opportunity for Helena Rubinstein Ltd.

Boris was passionate about the project, lobbying Madame to buy the patents, setting up a special space in the Surrey factory for the machinery and shopping with Ceska to buy silk. He later said, 'That powder was my child. I believed in it,' waxing lyrical about the production process. 'Silk is a transparent tube, and when it's micronised, you get little balls, equal-sized, with a hole in the middle. If there is dryness on the face and moisture in the air, the moisture goes into the holes and keeps the skin moist. It gives an ethereal look . . .'

It was an expensive and labour-intensive process, with the silk having to be dissolved in dilute acid, cooked in a vat under pressure and then neutralised with alkali. The mass, described by Boris as 'looking like mud sausages', was then passed through a boudilure, revolving at 10,000 rpm, which micronised it to the finest possible level. The Rubinstein Silk Powder compacts contained 30% pure silk. Boris knew it was an attractive product, with good department-store potential at a time when luxury goods were just re-entering the world of the British consumer. To Helena's credit, she supported Boris and Ceska wholeheartedly over the project, although he would fall foul of the New York board of directors. 'It was planned to make it a worldwide product, but Oscar Kolin never wanted the silk powder – in America or anywhere else,' wrote Boris. 'The American company would have been quite happy to have killed off the free-standing overseas business controlled by Madame.' Due to the silk additive in the powder, Oscar Kolin claimed he had the FDA to contend with, and also felt the line was too expensive. In the meantime, it became a European bestseller. Eventually, America packaged Liquid Silk, a bottled moisturiser based on the same concept; this and Liquid Dry Skin Moisturiser became, according to Jerry Emerman, sales promotion manager at that time, 'hot items'.

The cachet of having 'London-Paris-New York' on domestic product was of inestimable value to American manufacturers. Charles Revson, for example, years before he had any meaningful European subsidiaries, would have the actress Barbara Britton, 'the voice of Revlon', introduce their sponsored television shows by saying: 'If it's the finest of its kind it's by Revlon – Revlon London, Paris and New York.' Helena Rubinstein knew that what she launched in Europe had an effect on what they sold in America and continued to use London and Paris as a conduit of ideas until she died.

The Maharani of Baroda, in the meantime, was living an exotically expensive life in Paris and London, often selling off her jewellery to fund it. Boris Forter subsequently met Sita Devi, who he says 'was living with a jockey in her apartment in Grosvenor Square'. He met the Maharaja too, who lived a lonely existence, mainly in London, until he died in 1968. The rumour that Helena Rubinstein owned the missing Baroda pearls persists to this day. Whether Boris ever took Helena to peruse, or to buy, any of Sita Devi's sublime jewellery we will never know. One thing for sure came via Baroda, however – the formula for the Silk Face Powder.

The powder was used in an extensive advertising campaign as the decade turned. Advertising being a requirement for success in the cosmetic industry, it was also much on the mind of the ambitious Mrs Lauder in the late 1940s. She had amassed sufficient profit to consider a campaign, but a top advertising agency told her her budget was too small. At this point, Mrs Lauder developed what would rapidly propel her business to success. She put her budget into mailshots, sampling, and gifts-with-purchase. The latter was not a new idea, having been attempted unsuccessfully a few years earlier by Charles of the Ritz, but Mrs Lauder sensed the time was right and made it work. The system is still going strong today.

In cosmetics, sampling was nothing new, but even the giants like Rubinstein and Arden rarely produced 'luxury' size samples. Their handouts were quite meagre phials of fragrance or small sachets of cream. Mrs Lauder thought big, and packed her product into miniatures that were exact replicas of her full-sized product. She also gave gifts of alternative items when a customer had bought a full-size pack, and as everyone loves getting something for nothing, it was a roaring success. She had, by now, come to the attention of Elizabeth Arden.

By 1949, Elizabeth was yet again having trouble with her creative team, where Helen Golby was no longer flavour of the month. Over at Revlon, on the other hand, Miss Golby's replacement, the dynamic Kay Daly, was becoming a force to be reckoned with. Elizabeth was also having trouble with the new formula for an Arden bestseller, a foundation cream called Sleek. 'We have many complaints which are getting us in bad trouble with the insurance people. We have found that 2% of people are allergic to thioglycerol, according to our doctors. I am having it all called back as rapidly as possible, and will replace it with the original formula,' she told Teddy.

As if this wasn't enough, she had building problems too, with the salon in San Francisco delayed due to expensive, albeit innovative, fittings. 'You will be interested to hear we are putting in a Roman bath – exercises will be done under water against pressure, and we are going to have a machine that makes waves . . . a great publicity stunt as well as making arms and busts as small as possible.' Finally, however, she found an executive who pleased her. Carl Gardiner joined Elizabeth Arden Inc in 1949, and never left. 'Mr Gardiner is a treasure,' she said, 'and growing more valuable all the time. I just hope he won't go temperamental on me like Castillo.'

She was doing Castillo a great injustice in making this comment, as the 'temperament' in question was for Miss Arden's benefit as well as his own. Elizabeth's designer had, by 1949, been offered a tempting opportunity in Paris, and had hoped that Elizabeth would back him. Couturier Robert Piquet had offered a partnership and first refusal on buying his business. Piquet had been unwell for some time, and was anxious to retire to his native Switzerland. He had, in the style of Hattie Carnegie in New York, run a house that employed extremely talented designers to execute work under his label, at the same time influencing and encouraging them with his quiet, refined and ultra-sophisticated good taste. Christian Dior, Balmain and Hubert de Givenchy all worked for him, and when Castillo was offered the opportunity to buy the business, it had a turnover of 26 million francs. In the French manner of the period, 16 million francs was 'non-published profit' – cash in hand. The production cost for a seasonal collection was 5 million francs. The whole was for sale to Castillo for 50 million francs (about $100,000 in 1949).

He tried hard to persuade her, lunching with Gladys to explain his ideas and telling Elizabeth, 'I see now after all my experiences in America that the houses here in Paris are working on a very old basis and sooner or later are all doomed to death . . . Having this useful and interesting laboratory here, we could send styles and accessories often for the American Arden salons, and in the shop here in the "Rond Point des Champs Elysées" there could be a wonderful opportunity for preparations and perfumes.' It was a directional idea. The only trouble was, Miss Arden didn't like it. 'Castillo is going to get a tough letter from me about Piquet,' she wrote to Gladys. 'He must give up all these crazy thoughts if he is to continue with us.'

She was shortsighted. If she had gone along with the imaginative scheme, hers would have been the first luxury cosmetics house to wholly own a fashion brand of status, and the synergy between the two could have resulted in the formation of a powerful business. Instead, she preferred to produce clothes under her own name, reluctant to share anything with anyone, however talented. She failed to understand that the name of Elizabeth Arden was so powerful that to endorse another brand would have done her no harm at all. M. Piquet never found a buyer. He closed his house in 1951, retiring to Switzerland, where he died in 1953. Castillo did one further collection for Miss Arden, leaving in 1950 for Paris, where he joined Lanvin.

As the 1950s loomed, new methods of promotion were springing up. For those who could afford it, colour advertising was taking precedence over black and white. Lucrative 'designer' fragrances were becoming increasingly important; fashion shows and promotions were part of everyday life in the top stores; customers were getting used to receiving a pamphlet with their monthly store account bill, and advertising agencies were pushing television to their clients. The 1950s was the decade the beauty business grew up.

Helena Rubinstein, aged sixty-three. Richer by six million dollars and charged-up to reconquer America. She's photographed on tour with one of her African carvings loaned to MoMA for their 1935 'Negro Art Exhibition'. A very young Ernestine Carter was assistant curator at the exhibition and later confessed that the French shippers, at a loss as to how to pack the complex statues, had 'often removed heads, arms and feet to fit them into the crates'. Mrs Carter and her colleagues had to put them back together again, hoping they got it right

Edward W. Titus who, wrote journalist Wambly Bald, 'only sold books to people who loved them as much as he did'. Titus is shown in his first floor apartment, above his book shop in rue Delambre, Montparnasse

The Bangwa Queen. Helena's favourite – and most valuable – African carving, photographed by Man Ray in Paris, *circa* 1930. He posed 'the Queen' with one of his favourite models, Ady

Madame with her beloved younger son Horace, photographed at her Paris apartment, *circa* 1952

Miss Arden takes to the airwaves for an NBC radio show with Baron Wrangel and the Ritz-Carlton orchestra in 1934. She yearned to have her own show, and subsequently signed to sponsor an Elizabeth Arden show with CBS, featuring Eddy Duchin's orchestra

Madame on the radio in 1933 for a series of interviews on skin-care and beauty regimes, accompanied by her own press photographer to record the event. Her wonderful hat is by Schiaparelli – but the sound recording was less than wonderful. In part because she was always uneasy broadcasting live, and also because of her accent which listeners found hard to decipher

LEFT: Helena tried for years to persuade Picasso to paint her portrait and eventually sat for him in 1955 in the South of France, coming away with, if not her painting, then this picture as a souvenir

MIDDLE LEFT: Madame in posed repose on her famous Lucite bed. she was more normally to be found propped up on pillows holding a 'breakfast in bed' meeting with her senior staff at around 7.30 a.m. each morning while in New York than dressed and jewelled for a publicity picture

MIDDLE RIGHT: Helena with her friend, the artist Casimir Marcoussis. They are posed in front of a vast wall panel he executed for her Quai de Bethune, Paris, apartment in 1936

Madame in her Balenciaga red brocade dress at a party she hosted at her Grafton Street Salon in London in 1958 to celebrate her portrait by Graham Sutherland. Left to right – Viscount Hambledon, Lady Hambledon, Mr Douglas Cooper, Madame, Mrs Artur Rubinstein, Kathy Sutherland, Artur Rubinstein, Graham Sutherland

Helena had a great fondness for Yves St Laurent and followed his career from Dior to the launch of his own house in 1962. She's photographed here with him after his couture show in the autumn of 1962

Front row at the show. Madame always had a front row seat at the Paris shows, and an especially favoured one at Dior. Here she is sitting next to Marlene Dietrich at the second show designed for the House of Dior by the young Yves St Laurent in the autumn of 1958

Madame always said this was her favourite photograph. She's wearing a purple taffetta skirt with a white silk shirt and cashmere shrug, posing at her New York apartment, *circa* 1957

Helena with her second husband, the genial Georgian Prince, Artchil Gourielli Tchkonia, photographed at her New York apartment, *circa* 1950. Her 'official' press pictures would be carefully retouched, trimming inches off the upper arms and waist. This informal one shows her battle with the bulge

Madame with her niece Mala at the American Trade Exhibition in Moscow in July 1959, where Helena Rubinstein Inc exhibited with their own stand. By now, she was travelling with a full-time nurse in attendance

Patrick O'Higgins, Madame's personal assistant for fifteen years, photographed with American socialite Brenda Frazier, *circa* 1955

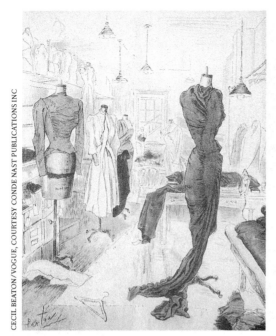

Miss Arden hired her old friend Charles James to design custom-made clothes for her New York Salon in 1944. Cecil Beaton drew the atelier for an editorial feature in American *Vogue* in December of that year . . . by which time James had already left

Elizabeth Arden sponsored the Duchess of Windsor Ball in New York in 1953, when Miss Arden coerced Wallis to wear an Arden gown – designed by Jean Desses – for her portrait picture for American *Vogue*. The duchess had originally decided on Dior

Miss Arden being escorted by Count Sarmi, her resident fashion designer, during the 1950s. All her designers – Charles James, Castillo, Count Sarmi and Oscar de la Renta, had to do 'escort duty' – or 'extra mileage' as James described it

Elizabeth with a young Oscar de la Renta, hired as her in-house designer in New York in 1962

Blue Grass... for a heart stirring Christmas

Elizabeth Arden

Elizabeth Arden Graham was never happier than when out with 'her babies' as she called her horses. She's leading a particular favourite, Jewel's Reward, into the winner's circle at Belmont Park in October 1957. Jewel's Reward subsequently became famous for biting the hand that fed him when he nipped the tip off Miss Arden's little finger. When Madame heard the news, she famously said, 'Tell me, how *is* the horse?'

Horses were used to promote Arden's signature fragrance Blue Grass for decades. Her management were originally against naming the new perfume after the 'Blue Grass' of Kentucky, telling her that women wouldn't associate glamour with horses. They were wrong. It was an all-time bestseller and remains on the line to this day

Elizabeth Arden Graham's proudest moment – in the winner's enclosure when her horse Jet Pilot won the Kentucky Derby in 1947. Left to right – her horse manager Leslie Combs, Mrs Graham, 'Silent' Tom Smith, her trainer, and her jockey, Eric Guerin on 'the Jet', draped with the Derby winner's famous blanket of roses

Miss Arden at her Irish castle, Barretstown, where her horses were trained by Stuart Murless. She's with two of her fillies – Canticle by Sovereign Path out of Lunestone, and Honey Fun by Alcide out of Honey Flower

Miss Arden's old friend Henry Sell was appointed editor of Hearst's *Town & Country* magazine in 1949. Maria de Gramont, by this time working for Elizabeth's sister Gladys, hosted a glamorous party to welcome Henry back to the Paris collections. Among the guests were (front row) artist Etienne Drian; (middle row on the left) Elsa Schiaparelli, Gladys de Maublanc, Countess Marie Blanche de Polignac, Maria de Gramont and fashion designer Jean Desses. Henry Sell is in the middle of the back row, with Christian Dior on his left

Elizabeth with her sister, Gladys de Maublanc (left). 'Gladys was more brittle, a little more soignée, said a friend. In the background is company sales vice president Jack Treat. He had all the criteria Miss Arden required in her staff – he was handsome, charming and very tall

Madame Rubinstein aged seventy-nine and giving it all she's got, wearing satin, sables and pearls, posing for Cecil Beaton in 1951

CHAPTER TWENTY-ONE

THE FABULOUS FIFTIES:
TWO BEAUTY QUEENS AND THE
MAN WHO WOULD BE KING
London, Paris, Rome, New York
1950–1955

RIVERS OF BLOOD-COLOURED lipstick and nail polish flowed between Arden, Rubinstein and Revlon in the first half of the 1950s. By mid-decade, Revlon was a public company, launched on the back of a successful promotion that Madame Rubinstein had rejected two years earlier. By that time, another serious player, Estée Lauder, had thrown her hat into the ring, but the war kicked off with the battles between the two reigning Beauty Queens and the man who would be King.

Helena was in hospital in London in early 1950, forced to rest following a bout of her recurring phlebitis. As usual, she spent the time writing letters, amongst them an identical missive to Roy, Horace and Oscar. 'I feel,' she said, 'the time has come when it would be prudent . . . to give some serious thought to what would result if anything more serious were to happen to me than an inflammation of the legs . . . I sometimes wonder whether any one of you has an idea of how complex and many-sided a business it is, and whether you would have any idea as to how to go about coping with all of the infinite problems that exist, not only in the US but all over the world?' She warmed to her theme. 'I am going to ask each one of you to put down your thoughts on paper. You may work separately, or together. If you could do it together, it would of course be wonderful . . . this would mean giving each other credit where credit is due and agreeing to share, or rather divide, responsibilities.' Realising this was unlikely to occur, she continued, 'On the other hand, if you would care to give me a confidential personal report, indicating just how you would go about running the business in all its phases if you had an absolutely free hand . . . I shall be pleased and interested to hear what you have to say, and you may be assured that anything that is written to me in confidence will be treated in complete confidence.'

Since she had spent the last fifteen years exchanging correspondence about the men in question, often sending their letters to other managers around the world annotated with her scribbled notes, the chances of their reports being kept private were remote. Her letter rattled them, especially as she indicated for the first time that she might have to consider bringing in a high-powered executive from outside the family.

Over at Revlon, where Revson's two brothers were still on board and a host of new directors had joined the company, there was no question whatsoever of anyone having a free hand. Charles checked everything. His obsessive streak manifested itself in his stranglehold over meetings, which could go on for hours. Grace Gilbert, who worked for Revlon in packaging and design in the 1950s, recollects that 'a lot of those sessions lasted a full day'. On the other hand, she says, 'As the business was worth $55 million and our department also represented control of the display units, a one-day-a-week meeting didn't seem out of proportion . . .' After a lifetime in cosmetics, Grace still maintains that decade was the most stimulating: 'Those years were the most creative, competitive and exciting – Revlon was creating unforgettable ads and the competition was busily engaged in nervous energy, each trying to "best" the other.'

Charles Revson monitored advertising as assiduously as he monitored sales. His competition, the two battling ladies whom he was determined to eclipse, were also concentrating on advertising – or in Arden's case, the lack of it, as she was temporarily without an agency in New York. Teddy had hired Coleman, Prentice & Varley to handle Arden's creative work in London whilst Madame hired the sophisticated Englishman in New York, David Ogilvy, to handle her account, with Horace as co-ordinator. Technically, Horace was supposed to manage the advertising spend, with his creative input co-ordinated by Sara Fox, which meant it took weeks to reach any decision as Horace would wander off on trips, ignoring all pleas to communicate with the team. Helena still wanted to see material, but as she, like Elizabeth, was away from the office so much, it was hard to keep her in the loop. She wrote to Ogilvy: 'I have heard very little from Horace since I left New York . . . I have also heard very little from *you* and all this concerns me very much.'

Revlon, on the other hand, took their advertising very seriously and had spent money in the media from their beginning. In the lean years, Charles borrowed privately to fund the spend when his bank wouldn't give him a loan. By the early 1950s, with a more assured cashflow, Revlon wanted to show they were *cool*, so launched a campaign, developed by Norman B. Norman and Kay Daly, of such eye-catching brilliance that it has become textbook material for students of the 'clever sell'.

The first warning that Revlon were emerging as a fighting force came with an ad in the *New York Times*. Smoke curled from the edges of the burning hole in the centre of the page. The headline simply said, WHERE'S THE FIRE? That's it. No text. No prices. No copy. No signature logo. A few days later, Revlon's latest lipstick colour, Where's the Fire, hit the stores running.

Helena retaliated by organising a public relations coup which went to prove she was still the 'battling warhorse' of publicity campaigns. 'Prince and Princess Gourielli' were at home at their new 'art gallery' in the autumn of 1950. That is to say, Helena had decided to open up the third floor of her triplex as a gallery and had promised to showcase the work of emergent young American artists. Apart from enabling her to charge alterations to the space to her promotional budget, the project was a vehicle for a press launch. The publicity resulting from the series of parties, titled 'Five Enchanted Evenings', and held to benefit Hospitalised Veterans Music Services, could have covered the walls of all thirty-eight rooms and ten bathrooms in her New York home. Social coverage showed an assortment of New York grandees peering at Helena's replica 'Montmartre studio' complete with a Toulouse-Lautrec canvas casually propped on an easel.

More significant were the reviews from the art magazines and newspapers, particularly *Art News*. This august publication took a benevolent view of Helena's magpie collecting. 'There were', said the writer, 'drawings by Degas, Modigliani, Picasso and Tchelitchew on every turning, corridor, in the bathrooms, behind the bar . . . the collection of Helena Rubinstein has a masculine force, a "damn the torpedos" feeling that is consistent with her taste. Her Derains . . . sit alongside a group of unusually strong Laurencins and an *entire* wall of Dufys, all dedicated to Madame Rubinstein.'

Such recognition pleased Helena, firstly because she truly loved her pictures but secondly because the publicity created sales pleased her bankers. Madame was of the school of tycoons who welcome publicity.

Investors and bankers like reading about the business they support, it creates confidence. As far as her consumer was concerned, if a woman couldn't own a picture herself, she was going to buy a lipstick from Helena Rubinstein who did. What's more, she'd bought them with money earned from her own efforts. Her women customers liked that.

Over at the Revlon headquarters, Charles was redecorating as usual. He knew nothing about art, other than what he liked, and he didn't like what his decorator presented him with. On viewing an exquisite set of eighteenth-century Piranesi etchings, he was heard to remark, 'Shit, couldn't we get the artist back to put a little colour into 'em?'

Both Arden and Rubinstein excelled at corporate sponsorship, with Arden in particular having a reputation for skilled selection in this area. One such event was the Polish Ball, held annually in New York, and chaired by Artur Rubinstein. For years, Helena had been their chief benefactor, but mysteriously, in 1950, she declined. The vacancy was immediately taken up by – Elizabeth Arden. Mala told her aunt, who was travelling at the time, 'The Polish Ball this year is sponsored by Arden. I think, however, that your name and mine is on the sponsor list. I notified the committee that you will not be in town for Artur Rubinstein's party . . .'

The media adored Madame's New York apartment, which had become a favoured location for photographers. Helena was happy to lend it to Bergdorf Goodman for a fashion shoot for *Vogue* to celebrate the store's golden anniversary. The event committee, raising funds for cancer relief by planning a show and dinner at the Plaza, included Mrs E.F. Hutton, Gertrude Lawrence, Mrs Vincent Sardi, Mrs Winston Guest and Nancy Moreland. They were photographed by Avedon, suitably gowned by Bergdorf and appeared in *Vogue*, the location credited to 'Princess Gourielli, Madame Helena Rubinstein'.

Madame's art collection attracted the attention of a host of visitors to New York and she would often oblige them with a private view. Late in 1950, Sir Osbert Sitwell and his sister Edith put in a request to visit and Helena organised a lunch party in their honour. The guest list included Artchil, David Ogilvy, Mala and Horace. Adding artistic interest to impress the Sitwells was painter Paul Tchelitchew and also invited was a debonair young man Helena had recently met at a party given by Fleur Cowles, Patrick O'Higgins. O'Higgins, who was working on Cowles's magazine *Flair*, had vivid memories of the lunch, particularly as Madame Rubinstein told him, '*Flair* won't last — you'll see, too expensive to produce, she'll have to close it down.'

He stayed in touch with Helena and when, as she had prophesied, *Flair* was closed, told her he was out of a job. In 1951, Horace was staying with his by now ailing father in Cagnes-sur-Mer. Titus died that summer, and, worried how it would affect Horace, Helena tried to think of things to 'keep him busy, to cheer him up'. She invited him to join her in Paris for a series of parties she was hosting and to take the cure with her in Austria. 'I had a note from Patrick O'Higgins,' she told Horace. 'I wrote him suggesting that you might like to meet or invite him to stay with you . . . if I did wrong, I am sorry.'

By the autumn, O'Higgins was on board at Helena Rubinstein Inc, with a desk squeezed into a cubbyhole outside Madame's office, trying to fathom her complex family relationships and the often eccentric methods of conducting business meetings *chez* Rubinstein. Coping with strong women was a forte of O'Higgins, who had worked for both Carmel Snow and Fleur Cowles. Patience also being his forte, he became captivated with the bejewelled, tiny tyrant, staying at her side virtually until the day she died.

Following her ex-husband's death, Helena herself was grieving. Memories of the man who had obsessed her were painful. She sought solace by seeking to have her portrait painted by the artist who was a link with her early life with Titus in Montparnasse, someone they had both known and admired — Picasso.

The idea of Picasso doing a portrait of Helena had been brokered to him by their mutual friend, Marie Cuttoli, but in 1951 even Picasso's favoured patron couldn't put him in the mood to paint Helena. The Cholly Knickerbocker column got an advance on the story. Unfortunately, Patrick O'Higgins rather over-enthusiastically called Igor Cassini, tipping him off about the supposed sitting. Artchil sent a message to his wife, who had remained in France. 'Patrick gave news to Cassini and he wrote about you and Picasso in his column. How are you doing with him?' The answer was that she wasn't doing at all well and was rather cross about the whole idea. Besides, there were other things on her mind, chiefly the defection of one of her top sales managers, George Carroll, to Elizabeth Arden.

She need not have worried. Less than six months later, Mr Carroll was dining with Horace, asking for his old job back. Carroll explained he had 'left' Arden. Miss Arden on the other hand maintained she had fired Mr Carroll, describing him as 'a hopeless drunkard'. At any event, Helena relented, taking him back at $35,000 a year, partly because Horace wanted him and partly because she felt he might have inside information on Elizabeth Arden, which made him useful. It might have been more useful if Mr Carroll had spent six months at Revlon, rather than Arden, as he could have forewarned his boss about their upcoming lipstick promotion. As it was, this caught everyone by surprise.

This promotion, launched in autumn 1952, set the whole of America talking. They called it 'Fire and Ice'. The Fire and Ice campaign was a benchmark in cosmetics advertising, marking the moment that the two most significant words now used in the industry were first mooted – *sex sells*. The campaign featured Dorian Leigh, one of the most beautiful models in the business, whose sister was one of the other most beautiful models in the business, Suzy Parker. Dorian was photographed by Richard Avedon, in a picture styled by Kay Daly, Revlon's resident creative supremo, wearing a figure-hugging silver-beaded turtleneck sheath dress, which left little to the imagination. It was worn with a black taffeta ruched cape, which Kay had had copied from something similar by Balenciaga, falling off her shoulders. Dorian's long fingers playing over her face, nails painted fiery red, her other hand falling over her hip, the picture oozed sex appeal. Avedon, who has a unique way with models, relaxed Miss Leigh enough to forget that her dress was a tube pinned at the back – the little man who sewed on the rhinestones having run out of time – with just a few safety pins between the success and failure of the shoot.

It wasn't Avedon's picture alone that made the impact, it was the double-page spreads booked in the media, with the facing page listing a panel of questions, which proved utterly irresistible both to American women and the American press. The strapline asked: 'Are You Made for Fire and Ice?' You were if you could answer 'yes' to eight of eleven questions:

Have you ever danced with your shoes off? Did you ever wish on a new moon? Do you blush when you find yourself flirting? When a recipe calls for one dash of bitters, do you think it's better with two? Do you secretly hope the next man you meet will be a psychiatrist? Do you sometimes feel that other women resent you? Have you ever wanted to wear an ankle bracelet? Do sables excite you, even on other women? Do you love to look up at a man? Does gypsy music make you sad? . . . Do you close your eyes when you're kissed?

In largely conservative America in the early 1950s, the older generation still held memories of the Depression and wartime shortages. Younger consumers had begun to realise that spending money wasn't a sin, but even so, such blatant references to sensuality were rare and the impact of the campaign was immense. Radio DJs, pundits, newspaper editors, celebrities – *everyone* was talking about Fire and Ice.

Whilst Revson was sweeping the board with what was basically yet another shade of red, Miss Arden was having trouble with a new lipstick formula. She had hoped that her new chemist could come up with something different, but disappointingly his samples were pronounced as 'bitter to taste', 'has a heavy consistency', 'wears off' and 'has tendency to patch' by her testing panel. Miss Arden would use various members of her staff to try out new products, resulting in visitors to the offices sometimes bemused on finding typists wearing blue mascara on one eye and brown on the other, or pink polish on one hand and red on the other. (Charles Revson tested his nail polish too – by wearing it himself – and was noted for being a superb manicurist). It got worse, with Elizabeth writing to Teddy: 'We are having *such* a bad time with lipsticks. After two months they are going rancid. I discovered this on my return home, having left the very latest ones on my dressing table. When I left, they had a smooth, wonderful consistency. Then for them to go rancid . . . it's just too shocking!' Elizabeth moved to put more coconut oil into her French formula, which she said 'is guaranteed not to turn rancid'. A frenzied search ensued for a new chemist. Furious with her laboratory staff, Elizabeth said, 'I *must* get a good chemist. Mr Couch is too old and is never in the lab . . . Dr Larson has tonsil trouble and is in hospital . . .' A top priority was to remix an Arden staple, a cream foundation called Basic Sheen, into a liquid, but she had been having problems. 'In liquid form it goes black in the bottle,' she said, '*why* can't we get it right? If Germaine Monteil can produce a good lotion, what *is* the matter with our laboratory?'

Meanwhile, Madame Rubinstein was cross that her staff were thinking of nothing else but lipstick. 'I was asked to attend a meeting on Torero Pink – our lipstick shade promotion for next season. I was shocked to see how many people were spending so much time on one little item which cannot bring us real profit,' she lectured. 'If all this effort and energy were being put into a $10 item, it would make sense to me . . .'

Miss Arden's worries weren't just about lipsticks. Her fashion salon was not performing to expectations. Since Castillo's departure she had experimented with various designers, including Greek designer Yanis Evangelides. She went off him when she heard his niece was an Arden treatment girl in London, this being too close to home for her liking, and she felt his clothes were dated. 'Our new designer is a great disappointment,' she grumbled. 'Evidently he thinks he's designing clothes for Queen Mary!' Help had to be drafted in fast and, as usual, sister Gladys rode to the rescue and lunched with Jean Desses in Paris. At the time running his own couture salon, Desses was interested in the American market and agreed to do a 'private' collection for Miss Arden. Covering her options, Elizabeth also bought model originals from Jacques Griffe, who had learned his craft working for Madame Vionnet. It was on Desses, however, that she had pinned her hopes.

With her show approaching she told her sister, 'I hope to goodness Desses will have all the clothes over in time – you know it takes three days to get them out of customs. Ask Desses not to have the bill exceed $14,000. I think he should come down a little in his prices . . . these models are for our wholesale collection and should not be too elaborate.' When the gowns were unpacked, Elizabeth was horrified. 'It seems primarily a couture collection, not at all suitable for wholesale. The evening dresses are frightfully expensive to produce. One voluminous, bouffant gown of black net over white net has an embroidered bodice of black pearls, paillettes and a kind of jewelled lace *entirely* done by hand. A quick estimate indicates it would cost about $140 to reproduce the work, and the jewels would have to be brought over from Paris . . . if they were made for us Mr Pelusio thinks each pearl would cost us five cents! Have you *ever* heard of anything so ludicrous?' Wisely, Gladys kept her counsel. She knew her sister would change her mind. The day before the show, Elizabeth was panicking, telling Gladys, 'I'm so afraid all our efforts have been in vain . . . I've ordered seven models from Jacques Griffe.' The day after, she wrote, 'It all went very well yesterday, lots of enthusiastic comments from buyers and press.'

The transatlantic relationship between Miss Arden and Jean Desses continued until 1951 when, at the suggestion of Carmel Snow, she hired Count Ferdinando Sarmi. Snow had admired his work assisting Fabiani in Florence and Elizabeth, who instinctively felt Italy was going to represent the Zeitgeist in the 1950s, was delighted to employ an Italian aristocrat. Count Sarmi lasted with Elizabeth for seven years, his first year perhaps the happiest, as he didn't speak much English and couldn't get involved in arguments.

Having invested heavily with Desses, however – the two remained friends thereafter – Elizabeth wanted her pound of flesh and contrived to get it by bringing pressure to bear on the Duchess of Windsor. Wallis was a client at Arden's Paris salon, where she would go each week for waxing, massage, a manicure, a Vienna Youth Mask, a special dose of Miss Arden's Bylines (said to 'freeze' forehead frowns), a pedicure and so forth. Such a regime was expensive – and the duchess didn't pay. Gladys was delighted to waive her bill in exchange for the publicity value. Elizabeth decided it was payback time.

Elizabeth Arden was sponsoring the Duchess of Windsor's Ball, to be held in January 1953 at the Waldorf Astoria in New York. There would be a de luxe show of 'Elizabeth Arden' gowns, designed by Count Sarmi, shown with furs by Maximilian, and the show sets and choreography done by Cecil Beaton. A group of New York's VIP ladies were modelling, including Clare Booth Luce and Mrs Cornelius Vanderbilt Whitney. *Vogue* planned to photograph Wallis, previewing the gown she would wear at the ball, and she had elected to wear Dior for her sitting. Whilst it might have been impossible to have her wear a dress by such a newly launched designer as Sarmi, Miss Arden deemed she should wear Desses.

Wallis was duly told she would be presented with a full invoice from Elizabeth Arden for her myriad treatments, and get no more for nothing. The duchess capitulated and the resulting picture of Wallis, wearing a coral faille and jewelled silk organdie gown, duly appeared in *Vogue* with a caption saying, 'chosen from the Elizabeth Arden Collection'. Elizabeth enjoyed the ball. She sat at the top table with the duke and duchess, and the omnipresent Elsa Maxwell – Wallis Windsor, in her eyes, having 'settled her account'.

Competition between Arden, Rubinstein and Revlon as to who could bring out the latest, and best product was intense. When Rubinstein introduced a new hormone product, Arden retaliated with something similar. Unfortunately Elizabeth, who liked to test all new creams, reacted badly to it. 'Teddy,' she wailed, 'we must get the new hormone cream right. My face broke out in several places, but I ate strawberries for three days running, so I can't tell whether the eruptions were due to the cream or the strawberries. Two big eruptions on the side of my mouth were particularly annoying, so I just smoothed on Spot-Pruf cream and a little Muscle Oil after that. Then I removed it with Velva Cream, followed by Velva Smooth Lotion and used Lille de France lotion as my make-up base. It really did the trick!'

If new products weren't forthcoming, the favoured trick was to give an existing product a new name and re-package it to an unsuspecting public, releasing it as having a 'new and improved formula'. It's said that Helena Rubinstein's Deep Cleanser was a reworking of her original Valaze formula and certainly, in the early 1950s, Elizabeth Arden Inc was experimenting with one of her favourite products, Firmo-Lift Treatment Lotion. She had reduced the oil content by 6% and her satellite countries, who made up their formulae locally, were unhappy. 'Firmo-Lift with only 30% oil, instead of 36%, has become more drying, more astringent and less beneficial. It dries quickly on the face and needs constant re-application in order to mould, without stretching the skin,' she was told by her London chemist.

Charles Revson rarely cut back on oils in his treatment creams and foundations, even going so far as to withdraw Sheer Radiance for over three months so the product could be made a little oilier. He knew that women *liked* a high oil content – it was more sensual when being rubbed into their skin. 'Make-up time is women's play time,' he continually lectured his sales force.

Madame Rubinstein meanwhile was becoming concerned about turnover in the US. 'I cannot help recall that I was told that Revlon considered us their chief competition about two years ago,' she said. 'I am afraid they have forged way ahead of us, and would not consider us their chief competition now . . .' Revlon's first attempt to conquer the all-powerful treatment-cream market came with Moon Drops, a not wildly successful cream, thought to have been 'bland'. Credibility in Revlon's skin-care range only took off with the launch of Eterna 27, named, says Grace Gilbert, 'because Charles thought 30 was too old, 25 too young and so between 27 and 28, 7 was a better number and it got named 27!' Beside herself with anger at what she saw as a successful invasion of her territory, Madame Rubinstein could be found hovering near the office window, shaking her fist at Revson's office directly across the road. 'The nail man is destroying our business,' she screeched. Oscar tried to soothe her. 'Now, now, Madame, don't worry, Eterna will soon be "returna" – the stores won't like it.' Apparently Helena snapped out of her mood immediately. 'Rubbish. Of course they will – it's a good name.' Oscar was silenced.

By 1952, temporarily out of favour with his mother following a blistering argument, Horace had retreated to the South of France to lick his
wounds. The drama, causing much gossip at head office, was mainly due to
a scandal involving a black girl he had been having an affair with. She had
a gangster boyfriend who decided to blackmail Horace over the affair.
Horace apparently retaliated by having gangster and girl kidnapped, and
ended up being arrested. The fracas cost Madame dearly in legal fees. 'Only
Horace could be so stupid as to try to kidnap a gangster,' muttered his
mother.

The row had been exacerbated by the perennial problem of 'what to do
with Gourielli' – not Helena's husband, who happily pottered around playing cards and backgammon, but what to do with the House of Gourielli, the
range that still bore his name. Artchil quite enjoyed being seen as the head
of a cosmetics division, but he was useless at it and simply did as he was told
by his wife. From time to time, he came under the influence of people who
thought they knew how to revive the ailing product – mostly packaging
designers, who stood to make a hefty profit out of change. Helena had been
procrastinating; now she had to make a decision. When Horace mentioned
to Artchil that he was in the South of France researching a new, up-market
fragrance not merely for Rubinstein, but for Gourielli as part of a revamp
brief, it set off an explosion in the chain of command at Rubinstein Inc.

The prince sent a note to Helena, and copied it to the board of directors.
Helena was furious, replying, 'I simply cannot understand why you sent this
memo without showing it to me first. You have no idea how much time,
energy and thought I give to Gourielli . . . the whole business has been a
source of grief and heartache to me and it seems to me the more I do, the
worse complications I get into.'

Thanks to the argument, changes at Gourielli were finally approved.
Horace was invited by his mother to make design proposals for the East 55th
St building and to have an input on the advertising campaign. By now,
Horace had come to see David Ogilvy as his saviour. When Ogilvy took on
the Rubinstein account, it's unlikely he had the faintest idea he would
become so swept up in family politics. From the correspondence between
Ogilvy, Helena and Horace, Ogilvy certainly seems more like a psychiatrist
than an advertising agent. Horace's idea to focus Gourielli entirely on men's
products and fragrance having been agreed by his mother, Horace worked
on the creative concepts whilst in the South of France. Drafts for layouts

were put up for consideration and Horace wrote to David Ogilvy, 'I tried to persuade Mother to come down this weekend but, alas, we keep being put off by her other preoccupations, which seem to take precedence. At all events, I have spent a week in Paris with her and am therefore in a position to guide you somewhat . . .'

The preoccupations had included, naturally, shopping. Five handbags at Hermes, a clutch of dresses at Dior, a dozen or so pairs of shoes at Roger Vivier. She could spend $15,000 on herself in a single afternoon. Helena liked to go to the couture shows, usually accompanied by her 'maid' – actually one of several talented dressmakers she employed, all with photographic memories, who would run up several useful copies of her favourite suits – 'cosh-tumes' as she called them. The invoices for what she did buy, including her jewelled Balenciaga gowns, would be sent to the Paris office for payment. She'd then take a copy of each bill from Mr Ameison, the financial manager in Paris, and give it to the company accountant in New York, Mr Levande, resulting in a double reimbursement for cash spent on her 'working wardrobe' whilst in Europe.

Rich as she was, money obsessed Madame, and her early phobias about avoiding income tax still haunted her. Boris Forter was shopping with her one day when a couple of two-shilling pieces rolled out of her bag. 'Ha! I've been wondering where they got to,' she said. An incredulous Forter remembers her beaming with pleasure. There was very little Helena didn't charge back to her business, yet the richer she got, the more miserly she became. In Paris at that time, the daily allowance given to her cook/housekeeper for food for five was a meagre 5000 francs per head (in old francs worth around $10), but if the guest list included the press, or visiting celebrities, the budget went up. The most memorable meal recollected by Patrick O'Higgins, who came to accept the Quai de Bethune cuisine as being usually excruciating, was at a lunch party for, amongst others, Edmonde Charles-Roux of *Vogue*, Hubert de Givenchy, Baron de Rothschild, Janet Flanner, Marie Louise Bousquet and André Malraux. The writer, Resistance hero and politician was also an expert on African art and had asked to see Madame's collection. Helena considered him important. Patrick was amazed to see gold plates materialising out of her safe, enormous tins of caviar appear from a cache in her bathroom, and Eugenie flexing her cooking muscles on coquilles St Jacques, fillet of beef and artichokes, washed down with Dom Perignon. He savoured the memory when, staying with Madame at Stella's cramped flat in

Cannes a few weeks later, they ate sauerkraut, greasy sausage, bread and dry Camembert, all piled on the same plate, precariously balanced on a card table where a bridge four would soon be established for a marathon game.

Meanwhile, Horace was full of ideas to photograph Helena in Grasse, ostensibly against a background of jasmine flowers, indicating that Gourielli fragrances were sourced from original flower essence. Helena winced at this. She hadn't envisaged a pure, essence-based fragrance for the Gourielli range. 'Synthetics', she always said about fragrance ingredients produced in a laboratory, 'are so much cheaper.' With skin care in mind, Horace proposed a strapline to David Ogilvy – 'Here's Important News for Men with Skin Problems' – admitting it had been rejected by his mother. As Madison Avenue's advertising hero was digesting this good news, Horace offered instead: 'Artchil Gourielli Solves a Male Dilemma', and copied this to his mother. Helena scribbled a note in the margin: 'Take this up with me first' and mailed it to the bemused Ogilvy. Fortunately for Artchil's reputation, the phrase that intimated he might be struggling with his manhood was quietly forgotten.

Persuaded by Horace that Gourielli could become a perfume and men's-line brand in its own right, Madame had become enthused about the concept, suggesting a range of handpainted glass bottles that she had seen at Lord Audley's that would, she had decided, 'very well lend themselves to custom-blended perfume, which we may be able to launch at Gourielli'. By now she was convinced that a revamp of Gourielli was not just necessary, but essential. She'd just heard about Arden for Men.

With the rise and rise in the popularity of men's toiletries, Arden for Men was a timely move. In 1950, American men had spent $24,000,000 on aftershave. By 1953, they were spending $30,000,000 on this one product. 'The men's market', noted the *Wall Street Journal* in early 1955, 'is now calculated to be worth $150,000,000 a year.' The Arden range, packaged in grey and gold boxes, with a logo of a man on a horse, included aftershave lotion, eau-de-cologne, soap, talcum powder and, in an innovative move, aftershave balm for moisturising and lip balm. Her London office balked at the latter two items. Even Miss Arden, who felt strongly about men's face cream, wasn't quite ready to launch a male moisturiser commercially in England in the early 1950s. Not that this stopped her giving advice on skin care to all the British men that came into her orbit. Lord Montagu of Beaulieu, who met her around this time, recollects her urging him to take care of his skin. 'She told me I should use her creams for my own skin . . . she believed passionately in the idea of men using moisturiser.' Mainstream acceptance by men for a skin-care regime was well over two decades away. Even now, it's rare to find a man whose facial care involves much more than aftershave balm, but this niche, always seen by cosmetics manufacturers as having 'big potential', was attracting much attention *circa* 1953.

As plans for the relaunch of Gourielli developed, the projected sales revenue was set at $1,200,000 for the year. Horace was furious that the advertising spend was nominal. He wrote a stinging letter to his brother. 'I take off my hat to *nobody* in the organisation where merchandising and promotional acumen is concerned. I cannot see how, with a limited advertising budget, one can hope to meet the Gourielli forecast. Roy, it is a source of never-ending amazement to me how "sales forecasts" are continually accepted without any kind of serious analysis as to just precisely *how* they are supposed to be arrived at.'

Meanwhile, at Rubinstein's New York head office, plans for a new factory fuelled anxiety in Horace. As creative director, he shouldn't have been worrying about building costs, but he fired off a letter to Helena's lawyer, Harold Weill: 'Personally, I should have thought that before planning such a large expenditure of money for the erection of a new factory, it would have been realistic, if funds were short, to plan a strong, long-range sales programme, enabling the company to utilise the production capacities of such a factory on a profitable basis.'

The factory in question, having cost some $4 million, opened in February 1953 at East Hills, Long Island. The site covered 20 acres, it had parking space for 200 cars, a railroad siding, loading facilities for 45 trucks and sunproofed, air-conditioned offices, with a cafeteria for staff, totalling 1000 in number. It was also, according to a trade journal review, equipped with soundproofed offices. Given the arguments between Helena, Horace, Roy and Oscar, it's probably just as well.

Madame wasn't there for the official opening, having contracted pneumonia whilst visiting Europe and being confined to her hotel bedroom in Rome, with an uneasy Patrick O'Higgins in attendance. So ill he thought she might die, Madame rallied when given a course of newly introduced antibiotics, which impressed her so much she bought shares in the pharmaceutical company. She paused in Rome long enough to commission a promotion involving paintings by twenty young Italian artists, including Antonio

Music. The result was a successful exhibition which toured the US for over six months, receiving rave reviews. Helena went home to discover it wasn't just 'the nail man' giving her problems. Whilst she had been away, Estée Lauder had also become a potent force, helped by a potent perfume.

Lauder's Youth Dew, originally sold as a highly fragranced bath oil, launched at Bonwit Teller in 1953, seemed to satisfy a desire for a strong, intense scent amongst American women, who took enthusiastically to the new product. The scent of a Youth Dew woman could be discerned across a crowded room, the effect having the same impact that Giorgio would create thirty years later. You loved it or loathed it but you couldn't ignore it. The fragrance was the result of Mrs Lauder's close friendship with Arnold Lewis van Ameringen, a Dutch-born industrialist whose company, which would evolve into the mighty I.F.F. – International Flavours and Fragrances – was the leading exponent in developing aromatic chemicals, the 'synthetics' so admired by Helena Rubinstein. Van Ameringen was a very useful friend to Mrs Lauder. Youth Dew became her leading 'gift with purchase' item at the top stores, and so powerful was its allure that within months the Lauder turnover at Neiman Marcus went from a few hundred dollars to $5000 a week.

Miss Arden was distinctly unamused with Mrs Lauder, calling her 'the woman down the road.' Elizabeth thought Youth Dew unspeakably vulgar and she thought Mrs Lauder unspeakably vulgar too, being caustic about her social climbing, causing her decorator to remark – rather bravely – 'Look at the pot, calling the kettle black.' Arden finally had a new perfume of her own, called My Love, which had been trialled in France and was due for launching in the USA in 1953, with packaging and advertising illustration done by the cult artist Jean Cocteau. When the first commercial batch arrived in New York, however, she flipped. 'The perfume is not the same as the first sample Gladys sent me. I think the chemist found it so good he is keeping it for Dior! Everyone loved the first sample, people literally followed me around and asked when they could buy it. Teddy, I am worried. I wonder if Gladys reduced the perfume man in price so much that he has omitted one of the ingredients?'

It was the success of Youth Dew that rankled with Miss Arden, whereas it was the reinvention of Mrs Lauder's persona as not being Jewish which infuriated Charles Revson. He once famously yelled, 'Her name's not Estée, it's *Esther*! Esther-from-Brooklyn.' No one had the courage to say it was

Esther from Queens. When Charles was in a temper, as with Madame and Miss Arden, it was best to ignore it and hope it would blow away. Estée Lauder's hard-earned success, however, did not blow away. With it came her ability to redesign her past, including telling the media her mother was born in Vienna, a story she clung to relentlessly. Other reports said she was a Catholic, with mixed Hungarian and Austrian blood – something she rarely denied, even once going so far as to produce a 'relative' who was a Catholic nun. Telling fairytales was something Mrs Lauder shared with Madame, just as Helena had painted a rosy glow about her parents' life some fifty years earlier, Mrs Lauder's version, as told to *Women's Wear Daily*, was that she had grown up in a 'luxurious home in Flushing, Long Island, with stables, a chauffeured car and an Italian nurse'. Corona Avenue, where she lived in an apartment above her father's hardware store, was never mentioned.

From the 1940s throughout the 1950s Estée Lauder was a hands-on, dynamic saleswoman virtually in sole charge of all her retail outlets. Interestingly, it was this very personal approach which did her the most good. The store cosmetics buyers were almost always women, whereas the sales staff for the big brands were almost always men. Demonstrators, training managers and counter staff were women, but men were in charge of sales, delivery dates and discounting terms – and they sold hard. These men were not just motivated, they were *driven*, and being bombarded by them could sometimes be quite wearying. Store buyers were no shrinking violets, particularly in the cut-and-thrust of American retailing, but it was pleasurable, for a change, to do business with a woman. Estée Lauder and the lady buyers established a real rapport. She talked to them non-stop about her product – she talked about little else – but she also talked to them as a woman about women's things. Girl talk about home, husbands, children – Estée being the mother of two sons, albeit left at home with her husband – college, camp and vacation plans. It made a difference. After giving a product pep-talk to the sales staff at stores, she would take the women out to an expensive dinner and make a fuss of them. If the laughter got a little raucous, so much the better. Mrs Lauder *lived* her business and her business was selling. She had an overwhelming, all-enveloping personality, and in the 1950s was considered to be particularly attractive – small, blonde, busty, bubbly. Denizens of the industry would remark that she reminded them of how Elizabeth Arden had been thirty years earlier . . .

By this time, Miss Arden rarely saw a buyer. 'She would from time to time make a state visit,' says Angus McCall, who looked after the top stores in London and Ireland. 'But it was carefully planned and she would only meet the top management.' The London business was run on deeply traditional lines. 'It felt just like the Brigade of Guards,' says McCall. 'When I first joined even I couldn't meet a store buyer unless I had been personally presented by Mr Haslam.' Whilst Elizabeth may not have dropped in to see buyers, she maintained contact with store owners, especially important stores like Neiman Marcus in Dallas, Texas, where Stanley Marcus had been one of her first guides through the maze of the fashion industry and where she had received a Neiman Marcus Award for 'distinguished services' to the industry in 1939. In 1957, it was the turn of an ageing but revitalised Coco Chanel to be honoured, and Stanley Marcus and his wife organised a private barbecue at his brother's ranch, Blackmark Farm. The only trouble was that Chanel had developed such bizarre eating habits she rarely ate at all, and couldn't bear the smell of pungent food. The aroma of spare-ribs and hot sauce, onions and spicy beans made her feel sick, so she simply dumped the entire plate on the ground underneath her seat. For Elizabeth Arden, sitting next to her, the evening began quite well – Coco owned racehorses herself, and they were able to compare notes on their 'babies'. It ended badly when Chanel's spiced food was tipped – all down Elizabeth's legs and over her shell-pink kid pumps.

There was no such drama at the intimate supper Diana Vreeland hosted for Chanel on the same trip, when Helena appeared for coffee and the two old friends locked themselves into Reed Vreeland's study with nothing but a bottle of champagne to sustain them whilst they talked for hours. No formalities existed at Helena Rubinstein's offices anywhere in the world either, apropos her meeting store buyers. By that time, Madame had delegated such duties entirely to her sales managers. Not that Boris Forter was seeing too many buyers in England, as Rubinstein's store presence was waning. To compensate, he had diverted activity to South Africa, where he operated a flourishing market, shipping raw materials from England, along with the product instructions, and having the Rubinstein range made up by an independent manufacturer.

By the summer of 1953, the Long Island factory development costs were taking their toll and Rubinstein's corporate borrowings were up to $2 million. Madame felt with judicious paring down on expenses the loans could be repaid much earlier. She said: 'This is one thing that has to be made clear to Horace. He has very extravagant ideas, some of which are quite good because they will dress up the line; at the same time it is more important to put our strength and effort behind less costly staple products which can bring us in big volume.' She was increasingly worried about her younger son's behaviour – dealing with Horace had driven Sara Fox almost to the point of nervous collapse. Madame wrote to David Ogilvy about her son, 'I so hope that you will be able to try and persuade him not to start new things again all the time.'

It wasn't to be. Horace wrote to her, 'I have as fertile imagination as anyone but whilst imagination can still be employed to promote certain items we sell, I am convinced that for most of our bread and butter items we need more, and better, laboratory research. This should be directed by somebody who understands the objectives and steers it in the directions that will do us the most good . . . I would like to take over this job myself.'

In despair, Helena washed her hands of Horace, who was supposed to be masterminding the House of Gourielli and seemed to be doing anything but. She took herself off to Mexico whilst Patrick O'Higgins and her newest protégée, Eleanor McVicker, the ex-beauty editor of *Harper's Bazaar*, were put to work on the project to revamp the building on East 55th St. Fixtures and fittings were ordered for a deluxe barber's shop, where the staff of ten were trained to give scalp treatments and 'vitamin-complex' shampoos, along with offering discreet colour. At Patrick's suggestion there was a 'sun-shop' offering tanning treatments; men could have mud-pack facials and a 'milk-protein' skin treatment, whilst Gladys Madison, the resident star manicurist, buffed and polished the nails of executive men to gleaming perfection. The ground-floor gift shop was restocked as a men's boutique, selling expensive 'executive' gifts alongside cashmere sweaters, gold chain belts at $30 an inch, Egyptian cotton trenchcoats for $125, Moroccan-inspired silk robes and striped silk 'lounging jackets' starting at $50 each. A ticker tape machine was installed so that clients could check their stocks, and food was sent in to order from the kitchens of the St Regis Hotel next door.

Madame herself, back in New York but confined to hospital in one of her increasingly frequent bouts of illness, monitored the opening plans from her sickbed. It was rumoured she had cancer and her family hovered in the wings. Lines of succession were much discussed, as was inheritance of her fortune. Not unsurprisingly, given his ability to have good ideas, it was

Horace who came up with a masterstroke which enabled Helena to do something she adored – minimise paying tax. In 1953, whilst O'Higgins was busy planning the merchandising of Gourielli, Horace suggested forming a Foundation. His memo said, 'The two main objectives would be to sponsor and guide, insofar as possible, worthwhile scientific projects of benefit to mankind as a whole – many of which, however, would have immediate and specific application to the Helena Rubinstein company.' In particular, Horace highlighted the 'threat of cancer in relation to absorption of materials through the skin', which he deemed a real danger and one worthy of research by a cosmetics company . . . who after all were feeding materials through the skin. He also talked about 'prolongation of life in both its general and specific aspects', then, as now, longevity being a subject of deep interest to those reluctant to surrender youth and beauty.

If these ideas seemed farfetched to his mother, his second objective was more succinct. He suggested initiatives to 'sponsor and guide certain cultural projects, largely in the fields of design, specifically applied arts, industrial design, textiles, graphic arts and so forth, plus colour – both physical and psychological phenomena'. Horace believed such endeavours could be tax-exempt, explaining to his mother that he felt 'such persons as Patrick O'Higgins, his assistant Allan Kurtzman, and myself can have our salaries applied to this Foundation, thus relieving the company payroll'. Madame grasped his point immediately and the idea was put to her lawyers and professional advisers who moved swiftly to set up the Helena Rubinstein Foundation. It never got as far as investigating cancers during Helena's lifetime, and there is little evidence of the 'lectures, publications and exhibitions' Horace dreamed of taking place. The Helena Rubinstein Foundation was, during her lifetime at least, a vehicle that channelled costs of various issues and donations near and dear to Helena's heart, mainly arts-related, through her business in a way that was nearest to her heart – as tax efficient.

The team in charge of Gourielli, meanwhile, were planning their opening party, which, given the awesome power of Patrick's address book, was becoming an important event. The budget was a constant thorn in Madame's side, even from her hospital bed. 'No dips,' said Helena, 'they'll stain the carpets.' She queried the champagne costs with Patrick, who visited her regularly and was ordered to brief her on 'what the family are up to while I'm not there to see it'. Artchil meanwhile fell foul of the efficient

Eleanor McVicker and retreated to Palm Beach until he was needed at the opening, muttering darkly about 'strong women'. The day of the opening dawned and flush with pleasure from the pre-publicity, with features in *Life*, the *New York Times*, the *Post*, *Time*, et al., Patrick presided over a group including his friend Truman Capote (whom he had persuaded to come by, promising him that Gore Vidal would *not* be there), two of the Gabor sisters, a surviving Dolly sister, Salvador Dali, a host of bright and beautiful New York socialites including Brenda Frazier, along with . . . Gore Vidal. Helena herself made a surprise appearance, dressed to impress, although looking frail. Flanked by a doctor and a nurse, she beamed with pleasure at the impressive crowd and returned to hospital clutching a plate of smoked salmon. When Eleanor McVicker and O'Higgins sent a dossier to Madame, cost-evaluating all the 'free ink' (press editorials as opposed to advertising) they had achieved, and showing the pro-rata value against pure advertising, the total came to $800,000. To their chagrin, their memo came back with a margin note from Madame saying, 'It should have been a million.'

Almost at once, the place started losing money. When the losses reached $50,000 there was a heated meeting at head office during which Mr Carroll remarked, 'The place is full of pansies.' Helena ignored it all. 'What to do? What to do?' she moaned. The decision was taken for her when, in the autumn of 1955, whilst Madame and Patrick were in Paris, Artchil suffered a massive heart attack and died. His funeral five days later, on 26 November 1955, was arranged by Campbell's, the service attended by the Russian coterie in New York, but not by his wife. She stayed in Paris, unable as always to cope with loss, swallowing her grief by retreating. She closed the House of Gourielli a few months later.

CHAPTER TWENTY-TWO

SHOW TIME
1955–1959

1955 WAS A BAD YEAR FOR Helena Rubinstein, but a good one for Charles Revson. It was the year his company went public, making him a multimillionaire, and it was the year the name of Revlon became known to virtually every person in America who watched television. With more than 28,000,000 sets in American households, that was a *lot* of people. Revlon had been persuaded to sponsor a quiz show aired by CBS called *The $64,000 Question*. They weren't the first beauty company to sponsor a TV show. Hazel Bishop, who had nurtured a successful lipstick line, had already earned significant brand recognition by sponsoring *This Is Your Life*. Charles Revson didn't even like television as a promotional medium. 'We sell colour,' he used to say, since all transmissions were then in black and white. But his advertising agency persuaded him that this particular show formula was right for Revlon. How right they were.

Several other companies had been pitched, including Chrysler, Lewyt Vacuums, even Helena Rubinstein. All had turned it down. It's said Helena rejected it because she disliked television, remarking scathingly, 'Only little people watch those awful machines.' Whilst she didn't own a television herself, the remark is probably apocryphal, as she was already in conversation with David Ogilvy about TV advertising.

Revlon took a thirteen-week option. It would last for four years. Every Tuesday night, from the first week of June 1955, contestants entered a sound booth, with 'Revlon' in neon italics over the door. Actress Barbara Britton, a vision in white tulle, presented the show and its live advertisements, and within a month *The $64,000 Question* was number one in the ratings. It was estimated that 55,000,000 people watched to see who could win the most money – all of them absorbing the message about Revlon. The show was so successful that Revlon agreed to sponsor a spin-off called *The $64,000 Challenge* which aired on Sunday night. Revlon's product-awareness recognition became light-years ahead of their competition's and, just a year later, company turnover was $85 million. Better still, the costs of sponsoring America's favourite quiz show were nominal. It cost the Revlon Corporation about $30,000 a show in production fees – prizes averaged $14,000 – and approximately $40,000 in network broadcast time. If a contestant made it to the $64,000 question and won, Charles personally appeared to present the cheque.

Revlon went public on 7 December 1955 at $12 a share, just six months after *The $64,000 Question* was launched. The television exposure did their share price no harm and Wall Street adored the company's high profile. Within weeks, their stock was trading at $30. It made Charles, who retained 52%, a multimillionaire, and his brother Martin, silent partner Charles Lachman, and a few handpicked employees with stock options, very wealthy men indeed. His brother Joseph, having sold his original 30% share to Charles a few months before, retreated into isolated retirement. Brokers continued to be excited by Revlon stock. Analysts who knew their numbers may have realised that Revlon's 'cost of goods' were spectacularly inexpensive – it was calculated their mark-up was 400%. By 1956, their shares split 2-for-1 and by the end of the year the company was listed on New York's stock exchange. If Joseph Revson had waited a while before parting company with the family firm, his holding would have been valued at $35 million.

While Revlon rode the crest of a wave, their competition, particularly Max Factor and Madame, could only watch and wail with frustration. The TV show hit Rubinstein's sales hard. By June 1956, monthly turnover was down like-for-like against the previous year by half a million dollars and by July, by a million dollars. Madame retaliated against Revlon's show by sponsoring a Sunday night programme starring Imogene Coca and Sid Caesar, but it did little good; they were past their prime and the show looked dated. At one point Madame was so incensed about Revlon copying her product that she bought shares and threatened to go to their AGM and complain. She never did. Nor did she sell the shares – they performed too well. Nothing it seemed could stop the relentless rise of Revlon.

Whilst 'that man's' success was irksome to Miss Arden, it didn't really touch her market. It wasn't until the end of the 1950s that Charles, concerned that his product was becoming too commercial, and yearning to be part of the speciality store business he secretly craved, established divisions to satisfy the upper-middle and even top end of the sales spectrum. The fact is, however, that he never really cornered that niche. He hadn't started there and, despite good attempts, he didn't end there. Only Elizabeth Arden, and later Estée Lauder, could claim the glittering prize of volume domination in the prestige cosmetics market during the late 50s and 1960s. Revlon had given up their chance when they took up popular TV . . . viewers were more interested in a one-dollar lipstick than expensive treatment creams.

Meanwhile, in Europe, blissfully unaffected by sponsored TV shows, Serge Heftler, owner of Dior perfumes, confident of their assured place in the up-market spectrum, launched into lipsticks, the beginning of what would become a fully fledged cosmetics line. A year later, they launched their fourth successful fragrance, Diorissimo, and following Christian Dior's death in 1957, M. Heftler sold out to Moet-Hennessy, who owned Moet et Chandon amongst other champagne marques, laying the foundations of what is now the mighty LVMH empire.

Although she would never have admitted it, Elizabeth Arden had a lot in common with Charles Revson. For example, they both had the most perfect colour sense. Charles, it's said, could differentiate between a dozen shades of black – a legacy from his early years working in the fashion textiles industry. One day, he was lunching at the Plaza and ordered a glass of skimmed milk. When it arrived he asked the waiter if he was sure it was skimmed. 'Yes,' said the waiter. 'Well, I know COLOUR,' yelled Charles at the hapless man, 'and this milk is yellow. Skimmed milk is blue!' Elizabeth knew at a hundred paces if a shade wasn't right. One infinitesimal differential in a tone of pink would cause an uproar. Staff were used to colour meetings with Miss Arden going on for the whole day under her eagle eye. Charles Revson would hold meetings that went on through the night, totally disregarding his directors' home life. Revlon wives were invited to lectures at head office where they would be encouraged to 'learn to type' so they could help with their husbands' reports, or 'to play bridge or go to the movies' in the afternoon so they didn't make demands on his time when he got home late. All this was accepted because, as Grace Gilbert puts it, 'Charles paid people beyond even their dreams.'

At Arden's New York headquarters, where she too paid extremely well, her executives were used to long meetings and the caprices of their boss.

Miss Arden would start a sales managers' meeting at 1.30 p.m., leave half an hour later for Belmont to see one of her horses racing in, say, the 3.00 p.m. race and another one at 4.15 p.m., settle 'her babies' into their stables, return to town, getting back by 6.30 p.m., and say to the men, still gathered around the table waiting for her, 'Where were we, gentlemen?' She had little time for corporate wives; she didn't care for wives at all, the exception being Katie Cross, who was just about her closest personal friend. For years, Katie had looked after her flowers via her work at the florist Irene Hayes, but in June of 1955 it was Elizabeth who was doing flowers for Katie . . . to be sent to her funeral. She was to be sadly missed by Miss Arden. Katie's death, after lingering cancer, would make Elizabeth finally feel the inevitability of encroaching old age. As far as other corporate wives were concerned, when she did dine with them, in particular on trips to Europe, a note would be sent explaining what colour gown Miss Arden would be wearing, the implication being they had to wear something different – preferably black – a colour, she felt, that acted as a good foil to her invariable pink.

Both Arden and Revson were monumental hypochondriacs, though Helena was no stranger to this habit. No one was immune from their advice on illnesses and cures. Revson, who was reported to have had a couple of minor heart scares in the late 1940s–early 1950s, was obsessive about maintaining a low-fat diet. In fact, he was a visionary in this respect, just as Arden was in respect of yoga and exercise, and several years before the University of Minnesota proved a definitive correlation between animal fats and heart disease in 1953, Revson was stripping the skin off his chicken and eating tuna in brine. He would hover near a buffet table, glaring at the food, mixing his own Maalox in a glass (he had shocking digestive problems) and grumble to his hostess about her menu. He gave up smoking overnight, having been a sixty-a-day man, never even lighting a cigar again.

Miss Arden loathed smoking. If a secretary or manager had lit up, and heard she was arriving in the building, they would hastily stub the offending weed out wherever they could. On one occasion, a panic-stricken employee stubbed her cigarette out in the desk drawer and forgot about it. It may have temporarily deflected Miss Arden's wrath, but it started a fire within minutes, causing the sprinklers to go off, which meant the building had to be evacuated. Miss Arden was not amused and, of course, the hapless girl was bounced.

Elizabeth had as many doctors as Charles Revson, and saw at least one daily, changing them every few months. 'It seems my illness comes from my throat and I now have Dr Ruskin,' she wrote to her sister, 'who says I must not talk because the blood vessels are involved from coughing. I am confined to bed without any talking . . . but feel better.' Presumably her staff felt better too as, for a while at least, she couldn't nag them. By the end of the month she had seen a new osteopath and a few days after that caught pneumonia visiting Canada. 'The place is just full of germs,' she said. Miss Arden worried constantly about germs. Yet when friends were ill, she visited them in hospital daily, taking fruit and flowers and giving endless advice. She worried about her sinuses (as did Revson), about her digestion, her circulation, her gout, her teeth, her low blood pressure and her heart. She had cranial massage for her headaches, and reflexology. Most of all, she worried about keeping up her high energy levels and had regular strong vitamin injections. The doctor of choice for energy-boosting shots at the time was Dr Max Jacobson – called 'Dr Feelgood' by his many society fans – whose amphetamine-based shots were taken by, amongst others, John and Jackie Kennedy. They were also taken by Elizabeth's old friend Charles James so it's likely Elizabeth tried them too.

Charles James, to the complete surprise of his friends, had married in 1954. Patrick O'Higgins was his best man and Gypsy Rose Lee, a long-time friend, the matron of honour. His bride, an heiress called Nancy Lee Gregory, had produced two children – which fascinated his friends even more – called Charles Jr and Louise, and Miss Arden, earlier rows forgiven, became godmother to baby Charles.

Elizabeth didn't take her health phobias to the same extremes as Revson, who had his blood pressure taken during meetings, yelling at his executives if it got too high, 'See what you guys are doing to me . . . I'm getting fucking *stressed out* here.' He had a full-time doctor on the payroll to give him an ECG each day he was travelling, and a personal trainer worked with him for an hour every single morning at his home, where he had installed a gym. Elizabeth worked with a yoga instructor and thought nothing of doing headstands, even when she was eighty. She too was violently anti-cholesterol and was a light eater although she never starved herself, believing women who were too thin didn't age well. Elizabeth was a standard 10–12 dress size, but if she wanted to shed a pound or two, her favourite reducing diet was rice served with stewed tomatoes without their skins, which she would eat three times a day. Being in the lucky position of running two of America's most famous health farms, where a raft of qualified quasi-medical staff were on hand to look after her when she visited, she did not go short of sympathy and health advice.

By the 1950s, her favourite was Maine Chance at Phoenix, handily situated between the East Coast and Santa Anita racetrack in California and her salons in Beverly Hills and San Francisco. Only open for the winter season, Phoenix attracted clients accustomed to wealth and luxury, such as Mamie Eisenhower, who visited annually, Clare Booth Luce, Ava Gardner and most of the wives of the men who were running American banking and industry.

Elizabeth could not often enjoy it, however. Her travel schedule was as punishing in the 1950s as it had been in the 1930s. By now, she had enthusiastically adopted air travel, although over two-thirds of Americans travelling domestically still used trains. Interestingly, Elizabeth never bought a company plane although she often availed herself of planes owned by her racing friends, and would charter a plane for short flights. Mostly she took commercial flights, booking out an entire row when, to her annoyance, sleeper seats were discontinued on long-haul services.

Being a senior executive in this privileged world meant a way of life most other executives could only dream of. Teddy Haslam, for example, disliked flying, so always used the *Queen Mary*, travelling first class and staying at the St Regis in New York. Angus McCall has fond memories of his transatlantic trips flying on the Stratocruiser, speeding at 325 mph, drinking gin and tonics in the cocktail bar where wartime bombs had been carried. Miss Arden always used Claridges when in London and the Ritz in Paris, whilst Oscar Kolin at Rubinstein preferred the Hotel Bristol in Paris. Boris Forter would persuade Helena to stay at Claridges on her rare visits to London and Charles Revson also used the hotel, commandeering 'the Royal Suite' for days at a time, with his executives on the floor below.

Travel, particularly if it was linked to 'exports', was one way of getting around the currency restrictions then still in place, and naturally, for those involved in perfumes, there was the obligatory trip to the South of France to 'check out Grasse' – conveniently, usually timed to coincide with an Easter break. One guest at the Carlton in Cannes recollects watching the managing director of Yardley sauntering through the foyer, the lining of his suit, his socks, his Panama hat-band, his shirt, tie, even his gloves, always in a sugared-almond Yardley colour – one day lilac, another pink, and his wife was co-ordinated in dress, hat and gloves to match.

Dining out on expenses was taken as a matter of course, especially when travelling, and sales managers were designated to look after visitors from head office and show them the best restaurants. Angus McCall thought it would make a change to take 'Duke' Wellington Cross to Pratts Dining Club when he was in London, and was rather startled when 'Duke', having dined well at the Duke of Devonshire's private club, took to the table top to do an impromptu tap dance and sing a song. 'As I remember,' he says, 'the members were absolutely enchanted.'

Dining well made up for the long meetings. Those close to Revson say he held such long meetings because he was lonely. He, like Elizabeth, had a real fear of isolation and was an insomniac. He would often phone executives, like Bill Heller, as late as 11.00 p.m. from his apartment in New York's Pierre Hotel, and ask him over. Often he would then have to stay the night, sometimes sleeping next to Charles, just as Irene Delaney or Miss Wonnacott slept next to Miss Arden, soothing her to sleep, so she wouldn't panic in the dark. Charles hated to go home, and would cruise the late-night drug stores, checking out what colours the hookers were buying. 'Creative research,' he'd say as he dragged another exhausted manager on the late-night tour. Miss Arden probably didn't know such drug stores existed, but she too would ring Jack Treat or Duke Cross, or even Henry Sell, at 11.00 p.m., or midnight, and insist they join her at El Morocco or the Stork Club, not leaving until 2.00 a.m. 'You were *always* on duty,' said Angus McCall. 'One never, *ever* knew what was going to happen at night and you simply couldn't refuse an invitation, however late.' Even then, she'd be up at 6.30 a.m. for the drive to Belmont to see her 'babies' on dawn exercise. Elizabeth compensated for lack of sleep by taking catnaps, and a fifteen-minute sleep in the car, on her sofa, under the hairdryer or even in her office on a chaise would invigorate her for another several hours.

Helena Rubinstein, on the other hand, was usually in bed by 10.00 p.m. The exception was when a good bridge game was in progress, but even then she would finish by midnight. She too suffered with insomnia, but took pills to sleep, waking up at about 6.00 each morning and starting her bedside meetings by 7.30 a.m. When she travelled, there were no luxury yachts, or sleeper seats on aeroplanes. Quite often she travelled tourist class, her tiny legs resting on her vanity case, stuffed with her jewels, her vast handbag – usually stuffed with wads of dollar bills – tucked by her side. On trains in Europe she preferred to sleep sitting up, rather than go to the expense of booking a couchette. She would wrap herself up in a huge sable stole and get out her torch so she could read, constantly tearing out pages that interested her from magazines, making a note to send an ad she admired to Miss Fox or Horace. Madame rarely went hungry, always packing a few hardboiled eggs, apples and chicken legs for her midnight feast, which would be pulled from a series of paper bags tucked in one or other of the many assorted pieces of luggage she carried.

According to Patrick O'Higgins, Helena had been diagnosed as a diabetic and her son Roy also suffered from the disease. Helena's low blood-sugar problems meant from time to time she would drop to the floor in a dead faint. This was alarming for whoever was with her, and panic would often ensue. Some handled the shock better than others. At Dior's salon in Paris, Monsieur Dior simply crouched down and kissed her hand, saying, 'Bonjour, princesse,' as though it was the most normal thing in the world for his clients to be flat on their backs. She'd wait a few minutes to get her breath back, then get up and carry on as though nothing had happened, but dreading the inevitable bruises.

In the days following her husband's death at the end of 1955 she stayed in bed in her Quai de Bethune apartment, alone with her memories, sometimes crying, sometimes morose, and becoming increasingly bad-tempered. Madame was moping. She cheered up when Marie Cuttoli telephoned with news that Picasso had finally agreed Madame could sit for him. The price to Cuttoli for brokering the arrangement was quite specific. The leading French politician Georges Pompidou and his wife had set their hearts on leasing an apartment in Helena's Quai de Bethune building. Marie knew that one would soon be vacant and the deal was done. In fact, Madame quite liked having the Pompidous as residents, particularly when he became Prime Minister and preferred to stay at Quai de Bethune than at his government residence. She would have a taxi waiting outside when his official car with outriders came to collect him each morning, slipping into the convoy speeding through Paris, calculating she saved money because her taxi would go through red lights as part of the Prime Minister's motorcade.

She wasn't quite so happy with her sittings for Picasso. Their first meeting started over lunch, with Helena decked out in an array of fringed and tasselled shawls, a gypsy blouse and tiered skirt in shades of red and yellow, apparently looking like a fairground fortune-teller. John Richardson describes the meetings between Madame and Picasso as fraught. 'Patrick put up a bit of a blot by bringing his camera . . . he was a rather good photographer and thought Madame would enjoy having pictures, but Picasso simply hated impromptu photographic sessions and it didn't go down too well.' The idea of painting Helena's portrait didn't go down too well either. Over the next few days Picasso sketched furiously. He drew her face, her neck, her hairline, her hands with their vast rings, even her mouth. He did over forty drawings but never completed one of her full face. Neither were the drawings used for a portrait. Richardson is convinced that Picasso, by now quite old himself, thought that if he completed a picture of Helena Rubinstein, he would die before her. They are, however, astonishing works. Richardson's personal favourite is the simple outline of Helena's head, her chignon just visible; no eyes, no nose, no mouth, just a blank silhouette.

As a friend of Patrick's, John Richardson was in a good position to see Helena's vast art collection at first hand. She often relegated pieces she had been told were worthless to the back of a cupboard, and from time to time gave them away to friends. In the early 1950s, Helena had given Patrick what she believed was a fake Cubist collage attributed to Juan Gris. By happy coincidence it caught Richardson's attention, and when he confirmed its authenticity, Helena invited him to cast his skilled eye over several of her other pictures with a dubious provenance. He discovered a series of large Juan Gris still lifes on paper, done when the artist had no money for canvas. Promptly arranging for a proper sale via Knoedler's – with the requisite commission built in for himself and Patrick – Madame became enamoured of Richardson, who always told her the truth and who from time to time would find the cash to buy early Picasso drawings from her. Helena had a grand passion for crisp dollar bills, which Richardson remembers well. 'Madame liked to use her bedroom as her office. We would sit side by side on her unmade bed, with a pile of dollar bills between us. Sometimes we would have to count them as many as six times before the figures would tally. Madame counted slowly out loud and every time she reached a hundred, she would puff out her lips and make a raspberry noise. Patrick, whose job it was to smuggle the dollars out of the country into Switzerland, wearing a moneybelt so capacious he looked pregnant, told me this meant Madame was happy.'

Whenever Madame was unhappy, or wanted to forget her troubles, according to one of her close friends, Leila Hirsch, she liked to take long walks. She would walk for miles, regardless of the weather, and adored exploring new territory. One such walking trip was taken in Ireland, where she was invited by her fashion-designer friend Sybil Connolly, whose clothes were a great favourite with Helena. Walking helped her clear her mind and plot strategy.

By 1956, long walks were the order of the day as she contemplated not only the slipping Rubinstein sales figures, but the fact that her salons were leaching money. The New York flagship, and Mala Rubinstein's Wonder School offering grooming and make-up classes, were now running at a grave loss, the trend for self-improvement having tailed off. Women, in New York at least, seemed to have learned to handle their own make-up and felt confident about their grooming without taking classes. Madame's demonstrators, just like Arden's, were very groomed, but as Claude Forter says, 'They all wore far too much make-up – more Gloria Swanson than Doris Day.' Women gained beauty courage in the 1950s. Surrounded by so many female filmstars, all wearing enough make-up to stock an average store counter, their heroines were beauties like Ingrid Bergman, Kay Kendall, Eva Bartok, Cyd Charisse, Elizabeth Taylor, Rita Hayworth, Kim Novak, Grace Kelly, Lauren Bacall and a young Audrey Hepburn, who starred in the ultimate fashion film of the decade, *Funny Face*. For young women who swooned as Marlon Brando rode his motorbike in *The Wild Ones*, or rocked around the clock to Bill Haley and the Comets and screamed at Elvis Presley concerts, the perfectly groomed look of their mothers was becoming . . . too perfect.

In 1957 Madame and Patrick set off on a world tour. They first went to Japan where Helena was to meet potential distributors in an attempt to tackle this lucrative territory. Taking time out to visit Kyoto, Patrick was delighted to find friends at the bar of their hotel. Hugger-mugger in their 'happy coats' were Cecil Beaton and Truman Capote. Fortunately for Mr Beaton, the trip did not necessitate yet another photograph of Helena, although it would inspire a revamp of her quite tired-looking picture gallery on the upper floor of her New York apartment. Beaton would later be hired to transform the room – for what Helena thought was an obscene fee – and took as his theme Japanese bamboo, building a trellis feature with flowerboxes underneath to display the pictures. 'Madame,' he grumbled to Patrick, 'is being chintzy with her pictures, I'm only being allowed one second-rate Picasso.' In the end she paid his fee, telling Patrick she couldn't bargain with him as 'he would gossip'! Beaton's light and breezy 'Japanese Winter Garden' art gallery, however, wasn't a success. The room, with its cloud-painted ceiling and white wicker chairs, had never looked more attractive, but the bamboo was attacked by beetles and the whole thing eventually had to be dismantled. After buying packets of pearls in Tokyo, and sending Japanese handprinted paper to Horace for packaging ideas, Helena and Patrick moved on to Hong Kong where Madame discovered the cheong sam and the delights of instant dressmaking, coming back to New York with dozens of dresses in startling pink, red and fuchsia brocade.

They then went to Australia. This was her first visit for nearly three decades and she was treated like royalty. For Patrick, the trip offered an intriguing insight into Helena's early years. For the press, it was the return of their very own heroine. She had her portrait painted, she gave interviews, she was wined and dined and attended a special lunch hosted by Mrs Myer of the famous department-store dynasty. Mrs Myer's daughter Marigold – now Lady Southey, and Lieutenant Governor for the State of Victoria – was at the lunch. 'My most vivid memory,' she says, 'is of the extraordinarily long rope of black pearls that Helena Rubinstein wore. They were memorable to me firstly because I don't particularly like black pearls, and secondly because I was impressed by the size and quantity of them. That string of pearls would have been worth a fortune . . . I also remember her black, shiny hair.' As ever when she travelled, Madame took her 'best bits' of jewellery with her, confident it would create an impression.

She would have had little opportunity to wear them when they went on to Auckland, New Zealand. Patrick was horrified, writing to his friend Amber Walker in New York, 'Ever been to New Zealand? It's rock bottom really, without one cheerful feature. Our hotel smells of stewed cabbage. Dinner ends at 7.30 p.m. The waitresses wear those awful starched bonnets like matrons in country hospitals. It's really ghastly. Where do people in a place like this hail from? They all look so pinched. I wonder why? Constipated no doubt . . .'

Patrick was by now weary of looking after Madame from early morning until night. He typed her letters, helped her with medication, escorted her to dinner, and had to put up with her grumbling that he was drinking too much when he poured a second glass of wine. As usual, packets of letters were forwarded from New York, with Helena dictating five-page replies. One missive was from Sara Fox, enclosing a stuffer for the new Rubinstein hormone treatment cream called 'Tree of Life'.

Tree of Life was Madame's pet product and she had monitored its development closely, instructing her promotional team to focus on its scientific qualities, and that it left skin 'baby soft'. She was appalled to be presented with an inexpensively printed, gold-coloured pamphlet with a picture of a mother and child. 'The picture is very misleading,' she thundered, 'it looks as if we are advertising a baby powder! I think it is cheap looking and hideous and I find it impossible to read the copy on gold paper . . . it has none of the style and elegance it should have. Tree of Life is expensive. The consumer has to feel it is unique and luxurious. I only hope that, somehow, these mistakes can be rectified.' Helena was fond of Sara Fox, but being responsible for all sales promotion material was now a huge task and she doubted Sara had the ability to handle it – whether assisted by Horace or not.

By this time, Horace was spending less and less time at work. His role had been reduced and, it was noted by staff, he was drinking heavily. Helena wasn't unsympathetic about Sara's problems, saying, 'I realise that we need a really strong and clever overall artistic director in charge of all the visual aspects of our business: photography, packaging, display, advertising. He should co-ordinate everything. This way I would never have unpleasant surprises.' She copied the letter to Roy, with a margin note saying, 'We are all the time more people, more worry and no one outstanding. I hope Roy that you will be a standby and take an active interest in these problems. It seems to me we are worse off than before . . .'

On her return to New York, Helena tried to talk to Roy about this and other matters, but felt he was avoiding her. 'I feel very sad that every time we make an appointment, most of the time you break it. I am terribly upset . . . we are just like two strangers in the business. I was hoping you will take a stronger and more aggressive interest . . . I don't want people to say that you are weak . . . I want them to feel that you are stronger than ever and that you concentrate on the business. With the name and reputation we have we should be doing three times as much business as we do . . .' Roy treated this as he had always treated messages from his mother, by ignoring it. Helena scrawled him a note saying, 'Your not answering my letter for five weeks certainly does not solve anything. You took offence where no offence is meant. Why should you bring yourself into this terrible state of nerves just because I pointed out to you your shortcomings? Can you not discuss business in a grown-up way, not like an immature child?'

By August that year she had a worse problem than falling figures. Horace had been involved in an horrific accident; he had been driving on the wrong side of the road, gone straight into an oncoming vehicle, and the occupants, a family of four, were badly injured. It got worse. Mr Gruberger, the driver and family breadwinner, subsequently died, triggering an aggressive insurance claim against Horace. Madame was desolate.

The following spring she was in Paris with Patrick when a call came through from New York. Horace was dead. He had been involved in yet another car crash and as a consequence, it's said, suffered a heart attack, dying in hospital the next morning. This time, she really suffered. Horace was her 'baby'. Creative, caring, careless but never cruel. She had loved him deeply and fought with him fiercely. Now he was gone.

Madame, to the outside world, took his loss bravely. Very few friends knew just how much she was hurting. Shortly after his funeral, Leila Hirsch, a friend of Helena's (the 'nice wife' of her favourite broker), visited Madame in her office. Helena shut – and locked – the door. 'Now I can cry,' she said, shaking with grief and sobbing as though she did not know how to stop. Leila stayed with her the whole afternoon, listening to Helena's outpourings about her lost son. She took her home that night, recollecting how dismally lonely Helena's vast, empty apartment, echoing with memories, seemed to feel.

Cecil Beaton came to Patrick's aid to create a diversion to shake Madame out of her lethargy. Beaton explained that Graham Sutherland had expressed an interest in painting her. Patrick layered on the charm: 'Sutherland has painted Churchill . . . Lord Beaverbrook . . . Somerset Maugham, but never a strong woman.' That did the trick. They went to London where Boris Forter made his customary fuss of the still-subdued Madame while Ceska nervously hovered in the wings, retreating to her favourite place, the seat by the high desk of the salon cash register in Grafton Street, where, Patrick observed, 'she looked like the rich owner of a flourishing delicatessen, tastefully dressed and jewelled, checking the receipts while nibbling on a pastrami sandwich'.

Helena first met Graham and Kathy Sutherland over lunch at their house in West Malling. They discussed the portrait, leaving the fee to be dealt with by Boris. The preliminary drawings were done in her suite at Claridges, where she sat enthroned on cushions, wearing her soon to be famous jewelled, red Balenciaga dress, her feet propped up on a complete set of London telephone directories. With the perception of all great portrait painters, Sutherland would later observe to Patrick about his memories of Madame:

> In many ways she was to me a real mystery woman . . . there was a good deal of talk about her youth. She asked me a lot of questions . . . made remarks about people . . . but was, for the most part, monosyllabic. We talked about Marie Cuttoli . . . about Marie Louise Bousquet . . . she spoke a lot about the business and how few people she could trust. But I have an acute 'sense' of her presence – even now – of the contained energy burning away behind the stillness. I sensed that she was suspicious of people and, in a curious way, even distrustful of herself – of her taste perhaps. My impression was strong in thinking that neither pictures, furniture nor objects meant more to her than a foil for her electric, contained and strong vitality. She had fallen you will remember and the blue-black of the bruises on her face might well have been maquillage! It was on the second visit that I discovered what to do, because at the time I was able to observe her buying – and bargaining – over a table-full of costume jewellery by the gross and I drew her, unaware of my presence, in her Balenciaga dress, looking like an empress . . . showing that rare, almost deprecating, but *enchanting* smile; it gave me the material in which I was able to work. She was, in a word – magnificent – minute and monosyllabic, with the force of an Egyptian ruler. She had a good many self-doubts and half-yearnings for some other life, half-glimpsed, which enabled her to say, 'I could do without all my money. If I were suddenly poor again, I could live perfectly happily.'

Madame was indeed badly bruised when she first sat for Sutherland. In a frantic rush to lose a few pounds ('I don't want to look *fet*,' said Helena) she had taken half a bottle of castor oil, several senna pills, hot grapefruit juice and vast quantities of strong black coffee. Not unsurprisingly, this assault on her system caused her to faint and she had fallen heavily, bruising her face, which she artfully painted out with as much make-up as possible. The shadows and lines, wrinkles and crinkles in the portrait of 'Madame Helena Rubinstein by Graham Sutherland' were laid bare for the world to see and observed by queues of people when it was exhibited at the Tate Gallery to great acclaim.

The moment Helena first viewed the result was a memorable one. Two portraits were propped against a wall at framer Alfred Hecht's workshops in the King's Road. The Sutherlands had tactfully retreated to Venice, leaving Madame, surrounded by a coterie including Patrick, Boris Forter, Ceska, Miss Simmons, the London publicity and advertising manager, and Eric Garrott, the firm's advertising consultant, to see the results. Sutherland had painted Madame both sitting and standing. She sat down abruptly when she saw them and her first words were to ask for a strong cup of tea. She probably thought the end of her world had come. Her first reaction was, 'I look so old . . . so savage . . . like a witch!' Assured by the group that the paintings were magnificent, she rallied enough to host a party a few weeks later at the London salon to show the portraits, attended by the Sutherlands, Douglas Cooper, the Artur Rubinsteins and Lord and Lady Hambleden amongst others. By the time the publicity from the Tate showing appeared, filling an entire filing cabinet in her New York office, she had mellowed about the portraits. She was flattered when she heard that the Queen and the Queen Mother had visited the Tate, and even more so when Lord Beaverbrook bought the standing portrait to hang in his gallery in New Brunswick, Canada, although Helena muttered that 'no one will see it up there' and grumbled about the costs of the sittings, especially as she had given the Balenciaga dress to Kathy Sutherland.

Clearly stung by the barrage of favourable publicity about Sutherland's painting, Miss Arden commissioned Simon Elwes to paint her portrait. She took him to the Four Seasons, along with Sir Victor and Lady Sassoon, their party of six, half-a-dozen of her closest inner circle of staff and Prince Aly Khan, who arrived, as always, dreadfully late but so full of good-humoured apologies that everyone forgave him. The relationship with Simon Elwes got off to a good start. 'I wore the red and white Nina Ricci dress and Mr Elwes is very charming and amusing,' Elizabeth told her sister. The second sitting went well too, but by the third she was changing her mind. 'I do not like the way he is doing it. He is putting in so much of the furniture that I look *totally* lost in the middle,' she grumbled. It got worse.

'Yet *another* portrait sitting. This is very exhausting. I am really quite tired of it.' Two weeks later she was still complaining. 'These sittings seem to go on for ever, I just wish Mr Elwes would *finish* this picture. I can't bear it anyway.' She loathed the final result. Elwes had a frame made in London, but there were no exhibitions of his portrait. The picture was never shown, and has not been seen since.

As the decade drew to a close, Madame travelled to Israel, establishing an art pavilion in Tel Aviv, contributing half of the $250,000 costs of the building, and, in a reciprocal arrangement, opening a factory. She lunched with Golda Meir and dined with David Ben-Gurion. She took a special stand, at considerable expense, at the American Exhibition in Moscow, travelling to Russia with Patrick, Mala and another essential companion – her full-time nurse.

Both Miss Arden and Madame Rubinstein struggled to come to terms with the exploding youth market and what the sweeping trends that influenced its growth meant to their business. In America 13,000,000 teenagers had, on average, $10 a week of disposable income, whilst it was calculated that Britain's 5,000,000 teenagers had a combined income of £8,000,000 a year to spend. They bought records – especially the new seven-inch EPs – and portable record players. They craved the new 'stereo' sound launched that year. They bought transistor radios, bicycles, cigarettes and . . . cosmetics.

There hadn't been much on the line at Rubinstein and Arden to tempt the fashion-conscious young, other than a rather violent package of hair dyes put out by Rubinstein Inc which, ironically, became a craze amongst a group of young Americans she vaguely knew were called beatniks. The Beat Generation, scornful of the consumerism of the Eisenhower decade, adored Alan Ginsberg's *Howl!* and read Jack Kerouac's *On the Road* while listening to cool jazz by Miles Davis. They dyed their hair white blonde or inky black, and swarmed to buy mascara and eyeliner, layering it on with a heavy hand. Their lips, however, were pale, even dead-white, more likely to be rubbed with Max Factor's Pan Stick or Miner's pearlised lip-shine than Rubinstein or Arden's rich pinks, reds and oranges. Cinema audiences were dropping as young people watched TV and flocked to coffee bars and jazz clubs.

As far as Miss Arden was concerned, however, her place in the cosmetics firmament was secure and she was given awards and honours galore in the 1950s, including the Lighthouse Award from the New York Association for the Blind for her 'enlightened policy of sub-contracting work to blind people'. She was awarded the Women's National Republican Club Presidential Campaign Award of Merit and invited to Canada for the dedication of the Dalziel Pioneer Park, planting a tree on the site of her childhood home in Woodbridge. The award that gave her most pleasure was the Grand Coupe d'Or (the Gold Cup) from the Comité du Bon Goût Française for her 1950s hit fragrance, Memoire Cherie. She hosted lavish parties in Paris and New York to celebrate her prize, the first time it had been awarded to an American woman. Madame didn't win any awards, but got a satisfying bonus when her share price rocketed from $39 to $49 – on false rumours that she had made a deal with Revlon to take over her company.

Elizabeth fussed over Patricia Nixon when the vice president's wife came into the New York salon to buy clothes designed by Count Sarmi (who had made her gown for the 1956 inauguration), and she fussed over the press release she issued when she fired Count Sarmi in January 1959, having heard he was planning to set up on his own. 'I am just horrified at such underhand behaviour when I have done so much for him, but at any rate, I am thankful to get rid of him,' she wrote. She didn't care for Mr Rockefeller's inauguration at Albany – 'There was such a crowd at the reception we couldn't even get in, and the ball in the evening was terribly crowded with lots of *dreadful* people.' Anxious to find a buyer for her fashion floor, Elizabeth tried to persuade Carmel Snow, by now pensioned off from *Harper's Bazaar*, to choose models at the Paris shows that would tempt her wealthy and largely traditional clientele.

Elizabeth carried on her weekly ritual of lunching with the power ladies of the press, although now it was Jessica Davies at *Vogue* and Nancy White (Tom White's daughter) at *Harper's Bazaar*, frequenting her favourite restaurants, the Côte Basque, the Colony, the Baroque, '21' and the Pavillon (where the maître d' ensured her table was far enough away from Charles Revson's to avoid sightline problems). She was always accompanied by one of her 'ladies', either her niece Patty, the well-connected Julia Lowell who ran the Arden fashion floor, or Mme Dendrammis, the wife of the Greek Consul General in New York, who had a job of amorphous assistant to Miss Arden. It's said that Elizabeth so terrified the poor woman that she took to popping into church on her way to work to pray for a peaceful day.

These women took on the role of ladies-in-waiting, rarely speaking, but nodding in agreement and being polite and ready to receive Elizabeth's cue to get up and leave, knowing her patient chauffeur Charles Noble would have the Bentley purring outside.

Having a good pedigree was still an essential for women wanting to join the Elizabeth Arden hierarchy. The Roman Princess Sciarra, for example, was recruited to work as 'international assistant' to Gladys, commuting to New York for the Arden fashion shows and ensuring her smart Italian friends supported Arden's initiatives in Rome and Milan. Elizabeth was also supportive to old friends, even though no longer part of her life, instructing Teddy Haslam to send £5000 to Maria de Gramont, now living in genteel poverty in the South of France. 'I still feel so sorry for her,' Elizabeth scrawled at the bottom of the note. She invited Maria's grandsons, Patrice and George, both living in New York, to suppers and parties. Surrounding herself with young people was one way the seventy-seven-year-old could feel young herself.

For friends — and relatives — who had spurned her, there was no sympathy. 'Patty's father is ill in Berlin,' she noted in her diary about her own brother Willie, later recording, 'Received a cable to say Patty's father died in Germany. Gladys is there with him.' His treachery had cut so deep, she couldn't even bear to mention his name. Her ex-husband's name was never mentioned either, although he was still vaguely working in the cosmetics industry. Angus McCall met him one night, drinking in the 'Old King Cole' bar at the St Regis in New York. 'He seemed a very personable fellow, actually, well-mannered and full of life,' said Angus. Knowing she never wanted to hear the name Lewis again, McCall discreetly forgot to inform her that their new chemist in London was called . . . Mr Lewis.

As social as ever, Elizabeth still delighted in attending balls and taking up her box at the Philharmonic. As usual, Elizabeth Arden Inc was a generous sponsor, supporting the influential Kips Bay Ball in New York and the 1959 new season's performance at the Boston Opera, giving a fashion show afterwards at the Ritz Carlton Hotel which she noted was 'very successful but my only complaint was that they served domestic, rather than imported champagne. It doesn't do.' She went to the 'April in Paris' Ball sitting with the Duke and Duchess of Windsor, escorted as usual by Elsa Maxwell, who by this stage was joined at the hip to the Windsors, along with the very social Mrs Winston 'C.Z.' Guest.

May and June that year meant her usual trip to Europe, where she went to London, Paris, Zurich, Berlin, Rome, Milan and back to England for the Derby, where she filled the Arden box, playing host to Sir Victor and Lady Sassoon amongst others. On Elizabeth's return, just as on Helena's, there was a party of office executives waiting to greet her, regardless as to what time her flight arrived. The Idlewilde Airport photographer, a news-service photographer and a staff photographer would join the throng and she would always be presented with flowers.

In June 1959, Miss Arden attended a lunch hosted by her PR consultant Count Rasponi at the Colony for journalist Constance Woodworth who had written a favourable story in the *Journal American*. Miss Woodworth captivated the lonely Elizabeth, who took to gifting her clothes and inviting her to dinner and the opera, often extending the invitation to Woodworth's lover of the time, Serge Obolensky.

Elizabeth Arden spent New Year's Eve of 1959 at a party hosted by Leslie Combs and his wife in Kentucky. She didn't feel well and left early. It was her birthday and she was seventy-eight years old. As midnight struck, the insomniac Elizabeth would still have been awake, resting fitfully in her white, satin-covered bed, tired and alone.

Helena Rubinstein spent the New Year holiday at her house in Greenwich. She spent most of the time writing memos, including one particularly sharp one to David Ogilvy and her executives supposedly in charge of creative activity: I would be obliged if, once and for all, our packaging design did not resemble Revlon, because we lose and they gain by it. I would really be sorry to think that our organisation does not have any taste or originality of its own. Our packaging should bear our own stamp, as should our handwriting.

Madame Rubinstein

CHAPTER TWENTY-THREE

LAST ACTS
1960–1962

I know what wages Beauty gives
How hard a life her servant lives

—W.B. Yeats

BOTH MADAME RUBINSTEIN AND Miss Arden will have remarked with glee at Charles Revson's embarrassment when *The $64,000 Question* became embroiled in the great quiz show scandals of the late 1950s. Producers were accused of rigging questions and feeding answers to the winners before the shows went on air. Even President Eisenhower got swept up in the criticism, calling the furore 'a whole mess' and demanding an inquiry. Charles denied any knowledge of such things, explaining to the Congressional House subcommittee investigation that his brother Martin had been in charge of the show. Flanked by one of the most expensive lawyers in America, Charles and Martin struggled to cope with the committee questions.

Charles was asked, 'You made a lot more from these shows than any of the contestants, didn't you?' He replied, 'Yes, we did.' He was then asked, 'Since you have branded these as deceitful practices, have you made any efforts or thought of any way to make restitution of that money to the American people?'

Charles Revson looked blank for a second or two, presumably caught on the hop, trying to understand if this meant he had to give customers refunds on their lipsticks. 'I would not truthfully know how to answer that question, sir,' he said, wincing as it was made quite clear that, in Washington at least, they felt the Revson brothers had profited from the racket, for which Shirley

Bernstein – Leonard's sister – as associate producer, took most of the responsibility. *If* Martin knew what was going on, Charles would have known too. Possibly not from a face-to-face meeting, as by the time the hearings took place, the two men were barely on speaking terms. Martin had left the Revlon Corporation in 1958 and, just a few months after the Congressional hearings in 1959, would cause more embarrassment to his brother by suing the company, claiming he was owed over $600,000, and delighting in informing the press about the harassment employees received at Revlon. The ensuing family rift was fierce. 'Brother? What brother? I don't have a brother,' Charles was heard to remark, just as when Elizabeth Arden's own brother died, she had said to her assistant, 'My sister's brother died yesterday.' Neither Revson nor Arden allowed rejection in their lives.

Charles, however, knew everything that was going on, in and out of the business. Such was his paranoia about the competition, and employee loyalty – plus his chief of security was an ex-FBI agent – that the Revlon Corporation had long been known to operate a system of wire-tapping. By the time Revlon was answering questions about the quiz show scandals, everyone had got used to the faint clickings on their company telephone lines, which would continue while Charles Revson was in control. Some tongue-in-cheek senior executives would lean down under their desks and call out, 'Can you hear me OK, Charles?' and when the company vacated the 666 building, janitors found a maze of wires behind panels. In the end, 'bugging' became as much part of Charles Revson's persona as Mrs Lauder's social climbing was of hers.

Stories had been rife about the tapping since 1955, when so many complaints had been registered about 'industrial espionage' between the cosmetics companies that New York State had set up special 'wire-tapping hearings'. The investigation into 'the illegal interception of communications' had been triggered by Hazel Bishop accusing both Revlon and Toni of spying on them, followed by Coty – by then part of Pfizer Inc – taking out an action against Revlon, claiming it 'had appropriated and used for its own purposes much of the advertising material used by Coty'. The Hazel Bishop management called in *über* wire-tapping expert Charles B. Gris to check their equipment; he found several bugs in place and testified on their behalf. Panic set in at several other cosmetics company head offices, where they realised they might have been vulnerable to the insatiable desire of competition to know what their rivals were up to.

At the early hearings, Revlon admitted staff calls were monitored, maintaining that the practice made for 'better service and staff relations'. George Beck, a flashy employee of a dubious nature, 'took the rap' for the wire taps, presumably being well rewarded for his pains. (Not that his wealth did him much good – Beck was later found murdered with wife number five, naked on their luxury motorboat.) At Helena Rubinstein, checks were made to see if bugs had been planted, as she would have put nothing past 'the nail man' when it came to stealing her ideas. Helena always operated her own system of internal security. When she was on the telephone, she would have someone else listen in on the extension as a witness. Madame would never have put in a system of wire taps, though – she would have blanched at the cost, and although Helena always grumbled that the competition were copying her, she never filed any formal suits, nor did Elizabeth Arden.

Elizabeth was altogether unconcerned about wire-tapping. One of her friends was J. Edgar Hoover himself, and they would sip cocktails together at the Stork Club, Hoover's favourite watering hole when he was in New York. She sent him vast Christmas boxes of Arden for Men, for which she always got a charming reply. Given Hoover's sexual inclinations he might have preferred Elizabeth Arden products, but Miss Arden clung to convention. Hoover, who wrote to her as 'my dear Elizabeth', enthused about her violent anti-Communist stance – she was very vocal on the subject – and had there been the slightest possibility that her offices or homes were bugged, he would have tipped her off and had them swept clean. It's said it was J. Edgar Hoover who so loathed Eleanor Roosevelt that he had started the rumour she was a lesbian, based in part on her friendship with Bessie Marbury, about whose sexual preferences Hoover was in no doubt. Hoover was also reported to be responsible for initiating the rumours about Adlai Stevenson's homosexuality during the 1952 elections, when Elizabeth had voiced the same opinion to Lord Montagu of Beaulieu. Hoover knew where all the skeletons were buried and if he chose to ignore Elizabeth's own friendship with Marbury, it was because it suited his purposes to do so. The very public anti-Communist pro-Republican stance taken by Miss Arden, one of America's most influential and wealthy businesswomen, kept her much more useful to J. Edgar Hoover than any debate over her long-dead friend.

As the 1960s started, and the stakes in the beauty game became ever higher, it's no wonder that Charles Revson wanted to know what his competition was up to. All the major companies watched their rivals like hawks.

They panicked if they heard a better product was on the line and all of them, in one form or another, copied each other. When Arden launched Veiled Radiance, Revlon brought out Sheer Radiance. When Revlon bought out a remarkably good lipstick called Futurama, Miss Arden sent her secretary to the pharmacy at the St Regis Hotel to buy three of them for analysis. Madame went one further. She so admired the product that she tried to get around the patent and produce something similar. 'Charles was *really* annoyed about that,' recalls Grace Gilbert, who moved from Revlon to Rubinstein, where she advised on packaging and display, in the 1960s. Grace was brought into Rubinstein by her ex-boss, Peter Ripps, who had joined from Revlon in the late 1950s. After working for both Hattie Carnegie and Revlon, she was a valuable asset at Rubinstein, where her memories of Madame, by 1960 frail but still feisty, are interesting. 'I saw an elderly woman, desperately trying to hold her own,' says Grace, 'surrounded by the proverbial Hollywood type of in-fighting family vultures. But she was still a woman who knew what buttons to push.'

The big issue for the cosmetics companies was the emerging trend for 'singing the sweet sound of science' to promote treatment creams. In an innovative trade presentation in 1960, American merchandising and advertising expert George J. Abrams, president of the Hudnut-DuBarry division of Warner-Lambert, entranced his audience by talking about developments in European skin care, in particular treatment creams using placenta, hormones, marine algae, polyunsaturates and other petroleum derivatives. Mr Abrams called such products 'charmaceuticals', describing them as a heady mix of pharmaceuticals and charm and explaining they 'plead for instruction which gives the department stores a virtual exclusive on their sale'. He meant that the cosmetics halls of major stores, by this time emerging as 'theatres of retailing', where a captive audience was in the hands of trained, uniformed and authoritative demonstrators, were the territory for these products to be nurtured and developed. The unique selling point of 'charmaceuticals' was their scientific edge, giving an aura of quasi-medicinal expertise. The independent pharmacy, run by people who actually knew about medicines, but which relied on goods in display cases, was not the natural setting for the dynamics of this revolution in skin care. At a stroke, manufacturers branding such products were able to charge premium prices.

The allure of creams was an intense one. 'The consumer,' says Grace Gilbert, 'was ready to be *enticed* with treatment products. Women's hopes rest in creams. For a cosmetics company, treatment creams represented then, as now, profits and long-term loyalty.' During the next few years, Elizabeth Arden brought out Crème Extraordinaire which advertising copy said, 'protects and re-directs'; Revlon promised their Ultima Cream would 'penetrate into the living cells'; Cosmetics Biotherm put out a product promoted as 'containing plankton, primal organisms in the living water of the earth'. Estée Lauder put out Re-Nutriv created to tilt head-to-head with the French Orlane company's B-21 which didn't just sound like a jet, it cost nearly as much to run as one, retailing at $75 for two-and-a-half ounces. Helena Rubinstein launched Deep Pore Bio Facial Cleanser and launched yet another hormone-based cream, this time called Ultra-Feminine Face Cream. The advertisement for this product showed Helena in a jewelled gown standing by a statue of Venus de Milo, the message being that great age imbued scientific wisdom, which, in turn, created great beauty. Whether the image of a rather fierce nearly ninety-year-old lady was the greatest asset to a campaign targeted at 40-something women wasn't up for debate. Madame liked it and no one dared argue.

Fragrance was also by now a valuable commercial product. When a fragrance was launched in the 1950s, along with perfume in a bottle and a 'hand-bag atomiser' came eau-de-toilette, solid perfume sticks, dusting powder in a fancy tub with a big swansdown puff, bath foam, boxes of bath cubes, jars of bath salts, tissue-wrapped soaps and bottles of hand and body lotion, all with the same scent. These products often came boxed in 'coffret cases', often quilted, embossed, richly coloured, sometimes even jewelled. They were an 'easy' gift, and if a fragrance took off, as had Arden's Blue Grass and Memoire Cherie, and to a lesser extent Rubinstein's Apple Blossom and Heaven Sent, it was a lucrative addition to the creams and colour cosmetics.

In 1960, Madame was planning to launch a fragrance called L'Affaire. Patrick was dispatched to Paris, with instructions to buy paintings by French artists to the budget of $10,000. 'That's ten pictures at $1000 a picture, Patrick,' came the plaintive message from Jack van Zandt, merchandise manager in New York, anxious about budgets for the sales promotion involving the paintings going on exhibition in department stores. 'The company would definitely prefer to retain ownership of the paintings after they have been used for publicity. Please investigate the possibility of having inexpensive prints made of the actual paintings. We would like to send these prints to the store buyers with Madame Rubinstein's letter announcing the introduction of our new fragrance line. All these materials will, of course, be sent out from Paris. Please get prices for 2000 prints of each and be sure to give Madame Rubinstein's best regards to all the artists.'

Whilst Helena wasn't on that particular promotional trip, it was still one of her great pleasures to spend time with artists. One journalist, who accompanied Madame to appointments whilst conducting an interview with her in Paris, wrote about spending time with the woman he described as 'the ageless little monarch'. He went with her to the studio of Camille Bombois, a well-known naif painter, then in his eighties. Bombois broke open a bottle of champagne whilst explaining to Madame that 'nothing was for sale'. His arms stiff with rheumatism, the artist who had been honoured for his bravery in the First World War and who had at one time been a circus strongman, then offered her a picture for $6000. 'Too expensive,' reported Helena, whereupon haggling took place, with Bombois refusing to compromise. The reporter left the studio with an empty-handed Helena, yet noted she was happy with her afternoon, despite the loss of a picture she had clearly hoped to buy.

Patrick's post brought him a letter from Sara Fox, alarmed at the wide scope of his brief. In case he had any doubts about her authority to instruct him, she wrote: 'I have been commissioned, after conferring with Mr Ripps, Mr Ogilvy, all the copywriters at the agency, all the copywriters here, *and* Mr van Zandt, to convey to you our combined thoughts with respect to the direction you should give to the young painters selected in connection with the launching of L'Affaire next season.' Clearly rattled by the name of the fragrance, Miss Fox said:

As you know, L'Affaire has a very strong sex connotation in this country, being almost synonomous with having a love affair . . . While it was our deliberate decision to choose a name with sex implications, because Americans are prudish concerning sex, we do *not* want the visual aspects to emphasise in any way any illicit or illegal inferences . . . We are seeking to portray L'Affaire as . . . being for a woman who should be able to see herself as either a wife, mother, sweetheart, mistress or seductress . . . we must ensure no tawdriness or overt sex insinuations creep into the whole presentation. Mr Ripps thought you should not even *mention* the name to the painters . . . we must have *no* nudes and no obvious sex situations. If you need any further elucidation, let me know.

Poor Patrick was sent running around in Paris, attempting to satisfy the bizarre brief from New York to keep sexual imagery out of a perfume called L'Affaire, when a few months later the birth control pill was launched in a blaze of international publicity proclaiming that 'women were now in total control of their own sexual freedom'. The fact that the Rubinstein company diverted so much attention to ensure L'Affaire was understood by both mothers and daughters, the nice *and* the naughty, only goes to show how much they had lost their way with what consumers and retailers were craving. Retailers wanted a strong, glamorous, sexy image to come through in every aspect of the product, from packaging to advertising. This was Revlon's forte, but sadly not Rubinstein's. L'Affaire bombed. This was a worry for the Rubinstein board, some of whom were getting alarmed about declining prestige store sales. The brand was a powerful presence in the smarter pharmacies and drug-store trade, but increasingly less visible at Bonwit's or I. Magnin. For what it was worth, Revlon were also suffering. *The $64,000 Question* had unleashed consumer sales at the lower end, but dented what Charles craved most, his reputation at Saks Fifth Avenue.

In an attempt to regain the high ground, to the astonishment of Miss Arden and Madame Rubinstein who were struggling with the costs of running such establishments, Charles Revson entered the luxury beauty salon business. The Revlon salon, opened in 1960, was something to behold. The actual development costs were well hidden from the stockholders, but they were reputed to be astronomical. The salon was on the second floor of the Gotham Hotel on 55th St and Fifth Avenue and, from the beginning, was fraught with problems. The fixtures were so heavy that the floors had to be strengthened. The glass doors were so heavy the ladies couldn't push them open. The sunken 'Pompei-marble' whirlpool bath was so large it took twenty minutes and 196 gallons of scented water to fill it. The pool was so deep there was a real threat clients might drown, so a maid-cum-lifeguard was on duty all the time. As it had to be cleaned after each session, it meant milk baths, salt baths or sulphur water baths were restricted to six each day, instead of the projected dozen. Ladies dressed in a Balmain robe on arrival (Revlon signed the franchise to distribute Balmain fragrance in the US) and put on gold plastic slippers. The coffee cups and saucers were so pretty that clients were known to slip them into their handbags, and once a set of gold taps in the bathroom were wrenched off and stolen.

Telephone jacks were littered around for clients to take personal calls. There was a kennels for their dogs. The six male, and apparently quite temperamental, hairdressers who all wore navy suits and ties *à la* Charles Revson – a deeply conservative dresser – used brass lacquered hairdryers which descended from recessed nests in the ceiling. The trouble was, their descent was quite likely to decapitate a client, so the stylists left them dangling most of the day, rather spoiling the effect Charles had wanted. The lighting for the boutique, hairdressing salon and treatment rooms was done by the designer who handled New York's Philharmonic Hall; nevertheless it was a mess. Generators broke down. Staff stormed out. The salon, naturally, offered credit accounts. On one memorable occasion a bill was sent to the right address – the wife's house – but in the wrong name, that of the mistress, which caused an uproar. Boris Forter in London would *never* have let such a thing happen, having a great respect for mistresses, whilst at Arden's London salon the awesome Miss Sallis, who had exercised total control in the accounts department for nearly forty years, rarely extended credit for more than twenty days without extracting a cheque, so brutally efficient was her department.

The Revlon salon tottered on for twelve years, costing an absolute fortune, until Charles washed his hands of it. Grace Gilbert says about the folly, 'It was the period when Charles was reaching out to show the world he had good taste and he was willing to buy it.' Well, he failed. Madame observed the salon in its early days when, back from Europe, she drove past with Patrick. 'Why, you naughty boy,' she said, 'you didn't tell me the nail man had built his own mausoleum.'

With Madame nudging ninety and Miss Arden seventy-nine, it might be presumed they were thinking of their own mausoleums, but they both felt they were immortal. Death was something Elizabeth rarely discussed, although from time to time someone would mention death to her. Her lawyers reminded her about her will, accountants would mumble about taxes and death duties, and occasionally a wholesale client would raise the subject, thinking about continuity of the brand. She ignored them all. One such brave man was Stanley Marcus. Neiman Marcus had the Arden line exclusively in Dallas; Mr Marcus says, 'It was a valuable franchise to preserve, so we were constantly at her mercy.' One day, he asked her about plans for the future. 'Death', he would later write, 'was a subject Miss Arden refused to contemplate and any reference to it met with icy silence. I'm confident that she was convinced she would never die, but would merely pass on into a Blue Grass-scented heaven, anointed by Eight Hour Cream.'

When those she knew died, Elizabeth was able to put their passing out of her mind quite quickly. However, as her dearest friends, family and long-term staff died, a small part of 'Florence Graham' died with them, even if Elizabeth Arden seemed to continue. She was upset to hear her cousin, Edith Tadd Little, was dying with cancer, sending $1000 to her family to help with expenses. The death of Miss O'Leary, one of her oldest treatment specialists, moved her to note, 'One more gone who was with me in the early days.' Her sister Lillian – Lollie – died, as did her niece Beattie. She grieved when her friend Prince Aly Khan died in a car crash, but nothing, absolutely nothing, affected her more than the death in early 1962 of Teddy Haslam. Her dear, devoted Teddy, who had been with her since 1921, was gone. She was devastated, flying to London immediately to attend the funeral at Putney Vale, where, according to Angus McCall, 'She took total prece-dence over everyone there, running the whole show.' Although her own health was deteriorating, Miss Arden was a fighter and despite several trips to hospital, including time spent in Lenox Hill suffering with kidney stones and pneumonia, she continued her routine and remarkable travel pro-gramme as though nothing was troubling her.

Elizabeth remained generous to old friends in need. When Maria de Gramont contracted inflammation of the lungs, Elizabeth invited her to rest at Maine Chance in Phoenix. The idea was that Maria would 'help out' in looking after clients, play bridge with them and give talks about history of art, but she was too ill and spent several weeks there in bed, too weak even to join Elizabeth in New York for a special dinner for Sir Victor and Lady Sassoon. Elizabeth didn't trust the skills of her temporary cook, so had Mr Kriendler at 21 send over a large carton of their sauce béarnaise to go with the steaks. Talk at dinner was about Mr Nixon and how he was doing in the fight against John Kennedy. The answer was, of course, not very well. 'I was not at all impressed,' Miss Arden remarked about a breakfast rally she had attended. 'He will *have* to do better.'

It wasn't just friends who benefited from Elizabeth's largesse, she extended it to a wide circle of acquaintances. When Elsa Maxwell was in the midst of one of her regular financial *crises*, involving a rather messy court case in Florida, Miss Arden came to her rescue with cash. By now, Elizabeth had adopted a talented Hollywood-based interior designer called Tony Duquette as one of her special favourites. Duquette had learned his craft in the visual display department of the speciality store Bullocks Wilshire, where he designed sets for Adrian, the king of Hollywood's fashion designers. He had been a devoted friend of Elsie de Wolfe, and kept Elizabeth in tune with gossip, prodding her from time to time to do favours for old – and still perhaps useful – friends.

Miss Arden had started 1960 extremely ill in Kentucky with pneumonia and, frustrated that she was unwell, hit out at everybody. She got through three horse trainers in as many months, fired two maids and two secretaries, and berated Leslie Combs for supposedly supplying her horse farm with inferior feed. 'I've seen the feed the horses are getting from Leslie's farm and it's just chaff,' she complained.

Madame hadn't been at all well herself in the summer of 1960 and was resting in Switzerland when she received a bundle of letters from New York which undid all the good of her treatment. Summoning a secretary from the Zurich office to her bedside, she fired off letters to Oscar Kolin, David Ogilvy, Sara Fox and her assistant Helen Wieselberg, Peter Ripps, Patrick and anyone else she could think of. The focus of Madame's wrath was the autumn campaign for one of Rubinstein's most popular and lucrative products, Mascara-Matic. Helena had bought the company some years before and developed the mascara wands quite painstakingly. Hers was the prototype 'roll-on' mascara and the product had been much copied. Ogilvy, Mather and Benson had produced an ad called 'Dancing Eyes' designed to launch a new series of *eleven* mascara colours, with a budget of over $140,000 and production costs of around $60,000, to be placed in glossy American magazines, the *New Yorker* and various newspapers. Helena had caught a glimpse of the layouts before she left New York, but when she saw the finished product she became incandescent with rage.

'When I saw the photostat for the ad "Dancing Eyes" I had a terrible shock,' Madame wrote to Miss Wieselberg. 'I have been forced to cancel it . . . had you explained this was to be a national campaign I would have turned it down. I did not realise there was so little copy and what there is, truly, is *meaningless.*' She berated Oscar, 'Every time I come to Europe, it seems something goes wrong with our advertising in New York and literally breaks my heart. How *could* everyone in New York permit such an ad? This is throwing money away in the most senseless fashion . . . the picture is ugly . . . the ad says nothing . . . the copy is zero . . . we are just playing into the hands of our competitors.' Sara Fox did little better. 'I truly hate to have to write this letter to you . . . but I think that it is a disgrace. How can we run such a flimsy, meaningless ad? The copy does not advance *any* new ideas or arguments. Twenty years ago, it would have been old-fashioned. Now, it is a tragic confession that we have nothing new to offer. I refuse to run "Dancing Eyes". If we have nothing better to say, then use the intelligent fear angle. Open women's eyes to the problem of caring for their eyes while embellishing them. Tell them *nothing* will show their age more than bad eye make-up!' She ripped into Mr Ripps: 'I have not slept since I saw the ad . . . I am not only concerned that our agency has produced such a trivial, old-fashioned and ugly ad, I am alarmed because this is further proof of lack of foresight on the part of *all of you* in New York.'

Madame saved her strongest complaints for David Ogilvy. 'If you cannot devise a good eye campaign, stay out of it altogether until we have something more worthwhile. You must push your people to greater effort . . . we must, since we have limited budgets and our competitors don't, break our heads to create something new . . . I know the skin better than anyone else and the skin around the eyes is most sensitive. Our products don't just embellish . . . they protect. Many colours are harmful to the eyes, that is why we have fewer, but they are all scientifically tested and we only use the best raw ingredients. [*Colourings used in cosmetics are universal, some causing more irritation than others. It is also the preservative in mascara that causes reactions in many cases.*] Please take a greater interest in what your agency does for us. I am surprised that you approved this ad. I am sad to have to write this letter . . . it is not to your credit.'

Sara Fox was the only one who stood up to Madame, writing, 'I am somewhat disappointed you cancelled the pages because you promised me before you left that you would *not* cancel any ads but would make comments for the future . . . I feel sure that if you see the final ad in full colour, you will agree it is *very* beautiful and will maintain our sales . . . It was considered by everyone that we do a fashionable and exciting presentation in order not to lose our customers to the other *fourteen* competitors at the last count that we now have.' Miss Fox had already tried to explain that times were changing faster than their product and their budgets, noting her concern about sliding department store business. 'It is necessary for us to bring out an interesting new product for department stores every six months at a price that is of interest to the better stores . . . we should certainly be able to afford *one* knowledge-able person who would think of nothing but top store business.'

At about this time, Estée Lauder, who thought of nothing *but* top store business, had really started to make her mark. The first luxury store outside New York she had tackled was Neiman Marcus, the fiefdom of Elizabeth Arden. Stanley Marcus remembers Lauder arriving to see him. 'She came swinging into the store like Sugar Ray Robinson,' he said, 'with vitality and a sense of urgency.' She didn't argue with her advertising advisers about pages, for the simple reason that she didn't have an agency. She didn't have the budget for colour either – even in the early 1960s there were only a dozen or so people on her staff – so she produced wonderfully elegant images in black and white, shot by Victor Skrebneski. Miss Arden countered by approving a superb campaign from her new agency, Trahey Advertising, with aristocratic overtones, shot in Kentucky and featuring subtle refer-ences to her horses, with lipstick colours like Saratoga Red. By the mid-1960s, Mrs Lauder had signed with AC&R (part of Ted Bates) whilst Revlon switched agencies relentlessly. When Batten, Barton, Durstine & Osborne had lost the Revlon account, worth $8,000,000 to the agency in 1957, *Time* reported the Executive Vice President as saying, 'I'm not weep-ing,' and described Charles Revson as the most 'feared, cheered and jeered advertising client' on Madison Avenue. Revlon got through nine agencies chewing up more than a hundred account executives in the process, over thirteen years, firing one – not unreasonably perhaps – because he had dirty fingernails.

Charles continued to be a scourge to magazine publishers, demanding his ads came first in the book – at the very least before his competitors. He wanted inside covers. He wanted back covers. He wanted Revlon cosmetics credits on fashion spreads. Eventually one publishing group, the mighty Hearst, found the courage to say Revlon couldn't come first in *every* issue – other clients were complaining. Revson replied that he would pull all his advertising. In the end, the harassed publisher negotiated that if Revlon advertised in black and white, they would come first. When Revlon had a colour page, it would be the first colour page, but other cosmetics ads in black and white could come first. As Revlon wasn't running black and white ads at the time, Charles sticking to his 'we sell colour' mantra and believing the public preferred colour pages, it didn't worry him. It should have. Mrs

Lauder only ran black and white, so her classy-looking pages opened first in *Harper's Bazaar*, where they made a big impression.

And Ogilvy Benson & Mather? In late 1963, David Ogilvy abruptly resigned the Helena Rubinstein account, which carried a $5,000,000 budget. Madame had been one of his first clients when he arrived on Madison Avenue; he had handled her account since 1950, had nurtured her son and continued looking after Rubinstein Inc when other agencies would have sought greater creative freedom elsewhere. David Ogilvy said little to the press about his resignation and his staff were forbidden to talk about it. All he would say was that 'Madame Rubinstein is a fascinating woman and I have the greatest possible admiration for her.' It was the end of an era. Revlon's advertising budget in the year Ogilvy resigned the Rubinstein account was $50,000,000 – ten times as much as Helena Rubinstein's.

For Helena, memories of people and events she had shared with Titus would come flooding back as Patrick worked on a serialisation of her life story for a London newspaper. She would have read with interest that Penguin in London were summonsed for planning to publish *Lady Chatterley's Lover*. Following their trial at the Old Bailey, when the jury voted the book wasn't 'obscene', Penguin's print run of 200,000 copies sold out on the first day of publication. 'Titus should have been so lucky,' she would have muttered to herself. Old acquaintances were dying. Ernest Hemingway in 1961, Jean Cocteau in 1963.

It was also the end of an era as far as mannered, old-money families were concerned. Even their fortunes were dwindling and the often modest, patrician members of 'old society' lacked the outward glamour of the brash, 'new-money' rich. Discreet Republicans observed the court surrounding Kennedy's bid for the White House and sighed. The so-called 'jet set', oil-millionaires, property developers, insurance salesmen, movie moguls, filmstars and Frank Sinatra's 'rat pack' were at the forefront of media attention. This crowd, along with the glitzy retailers who served them and the grand hoteliers, casino owners and restaurateurs who accommodated them, were taking precedence sponsoring charity balls, endowing buildings, parks and hospital wings and arranging debuts for their daughters. 'Celebrity' was becoming the name of the game.

When Cleveland Amory was writing *Who Killed Society?*, published with impeccable timing at the beginning of the 1960s, he called Elizabeth Arden for a quote. 'I don't think society means a thing any more,' she said.

'I've even noticed it with the horses,' meaning that the people owning, breeding and racing horses, not to mention people attending the track, were somehow becoming more flashy. The stakes were so much higher, the pace of it all unsettled her. In 1960, her Maine Chance stables made a loss of $937,100. In 1961 the losses were just over $921,000 and in 1962, over $750,000. Her heart may have been in the horses, but her health and impressive wealth were waning. Perhaps if she had retired from work at this point to concentrate on her stables she would have enjoyed her last years more. But Elizabeth couldn't contemplate retirement and travelled even more furiously. It was as though the effort kept her alive.

Just as for Miss Arden before her, for Estée Lauder, climbing the slippery slope of society was an integral part of marketing her brand and she decided early on to colonise Palm Beach as her launching pad. Palm Beach had been Miss Arden's territory for a long, long time. She still maintained an important salon there, where her manageress, Elisabeth Hockstead, masterminded the hair and beauty routines of the local rich. At one time Elizabeth had maintained a home in Palm Beach, but sold it during a financial panic at the end of the 1930s, preferring, when her horses were racing at Hialeah, to take an apartment at the Sea View Hotel in Miami. 'Mackie', the redoubtable Miss MacEwen, who had worked at the Palm Beach salon for forty years, would come down to do her facials. In Palm Beach she would stay with friends, in particular Mrs Stephen 'Laddie' Sanford. Mary Sanford was a larger-than-life character who went big-game hunting, played polo and carried a bag embroidered with the legend 'I thrive on Love, Leisure and Luxury'. Her house, 'Los Incas', was vast, Mr Sanford's wealth even more vast, and her generosity to charity bigger still.

Where for years Elizabeth Arden had hosted fashion shows and sponsored dinners, donating lavish cosmetics gifts, Estée Lauder now circled the arena like a hawk. Having moved from her first modest home in Palm Beach to a second, much more desirable property in 1964, she set about conquering the ladies' events by overwhelming them with product. Sharing Miss Arden's distaste for the sun, along with her tendency to larger than perfect thighs, Mrs Lauder was rarely to be seen in a swimsuit, preferring voluminous wraps and fussy, often veiled, hats. Also sharing Miss Arden's desire to be accepted by the 'society' she deemed so important, Mrs Lauder fought her way into Palm Beach grandee Mrs Munn and Mary Sanford's set. 'She courted me and I was flattered,' said Mrs Sanford.

'At charity events, she gave me presents . . . she was very aggressive . . . so socially aggressive.'

Mrs Lauder next set about conquering the ageing Duke and Duchess of Windsor, who always spent April, 'the little season', in Palm Beach, where the men who had made fortunes inventing some useful piece of machinery that kept America working, and their wives, who were often ex-showgirls of beauty and charisma, made a fuss of the ex-king and his 'American heroine' wife. The duchess had a fear of flying, as did Estée Lauder. Mrs Lauder, it's said, hearing that Wallis and her husband would be returning to New York by train, departing from West Palm station, booked a carriage for her husband and herself, arriving at *precisely* the same time as the Windsors. Photographers, arranged by Mrs Lauder, were at the station to record the event and the pictures of a beaming Estée, clinging to the arm of a rather pained-looking Wallis, were sent out over the wire. Estée Lauder's social pinnacle had been reached.

A few months later, Mrs Lauder was in Paris. August in Paris is a difficult time as a lot of salons and restaurants close down for the summer. She was due to dine with the Duchess of Windsor that night and had booked a hair appointment at the Elizabeth Arden salon. Unfortunately Miss Arden was upstairs at the time, going over decorating plans with Tony Duquette. When she heard who was downstairs she sent Duquette to throw Mrs Lauder out, regardless of the fact that her hair was still in rollers. Mrs Lauder left, her hair still wet and her face red.

Lunching or dining with Estée Lauder, whether in New York, Palm Beach or at her home in the South of France, was a complex affair. At her home, it was hard to find the food for the plethora of silver, crystal, linens and flowers that covered the table. Mrs Lauder was *very* keen on visual display and such opulence, even for a simple lunch, was how she liked to live. Recollecting the ostentation of Mrs Lauder's houses, Eleanor Lambert felt it was uncomfortable. 'Estée let her houses live her . . . she didn't live in them,' says Mrs Lambert. When eating out together, Estée was constantly swivelling her head to see who else was in the restaurant, so that she could table-hop and introduce herself.

Erica Titus Friedman, who lived with her second husband Bill in considerable style in Mougins, knew Estée Lauder well and often lunched with her during the 1960s. 'It was difficult for Estée to keep still,' says Erica. 'It was actually quite disconcerting lunching with her as she would bounce all over the place, particularly if she saw someone more important . . . or more useful . . . She would be saying something, but her eyes were all over the room.' Erica also knew Florence Gould, the undisputed 'queen of the Riviera' for nearly four decades, extremely well. Mrs Gould was as relentlessly pursued by Mrs Lauder as the Duchess of Windsor had been. 'Aah, yes, Florence,' says Erica, recollecting the fabulously rich, tiny blonde dynamo. 'She was a *particular* target of Estée's. I'm not entirely sure if she was as close to Estée as Estée liked to think. But you know, for all her pushing, you couldn't but help rather admire Estée Lauder. She tried too hard, but she was *very* determined.'

Whilst Miss Arden accepted the Duchess of Windsor, she was much more interested in her relationship with the 'real royals'. Angus McCall applied for her royal warrant in 1961 and at Christmas the company had to divert a full-time secretary to the task of wrapping and labelling the gifts sent to HM the Queen, the Queen Mother, Princess Margaret, Princess Alexandra, the Duchess of Kent and other ladies of the royal household. Elizabeth had a definite sense of protocol and was insistent that her London salon should close on Saturday, 30 January 1965, in honour of Winston Churchill's funeral, not merely in admiration of the man, but because his daughter, Lady Soames, was a valued client.

Elizabeth Arden was much in demand socially and delighted by it. She dined with Prime Minister Nehru of India and his daughter Mrs Indira Gandhi on their American visit in 1961, and was entertained by Prime Minister Robert Menzies of Australia on his tour to the US in 1962. She remained close to Mamie Eisenhower, who still visited Maine Chance whenever she could, and she took friends and visitors to her box at the Philharmonic. She lunched at Mrs Whitney's and dined with the Marchioness of Dufferin and Ava, and Loelia, Duchess of Westminster. There were relentless fittings for new clothes, but all too often she was wearing black, attending yet another funeral. In 1961 Carmel Snow (who had been selecting Paris couture models for the Arden collection since her retirement from *Harper's Bazaar*) died, followed by Elizabeth's close friend Constance Collier and worst of all, Maria de Gramont. 'I miss her already,' she wrote in her diary, 'she was so calm and peaceful and . . . beautiful.' She relied more and more on her public relations consultant, Count Rasponi, to escort her to parties and she was always pleased to go to the Rasponi home where their friends from Rome were fêted when in New York. 'The

Rasponis gave such a lovely cocktail party for Princess Maria Gabrielli and the Count and Countess Crespi,' Elizabeth noted in her diary.

Work filled her life, and when she felt sad, there were her horses. Every morning when she was in New York, she still went out to Belmont and most weekends she flew to Kentucky where Pat Young also spent more and more of her time, looking after the house and the horses. Yet another honour came, this time the Légion d'Honneur, which she received from the French ambassador in Washington. A few days before, she slipped and broke her wrist. Undaunted, she had a sling made in the same fabric as her satin-back coat to cover her cast. Nothing stopped her entertaining. She still hated to be alone, and filled her evening hours with guests. If she couldn't find friends, she roped in her staff, like Julia Lowell, or Florence Owens who ran her New York salon, both of whom played canasta with her long into the evening. For a woman of over eighty, she kept herself very fit, delighting in dance classes and still doing yoga, telling Diana Vreeland at lunch about a new yogi she had discovered. She also shopped for jewels, particularly pearls, treating herself to a double rope she spotted in a Parke-Bernet catalogue, and lunched from time to time with Jules Glaenzer from Cartier when he had something special to offer her.

In 1962 she did a little extra shopping. She bought picturesque Barretstown Castle outside Naas in Ireland's County Kildare. Now she was, quite literally, 'queen of the castle', complete with five-hundred acres of rolling, lush land and drifting woods, where she stabled fourteen valuable horses under the care of trainer Stuart Murless. Elizabeth paid $200,000 to buy Barretstown, bought, as so many of her extravagances, on a whim. Angus McCall recalls, 'She saw an advertisement for the property in an American magazine and called Gordy Yates asking him to give her a report.' McCall, who happened to be working in Belfast at the time, was dispatched to have a look. Passing back a favourable opinion, he was subsequently put in charge of liaison for the venture.

Over the next four years, Angus would watch as she lavished money on the castle: 'She spent a fortune on it,' he says. 'I was absolutely mesmerised by the costs, and you know, she only spent about a week or so there in the four years she owned it.' McCall had to escort Miss Arden over to Ireland, visits not without their problems. 'She had a hazy knowledge of geography to say the least,' he says. 'The first time she arrived she said, "Well, are we going over by train?" as though she imagined there was a bridge over the

Irish Sea.' Miss Arden never got to grips with Irish plumbing, having Tony Duquette, who was in charge of the décor, ship vast baths, bidets and shower fixtures from New York. 'In the end,' says McCall, 'the baths were so big and she was so small, that she had to stand on shoeboxes to get into her own bath.'

Duquette was a colourful character, and had a free hand to scour the local shops for antiques and traditional furniture, so he spent a lot of time in Ireland on his rich client's behalf. Goodness knows what the locals in the village of Ballymore Eustace thought about the flamboyant man, who was known to host parties dressed as a cardinal. 'The buying budgets', says McCall, still looking quite cross about it, 'got totally out of control. I queried what Duquette was spending with Gordy Yates, but he told me to keep well out of it and leave things alone.' Duquette, it seems, was so taken with the treasures he found in County Kildare that he had crate-loads shipped back to America, leaving McCall to reconcile the accounts and see what was for Barretstown and what was for Mr Duquette. As with all her homes, Barretstown was open to visiting friends, whether Elizabeth was in residence or not, and as always, it fell to Gordy Yates or Angus to make all the arrangements. 'I sat next to Mr Muir, the chairman of *Newsweek*, at a dinner in Washington last week,' she told Gordy, 'and he and Mrs Muir are in Ireland in August, so I want you to tell Mr Murless to expect them and to show them round Barretstown.'

Charles Revson went shopping as well in 1962. He didn't buy a castle but his purchase was a folly. The Revlon Corporation felt it appropriate that they enter the fashion business. In a move which amazed the industry, they purchased, for the vast sum of $12,000,000, the mainstream ladies' clothing manufacturer Evan Picone. Quite how Revlon felt this acquisition would enhance their up-market credibility is not clear. At any event, the project failed. Stylish women who yearned for slick lipsticks didn't feel the same way about easy-fit slacks, and four years later Charles sold Picone back to one of its original partners for just $1 million.

Revson didn't need a castle to entertain in; he would go on to buy his own palace for $3.5 million, albeit a floating one, with more guestrooms than Barretstown, not to mention sixteen bathrooms, twenty-two telephone extensions and a crew of thirty-one: his yacht, the *Ultima II*.

CHAPTER TWENTY-FOUR

THE FINAL YEARS
1960–1966

ADAME HAD HER OWN property moment in the early 1960s, buying an apartment in Ennismore Gardens in Knightsbridge, which became Ceska's London home and Helena's London base. Fleur Cowles suggested a decorator, a fashionable neighbour of hers in Albany, the elegant residence in Piccadilly – David Hicks. Hicks was a major name in interior design; he had an assured, if somewhat dictatorial hand, and had an impeccable pedigree by virtue of his marriage to Lady Pamela Mountbatten, younger daughter of Earl Mountbatten of Burma. 'Good name, good contacts,' Helena said to Patrick, 'useful, *and* he likes my colours.' He did indeed like the colour purple that Helena desired. At their first meeting, keen he remember exactly the shade she had in mind, she turned up the hem of her purple Balenciaga tweed suit and clipped off a piece.

With Madame back in New York, unwell and unable to travel, Patrick was left to co-ordinate with David Hicks, who was soon struggling with how best to display his client's eclectic collections without too much clutter. As Hicks was such a perfectionist (he left marks underneath objects he had displayed so when they were moved to be dusted, they would be put back exactly as he wished) his relationship with Madame was never going to be easy. By the end of 1960, she was tussling with his taste, writing to Patrick: 'I am honestly quite upset about the apartment . . . I know Mr Hicks could make some interesting pieces with the Chinese screens. Perhaps if you could explain everything to Mr Pallavicini he could be of help? I am really at a loss as to what to do about the apartment. Somehow I don't feel that there is anything startling about it and I fear the press won't find it of interest.' The opinion of the press as far as Madame was concerned was crucial. As her houses were where most interviews took place, she wanted them to reflect her dramatic persona. She would have been a modern interior designer's nightmare client. She needn't have worried. Her apartment, decorated in lipstick colours, attracted a lot of attention. So impressed was Boris Forter with the purple that he had the interiors of his latest, specially commissioned sports car upholstered in the same colour, describing it as 'French Violet.'

As Madame had by now reached such grand old age, she had become a source of fascination for the media. Patrick never failed to round up an interested journalist to undertake one of Madame's favoured personal interviews and the story rarely varied. She would wave a bejewelled hand expansively towards walls of paintings and pieces of sculpture and talk about her collecting. She would explain about her scientific training, she would talk about her travels and she would talk to them about their skin – usually saying it was dry and giving the writer a pot of cream: 'This is what I use, I know you will love it, take it please, try it . . . for me.' Invariably, the writers were enchanted, and invariably they wrote that she ran an empire worth $100 million, without knowing what the real figures were. Her reputation went before her: she was fabulously wealthy, feisty and frugal, and worked around the clock. Such interviews always went well, her staff in New York, should they be consulted, making the necessary sycophantic comments, murmuring obeisance about 'Madame'. She was, as had been the case for six decades, rarely out of the press.

Madame still travelled. It had become a compulsion, a way of life she couldn't change, and planning travel – keeping busy – kept her alive. Twice a year she flew to Europe. She went to Israel. She would spend a few days in London, in Switzerland, in Vienna and in Germany. She would stay awhile in Paris in January and July for the couture shows, and visit Italy. New developments in fashion, music and art fascinated her. She went to Yves St Laurent's debut collection in 1962, was photographed with the acclaimed designer and ordered a brocade cocktail suit. By this time, she was accompanied by both Patrick and a full-time nurse to monitor and administer medication. Amongst a cocktail of pills, Madame took librium morning and evening. She still suffered from insomnia, waking at six and going through her paperwork. Everywhere she went, whether taking off or arriving, there would be the ubiquitous photographer, arranged by her offices, and Patrick took advantage of every possible photo opportunity to keep her amused.

In 1963, having been in Rome, where she visited the set of *Cleopatra* and had her photograph taken with Elizabeth Taylor, she was leaving for America when she spotted jeweller Kenneth J. Lane at the airport. He had recently made a successful promotional ring for her, a large, quite glitzy affair with a lift-up lid encasing solid perfume. 'I spotted her with Patrick immediately,' says Lane, 'and went to say hello. She was very friendly and just as she was leaving, rummaged around in her vast handbag and pulled out a piece of paper she folded up into a little square. She pushed it into my hand saying, "Here, Rome's expensive, have a nice time." When I looked, it was a five dollar bill!'

Helena Rubinstein had become very out of touch with what things cost other people, although she knew exactly what things cost her and ensured it was as little as possible. She had spent her whole life getting what she wanted at the lowest possible price, whether by going to the vegetable market at Greenwich every Saturday just as they were closing, or having her secretary buy her stockings on mark-down at Bloomingdales. Staff who owned cars were roped in to drive her, food left at dinner would be served up for lunch next day. She abhorred central heating and her apartment was always chilly. One freezing morning when she was conducting her usual meeting nestled from the warmth of her bed, she said to the assembled group, 'Keep your coats on if you want to, but the cold will make you think.'

Saving electricity – 'electriks', as Madame called it – had become a pre-occupation. However busy she was, there was time to remind her staff of their extravagances. 'Madame Rubinstein was in the hair department Tuesday night until 7 o'clock,' wrote her secretary to Mr Michael, Rubinstein's star hairdresser in New York in 1959, 'and noticed all the lights were on throughout your floor, even though cleaners were working only in one room. She asked me to tell you to please pay closer attention. She said you probably weren't aware of the fact that it cost a great deal of money.' Madame had more money than she knew what to do with, but she knew to the dollar how much she had, and to the cent what company expenses were. Nothing at all could be spent without her approval. Memos had to be signed authorising the cost of photographic prints, of press mailings or catering bills. The word she liked to see best of all was 'discount', so much so that regular suppliers built costs up so they could mark them down. In 1962 she had a clutch of her paintings cleaned and reframed in New York: a Utrillo, two Chiricos, a Laurencin and four Marcoussis oils. The cost was $770.95 including the 'special 15% discount for Madame Rubinstein'. One ex-employee said, 'If Madame bought a packet of gum she would knock off half a cent.' Diane Moss, her great niece, explains, 'Sure, she loved a bargain, but you know she bought so much of everything – her shopping was a compulsion – that when people saw her coming they revised their prices upwards.'

Ever the workaholic, Madame entered her ninth decade immersing herself as intensely in the business as she had always done. In New York, her working day was complex, peppered with meetings, the morning sessions taken from her cluttered bed, surrounded by staff and paperwork. She gave rapid dictation, usually involving at least two of her 'little girls' as well as Patrick. By noon, she was ready for the office, and three afternoons a week went to her Long Island City factory. Madame worked each and every weekend, with executives permanently on call. One Sunday, when lunch had been delayed at the nearby Kolin household, Oscar's wife sent Diane to fetch her father home. 'I had to invent a pretext for calling' says Diane, 'he had been there for *hours* – but I winkled him out. We were just leaving when I heard her heels, clack-clacking down the corridor, 'Oscar, Oscar, just one more thing I've remembered . . .' Although often ill herself, she had very little time for ill health in others, and as her illnesses (real or imagined) were often a 'diversion' to create a drama or sympathy, she suspected that others might be doing the same.

Madame's unforgiving attitude to sickness was the cause of a serious breach between herself and Patrick O'Higgins in the early 1960s, nearly causing him to leave the company altogether. Deeply upset by the death of his mother, feeling isolated and tired, Patrick had contracted bad influenza in Paris and took to his bed in the Quai de Bethune apartment. Incapable of seeing he was genuinely stretched to the limits of his endurance, Helena berated him, saying he was lazy, weak and useless, calling him a 'no good bum'. Cut to the quick, Patrick, who had been devotedly loyal to her and deserved better, finally cracked. He checked into the American Hospital in Neuilly, where he was diagnosed with 'nervous exhaustion'. Borrowing $1000 from his close friend, Miss Arden's one-time designer Jean Desses, O'Higgins fled to Morocco for a well-earned rest.

One of the ways Madame exercised the control she craved over Patrick (and all men) was to keep him busy. She loaded him with work. 'Please, whatever you do, see to it that everything is finished before you leave,' she wrote. 'Maybe I am demanding too much of you, but I am sure you feel yourself you have a responsibility.' Another way was to keep him underpaid. Although he would often take a few days off from work after their European travels, staying with friends in various cities – such as Dickie Buckle in London – he had little money of his own for holidays. They argued bitterly about money. From time to time, sensing she had pushed him too far and fearsome he might leave her, she would give him a bonus. But given the breadth of his duties and his public relations skills, he was woefully rewarded, and it rankled. Patrick even discovered that Madame was allocated a company subsistence allowance whilst he lived at her apartment in Paris, but instead of donating it to the housekeeping budget, actually pocketed the cash herself. John Richardson says that Patrick came to terms with her miserly approach and that 'it amused him'. Somehow it seems doubtful that a grown man with a taste for the fine things of life, responsible for round-the-clock nannying of the head of a multimillion pound business, could not resent being kept on a shoestring budget.

Boris Forter would have agreed. He said, 'Her inner resistance to any superficial generosity was so great that she could brush off the feelings in her heart, which were always there because she was actually a kind person. But the inner resistance was generally the winner.' Boris also said that when Madame was in meetings in her later years she would often doze off. An understandable trait, given her age. 'There was only one little word which broke through that sleep and brought her brain back to functioning,' said Boris, 'and that was the word dollar or pound – I think even shilling would have done the same. It was absolutely comical to see that revival in her face the moment money was mentioned.'

When Patrick left her in 1963, however, it wasn't because of money. He left to regain some independence and to have some peace. Madame couldn't understand that people needed time to unwind from the pressures of work and, in Patrick's case, time to grieve for the loss of his mother. Madame had always pushed death behind her, pretending it didn't matter, swallowing her pain and suppressing her emotions. By now, she seemed to become even more resentful if her family or any senior employee relaxed away from work. Madame's sister Manka, having long retired from the fray, lived a rather more indulgent life, which was anathema to Helena.

When Ceska joined Manka and her husband on a holiday touring Italy, Helena became particularly grumpy. Manka wrote to her sister, 'We had a *marvellous* trip . . . visiting Florence and Rome and staying the longest time in Capri. Ceska stayed with us every day on the most glorious beaches . . . she was happy and looks very well. Often thought about you . . . what a pity you never have time to enjoy such a rest . . .'

The barb about her elder sister's regime did no good. Helena could have taken as many holidays as she liked, but she simply didn't want to. Helena's response was to write, 'I was disappointed not to have seen you and Ceska before I had to leave Paris. I thought you all *knew* I was leaving on the 8th for New York? I am angry about the stupid advertising Ceska is doing now in London . . . she could have come back a day earlier and talked over the business with me . . . everyone is much too much away from the business nowadays. Our competition is terrible, quite different than it was when you were with me . . . I wish I could forget the business like others, useless to complain to you about it.'

Sulking at having been left alone in Paris by both sisters, particularly as they were 'sunning themselves on a beach', an utterly worthless pastime *and* bad for the skin, Helena was doubly hurt at being bereft of Patrick's soothing presence. She became angry, making things difficult for everyone around her. Once back in New York, she berated Roy, who was nearest in the firing line. Helena had never had the relationship with Roy that she had with Horace. Following one particular meeting, resulting in an explosion of volcanic proportions, Roy stormed out and even Oscar yelled at his aunt. Attempting to make amends, Roy sent a note to his mother. 'I am so very sorry about what happened this morning. I know you didn't mean it . . . any more than I did by my leaving so abruptly.' Age hadn't calmed Madame's tantrums. If anything, they were more fierce. At one memorable breakfast meeting involving approval of packaging designs, she hated the new boxes so much she threw one of them across the room with such force she fell out of bed and broke her arm.

Madame struggled to make amends with her son and, in an exercise which must have taken several anguished hours, she composed a plaintive letter to him.

I would like to know why you bear such a resentment towards me. There must be a deepseated reason why you shun and avoid me. If this feeling stems from your childhood, you must not have a clear picture of what my life was like then. Life with your father was far from easy. He left me with the sole responsibility of you children . . . you and Horace always came before anything else with me. The business was only a means of seeing that you were both well provided for . . . I wanted you to have the best education and life possible. I never had a minute for pleasure like other people and I was forced to give my time to the business. I was always on the spot when you needed me . . . what have I ever done to you to cause you to behave the way that you do? You are my only son and you are very important to me . . . all I ask is that we be together often and have a good, strong relationship. When I point out the shortcomings in the business, I don't do it to be destructive . . . it is just that I am able to see things clearly, and I want what is best for the business. I don't think you and Oscar can run this business alone . . . we can make real strides if we work together and discuss problems. Oscar had no right to talk to me as he did . . . but I am a person who forgets things quickly and I don't bear malice.

Madame may have believed the last part, but no one else would, particularly Roy, who had listened to her resentment over her failed marriage to his father ever since he was old enough to remember. She was prone to jotting down hurtful comments and pulling the note out of her bag to show it to someone in the office: 'Look – look what he called me!' Helena would say. Nor did putting things that had hurt out of her mind mean she had forgiven or forgotten them. Six months after he left, Patrick O'Higgins went back to work for Madame, inexorably drawn to the domineering, impossibly demanding, yet curiously compelling woman he had devoted over twelve years of his life to looking after.

Whilst Madame attended Yves St Laurent's debut show in 1962, Miss Arden also had fashion much on her mind. The Elizabeth Arden Collection was in need of revitalisation and she wanted a resident designer to work, as Castillo and Count Sarmi had done in the past, based out of New York. Count Lanfranco Rasponi wanted one too. His public relations firm was paid a handsome monthly retainer to represent the Arden fashion division, which was in real danger of losing its way. It was getting harder to get the right press coverage and he might lose a client. The young man who subsequently joined her would later agree his time at Elizabeth Arden Inc launched his glittering career in America and beyond. His name was Oscar de la Renta, and he had been working in Paris as Castillo's assistant at Lanvin. Rasponi planned for de la Renta to meet Miss Arden informally by inviting him to join her table at a fund-raising ball for the Spoleto Festival at the Plaza Hotel. The idea of employing her ex-designer's assistant was – as Rasponi knew it would be – utterly irresistible to Elizabeth, and she hired him immediately at a salary de la Renta concurs was 'a fortune' – $700 a week.

Arriving at Elizabeth Arden – well briefed by Castillo – Oscar de la Renta immediately became at home in New York. Miss Arden was clearly fond of him – it would have been hard not to be as he is regarded as one of the most personable men in the fashion business. As a bachelor, he had to do his stint of 'escort duty'. As a designer, he had to tailor his creative ideas to what Elizabeth felt was 'her look'. He managed both with consummate skill and, for the main part, she was delighted. In a chatty letter to Gordy Yates – by now chairman and managing director of Elizabeth Arden Ltd in London – she said, 'Mr de la Renta showed me the first dress he has designed for the fall collection. It is beautiful – a very simple line – made exquisitely and of the most *wonderful* gold and pink brocade. Among all the fashion houses I have visited, there was nothing to compare. But we will have to watch carefully to keep our expenses to a minimum and make our designs very special, as the designers on Seventh Avenue are very smart.'

While the name on the label was 'Oscar de la Renta for Elizabeth Arden', Miss Arden gave Oscar de la Renta his own name on the engraved cards that were sent out by Mrs Lowell to the press and clients for his shows. The impressive media list who attended his first show included fashion editors and writers from the *New York Times*, *Vogue*, *Harper's Bazaar* and *Town & Country*, along with Constance Woodworth from the *Journal American* and Eugenia Sheppard, whose column in the *Tribune* was required reading by the smart set. In return, he gave much assiduous attention to the wealthy, often stick-thin and oh-so-social ladies who frequented Arden, charming them as much as he charmed Elizabeth. His shoulders were broad enough to cope with her tantrums, happily for Mr de la Renta's harmony in the work-place he liked pink, and when he moved onwards and upwards, some two-and-half years later, his career, and his place in the serried ranks of New York's super-chic, was assured.

There were other prestige salons where New York's smart ladies could have treatments – Lilly Dache in particular ran an impressive venue, where hairdresser Kenneth, who tended the tresses of smart, society women, worked. But none had the all-persuasive, enveloping top-to-toe hold on classy clients that Elizabeth Arden had.

In another clever, creative appointment, Elizabeth hired Pablo Manzoni as make-up artist at her Rome salon. Pablo was the star of the cosmetics firmament in the 1960s, in demand to paint the face of every actress in Rome and beyond. Not as easygoing as de la Renta, Pablo's was a more temperamental talent, but Miss Arden was shrewd enough to recognise his skills and was thrilled with the copious press coverage of Pablo's deft handiwork – his glitter, jewelled and gilded eye make-up was a work of art. Stung by de la Renta's departure, Miss Arden moved Pablo to New York permanently in 1965, where his creative skills could be more visible. The media simply adored Pablo, particularly Diana Vreeland at *Vogue*, who coined the phrase 'visagiste' to describe his skills. He was honoured with a Coty award – the first make-up artist to be nominated, despite the awards being sponsored by a cosmetics house.

Pablo, however, didn't share Miss Arden's passion for pink. By then, she had over one hundred shades of pink on the line in lipsticks and blushers, but, being a modern man, Pablo craved neutrals and pearlised, tonal shades. 'Elizabeth Arden ladies do *not* have beige lips,' she said witheringly to Pablo when the debate was overheating in a colour meeting, whereupon he threw the colour charts on the floor, and shouted in a huff, 'Pink – stink!'

Wallis Windsor would still call on Arden's services whenever she was in New York, visiting the salon for treatments and massage. Monica Smythe, Miss Arden's impeccable British secretary during the last years of her life, remembers vividly the time she was sent to take a peek at the duchess, resting in her treatment room, to check all was well. The duchess was fast asleep but, rather frighteningly for Monica, her eyes were wide open. By now Wallis had had so many facelifts, her eyes couldn't close. Pablo was on hand to do a special make-up for the duchess whenever required and, on one memorable visit to the Waldorf Astoria, persuaded her to try false eyelashes. The duke was patiently needlepointing whilst his duchess was being painted, but when Pablo dropped the eyelash strips on the dark-brown carpet and couldn't find them, rather than have Wallis get down on her hands and knees, he came over and rummaged around with a torch himself. After a fairly undignified scramble –

although most people would say the duke had spent his entire life at the feet of his wife – they all admitted defeat. At this point, Pablo simply cut up the remaining strip into 'individual' lashes, thus creating another trend, and the duchess sallied forth to her party.

1963 was *Cleopatra* year and cosmetics companies went mad with excitement, projecting a false eyelashes and green eye shadow boom. Whilst Madame had been on the film set in Rome, and busied herself promoting blue and green eye shadow, liners and mascara, Elizabeth Arden went to the New York première with Robert Lehman, who hosted a buffet party beforehand at Hampshire House. 'It's just as well we had something to eat as the film lasted for hours,' she told Gordy. 'The crowds were breaking down the barriers they were so excited. The film is certainly arresting and Rex Harrison is excellent, but I would not give you much for Cleopatra herself.' Elizabeth Arden ladies did not go in for heavy eye make-up and black wigs and she remained impervious to the craze, but over at Revlon it was another story. Hastily launching Sphinx Pink lipstick in a Cleopatra-motif lipstick case, along with Sphinx Eyes smoky kohl eye shadow 'with deadly ingredients' (not a phrase cosmetics companies would rush to use today) Richard Avedon, as usual, was brought in to shoot ads for the campaign.

Miss Arden planned to visit her Irish castle on 21 June, writing plaintively to Gordy, 'I hope you will be in Dublin to meet me and find me somewhere to rest my little head.' He was, naturally enough, waiting at the airport when she arrived with Monica Smythe, complete with photographer, flowers and rooms booked at the Russell Hotel. Angus McCall drove her out to visit the legendary racehorse Arkle who was retired at the Duchess of Westminster's stud, remembering 'that Miss Arden wore sensible shoes and walked for miles'. She also had her first taste of Irish poteen, which she didn't like, and soda bread, which she adored. It was, as usual, a flying visit. She had a horse running in the Hollywood Derby at Santa Anita, and flew from Paris to Los Angeles a few days later.

The world reeled in shock in November that year when President Kennedy was assassinated, although Madame grumbled when obliged to close the New York salon on the day of his funeral. Not all America's elite considered the funeral a reason to curtail their social plans. Mrs Elsie Woodward, for example, one of New York's premier hostesses, was wont to give regular Sunday evening suppers and Eleanor Lambert remembers she still held her soirée on the weekend that Jack Kennedy was buried.

Later that year, Madame went travelling but became ill and was confined to bed in her new apartment as 1964 dawned. Patrick, who had slipped away to Sicily for a well-earned break, wrote to his great friend Amber Walker, 'Madame is still in London. She has had double pneumonia, a heart attack, inflamed arteries . . . She was ninety-two on Christmas day and yet she has now completely recovered and dictates, on average, sixty-four letters a day. Two secretaries have already had nervous breakdowns and a third has developed a strange rash! I expect to be in Paris for the next three weeks at least, although I shall take a few quick side trips to see if the slap (i.e. slap the cream on) empire is holding together. I'm swamped with work but it seems to suit me.'

That same New Year in London, Mary Quant, who had represented the Zeitgeist of British fashion ever since she opened her first boutique on the King's Road in 1955, backed by Gala, launched her first cosmetics line. Quant introduced a startling simple range packaged in crisp silver and black, targeting the younger generation who, fed up with being carbon copies of their mothers, had eagerly taken to Quant's simple shift dressing. The range was an instant success.

The Arden look, in décor, fashion and cosmetics, was certainly not targeted at the young, although many a daughter was taken by her mother to Arden's salons for leg-waxing, eyelash-plucking and other treatments deemed essential for a young girl making her debut. Miss Arden spent the New Year of 1964 acquiring a building on Chicago's 'magnificent mile of golden retailing', North Michigan Avenue. With Tony Duquette still battling over Barretstown, she put Remisoff in charge of the interiors. The impressive salon was in Regency style, with touches of deco-simplicity, all black, white, gold and an accent of rich pink, with a mass of etched glass panels. Global business at Elizabeth Arden was holding up well, with London in particular turning in remarkable profits. Gordon Yates received a letter of congratulations about his 1963 sales figures which prompted him to write to Carl Gardiner at head office, reminding him Miss Arden had promised a pay-rise. 'My English salary,' he wrote, 'fixed in 1961, has fallen in value by twelve-and-a-half per cent in the interim.' Mr Yates, it seems, was a victim of poor British v rich American salaries and also a victim of his own work record. Having been with the company for over thirty-five years, it was hard to lay claim to the sort of salary that would be offered as a matter of course when Miss Arden was recruiting a new executive from a rival business.

New employees at both companies often wilted under tirades from the ladies in charge. Both had become even more forceful with age, even more iron-willed, and certainly more bad-tempered with those in the immediate vicinity. Madame turned her attention to a newish recruit in her advertising department, Mr Lockman. 'You have been with us for two years,' she thundered. 'I want to tell you what is wrong with you. You are too inflexible. You are too opinionated. You often see only your own point of view . . . you don't like taking advice or listening to other opinions. We are an international business and you must compare notes with me and Mr O'Higgins.' There was a brief to hire a new agency. 'I would like to meet with the agencies and hear from them what they suggest. I appreciate your drive, but I want you to realise that results are due to teamwork.' Teamwork with Madame (as with Miss Arden) meant everyone doing exactly as she said!

Madame even managed to get three burglars to do as they were told. In May 1964 she was resting in bed at her Park Avenue apartment. Her butler Albert brought her breakfast tray at 7.00 a.m. and, as usual, her bed was awash with newspapers, business reports, her handbag and an assortment of keys. Every morning, whenever she was in New York, her day started with a meeting at 7.30 a.m. attended by her lawyer, Harold Weill. By this stage most of their discussions were about her will, as Helena had taken to making changes and adding codicils to increase a dollar or two here and substitute a picture or piece of jewellery there. Poor Mr Weill, whom she called 'the young lawyer', was not so young any more. In his sixties and getting fed up with Madame's machinations, he put his foot down about the start time of the meetings, moving them to 8.30 a.m. Madame bargained the start back up to 8.00 a.m. The argument about this had reverberated so noisily around the office, that Madame's secretary, Nancy Goldburgh (who always arrived at the apartment by 8.30 a.m. herself), sighed, realising her boss would be in a bad mood the next day.

It seemed that Mr Weill himself was in such a bad mood about the argument that, for the first time in years, he didn't turn up for his meeting at all. Instead three young men, posing as florists, clutching a vast bunch of red roses, arrived at the building, smoothly persuading the doorman they were expected. When Albert answered the front door, he found three masked men, one flourishing a gun. Madame's maid and nurse were tied up and gagged and Albert was forced at gunpoint to guide them to her bedroom. He too was then tied and gagged and the robbers demanded the keys to

Madame's locked cupboards and safe, where presumably they hoped to find a vast cache of jewellery. They calculated without her iron will. Looking up at them, the tiny, indomitable Helena said, 'I'm an old woman. Death doesn't frighten me. You can kill me, but you can't rob me . . . now get out.' Whilst the burglars hesitated, she glanced down at her side and realised the keys to the cupboards were in her bag, so whilst the three robbers were rummaging through drawers, she slipped them down her nightdress. The three men split up, one heading for the dressing room, one going next door, the other searching her bag. He found $200 and put it in his pocket. When the other two, by now quite frustrated, burglars arrived back, panicking about the time, she pointed at their partner. 'He's got the cash from my bag, make sure you both get your share.' At this point, they yanked her out of bed, tied her to a chair and tried to gag her. The trio, however, had not calculated on Madame's ability to make herself heard, and she shrieked and screamed, pushed and pulled and made so much fuss that they probably began to regret their venture. Albert had by now struggled free. A few moments later, Madame's vocal and irate nurse appeared, and a short while after that, Nancy Goldburgh. The robbers fled, with just the $200. They were never traced.

Helena put a brave face on it. 'Fancy,' she said, 'they ran out with two hundred dollars and the flowers must have cost them $40!' After giving statements to the police, she put on her make-up and descended to the ground floor to greet TV crews gathered outside. 'I was robbed. It can happen to the best people,' she said. Patrick, by now on the scene, had been instructed to hire a limousine. Madame got in, claiming she was going to work, but had the driver go round the block before she wilted and went back upstairs to rest. Quite how the inept robbers missed the gold pill boxes, the Meissen dishes, or the Picassos and Braques hanging on her bedroom walls, or, as her daughter-in-law pointed out, the sables hanging in her wardrobe, is a mystery. They also ignored great heaps of baubles, probably not able to decipher what was valuable or not amongst the odd earrings, buttons, medals and cabochon stones. More sinisterly, she felt that she knew one of the young men. 'There was something about his eyes,' she would say later to Patrick. 'They seemed such *nice* boys.' The 'nice' boys clearly knew there was a window of opportunity that morning. She always felt that one of them at least may have worked for her office, and heard Harold Weill arguing about his arrival time. It was as though they knew they had half an hour before people arrived, and it unsettled her. She talked about the robbery for weeks afterwards, berating Mr Weill for not turning up, explaining every little detail to Rixie Marcus (the world ladies bridge champion who gave her masterclasses), and grumbling constantly to Patrick.

The robbery at Madame's apartment signalled a change in her outward bravura. She had the locks changed on all the doors and an intricate burglar alarm system installed. She slept badly, had panic attacks in the night and admitted to being afraid. For the first time in a long, long time, Helena Rubinstein felt vulnerable. She also felt old. She took to sleeping in a hospital bed set up in her bedroom, complete with oxygen tent. She also took to carrying her will around with her. This document, running to dozens of pages, bound in a leather folder, took on a new meaning in her life. She delighted in making margin adjustments, remembering a sweet 'little girl' who should receive a bonus and cutting out people who had offended her. To Patrick, it seemed that she was visibly wilting.

In the summer of 1964, they sailed on the SS *France* for Europe, where she stayed, listless and gloomy, at Quai de Bethune, stirring only to attend a press party at Combs-la-Ville where about two hundred people milled in the summer sunshine. Amongst them were Ernestine Carter and her husband Jake, who gravitated to the side of Madame, dressed in black, topped with her signature bowler hat (designed by New York milliner Mr John) with what Carter later described as 'a black gaze', standing entirely alone observing the crowds. Later that month, Patrick, concerned about her mood, suggested they go to Tangiers for a holiday, where heiress Barbara Hutton was planning to host one of her lavish parties. Entertainment was to be given by the young, ultra-hip Rolling Stones, and security by over five hundred 'Blue Men', nomadic tribesmen whose faces were dark with indigo dye. Neither Patrick nor Madame made it to the guest list, co-ordinated as usual by David Herbert, although Madame accurately predicted 'the rich one won't turn up'. She was right. Miss Hutton, in her barbiturate-fuelled haze, arguing already with husband number seven, was conspicuously absent from her own soirée. After a short tour when Madame visited places which struck chords in her memory, she settled back in New York for the winter to supervise the preparation of her official autobiography, a ghost-written book which gave Madame a command of the English language in print that she never had in life.

Patrick, as Madame's closest helper, was scathing about the final draft, telling her that, although it had been purged of the most boring passages and naïve statements, it still needed much more work. He told her, 'You cannot bring out a book, signed by you, which is sloppy, uninformative and generally unexciting. I am sure that it can be put in order very quickly. Pallavicini would like to illustrate it and have an exhibition around the illustrations, which is a good idea as the project can travel to stores for promotions.' Patrick laboured to pepper up the draft manuscript, working through piles of documents given to him by Madame, found littered in heaps in dusty files and shoeboxes. Madame clung stubbornly to *her* version of events, as she wanted to remember them.

In the spring of 1965 Madame was working in New York. She went to the Long Island factory on Tuesday 30 March, and again, briefly, the next day, but didn't feel well, actually suffering a slight stroke whilst at work. An ambulance took her to Park Avenue, where her doctor insisted she be admitted to New York Hospital. She suffered a more serious stroke that night from which she did not recover. Helena Rubinstein died at 3.30 a.m. on Tuesday 1 April, alone in her hospital room.

Front-page obituaries flooded every newspaper and reports about her death were on television and radio news. Madame would have been pleased. Miss Arden was less pleased, grumbling that Madame's age was mentioned, no doubt alarmed some bright reporter might start to talk about *her* advancing years. Newspaper reports were quick to point out that Madame's son, Roy Titus, Chairman of the Board of Helena Rubinstein Inc, would be 'assisted by her nephew, Oscar Kolin, who was Executive Vice President' and there was speculation in the trade that neither man felt comfortable with this plan. The *New York Times* explained to its awed readers that Madame had left a personal estate 'valued at over $100,000,000' and that her cosmetics empire 'had assets of over $17,500,000, owned factories, salons and laboratories in fourteen countries, had 30,000 employees and enjoyed a turnover of over $60,000,000 a year operating in over one hundred countries'. Helena Rubinstein Inc closed its factory, salon and offices on that Friday and Saturday to enable the staff, along with the demonstrators and store personnel who sold the range, to visit Campbell's and pay their final respects. The day after her death, while her family bickered about funeral arrangements, the share price in Helena Rubinstein Inc rose by $10, putting an extra $15 million on the market valuation of her American business, spurred by expectations of a takeover by Revlon. Roy Titus, when asked about his mother's art collections, told the London *Sunday Times*, 'The family would like to see my mother's art collections kept together in one place as a memorial. We have thought of turning her New York apartment into a museum to house all her treasures.' Within six weeks, however, the Plaza Art Gallery had catalogued and valued all her belongings in preparation for their disposal. Her executors decided to place her Park Avenue building on the market, whereupon it was bought by a New York attorney. A year later, as he was casting about for a home palatial enough to showcase his by now flamboyantly wealthy lifestyle, with his by now very fashionable third wife, Lyn, Madame Rubinstein's apartment was purchased by . . . Charles Revson.

Madame's will, covering some thirty-four pages, with no less than six codicils covering twenty-seven pages, left specific bequests to a long list of people. Not that many of them were too thrilled. Her Filipino butler, Albert, for example, was left a mere $1000 and an income from her Trust of a paltry $600 a year. Her French servants, after a lifetime working for her, were left a meagre lump sum of $3000 between them. Madame's maid in New York, Mathilda, inherited just $3000 and twenty-seven of her long-serving employees, $1000 each. Her sisters were left money and jewellery – Stella got the pearl necklace and Manka the cabochon rubies. Madame's niece Mala inherited the black and white pearls along with a Nadelman, a Derain and a Kandinsky. Patrick O'Higgins received $5000 and an income of $2000 a year for life, that particular codicil having been added when he had returned to her side some three years earlier. Boris Forter was left a picture by Graham Sutherland – which he later sold to buy another sports car. Mr Ameison in her Paris office got . . . nothing. Interestingly, she remembered her friends in the media more generously. Marie Louise Bousquet received $1200 a year for life, and Boston reporter Grace Davidson, who had so befriended Horace, received $3000.

Her immediate family were the chief beneficiaries. Horace's children and Roy's daughter Helena, and of course her nephews and niece, Oscar and Henry Kolin and their sister Mala, along with their families and the children of her sister Erna, were all left money. Even then, she tied up capital in a family Trust, clearly intending everyone should keep working for a living. Madame's American shares in the business, reported by the media to be 'tightly held by the family who controlled over 52%' and her overseas companies, along with property owned by the business, were left to the Helena Rubinstein Foundation. The Quai de Bethune building was sold, with Madame's apartment bought by Count Chandon of the champagne family, but Stella continued to live in her apartment at the landmark building at 216 Boulevard Raspail – the cause of so many bitter arguments with Titus – until she died. Similarly, Ceska remained at Ennismore Gardens until she too died some eighteen months later. For the moment at least, there was no word of selling the business, although Oscar moved swiftly to consolidate, making plans to close down the beauty salons and concentrate on wholesaling. Patrick was dispatched to Europe, specifically to co-ordinate inventories at Madame's properties, her sisters, it seems, having rather gone to pieces since Helena's death. Arriving back in New York he told John Richardson, 'Coping with New York seems much easier than in London or Paris. The atmosphere at the office is far less befogged . . . I was warmly received when I got back, and whatever feelings such a reception may camouflage, it's always pleasant to be looked upon as a prodigal, even a shop-worn one.' At this point he was still employed, albeit in a rather amorphous role. 'I will be going to Paris at the end of July to introduce Mala Rubinstein to the international press,' he wrote to John. Late that May, Patrick met Monica Smythe, Miss Arden's secretary, at a party in Newport. 'He was,' she says, 'very good company and we had a lot to talk about. But I do remember he somehow seemed older than I imagined, and you know, he didn't look at all well . . . quite worn out in fact.' He wasn't well. Doctors had found what he later would laughingly describe as 'an amoeba' in his intestines.

Patrick was due to fly to England for the publication of Madame's memoirs in the autumn of 1965, but by then his relationship with her family had deteriorated. The book, for which he had been prime instigator and as he cheerfully described 'handmaiden and fifteenth ghost', was launched without him. 'The family expressly forbade my trip, stating, tersely, that I was needed in New York,' he wrote to John Richardson. 'This is fiction. They *loathe* anyone being credited with anything.' How he missed Madame.

Miss Arden too had been really unwell for over a year, her iron will forcing recovery from two minor strokes. In April 1964 she had been due at Maine Chance in Phoenix to spend time with Mamie Eisenhower, but was confined to bed with a round-the-clock nurse at the Beverly Hills Hotel, comforted only by a telegram from Mamie saying, 'Have enjoyed every minute of my stay in the Garden of Arden. My deep affection, Mamie.' Rallying, despite the disturbing news that her niece, Ginny, was seriously ill, Elizabeth went ahead with plans to sponsor a ball in Newport that summer. She was starting to forget people's names, her left leg would swell up badly, her hands were stiff, her hair was thinning and she had to take strong nova-caine shots for pain. Miss Arden was, as always, good at disguising her discomfort. The super-efficient Monica, who had two assistant secretaries, took care of the morning mail and wrote most of Miss Arden's letters herself. 'She might glance at them, but you know, we knew what to say and how to handle things,' says Monica. There was, at this time, a telephone in her car. Emily Hutchison remembers being rather impressed by this early innovation. 'Oh, Elizabeth loved that telephone, she would chatter away from the car endlessly.' The ever-efficient Charles ran the car, recalls Emily, 'as though it were a shop and pharmacy. There was everything Elizabeth might need packed into the boot, including a change of clothes and several pairs of shoes.'

In August, Elizabeth was in Newport. 'I'm staying with the Wiley Buchanans,' she wrote to Gordy, 'who are hosting a dinner party for me, and then there is a luncheon and special games decathlon at the casino, with *all* the leading Newporters taking part.' The mayor of Newport gave her 'the Freedom of Newport' in honour of her sponsorship of the Elizabeth Arden International Ball, a fundraiser for the Preservation Society of Newport County, held at Marble House, the one-time home of the formidable Alva Vanderbilt Belmont, built for her at the staggering cost of $11 million back in 1895. Seventy years later, as Florence Nightingale Graham took her seat as the guest of honour in the awesome grandeur of Marble House, what thoughts must have flooded through her mind. America's reigning 'queen of beauty' had earned her place on the gilded throne once occupied by Alva Vanderbilt. Miss Arden had made her mark in business almost as powerfully as those early robber barons had made theirs. The men had founded empires and industries in steel, railways, coal, oil, property and banking. She had founded one in creams. It was no less significant. The pinnacle of accept-ance she had once so craved, was now hers by right.

Elizabeth arrived in Europe in September 1965, greeted at the airport in London by young Christopher and Caroline Yates, 'on duty' and lined up to present flowers to their father's boss. She spent time in Paris with Gladys and her new assistant, Comtesse Laura de Coursevilles, titles still being de rigueur for a job with the upper echelons at Arden. She dined with her friend Mrs Cabot Lodge, whose husband was the ex-US ambassador in Madrid, and lunched with yet another ex-ambassador's wife, Evangeline Bruce, talk-ing this time not about Madrid, but London, with Mrs Bruce tactfully urging her friend to relocate her salon to larger premises as she and her friends were finding the old space rather cramped. Back in New York, Miss Arden interviewed a young hairdresser who had applied for a job. Having worked 'on trial' with clients for most of the day, Maurice was given the task of dealing with Miss Arden's by now rather sparse hair. He remembers the occasion vividly. 'She arrived, dressed entirely in pink, with her alligator bag over her arm. Doing her hair was nerve-wracking I can tell you, but anyway she seemed pleased and said, "go home and shave the beard, you can start at 9.00 tomorrow morning." I loved my beard but I got rid of it that night. You couldn't have a beard and work for Miss Arden.' Over the next year, Maurice would often do her hair, agreeing that the rather orange colour she favoured 'was very fierce but that was the way she liked it'. He has fond memories of her: 'Sure, she was hard to work for, but she was a truly amazing woman.'

Miss Arden received the Kentucky Thoroughbred Breeders' Association's annual Ladies' Sportsmanship Award in October 1965, the second time she had scooped the honour. She entertained her old friend, designer Jean Desses, over from Paris for a working trip, hosting a party for him at her apartment and hiring New York's man of the moment, 'Killer' Joe Piro, the discotheque dancing genius, to give a demonstration of the Twist. She adored Piro, as did Jackie Kennedy, who hired him for a late-night party she hosted to honour John Kenneth Galbraith. Piro was on call again that year at Elizabeth's annual Blue Grass party at the St Regis Hotel, where she entertained press, suppliers, buyers and 'friends of Elizabeth Arden', and he acted as MC.

In March 1966, Elizabeth sponsored the Flamingo Ball at Hialeah, staying as usual at the Sea View Hotel in Miami, with Patricia Young in attendance. That summer, she made what would be her last trip to Europe, staying at Claridges in London en route to spend a few days at her Irish castle. She fell heavily in Dublin, and by the time she got to Barretstown was confined to bed for most of her visit. 'The gardener at the castle was a chap called Adams,' says Angus McCall, 'and he had the bright idea of taking up flowers to Miss Arden in her room. She was so delighted that she tipped him £20 . . . We all laughed at the idea of her tipping her own gardener for bringing her her own flowers, but you know, she really was very, very generous.'

Although confined to bed, Miss Arden spent a lot of the day on the telephone. The local exchange line at Ballymore Eustace was run by the sub-postmistress with the old plug-in system, involving a manual connection for each call. The poor woman struggled to keep up with the plethora of calls made from Barretstown that summer and told Angus, 'Ooogh, Mr McCall, I'm *that* tired and *that* busy, I haven't even had time to feed the hens since she came.'

Back in London, Elizabeth dined with her senior staff at Claridges, then at the Ritz in Paris, where Castillo, whose work once again formed the core of her New York fashion floor, visited her for fittings, disturbed to find her so frail. She flew back to New York, attending the gala opening of the new Metropolitan Opera House. She didn't care for the performance of *Antony and Cleopatra*, writing to Gordy that she also found the décor for the new building 'bordering on the vulgar, with the boxes, which were so rich and opulent, now very unattractive with *deplorable* colours'. She also grumbled to Gordy that 'Castillo is selling to Bonwit Teller's, which is *not* a very satisfactory state of affairs, however he is here part of this week and if we are to plan future collections with him, this "exclusivity" point will have to be cleared up first.' She lost that battle. Castillo insisted, quite properly, on being able to sell to other stores, whereupon Elizabeth sulked and said to Gladys that, 'I am going to buy from whom I like from now on, so my collections will no longer be exclusively by Castillo.'

She went back to the Opera House for *La Traviata* with sets by Cecil Beaton. 'The colours were lovely,' she told Gordy, 'but I did find the costumes rather old-fashioned.' She lunched later that week with Valentino and Princess Pignatelli, who were in town showing his collection. 'I missed seeing his presentation,' she said to Gordy, 'but I have asked Valentino to see Mrs Wonnacott on his way through London next week in case there is anything for the salon there.' Flying over to Beverly Hills for a charity show, she was dressing for a party being hosted for her by the Duquettes when she banged her knee badly. Ordered to rest by the doctor in attendance, she ignored him, and went to the party *and* hosted her show in the ballroom of the Beverly Hills Hotel the following day, her knee bandaged under her white satin Castillo gown, red satin slippers on her tiny feet, sadly, by now, unable to take to the dance floor.

Over the weekend of 15 and 16 October, Elizabeth went out to Belmont, staying quietly at her cottage there with Monica Smythe as her companion. She had been very concerned about one of her favourite horses, Buffles, who had flu. Not feeling well herself, she stayed in bed at her New York apartment on Monday morning dictating correspondence to Monica, with Pat anxiously looking on. It was becoming increasingly clear she was ill and Pat called for the doctor, despite Elizabeth's protests. An ambulance rushed her to Lenox Hill Hospital, a place she had generously endowed and where she had spent a lot of time. She would not linger there long on this, her last visit. In the twilight hours of 18 October 1966, Florence Nightingale Graham, known to the world as Elizabeth Arden, died of 'complications following a stroke and pneumonia'.

Three days later, over a thousand people jostled outside St James's Church, the pavement roped off as though the distinguished and glamorous guests arriving were attending a film première. It seemed to one observer that 'there were more cameras outside the church than in a television studio'. News reporters were enjoying a field day describing the roll-call of the great and the good of American society attending Miss Arden's funeral. In the crush, a well-coiffeured woman, in full mourning black festooned with diamonds, caught the eye of Monica Smythe, Miss Arden's British secretary, who was at the front of the receiving line. 'Thank you so much for coming today,' Monica murmured politely, not knowing who the woman was. '*She* wouldn't have said that if she knew *I* was here,' snapped back Mrs Estée Lauder, before turning to the news reporters and giving a strong sound bite: 'A great era has passed, leaving just us to carry on the fine tradition that Elizabeth leaves behind her.' Moving on into the church, leaning on the arm of her son, Mrs Lauder looked around the congregation before taking a seat next to Greer Garson. It was observed by an Arden employee that whilst the famous actress sobbed throughout the service, 'Mrs Lauder spent the entire time with a smile on her face.'

Miss Arden's death had been met with disbelief amongst her staff and her family. They had come to believe, just as Elizabeth had, that she was immortal. But she was made of flesh and blood, after all, and just as there are only two things certain in this life – death and taxes – she had faced one of them head-on and finally succumbed. It remained for her company and family to face the second. It would prove to be an unpleasant experience . . .

TAXING TIMES – THE AFTERMATH 1966–1989

I N 1926, FLORENCE J. LEWIS registered the patent for Puffy Eye Straps, a system she had devised for relieving swollen and sore eyelids. They were still in production forty years later, and many women (and men) working at Arden when Elizabeth died would have found them useful, whether their eyes were swollen with tears of grief, or tears of frustration.

For Carl Gardiner, who became president and CEO of the corporation when Miss Arden died, it was the latter. He tried hard to hold the business together under the awesome cloud of a tax bill estimated at over $35 million. Despite – or rather because of – being the sole owner of a corporation said to be turning over in excess of $60 million a year, Elizabeth had left her financial affairs in a woeful state. She had died rich, despite the costs of maintaining her lifestyle. Monica Smythe calculates that the cost of merely feeding and stabling her horses at that time was around $100,000 a month in America alone, without taking into account the horses in training in Ireland. But dying rich and funding payment of over $35 million in taxes are different things.

In her twenty-four-page will, Miss Arden looked after her horses rather better than her business affairs. She insisted they be sold, with those in training to go first, mares last and mares in foal only to be sold with their foals. She was generous to her family, with Gladys receiving $4 million, Gladys's son, John Baraba Graham – reconciled with his 'Aunt Elizabeth' by the time she died – $1 million, and her niece Pat inheriting $2 million, all her aunt's properties and the entire residuary after $1.5 million in bequests to staff and servants.

The executors – Pat, her aunt's lawyer, Howard Carter, and the Bank of

New York – were dealt a crushing blow when the tax bill arrived, whereupon they rolled up their sleeves and got on with selling the assets to meet the debt. Everyone watched and waited whilst lawyers made their killing as two bitterly contested, and costly, court cases were heard. The estate of Elizabeth Arden Graham was eventually settled five years later in 1971, by which time many of the people she had remembered in her will, people who had worked for her, in some cases for their entire lifetime, had given up hope of ever receiving their legacies. Elizabeth Arden may have left a large fortune, but in the end, all that was really left was the business that bore her name. By now, the unassailable position of that, too, was looking vulnerable.

First went Elizabeth's Irish castle, sold to Canadian millionaire Garfield Weston, who on discussing the price said, 'Remember, what I offer you today won't be what I offer you tomorrow.' Arden's executives, used to dealing with tough Canadians, swiftly agreed the deal. Elizabeth's beautiful Fifth Avenue apartment was snapped up by Charlotte Ford Niarchos, who had grown up in the same building, but she didn't keep it. Part of the bitter divorce settlement from her Greek shipping magnate husband Stavros included a sumptuous home on Sutton Place, so she sold the penthouse without ever having moved in.

Next went the horses, sold with almost indecent haste by Carl Gardiner and the board, quick to disassociate the Elizabeth Arden company from the ownership of three stablesful of racehorses. Fifty-six brood mares, twenty-seven yearlings and seven stallions from her Kentucky horse farm were sold by Keeneland, fetching $1,270,000. Twenty-two horses in training and eleven yearlings stabled at New York's Belmont track were sold, as were her twenty-three horses in Ireland. Elizabeth's Kentucky complex, with stables, land and mansion, representing her life's dreams, was sold in the summer of 1967, when the University of Kentucky acquired the property for $2 million. This acquisition held up settlement of Miss Arden's affairs for over three years.

In the early summer of 1967, California horseman Rex C. Ellsworth, in partnership with a Lexington vet, Arnold Pessin, made a bid for Elizabeth's lush, 720-acre blue grass estate. Word spread quickly that the pair had ambitious plans to open their own thoroughbred auction sales business on the site, in direct competition with the Keeneland Association. Ellsworth's offer of just under $2 million had, the duo believed, been accepted, when at the last minute Arden's executors backed down and instead confirmed a deal with the University of Kentucky who wanted to keep the horse farm open as an 'equine research' facility. The aggrieved pair immediately filed an anti-trust suit for $30 million, claiming that the county had conspired to block their purchase to protect what they desribed as 'the stranglehold' Keeneland held over the sale of thoroughbred horses in Kentucky. Insults were hurled from both sides. Keeneland's board of directors hotly denied any conspiracy and the executors of Elizabeth's estate denied they had deliberately blocked the sale. The case went to court in a hugely hostile atmosphere. Pessin and Ellsworth lost their case, but lodged an appeal.

Much to the relief of Arden's management, the appeal was eventually quashed in 1969. Kentucky University were left in situ, the horses stabled there being part of intensive animal health studies, with animal nutrition programmes taking place using feed grown on the farm. As Elizabeth had named her stables after her health resorts, it is fitting that her horse farm ultimately became a place where horses were put on diets, exercised to check their lung capacity and pampered with organically grown foods. She would have been pleased.

While battles were being fought over the ownership of her Kentucky home, its contents went on the block, making the estate $45,000. Money was also being pulled in from Arden subsidiaries all over the world. When Gordon Yates sent his year-end dividends at Christmas 1967, the amount was over half a million dollars. 'You may be sure it is much appreciated and is going to be a tremendous help to us in handling a part of the estate problem,' replied Carl Gardiner.

Two fires at the Arden 'Maine Chance' health resort in Maine finally decided the board to put the property on the market. The thousand acres of woodland, including Elizabeth's beloved farms where she raised her flowers and seeds, and where her shorthorn cattle had once grazed, were snapped up by a Boston business group who called themselves the Elizabeth Realty Trust. The new owners announced, 'Because of the glamour attached to the property and its name, we have to consider it as something pretty special, so we won't be making any hasty moves.' The Maine Chance resort at Phoenix remained operational. Elizabeth had instinctively put her finger on the precise pulse by combining health, fitness and diet with luxury and rest when she opened her original Maine Chance in 1934. There were rivals by the time she died, but for a while longer, Maine Chance in Phoenix reigned supreme.

Tackling the problems of ongoing costs within the business, one of the first things to go was the out-dated 'custom made' fashion floor. Mr

Gardiner replaced it with ready-to-wear, albeit expensive dresses, bought mostly from Castillo and Oscar de la Renta. De la Renta, by now winner of two Coty Awards, forged an even closer relationship with the company than he had enjoyed when Elizabeth was alive. His wife Françoise, the ex-editor in chief of French *Vogue*, was employed by Gardiner as a 'consultant on fashion and beauty', reporting directly to him.

The management at both Arden and Rubinstein took steps to consolidate. There were inevitable staff cutbacks and, in the case of Rubinstein, Oscar Kolin closed down the salons to concentrate on wholesale activity. Boris Forter, who had always got on well with Roy, remained in his job, although his future was uncertain, particularly when his closest ally, Ceska, died in 1968. Ceska was generous to Boris, his wife, son Claude and his other children, remembering them all in her will. There was much swapping of jewellery between surviving sisters and nieces, with bequests to her sisters Erna and Manka (the latter sharing a 'foundation' with Ceska, although the charitable beneficiaries were never made clear). Patrick O'Higgins left the company a year after Madame's death, to concentrate on his writing career, and decided to write a book about Helena Rubinstein.

At Arden's offices and salons, particularly in London, there was a natural cull due to retirement of ageing staff. Carl Gardiner, on commissioning an employee report, discovered that the average length of service was over thirty years. The redoubtable Miss Sallis had been guardian of accounts for over forty-three, Gordon Yates had been employed for over thirty-eight, Mr Harris and Mr Jones in export packing for thirty-two years, Mr Kimber in manufacturing for forty-three. All in all, there were over 160 employees at Arden's UK factory, salon and offices for whom working there had been a way of life. For a while at least, most of their jobs were safe, not least because Miss Arden was dead. She had tended to instantly dismiss anyone she didn't like the look of. Several went because they wore brown. Miss Arden loathed brown. Others went because they wore glasses. Woe betide anyone who grew a beard – it was forbidden. Job security for short men or tall women had been very suspect. Things were certainly calmer around the offices following 1966. Gina Ross, who worked at the salon at that time, vividly recalls what turmoil her visits had caused. 'Everyone was on tenterhooks for days before, and frozen with nerves when she was in the salon.' Previously, if Gordy Yates had wanted to protect an employee whom Elizabeth disliked, he would have had to give them the week off when she was due in town. Others had simply fled into the bathroom when she arrived in the building and once someone hid in a cupboard, getting trapped in there for over three hours. For all her foibles, however, Miss Arden was much missed. Death imbued her — as it did Helena — with almost mystical properties of courage and vision, generosity and kindness. People remembered what they wanted to remember, and for as long as they could remember, the indomitable ladies had been there. Now they were gone it left a huge void.

In New York, Pablo was given the title of Creative Director of the whole company, with his picture appearing on some of the packaging. Creative activity in the 60s, however, was originating in England. In April 1966, just a few months before Elizabeth died, *Time* magazine had written, 'In this century every decade has its city, and for the sixties, that city is London.' Arden's Bond Street salon — opened in that other decade dedicated to youth and beauty, the 1920s — struggled to cope with 'swinging London', the fashion and music capital of the world. Since Diana Vreeland had taken over as editor in chief of American *Vogue* — the most powerful job in fashion — in 1962, she had put her finger on the Zeitgeist of the British sense of style and featured its heroes and heroines on a regular basis. Penelope Tree, Twiggy, Jean Shrimpton, Terence Stamp and the Rolling Stones were the new icons. Laid-back shops like Michael Rainey's 'Hung on You' sold crushed velvets and tie-dyed linens to the hip sons and daughters of the stuffy rich. The mothers of the young, thin and sometimes rebellious debutantes of the day — no longer presented at court since the Queen had stopped the practice — were still core Arden clients, but though their daughters were still taken to Arden's for a leg wax, hairdressers like Arden's Michelangelo held little allure for a girl who wanted to have a geometric cut at Vidal Sassoon and drank Scotch and Coke at Sybilla's rather than tea with Mummy at Fortnum's. Girls wanted make-up, not skin care. Cleansing cosmetics off was much less appealing than layering them on, and false eyelashes reigned supreme. Aspiring models went to Max Factor's Bond Street cosmetics salon or to Lucie Clayton's for 'modelling and make-up classes'. In an attempt to seduce London's youth market, Arden employed a skinny-hipped, long-haired make-up artist called Pierre Laroche, who had a deft touch with the blusher brush and for a while was very famous — just as likely to be doing make-up for a male band as a female model.

Jacqui Brandwynne, who had been trained at Rubinstein, left to become the first ever female vice president at Yardley, making her mark by hiring

Jean Shrimpton as 'the face of Yardley' in the mid-sixties. Other top staff were headhunted for rivals, such as Leonce Pacheny from Rubinstein's Paris office who joined Orlane, by then a division of Max Factor. Helena Rubinstein Inc tried to do some headhunting of its own in 1966, offering Bill Mandel of Revlon the role of CEO, but Revson wouldn't let him go. Rubinstein consolidated their global business by pulling all the privately held satellites into its American company in 1969, with Oscar Kolin announcing to the media that this move made them 'truly international in scope'. The Rubinstein board agreed to buy 80% of Parfums Rochas for $25 million in 1970, only to have their plans quashed by the French government. Nevertheless, Helena Rubinstein announced to their shareholders year-end turnover of over $70 million and financial reporters noted 'the firm held its usual, formidable balance-sheet position.'

In 1969 they had launched Mykonos, a range eulogised as being 'the first time a complete product range has been marketed worldwide at one time'. International beauty editors were wined and dined on a boat moored off the Greek island of Mykonos, where helicopters circled and dropped carnations on to the deck – reminiscent of Madame's launch of Heaven Sent over two decades earlier.

Charles Revson didn't need to hire yachts for press launches. His own sumptuous vessel, the third largest in the world after those owned by Aristotle Onassis and Stavros Niarchos, with a stateroom larger than the US presidential yacht, *Sequoia*, cruised the Mediterranean with Charles and his third wife Lyn holding court. As befitted a woman who had made 'the best-dressed list', the media reported on Mrs Revson's wardrobe of cruise clothes as much as on the yacht's gold-plated cutlery and engraved Cartier stationery. The Revsons' guests, like Eugenia Sheppard, Eleanor Lambert, Aileen Mehle (who wrote the influential 'Suzy' column and would later become a non-executive director of Revlon Inc), and an impressive list of heavyweight social celebrities, guaranteed Charles the press coverage he seemed to crave, fuelled by his growing antagonism for Estée Lauder, who had by now honed her social aspirations to a razor-sharp edge. Revlon was now a seemingly unstoppable force in the global cosmetics industry, their figures for 1968 showing sales of $314 million and net profits of $31 million. Charles and Lyn were enjoying their place in the corporate, flaming, 'new-rich' sun.

On one of her trips on the *Ultima II*, Eleanor Lambert was refreshing her lipstick when Charles noticed her very pretty, vintage Cartier lipstick case. 'Why aren't you using my lipsticks, Eleanor?' he asked. 'Can you still *get* a refill for that?' When Lambert said she couldn't, Charles swept into action. 'He got on the phone right away,' she said, 'and organised it so that a special Revlon colour virtually identical to my favourite was fitted into my Cartier case. So generous.' I asked her what the others would have done. 'Well, let me see. Elizabeth would have said, "Such a pretty case, dear, may I see it?" She would have then had one copied to put on the line.' 'Helena?' I asked. 'Oh, I suppose she might have said, "Very nice. Cartier? I have lots the same."' Finally, I asked her about Estée Lauder. 'Oh, she would have said, "How lovely, may I borrow it?" She would have taken it away, copied it, put it on the line and sent it back, still empty, but with the copy of her own in an exquisite ribboned gift box.'

Although on her death Madame's stock had risen on rumours of Revlon buying her business, the only thing Charles bought belonging to Helena was her Park Avenue apartment, which took him over two years to convert and decorate to his 'gold with everything' taste. Patrick O'Higgins, who later went to dinner *chez* Revson, served by waiters wearing white gloves, said, 'The décor would have made Madame chuckle with glee. "Such a waste. So *nouveau riche*, so . . . Hollywood", she would have said.'

The cosmetics industry seemed to colonise New York's General Motors Building. The Estée Lauder company had over 123 offices on the 37th and 39th floors, including several for their newest 'star' brand, the hypo-aller-genic Clinique, launched in 1967. Revlon had over 600 staff in place on five floors – the top five floors, naturally – and in 1970 Helena Rubinstein moved in, the building taking on the trade nickname 'General Odours'. Oscar, Roy and Mala hired decorators to build them glittering, showcase offices 'with a focus on the future'. The foyer, reception room and each major executive's office incorporated more than a few touches of Madame, draw-ing from an extensive pool of antiques not included in her auction sales. There was a Venetian chandelier here, a carved eighteenth-century English mirror there. Even Helena's seventeenth-century oak refectory table, where she had used to sit on a high chair, her feet propped up on cushions, was used as a presentation table in Roy's office.

Everywhere, her portraits looked down on the relatives left handling their heritage. Roy had the sequinned Tchelitchew, Oscar the Graham Sutherland, Mala the Vertes. And there were modern pieces: furniture by

Marcel Brueur, Charles Eames and Knoll, with chairs upholstered in bold, spiced colours. In Mala's office, Victorian pieces owned by her aunt were painted white and re-upholstered in Thai check taffeta. Statues carved by Elie Nadelman were displayed either side of doors, just as over fifty-five years earlier they had presided over the space in Helena's first salon in New York. The family, however, were not to be in their glamorous offices for much longer.

At Arden, following her sister's death, word spread that Gladys would take over. She already owned the French subsidiary and media reports indicated she 'would run the world-wide business from Paris.' But Gladys was old and in 1969, feeling unwell herself she sold her shareholding in the French company back to the American board, trading her inheritance of $4 million from Elizabeth for a lump payment of $2 million, and retired, living quietly in Paris for two years until she died. And just as the Elizabeth Arden company was getting over one court case, another one, rather more serious, blew up. Carl Gardiner resigned abruptly in mid-1970, his departure veiled in uncertainty and gossip, whereupon Charles Bliss, chairman of the board of the Bank of New York, took over as president, sending a signal to the industry that Arden was, finally, up for sale. In September, the chemical and toiletries company, American Cyanamid, who had cast an eye over the business at the suggestion of Goldman Sachs, were formally approached to buy Elizabeth Arden. Management looked on with unease as the men in suits crunched numbers. Cyanamid were preparing to offer $35 million, with $28 million in cash, $4.5 million in stock and the remaining $2.5 million in the form of a contingency payment, which the Arden board wished them to pay over to Pat Young, Elizabeth's principal heir, who was still waiting for her money. Cyanamid refused the latter, but continued negotiations and papers were drawn up. Their executive committee passed the deal and delivered their offer to Arden's headquarters, indicating it merely needed the rubber stamp of a formal board meeting to be held on 7 October for the deal to be ratified.

At this point the giant pharmaceutical corporation Eli Lilly moved in, approaching Charles Bliss saying they too were interested. Realising time was short, Lilly, it appears, waived their due diligence and made an immediate offer. They went swiftly over numbers, and in the astonishingly quick time of two days came up with a figure of $38.5 million to buy the Arden business, with $20 million to be paid on the spot, clearing the way for Pat Young to receive her money. Charles Bliss was obliged to tell the losers the bad news. American Cyanamid were furious, claiming they hadn't been informed they were part of an auction situation, and rapidly moved to sue for compensation and loss of potential profit. In an attempt to undo Eli Lilly's acquisition, Cyanamid filed suits against Elizabeth Arden, the Bank of New York, Eli Lilly *and* Elizabeth's executors for $120 million, and subsequently against Goldman Sachs for the same amount. The legal action delayed settlement of Miss Arden's estate even further, and whilst it may have delighted expensive lawyers, it cost her heirs dearly. The case was eventually settled out of court for an 'undisclosed sum'. On Christmas Eve 1971, those still left alive got the Christmas present they wanted, the announcement they would receive their bequests.

Integrating an independent business into a mighty conglomerate is not easy, yet, in the beginning at least, Eli Lilly enjoyed owning Elizabeth Arden. Their executives particularly enjoyed visiting Europe and enthusiastically attended Wimbledon, taking the centre court seats Teddy Haslam had acquired for Miss Arden's business years earlier. Having implemented the handover, Gordon Yates, by now CEO of all the European divisions and Executive Vice President of the American parent company, retired. The London salon was relocated to a prestige, street-level site on Bond Street and offices at Arden's premises all over the world, particularly in New York, were redecorated at considerable expense. 'I think we've given Elizabeth Arden a little class,' said one Lilly executive to Duke Cross when walking him through the new corporate suite. Perhaps. But Miss Arden always felt it was her customers who had the class, and deserved the finest surroundings. Offices were where people worked. Interestingly, her own pine-panelled office above the salon in New York was left untouched. Even today, it remains virtually as it was when she worked there, as though none of the men controlling her company ever found the courage to change it.

The 1970's was the decade that saw conglomerates absorbing cosmetics companies as fast as Pablo used a make-up sponge. Cyclax, along with Lentheric Yardley and Germaine Monteil, were by now all part of BAT Industries. The charming building in London's South Molton Street, where Mrs Henning of Cyclax used to preside over her aristocratic clients, was sold, and became a hairdressing salon called Molton Brown. Eve of Roma had disappeared into Gillette in 1968, and Max Factor was part of the mighty Norton Simon. By 1971, the very popular Richard Salomon, head of Charles of the Ritz Cosmetics, who had built up that firm since he was a young man and taken it public ten years earlier, presided over the sales of Charles of the Ritz/Lanvin to the American giant Squibb. Salomon would later say that being president of a public company in the cosmetics industry, with an increasingly aggressive drive for profits and less and less time for, or investment in, creativity, was not a comfortable position.

In a move which critics said also showed an increasing drive for profits from advertising and less time for editorial creativity, the management at Condé Nast fired their famous, if ever more eccentric, editor in chief of American *Vogue*, Diana Vreeland, in 1971. '*Vogue*,' said Andy Warhol at the time, 'decided it wanted to go middle class.' In that same year, Coco Chanel died in her suite at the Ritz in Paris. Patrick O'Higgins completed and published his funny and affectionate book about Madame.

In 1972, 'Prince' Michael Evlanoff died in a nursing home where he had spent his last impoverished years, ill and alone. Ironically, the home was called 'Florence Nightingale'. The following year, Constance Woodworth, the journalist Miss Arden had so generously befriended, paid her back by writing a book about her life, co-authored with Alfred Allan Lewis. 'Constance Woodworth wasn't a very nice person', says Maurice at Arden's New York salon, 'and she didn't talk to the right people.' Neither Miss Arden's surviving niece, nor her nephew, were offered any continuing involvement with the corporation who had bought her business.

In 1973, Madame Rubinstein's family sold the business to Colgate Palmolive, receiving a top-of-the-market, boom price of over $143 million. 'It was', says Diane Moss, 'a hard decision for my father and the family to take, but it was the right time to sell, the business was becoming so very costly to run.' Following the sale to Colgate Palmolive, Madame's family retired from the cosmetics industry and Oscar Kolin became President of the Helena Rubinstein Foundation.

In 1973, in a blaze of publicity, Charles Revson signed gap-toothed American model Lauren Hutton to be 'the face of Ultima II' at a fee of $200,000 a year — the most money ever paid to a model on an exclusive contract in the beauty business. Two years later, in August 1975, Revson died of pancreatic cancer. There was no problem with the line of succession at Revlon as Charles had already hired Michael Bergerac, acknowledged as one of the brightest businessmen of his generation, as president, with a 'golden hello' of $1.5 million. By the time Revson died, Revlon was spending $65 million a year on its advertising from a company turnover in excess of $600 million.

For Colgate Palmolive, the acquisition of Helena Rubinstein would prove to be a disaster, not helped by their moving the entire business away from New York. In 1977 they launched Silk Fashion, a cosmetics line based on the original silk formula bought by Boris Forter and Ceska, with an extravagant soirée at the Villa d'Este Hotel on Lake Como, home of Italy's silk industry. The consumer response was less than expected. By 1978, Rubinstein's UK operation was merged with Pfizer's Coty and by 1979 it was reported Colgate's losses were running at $20 million, with debt standing at $50 million – and the business was for sale. L'Oréal emerged as a suitor at a price rumoured to be around $140 million, but talks broke down. The Kao Soap Company of Japan – then, as now, the world's largest consumer of cosmetics – were next to make an offer, with a figure thought to be in the region of $75 million, only a little more than half the sum Colgate had paid. This deal too collapsed. L'Oréal once again entered the arena, via their American subsidiary Cosmair. The price by now was rumoured to be down to $35 million. In the autumn of 1979, Colgate issued a statement saying the proposed deal had fallen through. They were left holding an ailing brand.

In 1980, Colgate Palmolive sold Helena Rubinstein to Albi Enterprises Inc, a small business operating out of New York, for a price that was observed by the industry to be 'petty cash'. Albi agreed a sum of $20 million, paying only $1.5 million on signing, with an additional $3.5 million to be paid in two equal instalments in 1981 and 1983, the balance being paid annually. It would be 1996 before Colgate were projected to receive the balance of their money, even then only a fraction of what they had originally paid. So desperate were Colgate to offload Rubinstein that they guaranteed domestic and overseas bank loans amounting to $43 million. Albi had acquired the rights for Giorgio Armani fragrances, which in the excitement of the Milan-based fashion boom years of the early 1980s, was a major coup. The film *American Gigolo*, starring Richard Gere alongside Revlon's model, Lauren Hutton, was released that year, and Gere's film wardrobe, exclusively by Armani, propelled the designer into orbit in the US – the timing for his fragrance distribution could not have been more perfect.

By 1984, L'Oréal had acquired Helena Rubinstein's business interests in Latin America and Japan from Albi. By 1988, they had bought up Rubinstein's operations worldwide. It had taken them nine years, and three failed attempts, but L'Oréal, at that time chiefly known in America for its hair-care products, eventually got the company they wanted, and with it, distribution of Giorgio Armani fragrances.

In 1988, Eli Lilly sold Elizabeth Arden to Fabergé. By 1989, Arden had changed hands yet again, when the Anglo-Dutch Unilever group bought both Fabergé and the Elizabeth Arden brand for $1.5 billion. The organisation that had been the recipient of Miss Arden's wrath when they enticed one of her best managers to run their Harriet Hubbard Ayer brand so many years earlier, now owned her business. She must have turned in her grave. They set about pruning what they perceived as 'dead wood', which in 1990 meant closing almost all the beauty salons around the world.

The staff at the salons were desolate, as were many of the clients, as so many of the Red Doors prepared to shut for the last time. In Chicago, at the last salon that Miss Arden had opened herself (having had the foresight to buy the freehold of what had proved to be a very useful building), the atmosphere was strained as they prepared to close down. The antique mirrors and Regency consoles had already been sold. The liveried doorman had long left. Valet parking had been discontinued. A forlorn Oscar de la Renta evening dress could be seen marked down from $4200 to $525. The chandeliers were looking dusty and the now shabby treatment rooms had an echo of emptiness. The shower rooms where Chicago's pampered ladies had enjoyed their 'Scottish douches' and showered in water scented with Blue Grass, courtesy of a handy tablet that fitted into the shower heads, were deserted. 'None of us are going to find *any* place with the panache and ambience we used to have here,' said a long-term employee tearfully as she contemplated looking for a new job, reluctantly accepting that the servicing of such a refined way of life was anathema to large corporations. Panache didn't deliver the profitability. The great era of the beauty salons as created by Elizabeth Arden and Helena Rubinstein had come to an end.

Epilogue

I N April 1990, twenty-five years after Helena Rubinstein's death, collectors and museum directors from all over the world gathered at Sotheby's in New York for the sale of the Harry A. Franklin Family Collection of African Art. The late Mr and Mrs Franklin had been passionate collectors and included in the sale were eight pieces they had purchased in Helena's 'benchmark' sale in 1966. The pride of the Franklins' collection was 'The Bangwa Queen', the statue Helena had so loved, the piece she had acquired without any cash changing hands, that had fetched $29,000 in the sale following her death. It sold that day for *three million, four hundred and ten thousand dollars*, making it the most valuable piece of African art to have been purchased in open auction in the twentieth century. You can see 'The Queen' today at the Dapper Museum in Paris, where she stands proud under plexi-glass, surveying the room. A small, stocky, sturdy figure, dancing with enthusiasm and exuding *awesome* power in her dual role as 'priestess and mother' . . . just as Helena Rubinstein once did.

In the same year, Sotheby's in New York sold the Brancusi sculpture 'La Négresse Blanche' which had been bought by Helena from the artist. It fetched $8 million. Madame always rather liked Brancusi. 'Clever. Good with his customers,' she used to say. So was she.

Following the death of Canadian tycoon Garfield Weston, Barretstown Castle was bequeathed to the Irish government. Today, horses still graze in the grounds and wealthy visitors dine at the castle. Now, however, it costs a *lot* to do so, and they are pleased to pay it. Barretstown is home to one of actor Paul Newman's Hole in the Wall Gang camps, where sick and terminally ill children spend a few happy weeks. Mr Newman's charity pays a rent of one Irish punt a year to the government. He put in over $1.5 million in seed money to start the cause, and plays host at the castle from time to time at fundraising dinners, where he charms the rich to part with their cash. The main door to the castle is still painted bright red, as it was when Miss Arden owned it. Elizabeth, who spent her life charming the rich to part with their cash and herself gave generously to children's charities, would be pleased.

At the end of 2000, Unilever sold Elizabeth Arden to Florida-based FFI Fragrances in a cash and share deal costing close to $240 million, retaining ownership of a block of the preferred shares, which gives them a holding of about 20%. FFI's chief executive officer, F. Scott Beattie, has changed the company name to Elizabeth Arden. Mr Beattie told *Women's Wear Daily*, 'Elizabeth Arden is one of the most classic beauty franchises in the US and internationally, and we're going to capitalise on that and grow it.' Nearly four decades after her death, her name and brand seems to have come home to someone who will cherish them.

The Red Door beauty salons and spas are being revived, as part of a global programme of expansion. Following in the tradition established by Elizabeth's friends, 'First Ladies' Mamie Eisenhower and Patricia Nixon, it's been reported that Mrs George Bush attends the Arden salon in Washington, a city where Elizabeth first opened her doors in 1913.

Elizabeth Arden's global sales now exceed $731.5 million a year and are growing. They are a small part of the global market in prestige cosmetics and skin care – calculated to be worth $30 billion a year and growing – but a large part of the history of the beauty industry.

Eight Hour Cream remains a worldwide bestseller. The Kentucky Derby, where Miss Arden had it rubbed on to her horses' legs, is now the richest, most glamorous social event in America's horseracing calendar.

At the time of writing, Catherine Zeta Jones has just been signed as 'the face of Elizabeth Arden'.

In 2000, *Forbes* magazine calculated the personal wealth of Mr Leonard Lauder, president of Estée Lauder, to be more than $3 billion. Estée Lauder is now a public company, with the Lauder family's shares worth more than

$6 billion and where a third generation is making its mark. Through its own brands and specialist acquisitions, Estée Lauder is estimated to control 46% of America's prestige cosmetics business, and in 2000 had a volume of $4.37 billion. Mrs Lauder herself, at the time of writing, lives in a twilight world at her home in New York. Erica Titus Friedman telephones from time to time to see how her old friend is, but accepts that 'it's never possible to talk with her now'.

Grace Gilbert says of Revlon today: 'If Charles were alive, he would probably laugh that sinister laugh that went through your spine, especially if you were the butt of it, and say, "even with all their bungling, they still haven't totally killed the legacy I left them."'

L'Oréal's sales in 2003 totalled 14.3 billion Euros. They have launched a costly promotional campaign to remarket the Helena Rubinstein brand.

Many of the rare books published by Edward Titus remain in the library belonging to his second wife Erica. The cultural heritage of the Titus name is remembered in New York, where 'the Roy and Nuita Titus Foundation' endowed the building of the Film Theatre at the Museum of Modern Art.

Madame's great-niece, Diane Moss, runs the Helena Rubinstein Foundation in New York with efficiency and skill, discreetly donating millions of dollars a year to help individuals, especially women and children, discover their potential. The Foundation allocates money to education, community services and the arts, primarily in New York. Her staff in the quiet suite of offices on Madison Avenue are under the watchful eyes of the portraits of Helena Rubinstein.

At the time of writing, over one hundred years since Helena Rubinstein's first cream included pink bark, 'Pycnogenol', the trademark name for pink bark extract, is being heralded as the latest in an arsenal of twenty-first-century anti-ageing ingredients, all promising 'miracles' in the quest for youth and beauty. Galen would have been amused, but not surprised. Neither would Elizabeth Arden and Helena Rubinstein, who made their fortune from treatment creams. Very little about the beauty industry in the twenty-first century would have surprised them, especially the money women are prepared to pay for products. In 1960, when Madame launched Ultra Feminine Face Cream, priced at $5.50 an oz, sales were off-target. When asked what the problem was, she remarked gloomily, 'Not expensive enough.'

Acknowledgements

It was never going to be an easy task to intertwine two lives, particularly such full and fascinating ones as those of Madame and Miss Arden. During the four years *War Paint* has taken to arrive from an idea to a finished book, I have been overwhelmed by the kindness and generosity of all the people who have helped make it happen. The editing process of a long story exploring not just two lines but an industry has meant some strands have had to be eliminated altogether. So, to those of you who helped me unravel mysteries, only to find they are not included, please don't be disappointed.

The joy of discovery has far outweighed the efforts made to glean some of the real background and personalities behind the public façade of Helena Rubinstein and Elizabeth Arden. Both of these remarkable women were experts at concealing what might dent their image. Both tugged the puppet strings of the media to brilliant effect, and both made their executives and families toe an iron line of discretion. My task in unravelling fact from fiction about their early lives has been helped enormously by the internet. To the friends I made around the world as I became a detective via my midnight messages, my heartfelt thanks.

My starting-off point, and the highlight of many trips for this book, which have taken me to India, Egypt, America, Ireland and France, was visiting Krakow and exploring Kazimierz. The young people who live in Kazimierz now – where the whole Jewish community is said to number only six hundred – gather to listen to the hauntingly beautiful music played at the time-warp restaurant, Alef, or eat at the Klezmer Hois, overlooking the lovely cobbled square of ul.Szeroka. I won't easily forget sitting over a vodka with local historian and author Henryk Halkowski whilst he explained the moving history of Krakow's Jews. Thanks in no small part to the power of film to tell a story, Krakow, the home of Oscar

Schindler's enamelling factory, is now on the tourist map and, taking pride of place by the doorway at the Klezmer Hois, is a letter saying 'thank you for looking after us and feeding us so well, love Stephen and Kate'. Part of *Schindler's List* was filmed in Kazimierz and as Spielberg's camera swept up ul.Szeroka, you can just see the Rubinstein family house on the left, where Helena – then Chaja – was born. My thanks also to Mrs William 'Zew' Schantz, whose husband was related to Helena by marriage. Mr Schantz was the youngest member of Oscar Schindler's list, and worked for Helena after the war, a period in their lives about which Olga Schantz shared her memories. Records of Krakow's Jewish community remain remarkably intact. Henryk took me to the city archives where we gently shook the dust off the copper-plate filled ledgers, becoming increasingly excited as they disclosed their details about Helena's parents, aunts, uncles, brothers, sisters and cousins. Many Polish-Jewish archives have been painstakingly translated and cross-referenced onto a database by a dedicated group of people, many of whom are volunteers, working for the Ronald S. Lauder Foundation Genealogy Project at the Jewish Historical Institute of Poland. In particular, I would like to thank Judy Wolkovitch, who in turn put me in touch with Dr Neil Rosen, author of *The Unbroken Chain*, and also introduced me to the indefatigable Alfred Silberfeld. Mr Silberfeld is a second cousin of Madame Rubinstein, and himself a noted genealogist, whose help has been of inestimable value. Other relatives who have provided background on Helena's family tree and filled gaps in tracking her early years include Catherine and Jacques Beckmann and Stella and Hank Marcus. Above all, I would like to thank Diane Kolin Moss, Madame Rubinstein's great-niece, who runs the Helena Rubinstein Foundation in New York and who was generous not just with her time and support, but with her archives, carefully maintained by Elizabeth Waterman. Most of the photographs used in *War Paint* are provided courtesy of the Foundation, for which I am truly grateful.

The mystery of Helena's time in Australia was largely unravelled by Trevor Jacobs. Mr Jacobs, who was born in Coleraine—and who sadly died without seeing the finished book—was a keen historian and local archivist. He shared the results of his meticulous investigation into Madame's life, from the official records of the time, coupled with memories of family stories from long ago. My thanks also to Professor John Poynter of the University of Melbourne, Sara Joynes at the National Library of Australia who set me off on my search into the Lamington family, Jan McDonald at the State Library of Victoria in Melbourne and Prue McDonald at the State Library of South Australia. Along with Elizabeth Hibbard at the State Library of Queensland

and Carol Galbraith at Australia's Native Plants Forum, they read and researched, advised and answered a huge list of questions.

Odette O'Higgins and her daughter, Marianne, generously allowed me to not merely read Patrick's letters and unpublished works, but to quote freely from them, also providing the picture of Patrick with Brenda Frazier from their family archives. John Richardson talked to me about Madame, Picasso and her paintings, and Kenneth J. Lane about Madame and her jewels. David Nash and John Marion described her 1966 art sales. At Sotheby's in New York, Mallory and Pete Hathaway and Vincent Plescia could not have been more helpful, and Jean Fritts introduced me to the compelling world of African Art. George Fehar, of OAN in New York, traced rare sale catalogues, as did Jeffrey Eger. Monsieur Christophe Tzara in Paris spoke of his father's collection, of growing up with African sculpture and memories of Charles Ratton. Jenny Tobias at the Museum of Modern Art in New York tracked down copies of their African Negro Art Exhibition and Elie Nadelman Exhibition catalogues. Observations on Madame's art collection were given by Ray Perman and Connor Macklin of the Grosvenor Gallery, as well as by David Nash and John Richardson. In respect of my attempts to understand the raw vitality of Montparnasse in the 1920s, I must thank Wilhelm 'Billy' Kluver and Julie Martin, co-authors of the incomparable *Kiki's Paris*. They were kindness itself, providing copies of their work, and of correspondence between Edward Titus and Bennett Cerf, along with many other contacts and advice. Through them I met Erica Titus Friedman. It was utterly enlightening spending time with her in Cannes, as well as great fun. She kindly allowed me to quote from her late husband's piognant letters. Thanks to an introduction by journalist Giles Chapman, I obtained unique insight into the character of Madame and her sister, Ceska, by meeting two of Boris Forter's sons, Claude Forter and Christian Wolmar. Boris Forter ran her London company from 1939 until 1971, and his eldest son Claude, who joined the firm in America after the war, provided reams of amusing copy, whilst Christian, who has transcribed hours of interviews with his father, generously gave me the transcripts. Nancy Carino in Greenwich, Connecticut discovered details of Madame's favourite house and Tony McAuliffe tracked down Grace Davidson's editorial text in a Boston library. Timothy Boettger, who specialises in tracing Russian nobility, worked hard in an attempt to establish the authenticity of the Gourielli title. Grace Gilbert, who worked for Hattie Carnegie, Revlon and Helena Rubinstein respectively, gave me a unique insight into the mercurial personality of the late, great Charles Revson and what working at Rubinstein was like. Captain Arthur Harris confirmed the sumptuous style of the Ultima II, recollecting several amusing stories which sadly there was no space to include.

In respect of Elizabeth Arden, my deep appreciation goes to Tiki Yates and his sister Caroline for allowing me to use family correspondence. Their father's correspondence with Miss Arden, and that of his colleagues and friends, has been an anchor to this book. Angus McCall's recall of the time spent working for Miss Arden was vivid and riveting. Lord Montagu of Beaulieu, the late Hon. Mrs Varley, Emily Hutchison, Eleanor Lambert and Joseph Wile added immeasurably to the reality of her personality, and Gina Campbell Ross, Priscilla Moynihan and Rosemary Barrington Wells gave me their recollections of working at the Arden Salon and office in London, as did Maurice – who still styles an immaculate coiffeur at Arden's salon in New York. Karen MacPerson, who worked for Miss Arden in Canada, added comment about the funeral, as did Monica Smythe (Lady Eyre), Miss Arden's private secretary during the last years of her life, who was a mine of helpful information. Geraldine Stutz added to my impressions about Bessie Marbury.

Edward Basset, the Chairman of Keeneland, advised me about Elizabeth Arden Graham's horses and provided background on Leslie Combs. Most importantly of all, he allowed the tirelessly helpful Phyllis Rogers to track literally hundreds of press clippings held at Keeneland's authoritative library, which were readily made available to me. Angus McCall shared hours of memories about his uncle, Captain Sir Cecil Boyd Rochfort, his mother Muriel McCall's Tally Ho stud in Ireland, and about Barretstown Castle and Tony Duquette. The management of the Elizabeth Arden Company allowed me unlimited access to their archives in both New York and London, where in particular Managing Director Susan Taylor and her PA Elinor Pritchard delved into the corporate past and current plans of the company on my behalf. In New York, my thanks go in particular to James Cantela, guardian of the archive, assisted by David Horak, who are lovingly cataloguing and restoring the pictorial treasures the company own onto digital format. Their skills have enabled me to show readers rare and fascinating pictures of Miss Arden and her work.

I'm grateful to my two hard-working researchers, Toto Lloyd in Paris and Jane Peyton in Los Angeles. Toto pored over magazines, translating texts from French, whilst Jane, who viewed 'Young and Beautiful,' also read my manuscript and made a mass of helpful suggestions. In Bombay, Sarita Pandit scoured archives, and in Thunder Bay, Ontario, Bill Martin – quite literally – traipsed through the snow to spend hours looking through microfiche records about the Graham family. In Cornwall, Isobel Pickering unearthed details of the Tadd family history and the fascinating – and often fatal – lives of the county's mariners. Sebastian Wormall at Harrods archives kindly uncovered information on Miss Arden's in-store appearances and about Mr Edward Haslam. Mr Eugene R. Schultz, the President of Frank E. Campbell in New York, checked their records concerning both funerals and burials, and is an archival historian *par excellence*. The friendly staff at the Surrogate Court in New York rushed to photocopy documents for me on Thanksgiving Eve in time for me to catch a flight back to London. Richard Tuske at the New York Bar Association pointed me in the right direction on the court case between American Cyanamid and Eli Lilly. William Keslar trawled the records of U.S. Steel, laying to rest the rumour that they offered for Arden's business. Jeffrey Brown at the Maine State Archives found copies of both Miss Arden's divorce documents. Mr Paul Cohen of Lehman Brothers gave me insight into their acquisition of the Helena Rubinstein Company in the late 1920s, and Richard Heller of *Forbes* magazine has taken me through the intricacies of today's financial data on the cosmetics industry in the context of this story. My particular thanks go to the ever-cheerful Janice Sherlock at the General Register Office in Southport who unearthed birth, marriage and death certificates of the Tadd, Graham and Titus family as I was battling against deadlines.

At the many libraries around the world which it has been my pleasure to use, I particularly want to thank Cynthia Cathcart, Director at the incomparable Condé Nast library in New York. My thanks also to Claude Zachary at the University of Southern California for information on Nicholai Remisoff, Yvonne Boyer at the Vanderbilt University, Tennessee, Stephane Houy-Towner of the Fashion Collection at the Metropolitan Museum of Art in New York, Richard Foster at the New York, Public Library, Leonore Benson at Fashion Group headquarters in New York and Annette Green of the Fragrance Foundation in New York. Richard May of Warner Brothers in Los Angeles unearthed information about Arden's film 'Young and Beautiful', and Bob Gitt, of UCLA Film and Television Archives, arranged the screening. Dr John Worthen at the centre for D.H. Lawrence studies at Nottingham University gave me guidance about the Black Mannikin Press and the publication of *Lady Chatterley's Lover* in Paris.

Endless people opened their address books, shared memories, made introductions and pointed me in the right direction, particularly Nicky Haslam, Luis Dominguez, Terry Mansfield, Susan Train, Nicholas Coleridge, Donna Christina, Shirley Giovetti, Tony Cash, Gregg Zachary, the Earl of Mayo, Lady Weidenfeld, David James, Katherine Stubenvoll, Celia Brayfield, Simon Rendall, Richard Channing and Mike Von Joel.

433

Alexandra Shulman and Suzy Menkes urged me to stop talking about the idea and write the story.

War Paint is about the lives – and lifestyles – of the two women who had such a profound impact on the origins of the 20th century beauty business, rather than a book about the beauty business itself. Miss Arden and Madame Rubinstein were united over the essentials required in the quest for beautiful skin – cleanse away grime, exfoliate dead cells, moisturise and keep out of the sun. It's wise advice. Although the evolution of the beauty industry since their deaths has been meteoric, I did not set out to write about what is true or false concerning the claims made by today's cosmetics manufacturers as they tread the paths of 'seductive science' to entice consumers.

In studying the history of the cosmetics industry, I must cite two superb books which for anyone with an interest in the subject are required reading. The first is *American Beauty* by Lois Banner and the second, *Hope in a Jar, The Making of America's Beauty Culture* by Kathy Peiss. For those interested in social history, *Fire and Ice, The Story of Charles Revson – the Man Who Built the Revlon Empire* by Andrew Tobias and *Estée Lauder, Beyond the Magic* by Lee Israel must be part of any reading list.

Finally, my own book was launched on its way by my agent, Lizzy Kremer at Ed Victor Ltd, and nurtured by my London publisher, Lennie Goodings at Virago, who believed in this project from the start, and tried not to wince as I turned in twice as much copy as she had expected. She was assisted by Elise Dillsworth, who took care of a host of technical and legal essentials too numerous to mention. Linda Silverman organised the pictures, the selection of which was masterminded under the discerning eye of my husband, Colin Woodhead. In America, I owe thanks to my supportive editor, Hana Lane at John Wiley & Sons.

Above all, my love to Colin and our sons Ollie and Max, with my thanks for everything you have put up with over the past four years and for being behind me all the way.

Notes and Sources

I have been fortunate to have been able to read and draw from the extensive correspondence between Miss Arden and her management team in London, which covers the period 1930–1966 and, thereafter, letters from Gordon Yates to Carl Gardiner at Elizabeth Arden Sales Corporation in New York, and to Eli Lilly, from 1966 to 1971, when Mr Yates retired. The correspondence includes certain letters between Miss Arden and her sister, Gladys de Maublanc, and between Mrs Yates and Madame de Maublanc.

In respect of Madame Rubinstein, correspondence made available for reference and research includes the private papers of Patrick O'Higgins and detailed correspondence between Mr O'Higgins and Madame Rubinstein. She herself provided Mr O'Higgins with letters and documents when he wrote the serial of her life story for the London *Sunday Times* and worked on updating her autobiography. Erica Titus Friedman kindly gave me permission to quote from her husband's correspondence.

In addition, the author was granted access to view extensive memorabilia, diaries and letters kept at the Elizabeth Arden archives at the company headquarters in New York, along with company records and sales material previously stored at the Acton, London factory archive, subsequently catalogued by Unilever. Many photographs for this book have been kindly provided by the Elizabeth Arden archives.

Diane Moss of The Helena Rubinstein Foundation in New York generously allowed extensive examination of their files and records and the Foundation has provided many of the photographs used for this book.

Abbreviations

EA – Miss Elizabeth Arden
LEA – Letter Elizabeth Arden

LTH – Letter Edward 'Teddy' Haslam
LGY – Letter Gordon Yates
LGdM – Letter Gladys de Maublanc
EAA – Elizabeth Arden Archives
MEA – *Miss Elizabeth Arden* by Alfred Allan Lewis and Constance
Woodworth, published in 1973

HR – Madame Helena Rubinstein
LHR – Letter Helena Rubinstein
LET – Letter Edward Titus
LHT – Letter Horace Titus
LP.O'H – Letter Patrick O'Higgins and P.O'H – Patrick O'Higgins
TBF – Tapes Boris Forter
HRF – The Helena Rubinstein Foundation, New York
MLfB – *My Life for Beauty* by Helena Rubinstein, published in 1965

Every effort has been made to trace copyright holders and to clear reprint permissions. If notified, the publishers will be pleased to rectify any omissions in future editions. Any omissions of fact or errors are the author's own.

Sources

Introduction

Toothbrushes, deodorants, hairwashing, see *Soft Soap, Hard Sell* by Vincent Vinikas, p xi. Krakow home life in Kazimierz *see* MLfB by HR p 13. Personality traits of HR confirmed in detailed interviews with long-term staff including Claude Forter and also TBF. On Arden, by interviews amongst others, with Angus McCall, also LEA. 'She had their desk removed', *Madame* by P.O'H p 47. 'Sometimes to tears', Angus McCall confirming Mr Haslam cried. 'Revolving door policy', widely quoted on Arden's employee relationships, originated in *Fortune*, August 1930. On HR's fractured relationship with her sons, LHR, LHT, LET, and interview with Erica Titus Friedman. See, also *Madame* by P.O'H, p 76: 'each was set on destroying the other'. On HR's fanatical thrift, TBF, *Life* magazine, July 1941, *Collier's*, 4 December 1948 by Hambla Bauer, LHR. Also *Madame* by P.O'H p 47: 'electricity is so expensive' and 'why don't they write on both sides of the paper?' on rummaging through wastepaper baskets. On Arden's insomnia, interview Angus McCall, plus LTH. Richest self-made women in the world, copy widely reported in business media including *Fortune*, August 1930, also *Fortune*, October 1938 on Arden: 'I am a famous woman in this industry'. *Famous Merchants* by Sigmund A. Lavine: 'she has probably earned more money than any other woman in America', p 103. On Rubinstein, *Life* magazine, July 1941: 'she is perhaps the world's most successful business woman'. *Profiles of Power and Success, Fourteen Geniuses who Broke the Rules*, by Gene N. Landrum: 'by 1950, Madame was listed as one of the ten richest, self-made women in the world', p 304. On Leichner, Coty and Rimmel, see *The Gilded Lily* by Terence McLaughlin. The careers of Annie Turnbo Malone and Madame C.J. Walker are brilliantly examined in *Hope in a Jar, The Making of America's Beauty Culture* by Kathy Peiss. Early American Beauty Culture reported by Anne O'Hagan in 'The Quest of Beauty' in *Munsey's* magazine, June 1903. On selling to department stores, LGD, also interview Mr Wile, Wolfe Wiles and background from various UK and USA department store archive records of the late nineteenth and early twentieth century, NYPL. On treatments in HR salons, *see* 'People Who Want to Look Young and Beautiful' by Allison Gray, in *American* magazine, December issue, 1922 and Jo Swerling 'Beauty in Jars and Vials', the *New Yorker*, 30 June 1928. Salon reviews, the *New Yorker*, 9 January 1937, American *Vogue*, *Harper's Bazaar*, February 1937 and on EA, American *Vogue*, April 1937. On early advertising, Arden, see *A Talent for Living: The Story of Henry Sell, An American Original* by Janet Leckie, pp 147–166. Use of illustrations by René Bouché, Bebe Berard, Jean Cocteau, Raol Dufy, photography by Baron de Meyer, Man Ray, Ralph Steiner. Product packaging design by Salvador Dali and Raol Dufy amongst others, interior design by Rue Carpenter, Nicholai Remisoff, data from EAA and HRF, also advertising in *Vogue*, *Town & Country*, *Harper's Bazaar* amongst others. They never met: *Life* magazine, July 1941, HR says 'we have nevair met, nevair'. Obituary, 2 April, *New York Times*: 'No one ever introduced us', Madame seemed quite wistful. 'Absolutely not, no, never', interview Angus McCall. Across a busy restaurant, *Madame*, P.O'H p 51. It was an equal contest between two giant personalities, p 90. On women's passion for lipstick see *Hope in a Jar* by Kathy Peiss, p 171 and p 245: 'by 1948, 80% to 90% of American women used lipstick'. *Lipstick* by Jessica Pallingston. 'Hot Lipstick' Emily Nelson, *Wall Street Journal*, 26 November 2001. The urge to decorate ourselves, see *A History of Make-up* by Maggie Angeloglou, *Cosmetics and Adornment* by Max Wykes-Joyce and *The Gilded Lily* by Terence McLaughlin.

1 Rivals Even in Death: 1965–1967

Information on Rubinstein's auctions, April 1966, from conversations with John Marion, David Nash, John Richardson, Kenneth J. Lane and descriptions from the Parke-Bernet Galleries Catalogues. 'Having received offers' private letter. On Peter Wilson, author's own recollections; see also *Sotheby's* by Robert Lacey, p 112, p 144, p 148. John Marion's skills, p 143, also *Madame*, P.O'H p 292: 'he was a wizard'. 'A Brancusi bronze, called Bird of Space, sold for £50,000 in 75 seconds', *Bruce Chatwin* by Nicholas Shakespeare, p 179. Further background on questionable taste of HR's pictures, *Madame*, P.O'H p 65: 'an art critic said unimportant paintings by every important painter of the nineteenth and twentieth century'. MLfB p 67: 'my collection today is partly good . . . partly not so good'. HR said, 'When I bought a picture because I thought I was getting a bargain, it most often turned out to be a mistake'. Some of her frames, *Madame*, P.O'H p 65. Family bequests identified from the will of Madame Rubinstein. Baroda Pearls, unsubstantiated, yet persistent rumour as explained to author amongst jewellery historians in London, Paris and Bombay. Missing furs: 'When Patrick, who had all the keys, was sent to Paris to do an inventory, he found all her furs missing', interview with John Richardson. On African art: 'We work from 9 to 8', *Bruce Chatwin* by Nicholas Shakespeare, p 177. On Rubinstein collection: 'African Negro Art', Catalogue for MoMA exhibition 1935, edited by James Johnson Sweeney. Press releases HRF. On relationship with Epstein, interview Erica Titus Friedman. Also MLfB by HR p 50: 'how wisely Jacob Epstein had advised me'. *Madame*, P.O'H p 66: 'What's his name, Jacob Epstein, started me off when I first lived in London. Pfft, that's how to collect . . . by the wagonload'. Further background: *Jacob Epstein Collector* by Ezio Bassani and Malcolm D. McLeod; *Travels in West Africa* by Mary H. Kingsley; Nelson Rockerfeller Collection: Masterpieces of Primitive Art; and *Kiki's Paris* by Billy Kluver and Julie Martin. Also *International Herald Tribune*, 'African Art Shatters Western Assumptions' by Michael Gibson, 2 June 2001. On the Bangwa Queen, Parke-Bernet Catalogue of the Helena Rubinstein sale, also 'The Harry A. Franklin Family Collection of African Art', Sotheby's Catalogue, New York, 21 April, 1990. 'Curators of the museum find it hard', comment from writer Greg Zachary on interviewing museum directors at the Volkerkunde. On Arden's attitude post-Madame's death, Ernestine Carter, *With Tongue in Chic*, p 177. On heat in her apartment, ibid p 176: 'I thought I would either faint or burst into bloom'. 'She was a magpie collector', ibid p 175. Mrs Carter's formidable personality, author's own recollections. 'Oscar Kolin was in Japan', interview with Claude

Forter. Background on the laying out of both bodies and of funerals courtesy of Mr Eugene R. Shultz, President, Frank E. Campbell's, Madison Avenue, New York. See also *Madame*, P.O'H pp 285–286 and MEA, p 21. 'A relative was observed wearing', interview with John Richardson. 'She was buried in a gown by Oscar de la Renta', *see* MEA, p 20. His tenure at Elizabeth Arden described in 'Oscar, The Style, Inspiration and Life of Oscar de la Renta' by Sarah Mower. On her passion for pink, interviews with Angus McCall, Monica Smythe (Lady Eyre), Emily Hutchison, Eleanor Lambert, LEA, LGdM. About Pablo, interview with Monica Smythe and MEA, p 20. Service sheet from London Memorial Service at St George's, Hanover Square. Miss Arden's legacies, information about her will published in the media and LGY. Litigation post her death, newspaper reports period 1965–1971 (cited in source notes on final chapter), also LGY, LGdM. Auction details, Parke-Bernet Catalogue, December 1968. Numerous Kentucky newspaper reports on Maine Chance auction, courtesy of Keeneland Library. 'She needed the money', interview with Emily Hutchison.

2   The Krakow Cream 1872–1896

Author has personally examined Polish birth records in Krakow City archives on ul. Sienna showing Chaja, daughter of Herz Rubinstein, dealer from Dukla and Gitel Silberfeld, daughter of Sale Silberfeld, was born on 25 December 1872. Her birth was illegitimate as her parents, although married 'under the huppah', had no civil ceremony. 'We lived in a large house near the Rynek', HR in MLfB p 13. In reality, census records prove Chaja and her family lived in Kazimierz, the old Jewish quarter of Krakow. On theory of Valaze formula, see *Madame*, P.O'H p 151. The legendary Modjeska, born Helena Modrzejewska in Krakow in 1840, had left to live in America by 1870, two years before Chaja was born. Gaylord Hauser's series of diet and healthy life-style books includes *Look Younger, Live Longer*. Prune whip recipe p 126. On diets, see *Madame*, P.O'H p 126: 'Madame was made for diets' and MLfB pp 162–185 titled 'eat your way to beauty'. On diet pills, LHR to Ceska: 'take pills to curb your appetite'. *The Art of Feminine Beauty*, p 139: 'I had oxygen injections to make hunger less noticeable'. On training, HR interviewed in Melbourne said, 'I trained under the best specialists in Europe'. On her strange accent, see *Fortune* magazine, August 1930, *Life* magazine, July 1941, *Madame* by P.O'H p 9: 'I couldn't make out her accent'. *See also* television footage of HR, particularly clips shown on 'The Beauty Queens', Channel 4, 1985. On the history of Krakow and on Polish history in general, references drawn from *Old Krakow* by Jerzy Dobzycki,

Krakow by Grzegorz Rudzinski, and *Legends from Kazimierz* by Henryk Halkowski. Also 'Kazimierz', the English language quarterly newspaper. Birth records of the majority of Gusta's children can be seen in the ledgers at ul. Sienna, as can census records, showing Chaja's father was a dealer in kerosene. Further assistance in tracing Chaja's family tree provided by Trevor Jacobs, Alfred Silberfeld, Catherine and Jacqui Beckmann, Stella Splitter Marcus, Dr Neil Rosen, author of *The Unbroken Chain*, the Ronald. S. Lauder Foundation Genealogy Project at the Jewish Historical Institute of Poland, Judy Wolkovitch and JewishGen. HR refers to her early love, Stanislaw, in MLfB p 18. Catherine and Jacqui Beckmann recall family oral history that Chaja lived with her aunt Rosalie Beckmann when she had to leave the family home. Passenger list from the *Prince Regent Luitpold* shows departure from Genoa. On HR's appalling memory for names, *Madame*, P.O'H p 41: 'mister, mister, what's-his-name?' Also p 47: 'her memory for names was zero'. Eva Levy's Divorce Petition, viewed by author, gives full details of her life with her violent husband, Louis Levy. John Silberfeld, whilst in Australia, ran a jewellery business in partnership with Maurice Shaumer, at 192a Swanston Street, Melbourne. Stella Splitter Marcus confirms her family ran a fur business in Vierma before moving to Antwerp. Photo HR in Vienna 'swathed in furs' courtesy of HRF. 'The Mascara Countess' reference, LHR to Ceska. On mascara formula, see also *Madame*, P.O'H p 144.

3   The Beauty Wizard of Oz 1896–1905

Have the world believe – HR's version of her journey to Australia, *see* MLfB p 23. She was quite shameless. In *The Art of Feminine Beauty* p 13, HR said, 'a girl of 19 who wasn't obliged to work for a living'. In reality she was 31 and penniless. Also p 4: 'my two grandfathers had extensive mining and banking interests and my father went into the exporting business'. She didn't like her life in Coleraine. HR to P.O'H: 'even if everyday only had twenty four hours I worked fifty' *Madame*, p 78, also 'I hated Australia, my relatives', p 78. 'I was hungry, lonely, poor in that awful place', p 247. On travellers meeting ships at India's docks, interview with Sharada Dwivedi, co-author of *Lives of the Indian Princes* and author's own research in *Times of India* archives in Bombay. HR owned copious amounts of Indian jewellery. Parke-Bernet Sale Catalogue describes in detail that part of her Indian jewels put up for auction. Coleraine in 1896: trade lists from Wise, Victoria Towns Directory. HR's entry in the *Australian Dictionary of Biography* by Professor J.R. Poynter of Melbourne University. HR on family tension 'What's a bugger?', see *Australian Dictionary of Biography* entry as above. About her uncle, 'he took liberties', *Madame*, P.O'H p 146. 'My own skin was', HR in *The Art of Feminine Beauty*, p 12. Lanolin as a staple ingredient in face cream, see *Cosmetics and How To Make Them*, Bushby 1936, pp 67 and 82. Cynicism abounds. 'She invented that cream from Poland', see *Beyond The Looking Glass*, Kathrin Perutz, p 40. On moving to Brisbane, HR in *The Art of Feminine Beauty* p 12. On moving to Melbourne, HR in MLfB p 25. On Steve Fairbairn see Fairbairn of Jesus. Further information from Friends of Rowing History and National Rowing Foundation. *Beauty Millionaire* by Maxene Fabe p 28: 'HR became Governess to the family of Lord Lamington'. On Lamington family and nurse Fanny Rod, information from the Cochrane-Baillie Lamington Papers, Glasgow. Naturalisation papers signed by Helena Juliet Rubinstein in 1907. On Toowoomba's forests, information provided by Australian Science and Technology Heritage Centre, the Australia Woods and Forests Department and Lamington National Park, Queensland. Establishment of the Federation described in *The Age*, 16 February 2001. Life in Melbourne and hotels in the city, see *Duchess, The Story of the Windsor Hotel*, by Chrystopher Spicer. Michaelis family information, courtesy of Trevor Jacobs (whose wife was a great grand-daughter of Mr Michaelis). On relationship of HR as nanny in the household, letter Dr Harvey Shannon, great-nephew of John Silberfeld. On Abel Isaacson, see *Madame*, P.O'H p. Further data drawn from letters between Abel Isaacson and Patrick O'Higgins. Winter Garden Tea Rooms, *Australian Dictionary of Biography*, entry by Professor Poynter. HR's age listed as 27 on her naturalisation papers, SLV, when she was actually 35 in 1907. Felton, Grimwade & Co. was an important pharmaceuticals and manufacturing company. On the Valaze formula, Maxene Fabe wrote 'once HR possessed Dr Lykusky's formula', *Beauty Millionaire* p 40. Unsubstantiated, but logical evidence points to Felton, Grimwade analysing and re-configuring her first formula. The Felton Bequest, founded in 1904 with a gift of £383,000, purchased William Dobell's portrait of HR in 1964. Early advertising on Valaze in variety of publications including *Table Talk*, the *Australasian*, the *Australian Home Journal* and the *Lone Hand*. HR talks about Madame Curie in MLfB p 26. There was a Doctor MacDonald in Coleraine who may have contributed to HR's knowledge on skincare, hence her using the name of Miss MacDonald. Otherwise, on early financing, Morty Michaelis was in a position to assist, as were Felton, Grimwade. Erica Titus Friedman claims Edward Titus was an early investor. On the power of editorials, HR to P.O'H: 'a good free write-up is worth ten ads', *Madame* p 120. Trade mark applications SLV. Rubinstein advertising mentions both 'Carpathian Pine Bark' and 'Carpathian Mountain Herbs'.

Abel Isaacson was clear she made the cream herself at the salon premises. Nellie Stewart's endorsement featured in Australian media. HR clung relentlessly to the description her cream was a 'skin food' until FDA 1938 legislation forbade the description. HR identified 'dry', 'normal' and 'oily' skin in Australian advertising and her Guide for Beauty pamphlets 1905–1908. Alfred and George Cummins signed her 1905 Trademark papers.

4 Rise of a Rival 1839–1907

Myth of the romantic elopement of Florence's parents can only have originated from her personally. The *New Yorker*, 6 April 1935 'Profiles Glamour Inc' talks about it with authority. Along with the fact she was born in Woodbridge, that her mother died young and her father was a farmer, little was ever known, or checked, by the press about Arden's early life. Her sisters and brother toed the family line. Birth records of Susan Tadd traced via General Register Office. Marriage records of Susan Tadd to William Graham in Canada registered at Thunder Bay, Ontario. Susan's family home, Churchtown Farm, still stands, opposite the church, Lanteglos by Fowey. Captain Samuel Tadd's diaries, along with Arden's family tree sent to Cornish historian Isobel Pickering by Constance Brothers and Sally Little Behr, Arden's second cousins, and provided to author. Shipping records traced at Fowey Library. Samuel Tadd's will traced by Constance Brothers. Birth records of Thomas Turvey traced via General Register Office. Census records filed at Thunder Bay show William Graham listed as a peddler, resident in Woodbridge. On Mrs Lauder's age, see *Beyond the Magic* by Lee Israel p 28. Leonard Lauder on age, see *Estée, A Success Story* by Estée Lauder, p 7. Jane Turvey's financial support for her grandchildren indicated in family records made available to author. Further information on Fowey see *Shipbuilders' Port of Fowey* by Ward Jackson. Birth dates of all five Graham children traced at Thunder Bay. On EA's over-heated houses, interview with Emily Hutchison and Angus McCall, see also *With Tongue in Chic*, Ernestine Carter p 176. On stuffing paper in her shoes see MEA by Lewis/Woodworth p 32. On EA's support for Syracuse University, LEA. '4,000 millionaires' from *The American Century* by Harold Evans, p 76. Background on Harriet Hubbard Ayer largely drawn from *The Three Lives of Harriet Hubbard Ayer* by her daughter, Margaret, with Isabella Taves. In 1893, Mrs Ayer was committed by her family as a lunatic. Following release, she lectured in Chicago in 1894 on her '14 months in a madhouse' which launched her career as a journalist. Details on her trial, see the *Herald*, April-May 1889, including gloating headline 'she was crazed by drugs'. Mrs Ayer's columns were used as background for her 1899 book, *Health and Beauty*. Her innovative beauty treatments included oxygen inhalation and electric currents for removing wrinkles. On 19th century cosmetics habits of society ladies see *Hope in a Jar*, Kathy Peiss, pp 38, 54, and *American Beauty*, Lois W. Banner, p 133. Strict Victorian moral principles determined rules on cosmetics. Rice powder, a pale complexion (often helped along by face cream containing arsenic), waxed and dyed eyebrows were acceptable. Paint was not. See *A History of Make-Up*, Maggie Angeloglou pp 97, 98. On the hierarchy of New York's elite, see amongst others, *The Social Ladder*, Mrs J.K. Van Rensselaer; *Incredible New York*, Lloyd Morris; *The Vanderbilt Legend*, Wayne Andrews; *Farewell to Fifth Avenue*, Cornelius Vanderbilt Jr; *The Astors*, Virginia Cowles; *Great Hostesses*, Brian Masters; *'King Lehr' and The Gilded Age*, Elizabeth Drexel Lehr and *New York in the Elegant Eighties*, Henry Collins Brown. Cady Stanton Smith on women of fashion; *American Beauty*, Lois W. Banner, p 22. William D'Alton Mann's scandal sheet *Town Topics* was as infamous as it was famous. See *Incredible New York*, Lloyd Morris p 256. On Mamie Stuyvesant Fish, *After All* by Elsie de Wolfe; *Great Hostesses*, Brian Masters; *Always In Vogue*, Edna Woolman Chase; *'King Lehr' and The Gilded Age*, Elizabeth Drexel Lehr; *Incredible New York*, Lloyd Morris. On Stanford White and his work, including houses for Mrs Fish and Rita Lydig, see *Elsie de Wolfe, A Life in the High Style*, Jane S. Smith; *Stanford White* by Charles C. Baldwin; *Morgan* by Jean Strouse; *The Glass of Fashion*, Cecil Beaton; *Who Killed Society?* by Cleveland Amory. The Floradora review was legendary, see amongst others, *Incredible New York*, Lloyd Morris and History of the Musical Stage by John Kenrick. On the British Blondes and Lydia Thompson see American Beauty, Lois W. Banner pp 65, 114, 121–25 and *Encyclopaedia of The Musical Theatre* by KF Ganzl. Mamie Stuyvesant Fish and her hair, King Lehr, Elizabeth Drexel Lehr. On Lillian Russell, *Lillian Russell, The Era of Plush* by Parker Morell; *Duet in Diamonds: The Flamboyant Saga of Lillian Russell and Diamond Jim Brady* by Richard O'Connor and *Incredible New York* by Lloyd Morris. The impact of the Gibson Girl is covered extensively in *American Beauty* by Lois W. Banner; see also *America's Great Illustrators* by Susan E. Meyer; HR making comment MLfB p 56; *The Gilded Lily* by Terence McLaughlin. EA wrote to Teddy Haslam about The Colony Club. On The Colony Club, Elsie de Wolfe's memoirs *After All*; *Elsie de Wolfe, A Life in The High Style* by Jane S. Smith; *My Crystal Ball* by Elisabeth Marbury; *Always in Vogue* by Edna Woolman Chase; *Who Killed Society?* by Cleveland Amory.

5   Madame on the Move 1905–1914

'When I returned to Krakow', MLfB p 32. Henryk Halkowski confirms Kazimierz was, by the early 1900s, largely occupied by the deeply religious or the poor. Those who could had moved out. Pauline Rubinstein Hirschberg and her husband lived in Paris. Their daughter Marcelle would later work in HR's business. Ceska and Lola's passage traced on passenger lists of the S.S. *Karlsruhe*. HR again joined at Genoa. Dr Kapp at Wiesbaden seems to have been HR's early mentor, so much so she claimed Ceska 'trained in chemistry in Berlin with the celebrated Dr Kapp', MLfB p 29, but Ceska had never left Krakow before she went to Australia. On Marienbad, *King Edward the Seventh*, Philip Magnus, p 263: 'the Prince enjoyed a month's cure at Marienbad' (the Princess of Wales preferred Wildbad p 107). Further information on spas, *The Technology of Orgasm* by Rachel P. Maines pp 72–81. Elsie de Wolfe and Anne Morgan at Brides-les-Bains, *My Crystal Ball*, Elisabeth Marbury p 263. Marmola thyroid extract as life-threatening, *American Chamber of Horrors*, Ruth de Forest Lamb pp 5–9, 14. HR selling diet pills, interview *The Australasian*, 30 January 1909. On experiencing treatments, ibid. On Yardley, Guerlain, Coty, Rigaud, Rimmel, Mrs Henning of Cyclax and Willie Clarkson, see *The Gilded Lily*, McLaughlin, also *Cosmetics and Adornment*, Wykes-Joyce and *A History of Make-Up*, Angeloglou. 'Mlle Rubinstein and her two Viennese assistants', interview *Table Talk*, December 1905. Co-tenants at 274 Collins Street, Sands Directory. Nellie Melba, interview the *Australasian*, 30 January 1909 and MLfB p 30. Salon décor, interview *Table Talk*, December 1905. HR 'establishing quick rapport' quote from Agnes Ash in *Beyond the Magic*, Lee Israel p 37. Homely, motherly approach, Hambla Bauer 'Beauty Tycoon' article in *Collier's* 4 December 1948. Skin-peeling, *American Beauty*, Lois Banner pp 213–14, 224; MLfB p 42. HR on clipping forehead muscles and plastic surgery, *The Art of Feminine Beauty* by Helena Rubinstein, pp 257–263. *See also* Gaylord Hauser's *Treasury of Secrets* p 269. Australian advertising 1 May 1907, *Australian Home Journal*, 1st November 1907, the *Lone Hand*. Meeting Titus. HR persisted in the fantasy they married in London when in fact they married in Australia in July 1908. Deeds of 24 Grafton Street held at the Marquis of Salisbury's Library, Hatfield House, examined by author. B.T. archives show Grafton Street telephone number registered as Mayfair 4611 in July 1908. Arguments on honeymoon, LHR. Her personal worth in 1908, LHR. 'He (Titus) had great charisma' letter to P.O'H from Grace Davidson. Quarrel jewels, HR in MLfB p 40: 'whenever we quarrelled, I would go out and buy more pearls'. On leaving Australia and New Zealand in 1908, HR may or may not have stayed in India, although no traces of branches or distributorship have been found in Delhi or Bombay. During author's interview with Mrs Titus Friedman, she explained HR targeting an aristocratic clientele in London was an idea instigated by Edward Titus. On 'Flame' d'Erlanger *see* MLfB p 44, and Cecil Beaton, *The Glass of Fashion* p 141. Misia Sert and relationship with HR see *Madame*, P.O'H p 91 and MLfB pp 53–54. Further information on Misia Sert, *The Life of Misia Sert*, Arthur Gold and Robert Frizdale, *The Memoirs of Misia Sert* and *Sacred Monsters, Sacred Masters*, John Richardson pp 3, 5, 7, 8–9. 'She wasn't nearly as useful', author's interview with John Richardson. Purchase of first Paris Salon instigated by Titus, LHR to Manka. Pauline took over daily running of 255 rue St Honore. Birth certificates of Roy and Horace Titus, General Records Office, Southport. Family rooms in Grafton Street were minimal, interview with Claude Forter: 'entertaining for more than six would have been impossible'. Although HR offered 'skinning', Frau Dr Emmie List has not been traced, neither has the supposed acne-sufferer who 'went to India and sent me Princesses', MLfB pp 42–43. As Lord and Lady Lamington were posted in Bombay from 1901 to 1908, it's possible Lady Lamington referred clients. Redfern, Charles Poynter, Creed, Madame Paquin, Lady Duff Gordon (Lucille), Worth, Poiret and Doucet, background from A History of Fashion, Black/Garland; a *History of 20th Century Fashion*, Elizabeth Ewing; *The Collector's Book of Twentieth Century Fashion*, Frances Kennett *McDowell's Directory of Twentieth Century Fashion*. See also *Poiret* by Palmer White and *Poiret* by Yvonne Deslandres. On Margot Asquith and Poiret, Ewing p 67. HR talks about Margot Asquith in MLfB p 43. La Revue Blanche, *Misia*, Gold/Frizdale pp 29, 30. Nathanson and Titus, MLfB p 53. Cocteau on Misia, The Nabis, p 287. HR's occupancy of house she called Solna never traced. HR and Titus however lived at Number One, The Terrace, Richmond. Scale plans and description of house at that time courtesy of present owner. Misia and Jo Jo Sert at Lady Ripon's house, Coombe, described by Beaton, *The Glass of Fashion*, p 298 also in *Misia*, Gold/Frizdale pp 158–159. Nadelman's first London Exhibition at Paterson's Gallery in Bond Street, 1911 see Lincoln Kirstein, MoMA Catalogue, Nadelman exhibition 1948. HR on Proust, *Madame*, P.O'H pp 92, 93. HR on Colette, MLfB pp 54, 55. 'They did little, extra things', HR to P.O'H, *Madame*, p 105. Colette's own beauty salon, *Secrets of the Flesh. A Life of Colette*, Judith Thurman, pp 394, 5, 6. On Galen and the symptoms of hysteria, *The Technology of Orgasm*, Rachel P. Maines p 24. Details of electronic massagers, pp 11–20, ibid. HR's first trip to America via the SS *Baltic*, Ellis Island records. Titus, with the boys, on the SS *Philadelphia*, Ellis Island records. On taking Elie Nadelman sculptures, MLfB p 58.

6 Florence Graham Becomes Miss Elizabeth Arden 1907–1914

Mrs Eleanor Adair's advertising in *Vogue* listed her New York salon at 557 Fifth Avenue. Florence Graham had spectacular massage skills, having stocky, square hands with virtually level fingers, considered essential for massage, from interview with Irene Delaney, the *New Yorker*, 6 April 1936. On massage and Mrs Hearst, author's interview with Eleanor Lambert. Florence Graham worked with Elizabeth Hubbard in 1909 from a suite of rooms at 509 Fifth Avenue, thereafter took over the lease herself. The building still stands, opposite the NYPL. Irene Delaney admitted Florence did free-lance manicures and 'worked around the clock', the *New Yorker*, 6 April 1936. Details on 'Arden', E.H. Harriman's estate in Orange County, courtesy of Columbia University. Florence Graham listed in NY telephone directory in 1909 living at 321 West 94th St off Riverside Drive. On salon financing, the only possible Graham relative with funds was Florence's uncle, James Liberty Tadd in Philadelphia. Employing her cousin Edith's relatives in the Depression described in family letters held by Isobel Pickering, in author's possession. On relationship with Ogilvie sisters, MEA p 55. On Ogilvie sisters, *Selling Dreams*, Margaret Allen p 22, 123, 163. It's fair to presume that Gladys Ogilvie, a milliner of some note, was pressed into training Lilian 'Lollie' Graham, who became a milliner at this time. Alva Belmont's role in the Suffrage movement chronicled in *Alva, That Vanderbilt Belmont Woman* by Margaret Hayden Rector. Consuelo Vanderbilt Balsan talks about her arranged marriage in her autobiography *The Glitter and The Gold*. Alva Vanderbilt Belmont's lifestyle reviewed in The Vanderbilt Legend by Wayne Andrews and *Incredible New York, High Life and Low Life of the Last Hundred Years* by Lloyd Morris. Miss Arden on the Suffrage march, 'I've been taking an active part in politics' MEA, p 61. Miss Arden's legendary temper confirmed by interview with Angus McCall, and Christopher Yates and Caroline Yates Parker reminiscing on their father's career. See also *A Talent for Living* by Janet Leckie p 158. Henry Sell to EA: 'our services are characterised by a burst of profanity and a slammed telephone'. EA sailed from Europe to New York on the SS *Caronia*, Ellis Island records. Tommy Lewis as silk salesman, *Beauty Millionaire*, Fabe p 86, also Yates: 'he was a brilliant salesman, hardly the gift of a bank clerk'. Value of domestic toilet goods reported in *New York Times*, 20 November 1928. On the growth of the American cinema industry *see*, amongst other books of record, *The Movies* by Griffith Mayer. HR devising make-up for Theda Bara, MLfB p 62. President Wilson on 'The Birth of a Nation', *The Movies* p 37. Use of eye make-up as well as lipstick was commonplace in Paris amongst showgirls and actresses; Mistinguett painted her eyes like 'blue stars'. By 1910 artists, models and women painters such as Hermine David, Pascin's lover, were wearing full make-up. Hermine's 'thin, powdered face from which, even for Paris, an extraordinary geranium-red mouth shone', Kluver/Martin *Kiki's Paris*, p 34. Edward Bok in 1912, see *Hope in a Jar*, Kathy Peiss, p 56, also Macy's manager firing salesgirl wearing make-up 1913, ibid, p 55. Lillian Russell went on to write beauty columns for a Chicago newspaper, but her salon folded as her career faded and she herself died in 1922.

7   The Women at War 1914–1919

Operating two salons in Australia, one in New Zealand, one in London and one in Paris meant full-time staff of at least five at each and more in London, but ancillary staff and production facilities in London, Paris and Sydney plus out-door workers for labelling and packing for mail order will have made up the numbers. Ellis Island records show Helena Juliet Titus arriving in October 1914. HR financial turnover explained in HR family letter. A letter to her British manageress, Rosa Hollay, dated 1914, shows her staying at the Hotel Marie Antoinette in New York, see *The Times*, 20 March 2002 (feature titled 'The Real Face of Rubinstein'). On the Paris artists joining regiments in the Great War, *The Bohemians* by Dan Franck, p 234 and *Kiki's Paris*, Kluver/Martin, p 64. Sibling arguments evident in HR's letter to her sister Manka, 'you came to me green'. On department store activity in USA, Grace Davidson wrote to P.O'H about Slattery's in Boston. American *Vogue*, 'On Her Dressing Table', June 1915. Elie Nadelman arrived in New York from Paris in 1914, his trip, according to The Whitney Museum in New York 'sponsored by his patron, Helena Rubinstein' (press release on 2003 Nadelman exhibition). Anne Morgan and Elsie de Wolfe's roles in the Great War described by Elisabeth Marbury in *My Crystal Ball. See also* de Wolfe's memoirs *After All* and *Elsie de Wolfe, A Life in the High Style* by Jane S. Smith. Details on Anne Vanderbilt, Anne Morgan and Madame Henri de Rothschild from *King Lehr*, Elizabeth Drexel Lehr. The leading plastic surgeon Sir Harold Gillies (according to Gaylord Hauser, he gave Elsie de Wolfe her first facelift) became a close friend of Elizabeth Arden. His seminal book *Plastic Surgery of the Face* was published in 1920, and his autobiography *Leaves From My Life* in 1927. Carmel Snow describes her time in Paris in her autobiography and refers to Chanel and Rodier pp 31–32. On Chanel in the Great War see *Coco Chanel* by Axel Madsen pp 80–82 and *Chanel* by Edmonde Roux-

Charles pp 140–180. On HR's New York and Greenwich properties, MLfB p 57. The West End Avenue apartment, *Beauty Millionaire* by Maxene Fabe, p 83. Grace Davidson writes to P.O'H about the Central Park West property 'where Madame lived until the late 1930s'. HR's paranoia about taxes is evident in all her correspondence. 'I had to pay nearly 12/-', *The Times*, 20 March 2002. John Oneal was left $1,000 in HR's will. John Richardson describes Titus as 'a Greenwich Village intellectual' in *The Sorcerer's Apprentice*, p 258. Artistic life in Greenwich Village superbly described in *Strange Bedfellows. The First American Avant-Garde* by Steven Watson. Nadelman exhibited his work at Stieglitz's famous 291 Gallery circa 1917 and HR remarks in MLfB, 'Eli Nadelman was launched in this country when I arranged for his first private showing', p 93. EA dropped 'Salon d'Oro' in 1915, re-locating to five sumptuous rooms at 673 Fifth Avenue and fitting her first Red Door. The St Regis was always her favourite hotel, interview Angus McCall, LEA, and see MEA p 80 on the Wedding dinner. Titus was a serial adulterer. The document outlining their legal separation, viewed by the author, confirms HR made financial settlement to her husband. EA's professional relationship with Mr Swanson is well documented. He was a chemist of distinction. Ardena Skin Tonic was launched in 1916. Sixteen years later costs were analysed by Consumers Research for *Skin Deep*. 'Fear Factor' advertising copy and 'tit for tat' squabbling copy against Rubinstein clearly evident in EA's campaigns in period 1914–20, see *Baʒaar, Town & Country, Vogue*. On Margaret Thilly and the Blaker Agency see *A Talent for Living* by Janet Leckie, p 153 on Leonore Buehler, p 155. EA's 'Madame Pompadour' delicate sales brochures of the period studied by the author, courtesy of EAA. On Dorothy Gray, see *Selling Dreams* by Margaret Allen, p 30. Also on Gray and Marie Earle, Ruth Maurer, Edna Albert, Peggy Sage and Kathleen Mary Quinlan, see *Hope in a Jar* by Kathy Peiss p 107. EA instigated an advertising campaign critical of competitors copying her in 1916–1917. EA adored dancing. On Vernon and Irene Castle, see Carmel Snow's autobiography, p 28, *My Crystal Ball* by Elisabeth Marbury pp 242–246 and *Modern Dancing* by Irene and Vernon Castle, with introduction by Elisabeth Marbury. On Irene Castle's influence on fashion, *The Glass of Fashion* by Cecil Beaton pp 90–92 and *Incredible New York*, Lloyd Morris, pp 321–322. *Georgia O'Keeffe. A Celebration of Music and Dance* by Katherine Hoffman explores the influence of the contemporary dancers of the time on O'Keeffe's art. Both Arden and Rubinstein were promoting 'anti-ageing' and 'skin-cell renewal' products in the period 1915–1920. HR on touring the US see MLfB pp 60–61. On her mistrust of the telephone, MLfB: 'to this day I cannot manage to dial a number correctly by myself' p 106. Ceska's naturalisation papers viewed by the author, along with correspondence on the issue of her father's nationality. Bernhard Silberfeld re-located from Antwerp to Melbourne on his retirement, living on Grey St, St Kilda with his daughter Eva. Ceska's marriage certificate, viewed by the author, shows her husband was a widower. Titus was unfaithful yet again . . . 'he couldn't keep his hands off the ladies. Madame stood it for years, but it made her grow harder'. HR's maid to P.O'H, *Madame*, p 86. Detective's report on Titus's infidelity in Chicago viewed by author. His excuses in LET. 'Lola' is Lola Beckmann, HR's cousin, who by now was operating a fashion shop in Chicago with a Rubinstein beauty concession on the upper floor. HR took a berth to Paris, contrary to her description in MLfB p 64: 'Edward and I laughed, played bridge, the thought of business far from our minds' . . . Titus did not accompany her.

8   Masters of Art, Mistresses of Money 1920–1926

1921 issue of *Harrodian Gazette* courtesy of Harrods archives. The Arden salon was above what is now Tiffany's in Bond Street. October 1922 Ellis Island records show Florence Lewis arriving back in New York. Her affectionate relationship with Teddy Haslam can clearly be seen in their correspondence, period 1931–1961, viewed by author. 'Get it out of your head', letter from HR to Rosa Hollay, published in *The Times*, 20th May 2002. HR to Hollay, ibid. Paris salon launched with extensive advertising campaign in 1924. Excess profits taxation schemes still in place post-war meant profitable companies advertised extensively. Gladys Graham remained in Paris until she died in 1971. On Wambly Bald and Montparnasse, see his columns 'On the Left Bank', 1929–1933, edited by Benjamin Franklin V. On the bookshop of Edward Titus, see *Kiki's Paris*, Kluver/Martin p 242. Titus remained close to Ford Madox Ford who often dined with him. Further background on Montparnasse drawn from *Paris Was Yesterday 1925–1939*, Janet Flanner; *A Moveable Feast*, Ernest Hemingway; *Paris Was Our Mistress*, Samuel Putnam; *Bohemian, Literary and Social Life in Paris*, Sisley Huddleston and *The Glamour Years — Paris 1919–40* by Tony Allan. 'Good with property', HR about Titus to Hambla Bauer in *Collier's* 4 December 1948. Fernand Leger on Montparnasse to Sisley Huddleston, Paris correspondent of the London *Times*. French *Vogue* opened on 15 June 1920 and *Gazette du Bon Ton* was merged with the title in 1925. On le Train Bleu and the Riviera see *Cote d'Azur Inventing the French Riviera* by Mary Blume, one of the best accounts of the age. EA was devoted to yoga, standing on her head each morning and evening. Celebrated Russian dancer Mikhail Mordkin appeared in the first Diagilev Paris season, then partnered Anna Pavlova in New York, where his Mordkin Ballet & Co eventually became the American Ballet Theatre. On Voronoff, HR quoted in the *New Yorker*'s 'Beauty in Jars and Vials' by Jo Swerling, 30 June 1928. On monkey serum and plastic surgery, HR quoted in the *American* magazine, 'People Who Want to Look Young and Beautiful' by Allison Gray, December 1922. Further information on Voronoff in Gaylord Hauser's *Treasury of Secrets*, p 8. Photo reference to HR in Tunisia with Lurcat courtesy HRF. 'She never gave him a moment', Eugenie to P.O'H, see *Madame*, p 96. HR's temper tantrums were described by Titus as 'violent', LET. His nephew Edward Ameison said, 'she's a hydra and of her nine heads, eight are constructive and one is destructive', *Madame*, p 80. Titus and his rue Delambre premises described in *Kiki's Paris* by Kluver/Martin. On HR's devotion to money, TBF. On The Jockey Club see *Kiki's Paris*, Kluver/Martin. HR's ownership of buildings discussed in letters between Titus and Helena. Josephine Baker's La Revue Negre described in detail by Sisley Huddleston. HR claimed to have created Josephine Baker's stage make-up. On Kiki – Alice Prin – *Kiki's Memoirs*, translated by Samuel Putnam, Black Manikin Press. The best contemporary sources come from *Kiki's Paris*, Kluver/Martin. She was also described by Wambly Bald and Sisley Huddleston. See also *The Bohemians*, Dan Franck. Elkuken's commission to undertake the Boulevard Raspail building described in detail in LET/LHR. See also *Kiki's Paris*, Kluver/Martin p 168. Helena herself said, 'I can't write French'. Titus would have been awed with the pedigree of Marie Laure de Noailles and at one point offered to publish her poetry, LET. For John Richardson's description, see *The Sorcerer's Apprentice*. On This Quarter, see Huddleston and also *Paris Was Our Mistress*, Samuel Putnam, pp 156–7. Putnam on Edward Titus, p 183. On Titus and his linguistic skills, interview with Erica Friedman Titus. Arguments about investment, letters HR/Edward Titus. To say the 1925 Arts Decoratifs Exhibition created the movement is an over-simplification – the style had been in fashion for over two decades and the exhibition had been planned for 1914, but world-wide impact was heightened due to better communications and marketing skills. Paris was established as a world centre of fashion and shopping, *see* Royal Academy of Arts Exhibition Catalogue for 'Capital of the Arts 1900–1968'. Dior's gallery in rue de la Boetie, *Dior in Vogue* by Brigid Keenan p 17. Marcoussis and his wife, Alice Halicka, were close friends of HR's. 'There's a beautiful picture', MLfB p 67.

9   Elizabeth and Tommy 1920–1926

Lady Islington, the noted interior designer, became a life-long friend of EA. Her social connections and powerful address book would have been of inestimable assistance in establishing a high-class clientele for the Arden salon. England, after America, was the most profitable centre of operation for Arden. Germany was third, reported in *Fortune* magazine, 1938. That Tommy Lewis was charming, author's interview with Joseph Wile, also Angus McCall, who met him post-divorce: 'I was struck by what a lively and pleasant chap he seemed to be'. I. Magnin was – and still is – regarded as a pivotal and influential stockist of luxury goods. *Fortune* magazine in 1930 examined Arden's figures for the previous decade. That Mr Lewis and Mr Graham had affairs with demonstration staff was identified by EA's private detective reports, LEA. *See also* MEA p 152" 'each time the detective returned it was to tell her about Tommy's infidelity with some other girl in the firm'. EA's passion for cinema, theatre, ballet and their stars is well documented. Showbusiness friends like Constance Collier made up the core of her entertaining and staff such as Duke Cross and his wife Katie, decorators and designers (Nicholai Remisoff, Tony Duquette, William Haines) came from the world of film and theatre. EA's passion for flowers was tempered with superstition. She never had twelve or twenty-four blooms in a bunch, only 11, 13, 23 or 25. On Revson and flowers, see *Fire and Ice*, Andrew Tobias, p 129: 'Charles sent two *enormous*, waisthigh vases of roses. One would really have been enough'. On the Yates's marriage, author's interview with their son and daughter, Christopher and Caroline Yates Parker. For Mrs Chase on EA, see *Always in Vogue*, p 322. On Texas Guinan, see *Incredible New York* by Lloyd Morris pp 326–329 and *The American Century* by Harold Evans, p 210. Products described in sales material of the period, EAA. Babani advertising in American *Vogue*. Arden's 1920s advertising was handled by The Blaker Agency, subsequently bought by Henry Sell. On the Ponds campaign, amongst various sources including MEA, see Hope in a Jar, Kathy Peiss, pp 105–6, 136–7. On Arden's budgets, National Advertising Records as cited in *Hope in a Jar*. EA believed in investment into ads and promotion on a major scale. Her philosophy on spending money is never better explained than in *Ladies Home Journal*, February 1932: 'Money must be spent. A miser who hoards his wealth is cutting his own dividends'. EA's letters are peppered with remarks about Jews in business. On Leonard Bernstein, Diaries, EAA. For Maury Paul and Café Society, see *Who Killed Society?* by Cleveland Amory, *Farewell to Fifth Avenue* by Cornelius Vanderbilt Jr and *I Married The World* by Elsa Maxwell.

10 In The Money – Helena 1926–1930

Statistics on volume of cosmetics sold in US during 1927 from *Soft Soap, Hard Sell* by Vincent Vinikas, p 59. HR's advertising during the 1920s still followed the text-led route she favoured pioneered by Titus. Factory space in the basement of Grafton Street described by Boris Forter, TBF. Maison Blanche, HR's house outside Cannes was rarely used, see *Madame*, P.O'H p 188: 'I hate this place, it cost me more than two hundred million francs to build and I've only spent six nights here!' Demolition of Collis Huntingdon house described in the *New Yorker*, 'Beauty in Jars and Vials' 30 June 1928: 'I liked the staircase, it's one of the finest I've ever seen,' she said. EA's advertisement 'On the staircase' ran in French *Vogue*, 1929. On writers in Montparnasse: 'they were easy to find', HR to Hambla Bauer, *Collier's* 4 December 1945, see also *Madame*, P.O'H p 182: 'they were meshugga'. Lilly Dache observing HR in a Talbot hat is taken from her memoirs: *Talking Through My Hats* p 211. All HR's wardrobe details taken from captioned photographs courtesy of HRF. Arden's client index cards, author's interview with Monica Smythe (now Lady Eyre). Richard Hudnut, Carmel Snow's memoirs p 38. Background on popular cosmetics from magazines of the era including *Ladies Home Journal, Vogue, Baʒaar*, the *New Yorker*, *NYPL* and *The World of Carmel Snow*. Beauty sector's advertising growth, *Soft Soap, Hard Sell* p 55. HR on jobs for women, interview in *An Outline of Careers for Women* by Doris Fleischman, 1928. Name change from Silberfeld to Silson, information from Alfred Silberfeld. 'Better they work' from *With Tongue in Chic*, Ernestine Carter, p 175. On Lee Libman, information from her obituary 17 June 1998, *Times Community* newspapers, Reston, VA. Cecil Beaton's observation in his diaries January 1938, from *Cecil Beaton* by Hugo Vickers, p 206. On HR's jewellery, author's interviews with Kenneth J. Lane and Diane Kolin Moss, also Parke Bernet Catalogue of Jewellery Sale, 1965. 'That's a ruby', HR to Hambla Bauer, *Collier's* 4 December 1945. On gifting jewels to the press, P.O'H, *Madame* pp 66–67. Sara Fox indexing her jewels found under the bed confirmed by Diane Moss. the *New Yorker* 30 June 1928 talked about HR's African Masks, her millionaire publisher husband and her nervous breakdowns. Share information on flotation of HR's company, *Moody's Manual of Investments 1928–1936*. Outline of the deal and HR's benefits, 'The History of Lehman Brothers' press release kindly provided by Lehman Brothers' New York archives. On HR's version of the Lehman deal, MLfB pp 71–73. Influence of Oscar Kolin described in letters from Horace Titus to his mother, viewed by author including, 'he should be put in his place once and for all. Why you are so afraid of him is beyond my comprehension'. Montparnasse property

opportunity described in letters to HR from Titus. The explosive relationship between HR and Titus is clearly evident from their correspondence, as
is her anguish and hysteria. Titus wrote about investment in This Quarter
which HR refused, and he wrote bitterly and aggressively about Osostowicz.
That HR did not inform her husband of the US sale is clear from correspondence: she only informed him a matter of days before completion,
despite negotiations having taken months to finalise. Lehman Brothers'
press release puts price to HR at $7.3 million. Titus claims it was $10 million.
On booming cosmetics industry, *New York Times* 20 November 1927 and
Soft Soap, Hard Sell by Vincent Vinikas.

11 End of an Era: Depression and Divorce – Helena 1929–1934
'Margin buyers were borrowing more than $8.5 billion . . . and lady
investors', Harold Evans, *The American Century*, p 231. On HR's share-
holders see MLfB p 73. Lehman's business development plans were
unquestionably altered by the Wall Street Crash. On the firm's venture into
cosmetics, author's conversation with Mr Paul Cohen at Lehman Brothers
New York. On proposed expansion of the business, *Sales Management
Magazine* 22 November 1930. Lehman's Press Release states, 'with the idea
of turning the Rubinstein business into a low-price mass production line,
Lehman bought a two-thirds interest'. On HR's personal view of Lehman
Brothers, see P.O'H *Madame* p 93: 'I knew they would make a mess of
things. What do bankers know about the beauty business? They tried to go
mass, to sell my products in every grocery store. Pfft! The idea wasn't so
bad, but the timing was all wrong, so they wanted me out of the way'. On
Edward Titus and *Lady Chatterley's Lover*, author's correspondence with
Lawrence scholar and biographer, Dr John Worthen. On Sylvia Beach and
the book, see *Sylvia Beach and The Lost Generation* by Noel Riley Fitch,
p 280. Black Manikin published *Kiki's Memoirs*, translated by Samuel
Putnam with introduction by Ernest Hemingway, viewed by author courtesy of Mrs Titus Friedman. Correspondence between Bennett Cerf of
Random House and Titus held by Special Collections, Butler Library of
Rare Manuscripts at Columbia University, generously made available to
the author by Billy Kluver and Julie Martin. Titus writes about arguments
between Putnam and Hemingway in his publisher's notes: 'I have a good
mind in joining the fray myself . . . but only to hit both on the head'. On the
Bangwa Queen's provenance, Parke-Bernet Catalogue of Helena Rubinstein's
African and Oceanic Art, 1965 and on the allure of collecting African art,
author's interview with Christophe Tzara and conversations with Jean Fritts
of Sotheby's and David Nash. Plans for refit of Grafton Street viewed by

author at Hatfield House archives. On Roy Titus as intern, TBF. Roy and Horace Titus as directors of Franc-Am Ltd, correspondence from their father, viewed by author. *The Art of Feminine Beauty* was published in 1930. The *Boston Post* feature interview appeared on 8 September 1930. Copies of correspondence between Titus and Frieda Lawrence are published in *Frieda Lawrence and Her Circle*, edited by Harry T. Moore and Dale B. Montague. It is author's own assumption that HR had a hysterectomy based on written comments made by Grace Davidson, Frieda Lawrence, Ceska Cooper, and letters from Titus on the 'long recovery period', plus HR's developing depression. With her company share price at an all-time low, HR bought the controlling interest in her business back for $1.5 million. That Titus was arguing with Marcoussis and Elkuken is evident from his letters to HR. Her bitter tirade against Anais Nin is in correspondence with Titus. The Jockey Club was demolished to make way for a modern building owned by Helena Rubinstein where her sister Manka had an apartment. The Boulevard Raspail apartment block still stands. Wambly Bald's final 'La Vie' column for the *Tribune* was published on 25 July 1933. Sara Murphy using her Helena Rubinstein lipstick from *Everybody Was So Young* by Amanda Vail. Anne Morgan and HR's donations to *Sylvia Beach appeal noted in Sylvia Beach and the Lost Generation* by Noel Riley Fitch, p 361. P.O'H says that HR bought Titus his house in Cagnes-sur-Mer, *Madame*, p 179. A significant part of F.H. Lem's collection of African art was purchased outright by HR and remained in Paris at her Quai de Bethune property. Harry Johnson's name first appears on the list of directors for Helena Rubinstein Inc in 1934, Moody's Manual of Investments.

12 Lipsticks and Lesbians 1926–1934

Details about Elisabeth Marbury's funeral from the *New York Times* 23, 24 and 27 January 1933. Her friendship with Eleanor Roosevelt, *Eleanor Roosevelt, Volume Two 1933–1938* by Blanche Wiesen Cook. p 10. Bessie Marbury's life examined in her own memoirs, *My Crystal Ball* and in Elsie de Wolfe's memoirs, *After All*. On her entertaining at Irving Place, *Incredible New York* by Lloyd Morris pp 254–255. Her literary talents and her own agency explored in detail in *A Talent for Living* by Janet Leckie. Her relationship with de Wolfe explored in detail in *Elsie de Wolfe* by Jane S. Smith and her life as a lesbian in *Ladies and Not So Gentle Women* by Alfred Allan Lewis. See also *Passing Performances: Queer Readings of Leading Players in American Theatre History* (University of Michegan, 1998) and *The Girls: Sappho Goes to Hollywood*, p 14 by Diana McLellan. On moving to Sutton Place, MEA p 128; *Elsie de Wolfe* by Jane S. Smith p 209. Edna Chase discovering Sutton Place, *Always In Vogue*, Edna Woolman Chase p 124. For Condé Nast's wife Leslie and Clare Booth Luce see *The Last Empire* by Gore Vidal, p 99: 'Clare ever experimental, allowed Leslie to seduce her, commenting afterward on the prodigious length and sharpness of Leslie's fingernails'. Mercedes d'Acosta writes about her friend Bessie Marbury as 'Granny Pa' at Sutton Place in her memoirs *Here Lies the Heart*. On D'Acosta's relationship with Marbury see *The Girls* by Diana McLellan pp 19, 31. Constance Collier, who became one of EA's closest friends, is described by McLellan as Eva La Galliene's 'old friend, mentor and lover', *The Girls*, p 41. Adolphe (Gayne) de Meyer joined *Vogue* in 1913, defecting to Hearst's *Harper's Bazaar* in 1922, poached by Henry Sell. On rivalry between the titles Mrs Chase said, 'after waiting for *Vogue* to discover and develop staff he (Hearst) lured them away with money often beyond their worth', *Always In Vogue* p 143. Carmel Snow, a devote Catholic as was Pauline Pfeiffer, was horrified by her affair with Hemingway, Carmel Snow p 55. Henry Sell meeting EA circa 1920 described in *A Talent for Living* by Janet Leckie p 150. De Meyer's campaign for Arden, using the bandaged head, ran for over fifteen years. On Marcel Gasteau of 'Marcel wave' fame, Alexandre Godefrey, the inventor of the hair-dryer, and Charles Nessler, who developed permanent waves, see *American Beauty* by Lois Banner, p 215 and also *Daring Do's: A History of Extraordinary Hair* by Mary Frasko. By 1924, barber's shops had installed ladies' chairs. By 1930, 113,000 women were working as hairdressers in the US *Soft Soap, Hard Sell* p 63. Antoine's life-story told in his memoirs *Antoine* by Antoine. Edna Chase remarked on 'the Holy Trinity of Paris: Antoine, Chanel and Reboux', *Always In Vogue* pp 158–160. On Antoine and Elsie de Wolfe's hair, see *Elsie de Wolfe* by Jane S. Smith p 201. On the question of EA's sexual proclivities MEA p 129. EA described as 'a dull little woman', *Elsie de Wolfe* by Jane S. Smith p 252. On Elsa Maxwell, see her own memoirs R.S.V.P. and on Elsa and Elsie, *Elsie de Wolfe*, pp 198–200: 'she was a younger, less refined version of Bessie'. 'Grand Duchess Marie' from *A Talent For Living* by Janet Leckie, p 90. Beaton's show at de Wolfe's gallery, see *Cecil Beaton* by Hugo Vickers, p 117. On Arden and Beaton and their argument over the photographs, 'she looked terribly tired' ibid, p 135. EA was unquestionably fond of Prince Kadjar, LEA, despite Haslam reporting his alcoholism to her, LTH. The Prince was charming, TBF. Correspondence between Sell and de Meyer over EA's perfume advertising published in *A Talent for Living* by Janet Leckie. Background on Nicholai Remisoff courtesy of USC archive. The Remisoff/Arden creative collaboration lasted until her death. Alva Belmont died in Paris on 26 January 1933. Bessie's will viewed by author. Mercedes d'Acosta on de Wolfe, see *Here Lies The Heart* p 72. EA purchasing Lakeside Farm MEA p 158. EA's unease about Cecil Beaton LEA. On EA's detective reports see MEA p 152 and LEA. It was reported Tommy Lewis received a favourable settlement, but papers filed in Maine show he received only $100.

13   Challenges and Changes 1933–1937

Survey details and Macy's, *Hope in a Jar* by Kathy Peiss, p 171. The National Industrial Recovery Act of 1933 initially called for codes of fair practice in beauty salons and hairdressers, supported by the NYFWC. Hedda Hopper describes her time working for EA in her autobiography *From Under My Hat*. EA's diaries viewed by author. HR: 'I'm a worker', *Collier's* 4 December 1945. She didn't like to be touched, *Madame*, P.O'H p 67. EA's beauty and medical regime evident from her diaries. Lady Weidenfeld shared Sir Artur Rubinstein's memories of HR with the author. Calvin Coolidge on luxury, *Soft Soap, Hard Sell*, Vinikas p ix. Information on toxic and dangerous cosmetics largely drawn from *Skin Deep*, by M.C. Phillips; *American Chamber of Horrors* by Ruth de Forest Lamb and *Everything You Want to Know About Cosmetics* by Toni Stabili. The Journal of the AMA identified Koremlu as containing rat poison in 1930. For Revlon's 'Ever On', see *Fire and Ice* by Andrew Tobias p 70. FDA's efforts to revise the 1906 Pure Food & Drug Act, see *American Chamber of Horrors*. Dr Harvey Wiley and the original 1906 Act FDA Consumer Fact Sheet, June 1981 by Wallace F. Janssen, FDA historian. Ceruse (white lead) used for centuries as a cosmetic was banned by the early act. It was being widely used in the USA both as a foundation and skin-whitener, in particular via a popular product called Laird's Bloom of Youth, which caused the death of a consumer in 1877, *Hope in a Jar*, Kathy Peiss p 10. Further reading on Benzoates and text by Dr William Jago in his Manual of Forensic Chemistry and Chemical Evidence from *Cosmetics Unmasked* by Dr Stephen and Gina Antczak. EA on Velva Cream and Orange Skin Food, the *New Yorker*, 6 April 1935. Chemicals used in cosmetics see *Cosmetics Unmasked*, Introduction, opening page. Personal care statistics Plunkett's Almanac. FDA budget explained in *Everything You Want to Know About Cosmetics* by Toni Stabili. On labelling claims, FDA Consumer Fact Sheet, 'Clearing Up Cosmetics Confusion', August 2000. On HR's relatives, authors extensive interviews with Claude Forter. EA/Harrods invitation courtesy of Harrods archives. Carmel Snow remembers Lois Long in her memoirs. Lois Long letter from *A Talent for Living* by Janet Leckie. HR uses her favourite *jolie laide* in *The Art of Feminine Beauty*. 1930's EA advertising images viewed in EAA. Revlon ad in the *New Yorker* illustrated in *Fire and Ice* by Andrew Tobias p 109. Diana Vreeland described Flame d'Erlanger, Perrara, Bebe Berard, her nail varnish and her suspicions about Charles Revson in *D.V.* pages 111–113. MoMA Catalogue on their African Tribal Art exhibition courtesy of MoMA Library. HR Press Release courtesy of HRF. Opening review of Max Factor's Hollywood beauty studio in *Time*, December 1935. Factor died three years later, his son Frank taking his name, becoming Max Factor Jr. 'Jake the Barber' Factor was a close associate of Chicago mobster Murray Humphries and ran the Stardust Hotel & Casino in Las Vegas throughout the 1950s, see *Illinois Police & Sheriff's News*, Bill Romer, on Las Vegas mobsters. On radio advertising, *Hope in a Jar*, Kathy Peiss, p 105. Most of EA's involvement with her radio show is explained in her letters to Mr Haslam. See also *A Talent For Living* by Janet Leckie p 158 and on Maury Paul, MEA p 170. In the US the Silver Purchases Act of 1934 imposed a fifty per cent tax on profits from silver, hence her desire to buy in Europe. Berlin was a favoured city for EA and she travelled there extensively from 1928 to 1938. Gordon Yates told Angus McCall the various stories about Goering. Listed ingredients of Eight Hour Cream from 2001 packaging. The original formula was developed by Mr Swanson. Boris Forter's recollections of the cosmetics industry in the Great Depression from TBF. On Condé Nast's financial hardship see *The Man Who Was Vogue* by Caroline Seebohm pp 303–306. Nast had borrowed $2 million from the Equitable Trust Corporation to invest into the Goldman, Sachs Trading Corporation. Post-crash, Equitable went under and shares in Condé Nast Inc went from $93 to $4.5. Mr Nast was ultimately left with debts of over $4,800,000. Germaine Monteil's business described by Boris Forter from TBF. Information on advertising in relation to sun products from brochures in EAA, *Vogue*, *Harper's Bazaar* and *Town & Country*. On Professor Jansion, see *Skin Deep* by M.C. Phillips p 105. Consumer's Research also analysed Arden and Rubinstein product, publishing the results in *Skin Deep*.

14 Maine Chance and Makeovers 1935–1939

VIP guests were entertained on the train by an accordion player, the *New Yorker*, 6 April 1935. Hauser Broth recipe: 'on Elizabeth Arden's Beauty Farm I made it part of the daily beauty ritual, I am convinced it is one of the best safeguards against premature ageing', *Look Younger, Live Longer* by Gayelord Hauser p 329. 'The poor dears' MEA Lewis/Woodworth p 159. Stanley Marcus on EA from *Minding the Store*,

p 314. EA's enthusiasm for Foster Blakely is evident from her letters to
Mr Haslam. 'The profits would stagger a Maharajah', *From Under My
Hat* by Hedda Hopper, p 243. 'His collar feels tight' ibid, p 245. Condé
Nast's British and French titles held up remarkably well in the
Depression with profits of $88,000 in 1934, but advertising revenues
globally were at an all time low in 1935, see *The Man Who Was Vogue* by
Caroline Seebohm pp 316–318. A salary of $35,000 in 1935 would be
worth over $445,500 today. EA is reported to have owned a hairdresser's
in MEA p 187. On hairdressing and lingerie, author's conversations with
Maurice and also Priscilla Moynihan. HR on meeting Artchil, MLfB p 77.
On investment into hormone treatments, *Beauty Millionaire*, Maxene Fabe
p 121. *Time*, 28 August 2000 reported that the value of cosmecuticals, that
is 'age specialist' products could shoot to well over $2 billion in the US in
2000 and were the fastest growing sector in the beauty industry. Gaylord
Hauser on hormones, *Look Younger, Live Longer*, p 169. On hormones,
Skin Deep, p 176. Vitamin Plus described in *A Talent for Living* by Janet
Leckie, pp 184–190. On Kate Lawson, Irene Delaney and Beattie's ball,
see *From Under My Hat* by Hedda Hopper p 244 and MEA, p 163. Louis
Sue and Quai de Bethune, *Art and Decoration Magazine*, Autumn 1937.
'Six hundred and twenty blacks', *Madame* P.O'H p 84. On the painting
Miracle Flower, see *Georgia O'Keeffe, A Celebration of Music and Dance*
by Katherine Hoffman, p 32. Review of Arden's Gymnasium Moderne,
American *Vogue*, April 1937. Hudnut's Success School featured in
American *Vogue* January 1939. 'Act more stupid', Mala Rubinstein in
conversation with Maxene Fabe, quoted in *Beauty Millionaire*, p 111.
Architectural report, the *New Yorker*, 9 January 1937. Salon review,
American *Vogue*, February 1937. Marie Cuttoli's rue Babylon apartment
is now the home of Yves St Laurent. Details on art award HRF. On the
fund-raising evening at Shakespeare & Company, *Sylvia Beach and the
Lost Generation*, Noel Riley Fitch, p 371. Harry Johnson joining EA
reported in *Fortune*, 1938. 'Madame herself is less than coherent', *Life*,
21 July 1941.

15   Princess of the Potions v Lady of the Lotions 1937–1939
HR talks about her stay in Switzerland in MLfB p 75 and to journalist
Irene Brin, observed by P.O'H, writing in *Madame*, p 126. HR: 'when you
work you have to eat', *Collier's* 4 December 1945. 'Platelicker-cleaner'
Life, 21 July 1941. 'She called her Caramel', P.O'H *Madame*, p 106. EA
talks about 'her dear friend Mr White' in letters to Mr Haslam and Tom
White and their affair is described in MEA p 220. On the uncertainty

over the Gourielli title, Timothy Boettger says, 'Gurieli-Chkonia never existed as a double name as far as I am aware in Georgia/Russia. Many people – some legitimately of the nobility and some not – assumed titles in emigration. The Machabelis were in fact princes, the Mdivani were not'. On meeting Titus, author's interview with Erica Titus Friedman. HR said 'she would be the death of him' P.O'H *Madame*, p 179. On Artchil, author's interviews with Diane Kolin Moss, and TBF. HR on Mrs Lauder's house quoted in *Estée Lauder, Beyond the Magic* by Lee Israel, p 59. *Fortune* magazine, 'I Am A Famous Woman In This Industry', October 1938. On Sonnenberg, P.O'H in *Madame*, p 206. EA complains about her dwindling share portfolio in letters to Teddy Haslam. District Sixty Five, *Fire and Ice* by Andrew Tobias, p 101. Condé Nast's party for Ilka Chase and Clare Booth Brokaw, *The Man Who Was Vogue* by Caroline Seebohm, p 343. EA's visit to the set of 'The Women' described in MEA p 185. Dr Erno Laszlo described in *Selling Dreams* by Margaret Allen, pp 132–133 and in *Elsie de Wolfe, A Life in the High Style* by Jane S. Smith p 313.

16   The Second World War – Part I 1939–1942

Almost all the information concerning Madame Rubinstein and her family and business activities during the war comes from the tapes dictated by Boris Forter, transcribed by his son, journalist Christian Wolmar. Forter ran the British office of HR from 1938 until 1971.

Elizabeth Arden wrote prolifically during the war, with her correspondence from the US seemingly subject to little delay. When America entered the war, most of her letters seem to have been delivered via various RAF officers on official duties in Washington who collected mail from Miss Arden, returning it to Mr Haslam and, it seems, vice versa. Unusually, there is very little evidence of any direct censorship whatsoever in their correspondence during the war years, although Haslam's letters were scaled down to contain less business information.

In her book, *One Girl's War*, Joan Miller describes working first in the advertising department and then in display, at Elizabeth Arden circa 1937–39, having acquired the job because 'Teddy Haslam had been an admirer of her mother's'. On the Gestapo visiting, footnote p 3. On Eve Andrews, an Arden employee classified by MI5 as being a 'disruptive character' ibid p 105. Edna Chase lunching at Claridges with Harry Yoxall and Teddy Haslam, *Always In Vogue* by Edna Woolman Chase, p 268. Regina Rubinstein's Australian naturalisation papers and entry documents into Australia seen by the author. Transfer of ownership of Bourjois explained in *Coco Chanel* by Axel Madsen, pp 244–245. Johanna de Knecht leaving Paris, see *Fire and Ice*, Andrew Tobias, p 75. Gordon Yates and his wife fleeing Germany described to author by their son and daughter. On Revlon turnover and the addition of lipstick, *Fire and Ice*, p 47. On Mickey Soroko, ibid, pp 68–69. Fire truck ibid, p 69. Government contracts and E. Insignia ibid, p 80. The gunpowder/facepowder quote is also taken from *Fire and Ice* by Andrew Tobias, p 81. Max Factor, Bronnley, Gala, Cyclax and Elizabeth Arden British advertising viewed by author in media of the time. EA's Velva advertisement, EAA. Claude Forter, Boris Forter's eldest son, confirms the Retty/Mumford trials. Pamela Churchill debts and Harrods, see *Life of the Party* by Christopher Ogden, p 92. Mrs Churchill and other notable clients of EA granted credit or given free treatments are noted in letters between Mr Haslam and EA. On Jock Whitney, see *The Life and Times of John Hay Whitney* by E.J. Kahn, Jr about *Gone With The Wind* pp 112–123. *Young and Beautiful* was eventually distributed in England by Warner Brothers. Access to the screening of the film, courtesy of Mr Richard May at Warner Brothers archive and UCLA. $300,000 in 1940 is worth well over $3,600,000 today. Mr Haslam's bonus of $5,000 would be worth $61,000 today.

17 The Second World War – Part II

Early in 1940, American *Vogue* ran a feature on items HR bought in South America in the winter of 1939 and exhibited at Lord & Taylor. Candido Portinari's portrait of Madame executed in 1939. Precision Hands Press Release courtesy of HRF. In her memoirs, HR claims she and Artchil sailed for New York on the last sailing of the SS *Manhattan*. It was in fact Titus and his new wife who sailed on this ship as HR was already in New York, author's interview with Erica Titus Friedman. 'Scene at Gourielli's – New York's latest Apothecary shop' American *Vogue* feature photographed by John Rawlings. Ostracised whilst working for HR, Tommy Lewis became close to Horace Titus, evident from Titus/Rubinstein correspondence. 'Military service transformed', see *Hope in a Jar* by Kathy Peiss, pp 253–254. Regina Rubinstein's correspondence with the Australian Government viewed by author. EA meeting President Roosevelt is described in a letter to Mr Haslam. HR comments in MLfB p 81: 'your war effort is to help keep up the morale of our women'. 'Operation Torch initiative described to author by an American serviceman. Salvador Dali painted Helena and Artchil circa 1942–43, author's interview with Diane Moss. Baron Kurt von Pantz painted HR twice, once in 1937 and again in 1944. *Les Editions Condé Nast* was put under the protection of the French Courts during the occupation when

French *Vogue* ceased publication. Michel de Brunhoff's nineteen-year-old son Pascal, fighting with the Maquis, was shot by the Gestapo on 10 June 1944. Aldous Huxley's screenplay on Madame Curie is described by Ilka Chase in *Past Imperfect*, p 245, as is her interview with EA on her radio show pp 225–226. Hortense Odlum, married to multi-millionaire Floyd Odlum who had a major investment interest in RKO pictures, was a close friend of EA. On Salvador Dali's windows for Bonwit Teller and Mrs Odlum, see *A Woman's Place* by Hortense Odlum, pp 165–166. Dali and his wife moved to New York during the war, where according to John Richardson 'Gala kept him slaving away on commercial projects, interspersed with glitzy portraits of society women in ball dresses posed "surrealistically" against desert island backdrops', *Sacred Monsters, Sacred Masters* p 296. On Paris fashion in the Second World War, see *Always In Vogue* by Edna Woolman Chase, pp 274–275 and Ewing's *History of 20th Century Fashion*, chapter seven. American and British *Vogue* issues of the period viewed by the author. Axel Madsen writes about Chanel and Hans Gunther von Dincklage in *Coco Chanel* p 239. Chanel, Misia Sert, Jean Cocteau and others who remained in Paris during occupation are described in *The Life of Misia Sert* by Arthur Gold and Robert Frizdale p 281: 'Sert's was the accommodating nature of the perfect collaborator – he soon became one of the most privileged people in Paris'. Sert saving Colette's husband Maurice Goudeket, ibid p 282. For further information on Colette and the war years in Paris, see *Secrets of the Flesh* by Judith Thurman. On the Gestapo and Quai de Bethune, HR to Andre Malraux: 'see the bullet holes? The Germans used the statues for target practice', p 137. EA wrote to Mr Haslam about her 'dear, dear friend Mr White'. See also MEA p 220: 'it was love'. EA's long, neurotic letters to Teddy Haslam about Evlanoff show her anguish and the extent of his debts. Serge Obolensky quoted in MLA p 224. Divorce documents viewed by author.

18   The Second World War – Part III 1943–1945

Description of the bomb damage to the Grafton Street building, TBF. The Nadelman bas relief panels decorating the salon were undamaged. Interestingly, Elie Nadelman himself was an air-raid warden in Riverdale New York. SOE training described in SOE Syllabus, Lessons in Ungentlemanly Warfare, Public Record Office. The missions undertaken by Sidney Jones are outlined in *SOE In France* by M.R.D. Foot. Further reading on the SOE: *A Quiet Courage*, by Liane Jones, herself a survivor. On Zew Schantz, author's correspondence with his wife, Olga Schantz. Gladstone's fraud described in letters to Mr Haslam, and in MEA p 235. His name was actually Maurice Goldstone, but EA preferred to call him Mr Gladstone. Ilka Chase on research help for her book, MEA p 234. Formula for scar cream, LTH. Fleur Fenton's fee of $7,500 in today's terms was worth over $86,500. EA wrote extensively about Charles James in her private letters. Further personal insight from an unpublished essay on James by P.O'H, courtesy of John Richardson. Additional reading on James: *The Genius of Charles James* by Elizabeth A. Coleman and *The Fashion Makers*, Barbara Walz and Bernadine Morris. Henry Sell wrote about Maria Hugo and EA: 'Elizabeth Arden for whom Madame Hugo works pretty much night and day', see *A Talent For Living* by Janet Leckie p 163. 'Extra mileage', Charles James to P.O'H, unpublished essay. Perfume ingredients: *Cosmetic Ingredient Dictionary* CTFA. 'Red light house' MEA p 231. On EA's cocktail party for Charles James, P.O'H, unpublished essay. The arguments between Oscar Kolin and Horace Titus were evident to senior staff, TBF, and to those within the family, author's interview with Erica Titus Friedman. Also HR wrote on returning to Paris in MLfB pp 82–83. Further reading on post-war Paris, *Paris Journal 1944–1965* by Janet Flanner and *Paris after the Liberation 1944–1949* by Antony Beevor and Artemis Cooper.

19 All the Queen's Horses and One of the Queen's Men 1932–1966

As well as drawing from the source of EA's extensive letters to Teddy Haslam on the subject of her horses, the author was granted viewing access of Miss Arden's files and records on her race-horses and stables held at the EAA in New York. In addition, author received a faultless series of press cuttings from the Keeneland Library in Kentucky. Further invaluable detail came from author's interviews with Angus McCall (Captain Sir Cecil Boyd Rochfort's nephew) and from Bill Curling's definitive biography of that indomitable trainer known to all as 'the Captain'. Citations are listed from the principle newspapers and racing periodicals which extensively charted Elizabeth N. Graham's devoted if quixotic approach to her horses. EA's letters feature much on 'Silent' Tom Smith and his son Jimmy. The author also wishes to gratefully acknowledge credit to Laura Hillenbrand's superlative book, *Seabiscuit*.

Kentucky Derby reports from the *Thoroughbred Record*, 10th May 1947 and the *New York Times*, Sunday 4 May, 1947. 'Weighing in at 1,450 pounds' from *Seabiscuit* by Laura Hillenbrand, p 70. 'The Indians called him the "Lone Plainsman"' ibid, p 20. 'There's next year's Derby winner', Leslie Combs II quoted in 'A Store of Two Derby Days' by Neville Dunn, *Thoroughbred Record*, 10 May 1947. 'I didn't win much', author's interview with Joseph Wiles. On Blenheim II, *Sire Lines* by Abe Hewitt. Jet Pilot's pedigree, 2001 Kentucky Derby Media Guide. Smith's ban covered extensively in LEA, also Daily Racing Form 19 October 1966. See also *Seabiscuit*, Laura Hillenbrand, p 332. Fred Johnson's invitation, LEA. Alfred Gwynne Vanderbilt at Adirondack Summer Art School, *The Vanderbilt Legend* by Wayne Andrews. Sam Riddles' personality made clear in his obituaries, particularly the *Thoroughbred Record*, 13 January 1951; the *Blood-Horse*, 13 January 1951; *Bloodstock Breeders Review*, 1951. On EA's trainers, variously reported, author cites specifically *Daily Racing Form*, 17 September 1984. 'Great Union', American Racing Manual. EA corresponded with her friend John Clark at Hialeah. V.R. Orchard's report filed with Mr Haslam's papers. On Leslie Combs II, see 'The Myrtlewood Heritage' by Rhonda L. Williams from the *Blood-Horse*, 14 April 1990 and The Combs Legacy, ibid, 21 April. On the Chicago fire, *Daily Racing Form*, 19 October 1966, *Time* magazine, 6 May 1946 and author's interview with Mr Ted Bassett III. See also *Louisville Courier Journal* magazine, 2 May 1982. Monte Parks story reported by Jim Bolus, ibid. Maine Chance Farm Records, *Daily Racing Form*, 19 October 1966. EA and Sir Cecil Boyd-Rochfort, LEA; also author's interview with Angus McCall. About the Coronation and Adlai Stevenson, author's interview with Lord Montagu. About Mrs Cowles, author's interview with Eleanor Lambert. Fleur Cowles on EA from 'She Made Friends and Kept Them' p 193. The late Hon. Mrs Varley recollected driving EA in conversation with the author. H.M. The Queen making comment about Aureole from *The Captain* by Bill Curling, p 171. Angus McCall told author the eiderdown story and about buying Administrator. On EA's Kentucky property: 'its rooms are colourful and completely feminine', the *Courier Journal*, 12 May 1957. Frank Lloyd Wright's prospective commission reported in the *Courier Journal*, 5 May 1963. For Boyd Rochfort's knee operation, see *The Captain* by Bill Curling, p 196 and on Lingfield and the Newmarket Stakes, ibid, p 197. Both topics covered in LEA. 'You seem to have no faith in me', *The Captain*, pp 197–8. Detailed version on file EAA. Jewel's Reward disqualified in the Flamingo reported in feature 'Sport of Queens' by Jack Ryan in *Family Weekly*, 29 April 1962 and 'Lady in a Dual Role' by Charles Morey in *Travers*, 1990. HR: 'how is the horse?' from *Madame*, P.O'H p 70.: On Jet Action, author's interview with Emily Hutchison. Mrs Whitney's quote has been widely used, author cites *Travers*, 1990. Jack Miller recollected EA in conversation with Jim Bolus for 'Beauty Cream on Racehorses' 2 May 1982, *Louisville Courier Journal*.

20 Post-War Warriors 1946–1950

Details on Mrs Lauder's birth in Corona taken from *Beyond the Magic* by Lee Israel, pp 8, 12. *Hope in a Jar* p 245 puts the figure at 80–90% using lipstick p 245, slightly less than the *New York Times* report, but the figures were still impressive. On the formation of Estée Lauder Inc see *Beyond the Magic* p 32. On John Schotz, ibid pp 18,19. For Revson's habit of changing receptionists, see *Fire and Ice* by Andrew Tobias p 96. On Bea Castle, author's interview with Grace Gilbert. Carmel Snow and Mrs Chase at Maine Chance Phoenix described in LEA and by Mrs Chase in *Always In Vogue*, p 322. Trunks to Gladys in LEA. HR to P.O'H: 'the magazine doesn't pay her much', *Madame*, p 108. Helena Rubinstein not only bought the arthritic Marie Louise Bousquet a car but left her an income for life in her will. EA wrote extensively about Castillo. For further information on Castillo, see Fairchild's *Dictionary of Fashion*, Dr Charlotte Calasibetta p 558; *Collector's Book of Twentieth Century Fashion* by Frances Kennett and MEA p 242. Serge Heftler, *Selling Dreams* by Margaret Allen p 134. Helen Golby at Revlon, see *Fire and Ice*, Andrew Tobias p 37 'in the early days he had an advertising director working for him whose fingernails were bitten and bloody from the experience'. HR and Mr Kolb, see *Madame*, P.O'H p 203. Boris Forter enthusiastically describes his acquisition of the 'silk' formula from Baroda in his taped memoirs. On Baroda's ancestors, the Maharajah Pratapsingh and Sita Devi, see *The Maharaja's Jewels* by Katherine Prior and John Adamson and *Lives of the Indian Princes* by Charles Allen and Sharada Dwivedi. Further background on Sita Devi and her son, Princey, *Tatler*, August 1985 and 'Death on the Riviera' by Sunil Sethi. Lauder's early entry into mail shots is described in *Beyond the Magic* by Lee Israel, p 36, and in Estée Lauder's autobiography, *A Success Story*, she talks about gifts and sampling on pp 32–33. Castillo wrote frankly to EA about Piquet and his business, letters viewed by author. Further background from *History of 20th Century Fashion* by Elizabeth Ewing; *McDowell's Directory of Twentieth Century Fashion* by Colin McDowell, pp 220–221 and Fairchild's *Dictionary of Fashion*, p 569.

21 The Fabulous Fifties 1950–1955

The story of Charles Revson and the founding of Revlon is described in the seminal book on his life, *Fire and Ice*, written by Andrew Tobias, which has been a major source of information. The author has also examined extensive press coverage on Mr Revson, including features in *Time, Fortune, Life, Newsweek* and other periodicals. I am indebted however for updated information and the unique insight given by Grace Gilbert, who worked variously for Revlon and subsequently, Helena Rubinstein Inc.

Where's The Fire? is described in *Fire and Ice*, p 117. Prince and Princess Gourielli's September launch of their art gallery reported in *Life* magazine and *Art News* amongst other publications. Revson on the Piranesi etchings, *Fire and Ice*, p 24. Bergdorf Goodman's anniversary sitting, American *Vogue*, 1950. HR told O'Higgins, '*Flair* won't last', see *Madame*, p 10. EA wrote to Mr Haslam about George Carroll. On the campaign for Fire and Ice, Dorian Leigh and Kay Daly, see *Fire and Ice*, pages 118–125, also *Selling Dreams* by Margaret Allen, pp 229–230. Background on Jean Desses from Fairchild's *Dictionary of Fashion*, p 560. EA wrote extensively about Count Sarmi. See also Fairchild, p 594 and MEA, p 270. (Ferdinando Sarmi went on to win a Coty Award in 1960, shortly after Miss Arden had fired him.) Duchess of Windsor at Arden Paris Salon, *The Windsor Style* by Suzy Menkes, p 147. On wearing an Arden gown for the *Vogue* sitting, *Gone with the Windsors* by Iles Brody, p 265: 'she wanted Wallis to wear a gown from Desses'. On Desses, the Duchess and the *Vogue* sitting, LEA to her sister. *Women's Wear Daily* reported the ball and gowns on Wednesday 7 January 1953. Revson and Sheer Radiance, *Fire and Ice*, p 38. 'It's a good name': P.O'H who witnessed the moment described it in an interview with Andrew Tobias, quoted in *Fire and Ice*, p 247. 'The scandal with the black girl', *Madame*, pp 179–80. Claude Forter confirms news of the scandal *flew* through the offices. According to P.O'H, HR said it cost her over $100,000 in legal fees to sort it out, *Madame*, p 179. The luncheon party at Quai de Bethune described by P.O'H in *Madame*, p 130. Men's toiletries market reviewed in the Wall Street Journal, 31 August 1955. Author interviewed Lord Montagu on his recollections of EA and her enthusiasm for men's skin care. Range information, EAA and interview with Angus McCali. The new Rubinstein factory reviewed in *Drug and Cosmetic Industry News*, February 1953. P.O'H on their trip to Rome, *Madame*, p 168. Brochure on the artists' exhibition viewed by author. On the launch of Youth Dew, *Beyond the Magic* by Lee Israel p 41 and in Mrs Lauder's own autobiography, pp 78–79. On Mrs Lauder's friendship with Van Ameringen, *Beyond the Magic* by Lee Israel, p 27: 'she had a boyfriend when she got the divorce from Joe, he became the head of I.F.F.'. See also *Coco Chanel* by Axel Madsen, p 266. A cosmetics buyer who used to work at Harvey Nichols made the 'love it, loathe it' remark to the author. Angus McCall recollects Tony Duquette saying 'pot calling the kettle black'. Revson saying to Harry Doyle 'her name is Esther from Brooklyn', *Beyond the Magic* by Lee Israel, p 62. On buyers, author's interview with Angus McCall. Stanley Marcus wrote about Chanel and EA in his autobiography *Minding the Store*, p 300. P.O'H describes the opening of Gourielli in *Madame*, p 210. HR's own description of the project, MLfB pp 85–86. Further information, the *Wall Street Journal*, 31 August 1955. On the Helena Rubinstein Foundation, *Madame*, p 293. Campbell's arranged Artchil's funeral at the Russian Orthodox Church on 26 November 1955. P.O'H describes the news of Artchil's death in *Madame*, p 215: 'I won't go to the funeral, we'll send a telegram'. HR records she was 'out of touch with the entire world for a month', MLfB pp 85–6.

22   Show Time 1955–1959

The $64,000 Question covered in depth in *Fire and Ice* by Andrew Tobias, see also *Selling Dreams* by Margaret Allen p 67. On Revlon going public and Joseph Revson's share, *Fire and Ice*, p 105. Jerry Emmerman, sales director of HR at that time, confirmed the failure of the Rubinstein sponsored TV show. On Revson at the Plaza, author's interview with Grace Gilbert. Revson's early training in textiles came from his time working at Pickwick textiles, *Fire and Ice*, p 29. On EA's meetings, author's interview with Angus McCall. *See also* MEA p 299: 'remain where you are, we'll be back shortly'. On corporate wives' dressing, interview with Christopher Yates and Caroline Yates Parker. Revson's digestive problems recorded in *Fire and Ice* p 41 and confirmed in author's interview with Grace Gilbert. On EA's anti-smoking stance, LEA and interview with Angus McCall, *see also* MEA, pp 273–274. Charles James and Max Jacobson 'Dr Feelgood' noted in *The Genius of Charles James* by Elizabeth A. Coleman. John and Jackie Kennedy and 'Dr Feelgood', see *A Woman Named Jackie* by C. David Heyman, pp 296–302. About Gypsy Rose Lee and Charles James, unpublished private essay by P.O'H. EA as Charles Jr's godmother, MEA p 233 and *The Genius of Charles James*. Revson's doctors and ECG, *Fire and Ice*, p 165. Revson's insomnia, *Fire and Ice*, p 22. HR travelling, *Cosmopolitan*, June 1959: 'Princess of the Beauty Business' by T.F. James. On fainting at Dior, *Madame*, P.O'H p 107. Pompidou at Quai de Bethune, *Madame*, P.O'H p 219. On Picasso, author's interview with John Richardson and *Madame*, pp 220–226. Richardson and Juan Gris collage, *The Sorcerer's Apprentice*, John Richardson, p 258 and author's interview with John Richardson. O'Higgins and about the money belt, *Sorcerer's Apprentice* p 259. 'Madame is hiking in the Irish peat bogs', private letter of P.O'H. About Cecil Beaton and Capote, *Madame*, P.O'H pp 241–242. See also *Cecil Beaton* by

Hugo Vickers, page 407 quoting '$5,000 fee'. HR's visit to Australia, letter from Lady Southey to Trevor Jacobs, viewed by author. Claim on the estate following Horace's accident evident from Petition for Ancillary Letters of Administration, Surrogate Court, State of New York. HR's grief following Horace's death on 18 April 1958, Leila Hirsch, interviewed in *Cosmopolitan*, June 1959 and in private letter of Patrick O'Higgins. On Ceska, *Madame*, P.O'H p 229. Letters from Kathy and Graham Sutherland to Patrick O'Higgins made available to author. Visiting Hecht to view paintings, TBF and *Madame*, P.O'H p 233. On Beaverbrook Gallery, *Madame*, P.O'H p 236. EA wrote in detail about Simon Elwes. On Mme Dendrammis, MEA, p 272. On Tommy Lewis, author's interview with Angus McCall.

23   Last Acts 1960–1962

Information from transcripts of the House Interstate and Foreign Commerce sub-committee Investigation into *The $64,000 Question*. 'Charles was asked', Fire and Ice, p 174. See also *Selling Dreams*, pp 68–69. 'My sister's brother passed away', MEA p 293. The New York State Joint Legislative Committee met to study 'the illegal interception of communications' in November 1955, detailed in *Selling Dreams* by Margaret Allen, p 64. 'You hear that Charles?' *Fire and Ice*, Andrew Tobias, p 210. Beck found dead, *Fire and Ice*, p 160. J. Edgar Hoover's scandal campaign about Adlai Stevenson reported under Freedom of Information Act. FBI files contain over 3,271 pages on Eleanor Roosevelt including many on her women friends. On 'Futurama', author's interview with Grace Gilbert. Mr Abrams and his speech on 'charmaceuticals' described in *Beyond the Magic* by Lee Israel p 46. Unpublished editorial feature on HR and Bombois from private papers of Patrick O'Higgins. Andrew Tobias describes Revlon's beauty salon in *Fire and Ice*, pp 221–223, additional background from Grace Gilbert. Patrick O'Higgins gave Andrew Tobias the 'Mausoleum' comment used in *Fire and Ice*, p 221. Stanley Marcus on Miss Arden and death in *Minding the Store*, p 314. On Revlon's advertising policies, *Time* magazine, 30 September 1957. Tony Duquette subsequently became president of the Elsie de Wolfe Foundation and guardian of her memorabilia. Stanley Marcus on Estée Lauder in *Minding the Store*, p 314. Revson's stance taken with Bill Fine of Hearst reported in *Fire and Ice*, p 248. Cleveland Amory quotes Miss Arden in '*Who Killed Society?*' p 53. Lee Israel reports on Mrs Lauder and Palm Beach in *Beyond the Magic*, p 54. Mrs Sanford quoted 'she courted me' on p 56 ibid. Gladys told Gordon Yates about the incident with Mrs Lauder and Angus McCall informed author. Mrs Lauder's 'table hopping' discussed in author's interview with Mrs Friedman. Revlon's acquisition of Evan Picone reported in *Fire and Ice*, p 228. Life on the *Ultima II* was described to author in conversation with Captain Arthur Harris, previously second mate on the yacht. See also *Fire and Ice*, pp 13–14.

24   The Final Years 1960–1966

The Ennismore Gardens apartment, decorated in lipstick colours, features in *David Hicks on Decoration* published by Macmillan. The author worked for David Hicks and can vouch for his perfectionist taste. Story on Forter's cars by Giles Chapman for the *Daily Telegraph*. Kenneth J. Lane recollected the $5 bill in conversation with the author. Madame never owned her own car, 'why buy something that will depreciate by 40% overnight?' she said repeatedly. Packaging designer Ladislas Medgyes created HR's illuminated Lucite bed. 'Keep your coats on' from obituary in *New York Sunday Herald Tribune* by Patrick O'Higgins. 'Oscar, Oscar, just one more thing', author's interview with Diane Moss. O'Higgins describes his collapse in *Madame*, pp 263–269 and in his private correspondence. Boris Forter wrote to P.O'H concerning HR's money fixation. 'She broke her arm' incident described by John Richardson. De la Renta fashion show invitation, EAA. His role described in MEA, pp 302–303. See also *Oscar de la Renta* by Sarah Mower, pp 60–63. Pablo screaming 'pink, stink!' ibid p 305. Pablo describes Wallis Windsor's make-up in *Instant Beauty*, pp 200–201. Kennedy funeral reported in *Madame*, p 262. O'Higgins writes about the robbery in *Madame*, pp 271–5. Further details, Rixie Marcus in conversation with Mr Terry Mansfield, kindly told to author. Ernestine Carter's memory of the French party described in *With Tongue in Chic*, p 174. P.O'H recalled the trip to Tangiers in *Madame*, pp 281–283 and in his private correspondence. 'Plaza Art Gallery' information, letter P.O'H to John Richardson. HR's will and codicils obtained from Surrogate Court of New York. Amongst the many obituaries on HR author wishes to cite the *New York Times*, 2 April 1965, *Journal American*, 1 April 1965, *Women's Wear Daily*, 2 April 1965, the *Daily Express*, 2 April 1965 and the *Sunday Herald Tribune*, 11 April 1965. Further details from *Madame*, P.O'H pp 288–9. Enid Hardwick recollected Count Chandon buying the Quai de Bethune apartment. O'Higgins' frail appearance described by Monica Smythe, who also detailed EA's deterioration to author. Christopher Yates recollected meeting EA at Heathrow. On memories of his employment, author's conversation with Maurice in New York. 'Killer' Joe Piro and Jackie Kennedy from *A Woman Called Jackie* by C. David Heyman p 446. Piro at The Blue Grass Ball, MEA p 306. On her last visit to Ireland, author's conversations with Angus McCall and Monica Smythe. From the many obituaries on Miss Arden, author would like to cite the *Palm Beach Illustrated*, October 1966, the *Lexington Herald*, 19 October 1966 and the *New York Times*, 19h October 1966. Mrs Lauder at EA's funeral described by Monica Smythe. 'She sat with a smile on her face', recollected by Karen MacPerson who worked for EA in Canada.

25   Taxing Times 1966–1989

Patent documents, EAA. It was variously reported that EA's personal and corporate tax obligation was between $35 and $37 million. The IRS refused to confirm the precise amount at the time of writing. Monica Smythe took the call from Galen Weston. Charlotte Niarchos purchase reported in MEA, p 315. According to Monica Smythe, Charles Noble, EA's chauffeur, went to work for Mr and Mrs Whitney who subsequently purchased Arden's apartment. Sale of EA's horses reported in, amongst others, the *Lexington Herald-Leader*, 20 October 1966 and ibid, 20 June 1967, clippings courtesy of Keeneland Library. Litigation on EA's horse farm widely reported but author particularly cites the *Lexington Herald-Leader*, 14 January 1969, the *Courier-Journal*, 30 January 1969 and the *Sunday Herald-Leader*, all courtesy of Keeneland Library. Castillo/Lanvin, Sarmi and de la Renta selling to Arden after her death, EAA and MEA p 316. Will of Ceska Cooper viewed by author. Auction of EA's Kentucky furnishings, *Lexington-Leader* 20 October 1967. Sale of Maine Chance, Mt Vernon, Maine reported in the *Lexington Herald-Leader*, 28 September 1969. All clippings courtesy of Keeneland Library. London staff service details, papers of Gordon Yates. EA's spontaneous firing widely reported and confirmed in author's interview with Angus McCall. Author met Pierre Laroche, having hired him to handle make-up for press fashion shows, circa 1971–72. On Yardley's 1960s expansion, see *Selling Dreams* by Margaret Allen, p 79. Leonce Pacheny, ibid p 105. Bill Mandel of Revlon and Rubinstein job offer, *Fire and Ice*, p 216. Oscar Kolin quoted in *Financial World*, 20 August 1970. Rochas deal ibid. On Mykonos launch, see *Selling Dreams*, Allen, p 223: '135 journalists were on a boat moored off Mykonos in Greece'. On the *Ultima II*, author's interview with Eleanor Lambert and conversation with Captain Harris. See also *Fire and Ice*, pp 13–14. Mrs Lyn Revson has never spoken to the media about Charles and declined to comment for this book, despite Mrs Lambert's best efforts to persuade her. O'Higgins wrote about Revson's changes to HR's apartment in *Madame*, p 293. Andrew Tobias writes 'Revson spent $3 million gutting it and redoing it to his gold-everything taste' in *Fire and Ice*, p 15. 'General Odours' building, author's interview with Claude Forter. About Estée Lauder's offices, *Beyond the Magic* by Lee Israel p 81. The redecorated Helena Rubinstein Inc offices featured in Architectural Digest, Spring issue, 1971. News of Cyanamid's prospective purchase of EA surfaced in the media in the autumn of 1970, via the *Wall Street Journal* on 30 September. Subsequently, wide-spread media reports outlining collapse of the deal and litigation instigated by Cyanamid appeared. Author cites in particular the *Wall Street Journal*, 8 October 1970; *Business Week*, 17 October 1970; the *Wall Street Journal* 21 October 1970. Reports on further litigation, including the suit against Goldman, Sachs reported in the *Wall Street Journal*, 2 February 1971 and in American Cyanamid vs. Elizabeth Arden Sales Corp. 331F. Supp. 597 in the Southern District of New York. Lilly's plans for UK evident in Gordon Yates's correspondence. Re-vamp plans, interview with Angus McCall. Richard Salomon's speech, see *Selling Dreams*, Allen, p 76. Annette Tapert and Diana Edkins wrote about Diana Vreeland, quoting Andy Warhol in *The Power of Style*. Diane Moss recollected the board's decision to sell the business during interview with author. Colgate's launch of Helena Rubinstein's 'Silk Fashion' at the Villa d'Este, with Veruschka riding into the gala party on a white horse, reported in *Selling Dreams* by Margaret Allen, p 223. Merging of British production with Coty at the East Molesey plant and world-wide company debt, ibid, p 90. Trade information on L'Oréal's first approach to buy Rubinstein, ibid, p 90. Kao Soap Company of Japan, ibid, p 91. Collapse of Kao bid and Cosmair's prospective purchase in 1979, ibid, p 94. Colgate's statement that negotiations had 'terminated' dated 27 September 1979, ibid, p 95. On Revlon hiring Lauren Hutton, *Fire and Ice*, Andrew Tobias, p 132. Revson's death, ibid, p 272. Appointment of Michael Bergerac, ibid, p 19 and *Selling Dreams*, pp 110–111. On Colgate selling Rubinstein to Albi, ibid, pp 96–97. L'Oréal's acquisition history of the company reviewed in *WWD*, 16 August 1994: 'L'Oréal began acquiring Rubinstein's businesses around the world in 1983, except the Israel company, owned independently by Israeli citizen, Gad Prosper'. 'L'Oréal completed the take-over of the Helena Rubinstein brand name in 1988' from *Mémoire de la Beauté Helena Rubinstein* by Catherine Jazdewski. On the Eli Lilly sale to Faberge, Susan Taylor, Managing Director of Elizabeth Arden UK today, says, 'it was all about big business buying glamour stock – then they realised there was more to it and often couldn't cope', author's interview with Mrs Taylor. On closing Chicago salon, report in US *Cosmopolitan* magazine, May 1990. See also *Chicago Tribune*, Style section, 10 October 1990, 'The Grand Old Dame Takes a Dive.'

Epilogue

Sotheby's catalogue of the Harry A. Franklin Family Collection of African Art, April 1990. Grace Gilbert quoted on Charles Revson. On Mr Leonard Lauder's wealth, *Forbes* magazine listing, Time 100: Builders & Titans — Estée Lauder by Grace Mirabella. Accurate statistics on the value of the beauty industry are notoriously flawed. Divisions between toiletries, 'personal care' including deodorants, hair-care products, nail care, fragrances, coloured cosmetics and skincare are blurred, especially as many corporations who produce both shampoo and skincare do not publish inter-divisional figures. Author's careful investigation into the prestige skin-care, anti-ageing and coloured cosmetics market leads her to estimate the present value to be worth in excess of $75 billion.

Bibliography

ALLAN, Tony: *Americans In Paris. An Illustrated Account of the Twenties and Thirties.* Contemporary Books, Chicago 1977

ALLEN, Charles and DWIVEDI, Sharada: *Lives of the Indian Princes.* Century Publishing Co. 1984

ALLEN, Margaret: *Selling Dreams: Inside The Beauty Business.* Simon & Schuster, New York 1981

AMORY, Cleveland: *Who killed Society?* Harper and Brothers, New York 1960

ANDREWS, Wayne: *The Vanderbilt Legend.* Harcourt, Brace and Company, New York 1941

ANGELOGLOU, Maggie: *A History of Make-Up.* N.Y. Macmillan Press 1970

ANTCZAK, Dr. Stephen and Gina: *Cosmetics Unmasked.* Thorsons, London 2001

ANTOINE: *Antoine.* W.H. Allen and Co., London

ASQUITH, Margot: *The Autobiography of Margot Asquith (Volumes 1 and 2).* Penguin Books, London 1936

AYER, Margaret Hubbard and TAVES, Isabella: *The Three Lives of Harriet Hubbard Ayer.* W.H. Allen 1957

BAKER, Nancy C.: *The Beauty Trap. Exploring Women's Greatest Obsession.* Franklin Watts, New York 1984

BALD, Wambly: *On the Left Bank 1929–1933.* Ohio University Press, 1987

BALDWIN, Billy: *Baldwin Remembers.* Harcourt Brace, New York, 1974

BALDWIN, Charles C.: *Stanford White.* DaCapo Press, New York 1976

BALLARD, Bettina: *In My Fashion.* David McKay & Co. 1960

BALSAN, Consuelo Vanderbilt: *The Glitter and The Gold.* William Heinemann Ltd. 1953

BANNER, Lois W.: *American Beauty*. The University of Chicago Press, Chicago 1983

—— *Elizabeth Cady Stanton: A Radical for Women's Rights*. Little, Brown and Company, Toronto 1980

BASTEN, Fred: *Max Factor's Hollywood: Movies, Make-up, Glamour*. Grantham Books, 1999.

BEATON, Cecil: *The Glass of Fashion*. Weidenfeld and Nicolson, London 1954

BEEVOR, Antony & Cooper, Artemis: *Paris: After the Liberation: 1944–1949* Hamish Hamilton, London 1994

BERNAYS, Doris Fleischman: *An Outline of Careers for Women*. Doubleday Doran, New York 1928

BETTINA: *Bettina*. Michael Joseph, London 1965

BIRMINGHAM, Stephen: *Our Crowd – The Great Jewish Families of New York*. Harper & Row, New York 1967

—— *The Rest of Us. The Rise of America's Eastern European Jews*. Little, Brown & Company 1984

BREWER, John and PORTER, Roy: *Consumption and The World of Goods*. Routledge, 1993

BRODY, Iles: *Gone with the Windsors*. The John C. Winston Company, Philadelphia/Toronto 1953

BROWN, Henry Collins: *New York in the Elegant Eighties*. Valentine's, New York 1927

—— *Brownstone Fronts and Saratoga Trunks*. E.P. Dutton, 1935

BURNE, Jerome: *Chronicle of the World*. Longman Group & Chronicle Publications, 1989

BUSHBY, Robert: *Cosmetics and How to Make Them*. Sir Isaac Pitman & Sons, London 1947

BUSHMAN, Richard L.: *The Refinement of America*, Vintage Books (Random House), New York 1993

CALASIBETTA, Dr. Charlotte: *Fairchild's Dictionary of Fashion*. Fairchild Publications, New York 1975

CALLERY, Sean: *Harrods – the Story of Society's Favourite Store* Ebury Press, 1991

CAMPBELL, Nina and SEEBOHM, Caroline: *Elsie de Wolfe – A Decorative Life*. Arum Press, 1993

CARTER, Ernestine: *With Tongue in Chic*. Michael Joseph, London 1974

CASSINI, Oleg: *In My Own Fashion*. Simon & Schuster, New York 1987

CASTLE, Mr. and Mrs. Vernon: *Modern Dancing*. Harper and Brothers, New York 1914

CHASE, Edna Woolman & Ilka: *Always In Vogue*. Victor Gollancz, London 1954

CHASE, Ilka: *Past Imperfect*. Doubleday, Doran and Company, Garden City 1942

—— *In Bed We Cry*. Doubleday, Doran and Company, Garden City 1943

CHISHOLM, Anne: *Nancy Cunard*. Sidgwick & Jackson, 1979

COLEMAN, Elizabeth A..: *The Genius of Charles James*. Holt, Rinehart & Winston, New York 1982.

COOK, Blanche Wiesen: *Eleanor Roosevelt. Volume Two 1933–1938*. Viking Penguin, New York 1999

COWLES, Fleur: *She Made Friends and Kept Them*. Harper Collins, 1996

COWLES, Virginia: *The Astors*. Alfred A. Knopf, New York 1979

CREED, Charles: *Maid to Measure*. Jarrolds, London 1961

CURLING, Bill: *The Captain: A Biography of Captain Sir Cecil Boyd-Rochfort: Royal Trainer*. Barrie and Jenkins, London 1970

DACHE, Lilly: *Talking Through My Hats*. Coward-McCann, 1946

DARE, Frances: *Lovely Ladies: The Art of Being A Woman*. N.Y. Doubleday, 1929

De ACOSTA, Mercedes: *Here Lies The Heart*. Reynal and Company, New York 1960

De COURCY, Anne: *1939– The Last Season*. Thames and Hudson, London 1989

De FOREST LAMB, Ruth: *American Chamber of Horrors. The Truth About Food and Drugs*. Grosset and Dunlop, New York 1936

DESLANDRES, Yvonne: *Poiret – Paul Poiret 1879–1944*. Editions du Regard, Paris 1986

De WOLFE, Elsie (Lady Mendl): *After All*. Harper, 1935

DREXEL LEHR, Elizabeth: *'King Lehr' and the Gilded Age*. J.B. Lippincott Company, London 1935

EVANS, Harold: *The American Century*. Jonathan Cape, London 1998

EVERETT, Felicity: *MAKEUP*. Usborne Publishing, London 1986

EWING, Elizabeth: *History of 20th Century Fashion*. B.T. Batsford, London 1974

FABE, Maxene: *BEAUTY MILLIONAIRE: The life of Helena Rubinstein*. Thomas Y. Crowell & Co., New York 1972

FAIRCHILD, John: *Chic Savages*. Simon and Schuster, New York 1989

FITCH, Noel Riley: *Sylvia Beach and the Lost Generation*. W.W. Norton & Company, New York 1983

FOOT, M.R.D.: *SOE In France*. University Publications of America, 1984

GAINES, Steven: *Simply Halston: The Untold Story.* G.P. Putnam's Sons, New York 1991

GILL, Brendan: *Cole.* Michael Joseph, London, 1971

GILOT, Francoise *Life with Picasso.* Virago, London 1990

GOLD, Arthur and FRIZDALE, Robert: *Misia: The Life of Misia Sert.* Knopf, 1980

GOODRUN & DALRYMPLE, *Advertising in America: The First 200 Years.* N.Y. Abrams 1990

GORDON, Lady Duff: *Discretions and Indiscretions.* Stokes, New York 1932

GRIFFITH, Richard and MAYER, Arthur: *The Movies.* Simon & Schuster, New York 1957

HAUSER, Gaylord: *Look Younger, Live Longer.* Farrar, Strauss and Company, New York 1951

—— *The Gaylord Hauser Cook Book.* Capricorn Books, New York 1963

—— *Diet Does It.*

—— *Be Happier, Be Healthier.* Farrar, Strauss and Young, New York MCMLII

—— *Good Food, Good Health, Good Looks.*

—— *Mirror Mirror On The Wall.* Farrar, Strauss and Cudahy, New York 1960

—— *Treasury of Secrets.* Farrar, Strauss and Company, New York 1950

—— *Here's How to be Healthy.* Tempo Books, New York 1934

HEMINGWAY, Ernest: A *Moveable Feast.* Arrow, 1996.

HERNDON, Booton: *Bergdorf's on the Plaza.* Alfred A. Knopf, New York 1956

HEYMAN, David: *Poor Little Rich Girl. The Legend of Barbara Hutton.* Hutchinson & Company, London 1983

—— A *Woman Named Jackie.* Carol Communications, 1989

HIGHAM, Charles: *Secret Lives of The Duchess of Windsor.* Sidgwick & Jackson, London 1988

HILLENBRAND, Laura: *Seabiscuit: The Making of a Legend.* Fourth Estate, London 2001

HOFFMAN, Katherine: *Georgia O'Keeffe. A Celebration of Music and Dance.* George Braziller, New York 1997

HOMBERGER, Eric: *The Historical Atlas of New York City.* Henry Holt and Company, New York 1994

HOPKINS, Harry: *The New Look. A Social History of the Forties and Fifties.* Secker & Warburg, 1954

HOPPER, Hedda: *From Under My Hat.* Doubleday, New York 1952

HUBBARD AYER, Harriet: *Harriett Hubbard Ayer's Book. A Complete and Authentic Treatise on the Laws of Health and Beauty.* Arno Press, New York 1974

HUDDLESTONE, Sisley: *Bohemian Literary and Social Life in Paris.* George G. Harrap & Company, London 1928

ISRAEL, Lee: *Estée Lauder: Beyond the Magic.* Macmillan, New York 1985

JAMES, Edward T. (editor): *Notable American Women – A Biographical Dictionary* Harvard University Press, 1971

JAZDEWSKI, Catherine: *Helena Rubinstein.* Assouline, Paris

JONES, Liane: *A Quiet Courage.* Bantam Press, 1990

JOSEPHSON, Matthew: *The Robber Barons,* Eyre and Spottiswoode, London 1962

JULIAN, Philippe: *de Meyer.* Alfred A. Knopf, 1976

KAHN, E.J. Jr: *Jock: The Life and Times of John Hay Whitney.* Doubleday, 1981.

KEENAN, Brigid. *Dior in Vogue.* Octopus Books, 1981.

KENNETT, Frances: *Coco – The Life & Times of Gabrielle Chanel,* Victor Gollancz, London 1989

KLUVER, Billy and MARTIN, Julie: *Kiki's Paris. Artists and Lovers 1900–1930.* Harry N. Abrams, New York 1989

LACEY, Robert: *Sotheby's.* Little, Brown & Co (UK) 1998

LANDRUM, Gene N.: *Profiles of Power and Success. Fourteen Geniuses who Broke the Rules.* Prometheus Books, Amherst N.Y. 1996

LAUDER, Estée: *Estée, A Success Story.* Random House, New York 1985

LAVINE, Sigmund A.: *Famous Merchants.* Dodd, Mead and Company, New York 1965

LECKIE, Janet: *A Talent for Living: The Story of Henry Sell, An American Original.* Hawthorn Books, New York 1970

LEWIS A.A. & WOODWORTH, Constance: *Miss Elizabeth Arden. An Unretouched Portrait.* W.H. Allen, London and New York 1973

LIEVEN, Prince Peter: *The Birth Of The Ballet Russes.* George Allen & Unwin

MADSEN, Axel: *Living For Design – The YSL Story.* Delacorte Press, 1979
—— *Coco Chanel,* Bloomsbury, London 1990

MAGNUS, Philip: *King Edward the Seventh.* John Murray, London 1964

MAINES, Rachel P.: *The Technology of Orgasm. 'Hysteria': the Vibrator, and Women's Sexual Satisfaction.* The Johns Hopkins University Press, Baltimore and London 1999

MANZONI, Pablo: *Instant Beauty: The Complete Way to Perfect Make-up.* Simon and Schuster, New York 1978

MARBURY, Elisabeth: *My Crystal Ball.* Boni & Liveright, New York 1923

MARCUS, Stanley: *Minding the Store.* Little, Brown and Company, Boston 1974

MARGETSON, Stella: *The Long Party.* Gordon Cremones, London 1974

MARLOW, Joyce (Editor): *Votes for Women. The Virago Book of Suffragettes.* Virago Press, London 2000

MARTIN, Richard: *Fashion and Surrealism.* Thames and Hudson, London 1988

MASTERS, Brian: *Great Hostesses.* Constable, London 1982

MAXWELL, Elsa: *I Married The World.* William Heinemann, London 1955

McDONAGH, Everett, G: *The Truth About Cosmetics.* N.Y. 1937. Published by The Drug and Cosmetics Industry

McDOWELL, Colin: *McDowell's Directory of Twentieth Century Fashion.* Frederick Muller, London 1984

McLAUGHLIN, Terence: *The Gilded Lily.* Cassell & Co., London 1972

McLELLAN, Diana: *The Girls – Sappho Goes to Hollywood.* Robson Books, 2001

MENKES, Suzy: *The Windsor Style.* Grafton Books, 1987

MILLER, Joan: *One Girl's War. Personal Exploits in M15's Most Secret Station.* Brandon, Co. Kerry 1986

MISTINGUETT: *Mistinguett – Queen of the Paris Night.* Elek Books Ltd., 1954

MOORE, Harry T. & MONTAGUE, Dale B.: *Frieda Lawrence and Her Circle.* Palgrave Macmillan, London 1981

MORGAN, Anne: *The American Girl.* Harper and Brothers, New York and London 1915

MORRIS, Lloyd: *Incredible New York. High Life and Low Life of the Last Hundred Years.* Bonanza Books, New York MCMLI

MYRDAL, Alva: *Women's Two Roles.* Routeledge and Kegan Paul, 1965

OBOLENSKY, Prince Serge: *One Man In His Time. The Memoirs of Serge Obolensky.* Hutchinson, London 1960

O'CONNOR, Richard: *Duet in Diamonds. The Flamboyant Saga of Lillian Russell and Diamond Jim Brady.* Putnam, New York 1972

ODLUM, Hortense: *A Woman's Place.* Charles Scribner's Sons, New York and London 1949

OGDEN, Christopher: *Life of the Party. The biography of Pamela Digby Churchill Hayward Harriman.* Little, Brown & Company, 1994

O'HIGGINS, Patrick: *Madame. An Intimate Biography of Helena Rubinstein.* Weidenfeld and Nicolson, London 1971

PALLINGSTON, Jessica: *Lipstick. A Celebration of a Girl's Best Friend.* Simon & Schuster UK, London 1999.

PARKER, Morell: *Lillian Russell, The Era of Plush.* Random House, New York 1940

PEISS, Kathy: *Hope in a Jar. The Making of America's Beauty Culture.* Metropolitan Books, Henry Holt & Company, New York 1998

PERUTZ, Kathrin: *Beyond The Looking Glass: America's Beauty Culture.* William Morrow, New York 1970

PHILLIPS, M.C.: *Skin Deep. The Truth about Beauty Aids – Safe and Harmful.* Consumer's research, Washington 1934

PUTNAM, Samuel: *Paris Was Our Mistress.* Plantin Publishers, London 1947

RAGAS, Meg Cohen and KOZLOWSKI, Karen: *Read My Lips. A Cultural History of Lipstick.* Chronicle Books, 1998

RICHARDSON, John: *The Sorcerer's Apprentice.* Jonathan Cape, London 1999

—— *Sacred Monsters, Sacred Masters.* Jonathan Cape, 2001

RIGDEN, Dennis (introduction): *SOE Syllabus. Lessons In Ungentlemanly Warfare World War II.* Public Records Office, 2001

ROUX-CHARLES, Edmonde: *Chanel.* Collins Harvill, London 1989

RUBINSTEIN, Helena: *My Life for Beauty.* The Bodley Head, London 1964

—— *The Art of Feminine Beauty.* Horace Liveright, New York 1930

—— *Food for Beauty.* Ives Washburn, New York 1938

SCHIAPARELLI, Elsa: *Shocking Life.* J.M. Dent & Sons, 1954

SEEBOHM, Caroline: *The Man Who Was Vogue. The Life And Times of Condé Nast.* Viking Press, New York 1982

SEELING, Charlotte: *Fashion. The Century of the Designer 1900–1999.* Könemann Verlagsgesellshaft mbH, Cologne 2000

SERT, Misia: *Misia and the Muses – the Memoirs of Misia Sert.* The John Day Company, New York 1953

SHAKESPEARE, Nicholas: *Bruce Chatwin.* Vintage Books, 2000

SHUKER, Nancy: *ELIZABETH ARDEN: The Cosmetics Entrepeneur.* Silver Burdett Press, Englewood Cliffs, N.J. 1989

SINCLAIR, David: *Dynasty. The Astors and Their Times.* J.M. Dent and Sons, London 1983

SLATER, Leonard: *ALY – A Biography.* Random House, 1964

SMITH, Jane S.: *Elsie de Wolfe, A Life in the High Style.* Atheneum, New York 1982

SNOW, Carmel (with Mary Louise Aswell): *The World of Carmel Snow.* McGraw Hill, New York 1962

SPICER, Chrystopher J.: *Duchess, The Story of the Windsor Hotel.* Loch Haven Books, 1993

STABILI, Toni: *Everything You Want to Know About Cosmetics.* Dodd, Mead & Company, New York 1984

STEWART, Charles Conger (Editor): *World Digest August 1935 Volume 11, No 8.* World Digest Publishing Company, New York 1935

STROUSE, Jean: *Morgan. American Financier.* Perennial, New York 2000

SULITZER, Paul-Kemp: *Hannah.* Poseidon Press, New York 1985

TAPERT, Annette & EDKINS, Diana: *The Power of Style.* Crown, 1994

TAVES, Isabella: *Successful Women and How They Attained Success.* E.P. Dutton, New York 1943

THURMAN, Judith: *Secrets of the Flesh. A Life of Colette.* Bloomsbury, 1999

TOBIAS, Andrew: *Fire and Ice: The Story of Charles Revson – The Man Who Built the Revlon Empire.* William Morrow and Company, New York 1976

TRASKO, Mary: *Daring Do's. A History of Extraordinary Hair.* Flammarion, Paris 1994

VAIL, Gilbert *A History of Cosmetics in America.* N.Y. Published by The Toilet Goods Association, 1947

VAIL, Amanda: *Everybody Was So Young.* Little, Brown & Co (UK) 1998.

VANDERBILT, Cornelius Jr: *Farewell To Fifth Avenue.* Victor Gollancz 1935

—— *Man of the World. My Life on Five Continents.* Crown Publishers, New York 1959

—— *Queen of the Golden Age.* McGraw-Hill Book Company, New York 1956

VAN RENSSELAER, Mrs John King: *The Social Ladder.* Eveleigh Nash and Grayson, London 1925

VICKERS, Hugo: *Cecil Beaton.* Phoenix Press, 2002

VIDAL, Gore: *The Last Empire – Essays 1992–2001.* Abacus, 2002.

VINIKAS, Vincent: *Soft Soap, Hard Sell. American Hygiene in an Age of Advertisement.* Iowa State University Press, Ames, Iowa 1992

VOGUE'S HISTORY OF 20th CENTURY FASHION: Viking, 1988

VREELAND, Diana: *D.V.,* Alfred A. Knopf, New York 1984

—— *Allure.* Doubleday, 1980

WALZ, Barbara and MORRIS, Bernadine: *The Fashion Makers*

WARSHOW, Robert Irving: *Jay Gould. The Story of a Fortune.* Greenberg, New York 1928

WATSON, Steven: *Strange Bedfellows. The First American Avant-Garde.* Aberville, New York 1991

WENDT, Lloyd and KOGAN, Herman: *Give the Lady What She Wants.* Marshall Field and Company, 1952

WHITE, Palmer: *Poiret.* Studio Vista, London 1973

—— *Elsa Schiaparelli.* Aurum Press, 1995

WYKES-JOYCE, Max: *Cosmetics and Adornment: Ancient and Contemporary Usage.* Peter Owen Limited, London 1961

Index

CPSIA information can be obtained
at www.ICGtesting.com
Printed in the USA
BVOW06s1642230717
490043BV00005B/171/P

9 781683 366485